THE

THEOLOGY OF LUTHER

IN ITS

HISTORICAL DEVELOPMENT AND INNER HARMONY.

Dr. JULIUS KÖSTLIN,

PROFESSOR AND CONSISTORIALRATH AT HALLE.

TRANSLATED FROM THE SECOND GERMAN EDITION

BY

REV. CHARLES E. HAY, A. M.

COMPLETE IN TWO VOLUMES.

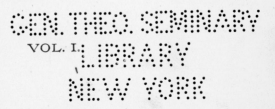
VOL. I.

PHILADELPHIA:
LUTHERAN PUBLICATION SOCIETY.

TRANSLATOR'S PREFACE.

THE life of Martin Luther was one so unique in its personal characteristics and so full of dramatic interest that we are prone to rest content with the contemplation of its outward aspects, and too seldom stop to trace the course of the full, deep current of religious thought that lay beneath it. Here and there in his career certain definite religious convictions are recognized by all as controlling his conduct and prompting his fearless utterances. The world knows what were the truths for which he stood at Worms and Marburg. But it is the task of the painstaking scholar to note the germination of the great initial conceptions which gave direction and form to all the subsequent thought of the Reformer, and to mark the natural stages of development by which this seed-thought grew until it covered the whole field of theological truth.

So admirably was this task accomplished by Dr. Köstlin in his exhaustive work, published in 1863, that scarcely an effort has since been made to traverse the same field of inquiry. The author's claim to recognition as the foremost Luther scholar of the world, resting largely upon this publication and his biography of the Reformer, and confirmed by numerous special contributions to the literature of the subject, is universally acknowledged.

It is impossible to estimate the influence which has been exerted by this lucid and complete exhibition of the doctrinal basis of Luther's tireless activity. It reveals his grasp of great fundamental truths and his fidelity to them amid all the changing phases of theory, and even while his own mind was yet struggling to free itself from the bondage of traditional error upon minor points. It has been for scholars a storehouse of historic facts elsewhere accessible to few, and has contributed in no small degree to the modern revival of intelligent interest in the defence and propagation of the vital principles for which Luther lived and with which his name has become inseparably associated.

It will be found a special excellence of the present volumes, that the author illustrates his assertions by the most abundant quotations from the entire range of the Reformer's writings. We have here, indeed, little more than a marshaling in logical sequence of the leading ideas embedded in the utterances of each successive period, and the tracing, by a masterly and impartial hand, of the unbroken thread of fervent conviction that unites them all and harmonizes the apparent inconsistencies which have ever made the theology of Luther to smaller minds an insoluble enigma.

The presentation of this work to the English-reading public is made with no polemical intent. It may furnish fresh weapons for valiant gladiators, but its tendency must be to remove misapprehensions and clear the way for an intelligent understanding of our Church's rich inheritance of doctrinal statement. We may not always find ourselves in full accord with the great Leader of the Reformation, but we owe it to his memory at least to study faithfully the positions which he maintained before venturing to assail them. Nor need we fear that the rejuvenated Church will ever swerve from the line of reverent loyalty to the Word of God marked out for her in the Theology of Luther.

CHARLES E. HAY.

ALLENTOWN, PA., *May 1, 1897.*

AUTHOR'S PREFACE TO THE SECOND EDITION.

As my friend, the publisher, has expressed a desire to issue in this Luther Jubilee year a new edition of the present work, which has now been for twenty years before the public, I have deemed it a duty to assist in the undertaking, cherishing as I do the hope that, as it was the first attempt to present a comprehensive and scientific exhibition of the Theology of Luther, it may be yet further serviceable in the same cause.

I had, from the first, announced the aim of the work to be purely historical, apart from all dogmatic or apologetic design. In this character, I venture to believe, it may, although Lommatzsch has since, in his *Luther's Doctrine from the Ethico-religious Stand-point, 1879*, undertaken to discuss and justly estimate the Reformer's teaching in a comprehensive and interesting dogmatic survey, yet maintain its place, and may not unfittingly accompany my larger and smaller biographies of Luther, now also about to appear in new editions.

With the exception of the treatise of Lommatzsch, there have appeared within the period named only separate discussions of certain leading features of Luther's theology, such as the excellent study, *The Mysticism of Luther*, by H. Hering, and Luthardt's brief review of the *Ethics of Luther*. These furnish no occasion for any essential modifications of my own conception of the subject, however valuable the contributions which they present for a new elaboration and critical estimate of the doctrine of the Reformer.

Many points upon which I was at first somewhat in doubt myself, and upon which I therefore especially hoped to be confirmed by the labor of others, have as yet received no further elucidation. Recent investigations, although furnishing rich material for the history of the life and activity of Luther, have, so far as I have observed, given comparatively little attention to the examination of his theology. As supplemental to my entire presentation of

(v)

the Theology of Luther, a full exposition of its relation to the immediately preceding theology of the later Middle Ages is certainly much to be desired. But although a number of eminent scholars have directed attention to this felt want, it has not yet been adequately met by any one.

Of the writings of Luther, the *First Lectures upon the Psalms* (published by Leidemann, 1876) have been given to the public since the preparation of the present work. They take their place, as I show in my *Martin Luther, his Life and his Writings*, Second Edition, Vol. I., p. 111, immediately after the *Annotations of the Psalms* spoken of in the present work, Vol. I., pp. 91 sqq. The larger biography above mentioned affords a continuous introduction to the study of all the separate writings of the Reformer from which I have here sought to deduce his doctrinal views.

J. KÖSTLIN.

Halle, April, 1883.

INTRODUCTION.

The great original instruments of divine revelation and heralds of divine truth exert an influence peculiarly powerful in consequence of the fact that their teaching is seen to be in fullest accord with their own lives. They have in their own inner and outward experience realized the truth of that to which they bear testimony. With the harmony manifest in the objective presentation of their doctrinal views corresponds that which is displayed in their entire Christian personality. Very gladly, therefore, will the historical study of their doctrine follow, as far as may be possible, the path upon which their perception and proclamation of the truth have advanced in such striking accord with their own lives.

This is true, in large measure at least, of all theologians who have ever drawn their inspiration from the original Word of Truth, and presented to the Church in fresh, impressive and suggestive form that which they have there discovered. Of none who could be named, however, is it more true than of Luther, as there is also none in whom we are able to trace more accurately the course of historical development in both doctrine and life.

Evidently, this must furnish us the starting-point in any presentation of the Theology of Luther. The germ of the latter we shall find already advanced to a remarkable degree of maturity in the personal development of the man at the time when he first appears as the advocate of reform (see Book I.). Yet, after this period, we must still present his doctrinal views as constantly advancing. That which had for him at this critical point in his career become a fixed and living certainty was yet to attain a more complete development only through the continuous pressure of historical events and in conflict with the papal theology and church (see Book II.). Even after the fundamental doctrines of his own theology, as over against that of the Papacy, had been fully established and clearly justified, a yet further advance in doctrinal statement was rendered necessary in various important directions, partly in pursuance of his opposition to the hitherto prevailing errors, partly, and especially, in consequence of certain tendencies which he now found it necessary to combat upon the territory of the Reformation itself (see Book III.).

It was just these historical occasions, also, which led to the preparation of the great majority of those writings of the Reformer from which his theological views are to be chiefly and most surely gleaned. It follows, hence, from the nature of the case, that our presentation of the Theology of Luther will serve, at the same time, as a historical introduction to his literary productions.

Finally, we propose in our last book to review in a systematic way the doctrine whose development we shall then have traced from one original fundamental principle, regarding it as a complete whole in its inner consistency, and, at the same time, to elucidate also more fully various matters of importance, the detailed consideration of which may not have fallen within the scope of the preceding historical study.

TABLE OF CONTENTS.

BOOK I.

THE INNER LIFE AND THE DOCTRINE OF LUTHER BEFORE THE INDULGENCE CONTROVERSY.

CHAPTER I.

LUTHER FROM HIS CHILDHOOD TO THE TURNING-POINT OF HIS RELIGIOUS DEVELOPMENT IN THE MONASTERY AT ERFURT.

CHAPTER II.

LUTHER AS TEACHER AT WITTENBERG UNTIL A. D. 1517.

BOOK II.

THE GREAT REFORMATORY TESTIMONY OF LUTHER, FROM THE PROMULGATION OF THE NINETY-FIVE THESES UNTIL THE DIET AT WORMS.— A. D. 1517 TO A. D. 1521.

INTRODUCTORY.

FUNDAMENTAL PRINCIPLES INVOLVED IN THE THEORY OF INDULGENCES.

CHAPTER I.

LUTHER'S FIRST GREAT UTTERANCES IN CONDEMNATION OF INDULGENCES.

CHAPTER II.

PAGE

CHAPTER IV.

BOOK III.

PRINCIPAL POINTS IN WHICH AN ADVANCE IS MANIFEST IN THE DOCTRINE OF LUTHER AFTER HIS RETIREMENT AT THE WARTBURG:—DEVELOPED IN OPPOSITION, NOT ONLY TO CATHOLICISM, BUT PARTICULARLY TO TENDENCIES WHICH APPEARED UPON THE TERRITORY OF THE REFORMATION ITSELF.

BOOK I.

———

THE INNER LIFE AND THE DOCTRINE OF
LUTHER BEFORE THE INDULGENCE
CONTROVERSY.

CHAPTER I.

LUTHER FROM HIS CHILDHOOD TO THE TURNING-POINT
OF HIS RELIGIOUS DEVELOPMENT IN THE
MONASTERY AT ERFURT.

VERY meagre in their scope are the accounts which we possess concerning the earliest period of Luther's development. In this period we must include his entire life up to the time when, in the monastery at Erfurt, the light of Gospel grace burst full upon his soul, and, silently and at first all unobserved, that germ began to develop whose unfolding is seen in the entire subsequent life and doctrines of the Reformer. Neither he himself nor his friends and contemporaries have here left us such detailed and connected information as we might desire.

In regard to his childhood, especially, we can learn but little. Yet that which we know is sufficient to enable us to trace even then, in a general way, a definite course in his development. It was, further, so far as we are at all able to judge, one peculiar tendency which, modified by outward circumstances and the means of spiritual culture enjoyed, controlled that course from the beginning. This it was which at last drove him into the monastery, reached there its culmination, and then led him with inward yearning and receptivity to open his heart to the influence of divine grace, by which he was aroused to new life and transformed in his inner nature.

1. EARLY YEARS UNTIL DEPARTURE FOR THE UNIVERSITY.
A. D. 1483–A. D. 1501.

FEW PLEASURES—STERNNESS OF PARENTS—EARLY SCHOOLING—
URSULA COTTA—RELIGIOUS INSTRUCTION.

We often speak of a " happy childhood." Luther himself, in his *Tischreden*, frequently exalts the condition which this expression is intended to define. He calls the life of childhood the

happiest and best.   He does not, however, thus exalt it merely
because of its freedom from earthly cares; but its chief advantage appears to him to lie in the fact that children do not yet
"suffer nor experience the terrors of death and hell, but have only
pure thoughts and joyful anticipations."   They believe, he declares, with perfect simplicity and without any doubting, that God
is gracious, and that the present life will be followed by one that
is eternal.   To his little son he says: "You are under the grace
of God and the forgiveness of sins, not under the Law." [1]   It is
well known, too, how Luther, in dealing with the little ones, loved
to dwell upon this happy trait of childhood character and to foster
it with gentle words of encouragement.   The effort to preserve to
children as far as possible this happy immediate consciousness of
divine grace and, from it as a starting point, to carry forward
their development in Christian life through maturing years finds
no contradiction whatever in the fact that he at the same time
manifested inexorable severity towards all outbreaks of youthful
folly and sin, and declared that he would rather have a dead than
a wayward son. [2]

But Luther had never been permitted himself to enjoy such a
happy time as he afterwards wished for all children and as he saw
his own children and those of his congregation enjoying.   The
experience of simply resting and walking in the goodness and
grace of God, under the eye of parents and instructors ever ready
to promote his gratification at the expense of their own, was, in
so far as we are acquainted with his boyhood, almost unknown to
him—certainly never so fully realized as to have furnished the
keynote whereby to regulate his future life.

His parents were distinguished by an earnest piety and a firm
purpose to so rear their son that he might prove an upright man,
well-fitted for his future calling in life.   He speaks of them,
especially of his father, with deep respect and warm affection.
When the news of the latter's death was brought to him, he
recalled with expressions of grief his "most tender affection" and
the "very delightful intercourse" enjoyed with him.   He confesses: "Through him my Creator gave to me whatever I am
and have; through his toils the Father of mercies supported me

[1] Luther's Deutsche Schriften, Erlangen Edition, lvii, 258 sq., 274.   Tischreden, Förstemann, i, 198, 211.

[2] Erl. Ed., lvii, 263.   Först., i, 202.

and moulded me such as I am." [1] Melanchthon lauds in the father " integrity," for which he was very highly esteemed by all upright people, and in the mother, especially modest worth, true fear of God and prayerfulness. [2] Yet among the many discourses of Luther upon childhood, the training of children, etc., which have been handed down to us, he has, in referring to the time of his own childhood, no example to produce of any gentle attempt on the part of his parents to implant or cultivate in him the genuinely happy child-temper. They can themselves have had no conception of it, and this fact coincides exactly with the prevailing character of piety and integrity witnessed in so many unpretending, worthy representatives of Christianity among the common people before the Reformation. Upon the other hand, he was deeply impressed by illustrations of a mistaken severity experienced at the hand of his own parents. Referring to this, he adds the quiet comment : " They meant it all for the best." They treated him, says he, so harshly that he became quite timid, his mother once beating him until the blood flowed for taking a little nut. He himself deduces from this austerity of his parents the most far-reaching consequences for his later development. " Their sternness and the strict course which they pursued with me led me afterwards to take refuge in a cloister and become a monk." [3]

Luther was very early sent to school, first at Mansfeld, to which place his parents had removed. He was at that time so small that he regarded it a kindness to be carried to school in the arms of a friend. [4] At fourteen years of age he was transferred to the Latin school at Magdeburg, and, one year later, to Eisenach, where some relatives of his mother were living. His experience in these places tended only to deepen the disposition which had been evoked by the strictness of parental discipline. Already at Mansfeld he appears to have become acquainted with the kind of school-masters who " deal with children just as an

[1] Luther's Briefe, De Wette, iv, 33.

[2] Vita M. Luther, in Vitæ quatuor Reformatorum, etc., praef. A. Neander. Berol, 1841, p. 3.

[3] Erl. Ed., lxi, 274. Först., iv, 129.

[4] In the year 1544 Luther still gratefully remembered that this act of kindness had been performed by Nicolas Oemler, who afterwards became his brother-in-law. See Briefe, v, 709.

executioner or jailer would treat a thief." He relates that he was once beaten fifteen times in one morning at school. [1] As, in speaking of this, he adds that children should indeed be chastised and punished, but that we should nevertheless still love them, it is evident that he was not able at that time to console himself with the reflection that he was still an object of affection. At Eisenach we see him burdened, in addition, with care for his daily support. It was here, as he, a poor scholar, was singing for his bread from door to door, that Madam Cotta showed him the kindness for which her name will always be preserved in connection with the history of the Reformer. Far more important than the outward support which her table afforded him must have been the stimulating sensation of love which her benevolent deed awakened within him. He had been made so timid by the "constant threats and cruelty of the school-masters," that he was overcome with fear even when gifts were kindly offered to him. [2]

According to the regulations of the Church, children were required to learn what are now the principal parts of our catechism, i. e., the Ten Commandments, the Apostles' Creed and the Lord's Prayer. Luther himself afterwards showed how the entire contents of the joyful message of salvation might be attached to these in a condensed form suitable for children ; and he regarded it as a matter of inestimable importance, that these fundamental articles of Christian doctrine had maintained their place in the Church. There were also hymns, well-suited to convey the word of salvation in simple but impressive melodies to the heart even of a child. Thus, for example, Luther mentions among the "excellent hymns" sung even under the Papacy, the familiar one in celebration of Christmas : "Ein Kindelein so löbelich ist uns geboren heute." [3]

But just in this connection, he reveals to us the deepest source of the spiritual poverty and inward distress under which he was compelled to suffer, both while under the care of devoted parents and when committed to the training of the Church. The real, soul-satisfying substance of that which was thus taught and sung

[1] Erl. Ed., lxi, 275. Först., iv, 130.

[2] Compare the story of the farmer who offered sausages to the school-boys, but frightened Luther away from him with his rough voice.—Enarr. in Gen. xliii. 23 ; Exeg. Op. Erl. x, 259.

[3] Erl. Ed., iii, 326.

may much more truly be said to have been concealed than to
have been brought to light. " Of all this," he says, " not one jot
nor tittle was understood, but the attention was at once directed
to something quite different." [1] Hungering souls were directed
away from Christ to Mary and the saints, and for spiritual food
were offered empty legends. Christ, upon the other hand, he
learned to know only as a stern judge, striking terror to the hearts
of men. Instead of the " great joy, which shall be to all people,"
and the announcement of the angel : " Unto you is born this day
a Saviour," the fires of hell formed the theme of preaching. [2]
He relates, for example, [3] that in his youth he regarded with aversion the verse, Ps. ii. 11, because he did not like to hear that
God is to be feared ; for he did not know that joy and hope may
be combined with fear, being ignorant of the difference between
the Saviour's works and ours.

We must, of course, not fail to recognize the fact that, despite
the obscuring of the Word of grace which had become almost
universal, there were yet many Christians of devout temper who,
in the decisive moment when struggling under deep conviction
of sin, laid firm hold for themselves upon the message of forgiveness assured in Christ and were enabled afterward to direct their
distressed brethren upon the same path. Luther himself was so
fortunate as to receive such assistance in the monastery. Yet
just this was the most important circumstance in the first period
of his life, that he had parents who, with all their well-meaning
fidelity toward their son, did not know how to impart to his inner
nature, as a preparation for life's journey, the fundamental testimony of the Gospel, and that he found that consolation at a later
day only after he had most deeply experienced the anguish of a
heart striving heavenward and yet unblessed by the experience of
divine grace.

Meanwhile, the boy and maturing youth had readily yielded to
the influence of his peculiar training. A spirit of timidity and
fear possessed him. What he endured was essentially the very
same terrors of the Law under which he well-nigh perished when
a brother in the monastery, and which he so impressively deline-
ates in his later sermons and writings. We find, upon the other

[1] Erl. Ed., iii, 326.
[2] Cf., e. g., Erl. Ed., i, 260 sqq; v, 336 ; xxiv, 347.
[3] Ex. Op. Erl., xviii, 111 (Walch here translates *adolescens* " Knabe ").

hand, no trace of any period in which he desired in bold self-assertion to cast off the yoke of human and divine discipline which so sorely oppressed him. Even the keen scent of enemies and revilers has been as little able to discover anything of this kind in the history of his youth as in that of his life at the monastery. When referring afterwards to the hard experiences of his childhood, he always does it without any bitterness, and he regards the trying nature of his outward circumstances, resulting from the limited resources of his parents, as a wholesome means of education for a worthy manhood. We cannot therefore imagine him, even as a boy, cherishing any embittered feelings, however closely concealed may have been the inward emotions of his peculiarly deep and fervent nature. It was his " singing and heart-felt prayer " which, as Mathesius reports, led Madam Cotta to conceive such a " yearning affection " for him.[1] Already in Mansfeld, Luther was " most commendably diligent and quick " in his studies.[2] But it was especially at the school in Eisenach that his fine intellectual endowment became manifest. He there rapidly outstripped all associates of his own age.[3]

Touching the relation of Luther during this period to the prevailing ecclesiastical life, we observe that, until his departure to Erfurt, there had never been suggested to him from any source the question, whether Christian integrity and religion might not be possible in connection with a freer attitude toward the formal requirements of the Church, or even in actual opposition to them. In Luther's father we recognize, especially from his bearing at the time of his son's entrance into the monastery, a man who possessed a strong, inflexible consciousness of paternal rights, even when he was thereby led to a position at variance with prevailing views in the Church. When young Martin against his wishes took that step, he insisted that the duty of obedience should have had more weight with a son than all prospect of the special perfection and special merit opening, according to the view of the Church, before a monk. He never, indeed, ventured to think of the vow, once assumed, as other than irrevocable despite all subsequent paternal protest. But, although no longer able to enforce his will, he yet for a long time stubbornly persisted in the manifestation of his

[1] Mathesius, Leben Luthers in xvii Predigten (herausg. von Rust, 1841), p. 5.
[2] Ibid.
[3] Melanchthon, Vita quat. Ref., praef. A. Neander. Berol, 1841, p. 4.

displeasure. It is safe to infer that the view of the moral significance and divine authority of the bond existing between parents
and children which lay at the basis of his deportment in this
instance must have been deeply impressed upon Luther from his
earliest childhood. That which the elder Luther, with a vigorous
immediate consciousness of his position as a father, practically
exemplified, the Reformer afterwards, in the light of the Gospel,
maintained with all his power as a fundamental divine ordinance.
It was, moreover, unfavorable opinions of Monasticism in general
which aroused the father's opposition in this special case. It may
have incensed him, as it afterwards did the Reformer, that any
should thus employ the goods of others to make themselves com-
fortable, instead of eating their bread in the sweat of their faces. [1]
At all events, as we have observed, he did not entertain so exalted
an opinion as to the holiness of the order as the Church endeavored to cultivate. He would rather have seen his son become
distinguished in some temporal calling. In harmony with this,
our own Luther afterwards himself most impressively taught that
it is possible to serve God in such a calling just as well as in the
so-called spiritual orders. He has given us, however, not the
slightest reason to believe that his father ever permitted his growing children to hear from him free criticism of the positions and
ordinances of the Church. It is in the highest degree improbable
that, had this been the case, he would have failed to speak of a
matter which would have furnished him such occasion for gratitude
to his father. The latter, probably, went quietly on his way as an
honest citizen, meeting the personal obligations resting upon him
in the Church, without troubling himself further about those things
which impressed him unfavorably in the church-life of the day, or
expressing himself at all in regard to them in the presence of
others, least of all in the presence of his own children. As early
as A. D. 1520, it was currently reported that the Reformer had
been born in Bohemia, educated at Prague, instructed in the books
of Wickliffe—and that his own father had acknowledged this. [2]
How eagerly would his enemies at that time have seized upon any
expressions of his father in the least degree heretical or unchurchly
in tone which could have been discovered. But even his evil-
disposed neighbors were never able to produce any evidence of
this kind.

[1] Erl. Ed., xxviii, 156. [2] Erl. Ed., xxvii, 75.

We know to what an extent, and for how long a time, the offences occasioned by the immoral life of the clergy had already before the end of the fifteenth century prevailed in Germany, and what loud complaints were everywhere heard. But not once in his boyhood days did Luther receive any decided impressions in regard to these, either because the state of affairs was at that time really better in the neighborhood of Mansfeld than elsewhere, or merely because Luther, for some reason, never happened to hear of such things. He could afterwards say [1] that he remembered that, when he was a boy, the priests, even though living in the same houses with women, were not suspected of fornication or adultery, and that it was only within his own recollection that the licentiousness of the priests had so fearfully increased.

During his attendance at the schools in Magdeburg and Eisenach, there had already arisen there, as at so many other places in Germany, at least solitary representatives of a tendency freer in its attitude toward the Church, yet resting upon a deep religious basis.[2] Among these was Andreas Proles, vicar of the Augustinian Order, who was laboring at that time in Magdeburg. Luther relates of him,[3] that he openly expressed his disapprobation of a certain opponent of Huss at the Council of Constance, who had craftily laid snares for the latter, and who had received from the Pope the decoration of the rose as a reward for the victory thus gained. Yet Luther, in this very connection, pronounces Proles a man of great reputation and faith. It is further known of him, that he was at one time actually excommunicated and threatened with imprisonment at Rome on account of expressions touching the Romish abuses. It is possible that, as he was specially active and highly-esteemed as a preacher, Luther may really, as is related, have heard him during his stay at Magdeburg. But that he, at all events, received no permanent impressions from the characteristic peculiarity of the man, is very plainly manifest from the way in which he at a later period speaks of him, *i. e.*, without any hint of such a personal relation to the one whom he so highly commends.

Far more decisive than the testimony of Proles, concerning

[1] Op. Exeg. Erl., ix, 260.

[2] Comp. especially Jürgens, Luther's Leben, i, 269 sqq., 295 sqq.

[3] Erl. Ed., xxiv, 24, 25; lxv, 80: Proles expressed himself thus in conversation with Staupitz, and the latter reported it to Luther.

the distress of the Church, must have been that of the Franciscan, Johann Hilten, at Eisenach. He is said to have proclaimed that the reign of the monks would soon be at an end, and that there would soon appear one whom they would be unable to withstand. He is even said to have indicated, in papers left at his death, the exact time when this one should appear, namely, in the year 1516. [1] Long before Luther's transfer to Eisenach, Hilten had been imprisoned in the cloister. The prophecy referred to is, upon the authority of the *Tischreden*, said to have been quoted by Luther as uttered while he was attending school at Eisenach; [2] and Hilten is said to have spoken it just as he was about to die. This makes it appear as a natural inference, that the matter had already at that time come to the ears of Luther as a student at Eisenach. But not only are the statements in the *Tischreden* themselves unreliable, inasmuch as Hilten certainly did not die until long after Luther's departure from Eisenach; but there is also preserved a letter of Luther, addressed to Frederick Myconius in the year 1539, in which he speaks in such a way of the prophecy of the monk (of which Myconius has spoken to him, requesting further information in regard to it), as though he had then for the first time heard of the matter. It is not to be wondered at if the cry of the imprisoned witness of the truth never reached the ears of the student Luther. Thus, in view of all the influences mentioned, which might be at all presumed to have affected Luther during his stay at Magdeburg and Eisenach, we must abide by the conclusion: " There has not yet been presented a single trace of evidence to indicate that he had been even remotely or slightly influenced from this side." [3] Much rather are we to assume the very opposite.

Luther relates, on the other hand, an incident of an entirely different character, which he remembered as occurring at Magdeburg when he was in his fourteenth year. [4] A prince of Anhalt made his appearance there in the garb of a bare-footed friar, with sack upon his back, bowed down to the earth, so wasted by fasting as to present the very image of death, begging for bread upon

[1] Cf. Apol. Confes. Aug., libri Symb., etc., ed. Hase, p. 277.

[2] Erl. Ed., lx, 28. Först., iii, 252.

[3] Jürgens, i, 298.   [4] Erl. Ed., xxxi, 239 sq.

the streets, and soon died in consequence of his strict mode
of life. Every one who looked upon him was overwhelmed with
a sense of reverence and filled with shame at thought of his own
worldly condition. Impressions of this kind may at that time
have exerted a peculiarly powerful influence upon the mind of
the susceptible youth, and contributed no little to the further
determination of his religious tendency.

2. At the University—Becoming a Monk.
A. D. 1501–A. D. 1505.

COURSE OF STUDY—MASTER OF PHILOSOPHY—OFFICIAL INFLUENCES—
HUMANISM—INWARD LONGINGS UNSATISFIED.

At length, in his eighteenth year, Luther entered the University
at Erfurt. The financial circumstances of his father had im-
proved to such an extent that the latter was able with the fruits
of his toil to furnish his son at least sufficient assistance to ensure
the prosecution of his studies. It was the expectation, as already
remarked, that he should prepare himself for a temporal calling,
preferably that of a lawyer. As introductory to this, he pursued
a course in philosophy, in the "old logicians and other liberal
scholastic and rhetorical sciences," as Mathesius says.

Thus Luther stood at that point in his career at which it commonly devolves upon the youth by his own responsible decision,
to an extent hitherto impossible to him, to give permanent
direction to the course of his inner and outward life. In this,
Luther enjoyed the greater freedom, inasmuch as his father, a
plain tradesman, could not be in position to estimate very accurately the tendency of his studies and the development of his
convictions.

But we have at this point no express information as to Luther's
student-life, except a few words of Mathesius and the scarcely more
satisfactory statements of Melanchthon. With these must be
considered the advantages afforded, especially at that time, by
the University at Erfurt. In regard to the latter, the question
will naturally arise, in how far he came in contact with them and
availed himself of them.

Of Luther's labors in the higher branches, Melanchthon reports
that, having reached the University filled with a burning thirst
for knowledge, he was there led into the subtle dialectics of the

period, and, by virtue of his keen intellectual vision, soon became a master in that field. As his spirit craved something more and better, he read most of the Latin standard literature, the works of Cicero, Virgil, Livy and others, absorbing not alone the words, but precepts and life-pictures of ancient times. His transcendent gifts secured for him the admiration of the entire University. Thus, at the age of twenty years,[1] the rank of Master of Philosophy having been conferred upon him, he began the study of law, in accordance with the advice of his relatives, who believed that his capable mind and his rich oratorical gifts should be trained for the service of the state.

How far may Luther already at this time have been led, through the philosophical lectures and writings with which he was constantly occupied, to the consideration of the fundamental questions of religious faith and knowledge? How far may he have been already led to note possible objections to the prevailing doctrines, or even to entertain actual doubts in regard to them?[2] The writings of the man whom we must regard as by far the most significant of the earlier teachers of that University and an important forerunner of the Reformation, JOHANN VON WESEL, were yet a subject of special study at Erfurt. He had been condemned as a heretic, especially on account of his attacks upon the indulgence business. He had, further, refused to recognize the spirit under whose control the holy fathers and doctors interpreted the Sacred Scriptures as identical with the Spirit through whom they had been originally revealed. He acknowledged nothing as a necessary article of faith which was not contained in the Sacred Scriptures. In his doctrine of the grace of God, we recognize, as afterwards in Luther, Augustinianism, as he maintained that grace may be imparted even without any exercise of the free will. In the Lord's Supper, he held it to be at least possible, that the substance of the bread should remain, while under its form the body of Christ was present.[3] He refused to grant to the Pope the title of "Vicar of Christ." These are all propositions from

---

[1] Mathesius, First Sermon (early in A. D. 1505.) Melanchthon in his account mentions the Baccalaureate instead of the Master's degree. Comp. Jürgens, i, 312.

[2] Cf. especially the development of this thought in Jürgens.

[3] Comp. especially his declarations so late as A. D. 1479 before his accusers, as reported in Ullman, Reformatoren vor der Reformation, i, 387 sqq.

which it might be inferred that Luther afterwards became his disciple. There is wanting in the writings of Wesel only the germ and clear central point of the doctrine of salvation as presented by Luther. At least fifty years before Luther's arrival at Erfurt, he had left to accept a position as preacher at Mentz; twenty years before that time, after almost two years' imprisonment, he had died, an old man sadly broken down by persecution. But as he had once "ruled the University at Erfurt with his books," so, says Luther, it was by the study of these that even he himself yet attained the title of Master.[1]

We are naturally interested in the teachers who labored at Erfurt in Luther's time. Of JODICUS TRUTTVETTER, under whose rectorate he was matriculated, he was able in 1518 to recall,[2] that it was from him that he first learned that only the canonical Scriptures are thoroughly trustworthy, and that all others are to be subjected to critical judgment. Of his teacher ("Institutor"), JOHANN GREFENSTEIN, a "learned and pious man," he even reports[3] that, at a time when he himself had little thought of ever becoming a priest, he had been told by him that Huss had been condemned to death by the ignorant tyrants without proof or refutation. It is beyond question, therefore, that a certain influence of this kind was exerted upon Luther by the two instructors just named. But how limited, even in its original energy, this influence must have been, compared with the entire attitude otherwise maintained by both men, is very clear from the cold and even hostile reception afterwards accorded to Luther's declarations against indulgences, not only by the other authorities at Erfurt, but especially by Truttvetter. It was, doubtless, only in secret that Grefenstein had ventured to express the opinion above referred to; for Luther, in the passage quoted, says that he feels authorized to mention him by name, inasmuch as he is no more among the living. And how very slight a lodgment—practically none whatever—such an influence can at that time have found in the mind of Luther himself, is manifest from the unreserved determination with which he immediately afterwards surrendered himself entirely to the service of the Church,

---

[1] Erl. Ed., xxv, 325.   [2] Briefe, i, 109.

[3] Erl. Ed., xxiv, 25.—Löscher, Reform. Akten, etc., i, 206, ventures only to say: "Luther *perhaps* heard also Grefenstein at Erfurt;" but it is hardly possible to think otherwise.

and with which he refused to harbor the thought of Huss's innocence. It must, indeed, have been a matter of great significance
for Luther afterwards that, when the reformatory spirit had been
independently awakened within him, he was able at once to recall
to mind utterances such as these as having fallen from the lips of
teachers so moderate in temper and held under such ecclesiastical
constraint. But it is to be observed, finally, that the writings of
Wesel by which we should have expected him to be most powerfully affected, *i. e.*, those in which were presented distinct reformatory principles, appear to have remained entirely unknown to
him. In the passage in which he refers to Wesel,[1] in the year
1539, he finds himself unable to assign any other reason for his
condemnation by the " desperate, proud murderers, the preaching monks," than that, instead of saying, " I believe that God is,"
he said, " I know that God is," just as all schools have held that
the existence of God is a matter of intuitive knowledge (Deum
esse per se notum sit). Evidently, therefore, he had even at that
time no knowledge whatever of Wesel's most important positions.
We must infer that the authorities at Erfurt, whilst wishing still
to honor the memory of their former celebrated teacher, expunged
and concealed but the more carefully on that account those
portions of his works by which they, as well as he, would have
been exposed to the charge of heresy.

It must be borne in mind that the original object of Luther's
studies would naturally lead him at this time to give his attention
first to the traditional Logic, then to the so-called Physics[2] and
Ethics, rather than to concern himself with the fundamental questions of philosophy and theology. Accordingly, it is only in connection with the continuation of his studies in the monastery that
Melanchthon speaks of his being occupied with the scholastics,
Biel and Occam.

With what interest and diligence he read the ANCIENT CLASSICAL
AUTHORS, is evident from the quotations from this source which
he was throughout his entire life so fond of weaving into his
writings wherever the connection would at all allow it. These
consist chiefly of sentiments from poets, especially those of the

[1] Erl. Ed., xxv, 325.

[2] His instructor, Truttvetter, published an " Epitome seu breviarium logice "
(1507) and an " Epitome seu breviarium dialectice." His chief work was the
" Summa totius philosophiæ naturalis, 1517.

Romish Church, and preferably such brief utterances as seemed to him to embody wholesome common-sense views of life or illustrations of practical wisdom. They remind us of the well-known saying of Melanchthon in regard to Luther's method in reading ancient authors. Such quotations meet us, for example, even in the sermons upon the Ten Commandments, published in 1516–1517,[1] which were entirely practical in their aim. We shall see what importance he afterwards, as a Reformer, attached to the study of these writers. He had little or no time to make their acquaintance at any later period of his life.[2] What he knew of them and had at his command must have been, at least in substance, a fruit of his early years at the University.

It is therefore the more remarkable that he was so slightly influenced by the peculiar spirit of the HUMANISM of that age, and that the further course of his life can in no sense be said to have been determined by it. It is well known that Erfurt was at that time one of the chief centres of Humanism in Germany.[3]

Before Luther's appearance at the University, humanistic studies had been there revived, especially through the agency of MATERNUS PISTORIS. NICHOLAS MARSCHALK, who, however, moved away in 1502, had rendered eminent service in promoting the study of Greek. He published, in 1501, the first book in the Greek language which ever issued from a German press. Already there were gathered around such teachers bold, ambitious, talented young men, who were soon afterward found winning glory for their own names. From the year 1503, there lived in the neighboring town of Gotha one of the most distinguished lights of Humanism, MUTIANUS RUFUS, who soon entered into intimate relations with men of like spirit at the University, especially with the younger among them.

Whilst we do not know that Luther himself attended the lectures of a Maternus, or any teachers of that class, it is at least certain that he was on terms of intimate friendship with a number of young men who were zealously engaged in the humanistic

[1] Op. Exeg. Erl., Vol. XII. Cf. *e. g.*, pp. 169 sqq.

[2] Cf. Briefe, ii, 314 (in 1523): Saepius indignor mihi, hac aetate et his moribus non permitti tempus aliquando poëtas et rhetoras versandi.

[3] Comp. Jürgens, i, 448 sqq. But especially for the following section, comp. Kampschulte, die Univers. Erfurt in ihrem Verhältnisse zu dem Humanismus und der Reformation, Part I. 1858.

agitation. The most enduring friendship of his Erfurt days was that of JOHANN LANGE. The latter was distinguished for an acquaintance with Greek remarkable for that day, which he probably acquired through Marschalk. When Luther in 1516, in the exercise of his authority as Vicar of the Augustinian order, appointed him Prior of the monastery at Erfurt, he commended him by letter to Mutianus with the remark, that Lange was already known to the latter as a Greek and Latin scholar.[1] GEORGE SPALATIN, whose relations with Luther also reach back to the time when they were together at Erfurt, was on intimate terms with Mutianus, received his first appointment through the mediation of the latter, and upon his recommendation was selected as tutor of the electoral prince. Luther was at that time intimate with yet another man who attained eminence as one of the most zealous and talented among the younger humanists, CROTUS RUBIANUS,[2] who had entered the University at Erfurt as a student in 1498, and received the bachelor's degree in 1500. He himself speaks of his association with Luther at Erfurt in a letter of October, 1519, in which, greatly delighted at the public appearance of the latter as a Reformer, he renews his friendly relations with him.[3] He writes (in Latin) : " With the closest intimacy we together devoted our toil at Erfurt to the noble arts in the days of our youth, at which time, amid similar habits, the very firmest foundations of friendship are laid. A thunderbolt from heaven drove you from our band of associates, most deeply grieved by your departure, within Augustinian walls. Although since that time our intimacy has been slight, my heart has always remained yours." In a later letter (April 4, 1520), he observes : "You were the musician and erudite philosopher of our old circle."[4] This friendly intercourse continued for quite a long time. Thus Luther, in 1523, printed as a preface to one of his writings a letter addressed to Crotus. At about the same time Luther spoke of him as " our most genial Crotus."[5]

[1] Briefe, i, 22.

[2] Jürgens appears to have no knowledge whatever of his relation to Luther.

[3] Ulrichi Hutten opera. ed. Bocking, 1859, i, 309 sqq.—Mieg, monumenta pietatis et literaria, etc. Frankf., 1702, i, 12 sqq.

[4] Ulr. Hut. Op., i, 340 (from a letter never before printed).

[5] Briefe, ii, 358 sqq. Compare the forms of address : " Optime Crote," " Mi Crote," Briefe, ii, 313.

We do not, however, find any evidence that Luther cultivated further intimacy with the circles of humanists during his student years,
nor that they took particular notice of him.   He is not mentioned
in any of the many letters and poems of the day, issuing from the
circle of Mutianus and the Erfurt humanists, which have been
preserved to us.   We cannot, for example, discover that he was at
that time even upon terms of friendship with COBAN HESS, whose
name was entered upon the roll at Erfurt in 1504, and who there
quickly attracted the attention of the humanists.   At a later date
the two became very intimate.   Hess asked permission in 1523
to dedicate to the Reformer a poem which he had composed and
was about to publish: and Luther was afterwards particularly
pleased with his poetic rendering of the Psalms.   He calls him
" a royal poet and a poetic king." [1]   Luther's letters of this
period give no indication, however, that the relations with Hess
had been already established at Erfurt.   ULRICH HUTTEN, having been acquainted with Crotus at an earlier period, was by
his influence drawn to Erfurt, but not until the year 1506, at
which time Luther had already been withdrawn from his earlier
associates by his entrance to the monastery.   We know nothing
more concerning the beginning of the relations of Hutten and
Luther than that they corresponded as early as 1520.   None of
Luther's letters to him are extant. [2]   With Mutian it is evident
that Luther entered into no personal relations during his student-
life at Erfurt.   In the above-mentioned letter addressed to him
in 1516, he describes their " mutual friendship " as one of such
recent origin that he did not feel himself authorized by it, upon
the occasion of a brief sojourn in Gotha, to call upon the distinguished man.   And, far from attempting to make use of his own
classical studies, of which Mutian might possibly have some recollection, as a point of contact between the two, he, in addressing
the learned, highly-cultivated man, describes himself as " that
rustic Coridon, Martin, barbarous and always accustomed to
cackling among the geese."

How much can we now really recognize of any influences

---

[1] Briefe, ii, 312; iv, 137.—Comp. also iii, 306; iv, 6; v, 74 (Letters from
the years 1523–1537).

[2] Comp. Briefe, i, 445, 451, 468; vi, 20, etc.—Upon Hutten's arrival at
Erfurt, comp., together with Kampschulte, also Strauss, Ulr. v. Hutten, i
23 sqq.

which, during his stay at the nursery of Humanism and his intercourse with the young friends named, that movement itself may
have exerted upon him, or of the part which he may himself have
borne in promoting it?

That it attracted him as well as others, and that he was capable
of appreciating it, is manifest from what we know of his reading
of the classics, and also from the friendships which have been
mentioned.   Nevertheless, its real influence upon him appears to
us, as already indicated, to have been comparatively very limited.

If we confine our inquiry to his study of the ancient languages
and authors as such, we observe that his knowledge of Greek does
not appear to have been as yet acquired to any great extent.
This may, indeed, be in great measure accounted for by the departure of Marschalk, the teacher of this language, some time
before.   But we have already seen from his letter to Mutian how
little he felt himself at home in classical Latin.   It is probably
not without significance, that Crotus in the above-quoted passage,
in which he speaks of Luther's eminence as a philosopher, says
nothing of his philological attainments.   His own inclination evidently led him, even when associating with these friends, to prefer
the investigation of the truths of philosophy.   Even in the reading of the classics, it appears, as we have already remarked, to
have been chiefly the contents, and particularly the rules prescribed for the wise conduct of life, that attracted him.   Confessing, at a later date, that he was not well-versed in Latin, he yet
indicates that he may, indeed, at one time have known a little
more about it. [1]   It is clear, too, from his letters to Crotus, Hess,
Mutian and Erasmus, that he was by no means lacking either in a
due appreciation of the elegance of diction for which they were
so justly noted, or in the ability to develop to no small degree a
similar style in his own writings.   Nor can we fail to note very
distinctly in his later life the formal advantage derived from
classical studies for the apt, easy and harmonious arrangement and
employment of the subject matter of teaching.   But he was, nevertheless, always fond of representing himself, in comparison with
such men, as we have already seen in the case of Mutian, as a
barbarian upon this field of culture.   The effort to attain a
proper form of diction was always with him far overbalanced by

---

[1] Briefe, v, 211 (1539); Ego latine neque peritus, ac, si peritus fuissem,
desuetudine ⸺ ⸺ ⸺ imperitus.

direct and purely religious interest in his theme. His language never seeks a beautiful form; but either, when assuming it, does so as the natural and unpremeditated expression of clear, vivid ideas, or, as much more frequently, neglects the form altogether, under the weight of the thoughts that fill his mind, and the pressure of powerful and intense inward excitement. Then, too, along with the results of classical culture, his language displays, to an at least equal extent, the influence of his natural, spontaneous mode of expression and his constant intercourse with the common people, from whom he sprung and in whose interest he was called upon to speak. Just in this we recognize again a peculiar higher destiny, which did not permit him to enter any more deeply than he did into the humanistic movement. We know to what an extent others were by this very means deprived of ability to work directly upon the common people.

But the chief matters of moment for us here are, after all, the significance of the humanistic studies for the cultivation of a free, clear intellectual vision, by which afterwards, in the sphere of religion, the distinction between self-evidencing truth and error firmly entrenched in tradition should be readily detected, and before which the restrictions imposed by deeply-rooted opinions and mere empty authorities must vanish; and, particularly, the free criticism of the scholastic character of the prevailing philosophy and theology, to which the spirit, form and contents of the classical literature inevitably led, and which was itself further led to direct assaults upon ecclesiasticism and tradition in general by the very fact that it proved such an occasion of offence to the champions of the existing church life and traditions. Luther himself afterwards [1] compared the renewed interest in the languages and sciences to a John the Baptist preparing the way for a new revelation of the divine Word. On the other hand, we must always, when thinking of the relation of Humanism to the Reformation, keep in view also the traces of a secularized spirit, which inclined many, even among the German humanists, to a renunciation, not only of the prevailing ecclesiasticism, but of the Christian faith and Christian life in general.

It is to be particularly noted, however, that in the immediate circles at Erfurt there was as yet, so long as Luther studied there, no manifestation whatever of a tendency in Humanism hostile to

[1] Briefe, ii, 313.

the Church or even to Scholasticism. A marked characteristic of Maternus Pistoris was his peaceable and even friendly attitude toward the representatives of the old system, while the latter looked without distrust upon the new life and activity, and even regarded it with favor. Thus Göde, the teacher of ecclesiastical jurisprudence, although clinging tenaciously to tradition and afterwards manifesting great hostility toward the Reformation, encouraged the young poets and was greatly admired by them in return. In the soul of Mutian,[1] indeed, the tendency referred to had already appeared and was gaining strength ; in fact, we have expressions from him in which he manifests, not only an exalted independence of ecclesiastical ordinances, but a spirit which threatens on philosophical grounds to refine away the specific content of Christianity itself. But, upon the other hand, he himself again recoils from such a possible conclusion, not only recommending evangelical and theological studies in contradistinction to those purely secular, but himself also personally resuming the observance of religious and ecclesiastical exercises. Thus his friendship could be sought not only by the humanists at Erfurt, but even by such a man as Göde. It was only in later years, after Luther's entrance into the monastery, that he conceived a bitter aversion toward the barbarians, sophists and scholastics, which his young friends at Erfurt, eager for the conflict, made their own. Yet, among the young men who stood in peculiarly close relations with him, many remained, even after this, faithful to a genuine churchly position. Thus, notably, Luther's friend, Spalatin, of whom it is related that before entering upon his position as tutor in 1509 he read mass for thirty days, hoping thereby to win blessing from heaven. Of all the men hitherto named, Crotus was doubtless the most strongly inclined toward the tendency of which we speak. Already at the time of his association with Luther in 1504, he induced the youthful Hutten to escape from the cloister Fulda, or at least rendered him assistance in doing so. In the opening assaults of the followers of Mutian upon the old system, he was at once brought into prominence by his keen and ready wit. That, nevertheless, with all his aversion to the prevalent ecclesiasticism and with all the boldness

---

[1] What Strauss has to say of Mutian's ecclesiastical and religious standpoint, in his " Ulrich von Hutten," is one-sided, as may be very clearly seen from the evidence presented by Kampschulte.

of his ridicule, he yet retained even to a later day, and upon
occasion manifested, a deep religious interest, is proved by his
letters to Luther after the breaking out of the indulgence controversy. We should by no means be justified in accounting it
a mere accommodation to Luther's style, that, together with quotations from classical authors, he addresses to him also encouraging words of Scripture and, with a distinct acknowledgment of
human sinfulness, joyfully embraces the evangelical doctrine of
justification by faith in opposition to the merit of human works.[1]
He afterwards, indeed, when the hour of real conflict had come,
displayed the lack of depth in his convictions, and especially the
absence of a deeper ground of faith and life, by shrinking from the
struggles and sacrifices involved and becoming an humble servant
of the archbishop, Albrecht of Mentz. Luther then denounced
him as an Epicure and a flatterer of the ecclesiastical princes.[2]

In regard to Luther himself, it is, first of all, beyond question
that he never suffered himself by his association with any of the
humanists to be diverted into any path hostile to Christianity in
general, still less to be inclined toward the adoption of frivolous
views of life. When we find him afterwards, as a Reformer,
speaking always with deepest Christian earnestness even in his
intercourse with the cultured men of the world who were on
terms of friendship with him, and habitually charging with Epi-
cureanism as the ground of their conduct those humanists who
from an original participation in the reformatory movement had
passed over to a position of indifference or hostility, it is impossible for us to think of him as a man conscious of having himself
once walked in the paths which he now denounces. Of his Erfurt
friends, it is certain that Johann Lange was upon terms of closer
intimacy with him by far than any other; and it is just he who
from this time forward stands pre-eminent for his genuine Christian character. It was in view of this that Luther appointed him
to the position of Prior at Erfurt. In his letter to Mutian, while
mentioning the classical culture of Lange, he commends him far
more highly as a " man of pure heart." We recall also, in this
connection, what has just been said of Spalatin.

---

[1] Comp. the two letters above quoted, especially the second (1520). To the
interval between these two belongs the one quoted by Böcking, 307 sqq., and
by Mieg, 11 sq. (1519).

[2] Briefe, iv, 311 (1531).

But even those features of Humanism, which were calculated to prepare the soil for a genuine evangelical awakening, and which really rendered this service in the case of important later champions of the Reformation, exerted their influence upon Luther only to a very limited extent. They utterly failed to shake his confidence in the position which led him to submit himself unconditionally to the faith and authority of the Church. It is in perfect harmony with the observations already made as to the condition of affairs in general at Erfurt, that he did not at all obtrude his position in a blunt, offensive way upon others, but rather occupied himself with more general scientific investigations, yet maintaining at the same time undisturbed his own convictions. That this was really the case, is proved by his adoption immediately afterward of the monastic life. In taking this step, he is evidently not returning to views which he had at one time abandoned, or in which his confidence had ever been shaken; but before the influences of humanistic study had even begun to affect his ecclesiastical convictions, they were neutralized by a tendency in his religious life and in his religious and ecclesiastical intuition which they had never been able to suppress, and which now for the first time fully asserted itself. The influences referred to were not, however, upon this account fruitless. They made themselves felt after the great revolution in the faith and inner life of Luther. The studies at Erfurt no doubt contributed very materially to the freshness and clearness of intellectual vision which he afterwards displayed. But it was another power which *originally* broke the fetters of his spirit and brought about that revolution itself. In the case, likewise, of every separate article of the ancient faith which he afterwards came to regard as delusion and superstition, the original impulse to a bold rejection came, as we shall further see, not from any objections of general intellectual culture or science, but directly from the central point of his own religious life.

Summing up briefly our results as to the scientific influences under which Luther developed as a student, we find that they afford important preliminary conditions for the proper equipment of the future Reformer; but, so far from having originally incited him to reformatory temper and activity, they were not even able to render the service for which they were providentially appointed, until a tendency which in spite of them maintained itself within

him had completed its development, and had been overcome
without their assistance by means of an entirely different character.

Calling to mind, finally, the few details within our reach touching specifically Luther's INNER RELIGIOUS LIFE itself during the years
in question, we must give prominence to the statement of Mathesius, that he began his studies every morning with earnest prayer
and church attendance, observing already at that time his maxim :
" To have prayed diligently is to have studied more than half the
lesson." We have evidence of the constant, warm, religious interest, which inspired him even during his philosophical course and
made him long for fuller satisfaction than the Church afforded, in
the great joy with which he, when a bachelor of philosophy, twenty
years of age, in the library at Erfurt, grasped the first complete
copy of the Bible upon which his eye had ever rested. He declared that he would count himself perfectly happy could he
but be permitted to own the book himself. He soon afterwards
bought a postil, which contained at least more extracts from
Scripture than the commonly-read pericopes from the Gospels.[1]
He himself declares :[2] " I was for fifteen years a monk, *besides
the time I had lived before that*—and yet I was never able to draw
comfort from my baptism, but always thought : O, when will you
ever become pious and do enough to make God gracious to
you? And it was such thoughts that drove me to become a
monk." He here represents the spiritual condition described as
extending also over the period of his student-life. But this distressed state of mind cannot have been manifest at that time, at
least not in any open, decided or effective way, in the presence of
his acquaintances and friends. His resolution to enter the monastery was a complete surprise to them. Association with such
young men as Crotus can scarcely be conceived of as possible,
unless his spirit, with all sense of inward oppression, had been
capable also of free, fresh youthful excitement, and in such company enjoyed it. His friends must have recognized in him,
despite the moral earnestness of his bearing, the " lively and
cheerful young comrade " which Mathesius in the context of the
above-quoted passage declares him to have been. But it is by
no means irreconcilable with this, that the timid, restless state of

[1] Mathesius, p. 6. Tischreden, Först., iii, 229.—Erl. Ed., lx. 255.—Colloquia, etc., Cod. chart. bibl. duc. Goth. (in Jürgens i, 488.)

[2] Erl., Ed., xvi, 90.

mind referred to should have nevertheless furnished the key-note of his hidden inner life. Thus, with all the quickening power which the pursuit of the fine arts and liberal sciences and association with like-minded companions exert upon a youthful spirit, the lack of true, abiding peace may nevertheless make itself constantly felt; and this feeling will but the more effectually lay hold upon and overpower a noble soul, the more clearly the latter shall realize that these efforts and pursuits, so noble in themselves, are not able to satisfy the divinely-implanted impulse toward higher things nor to quench the spiritual thirst. But Luther had been hitherto unable to find at Erfurt either counsel in his spiritual distress or means of deliverance from it. He had not during his stay at Erfurt, he afterwards assures us,[1] listened to a single genuine Christian lecture or sermon. We recall the expressions already quoted in regard to the state of affairs under the Papacy, which he had himself experienced. The passage in the Psalm which commands us to fear God, he hated when a "youth." This points particularly to his student-years. Christ, as the one true Advocate and Mediator, was hidden from the eyes of those who prayed. When Luther's life was threatened by an accidental injury, he called upon the Virgin Mary in his distress, and would have died, he afterwards relates, depending upon her.[2] He would have thought himself most highly favored at that time if he "could have heard a Gospel lesson, or even a little Psalm." Only for a moment had he been permitted to handle with delight that Bible in the library. "How deeply," he exclaims, "was the Scripture buried there, while we were so exceedingly hungry and thirsty for it, and there was no one to give us anything from it."[3]

Suddenly, and under the pressure of peculiar occurrences, Luther at length dropped his secular studies and hastened to the cloister. In his own writings we find no account of the outward circumstances. We have, however, no reason to doubt the report found already in Mathesius;[4] the incidents there recorded were afterwards combined and further adorned by legendary tradition. First of all, it is said, a good friend of his was fatally stabbed. Then " a heavy storm and a dreadful clap of thunder greatly terri-

[1] Briefe, iii, 228.

[2] Colloquia, etc., cod. chart. Goth., in Jürgens.

[3] Briefe, iii, 228.   [4] In the first Sermon.

fied him," and, "deeply alarmed in view of the wrath of God and
the day of judgment," he resolved and vowed to enter the monastery.[1] The mention of the thunder storm fixes the time within
the limits of the summer season. We know, too, that Erfurt
suffered in that same summer from a visitation of the pestilence,
which became so severe that students and teachers fled from the
town. It might be supposed that this had something to do with
Luther's serious and timid frame of mind; but he had already
entered the monastery before the flight occurred, for Crotus, who
was evidently in Erfurt when Luther took that step, was among
the fugitives. But we know enough of Luther's whole previous
course of life to recognize how fully he had been prepared by his
inward development for the step which he now took. Even he
himself traced it back to the experiences of his childhood. From
his very earliest days, the tendency which now under deep impressions so powerfully asserts itself and tears him away from the
path which his chosen studies appeared to have marked out for
him had been taking root in the deepest foundations of his inner
nature. This accounts for the firm determination with which he
clung to the resolution now at length formed, and carried it out
so quickly and independently, as though filled with anxious dread,
lest anything should yet cause him to hesitate in its accomplishment. Thus he was, for example, particularly careful not to
secure his father's opinion before carrying out his design, which
was according to the judgment of the Church perfectly right and
proper (" recht und wohlgethan "), since the service of God,
required in the First Commandment, takes precedence of the
Fourth Commandment.[2] He himself represents to his father
that he has been called into the cloister " by means of a terrifying manifestation from heaven," [3] meaning evidently, in particular,
the impression received in the thunderstorm.

[1] Compare especially also the passage from the letter of Crotus: Te redeun-
tem a parentibus *coeleste fulmen* veluti alterum Paulum ante oppidum Erfurd-
ianum in terram prostravit atque intra Augustiniana septa compulit, etc.

[2] Erl. Ed., x, 379 sq.

[3] Briefe, ii, 101.

3. In the Monastery—Self-Righteousness and the Righteousness of God.
A. D. 1505–A. D. 1508.

DELUSIVE HOPES—ZEALOUS TOIL—STUDIES—DISTRESS OF MIND—PRIESTHOOD—PREDESTINATION—HELP FROM SCRIPTURE—COUNSEL FROM A BROTHER—STAUPITZ—GERSON—AUGUSTINE—THE " RIGHTEOUSNESS GF GOD "—RESEMBLANCE TO ST. PAUL.

Luther himself has, in the language already quoted, explained to us his object in assuming monastic vows. He hoped in this way to become pious and by good works secure the favor of God. He often afterwards made reference to the thoughts which then controlled him. Whenever he speaks of the fascination exerted upon the minds of others by Monasticism, or of the illusions by which so many an upright, energetic Christian has been drawn within its toils, we realize to what an extent his utterance is prompted by the recollection of his own experience. To the monastery he was allured by the precious promises whose fulfilment was commonly supposed to be assured to all who entered such an institution, namely, " that the prayers offered by them should certainly be heard and answered, and whatever they might do should be well-pleasing to God and approved by him." In view of the obligations of ordinary Christian life, he had felt himself a sinner, a debtor, a child of wrath and condemnation. Now he was to enter a calling " which was far above the Ten Commandments," in which he should exercise himself in " far more and better works than those commanded in the Gospel." By this means he hoped finally to secure and merit the grace without which he must despair, and to blot out his sin and guilt.[1] Luther afterwards [2] describes the monastic ideas as a sweet allurement, a hellish, poisonous pill coated with sugar ; since it was exceedingly sweet to hear, and had a very agreeable taste to the reason, that a Christian could make himself pious, full of spiritual life and blessed, before Christ and his Holy Spirit should come near. " Yes," says he, " we wanted to climb up to heaven and slip into the kingdom before He should know what we were

[1] Cf. Erl. Ed., xlix, 314; xliv, 190; xlv, 154.
[2] Erl. Ed., xxxi, 279 sq.

about." In his own case, however, when fleeing to the cloister, this impulse of natural self-sufficiency was far overbalanced by the pressure of the inward distress from which, in the light of his entire previous religious education and training, he knew no better means of deliverance. Thus he could say of himself : " I did not become a monk from choice or free will, much less for the sake of my stomach and good living; but in the midst of alarm and terror of death, I was compelled and forced to make the vow." [1] Yet he could also at the same time account the resolution then formed as sinful, since he would not have suffered himself to be misled into the adoption of such means, if he had not, despite all the terrors that alarmed him, concealed and cherished in his heart a secret pride. What he at that time imagined to be a service of God, he afterwards recognized as idolatry, a service of self.

With unremitting energy he now devoted himself to all the exercises by which it was supposed that sin could be crucified, perfect holiness attained, and the grace of God won. He had no occasion to fear contradiction on the part of any one who knew him at that time, when he afterwards described how he there watched, fasted, froze, prayed, tortured and mortified his body, abused and tormented himself, trying to render obedience and make his flesh pure.[2] It is related, that the more he excelled the other monks in diligent application to study, the more exacting were the humiliating services demanded of him as a novice in the cloister, until it became necessary at length for the University to intercede in his behalf. According to a statement in the *Tischreden*, he was, even after entering the priesthood, not exempted from the duties of begging and " going to the villages for cheese." [3] But he never in later times, when he had learned to execrate and abhor the whole system of monkery, showed any ill humor in view of these personal humiliations. How submissively must he then have endured them in the days of his bondage ! To what extent he went in the matter of fasting, Melanchthon often afterwards observed with amazement—testifying that he upon one occasion neither ate nor drank anything for four days

---

[1] Briefe, ii, 101.

[2] Comp., *e. g.*, Erl. Ed., xlviii, 317; xlix, 27, 300.

[3] Erl. Ed., lx, 309. Först.,iii, 336.

in succession, and that a small piece of bread and a herring often satisfied him for an entire day.[1] He could himself testify : " It is true, I was a pious monk, and so strict in the performance of my duties that I can say : ' If ever a monk reached heaven through monkery, I would surely have entered there.' All my friends at the cloister will bear witness to this, for if it had lasted any longer, I should have tortured myself to death with watching, praying, reading and other work." [2]

It was but natural that he should now utterly refuse to harbor any thought which might threaten to disturb his unconditional acquiescence in the Romish ecclesiasticism and its decisions touching heresy. We recall the expression which he had once heard from the lips of Grefenstein in regard to Huss. A book containing some sermons of Huss now fell into his hands in the cloister library. Curious to see what the arch-heretic had taught, and feeling justified in the investigation since his book had been there preserved unburned, he found so much that he was filled with amazement, and wondered why such a man, able to handle the Scriptures in such a Christian spirit and so power-fully, should have been burned. But, as the name of Huss rested under such fearful condemnation that he thought the walls would become black and the sun be darkened if it were even men-tioned, he closed the book and went away with a bleeding heart. He found some consolation in the thought, that Huss had perhaps written these things before he became a heretic.[3] Luther after-wards declared [4] that he was when a monk such a rabid papist, that he would have been ready to murder all who should by even the smallest syllable refuse obedience to the Pope, or at least would have found pleasure in their murder and would have helped to accomplish it.

At the same time he applied himself with all diligence to the study of the scholastic writers. Nominalism was the ruling system of philosophy at Erfurt. Luther himself, whilst able afterwards in the presence of his enemies to claim a thorough acquaintance with all the leaders of the scholastic theology, yet followed, in the main, the Nominalists, Gabriel Biel, Peter D'Ailly and William of Occam. The two first named, according to the

[1] Vita Luth., p. 5.   [2] Erl. Ed., xxxi, 273.
[3] Ibid., lxv, 81.   [4] In the preface to his Latin works.

testimony of Melanchthon, he knew almost by heart. He preferred the acute-minded Occam to Thomas Aquinas and Duns
Scotus. Nominalism had in Occam already displayed, as a
natural result of its essential character, an inclination toward a
critical, skeptical tendency. His dialectics threatened in the
end to refine away the very dogmas which he was yet with unswerving orthodoxy laboring to expound. In the sphere of
ecclesiastical theology, Occam already, and, after him, D'Ailly,
had pronounced against the supreme power of the Papacy. We
may well believe that the acquaintance which Luther here gained
with Occam in particular may have subsequently exerted a
decided influence in the formation of his reformatory convictions.
The latter remained for him without doubt " the chief and most
highly-gifted of the scholastic doctors." [1]   But it was through
influences of another kind that the doctrine of the scholastic
writers, and especially that of the Nominalists, affected most
deeply his life and faith as a monk. The theological principles
which it inculcated directly confirmed him in the striving after a
righteousness of his own. This mock-theology (*theologistria*)
taught him that human merit must avail upon the way of salvation ; that the commandments of God may be perfectly obeyed, at
least with respect to the substance of the deed, even if not according to the intention of Him who gave the commandment ; that
man may with free will decide one way or the other ; that the
will by its natural powers can love God, etc.[2]

Thus did Luther seek his salvation at the monastery.   But the
more strenuously he exerted himself to attain it in this way, the
farther was he from finding it.   Upon the contrary, the inward
assailment against which he had sought protection now reached
its culmination.

The promises touching the grace assured to the monastic state
were discovered to be most sadly false.   He was never able,
says he,[3] to convince himself that his works, even when most
diligently performed, were well pleasing to God.   He never,
with all his self-mortification and chastity, reached an assured
conviction that God was graciously inclined toward him.   He

---

[1] Respons. ad artic. Lovaniens, Luth. Op. Jen. (1556), T. i, 501 b.

[2] Briefe, i, 304.

[3] Erl. Ed., xlix, 314, 168; i, 103; xvii, 139.

was never able to realize that his strict life had been of any help to him, or that it gave him any claim to heaven.   Never, despite the greatest diligence in prayer, confession, etc., had he ventured to believe that he possessed the Holy Spirit, or even that his prayers were heard.   The reason of this was, that by this very working and doing he was seeking his own righteousness.   But he was always pointed, says he, to these works of his own.   It was in this that he afterward recognized the characteristic feature of papal doctrine.   Thus, he was expressly taught that no one can be assured of the favor of God.   The Pope, says he, had utterly forbidden such assurance, and was accustomed to quote, for the sake of appearance and as a pretext, the passage in Eccles. ix. 1 (Vulgate) : " No man knoweth whether he is worthy of love or of hatred."   In this Luther afterwards saw the reason why all his praying failed to profit him.   He had never prayed with the confidence that his prayer was well-pleasing to God ; but his thoughts had always been turned upon the reflection that he had kept his vow of obedience to his Order and the Church, had read his mass, and said his appointed prayers.   Three elements of devotion were held to be necessary to constitute a proper prayer, namely, the *material*, that the words of the prayer be repeated by the mouth ; the *formal*, that there be an understanding of that which is read ; the *emotional*, that the heart breathe a sigh and say, " O Lord, help," etc.   But no one knew anything about coming to God in the name of Christ, as chickens nestling beneath the wings of the hen.   Instead of this, men placed confidence in their own righteousness and in the merit of their prayers, which were right and precious because the petitioner had understood the words and desired the blessings asked for.   With all this, the heart remained without faith and full of despair.   Luther still heard, indeed, from the pulpit of a blotting out of sin and debt, accomplished by the Redeemer.   But this was supposed to have reference only to original sin and to the grace of baptism, once bestowed but forfeited by subsequent transgression.   Satisfaction must then be further rendered by the sinner himself.   " My heart," says he, " was poisoned by this popish doctrine, that I had polluted my baptismal-robe, had lost Christ and my baptism, and must now help myself." [1]   It was in view of this loss that the mo-

[1] Erl. Ed., xliv, 124, 127; xvii, 139, 140; xliv, 354.

nastic life and " monastic baptism " had been highly commended
to him.　He at one time heard a most highly esteemed Dominican
friar declare that, " even though one should regret the assuming
of his cloister-vow, or if one should have lost all his former good
works, it would only be necessary to turn about again and form a
new resolution, and the offender would then be again as pure
as though fresh from his baptism, and that thus new baptism
and innocence could always be again secured.　" There we young
monks sat," says he, " with gaping mouths and nostrils, overcome with devout feelings in view of such a comforting discourse ;
and thus this opinion became prevalent among the monks." [1]
But he himself was only too soon compelled to taste the poison
that lay beneath this sugar-coating.

Driven to doubt the grace of God, Luther was at once filled
with dread of judgment and perdition ; bidden to look to his own
works, he saw at once impending over him all the terrors of the
inflexible divine Law, in accordance with which the heart and life
of man are to be judged.　He fled from the God whose grace
he sought in vain to secure.　Thus it is, he afterward declared,[2]
with all who try by their own working to satisfy the divine
requirements, and who must yet feel that they cannot keep the
Law.　He was himself, says he, once such a pupil of the Law.
What had he to hope for from his prayers, if the acceptance of
these was to be dependent upon his own purity and his own
merit?

He fled for refuge to supposed available mediators before God,
seeking to find outside of himself a " rock and foundation for
prayer " ; but he selected for this purpose " not Christ, but St.
George, St. Vincent, etc."　Seeking thus to find protection against
the distress occasioned by his sins, he followed an impulse which
he afterwards recognized as itself essentially sinful.　" Nature," says
he, " is altogether too much inclined to flee from God and Christ,
and to place confidence in men." [3]　Christ, on the contrary, now
assumed for him entirely that character in which, as he says, the
Saviour was by the perversions of the Papacy commonly made to
appear.　" I did not," says he, " believe on Christ, but regarded
Him only as a stern and terrible judge, as He was seen in paint-

---

[1] Erl. Ed., xxxi, 280.　　　　　[2] Ibid., xlvi, 73.

[3] Ibid., xliv, 355 ; lxv, 120.

ings, sitting on a rainbow." Even when he thought of Christ as hanging upon the cross, he found no comfort there; for he had forfeited the grace of the cross of Christ, sinning directly against it, and thought that he must first of all regain the friendship of the Lord by his own works. He declares, upon the other hand : " When I beheld Him upon the cross, He appeared to me like a flash of lightning ; when His name was mentioned, I would rather have heard the devil's name pronounced ; I shrank back in terror when I saw His picture, closed my eyes, and would rather have seen the devil." He therefore turned again to the saints and to his own works and merit. He testified at a later day : " I did all this, not for the sake of money or property, but for God's sake." He did it, he declares, in ignorance, and always " went about as in a dream. But nevertheless it was idolatry." He was yet to experience, to the last degree, the anguish of soul which is the inevitable accompaniment of such a course of life.[1]

But with all his striving thus by his own efforts to attain perfection and holiness, he did not even feel that he was making any progress in this direction. " I was very much in earnest," says he, " in the determination to become pious ; but how long did it last? Only until the mass was ended. One hour afterwards I was more wicked than before." " Even when we tried to be chaste, and tortured ourselves with fastings, the more we sought to guard against sinful lust the more did it assail us." The multifarious trifling regulations of the Church and the Order afforded the misled conscience, moreover, constant occasion to accuse itself of transgression of the divine Law, when there was in truth no ground for such accusation. The alarmed conscience invented sins where there were none. Luther afterwards, taught thus by his own experience, gives warning against " whimsical sins," and against " wanton sins, half-sins and imaginary sins." [2]

Luther was ordained a priest in 1507. His father, though still unreconciled, was present at the attendant festivities, but, when assured by his honored son that the latter had entered the monastery in obedience to a higher call, responded : " God grant that it may not prove to have been a delusion and an apparition of the devil." This response, Luther afterwards confessed, pene-

[1] Erl. Ed., xlix, 27 ; xlv, 156; xliv, 127.
[2] Ibid., xlviii, 201, 263. Jena, ii, 540.

trated to the depths of his soul, as though it had been spoken by
God himself. But he " closed and barred his heart against the
thought as well as he could." [1] He pressed forward with zeal
upon the path upon which he had entered, and his heart continued to throb and tremble in the vain endeavor to secure the
favor of God.[2] It was for him a matter of the very gravest moment, that he was now counted worthy to hold mass and thus
bring sacrifices to God for the living and the dead. This appeared to afford him the opportunity of performing an especially
excellent meritorious work of devotion. He had no rest, therefore, unless he held mass daily; which he most conscientiously
did, as he has himself testified.[3] We have already seen how his
thoughts had been turned in this same direction, when seeking
in his prayers to meet the approval of God and gain a gracious
response. Now, in administering this awfully holy ordinance,
he realized in his soul but an increased sense of responsibility and
a deeper sense of guilt. How should he, himself so impure,
worthily administer it? He was overwhelmed with terror, when
he for the first time undertook to present the offering before God
with the words: " We offer to Thee, the Living, the True and
the Eternal." How should *he* address the supreme Majesty?
Here came again, especially in the administration of the mass,
the multitude of trifling yet strictly prescribed forms. It was
represented to him as a most grievous sin to omit even a single
word, or even to stutter in repeating the words of institution. In
the *Tischreden*, he relates that he almost died during the administration of his first mass; for his whole concern was for his own
personal worthiness, and lest he should omit any of the prescribed
gestures or ceremonies.[4] He was subject to conflicting inclinations. He thought it a duty to celebrate mass as often as possible, and yet, as he afterwards acknowledges, he never celebrated
it willingly.[5]

While Luther was thus deeply concerned for his salvation, his
profoundly penetrative and inquisitive spirit was led back to the

---

[1] Briefe, ii, 101.   [2] Erl. Ed., xlv, 156.

[3] Op. Exeg. Erl., x, 232.—Erl. Ed., xvii, 139.

[4] Op. Exeg. Erl., vi, 158—Erl. Ed., xxviii, 65—Tischreden, Erl. Ed., lix,
98; lx, 400 sq.

[5] Erl. Ed., xix, 39.

final, supreme, unfathomable questions touching eternal, divine fore-ordination or predestination, according to which the final destiny of every soul has been already determined in advance. He afterwards described this as the most terrible and dangerous snare with which the devil can entangle alarmed consciences to bring them to despair and ruin. He was himself at that time, he says, caught in it, and would have been drowned and would have long ago sunken into hell had not God sent him Gospel consolation.[1]

He was in great danger at this time, as he afterward declared, of being worn out in body and soul and perishing from sheer exhaustion. He learned from experience what is meant by " broken bones " (Ps. li. 8), an expression which none of his associates in the cloister were able to explain to him ; for he recognized in the words of the Law " the wrath of God and eternal death." [2] Melanchthon relates [3] that he was himself upon one occasion a witness of the power with which such deep, grievous thoughts concerning the wrath and the decree of God assailed and overpowered him. During a conversation upon this subject, he arose and, entering an adjoining room, cast himself upon the bed, crying out repeatedly : " He hath concluded all under sin, in order that He might have mercy upon all." It is well known how he upon one occasion, overcome with melancholy, shut himself up for some days in his room without admitting any one, and, when his friends at length broke open the door, was found lying in an unconscious condition upon the floor. This did not, indeed, occur during his life at the monastery, but within a few years afterward ; but we may infer from it what must have been his inward experiences at that earlier day, when he was yet in ignorance of the Gospel.[4] Hieronymus Duengersheim, of Ochsenfahrt, who afterwards became an opponent of Luther, relates an incident as occurring during the cloister-life of the Reformer, which, as the reporter was a contemporary and quotes his authority, must have had at least some foundation in fact, and in which we cannot but recognize a violent outbreak of the most fearful inward conflict and agony of soul. The narrator declares, that

[1] Briefe, v, 513—Op. Ex. Erl., vi, 296.

[2] Op. Ex. Erl., xix, 103.   [3] Vita Luth., 5.

[4] Seckendorf, Historia Lutheranismi, Lib. I, Sect. viii, Add. 3 ; comp. Jürgens, 286.

Dr. Johann Natin, the father in the Augustinian monastery at Erfurt to whom he frequently appeals in other connections, and with whom Luther for some time after his stay in Wittenberg sought to maintain friendly relations,[1] did not afterwards attempt to conceal the fact, that, as the Gospel lesson containing the account of the man possessed of the devil (Matt. xvii.) was being read in the church at Erfurt, Luther fell down in the choir and raved like one possessed.[2]   Luther himself, in the early period of his reformatory activity, speaks of pangs of purgatory which the living are already called upon to endure.   In evidence, he appeals to a certain sufferer of his acquaintance.   We shall make no mistake if we see in the latter the Reformer himself, speaking after the manner of the apostle Paul in 2 Cor. xii. 2.   He says (in Latin) : " I knew a man who declared that he had very often endured such torments, for a very brief interval of time indeed, but so great and so infernal as to be beyond the power of tongue to tell, of pen to write, or of any one, without himself experiencing, to believe ; so that, had they been continued, or had they lasted for a half-hour, or even for the tenth part of an hour, he would have utterly perished and all his bones would have been reduced to ashes."[3]   We readily believe him, when he afterwards assures us that he would then willingly have given up his life if he could thereby have purchased peace with Christ.[4]

We have dwelt the longer upon these experiences of Luther, because in them lies the key to the entire method with which he in consequence grasped, maintained, and in his teaching expounded, the truth revealed in the Gospel, starting always from a definite central position and proceeding preferably in certain definite directions.

He who lacks a spiritual understanding of that truth, viz., of the divinely appointed way of salvation, will either attribute Luther's experiences to physical disease, and be compelled, accordingly, to recognize also in the entire subsequent life of the Reformer, not only the after-effects of his youthful infirmities, but also constantly recurring new attacks of mental malady in

---

[1] Comp. Greetings to him in letters until 1520.   Briefe, i, 99, 256, 283, 397.

[2] Seidemann, Lutherbriefe, 1859, p. 12.

[3] Resolutiones disputationum de virtute indulgentiarum.   Löscher, ii, 217.

[4] Op. Ex. Erl., xx, 2S1, 282.

the midst of the most vigorous and healthy intellectual activity; or he will deem it necessary to search for some very special sins or sinful impulses as the cause of the persistent consciousness of guilt. We have already heard from Luther himself how far he was from being satisfied with his attempts at moral advancement during his monastic life, and how he was compelled to struggle against the power of sinful impulse. He gives prominent place, too, in this connection, to that particular impulse which tempts to the violation of the vow of chastity.[1] But it is by no means to be inferred from this that the power of sin and of the flesh was greater in him than in any other persons then or now attempting to walk in the way of legality and self-righteousness. He himself, on the contrary, always represents what he experienced in this respect as something from which no one making such attempt could be exempted. Over against fleshly lust in particular, there was in his case always found the most intense intellectual activity. If we discriminate between sins of the lower, or fleshly, and those of the higher, or intellectual life, his natural disposition, beyond all doubt, inclined him much more strongly toward the latter. No enemy among the contemporaries of the Reformer was able to raise any evil reports in regard to his past life in the former respect, although one did venture to accuse him of a certain stubbornness of opinion and controversial temper.[2] When, at a later period, Luther resolved to marry, he manifested a remarkable deficiency of carnal passion.[3] But, on the other hand, as a monk, while condemning himself, he was by others, and especially by those constantly associating with him, regarded as a model of holy living. Thus Dr. Natin, as Duengersheim further testifies, lauded him as one who "was, like another Paul, wonderfully converted to spirituality."[4] We can, therefore, as did he himself, see in his suffering nothing but that keenest sense of the vanity of all human striving, combined with consciousness of guilt and

[1] Cf. also Op. Ex. Erl., xx, 281 :—Eram alligatus contra naturam ad im purum coelibatum.

[2] Thus Oldekop, of Hildesheim, in the extracts from his Annals of the year 1508, in Lüntzel, Annahme des ev. Glaubensbek. von Seiten der Stadt Hildesheim, 1842, p. 154.

[3] Briefe, iii, 13.

[4] Seidemann, Lutherbriefe, 12–13.—Cf. Luther, Op. Ex. Erl., vii, 214: Tota vita mea erat speciosissima in aliorum oculis.

desert of punishment before God, which every one must have experienced before finding his Saviour in faith, and which is but the
more deeply felt, the more sincere the moral purpose, the more
earnest the effort, the more vivid the consciousness of the severity
of the divine Law. Men may call it pride for which he was compelled so painfully to atone ; but it was essentially the same pride
which runs through all self-righteous thought and conduct. The
peculiar providence of God in Luther's case consisted only in this,
that he was by it first so deeply and completely subjected to this
feeling of vanity and guilt, apparently so utterly abandoned to it,
in order that he might then also bear testimony to the entire and
full significance of grace. Most deeply did he realize in his own
experience that which Melanchthon heard him utter in tones of
distress : God concludes under sin, in order that He may have
mercy [p. 57]. He afterwards said, with special reference to his
own experience : " One must sit under the Law as in a sweating-
bath, suffering anguish and distress, in order that the Gospel may
have the right taste afterwards." [1] It was a circumstance, moreover, of far-reaching importance, that the encouragement which
he might have received from individual Christians of a more evangelical type, such as he afterwards found even under the papal
dominion, had been entirely denied him in the early portion of
his career. It was the Church then dominant whose doctrine
and practice in regard to the fundamental questions of salvation
he was thoroughly to test in his own experience, for it was by her
that he had been so unhappily led astray. He recognized, therefore, in the delusive fancy of self-righteousness the fundamental
error of the entire ecclesiastical system which he was called to
oppose, and was not tempted to waver in his judgment as to the
general character of the Papacy and its doctrines by the discovery of individual souls who amid all the darkness yet found
the light, nor even of such dogmatic formulas as presented the
error in question with some degree of moderation and prudence.

As over against the spiritual trials which he endured, and the
errors of the prevailing doctrines, which kept him in bondage in
this miserable state, it was always the Scriptures that brought to
Luther light, deliverance and life. We are told that, while yet
a novice in the cloister, he had in response to his own request

[1] Erl. Ed., xlviii, 202.

received a copy of the Bible in Latin, and had read it through with deep earnestness and prayer, committing a considerable part to memory. It was afterwards, indeed, taken from him by the brethren, and he was instructed to devote himself entirely to the study of the wisdom of the schools ; but he got possession of it again whenever he could, and always applied himself faithfully to its perusal.[1] Melanchthon mentions, as portions read at this time with special interest, the writings of the prophets and apostles.[2] We shall hereafter have occasion to speak of the confidence with which he himself frequently insists that the Scriptures are clear enough in themselves ; that they carry their own light within themselves, shedding it upon the souls of men by the power of the Spirit, without needing for their illumination the comments of the Church Fathers and teachers ; and that the experiences of life, above all, spiritual temptations, are intended to prepare the soul for the reception of this light, and to lead it to a proper under-standing of the Word. Thus, in his own case, he declares that the assaults of temptation led him to study his theology carefully and with ever increasing thoroughness ; that without these he could never have learned to understand the Holy Scriptures ; that the Pope, the universities and learned men, and through these the devil, by constantly importuning him, drove him to the Bible ; that he read it diligently, and thus at length reached a proper understanding of it.[3]

Nevertheless, it would be an error to regard the mere written Divine Word in itself as the source whence Luther derived help in the time of his greatest need. We have already observed that he had enjoyed occasional opportunities for the study of this from the very beginning of his cloister-life. But for him no ray of saving light had as yet arisen from it. The explanation of this is not to be found merely in the defectiveness of the trans-lation which fell into his hands ; nor only in the misleading expositions of the Roman Catholic commentators at his com-mand ; nor in the influence of the entire doctrinal system of the Church, by which his apprehension of scriptural statements was limited in advance : but the very condition of his own mind, which impelled him to seek comfort, beclouded also his vision of

---

[1] Mathesius, l. c.   [2] Vita Luth., 5.

[3] Tischreden, Erl. Ed., lvii, 99.   Först, i, 76.

the essential germ of saving scriptural truth, the testimony of the love and grace of God in Jesus Christ. Those passages of Scripture in which he found utterances of wrath and judgment were ever floating before his eyes. Even those in which he afterwards recognized a direct message of salvation were transformed for him into terrifying announcements. It was the spoken word of Christian brethren and fathers, or rather, a divine word presented to him through the medium of their lips, by which he was at length lifted out of his distress ; and then, gradually proceeding from this as a central point, he learned to grasp the entire message of salvation. The exclusive authority of the Scriptures for him—as he himself afterwards represents his own relation and that of all genuine Christians to the divine Word— and his conviction concerning the central point from which they must be viewed in order to rightly comprehend them did not depend upon his regard for these particular men or their office. The firm conviction of the sufficiency and the true sense of the Scriptures was wrought within him by the inner power of the Scriptures themselves and of their own light, which power he was by the grace of God permitted to experience in his own soul. He saw, indeed, in the service rendered by such brethren a divinely appointed, gracious guidance to that fountain, which should then by virtue of its own power refresh, invigorate and make sure of the enjoyment of God's grace all who should seek to draw directly from it. It always remained for him, too, a matter of special importance that, when God should through the mouth of such brethren send to a tempted brother the testimony of his grace, this should be offered by them to him, and appropriated by him directly and personally as a separate individual message and as meant just for him. We shall see that the Reformer's subsequent doctrine touching the application of redemption was essentially influenced by these experiences, particularly those through which he passed while yet at Erfurt.

Melanchthon and Mathesius tell us of an aged brother in the monastery, through whom the Word of grace in this way first found deep and effectual lodgment in his heart. The name of the man has been forgotten ; but in his blunt utterance we may see the starting-point of Luther's evangelical life, of his testimony in behalf of the Gospel, and of his awakening to the work of the Reformation. Luther having retailed the story of his temptations, this brother pointed out to him the meaning of faith, and of the words in the so-called Apostles' Creed : " I believe in the forgiveness of sins," explaining that we must not only believe in general that some persons are forgiven, which even the devils believe, or that David and Peter have attained forgiveness, but that it is God's commandment that every one should believe in for- giveness for himself.   His father confessor then directed his atten- tion also to a passage in a sermon of St. Bernhard, in which the latter likewise insists upon faith in such forgiveness of sins through Christ, and, in support of his position, appeals to the saying of St. Paul, that *man is gratuitously justified through faith.*   Luther himself, upon one occasion, speaking of the " teacher " to whom he had told his troubles (without doubt this same father con- fessor) relates that he was powerfully impressed by the question of the latter : " Do you then not know that the Lord himself has commanded us to hope (*i. e.,* in his forgiving grace) ?"   He was now convinced by this one word, " commanded," that he ought to believe the absolution ; he had, indeed, often heard it before, but without applying it in faith to himself.[1]   It was there- fore in the form of the *obedience of faith,* or *subjection* to the way of salvation graciously offered and *commanded* by God (comp. Rom. i. 5 and x. 3), that saving faith arose within him.   In reality, just at this point was attained the complete and decisive subjection of the Ego, in whose profoundest depths, despite all supposed humility and despairing self-abasement, the pride which strives to attain a righteousness of its own had hitherto main- tained its sway.   This it had been, which, without any conscious- ness of the fact upon Luther's part, had closed his heart against a real reception of the Word of grace.   Thus, again, the funda- mental experiences of Luther enable us to understand why he was afterwards so fond of representing the heart-felt, unconditional confidence in a merciful God, which presents the direct opposite of man's own working, as the fulfilment of the First Command- ment, and self-righteousness, upon the contrary, as a fundamental transgression of it.

For the greatest advancement in his believing knowledge of the way of grace and peace, he had now to thank JOHANN STAUPITZ. The latter in 1503 had been elected Vicar-General of the Augus-

[1] Op. Ex. Erl., xix, 100.

tinian Order. Upon his visits to the monastery at Erfurt, he
became interested in Luther. He admonished the prior to treat
the studious monk with less rigor, and to allow him more time
for his studies. But especially did he manifest a paternal interest
in the spiritual troubles which the latter himself confessed to
him. Luther often, in his later life as a Reformer, finds occasion
to speak of the encouraging and instructive words of counsel
received from him. Very often, too, in the directions which he
himself afterwards gave to other souls, we catch again the very
words which he has reported to us as heard from the lips of
Staupitz.

Unfortunately, all the publications of Staupitz which have been
preserved to us bear a later date, as, for example, his little tract
upon Predestination (1516), his *Von der holdseligen Liebe Gottes*
(1518), and doubtless also his *Von unserem christlichen Glau-
ben.*[1] It is a question whether the living seed, which under his
quickening influence had grown so vigorously in Luther's soul,
had not meanwhile also borne fruit in his own life. The two had
since then maintained an intimate acquaintance ; and we shall see
how far the development of Luther's evangelical views had already
progressed by the year 1516. Hence the precise theological position of Staupitz during the time when Luther's relation to him was
one of pure receptivity cannot be determined from these writings.
Nevertheless, from all that we know of him, we can at least clearly
enough discern how well-fitted, on the one hand, were his religious tendency and his theological views to exert such quickening
influence upon Luther at that time, and, on the other hand, how
far short they fell of attaining the intelligent faith to which the
latter under their stimulus advanced.

If we take into view the contents of these later writings, it
might at the first glance appear that Staupitz had in them already
announced, at least in its essential features, the entire fundamental truth touching salvation, and that there was lacking only
the thorough-going open conflict with the opposing errors then
dominant in the Church. In treating of God, His love is exalted
above everything else. He is declared to be Love itself, than

[1] The two last-named were republished by Joh. Arndt, and afterwards again
appeared as reprints (Strassburg, 1624; Frankfurt a. M., 1692); *Von der
holdseligen Liebe Gottes* recently again in Stuttgart.—I have unfortunately
not had access to the tract upon Predestination (see extracts in Jürgens, i, 59.)

which nothing more love-like (*lieblich*) can be experienced, and which makes love-like everything upon which it falls. The entire life of true Christians as such, or life in the state of salvation, is made to depend upon the fact that this love of God is poured out through the Holy Spirit into the hearts of the elect. The whole weight falls upon this act of grace. *Not our works,* which we do before God, nor the love which *we* have toward God, are the ground for our hope of attaining salvation or the glory of son-ship with God ; but only the love which God cherishes toward us, the works which He works in us. It is only through the revela-tion of His love to us that our love to Him is born. Our works then, their relation being that of fruit to tree, merely give a com-forting presumption that the hope is in us. Christ is represented as the One through whom the merciful God pours His love into the hearts of men ; this love then (evidently the self-existent, essential Love, which is God Himself) before all graces and gifts and *without any merit of our own,* being given to us for righteous-ness. But he who, through this love, possesses true love to God will then certainly keep all the commandments of God. It is the end of the Law, since, where it is, evil-doing cannot continue. We have thus briefly stated the fundamental thoughts of the sec-ond of the writings above named. The last-named brings into direct view those doctrines which Staupitz had occasion to pre-sent to Luther in the hour of his distress, and which afterwards constituted the chief subjects of the latter's testimony. In it Staupitz himself endeavors to exercise brotherly love toward others, and render them such assistance that they may not lose the only comfort of the elect. Like Luther's aged friend in the monastery, he represents it to them that they are in duty bound to believe in God and His promises, and that we must not only believe that God became man, but that He did so for our good. More definitely still, he insists upon faith in Christ as the sin-bearing Lamb of God ; and he declares of such faith that it puri-fies the heart, *justifies,* produces sonship to God, and saves without the works of the Law. To a man disturbed by doubts of his predestination he represents, that whoever believes on Christ is certainly saved and predestinated to salvation, that further than this we have no occasion to ask, and that it is not in our place to inquire why the Father has thus predestinated one and not another.

5

The passages quoted from the last-named writing would really
dispose us to regard the author's position as identical with that
of the Reformer Luther, and merely to inquire further in how far
Luther himself, in formulating his views, had fallen back upon the
teachings of his former instructor. A closer view will, however,
lead us to a different conclusion. This will be already apparent
if we but place side by side the two publications before us. They
both certainly had their origin in one and the same period of the
life and development of Staupitz, namely, in the time when Luther
was already preaching the Gospel with clearness and power, and
when Staupitz still maintained constant and close intimacy with
him. The last-named cannot be placed earlier than the other
(*i. e.*, not before 1518), for in it the coincidence with Luther's
teaching is much more marked; and the intimacy of the two men
continued but a few years longer, having no doubt been seriously
interrupted when Staupitz removed to Salzburg, which appears
to have been as early as 1519. But how striking now, since both
these writings were certainly prompted by the same spirit, is the
difference between them in the very point which here is of chief
importance to us, *i. e.*, in the explanation of the significance of
faith. Faith is only briefly mentioned in the former, when it is
said that the indwelling Holy Spirit awakens in the first instance
the light of faith. Yet it is in this tract that the attempt is
made to develop in far more comprehensive way than elsewhere
the entire theological position of the author. The last-named
document, keeping in view the single purpose already mentioned,
is of a thoroughly practical tendency. We must therefore conclude that in the connected, radical apprehension and presentation of doctrine the specific significance of faith, after all, in the
case of Staupitz fell into the background as it never did for
Luther. His own religious experience and his knowledge of
Christian experience in general drove him, indeed, again and
again to lay all stress upon it, as over against the assaults of
temptation; but in his general theological system it had not
been able to win for itself the proper position, nor to suitably
adjust itself to those elements which disputed its claim. He fails
here to look carefully for that in the subject by which salvation
is really and fundamentally appropriated. The whole weight, in
his presentation, falls simply upon the divine working, which
itself produces even this appropriation. It is, indeed, granted

that for the inner Christian life the light of faith is the first requirement. But that life itself in reality begins with the love which is born of the Love from above, and the presentation of it (cf. Cap. 11 of the first document) proceeds at once to deal with progress in love and the perfection of love, by means of which the spirit of the one so loving becomes one spirit with God : faith, meanwhile, is not again taken into consideration in the first tract. We will find it entirely different with Luther— for example, in his *De Libertate Christiana,* which might otherwise, on account of its decided mystical tendency, be most appropriately classed with this of Staupitz. Instead of presenting faith as a positive apprehending and receiving of the objectively presented salvation and Saviour, Staupitz speaks constantly rather of a renouncing of self by the subject, of a simple waiting upon God in complete obedience and perfect resignation, and, finally, of a " perfect empty-making of the spirit." But in the second tract also we see the predominant zeal for essential inner union with Christ, as opposed to that which has been said before of justifying faith upon an objective Christ, manifesting itself at last in such a way as to even threaten an impairment of this unvarying significance of faith and of Christ himself. Staupitz there speaks of that most complete union, in which the believer has surrendered himself entirely to God, emphasizing *only* the Christ *in us ; in us,* not outside of us, is he now our wisdom, righteousness, etc. We shall see how closely Luther himself afterwards approaches the thoughts of Staupitz, and yet how his doctrine of justification, with its unwavering consciousness of the necessity of an objective atonement, avoids this danger. Finally, in the first-named of the above writings, namely, that upon Predestination, Staupitz still presents some of the very conceptions against which Luther afterward contended. Inasmuch as he traces the real existence of the life of salvation back to the infusion of love through grace, he at the same time regards faith in and of itself as yet a dead thing. Love must awaken it to life. He speaks, after the manner of the scholastic theology, of faith as fashioned (*formata*) by love. Even an utterance of Staupitz in which Luther acknowledges that he himself received the first real clue to the understanding of Christian repentance, and which we shall soon see him cordially endorsing, may yet, when interpreted in the sense in which Staupitz probably meant it, bear additional testimony that his view was such as we have been compelled to represent it. As Luther was upon one occasion talking with him about the torturing of consciences by the endless and insufferable requirements in regard to confession, the latter declared that true repentance is that only which begins in love to righteousness and to God.[1] It was of great significance for Luther to find himself directed, not to the wearisome, outward, human works of merit, but to the inward turning of the soul toward God. He learned, as he declares, under the suggestion of this brief remark, to conceive of repentance, according to its original scriptural name ($\mu\epsilon\tau\alpha\nu\omega\alpha$), as a change of the inward nature. But we yet look in vain for the essential emphasizing of the faith which alone responds to the impulse of grace coming from God Himself; and, in view of what has been already said, we dare not regard this as merely accidental, but must see in it a note of distinction between the general doctrinal conception of Staupitz and the peculiar, deeper apprehension and teaching of Luther. Staupitz, with these characteristic views, stands as yet essentially upon the basis of the hitherto-prevailing practical Mysticism, which was deeply religious and full of vitality, but which had not yet attained to a clear consciousness of fundamental doctrine, and, in consequence, not yet to reformatory light. We shall have occasion also to observe how Luther still continued by the independent study of this system to add depth to his own views, but we shall, at the same time, see how he, though powerfully aided in his progress by it, yet at once stepped out beyond it upon the ground of evangelical truth and the scriptural teaching of justification by faith.

Yet how well Staupitz, with his deep, direct sense of religious need and of the fountain of pure grace and love revealed in God, understood the art of guiding the distressed conscience is plainly shown in his treatment of Luther. He pointed him away from his own working and self-torture to that grace which stood ever revealed to his own gaze in Christ and his atoning death. He especially tried to restrain him from the distressing " speculations " in regard to predestination, comforting him, as Luther himself tells us, with the counsel: " Look upon the wounds of Christ and his blood shed for you : from them predestination will shine out

[1] Briefe, i, 116 sq.

upon you." [1] It was thus Staupitz through whom God saved him from the condition in which he would otherwise have been " drowned." We shall find that all the counsel afterwards given by Luther himself to those assailed by spiritual temptations pursued exactly the line of this exhortation. His sorest troubles of conscience, indeed, as he relates in the *Tischreden*,[2] were far too deep for the experience or comprehension of Staupitz : he could find no confessor who knew anything about such difficulties, and this added greatly to his depression. But Staupitz was able at least to assure him that such trials were good and necessary in order that he might be made useful in the world. They seemed to be, said he, more necessary for Luther than eating and drinking. This led the latter to think of the thorn in the flesh which the Apostle Paul was compelled to endure (2 Cor. xii. 7), and he at length came to understand that he must learn (as he afterwards exhorted others) to *endure* temptation. When Luther was tormenting himself with his " imaginary " sins, Staupitz reproved him for that sort of conscientiousness, telling him that he wanted to be an imaginary sinner and to have Christ as an imaginary Saviour ; that he must accustom himself to think of Christ as a real Saviour and of himself as a real sinner; that God was not dealing in play or fiction, nor making sport, when He sent His Son and offered Him up for us ; and that, if he wished to be free from his sins, he must have a list of genuine sins, and must take them to Christ with prayer for His assistance.[3]

Staupitz had undoubtedly struck the right point in this reproof. All such self-inflicted suffering arises from the fact that the heart of man, instead of depending entirely and simply upon God and His plainly-revealed will, busies itself with its own works, and thus, in the midst of its self-torture, and with a show of zeal for God's Law, secretly seeks the gratification of self. A perverted conscientiousness has its roots in the same disposition which prompts men to strive after righteousness by means of their own works. Here, too, the self-reliant heart fails to find the grace of God as it is in its essental nature and as it is freely offered to all. When, finally, Luther laments that his good resolutions always

---

[1] Op. Ex. Erl., vi, 296, 297.—Cf. Tischr. Erl. Ed., lx, 160 sq.—Först., iii, 160.—Briefe,v, 513.

[2] Erl. Ed., lx, 128, 136. Först., iii, 135 sq., 141.

[3] Briefe, v, 680. Tisch. Erl. Ed., lviii, 182. Först., ii, 23.

came to grief, Staupitz declares that he too has lied to God a thousand times in his promises to become pious, and that he will no more form such a resolution, since he sees very well that he cannot keep it.[1] He always thus directed him away from thoughts of self to the grace of God. Even the very boldest expressions which Luther himself afterwards employed when treating of this subject remind us forcibly of words heard at this time from the lips of Staupitz.

But it was, after all, in the *Sacred Scriptures* that Luther discovered the source from which he might derive a full and independent knowledge of saving truth; and, himself already preferring the study of these to that of any other authorities, he found in Staupitz again a timely counselor, confirming his inclination and exhorting him to endeavor to gain a thorough textual and local knowledge of the Word of God.[2] From the way in which Staupitz (for example, in the treatise, *Von der holdseligen Liebe Gottes*) speaks of the letter, not only of the Old Testament, but of the New as well, presenting it in contrast with the spirit as killing, we might be led to fear that he had not only been driven beyond the limits of human and scholastic learning to the Word of God, but had fallen also into the error of a fanatical, spiritualistic conception of the light of the Holy Spirit, exalting himself under such supposed illumination above the firm foundations of the divine Word. As evidence to the contrary, however, we recall the weakness which he displayed in shrinking from a decisive support of the evangelical doctrine as against the ruling ecclesiasticism, and the fact that all his devotion to the Scriptures did not suffice to equip him with valor and fortitude for the conflict when once the open breach had been made. Yet, sensible of the dangers to which the unaided powers and opinions of men are exposed, his pure religious feeling kept him bound in humble submission to the written Word. We are, said he at one time to Luther, even in that which we know and understand most thoroughly, so exposed to error injurious to ourselves and others that it is necessary for us to pursue the study of the Holy Scriptures with the greatest diligence and with all humility.[3] Impelled by

---

[1] Erl. Ed., xlviii, 201. Op. Ex. Erl., Comm. ad Gal., iii, 21.

[2] Seckendorf, Lib. 1, Sect. viii, Add. 3.

[3] Op. Ex. Erl. Comm. ad Gal. i, 170.

this feeling, he faithfully maintained this high estimation of the
Scriptures as opposed to all human traditions and all scholastic arts
and sciences, just in so far, however, and just as long as he could
do so without engaging positively in the great conflict.   Thus he
at one time quoted approvingly to Luther a saying of the Elector
Frederick the Wise, to the effect that all sermons which deal in
such traditions and such subtleties and refinements are beyond
measure frigid and weak, and that the Scriptures alone by their
majesty and power, without any help from us, cast down all
opposing bulwarks and compel recognition as a voice from
above.[1]   It was in this spirit that Staupitz at that time influenced
Luther ; and he observed with amazement the rapid progress of
his pupil in the line of study thus commended, regarding him in
consequence as superior to all others.[2]

Further, Luther found in the writings of at least ONE theologian
some instructions calculated to allay his distress of mind.
Melanchthon mentions, after the books of the scholastics above
named and of D'Ailly, those of GERSON as among the works
diligently studied by Luther in the monastery at Erfurt; and
the latter himself long afterwards testified[3] that Gerson alone
among the teachers of the Church, not excepting even Augustine,
had written of spiritual temptations as distinct from those of
the flesh, and that he alone therefore could comfort and strengthen
distressed consciences.   He qualifies his praise, however, by
declaring that the latter had not yet advanced so far as to be able
to offer the consolations of the Gospel through Christ ; that he
had only by a mitigation of the laws made the distress more
tolerable and endurable.   St. Paul, on the other hand, he declares, knocks the bottom out of the cask at a single stroke when
he says plainly : Let no man trust in the law, by whose works no
flesh shall be justified ; but let every one trust only in Christ.

The light of the Gospel had broken upon Luther's soul.   In
the midst of his continued inward experiences and difficulties,
he learned to derive more and more of this light from the Scriptures, and, in turn, through its illumination to understand the
latter.   It is manifest from all his later writings, and from his
entire method in presenting the truth, that it was particularly

[1] Op. Ex. Erl., xiv, 67.   [2] Seckendorf, l. c.

[3] Erl. Ed., lx, 88 sq.; lxii, 121.   Först., iii, 106 sq.; iv, 393 sq.

the writings of St. Paul, as was to be expected from their peculiar contents and character, which attracted his eager attention and contributed to his further understanding of the way of salvation.

Here we find ourselves again unfortunately without such further details as would enable us to follow more closely the constantly advancing steps in Luther's apprehension of saving truth. Especially must we regret the lack of more precise information concerning his earliest acquaintance with that teacher of the ancient Church to whom he was indebted for the most powerful further impulse to the understanding of the significance and sole efficacy of the grace of God, namely, St. Augustine.

It was the thought of the *divine righteousness* which filled Luther with such violent qualms of conscience. In view of this he felt himself to be only a poor sinner, resting under condemnation. Wherever he read in the Scriptures anything concerning God's righteousness, he understood the words as indicating that attribute of God, by virtue of which He metes out to each of us, as demanded by His Law, a reward according to the merit of our works—and this meant for him only merited perdition. Hence, he trembled with fear when called upon to pray in the words of Ps. xxxi. 1 : " Deliver me through thy righteousness." He declares that he hated this word with his whole heart. He had the same feeling when he read the testimony of Rom. iii. 21, concerning the righteousness which is revealed in the Gospel. He declares in the *Tischreden* that he for a long time did not know to what he was coming. He had a sense (smelt), indeed, of something near at hand, yet undiscovered, but he did not know what it was. Then, at length, his attention was arrested by the declaration in Rom. i. 17 : " The just (righteous) shall live by faith." This helped him ; he now saw what Paul meant also in the previous verse (and likewise in Chap. iii) by " righteousness." He apprehended thus the righteousness of faith, the righteousness of the Gospel. He now understood the " righteousness of God " in the *passive* sense, *i. e.*, not as that by virtue of which God is righteous and condemns the ungodly, but as that with which God endows us, makes us righteous, justifies us— as a work wrought in us by God in his mercy. Luther afterwards upon several occasions observed that he was led to this discovery chiefly through the writings of Augustine. He mentions particularly the latter's *De spiritu et litera*, in which he describes the righteousness of God as that with which He endows man. We discern very clearly in the Reformer's earliest writings, and no less plainly in those of later date, that it was from this point onward his most earnest effort to gain further light upon the most important and vital question which agitated his mind and upon the true sense of the divine testimonies.[1]

In the above-mentioned Preface to his Latin works (1545) he relates, however, immediately after reporting his negotiations with Miltitz (which occurred in the year 1518–1519), that he undertook again in that same year the exposition of the Psalms. He now felt himself better prepared for this because of his diligent study of the Epistles to the Romans, Galatians and Hebrews, which he had expounded in the course of lectures just completed. He had earnestly sought to gain a proper understanding of the Epistle to the Romans, and had hitherto found no greater difficulty in his way than the *one word* touching the " righteousness of God " (Rom. i. 17) which is revealed in the Gospel. He felt an aversion to this word, because he understood by it the " active righteousness " of God. Describing his condition at this time, he says that, although beyond reproach in his monastic life, he yet realized that he was a sinner before God, and sought to reconcile Him by himself rendering satisfaction for his sins, and that it was on this account that he was secretly offended at the righteous God. Nevertheless, he held fast to these words of St. Paul, and meditated upon them day and night, until at length he caught their meaning by comparing the words immediately following : " The righteous shall live by faith." Now he recognized the righteousness spoken of as "*passive*." Immediately he felt as though he had been born anew. Paradise stood revealed to his view. He then ran through the whole Bible, understanding other passages everywhere in accordance with this same rule of interpretation, *e. g.*, the work of God as that which He does Himself, His wisdom as that by which He makes us wise, and thus also His strength, salvation, glory, etc. Afterwards, he read also Augustine's *De spiritu et litera*, and there unexpectedly found the same explanation of the " righteousness of God." Strengthened by these new

---

[1] Op. Ex. Erl., x, 155; xiv, 207; xix, 24; vii, 74.—Tischr. Erl. Ed., lxviii, 336, 404. Först., ii, 143, 197.

thoughts, he applied himself again to the exposition of the Psalms ; but his work upon this suffered an interruption through the calling of the Diet at Worms.

Luther has in this Preface briefly and clearly described the course of his development, just as we have traced it by a comparison of numerous other statements in his writings. But what shall we think as to the time, in which he here seems to locate the experience in question? He is correct in his recollection of the year in which he began his new exposition of the Psalms, or in which, at least, he first published a portion of it. The explanation of Psalms i.–v. appeared in 1519, with a dedication to the Elector Frederick, under date of March 27. In the annotations of Psalm v. in this publication we find the above-cited reference to the definition of the " righteousness of God " in Augustine's *De spiritu et litera*.[1] Now it was in 1513–1514 that he held his first lectures upon the Psalms, of which we shall have further occasion to speak. Was it really, as would appear from the account in the Preface, only at a later period that he attained the conception of the righteousness of God which was of such prime importance to him, and then happened to find the passage in Augustine?

The supposition is most plainly contradicted by the earlier writings and expositions of Luther himself, published before 1519 and 1518. An explanation of the Penitential Psalms, which was ready for print as early as March 1, 1517, defines the righteousness of God as the grace by which God makes us righteous, and quotes the Epistle to the Romans in confirmation. In full accord with this, we find annotations to the Psalms in Luther's own handwriting, which were beyond doubt (as will hereafter appear) made by him in connection with his first course of lectures ; for example, under Ps. li. 14, " thy righteousness—with which thou makest righteous—not mine, nor that of the Law," although under Ps. xxxi. 1 (see above, p. 72) another interpretation is given, namely : God as a righteous judge of the suffering Christ, whom men hold to have been justly crucified. In the same sense, we find Christ spoken of in the same publication and in various letters as " our righteousness." Still further, He is declared to be, in so far as He dwells in us, the " righteousness, wisdom, strength, etc., of God." [1]　In regard to Luther's acquaintance with Augustine, and especially with the latter's *De spiritu et litera*, it is to be observed that he appeals particularly to this as early as 1516 in support of his own view of the Pauline conception of human righteousness.[2]　In the above-mentioned manuscript of the years 1513 sqq. we find evidence of a most diligent use of Augustine's *Exposition of the Psalms.*

From the foregoing, it is beyond all question that Luther was confused in his recollection as to the time of the events reported in the Preface to his Latin works.　It is, moreover, inconceivable that, after the help that had been given him in his spiritual troubles at Erfurt, he should have yet so long remained in darkness and uncertainty in regard to the proper conception of the righteousness of God.　Did not the father confessor there point him to justification by faith?　It is to be supposed, too, even without direct evidence, that he as an Augustinian monk must, when in the monastery at Erfurt, have already given special attention to the writings of Augustine.　Yet we dare not depend too much upon such a supposition.　He himself says, in connection with the above appeal to Augustine: [3] "Not that I am inclined in consequence of my professional study to approve the noble Augustine, who found not even the least favor at my hands before I happened upon that book of his."　Still, we have no reason to doubt the report of Melanchthon, that he had already during his life at Erfurt discovered the books referred to and forthwith made them a leading subject of study.　Melanchthon says that he began to read them there, and found in them, especially in Augustine's *Exposition of the Psalms* and his treatise, *De spiritu et litera*, many clear statements.　From this time forward he held Augustine in far higher esteem than any of the other teachers of the Church, on account of his testimony to the grace of God as the exclusive source of salvation, although afterwards noting with most decided displeasure the absence in his writings of a full and correct expression of evangelical doctrine.[4]

We are not able to determine more definitely the precise stage

---

[1] Erl. Ed., xxxvii, 430.　Walch, Luther's Schriften, ix, 1845, 1686.—Briefe, i, 17.—Erl. Ed., xxxvii, 141.

[2] Briefe, i, 39.　　　　　　　　　　[3] Briefe, i, 40.

[4] Cf. Erl. Ed., xxx, 107 et al.—Per contra, e. g., ix, 233 sq., 339 sq., 347 sq.

of development attained by Luther during his stay at Erfurt in his new and delightful apprehension of the truth and in the new life awakened within him by the message of salvation. It may have long appeared as though the sun of divine grace were engaged in a yet doubtful conflict with the deep darkness which enshrouded his soul. The illuminating rays may at first have seemed to penetrate the gloom only in rare and brief moments. At later periods, even long after Luther had been led to rejoice in a full knowledge of saving truth, there were again and again violent and distressing fluctuations in his inner moods. It was, at all events, by very gradual stages that he advanced to enlarged views of truth. Even after he had appeared as a Reformer upon the field of conflict, we yet note by what slow degrees the light shone out from the central point of his apprehension of saving truth upon various other points of doctrine. It was Luther's way, while penetrating with his whole soul and all the power of his mind to the very foundations of this central truth, and, with it in view, reading anew the inspired testimonies, to allow the light to diffuse itself more widely by its own force, the germ implanted to unfold further by its own inner energy, bursting through one bond of error after the other. With all his zeal for advancement in knowledge, he is never restless nor in undue haste. Especially was it not at all his disposition to allow himself to be controlled or carried away by an expressly negative, polemical interest or critical impulse. He merely followed quietly and submissively the promptings of the positive impulses within. He feels no direct or personal craving to go beyond this and engage in public controversy. It is only when, after long years of deep meditation, investigation and development, an insufferable evil in the Church had compelled him, in view of his official responsibility, to enter the conflict, that the opposition which he unexpectedly meets carries forward his conviction finally to a bold and polemic, but even yet only gradual, unfolding of its natural consequences. Only thus can we explain his attitude up to the year 1517 ; and it is, beyond doubt, in this way that we must understand especially the beginnings of his evangelical development at Erfurt. But the light had there already risen upon him which was to seek ever further diffusion ; in his heart and mind had been implanted the living germ with an energy and power that were a sure prophecy of growth. Such growth, moreover, was to be especially promoted by the continued conflict with spiritual temptations. The means which, in connection with zealous devotion to the inspired Word, certainly contributed at this time already to the moulding of his inner life, were those which he himself afterwards often briefly designated as " prayer, meditation and temptation." [1]

We have already mentioned a testimony to Luther's character as a monk, in which he is described in his " spiritual " monastic life as another Paul.   Friends of Luther were able to trace in the powerful voice from heaven, by which he was so suddenly impelled to enter the cloister, some resemblance to the calling of the Apostle.   Thus Crotus, in the letter already referred to,[2] reminds him how a lightning-stroke from heaven had cast him like another Paul to the earth.   We may observe the resemblance in other particulars.   In the monastery he first learned thoroughly from his own experience, like Paul, how little man can accomplish by all the righteousness of the law and the most perfect conformity to it.   He had learned to join in the lament : " O, wretched man that I am !   Who shall deliver me from the body of this death?"   He had learned, too, like Paul, to count that which was gain to him as loss and as dung, that he might win Christ and righteousness through faith in Him, namely, the righteousness which is imputed by God to faith.[3]   We have observed that Luther assigned to Augustine, as the great herald of grace, the highest position among the teachers of the ancient Church. It is well known that the latter was also led to the acceptance and proclamation of this doctrine by the course of his own inner life.   But in Luther we find a yet further resemblance to the Apostle in the fact that, before experiencing the grace of God, he had not, like Augustine, been entangled in the net of openly sinful and carnal life, but, on the contrary, had contended against such temptations with all his native moral energy, and had won for himself a reputation of spotless purity.   The peculiarity in his case was the existence of the deepest consciousness of sin and sense of guilt in connection, not with any specially striking manifestation of the power of sin, but with the most intense striving

---

[1] Oratio, meditatio, tentatio : E. g., Erl. Ed., i, 69, and lxiii, 404, in Preface to German Works.

[2] Vid. pp. 39, 48.

[3] Phil. iii, 6–9.   Rom. vii, 24.

after righteousness. Thus was he prepared to become the greatest, or rather, indeed, the first great, clear preacher of the righteousness of faith sent to the Christian church since the days of
the Apostle Paul.

CHAPTER II.

LUTHER AS TEACHER AT WITTENBERG UNTIL A. D. 1517.

SECTION I. BEFORE RECEIVING THE DEGREE OF DOCTOR OF
THEOLOGY.

LECTURING UPON PHILOSOPHY—THEOLOGICAL VIEWS—ASSOCIATES—
ADVANTAGES OF WITTENBERG—BACHELOR OF SCRIPTURE—PREACH-
ING—STUDIES—JOURNEY TO ROME—RETURN TO WITTENBERG.

IT was mainly upon the recommendation of Staupitz that
Luther was in 1508 called to a chair in the newly-established
University at Wittenberg. It was at this place, and on account
of the office which he here filled, that he was publicly to proclaim
the evangelical views and convictions whose germ had been first
implanted in his mind during his quiet life at the Erfurt monastery, and to begin the conflict with the ruling Church and its
theology. What most impresses us, however, in his life and
activity at Wittenberg for a number of years, is the silence in
which he must now have carried on the toil and conflict in his
own soul.

The chair to which he was at first appointed was one of Philosophy. He was to lecture upon the dialectics and physics of
Aristotle. Very soon after accepting this position, he declared to
a friend that he would, from the first, have been very glad if he
had been permitted to exchange philosophy for theology, since
the latter has to do with the kernel of the nut, the substance of
the wheat, and the marrow of the bone. Still, he acknowledges
that God is God, and will guide him ; man is often—yes always—
deceived when he trusts in his own judgment.[1] It is evident from
this how eager Luther was already at this time, not only to investigate for himself the deepest problems of Christian knowledge,
but also to impart to others the convictions to which he had been

[1] Briefe, i, 6.

led. He must have been satisfied in his own mind that he had indeed found a way out of the darkness which had formerly enveloped him when meditating upon divine things, and that he would be able also to direct others, however much of labor and conflict this might yet involve for him. It is worthy of note, further, that he as yet expresses no dissatisfaction in view of his limitation, within the sphere of philosophy, mainly to Aristotle.

That he, in connection with this, still pursued as far as he was able, at least for his own satisfaction, the study of theology, might be safely inferred from the above declaration. That he did so, Melanchthon positively asserts.

This is, however, all that we can with certainty affirm as to the stage of his development during the first years at Wittenberg. He declared in the year 1521,[1] that he had held himself in check for more than ten years, although during all that time it had seemed to him that much in the papal Church and in the theology of the Universities was perverted and contrary to the will of Christ. He restrained himself with the thought, that if such were really the case, there were always enough theologians who would not keep silent. This declaration, however, leaves us still in great uncertainty as to the extent to which these suspicions had already taken shape in his mind at the beginning of the years mentioned. It brings us, reckoning backward from the beginning of his open assault upon the prevalent abuses and errors, to the time of his stay at Erfurt, or, at least, to the early years of his teaching at Wittenberg. It could not, indeed, well be otherwise than that with the first apprehension of righteousness as granted only by free grace to faith there should be united an aversion to doctrines and ordinances which seemed to stand in conflict with this. But to how great an extent, and with what power, firmly-rooted views and customs at first continued to maintain their hold upon Luther's mind will be strikingly manifest when we follow him in his journey to Rome. He himself often assures us that it cost him much time and great exertion to carry out his knowledge to its most important consequences. He endeavored at that time, as we must infer particularly from this journey to Rome, not only in dealing with others, but, above all,

[1] Jena, ii, 401 b.

in seeking to satisfy his own mind, to silence these suspicions by the thought that it was the duty of others rather than his own to give expression to them—that he, with the uncertainty yet attaching to his own views, must be content with that which these others approved. Especially must we conclude that he thought it necessary to hold fast to the existing ecclesiasticism and its ordinances. The pure grace of God had been revealed to him as the fountain of salvation; but he yet sought diligently to satisfy his thirst from the channels through which the Church seemed to convey to him the gifts of grace. In faith he sought the grace of God; but he at the same time endeavored, as far as possible, to observe the ordinances upon which the possession of grace was by the Church made to depend, seeking also in this way to meet the will of that God from whom as righteous he now no longer fled, but whom he sought as gracious, yet whose grace he had not yet learned to apprehend as freeing from such yoke of bondage. With an indistinct but earnest desire to fulfil all the conditions of salvation, he may have thought that, while the one ought to be done, the other ought not to be left undone (Matt. xxiii. 23), but rather accepted and fulfilled with humble and conscientious fidelity. The indistinctness here manifest is a characteristic indication of the course of his development.

The new University at Wittenberg was at that time probably better adapted than any other for the encouragement of a free and independent advance in philosophy and theology. The greatest intellectual light of which it could boast, MARTIN POLLICH, of Melrichstadt, a Doctor in three faculties, a man who had rendered valuable service in the founding of the University, and who was highly esteemed by the Elector, had already before the arrival of Luther advanced to the assault upon Scholasticism. He anticipated that the pursuit of classical studies would lead to the greatest advance in theology. He complained of the extravagant estimate placed upon Aristotle.[1] An expression of Pollich in regard to Luther, which his brother frequently repeated to Mathesius, and which has also been preserved by Melanchthon, may serve to show what impression Luther made upon him, and, at the same time, how highly he himself esteemed the significance

---

[1] Cf. here and for the following account: Jürgens. ii. Löscher, Reform. Akten, i, 87 sqq.,313 sqq.

of scriptural studies. " Luther," said he, " will overthrow the scholastic theology now prevalent, and reform the Church; for he plants himself upon the writings of the prophets and apostles, and stands upon the Word of Christ, which no one can overturn either by philosophy, or by sophistry, or by scholastry, etc." It is by no means to be inferred, however, that such a spirit as this was so prevalent at Wittenberg as to captivate and carry away a newcomer. STAUPITZ, whom Luther now met as teacher of theology at Wittenberg, through whom he had himself been brought thither, and to whom he certainly upon his arrival attached himself more closely than to any other, was himself, despite all the encouragement which he gave to an evangelical tendency, decidedly averse to every forward movement and to every disturbing agitation. Certainly, no such offence was to be expected on the part of TRUTTVETTER, Luther's former teacher, who had also been secured as a professor at Wittenberg, and remained there until 1519. He occupied a position of special prominence and influence at the time of Luther's appearance. Younger theologians of Wittenberg, who afterwards devoted themselves with zeal to the promotion of the Reformation, were impelled to such activity by the impulse which they received from Luther several years after the time of which we now speak. Among these were BODENSTEIN, of Carlstadt, who was made Bachelor Sententiarius (Bachelor of the Sentences of Peter Lombard) in 1509 and Doctor in 1510, and AMSDORF, who was made Bachelor of Scripture in 1507 and Licentiate in 1511. Carlstadt especially, who, on the basis of the impulse thus received, so passionately sought to force himself into prominence as a reformer, was still at that time wholly devoted to the study of the scholastic theology; it is said that he never saw a Bible until after he had received his doctor's degree.[1]

It was, however, not the theological, but the legal, faculty which had up to this time chiefly flourished at Wittenberg, and its chief light from 1509 onward had been HENNING GÖDE, teacher of canonical law, a decided Romanist. Luther found warm friends in CHRISTOPH SCHEURL and HIERONYMUS SCHURFF. When he afterwards decidedly and in open controversy proclaimed the evangelical doctrines, they, from the first, stood cheerfully by

[1] Erl. Ed., lvii, 35.

him.[1] But we find no indication whatever that the convictions of the latter, who was but a few years older than Luther, had at that time assumed a fixed and independent character; whilst the former in the following year writes in entire harmony with the Church's views in support of the priesthood, mass, etc., entertaining, at the same time, a high opinion of the humanistic studies.

Wittenberg had as yet no prominent teacher of the Ancient Languages. . It was only after the arrival of Melanchthon, in 1518, that it became celebrated as a seat of classical learning. Among the humanists who up to this time had been permanently located at Wittenberg, or who had occasionally in passing stopped to deliver lectures there, there was none with whom Luther could have entered into closer relations.

The University of Wittenberg was thus a peculiarly favorable place for a teacher of philosophy and theology who felt impelled toward a free and independent development and expression of his convictions. All the more independently could such an impulse be obeyed if kept free from the pressure of outward influences, even of such as might seem to harmonize entirely with it. Thus, too, it was possible for this impulse in Luther to advance by gradual and seemingly slow steps, in accordance with the entire constitution of his mental and moral nature and the previous course of his inner life.

From March, 1509, he was Bachelor of Scripture, which required him to lecture for at least six months upon the Sacred Scriptures.[2] But we have no report of any lectures of this kind as then delivered by him. Melanchthon makes the first mention of such after his promotion to the doctorate.

When he began also to preach in Wittenberg is uncertain. The reports, which indicate the years 1508 or 1509 for this, also represent him as already pastor of the city church, and, while not on this account to be utterly rejected, are yet unreliable. It was not until 1516 that he accepted the latter office as an assistant of the regular pastor. Up to this time he had preached in the dining hall of the Augustinian monastery. The Elector had already heard him preach before he became a doctor, and, as

[1] Cf. in regard to Scheurl, Briefe, i, 49 sqq., 78 sqq.; in regard to Schurfl, Ibid, i, 108.

[2] Cf. Jürgens, ii, 251.

Melanchthon relates, was deeply impressed by his power and eloquence. Luther himself confesses in the *Tischreden* that he at first greatly dreaded this duty, and only upon the urgent request of Staupitz ventured to undertake it. He afterwards recalls with what conscientious prudence he yet, especially when in the pulpit, expressed his convictions.[1]

From that which we know of Luther's earlier studies at Erfurt, and from the later utterance already quoted, in which he deeply laments the lack of time for the study of the ancient classics, we may infer that he now gladly availed himself of the opportunity for such pursuits. The study of Greek and Hebrew became a special duty in connection with his biblical lectures.[2] But it is very doubtful whether he could even now find much time for humanistic studies. It is very certain that he did not, at all events, apply himself expressly to them. In this connection we repeat the statement already made, that it was not at all from such studies that Luther derived the impulse for the development of his reformatory views. The above-mentioned Oldekop, who was not kindly disposed toward Luther, reports, evidently with a touch of ridicule, that "the students were fond of hearing him speak at Wittenberg, since his like had never been heard, so bravely did he Germanize every Latin word."[3] It was doubtless his chief aim, not to make a show of great philological attainments, but to bring the subjects of his philosophical and theological discussions fully within the comprehension of his readers. Great importance in determining Luther's precise position at this time would attach to a letter in which he, in referring to the conflict between Reuchlin and the theologians of Cologne, declares himself as decidedly in sympathy with the former, provided we were assured that it had been written in 1510 (as Löscher, Walch and De Wette think) ; but we must, with Jürgens, place this in a later year (according to Aurifaber, not earlier than 1514).[4]

To this transition period in Luther's life belongs his JOURNEY TO ROME. This must, beyond question, be regarded as an event

---

[1] Cf. Jürgens, ii, 254 sq.; iii, 75 sqq.—Tischr. Erl. Ed., lix, 185 sq. Först., ii, 369.

[2] Cf. Melanchthon's report, l. c., p. 7.

[3] Lüntzel, l. c., p. 154,

[4] Briefe, i, 5 sqq. Jürgens, ii, 522.

of the very deepest significance in his career. It sets before us in clear light the point of view which Luther at that time still occupied, and it, with the accompanying experiences, was peculiarly fitted to lead him to a more advanced position, and, for the time being at least, quietly to relax the tension of bonds in which he might otherwise still have been held with an unshaken confidence and unquestioning obedience but which he as a champion of the Gospel would so soon afterwards be called upon to cast off without hesitation or scruple. But, unfortunately, we find in Luther's own writings very little reference to this journey or to its significance for him ; and the traditional accounts, even when professing to have originated with contemporaries and friends, and to consist of reports from his own lips, are full of uncertainties.

The journey was probably made in the year 1510, the weight of authorities, including Luther's own written statements, favoring that date, although Melanchthon says that it occurred three years after his appointment at Wittenberg, i. e., in 1511.[1] Luther himself is said to have spoken of the journey as undertaken in fulfilment of a vow. Already as a boy, and again while at Erfurt, he is said to have vowed that he would go to Rome and become pious.[2] Melanchthon and Mathesius know nothing of this. According to them, he was sent to Rome upon some business connected with the monastery.[3] The testimony of his opponent, Cochlæus, also points in this direction ; for, although we must consider as malicious and incredible, in view of the personal relations of the two men, his more detailed statement, that Luther desired to awaken opposition at Rome against Staupitz, the Superior of his Order, on account of some measure adopted by the latter, it is yet evident everywhere that business of the nature indicated was generally known at the time to have given occasion for the journey. Had Luther really been led to the undertaking for the fulfilment of a vow, or had he even been influenced to any

---

[1] "Anno Domini (ist mir recht) 1510," etc. Erl. Ed., xxvi, 125 ; "Anno 1510." Erl. Ed., xxxii, 424. Cf. my notice of the article of Brandes, *Luther's Reise nach Rom*, 1859, in the Gött. Gel. Anz., 1860, pp. 601 sqq., as also in connection with the following paragraphs.

[2] Cf. Jürgens, ii, 271 ; i, 322.—Cf. also, as evidence of the caution with which such reports are to be received, Jürgens himself, i, 156 Anm.

[3] Mathesius : "Von seinem Convent."—Mel.: "propter Monachorum controversias."

considerable extent by such a motive, it would of course have furnished us a proof of the remarkable power which the old religious and ecclesiastical prejudices still exerted upon him. But why should he, during the years when he was certainly much more fully under the dominion of these prejudices and impelled by them to all manner of undertakings supposed to be savingly meritorious, so long have postponed the fulfilling of such a vow? And why does he make no allusion in any of the numerous passages in his writings in which he speaks of the traditionary zeal for journeys to Rome to the (supposed) fact that he had at one time allowed himself to be carried away by it? This silence is the more remarkable, as he is especially fond, when speaking of monkish customs and false holiness, of referring for illustration to his own earlier life and experience. It is possible, we may admit, that he may at some time have used some such expression as is attributed to him—may have said that he had often in his earlier years of darkness formed such a resolution and was very glad even yet for the opportunity to carry it out. But of a formal vow we are not to think ; we must look elsewhere to discover the real occasion for the journey.[1]

Luther himself testifies, however, how faithfully and zealously he employed upon the journey all means by which, according to the teaching of the Church, he could promote the salvation of his own soul or the souls of others. Speaking at one time of the making of pilgrimages, once so popular, he says : " It was in no commendable spirit that we undertook them, just as it was with me at Rome, where I was also such a frantic saint." In proof of this he cites, not the journey to Rome itself, but his conduct while there. He goes on to say that he ran about to all the churches and shrines, believing all the false and vile stuff (*das Erlogene und Erstunkene*) that he heard. He held a mass or two while there, or perhaps ten of them, and was almost sorry that his parents were not dead, so that he might by his masses and other excellent prayers deliver them from purgatory. There was a saying at Rome, that

[1] Cf. also Georg Mylius (Preface to Rom. in Lindner, C. F. Junii Compend. Seckendorfianum, etc., 1755, pp. 40 sq.), who relates what he professes to have heard from the lips of Luther's own son, namely, that Luther was *compelled* [evidently by instructions from his superiors] to journey to Rome, but undertook the enterprise the more willingly, because he hoped by visiting the holy places, etc., to find peace and comfort.

any mother was blessed whose son should read mass at St. John's on Saturday. Very gladly would he have made his mother blessed, but he could not force his way through the dense crowd.[1] As the strongest evidence of the faith or superstition by which he was controlled, it is related that he climbed upon his knees, as was then and is still prescribed, the holy stair-case which is said to have been brought to Rome from the judgment-hall of Pilate at Jerusalem.

There is not the slightest trace of evidence that he had any thought of pursuing, even incidentally, scientific ends while upon his journey—that he made any attempt to reap advantage from contact with the Italian Humanists, or had any intercourse at all with them. The thought of such a thing was far from his mind.

But as he was reverently toiling up the steps of Pilate's stair-case—so runs the traditional account—there appeared to sound in his ears, as with a voice of thunder, the words : " The righteous shall live by faith," and this inner voice followed him throughout his entire journey. In view of all that we already know of Luther's development, we can by no means conclude that the hearing of this voice marked a prominent turning-point in his life (even Maurer, in his *Life of Luther*, lays too much stress upon it). It would harmonize, however, perfectly with the course of that development, if, just at the time when he was enjoying the privilege of performing the works of merit to which had been attached the very richest promises of reward, the con-tradiction between the higher light which he had attained and all efforts of this sort, together with the hopes based upon them, impressed his mind with a force never hitherto experienced.[2]

But how startling the revelation which now came to him of the character of the holy place whence he thought to see streams of salvation pouring out upon the Church ! The strongest impression which he took with him from the city of the Pope was evidently that it was the seat of the gravest and most fearful abuses. When he, at a later day, denounces the venality of the saints at Rome,

[1] Erl. Ed., xi, 284.—As to the church (St. John's) cf. Meurer, Luther's Leben 2 Aufl. § 37 Anm.—As to the masses celebrated, Erl. Ed., xxvii, 20; xxxi, 327.

[2] Cf. also Mylius, l. c.—The Stair-case is the Santa Scala in the Capella Sancta Sanctorum; it is a plain error to locate it in St. Peter's Church.—Cf. Gött. Gel. Anz., l. c., p. 610 sq.

the licentiousness of the holy leaders of the Church, the unbelief and frivolity of those who stood as the very pillars of the Catholic faith, he is only telling what he himself discovered, appealing in support of the charges to his own experience. He heard priests at the mass openly making sport with the words of consecration. He could not escape the thought : If men talk thus openly and publicly at Rome, and if even popes and cardinals thus hold mass —how shrewdly had he not been deceived by them ! Above all was he shocked by what he heard of licentious corruption—of • Sodomitic abominations never yet mentioned in German ears. Cardinals who cultivated at pleasure impure relations with women, he saw honored on this account as holy men.[1] He heard it said at Rome : " If there is a hell, Rome is built upon it." Certain cardinals even, he was told, had declared : " It cannot continue thus ; there must be a break." [2] It was these revelations which afterwards led him often to say that not for a thousand guldens would he have missed the seeing of Rome and discovering with his own eyes how the popes and bishops had deceived the world.[3]

" But when God had now brought him safely back to his cloister at Wittenberg," reports Mathesius, " he went on studying and discussing." However forcibly his heart must have been impressed and agitated by the abuses which, instead of the anticipated blessings, had forced themselves upon his attention, yet the suspicions aroused within him were not powerful enough to overcome the earlier views of ecclesiastical order which had so long been fixing themselves in his religious nature, nor to demand expression in spite of the conviction that it was not in his place to criticise these things as there were enough others whose duty it was to attend to such matters. These suspicions must be lulled to rest, until Luther's religious views should be positively fixed and should by their own natural development have reached such a degree of maturity as to have no further need of the old ecclesiasticism, and until he should be compelled, in order to maintain his position, to come to an open breach with the latter.

Meanwhile, he simply went on in the discharge of his official

[1] Erl. Ed., xxxi, 327 sq. Op. Ex. Erl., iv, 261, 264. Erl. Ed., xxxi, 72; xxv, 32. Cf. Luther's epitome of the abominations in the words of a poet, Erl. Ed., xxvi, 129 sq.

[2] Erl. Ed., xxiii, 10 ; xxvi, 131.

[3] Mathesius Pred., 1: Tischr. Erl. Ed., lxii, 441. Först., iv, 690.

duties at Wittenberg.   We have not the slightest intimation from any source that he aroused suspicion by critical remarks of any kind.

A new official appointment now furnished the occasion for the first expression of these views in systematic form in theological lectures and writings   This became his duty when he was made a Doctor of Theology.   But he even then at first moved simply and plainly forward in his positive course—full of courage and ready to defend his evangelical convictions, but never dreaming that he should be compelled in their defence to take up arms against the Romish Church.

SECTION II. AS DOCTOR OF THEOLOGY—UNTIL A. D. 1517.

1. Entrance Upon New Office—Positive Teaching.

LECTURES—PRAECEPTORIUM—FIRST EXPOSITION OF THE PSALMS—
DISPUTATIONS—LETTERS—" GERMAN THEOLOGY."

On the 19th of October, 1512, Luther was solemnly invested with the title of Doctor of Theology.   He accepted it only after Staupitz had most strongly urged him to do so, declaring then that he yielded only in obedience to the Vicar and other fathers of his Order, and calling God and his conscience to witness how unworthy of such an honor he felt himself to be and how little he coveted it.[1]   The responsibility which he had now assumed with a heavy heart afterwards gave him firm courage and confidence in his public confession and in his conflicts.   He felt conscious of authority to act, in virtue of the office which had been conferred upon him.   To this consciousness we may attribute the calmness and decision with which he from this time forward in his lectures and writings presents the evangelical truth as fully as he has himself apprehended it.   The same sense of responsibility must have stimulated him to the effort to attain yet greater clearness and more thorough understanding of it.

As to his LECTURES, we note first the report of Melanchthon, that he, as Doctor, " began to expound the *Epistle to the Romans*, then the *Psalms*."   Oldekop, on the other hand, in

----
[1] Briefe, i, 9 sq.   Erl. Ed., xxxix, 256.

1513, simply says [2] that Luther had then just published his first book, namely, a "*præceptorium*," treating of the Ten Commandments, and had at the same time begun to lecture upon the Psalter. In the year 1515 he relates that he had himself removed in the preceding spring to the University of Wittenberg, and that "about that time" Luther had begun to lecture upon the *Epistle to the Romans.* This still leaves room, however, for the question whether Luther had not perhaps already at an earlier period given public expositions of that epistle. We come then to the statement of Luther in the preface to his Latin works, *i. e.*, that he was encouraged to undertake his second exposition of the Psalms by the reflection that he had "now" had fuller preparation through the lectures which he had since delivered upon the Epistle to the Romans, etc. This clearly favors the location of the latter between the first and second courses of lectures upon the Psalms. The essential and unquestioned fact, that it was mainly from the Epistle to the Romans that he from the beginning gained the needed light for the elucidation of the scriptural doctrine of salvation—and this, in fact, as we shall see, in his *First Exposition of the Psalms* as well as elsewhere—may give color to the supposition that he began his public elucidations of the Scriptures with that book. If he did not, however, do so, we must regard it as an indication that he did not as yet feel himself fully competent to undertake the public exposition of the book which for him excelled all others in importance—that, despite the light which he had gained upon its leading doctrine, he did not as yet venture to attempt the elucidation of its entire contents. On the other hand, we can easily understand how the Psalms would naturally seem to offer him suitable material for treatment. They afforded —and he always so regarded them—an expression of the deepest agitations, emotions and struggles which he experienced in his own soul, and which mark the inner life of all truly religious natures. Presenting at once testimony and instruction, they set forth how in the midst of such experiences the soul should aspire to fellowship with God, and how God reveals Himself to it with His salvation.

As to the contents of the "*Præceptorium*" referred to, we have no further information. Oldekop says it "was full of instances

[2] Lüntzel, l. c., p. 156 sq.

(Zufälle), and materials for disputation." So far as we can judge from Luther's earliest exposition of the Psalms, and particularly from his sermons upon the Ten Commandments (after 1516), his investigations and disputes had already at that time concentrated themselves entirely upon the fundamental questions of salvation. The "materials" of Oldekop must therefore have had relation, not to mere questions of casuistry, but to sin, justification, grace, etc.

The earliest work from Luther's hand which has been preserved to us is, as already stated, an *Elucidation of the Psalms*, the greater portion of which, at least, dates from the years 1513 and 1514, when he delivered his first lectures upon this portion of the Bible. There is yet in existence a Latin Psalter (Vulgate text), published in Wittenberg in 1513 (VIII. ante Idus Julias), upon the margin and between the lines of which are running glosses and longer comments in the handwriting of Luther. Luther presented it to his friend, Jacob Propst, and it is preserved in the Wolfenbüttel library. A German translation has been published by Walch.[1] The external arrangement of the book is characteristic, revealing the method which Luther commonly pursued at that time in preparing his exegetical lectures. In the same way, according to the report of Oldekop, he had had a special copy of the text of the Epistle to the Romans printed by the publisher of his Psalter (J. Gronenberg) for his use when lecturing upon that epistle, the lines being set far apart to allow the insertion of glosses. That the annotations in the Psalter referred to really date, substantially at least, from so early a time, is attested by their entire character and contents, when compared with documents of but little later origin, especially with elucidations of the Psalms appearing in the years immediately following. By the end of February, 1517, Luther had completed an exposition of the *Penitential Psalms*, which was at once given to print.[2] In this he already displays a greater freedom in dealing with the Vulgate version (although even in the former volume he had here and there appealed to the original text). He shows, too, a greater caution in the use of allegorical

[1] Luther's Werké, ix, 1474 sqq.—Cf. the statement of Walch in the Preface, pp. 25 sqq., and that of Jürgens, ii, 438 Anm.

[2] Briefe, i, 52. Erl. Ed., xxxvii, 340 sqq.

interpretations and in the immediate application of passages in
the Psalms to Christ : under the Sixth Psalm, for example, which
he had designated as a prayer of Christ, he now makes no reference to such an application.   Verses which in the former were
but briefly commented upon now receive annotations of most
important and significant character, *e. g.*, Ps. li. 8, upon the inward
imparting of the forgiveness of sins, and Ps. cxliii. 12, upon Christ
as our righteousness.   Nowhere, on the contrary, do we find in
the former volume any expressions which reveal an advanced
stage in the conception of evangelical truth, as compared with
this treatise upon the Penitential Psalms.   This latter, moreover,
is evidently, for the most part, the result of entirely independent
labors, and not a product developed from the earlier annotations,
from which these were again in turn enriched.[1]   All that has been
said applies, and with even greater force, to the *Operationes in
Psalmos*, which Luther after 1519 published in connection with
his second course of lectures upon the Psalms.   Furthermore,
if we compare the Annotations with literary remains of the period
before 1517, we will observe no progress of the nature indicated.
On the contrary, there runs through the former a peculiar conception of the Mosaic Law (to be more closely examined hereafter),
which in the latter appears only in an essentially modified form.

Luther no doubt frequently revised the Annotations in question.
Among those originally made are others inserted by his own hand
in different ink.   At the end of the year 1516 a book-dealer re-
quested for printing his " Dictations upon the Psalter," by which
he doubtless meant the glosses suggested to his hearers during the
first course of lectures.   It was his intention at that time, after
his " Pauline lecture course," to devote himself entirely to this
work.   The form in which they have reached us corresponds
exactly with his own designation of them as " not collected in
such shape that they could be printed in his absence." [2]   He

---

[1] But compare, on the other side, Erl. Ed.. xxxvii, 370, under Ps. xxxviii,
with the words of Walch, ix, 1750.

[2] Briefe, i. 47.—Löscher, Reform. Akten, i, 212, infers from the fact that
the " Dictations " were, according to the letter in question, ready " for printing " (as we have seen that they were not), that Luther had not lectured from
them until 1515.—But it is evident that the request may not have been made
until after a longer interval, and it is furthermore quite possible that the desire
of the publisher may have been previously and repeatedly expressed to him.

may already before that time have made occasional additions to them ; but from the very expression we may infer that his attention had then already been entirely demanded by other courses. He was therefore never able to carry out his intention, and must, instead, have applied himself at once to a new series of comments, covering only the Penitential Psalms. At all events, we find the very thoughts which are of chief significance for us, namely, those touching righteousness and grace, running so uniformly through the Annotations as the fundamental ideas of his entire doctrinal position, that they must of necessity have belonged to the original draft. We may, therefore, without hesitancy declare, with Johann Wigand, who had himself seen this book, that we have in it " the beginnings of Luther " (*initia Lutheri*).[1]

The richest source from which to gain a knowledge of Luther's views of doctrine at this time is found, however, in SERMONS, which have been preserved in Latin. First in importance are those *upon the Pericopes* for the Sundays and festivals from St. Martin's Day (November 10), 1515, until the summer of 1517 ;[2] then, the series in which Luther, from the summer of 1516 until St. Matthias' Day (February 21), 1517, treated the Ten Commandments after commenting upon the Pericopes, and which were with his approval published as a connected whole in 1518.[3] We have already mentioned the little treatise upon the *Penitential Psalms*. It was designed " not for cultivated minds, but for the rudest." [4] An *Exposition of the Lord's Prayer* was given by Luther in 1517. It was first published in 1518 by a hearer, who had taken it down at the time. Luther himself then prepared it for publication, in order " to explain his views yet further," and published it within the same year. Even this edi-

---

[1] Walch, ix, Pref. p. 31.

[2] First published by Löscher, Reform. Akten, i, 231 sqq., 745 sqq.—In regard to the years in which they were delivered, cf. Löscher, i, 745. The sermon on St. Martin's Day, which Jürgens (iii, 71) quotes as from the year 1516, belongs to the year 1515. The sermon on St. Martin's Day, 1516, may be found in Löscher, p. 756, as also one upon the Ten Commandments.—Op. Ex. Erl., xii, 104. Löscher, i, 654.

[3] Op. Ex. Erl., xii, 1 sqq. Löscher, i, 577 sqq. Löscher has trom a MS. indicated the days on which they were delivered.—Luther sent them in German and Latin (Briefe, i, 61) already on Sept. 4, 1517 (in MS. form, therefore) to a friend for use in the pulpit.

[4] Briefe, i, 51 sq., 259.

tion contains nothing which might not be accepted as the view
of Luther in the spring of 1517.[1] Finally, mention must be here
made of a *Sermon upon I John* v. 4, which Luther prepared for
his friend, Propst, of Litzka, or Leitzkau, to be preached by the
latter at the Lateran Council, 1516.[2]

Luther frequently made his discoveries of truth and the questions which arose in his own mind the subject of DISPUTATIONS.
Oldekop repeatedly charges him with a fondness for disputing.
Mathesius, too, speaks of protracted disputations of Luther. Of
the earliest of these we have no record preserved. It must remain
an open question, therefore, whether in conducting them he
always, as Mathesius reports, maintained with great decision the
proposition that the true faith is to be learned, not from Aristotle,
but from the Holy Scriptures.[3] We have, on the other hand, two
very important series of theses from the years 1516 and 1517 ;
the one entitled, *De viribus et voluntate hominis sine gratia
contra doctrinam sophistarum*—and the other maintaining the
Augustinian doctrine of grace, especially against Aristotle. He
presented these as subjects for debate when presiding at disputations preparatory to academic promotions.

In 1516 Luther published, with a short preface, a part of the
so-called " GERMAN THEOLOGY," under the title : *Was der alte
und der neue Mensch sei*, following this, in 1518, with a publication of the entire collection with a new preface.[4]

The LETTERS of Luther, which from this time onward are more
numerous, are of very great importance in our investigation.

Such are the original sources by the aid of which we must
endeavor to trace the development of Luther's views until the
breaking out of the controversy upon indulgences. Along with
the positive contents of his teaching, his polemic bearing toward

---

[1] Later Edition: Erl. Ed., xxi, 156 sqq. Löscher, 328 sqq., 539 sqq.—Cf.
Briefe, i, 34, 60, 63.

[2] Löscher, i, 221 sqq.

[3] Jürgens (ii, 487–8) wrongly quotes Mathesius as saying that Luther was
"denounced as a heretic at his first disputa ion." Mathesius says this only
with a general reference to the years before the indulgence controversy.

[3] Erl. Ed., lxiii, 235 sqq—Theologia deutsch, Stuttg.. 1851 (publ. by Pfeifer).
Cf. the references in the preface of this work. Walch, xiv, 20 sq., 205 sq.,
and, following him, Jürgens iii, 268 sqq., wrongly place both prefaces in
the year 1516; and Jürgens understands the first document to have been, not
the " German Theology," but merely something similar to it.

Aristotle and Scholasticism comes into special prominence ; while, on the other hand, the influence of mediæval Mysticism in giving shape to his general conceptions of doctrine is very marked. For the determination of his attitude toward the various ecclesiastical parties, and of his tendency in general, great significance attaches to his relation to Humanism, as illustrated in his utterances in the Reuchlin controversy.

2. DOCTRINE OF THE FIRST EXPOSITION OF THE PSALMS.

THREEFOLD SENSE OF SCRIPTURE—THE "RIGHTEOUSNESS OF GOD"
—FAITH—"MERIT"—CONCEPTION OF GOD—LAW AND GOSPEL—
SAINT WORSHIP—SACRAMENT OF THE ALTAR—EXISTING CHURCH.

We proceed, therefore, first of all, to a careful examination of the "Initia Lutheri," his *Annotations upon the Psalter*, noting particularly the simple, fundamental doctrines touching salvation, which, firmly coherent in their mutual relations, here already found expression in a positive though undeveloped form. He himself, in the preface to his Latin works, says of his first printed publications, that the reader will observe how many and what important articles he at that time still humbly granted to the Pope, which he afterwards came to recognize as blasphemy and abominable errors. At another time he went so far as to say that even after he became a Doctor he knew no better than to imagine that his monk's cowl was pleasing to God and the way to Heaven.[1] We, upon our part, while not failing to observe the "articles" referred to, but, on the contrary, regarding it as characteristic of Luther that he should be able only by a very gradual process to abandon the concessions made, can yet by no means, in the light of these explanations of the Psalter, speak of him as Doctor in such terms as he employs in the second passage quoted. Above all are we compelled to recognize the fact, that, despite all the prejudices which bound him to the doctrinal system of the Church, the evangelical principle which ever after formed the basis of his entire reformatory testimony had already at that time become with remarkable clearness the central point in his convictions.

It might at first glance, indeed, appear to us that Luther was,

[1] Erl., Ed., ix, 15.

in his treatment of the Holy Scriptures, in which he felt vigorous though as yet unsteady pulsations of the truth, still entirely bound to the old school of theology. He starts out, in the traditional way, with the adoption of a THREEFOLD SENSE in the interpretation of Scripture. In his prefatory remarks [1] touching the allegorical, tropological and mystical interpretations, which he in the body of the work constantly seeks to discover, he leaves no independent significance whatever to the simple, literal, historical sense. We must discriminate, he says, between the quickening spirit and the killing letter. We dare not be content with the latter, since it has been " emptied " through Christ.[2] As far as possible, he regards all the contents of the Psalms as declarations of Christ concerning Himself, rejecting the views of Nicholas Lyra whenever they fail to harmonize with this principle.[3]

But it is not his aim to find abstract ideas and dogmas by means of the allegorical and mystical interpretations. The chief sense is for him the tropological, the testimony touching Christian life and for its benefit. Everywhere he reads : " I am he that teacheth thee what is useful ;" and the " ways " which God teaches are the ways of the Gospel, as the message of salvation and grace.[4] As the fundamental conception in his apprehension and presentation of the doctrine of salvation, the idea of righteousness now already presses everywhere into the foreground. This corresponds, as we have seen, to the course of his own development. We have already noticed his preference for the study of the writings of Paul, especially the Epistle to the Romans, and we are not surprised to find that the quotations which he now makes from other books of the Bible consist mainly of passages originally found in this epistle, and treating of righteousness.

Luther has in one passage drawn a distinction between RIGHT-EOUSNESS IN GENERAL and SPECIAL RIGHTEOUSNESS, and of the latter he now declares that it is possessed by no man. He means by the term what he elsewhere calls the righteousness of God. To this he finds testimony throughout the entire Psalter. It is always for him the righteousness, " *by which God makes men righteous* " (cf. supra), not human righteousness or that of the Law, by which

---

[1] Walch, ix, 1478 sqq.—Comp. Jürgens, ii, 438 Aum.

[2] Walch, ix, 1512.

[3] Thus in the passage cited, Ibid., 1918.   [4] Ibid., 1896, 1653.

men may become righteous before God. "The righteousnesses of the Lord are righteous, because they make righteous." This he sees in almost every passage in which a psalmist says, " my righteousness," or, in address to God, " Thy righteousness." He never interprets the word as referring to right conduct of the psalmist in his own works. This righteousness, further, is imputed to *faith ;* " the righteousness of God " is for us " the righteousness of faith." When it is said that " righteousness shall arise," the reference is to an arising of faith, by which we are made righteous before God. This, again, is one with the righteousness of Christ ; and the faith which makes one a partaker of this is the faith that rests upon Christ : *through Christ, in faith upon Him, we are made righteous.* The righteousness of God is defined directly as this faith in Christ itself. This determines, further, Luther's conception of the judgment which God proclaims to the whole race. When it is said (Ps. xcviii. 9) : " He shall judge the world with righteousness," it is the righteousness of faith, by which alone we become righteous before Him. When it is added : " and the people [Luther : the believing] with equity," it means that He will have no regard for the person of any, that He will remove the distinction between Jews and Gentiles, having appointed for all a righteousness of faith. Evidently Luther has here in mind the passage Rom. iii. 30.[1]

Throughout the entire work runs a vein of hostility toward self-righteousness and legal righteousness. In almost every instance in which complaint is made concerning the enemies of God and of the pious, the psalmist (or Christ speaking through the psalmist) has in view, according to Luther's conception, the carnal, self-righteous, Jewish and Judaizing disposition which rejects the salvation offered in Christ and refuses to understand or accept the true righteousness. He quotes, as already stated, especially those passages in the Epistle to the Romans which testify in behalf of the righteousness of faith and self-righteousness, as also, for example, the important passage Eph. ii. 8.[2]

FAITH is defined in general (according to Heb. xi. 1) as an " evidence of invisible things ;" that is, we have in the present life

---

[1] Walch, ix, 1532, 1771, 1845, 1612——1535, 1642, 1731sq., 1987——1612 sq., 1703, 1770 sq., 1969——2191, 2179, 2181.

[2] Ibid., 2387.

7

not the realities themselves, but testimonies to the realities. But the testimony in question is good news. It must be appropriated in faith. Hope is then represented, in intimate relation to faith, as hope in the mercy of God.[1] He cherishes, however, a despair of self and of man's own power, amounting to a complete abnegation of man's own righteousness; and this is based upon a deeper spiritual conception of the *Law* and of *sin*. The Law, according to this conception of it, not only, like that of the Jews, sets its face against open sins, but it binds the soul in its hidden life before God. Every transgression of this is already sin. As soon as we turn our hearts toward created things, we have already turned our backs upon God. We thus commit sins, of omission at least, even when we are doing what is good, and the number of these, according to Psalm xix. 13, we cannot ourselves understand; for we are bound to love God with our whole hearts, and yet we seldom or never do so. We must, therefore, in order that we may be able to receive the grace of God in faith, be prepared through chastisement by means of the divine Word, and through troubles which God sends upon us. The flesh must be crucified. The saints must become, and always remain, bitter to themselves, in order that the mercy of God may become sweet to them. The soul becomes silent before God, because it knows of nothing more of which to boast, and every mouth is stopped (Rom. iii. 19). Luther, in one place, declares of this self-humiliation and self-condemnation, as is commonly said of faith, that it is accounted as righteousness before God.[2] But when he endeavors to present specifically that by means of which salvation itself is actually attained, he always mentions faith as that positive turning to the grace of God, for which the surrender of self is the negative condition and presuppositon. Faith is the central point, the marrow, the " short path."[3] It is to be observed, however, on the other hand, that he does not attempt to define strictly the conception of the positive essence of faith itself. As related to the grace of God, to which man on his part can bring nothing, faith presents itself as a simple accepting of that which

---

[1] Walch, ix, 1835 sq., 1612, 1702 sq., 1708.

[2] Ibid., 1708, 1614, 1667, 1890, 1929, 2086, 1965, 1907, 1909, 2167.

[3] Ibid., 1565.—In the same way, p. 1703, the Gospel is said to guide in a short path to eternal happiness.

is offered.   But along with this, love also is placed in the very beginning of the Christian life[1] ; as when it is said to be the beginning of such a life " to know and to love that which belongs to faith."   Even the expression, " unformed faith," to which the scholastic theology, as is well known, set in contrast, as justifying, the faith "formed " by love, meets us in one place—in a connection, however, in which the way of justification is not the subject of discussion, but in which the author is merely lamenting that the faith of his day was so often ineffectual.[2]   At a later day, Luther, in the interest of the view which holds faith as of itself justifying and as having in itself its own life, vigorously opposed the whole conception of faith as unformed (*informis*) and formed (*formata*.)

If we now scrutinize more carefully that righteousness, by which God in Christ makes us righteous, it will be found to embrace, first of all, THE REMISSION OF THE GUILT, under which the believer groans.   Sin is not imputed.   Luther holds the first signification of the passage 1 John iii. 9 (" he that is born again doth not commit sin ") to be, that the sins of such an one are not imputed ; that he is now also able to forsake sin, is but allowed as the second signification.[3]   Yet he never defines this righteousness in such a way as to limit its significance chiefly, or even approximately, to the single element of the remission of guilt, or God's acceptance of man as righteous.   Without attempting any sharper discrimination of the elements embraced, he uses the term in general in such a way as evidently to include in it the IMPLANTING OF A DISPOSITION IN HARMONY WITH RIGHT AND WITH GOD'S WILL and a consequent RIGHTEOUS BEHAVIOR on the part of man.   It carries with it particularly the idea that man is " made righteous'' (*justificetur*).   It is this new attitude, this new behavior of man, that he has in view when he speaks of righteousness as a righteousness " in the spirit before God."   It is a state of righteousness in man's own inner nature, a righteous behavior from simple righteous disposition.   The opposite idea is hypocrisy, or that one should only outwardly with the hand do what is righteous.[4]   We shall find this conception of righteousness, in which Luther betrays particularly the influence of his favorite teacher, Augustine, still further

---

[1] Thus at least, Walch, ix, 1900.   [2] Ibid., 2010.

[3] Ibid., 1717.   [4] Ibid., 1613, 1923.

prevailing in his writings.   It is everywhere dominant in his *First Exposition of the Psalms.*

With this righteousness comes PEACE.   Christ himself, in whom we are righteous, is our Peace.   In Christ we have further, according to Psalm li. 13, the "free" (*freiwilliger*) spirit, *i. e.*, the spirit of liberty, as opposed to the spirit of fear, the servile spirit of the Law.   This spirit makes free servants of Christ.   Thus the Gospel is in Psalm lxviii. 10 called a plentiful (free, *freiwilliger*) rain, whereas the Law was a violent force drying up the land.   As the Gospel of God guides through faith in a short path to everlasting happiness (vid. supra), so God also makes in His Word an easy path, that we may be enabled to exercise the virtues which He approves.   Luther has now learned to regard the exhortation of the Second Psalm, which once so greatly distressed him (*i. e.*, that we should serve God with fear and rejoice with trembling), as an expression in harmony with the Gospel.   The fear there spoken of is now for him one that fills the very heart : it is a joy to the heart to fear God.   The punishments which God ordains, he no longer regards as simply punishments ; as a result of the suffering of Christ, they redound further to the "amendment and merit" of men.   He gives the assurance that even when the saints of God are called upon to endure temptations, He is not angry, although to outward view He may seem to be so.[1]

When man lives thus in the Spirit and in faith, his life is also WELL-PLEASING TO GOD.   But that which we have heard Luther declare in regard to the defectiveness of man's love to God and of his *good works* applies none the less, in his view, to believing Christians.   Furthermore, in every good work of ours, God does to us more good than we ourselves accomplish.   Still further, no work of the believing and regenerated is valid or sufficient in itself, but only in so far as God in His grace accepts it as valid.   Not only for those who seek to enter upon the state of salvation, but also for such as already enjoy the grace of God, man's own righteousness is strictly excluded.[2]

In the same spirit Luther declares in regard to his fundamental conception, namely, that of "the righteousness of God," that

[1] Walch, ix, 2096, 1844, 1946, 1950——2102——2142, 2143.

[2] Ibid., 1615, 2158, 2262.

man must put this on, but cannot do so fully in this life ; and hence no man living is righteous before God, since there is no one who does not sin. By the righteousness of God which is to be put on, Luther here means again righteousness implanted in the individual as moral character and moral life. But no one is righteous by virtue of this implanted righteousness. When, on the contrary, the forgiveness of sins is in question, he constantly avers that this is now complete. In this respect, faith makes truly righteous already in the present life, and it does so just because the forgiving is always bestowed upon faith from pure grace, and not by virtue of our own works, nor even by virtue of the exercises begotten in us by grace. Freely and gratuitously does God ever forgive all offences. He covers over daily faults. He heals now all our diseases, in that He forgives our inability to do good and our inclinations to evil.[1] In this we must of course recognize a limitation of what Luther has said (vid. supra, p. 99) in connection with 1 John iii. 9 concerning the ability to refrain from sin as granted to the regenerate.

In isolated passages we read, as above, of a " *merit*," for the attainment of which God overrules sufferings. There can in this be no lingering thought of any endurance of suffering as establishing for Christians a personal claim upon God. Even at a later day, Luther now and then unguardedly employed the word " *meritum* " without attaching any such meaning to it. To "merit" means for him in such connections only to secure or gain the blessings of salvation. The very fact that Luther so unconditionally excludes, even in the case of the regenerate, all efficacy of human efforts draws already, though unconsciously to himself, a remarkably clear line of distinction between his view of the order of salvation, as this is constantly presented in his *Exposition of the Psalms*, and that of Augustine, whom he yet quotes with unusual frequency in his Annotations, and whose influence upon his own conception of the righteousness of God, so gratefully acknowledged by him, has recently claimed our attention. He no longer speaks of " *Genugthuungen*," the rendering of satisfaction by means of alms or other good works, by which the regenerate must do penance for new sins. They, too, have been superseded by the " short path " of faith.

[1] Walch, ix, 2506, 2218 sq.

It will be in harmony with Luther's own doctrinal method if we *from this point of view* regard the conception which he entertained of GOD'S OWN CHARACTER AND BEING and his objective COUNSEL AND ACTIVITY. It is plainly evident throughout the entire course of his explanations that, in view of his own religious need, and the general need which he presupposes in his readers, he is primarily concerned to present, not opinions or theses upon God Himself, but our own relation, particularly the relation of our moral life, to God and God's doing for us, to us, and in us. It is very characteristic of these initial lectures that he never allows himself to attempt an express development of these topics. We are reminded, as we read his lectures, at every point of his designation of the tropological sense as the most important, and his constant reference to the teaching of " what is useful " to us (p. 96). In the development of his views in the writings now under observation there may always be traced this same underlying purpose, as afterwards also, for example, in Melanchthon's first draft of his *Loci*. The conception of God Himself, however, which his writings reveal took shape in his mind in entire accordance with the testimony which he found in the Gospel as to the doings of God, and with the life and experience of believers themselves.

Accordingly, GRACE and MERCY are the traits which are everywhere prominent in Luther's conception of God. In a still more general way, he at one time speaks of God as the essentially Good Being, who must therefore be praised for His own sake, and not only on account of His outward gifts to man.[1] This goodness he then sees in active operation as free mercy, seeking to secure for sinners righteousness and salvation. Yet ever hand in hand with the workings of grace goes the exercise of holy JUDGMENT. The old man must be condemned and crucified. Thus within man himself judgment must be executed, just as righteousness is imparted to him in faith ; and in this process man learns to know himself. It is thus that this righteousness and this judgment are the bulwarks of the throne of God (Ps. lxxxix. 14).[2] Further, there hangs over the carnally-minded the judgment which condemns flesh and sin, separating those who walk in the Spirit from those who walk in the flesh. It will be finally most distinctly revealed in the Last Day upon those who have done good in the

[1] Walch, ix, 1860, 1861.   [2] Ibid., 2120, 2193.

spirit and upon those who have done evil in the flesh.[1] Thus
Luther maintains the holiness and righteousness of God with all
the earnestness with which the original impression of these divine
attributes had filled his soul, whilst, at the same time, the fundamental aim of God in His dealings with the race is always presented as tending toward the revelation of mercy and the imparting of that righteousness of God which He bestows on man.
Several remarkable passages, in which he speaks of the wrath of
God, are worthy of special notice in this connection. He represents the Scriptures as often speaking of a most fierce and relent-
less wrath, which in Psalm lxxiv. 1 is called " furious wrath ;" but
declares that wrath is never altogether without goodness. In
one place, indeed, conceiving of wrath as an objective power
called into being by sin, and as equivalent to death, he declares
in bold language that God Himself hates wrath, *i. e.*, death, and
is angry at it : for He did not make death, and has no pleasure
in the destruction of the ungodly, but has pleasure in life and
loves it ; He makes alive and holy, in order to destroy death.[2]

It is, further, essentially characteristic of Luther's conception
of God as merciful, that he always contends that God in the exercise of His mercy acts wholly and unconditionally upon the
impulse of His own nature—that the work of salvation is purely
and alone His work, a work of His divine and therefore eternal
will and decree. That God is influenced in the exercise of mercy
by human deed or merit, he denies, not only in reference to man
as fallen into sin, but in general and on antecedent grounds. He
maintains that the mercy of God has existed from all eternity.
No man has merited it ; for all men are later in their origin.[3] We
shall in the later writings of Luther find a much more thorough
presentation of his view of the unconditioned character of the
divine will and working. It stood in direct connection with his
deep religious consciousness of his own inability and unworthiness
before God. In the fact that it was developed under the strict
and constant control of such a sentiment, we may see again the
special influence of Augustine. This view maintained its place
also amid all the later advances in his theological positions. But
from the way in which he actually employs it, we at once again
discover the religious root from which it sprang. It thus becomes

[1] Walch, ix, 2200.   [2] Ibid., 2206, 1682.   [3] Ibid., 1651 sq.

evident that it had its origin, at least in its *essential basis*, not in any philosophical or metaphysical process of thought, but in the sphere of religious interest ; and, still further, not in a general sense of the divine power, but directly in personal submission to that mercy from whose free exercise alone he felt that he could hope to receive salvation, and with which, if weakened in the least in its unconditioned character, the certainty of his own salvation threatened to fail him.   We may already observe, accordingly, that he never speaks of this unconditioned character of the eternal divine will except when treating of the original foundation of salvation.

The WORK OF CHRIST is thus only a carrying out of the divine will.   In Christ, says Luther, God seems to have called to mind again, as it were, what had really been from all eternity (by which, of course, He means only to present the matter as it appears from a human point of view).[1]   But this interposition of the eternal mercy realized in time does not, because thus subordinate, retreat into the background.   The fact is just the opposite. It is remarkable how seldom Luther speaks of the eternal decree. The eye of his faith is, upon the contrary, always directed upon the incarnate Christ.   To Him he constantly points his hearers. In the effort to become a partaker of salvation, and to be sure of his part in it, he holds simply to Him in whom he finds the Holy Scriptures testifying that Eternal Mercy offers itself to men, and in whose person, life and death he sees the revelation of that mercy.   The conception of Christ's nature and work stands again in close relation to Luther's fundamental idea of the " righteousness of God."   It is just the latter which is bestowed by Christ and in faith.   Here, too, as in Luther's conception of that righteousness in general, the thought is, first of all, of the blotting out of guilt, but at the same time, also, of the imparting of righteousness to the inner nature.

If, indeed, we but seldom meet with abstract speculations in regard to the divine nature in itself considered, we have, on the other hand, abundant references to it as the definite object of faith.   After this he strives, into this he penetrates, in this he moves, just as does that saving faith itself which unites the subject with his God.   *Christ* is the essentially righteous One ; from

[1] Walch, ix, 2097, 2098.

His essential righteousness flow all His works.[1]   Further, in order that He may be able to make righteous before God, if for no other reason, He must Himself be God.   God gives His glory to no other; hence, *He* can be no other to whom is given righteousness in order that He may make others righteous (cf. John v. 26).[2]   The humanity of Christ is only, so to speak, His back; His divinity is His face.[3]   On the other hand, the institution and impartation of the salvation which He brings for us is attributed directly to His humanity.   By virtue of His human nature, He is the rock upon which His congregation on earth is builded, the foundation and corner-stone of His whole Church—far above all men and angels.[4]   We observe a special fondness for the tracing of those strictly human features in the life of Christ in which His mercy toward us is displayed; as, for example, when it is said that He may often at other times have wept in the night, as at the grave of Lazarus.[5]   At the same time, it is mainly as the One who has borne our sins that He is presented to our view.   We may refer, for illustration, to His weeping, which nothing but our sins occasioned, and, especially, to His last sufferings and death.   It is here that the consciousness of the primitive divine wrath directed against sin asserts itself in its full strength.   In many sentences, scattered through the entire work, we find already a complete expression of that very deep view of the *sufferings of Christ* as due to the wrath of God which remained a distinct characteristic of Luther's teaching.   It was punishment, which He there endured.   He saw the wrath of God, and therefore wept and prayed for us.   In order to suffer thus, He took upon Himself infirmity from the sole of His foot to the crown of His head.   Confessions of sin uttered by the psalmists are to be regarded as spoken directly by Him.   He, made to be sin and a curse for us, confessed our own sins before God.   The death which He suffered was that appointed for Adam : He reaped what Adam sowed.   He even tasted hell, but did not exhaust its misery.   The ungodly must drink the dregs, and can never fully drain the cup.   Believers now, on the other hand, shall never taste of it.[6]   This language is meant to convey the idea of actual inner suffering.   Luther wishes to present the suffering Saviour as

[1] Walch, ix, 2c97 sq.   [2] Ibid., 1984.   [3] Ibid., 2066.
[4] Ibid., 1949.   [5] Ibid., 1515.   [6] Ibid., 1525, 1590, 1762, 1750, 1959, 2305.

having become entirely like the human soul tormented under the burden of sin. Yet, since He was cut off from every source of comfort and utterly forsaken in His agony, the divine power sustained Him in the midst of His suffering.[1] But there was in this awful experience nothing left to Him but the *hope* that God would help Him and raise Him up again, and even this hope filled Him with anxiety.[2] Luther even ventures, placing the language of Psalm lxxi. 9, concerning the failing of strength, in the mouth of Christ Himself, to interpret the strength there referred to as equivalent to "the faith by which I have overcome the kingdoms of the world," and the failing of this strength is said to have occurred while the Saviour was hanging upon the cross.[3] Referring to the disturbance and perplexity of the heart under the multitude of sins, spoken of, for example, in Psalm xl. 14, he declares that this occurred to the fullest extent in the case of Christ, even as He also experienced the highest joy.[4]

We find ourselves thus brought to consider the process which must go on also in our own hearts. Christ has taken upon Himself that which sin would have brought upon us. Within ourselves also, therefore, must be constantly executed a judgment against sin. Yet this is conceived in such a way that there is no thought of salvation as wrought out through any endurance or suffering of our own. Salvation, on the other hand, is made to depend entirely upon the sufferings of Christ, and to demand such sufferings upon our part only as a negative condition for its application to us. It is further maintained, that the believer shall no longer experience at all the wrath of God, nor taste of hell, since this has all been endured for him by Christ. As in this manner a fellowship is represented as established between Christ and us, according to Luther's view, we should naturally expect to find, on the other hand, a presentation of the corresponding truth that the entire fullness of Christ's resources (blessings), and even of His own nature, is transferred to us and the life of believers becomes His life. But in the publication now before us such a view has not yet attained the least recognition. This is the more

---

[1] Walch, ix, 1590.—Yet it is to be observed that Luther, in explaining the language of Psalm xxii. 1, "Why hast Thou forsaken me?" merely says: "Given into the hands of the Jews, when Thou withdrewest from me the help of the divine nature" (der Gottheit).—Vid. Ibid., 1628.

[2] Ibid., 1958. [3] Ibid., 1979. [4] Ibid., 1773.

remarkable since it is so fully presented in the later writings of the Reformer. It is to be observed, in general, that we here find as yet no such treatment of inner communion with Christ as is afterwards accorded to the subject, and, particularly, no such emphasis upon communion in the possession of His blessings and life. It is very often declared, indeed, in connection with the interpretation of psalms as personal expressions of Christ, that He is speaking also at the same time in the name of His Church, especially when He speaks of His sufferings, confesses His sins, etc. We should, it is said, pray such psalms " in Christ," combining our own emotions with His, and saying, Amen.[1] A similar view is to be taken of the passages in which He prays for or announces His own victory or resurrection. But still there is no express treatment of the theme of personal communion with Christ; and it is usually rather " the Church " than the individual which is regarded as the subject in whose name, together with His own, Christ is said to pray. In the appropriation of salvation by believers, the reference is everywhere to the idea of " righteousness." It is this which is represented as bestowed by Christ, and, with this, the forgiveness of sins, the new inward disposition, the new graces—not, therefore, Christ Himself as living in us. Luther repeatedly, in presenting the view of the language of the Psalms as uttered by Christ at once in His own name and in that of the Church, declares that, according to Augustine, Christ and the Church are one flesh, as bride and bridegroom.[2] This is a figure of speech to which we shall at a later period find him attaching the fullest development of the idea of personal communion. But it is on this account only the more remarkable how little use he here makes of the proposition of Augustine in his own comments, and, especially, how utterly he fails to employ it as applicable also to the relation of Christ to the individual soul. This furnishes us, incidentally, another evidence as to the early date of the present document.

Returning now from this point to the consideration of that exhibition of divine energy, in which Eternal Mercy is revealed in time, we shall find the salvation instituted by Christ and dependent upon Him represented as brought to the individual by means

---

[1] Thus under Psalm xxxviii. in Walch, ix, 1750.

[2] Walch, ix, 1750, 2337, 1772.

of the GOSPEL, which God proclaims through His messengers. It is this which makes justified men.[1] It has its continued being, as it originated, from pure mercy, and not from our works and merits.[2] Even the *effective working of the Gospel* in the individual is again traced back to eternal and solely-regnant mercy. As this was in existence before man was created, it is said : " Blessed is the man whom Thou *from eternity hast chosen*, to be reconciled to him, and whom Thou hast also accepted in the time of grace ; for such an One shall dwell in Thy courts as an heir and a son." [3] *Faith itself* is then directly described as wrought by God. " Faith, in which everything good is embraced, is a *gift of God*." God, it is said, gives righteousness, since He bestows faith.[4] We are to interpret in the light of these declarations the further proposition, that in the reception of the Gospel by the individual God must " directly inspire and teach man." [5] Yet, however positively Luther now and in later years speaks of the divine working as the only factor in the origination of our faith, without even designating as an affair of the human subject the acceptance of that which God does ; and however decidedly the doctrine of unconditioned election is for him combined with this conception, and even openly professed,—it is nevertheless already evident that the chief stress in the elaboration of his views is not laid upon this point. He appears, upon the contrary, to have purposely refrained from entering any further upon the discussion of predestinarian conclusions or premises. This brings to view again the practical religious central point of his own entire apprehension of truth, and the practical religious tendency of his teaching. He is concerned, first of all and above all, to know and testify the truth which man must accept in order to become righteous and be saved ; and this is for him, not the doctrine of the objective eternal decree itself, not the docrine of the divine act which works faith in the subject, but it is Christ held up to our view and the message of His work of salvation announced to us. Because he looks upon Christ and lays hold upon the message announced, he is well content to be an object of the gracious divine decree. It is his effort, by simply pointing his hearers in this direction, to promote the divine working upon their souls. He knows that

---

[1] Walch, ix, 1703.   [2] Ibid., 2127.   [3] Ibid., 1925.

[4] Ibid., 2331, 2193.   [5] Ibid., 1981.

God Himself, in carrying on His work of grace, asks of us no further service than simple testimony to the truth. He quietly lays aside the difficult theoretical problems which arise in connection with the positions indicated. Even self-glorying he rebukes, not so much by presenting the unconditioned character of the divine working in itself, as by holding before his hearers, upon the contrary, on the one hand, man's own sin and guilt, and on the other, unmerited grace as revealed in Christ—in a word, by simply preaching faith as capable of bearing to grace only a relation of pure receptivity. In this, again, we note clearly the great difference between Luther and his teacher, Augustine. We are reminded, on the other hand, of the counsel received from Staupitz at the time of his early spiritual troubles about predestination.

The problems in question are thus, indeed, left to stand unsolved. It may be objected, that we should strive to find a definite solution of them with which the demands of the practical religious interest of which we speak may be seen to be in harmony. It would not, however, be in place for us here to pursue this problem farther, but it is for us merely to record, as matter of history, in how far Luther, for himself or in behalf of others, entered into these discussions or avoided them, and how, accordingly, we are to estimate the peculiar features of the doctrinal position which he maintained. We shall hereafter find him led upon various occasions to much more positive explanations and elaborations in regard to the unconditioned divine decree and working. But his manner of dealing with these questions, seeking to avoid the suspicions which they are calculated to arouse, will be found to be always in keeping with the attitude which he assumes in these first expositions of the Psalms. His fundamental interest will always be seen to be precisely that which now dominates him. The question will hereafter arise in how far he at any time, while maintaining this interest, enters into the doctrinal investigations and accommodations whose absence is already here so noticeable.

In intimate connection with the doctrine of the way of salvation thus developed, we find yet one further article which demands our attention, and which reveals, upon the one hand, very plainly the continued influence of the dominant theology, and especially that of Augustine, upon Luther, whilst, on the other hand, affording us a preliminary announcement of the path which he afterwards marked out for himself as demanded by his own fundamental principle. We refer to the doctrine of the relation between LAW and GOSPEL. In examining this we shall find ourselves also brought back to a further consideration of those views of Luther touching the *sense of Scripture* to which our attention has already been directed.

The Gospel, as the word of grace, justifies; it leads by the short path of faith to eternal happiness.[1] The Law is now set over against Grace. It is considered as demanding from us efforts of our own. Thus it is said, according to Rom. iii. 21, that righteousness is revealed without law; the Law can do nothing to make better. The Mosaic Law is said to crucify the heart, since it increases the remembrance of sin; the "righteousnesses of the Lord," upon the contrary, rejoice the heart, since they make righteous. Thus Grace is the morning; the Law is the evening and the night (under Psalm v. 2).[2] Thus far all is in perfect keeping with the Pauline mode of thought, and, we may add, with that which afterwards characterized Luther.

But, together with this, we now find an expansion of the conception of the Law. It is made to include even the Gospel itself, as "New Law." Christ Himself, as the originator of the Gospel, is called a lawgiver. The Gospel is thus spoken of as the "law of faith," with appeal, indeed, to Rom. iii. 27, but especially, also, in so far as it reveals God's will concerning our moral conduct. While man meditates upon the law of the Gospel, his steps shall be conducted onward from one virtue to another.[3] Upon the other hand, we find the conception of the Gospel at the same time enlarged, the term being applied to the entire sum of the divine requirements, as these meet us in the New Testament revelation. These two elements also, the proffer of salvation and the divine requirement, appear in the closest mutual relation, inasmuch as the "New Law of the Gospel" has taken its origin, not from human works, but from Grace, and as God Himself grants the power of fulfilling the requirements.[4] Even the chastening, punitive, condemning Word of God, as this is perfectly revealed in the new covenant, is included under the term, Gospel. Thus the *wrath* of God is said (with appeal to Rom. i. 18) to

[1] Walch, ix, 1703 sq.   [2] Ibid., 1516, 2037, 1650.
[3] Ibid., 1655, 1608 sqq., 1550, 2089, 1746.   [4] Ibid., 2127, 2089 sq.

be revealed by the Gospel, since men did not before know that they were under such wrath. The same testimony which directs to Christ convinces those who do not make proper use of it that they are sinners.[1]

In short, the whole New Testament revelation is defined as " Gospel." It is the same thing as the New Law. The opposite conception is the Old Law; and this again is conceived of as identical with the " Law of Moses." " There are two kinds of years : one is the year of the Old Law and the other the year of the New Law. The incarnation and the sufferings of Christ lie midway between these years of the Old and the New Testament." In so far, therefore, as the Gospel and the Law are in general expressions opposed to one another, we must in Luther understand by the latter only a Law in the narrower sense of the word.

As the divine demands are thus included in the scope of the Gospel ; so, reversing the case, we are to understand, as embraced under the Old Law, or Law in the narrower sense of the word, also the foreshadowing and prophecy of salvation itself, though yet veiled under figurative language. Of the contents of the " clear " New Testament commandment, which is the same thing as the " righteousness of the Lord," it is said, in a very general way, that in contrast with it the " Law " yet veiled the eyes with figures of speech, as the face of Moses was covered with a veil (cf. 2 Cor. iii. 13). What in the " Law " was but a word is now a work. Then it was a promise, now it is fulfilment; then it was a sign, now it is the thing itself ; then it was a type, now it is the truth itself : and the " work of the Lord," meanwhile, falls " midway between the years " (vid. supra). Similarly, it is said that Christ now fulfils what had been prefigured in the " Old Testament." The Law and the Old Testament are regarded as one.[2]

If we now inquire in what, according to the above, Luther makes the essential difference between the Gospel and the Law, or between the Old and the New Law, to consist, we may find an appropriate starting-point in meeting the inquiry in the proposition just cited, i. e., what there was word, is here work. More fully, it is to be said, that in the former Luther sees a Word, in which reposes, indeed, already the divine content of the Gospel,

[1] Walch, ix, 2137, 2037.   [2] Ibid., 1929, 1851 sq., 2181.

but which does not yet communicate what it possesses, remaining, upon the contrary, for man only a word, and therefore a bare *letter*. In the latter God Himself works for the communication and establishment of that which had there been already promised to men and was required by them; and He does thus, further, through His Spirit. He now, as we have seen above, inspires directly, and His Spirit makes alive and strong. It is the grace of the Spirit which now makes the heart willing, whereas the letter of the Law made it indolent.[1] We have observed that the righteousness of God, as a spiritual disposition and life, is regarded as the opposite of a merely external activity. But it must be remembered that this conception, too, was regarded as already essentially embraced in the Law or under the letter. " The New Law lay already in the Old." " The Law, spiritually understood, is the same as the Gospel." The Old Testament Scriptures were already " pregnant with the Spirit." The perverted Jews ripped them open before the time of delivery (after Psalm xii. 1) and destroyed what was perfect in the Law, namely, the Spirit.[2] But the New Law was at that time yet waiting for the coming of the deliverer, through whom it should be brought to light and revealed. Now for the first time were revealed the fountains of living water, or the books of the Old Law freed from the shadows of the ancient types.[3]

In thus contrasting the Spirit and the Letter, Luther appeals expressly to utterances of St. Paul, especially to the third chapter of Second Corinthians. But if we examine closely we shall detect here a mode of apprehension which differs not only from that peculiar to St. Paul, but also from that which he himself afterwards adopted. We may best observe the peculiarity by a direct comparison with the Pauline view. When St. Paul declares the Law to be incapable of saving men, he has in view chiefly the holy requirements of God (without grace and in contrast with it), *i. e.*, in the Mosaic Law mainly the distinctly moral commandments, including, however, also the testimony in the voice of every man's conscience corresponding to the demands of the positive Law. He regards the Law as in itself holy and good and given to minister life. The reason for its remaining a bare

[1] Walch, ix, 1981, 2314.   [2] Ibid., 2356, 1558, 1561, 1563.
[3] Ibid., 2356, 1595.

letter, powerless and working death, lies on man's side, in the
sinful flesh. It is in this light also that the matter is viewed in
the first-cited utterances of Luther, in which he declares that no
one becomes righteous through the works of the Law. But if we
carefully consider his entire discussion of the subject, we shall find
it nevertheless characterized by a view which, while distinctly recognizing the power of sin in men themselves, yet attributes the
weakness of the (old) Law and its inability to produce life essentially to its *objective form*, viz., the definite form of the *Mosaic*
Law. He has constantly in view that peculiarity of this Law by
virtue of which it becomes itself, through its " letter," a means
of directing to a bare external, sensuous activity those who have
not yet been led to comprehend its inner spiritual meaning. Of
the letter in general, he says, that it consists of everything which
has to do only with the body and the senses, not with the spirit.[1]
But the Letter and the Old Law are in his thought identical. Of
the Jewish Church he declares, that it knows no spiritual transgressions, but only those which are outward and sensual ; while, upon
the contrary, it is only the New Law which purges from the
hidden sins that lie in the soul.[2] To the " reality of the divine
righteousness," which consists in humility, self-accusation, etc.,
he opposes the shadows of the Law in its righteousness.[3] Here
we may recall, too, the above-quoted expression in regard to the
" figurative language " with which the Law veiled the eyes of men.
Luther even bluntly declares that the Law of Moses gave instruction only to the outward senses.[4] Everywhere in these utterances
of his we may detect that peculiar conception of the Law which
combines without distinction those two features of its contents, by
virtue of which it, on the one hand, makes demands upon the
individual, and, on the other, in its cultus prefigures the future
work of salvation. Even the external, historical contents of the
Old Testament and its declarations in regard to the outward
working of God in nature fall for him under this conception of
the Letter. He utters a very deep thought and full of true meaning when he declares that by all the works and deeds of God
recorded in the Old Testament was foreshadowed what should in
the future come to pass through Christ.[5] But the utterances of

[1] Walch, ix, 1510.   [2] Ibid., 1614.   [3] Ibid., 1842.
[4] Ibid., 2357.   [5] Ibid., 1932.
8

the Old Testament in regard to these are not accorded their true significance, since the Letter is regarded as only the shell of spiritual truth. All this is connected very closely with the allegorical interpretation which Luther extended as far as possible. By this he would release the Spirit from the bondage of the Letter. But, on the other hand—and we call especial attention to this fact—it is never clearly indicated what was, before the revelation of grace, the relation of man to the divine Law itself, leaving out of view the " figurative " character of the latter. Only of this Law in itself can it be said that it " increases the remembrance of sin and takes captive with distress," as we have heard Luther so emphatically declare (vid. p. 110). Yet immediately upon this declaration follows the other expression referred to, which lays all stress upon the " figurative character " of the Old Testament language.

The manner in which Luther thus combines different views of the Law is no doubt to be explained, on the one hand, by the influence of the writings of St. Paul and his own personal experiences, and, on the other hand, by the preponderating power still exercised upon him by the traditional modes of doctrinal expression, and particularly that of Augustine. We know how highly he esteemed Augustine's treatise, *De spiritu et litera*, on account of its teaching concerning righteousness; and in this treatise we find the very conception of " the Letter " which we have above noted.

It will help us to understand the course of Luther's development if we now call to mind the ways in which, it would appear, the view then entertained as to the Law and the Gospel might have further led him.

What value, it may be inquired, does the Old Law then yet possess for us? Its *peculiarity*, as compared with the New Law, appears, by this view, to consist entirely in the fact that it *veiled* what has now been made manifest. Why then still go back to it, since that which was valuable in its contents is now accessible to us in the New Law in an entirely different form—why back to that Letter which has been " emptied " by Christ? In regard to the Old Law as a body of moral requirements, if we take the term, " Gospel," in the wider sense of Luther, and the term, " Law," as opposed to " Gospel," in the narrow sense (as the Old Law), the question will be : Why still preach the Law at all, and not merely the Gospel? We shall hereafter see how, in Luther's later conception of the difference between Law and Gospel, the preaching of the Law as such demanded and secured its rightful place.

Again, it may be asked : What is to be thought of the original value of that " Letter," whose sole peculiarity thus appears to lie in the fact that it is a veil of the truth and withholds the revelation of the latter. We find, indeed, remarkable expressions bearing upon this point. Luther, for example, already frequently speaks of the Old Law simply as one in which God has taught men. He quotes from Psalm ciii. 7 the declaration that " God made known His ways unto Moses and His will to the children of Israel ;" and he describes even the " ceremonial law " as being the testimonies of God.[1] But then, again, he uses the strong expression in regard to the " Law of Moses," that it is not an unspotted law (Ps. ci. 2), and that the only unspotted law is that of Christ. Of the origin of the Law, he declares in commenting upon Psalm lxxviii. 1, in which God speaks of the " words of his mouth," that the mouth of Moses and Aaron was a strange mouth, and that only now, in the Gospel, does God open His own mouth, since He no longer desires to speak through a strange mouth in shadows and figures. He even contrasts that " Law " which veils the eyes with figurative language directly with the " commandments of the Lord," without calling also the former a law " of the Lord." In one passage he combines in one conception " the Law of Moses " and " human law", declaring that they have not led into the truth, but into the digression of figures and the by-way of ceremonies.[2] Had then, really, that form of the Old Law, by virtue of which it was Law as contrasted with Gospel, its origin in the transmission of the Mosaic revelation through human organs, and in the consequent defects and weaknesses? Upon this point we observe an undeniable lack of clearness in the utterances of Luther. It is evident, too, that the subordinate position which he here seems in danger of assigning to the Law as a consequence of its origin has an intimate connection with Luther's peculiar deep consciousness of the fact that only evangelical grace can save, that the Gospel only can avail in the actual achievement of salvation. He was thus led to expressions

---

[1] Walch, ix, 1220, 2196.   [2] Ibid., 2201, 2035, 1612, 1651.

touching the Old Law, into which the traditional conception of
"the Letter" by which he was still controlled did not indeed
fall, but only because it had not so conceived the value of the
Gospel as he had.   There appeared reason to fear that he should
approximate the positions of the ancient Gnostics against the
Law.   But the combination of ideas noted was inevitable under
the circumstances, resulting from the fact that he, while maintaining the evangelical position attested by his own consciousness,
was yet at the same time influenced by the prevalent views upon
the subject.   He was afterwards, however, driven by the consider-
ations which constituted the central point and basis of his own
evangelical convictions to overcome this disturbing influence.
His peculiar consciousness of sin and guilt leads him to perceive
more clearly that it may be said of *all law*—of every revelation
of the divine requirements, and not only of such as presented
under the garb of ceremonies—that it cannot bring justification
and life, but is powerless for such a purpose, and can, on the contrary, but work death.   He then clearly sees that the explanation
of this fact lies, not at all in the form of the Law itself, but in
the sin and carnal nature of man.

The view which we have been discussing gives occasion, on the
other hand, to fear evil results as to the authority of the Gospel
itself.   If the weakness of the Old Law is conceived as bearing
such an essential relation to its outward form, and if the saving
Gospel is regarded as already included in the contents of the
general moral requirements of the former, it may well be asked
whether it will be possible to maintain with sufficient distinctness
the peculiar significance of the preaching of salvation as contrasted with the preaching of the divine commandments.   Is not
the saving efficacy which is ascribed particularly to the Gospel
to be attributed likewise to the *preaching of the Law*, now that the
obstructing veil which rested upon the Old Testament presentation
of the divine commandments has been removed?   We recall in
this connection the then prevalent theory of the theologians which
applied the declarations of St. Paul against the righteousness
gained through the Law, and against the works of the Law, only
to the Mosaic Law in its ceremonial character, and which attributed, on the contrary, to the preaching of the perfect revealed
commandments of God an efficacy for the achievement of righteousness itself, and thus also of salvation.   When, therefore,

Luther proceeded to present the Gospel as in opposition to the commandments of men, *i. e.*, the outward ecclesiastical ordinances, declaring that the latter could not of themselves lead to justification, it might be asked at the outset whether he did not do so simply on account of their ceremonial form.   He seems, it might be said, to have in view, at the same time, the *divine* commandments when he declared that the commandments of Moses and of men lead not into the truth, but into the by-way of ceremonies. But Luther, in the gradual unfolding of his doctrinal views, never approaches this path of danger.   When he points men in simple faith to the Gospel, the object of the faith by which they are to be justified is yet ever for him the testimony of reconciling grace, not merely the New Law as the essential contents of the perfect commandments.   Thus distinctly does the basis and central point of his convictions already manifest its power.   It was yet to lead him, still further, to a clearer discrimination of the elements embraced in. what he now designates as the Gospel, *i. e.*, to separate the distinctive message of salvation, which works life, from the New Testament commandments, which are designed, in connection with the now properly understood requirements of the Old Testament, to convince men of sin and the wrath of God and to guide in their new course of life those quickened through the message of salvation.   Only *that message* itself does he afterwards call " Gospel."   In this we see again an immediate result of that fundamental consciousness of the exclusive efficacy of saving grace which has been already noted.

Luther's conception of the Letter in contrast with the Spirit leads us, finally, to the consideration of the Divine Word as presented in the New Testament, inasmuch as this also lies before us primarily as an outward word or letter.   The question here arises for us, especially in view of the passage already quoted, in which he says that God Himself must directly inspire and teach man.   He declares further in the same connection : " Even the Gospel in words and letters is an imperfect law, unless God at the same time teach it inwardly, but it is the Spirit that quickens."   What is here the relation of SPIRIT and WORD?   Two questions naturally present themselves : first, may there not be also a direct inspiration of the Spirit, unconnected with the outward Word, and even leading beyond the contents of the latter ; secondly, may not the Word, on the other hand, be offered to a man without any reason being thereby given us to expect that God will really make it inwardly effectual for the one to whom it is thus offered? The *Exposition of the Psalms* never enters upon the discussion of these questions. The agitation occasioned by the fanatics who attached themselves to the Reformation led afterwards to a definite response to the first question. Meanwhile, Luther's practical way of dealing with the Scriptures sufficiently attests how little, if at all, he was inclined to that by-way of error. As a matter of fact, he holds to the divine Word with thorough self-surrender, without stopping to justify himself by furnishing answer to the questions before us. This was a natural result of his own previous personal experience, in which he had found light and peace through such unquestioning submission to the Scriptures. The second question calls to mind an expression of Staupitz, whose views were at so many points closely related to those of Luther. He declares in his little treatise, *Von der holdseligen Liebe Gottes*, when expanding the thought that the love of God must come through the Holy Spirit, that no man can learn from another to love God above all things, nor can this be learned from the letter of the Scriptures; that the letter is, on the other hand, a means of driving men through fear to grace and to the Spirit. This is expressly declared to be true even of the letter of the New Testament, when not accompanied by grace. " Although it brings Christ before the eyes and His teaching to the ears, yet, since it is not able to bring the Spirit of Christ into the heart, it serves only to bring grievous death." The question here confronts us how far this Spirit, upon His part, is willing to work always with and in the Word. This question, for both Luther and Staupitz, stands in close connection with that already discussed, concerning the unconditioned working of grace in general. If the Word remains for any man a bare, killing letter, is the reason to be found in the will of grace itself? The whole later doctrinal development of Luther will bring us back to this question as one of its most difficult problems.

We have now enumerated the most important particulars in which we find a positive presentation of Luther's doctrinal position in his first lectures upon the Psalms. They fully justify us in recognizing the latter as the " *Initia Lutheri*," as well in view of the new light which had already risen upon him as in view of those aspects of his teaching which had not yet been brought into harmony with it. The thorough coherence of all these separate particulars confirms us also in the conviction that they must all have belonged to the doctrinal position of one period, namely, the first years of Luther's theological teaching.

We must, finally, direct particular attention to those ECCLESIASTICAL TEACHERS in whose writings he at that time thought it necessary to seek for help in deepening his understanding of saving doctrine imbedded in the Scriptures. We have already had repeated occasion to call attention to that which is the most important thing to be noted in this connection, viz., his use of the writings of *Augustine*. Again and again are the words of this church father quoted, whereas only occasionally do we find appeal taken to any other teacher of the Church. He quotes *Cassiodorus* now and then in fixing the meaning of biblical words and ideas, and, upon external exegetical points only, *Jerome*. He appears to have had *Lyra* often or constantly at hand, but the exegetical principles originally adopted in his work must have made this writer uncongenial to him. For the linguistic conception of single words, on the contrary, we find him already calling in the aid of *Reuchlin*. As teachers who were capable of testifying in matters touching the inner religious life, we find frequent mention of *St. Bernhard*, and, after him, of *Hugo* of St. Victor and *Bonaventura.*

As the use of Augustine is peculiarly characteristic, so, upon the other hand, is also the entire neglect of the Scholastics, with the exception of those just named, whose mystical elements commended them to his attention. It is worthy of special note that as yet we have no quotations from Tauler, whose mysticism Luther soon afterward most fully imbibed. Evidently, he had not yet become acquainted with the writings of the latter. This corresponds with what has been already said of the failure of the *Exposition of the Psalms* to enter at length upon the view of the mystical communion of the soul with God and Christ, and we have thus another evidence of the age of that work. We find, on the other hand, nowhere any trace of a direct polemical attitude toward the Scholastics. Luther does, however, already oppose at least that one proposition of the master of Scholasticism, Aristotle, which he even pronounces a fundamental perversion of the doctrine of salvation, viz., that we become righteous if we practice righteousness. It is for him, on the contrary, the fundamental doctrine of saving truth, that there must first be a righteous person before there can be any exercise of righteousness:[1] and no one can become righteous except as God makes him so out of grace through faith.

That he shall be led to place himself in open conflict with the doctrine prevalent in the Church, Luther has at this time, so far as we can see, not the slightest anticipation. He is aware that the self-righteousness which he always zealously condemns is widespread in the Church; he sees especially many members of the monastic orders ensnared by pride.[2] But he never permits a suspicion to enter his mind that propositions detracting from the divine testimony touching the freedom of grace and the righteousness of faith could be authorized by the Church itself.

Yet much less can it be said in regard to any other points of doctrine, that he had any thought of departing from the prevalent ecclesiastical dogmas or ordinances. We find, in general, beyond that unfolding of the fundamental doctrine of salvation which was Luther's aim throughout the entire *Exposition of the Psalms*, only slight reference to the remaining articles of Christian faith and morals. The few instances that occur stand by themselves, having no vital connection with the general course of treatment. We cannot, therefore, positively affirm that these separate expressions belong to the original basis of the work and to the stage of doctrinal development which it represents. There is, however, nothing in them which is not perfectly consistent with such a view. It is, nevertheless, an obvious fact that upon this broader field the evangelical central point of Luther's convictions had as yet exercised very limited—rather, let us say, very little *positive* and *conscious*—activity. Unquestionably, we may here make application of his confession in regard to the articles which he for a time humbly granted to the Pope although they afterwards became an abomination to him. At all events, we must regard it as very significant that he so seldom finds occasion to speak of the matters in question. He must have regarded their importance as far inferior to that of the fundamental doctrines, which he urges upon every opportunity. All that has been said holds true when applied to the very first draft of his work. He did not at a later day strike out from his manuscript as false

[1] Walch, ix, 2099.   [2] Ibid., 1893.

or wrong anything originally written.   It is for us, therefore, to
observe in what way and from what point of view he already
regards and applies those articles of doctrine which he as yet
accepts without any hesitancy, but which he afterwards rejected.

We have seen how he directs faith always and entirely to
Christ, as the Mediator of salvation.   At this point the question
naturally arises as to the attitude which he maintained toward
the WORSHIP OF THE SAINTS.   It was only at a rather late day, as
we shall see hereafter, that he advanced to a positive rejection of
this custom, *i. e.*, not until his open conflict with the Romish
Church had been already long in progress.   For the present we
find no deprecating word in regard to it.   But, on the other
hand, one must look very far to find any mention whatever of the
saints.   He refers in one place to " the example of Saint Agatha
and others," but he mentions her only as an illustration of faith
in Christ and suffering for Him, not as an object of worship.[1]
He may have had in view chiefly the abuses which were connected
with the retailing of legends, when he declared that God gave
His Word to the Evangelists, *i. e.*, not the fable-mongers, but
those who preach good things and the peace of Christ.[2]

He recognizes the " SACRIFICE OF THE ALTAR."   But he discusses
it (although without any polemic reference to that conception of
it which regards it as an atoning sacrifice) only in the light of a
praise-offering, in illustration of Psalm l. 23 : in it the vows and
praise of all should be offered up.   He further declares, that it
belongs only to those who in and with it offer up themselves also
in the administration and power of the sacrament, since it is not
enough that one should have pleasure in it as in an *opus operatum*.[3]   Evidently, the denial of the efficacy of the sacraments *ex
opere operato* was a thought already at that time not remote from
Luther's mind.   He declares, further, that the Church must also
constantly sanctify herself, that she may be an offering to God.[4]

The MORAL LIFE of the believer appears to Luther mainly as one
of suffering and conflict.   We find as yet no expression of the
lofty and bold consciousness of that freedom which the Christian
enjoys in the possession of the righteousness of God, and in which
he regards even secular ordinances and ranks as hallowed by God,
even in worldly things seeking to meet the divine approval in

[1] Walch, ix, 2309.   [2] Ibid., 1947.   [3] Ibid., 1839.   [4] Ibid., 1971.

serving God and his fellow-man.   But of any value attaching to
the " monk's cowl " in the sight of God, or of its being " the
way to heaven " (supra, p. 95), we find no hint anywhere.
Only in one passage, under Psalm xlv. 15 (" the virgins that
follow her and her companions shall be brought unto " the King),
does he speak of the virgins who are such " in body and inward
disposition," declaring that they are here particularly mentioned
as a special ornament of the Church, and that the " companions "
are *all* believing souls, widows, married, etc.[1]   Speaking of temptations at one place, he says that they are fools who try to overcome these by flight or other such means ; that we must, on the
contrary, flee to Christ and strengthen our hearts for resistance
by believing contemplation of Him.[2]

Of the EXISTING CHURCH Luther has no other idea than that it
is absolutely one with the Church of Christ or the body of Christ.
—that he who stands in the fellowship of Christ and His salvation
must submissively attach himself to her.   He utters many warn-
ings against " the heretics, who seek to catch the souls of men in
their net."   He says of them, that they usually start with utterances of their own reason, but that they are particularly dangerous
because they misuse the language of the Scriptures themselves in
the interest of their lies.   He classifies them, further, with all
ungodly men who prefer their own to the divine wisdom and
righteousness, and particularly with those who set up their own
righteousness and place a low estimate upon the righteousness
of God.[3]

Whilst he repeatedly complains of abuses into which the
Church, and even popes and bishops have been led, and of gross
offences originating with members of the monastic orders and
lofty prelates,[4] there is not the most remote suggestion of a consciousness on his part that he himself might be called upon to
enter the lists against these as a Reformer, or even of a suspicion
that the Church had in consequence of these ceased to be the
one true Church, or that it was not still the simple duty of every
single member of that Church humbly to suffer and to toil with
her.

Everywhere we find embraced in his view of the Church an

[1] Walch, ix, 1807.   [2] Ibid., 1904.
[3] Ibid., 2488-90.   [4] Ibid., 1786, 2208.

acknowledgment of the validity of the priestly office and its hierarchical organization. " They that ride upon the sea " (Ps. cvii. 23) are the bishops and priests; the ships are the individual congregations. The " hedges " of the nations (Ps. lxxxix. 40) are the prophets, bishops, popes, Levites, priests and elders. By the " strongholds," in the same passage, we are to understand the subordinate officers of the Church. He accepts also the historical premise upon which the Papacy is founded, namely, that Peter was already in his day the chief bishop.

But the Pope is never referred to as the chief head of the Church, this title being reserved for Christ alone. The dispensation of salvation is never traced to the definite hierarchical order as such, nor, when treating of the former, does he even expressly think of Rome. The outward, legal order of the Church is never emphasized. On the contrary, the men whom God, or Christ, sends to His Church as messengers, or leaders, or shepherds, are regarded as essentially teachers, who are to bring His Word to the congregations. Thus, for example, the " work " (business) which in Psalm cvii. 23 is parallel with " riding upon the sea " is understood as the work of Christ, which is prosecuted when His Word is preached and urged upon the attention of men. The Word here referred to is the Gospel, in contrast with the Law and the Letter. Luther directs his language also unmistakably against a perverted zeal on the part of those holding official position in the Church of his own day, when he understands by those who " build in vain " upon the house of God (Ps. cxxvii. 1), Pharisees and Scribes, who by their teaching of the Law tear it down rather than build it up, and by those who " watch in vain," such as would keep guard over the city of Christ in a carnal way by teaching the letter of the Law. We are here again reminded of his comment upon " human law," with its round-about way of ceremonies. Of especial significance for us are his comments upon Psalm lxxxiv. 5. It is very easy, he there says, to establish laws, but only God can give the power to keep them. Therefore prelates and bishops should not be so ready to multiply laws, but should remember that they are not able to impart strength for the observance of such requirements, and that at the present time everything is full of laws and snares for the conscience. Yet with all this, he cherishes no doubt of the *validity* of such ordinances. If, therefore, a bishop or prelate commands anything, men are

before God and heaven bound to obey. He applies to this case
also the authority to bind conferred by Christ, merely adding the
remark, that if such a law be not a good one, God can recall
it again.[1]   It is easy to detect how all these declarations grow out
of Luther's fundamental conception of the divine work of salvation and its application to individual souls.

Of special significance, finally, as indicating his conception of
the essential nature of the Church, is the distinction which he
already in one passage draws (although but briefly and incidentally) between real and merely outward members of it.   He
there declares that some are in the " honor " of Christ (Ps. xlix.
20) and of the Church, since they understand spiritual and divine
things.   Such are numerically and deservedly in the Church;
others, who do not understand such things, are in it only numerically.[2]

We thus recognize already, in connection with all the doctrinal
points here touched upon, a certain influence of the light that
has arisen in the soul of Luther.   Our attention is directed,
further, in each instance, to that particular point at which this
light at a later period broke through and purified the ecclesiastical system which yet enveloped it.   Yet it is none the less to be
constantly observed, that Luther himself up to this time manifests
no disposition whatever to apply the results attained directly
against this system, nor any consciousness of the consequences to
which they must lead.

With respect to these first lectures of Luther (in connection
with those upon the Epistle to the Romans) Melanchthon could
afterwards testify[3] : " He expounded those biblical writings in such
a way that after a long, dark night a new light of doctrine appeared to arise for all persons of piety and understanding.   Here
he taught the difference between Law and Gospel.   Here he
refuted the error then dominant in schools and in sermons, that
man by his own works can merit for himself the forgiveness of
sins, and by means of legal discipline be righteous before God.
He appealed again to the Son of God.   He directed, as John the
Baptist had done, to the Lamb of God, who has borne our sins,
and showed that for the sake of the Son sins are forgiven, and
that this blessing is to be accepted in faith."

[1] Walch, ix. 2089 sq.   [2] Ibid., 1831.   [3] Vita Lutheri, p. 6.

3. DEVELOPMENT OF DOCTRINE FROM 1515 TO 1517—UNDER THE
   INFLUENCE ESPECIALLY OF GERMAN MYSTICISM.

All the material which the further writings of Luther afford us
for the determination of his theology and its development during
this period may now be embraced in a single section.[1]

We must, in order to follow the course of his development, first
of all look separately at the few sermons remaining from the
year 1515.

a. Sermons Dating from the Latter Part of A. D. 1515.

RIGHT USE AND INTERPRETATION OF SCRIPTURE—SELF-RIGHTEOUSNESS
CONDEMNED—THE ETERNAL WORD—MYSTICAL IDEAS.

The *Sermon on St. Martin's Day*, of which, however, but a fragment has been preserved, relates to the right use of the Scriptures.
It presents no other general principles bearing upon this subject
than those already expressed by Luther in his *Exposition of the
Psalms*. We are to refer everything, it is said, to Christ, and thus
press forward from the flesh and the letter to the spirit. The
sermon itself affords an example of quite bold allegorical interpretation. But we now hear Luther for the first time expressing
a definite consciousness of the danger into which it is possible to
fall, if we make the *Scriptures*, in such a way as he advocates, the
source of knowledge. He now already attempts to guard against
this danger by the application of the principle which served the
same purpose at a later day, when he was opposing ecclesiastical
tradition upon the basis of the sole authority of the Scriptures.
The latter, he declares, may indeed be stretched and led. Only
no one should lead them according to his own feelings, but they
should be led up to the fountain, *i. e.*, to the cross of Christ.
Then the result will be right. " Preach one thing, the wisdom
of the cross." He does not in this merely seek to set up an
objective rule of interpretation, but he is above all concerned for
the inner temper and disposition of those who use the Scriptures.
By such a preaching of the cross, he conceives, will man learn

[1] Cf. Dieckhoff (Luther's Lehrgedanken in ihrer ersten Gestalt), in der
deutschen Zeitschr., 1852, N. 17 sqq, and Harries, in den Jahrb. f. deutsche
Theol., 1861, vi, 714 sqq.

" to distrust himself and to hope in Christ." [1]   This fragment
of a sermon has a double interest for us, since, in addition to the
significant character of the subject discussed, it contains the first
deliverances of Luther which have been preserved in the German
language.

In the sermons preached at Christmas we meet again polemic
utterances against *human righteousness* and human merit.[2]   We
must take refuge beneath the wings of the hen, *i. e.*, Christ
(Matt. xxiii. 37), in order to receive what we lack from His fullness.   We shall be able to treat more fully the topics connected
with this position in connection with the contents of the further
documents of this period.

We must here, however, examine more closely, on account of
its distinctive character, a discussion of *Christ as the Word of
God*, found in a sermon upon John i. 1 sqq.[3]   In Luther's later
writings, also, we find the deepest views upon the nature and
significance of the Son of God presented whenever he comes to
speak of this fundamental article of faith and of apostolic testimony.   But he never afterwards entered so fully as here into the
strictly philosophical and metaphysical discussion of the theme.
He was accustomed to pursue it only so far as required by his
immediate religious interest.   We have here a striking evidence
how deeply he had been interested in speculative studies, and
how little inferior he was in capacity for their pursuit to the
scholastic theologians who claimed to be masters in this depart-
ment.   It is, of course, the philosophy of Aristotle of which he
here chiefly seeks to avail himself.

He maintains, first of all, the unity of essence between the
Father and the Son, together with their difference in person,
against the Arians and such false logicians as conclude : Whatever
is God is the Father ; the Son is God : therefore the Son is the
Father.   He undertakes to present a better refutation of this
conclusion than D'Ailly has done.   In the attempt, he enters into
logical discussions such as he never afterward felt himself called
upon to pursue.

He professes, indeed, already to explain the name " Word,"
as he does in his later writings, chiefly from Scripture, *i. e.*, by a
reference to Gen. i. 3.   But he at once proceeds to a philosoph-

[1] Löscher, 269.   [2] Ibid., 244, 238.   [3] Ibid., 231 sqq.

ical analysis of the nature and significance of the " Word." He
notes the use of the term in a two-fold sense. In the proper
sense, it stands for the inner word; and it is thus applied to the
Son of God in John i. 1. The word in this sense is found only
in the most perfect form of being, *i. e.*, in that endowed with
reason and understanding; as it is said, for example, in regard to
the thoughts of a man : " he speaks with himself in his thoughts,"
or, " my heart tells me that." Thus also, he declares, God
speaks in His heart, and it is to this Word that John refers. He
is counsel, wisdom, truth, divine thought; and hence Christ is
called the wisdom and truth of God. Of this Word Luther now
declares at the outset, that it remains in God and cannot be
poured out beyond Himself (*effundi foras*). A sending forth
(*mitti foras*) however occurred, inasmuch as it united itself with
flesh, or humanity, thus becoming likewise the visible Word. We
are thus led to consider the significance of the word as external.
The external word, says Luther, exists for the sake of others; in
it we converse with others. In applying this then to Christ, he
includes in the conception of this " word " the incarnation of the
Word and its diffusion through preaching, since by the latter
means Christ Himself descends like rain (Ps. lxxii. 6) upon the
nations.

But Luther dwells yet further upon the " word " in the proper
sense of the term. He defines more closely its relation to the
human spirit by discriminating between the reason (*ratio*) and
the intelligence (*intellectus*)—a distinction which to many philosophers indeed, he declares, seems absurd, but which is in accord
with the Scriptures. He explains as follows : " Intellect is a
property of invisible and eternal beings, who make others happy ;
which, as I understand, Augustine designates as the superior
portion of reason, or the man, just as the inferior (portion of)
reason is the woman, which is occupied with temporal affairs,
which presides over all the works which are prosecuted on earth
with wonderful skill and industry, not caring whether they are
pleasing to God or promotive of the happiness of future beings."
We shall have occasion hereafter to recur to the significance of
this distinction in determining Luther's doctrine concerning man.
In the present connection, the aim is merely to define the place
of the " word." Of this it is now declared, that it belongs properly only to the intellect, since it is a stable, real and eternal, not

a vain, *cogitatio*. The work of the reason (*ratio*) is to be called rather thought than word, as when, for example, it is said in the Psalter that the thoughts of men are vain. But the chief interest of Luther is confined to the effort to find analogies to the inner speaking and producing of the word in all existing things, including those not endowed with reason, nor even with life ; and then to show how, by such a representation of this inner speaking and producing, the Church's definitions concerning the relations of the persons in the Trinity may be justified. Everywhere, he declares, we may find something which in its own way, though it be but imperfectly, corresponds to this word. His meaning may be briefly expressed as follows : He finds analogies in the inner vital acts of every living thing, even in the inner motion which is imparted to anything whatsoever. As, for example, the thought of a rational creature is a rational word, a rational sensation, a rational life, a rational motion ; so, also, the sensation (*sensatio*) of a sensuous thing (*res sensualis*) is its inner tendency (*intentio*), or a sensuous word, a sensuous thought, a sensuous life, a sensuous motion. The sense, or sensation, gives to this thing according its own nature what the intelligence (*intellectus*) gives to the intelligent being—and what the life gives to the living thing, and the motion to the thing that is moved. We may, therefore, not only apply what is said of lower orders of beings to those which are higher, but may also reverse this process. Thus we may not only describe the word as intellectual life, sensation, motion, but may also call the life of the living thing its word, and the motion of the thing moved its word, sensation, life. In these inner transactions Luther sees therefore an act in which the things produce themselves, transport themselves into something in which they were not before, multiply themselves within themselves, whilst yet at the same time remaining in themselves. The intelligence, dealing and speaking with itself, brings forth the word inwardly, and thus originates from within itself a vital act, an intellectual sensation ; through its thought, it attains to that in which it has not been before (*profecit in id, in quo prius non fuit*). The same may be said of a sensuous thing : in sensation it shows and arouses itself, puts life into itself to a certain extent, and brings itself forth. Likewise a living thing, when it grows, blooms and produces fruit, goes forth out of itself. Even the thing moved grows to a certain extent, and becomes what it was not before, or attains to that in which it was not before ; but whilst thus multiplying itself, it yet does not depart from itself. Similarly God, while knowing Himself, addressing Himself, receiving sensations from Himself, pouring Himself out (*profundit*), moving Himself in an intelligible and super-intelligible way, nevertheless remains the same, and yet none the less multiplies Himself. At this point Luther introduces the proposition of Aristotle, that God Himself is an act of motion (*actus mobilis*) ; motion itself is the essence (*essentia*) of God. Similarly, the growth (*nascentia*) of a living thing is the living thing itself as such : to which he adds, that under the *nascentia* or *incrementum* he here understands every act of a living thing, just as under sense or sensation, every act of a sensuous or sensitive thing, and under word, every act of the intelligence. By " the living thing as such (*in quantum hujusmodi*)," he. further explains, he means —in so far as it is simply a living thing, not in so far as it is tree, plant, etc. ; and in this again he appeals to Aristotle. With this, he comes finally to define more definitely the conception of the Word which is said to be the Son of God. The word is the intelligence itself as such, just as the motion and the movable thing are one. The essential divine nature (*esse divinum*) is therefore itself the Word, proceeding (*descendens*) out of God Himself by virtue of an unutterable, super-intelligible motion ; the Son of God is the essence of God Himself. It is to be borne in mind also that everything attains its goal (*terminus ad quem*) not in accordance with its essential nature (*esse*), but by virtue of its motion, *i. e.*, not in so far as it is, but in so far as it is movable : Thus the divine intelligence, or God, multiplies Himself not through His essential nature (*esse*), but through His producing, which is in accord with the Trinitarian definition : Essence (*essentia*) neither generates nor is generated. Rightly, therefore, does Augustine pronounce the *mens, memoria* and *voluntas,* or the *mens, notitia* and *amor,* to be one life and yet three lives. In precisely the same way may it be said of a lifeless thing : Thing, motion and rest are one and yet three : out of its essential nature (*esse*) flows the motion, not in so far as it is, or exists, but because, while it is a thing, it is also movable. Out of this essential feature, *i. e.*, its movableness, flows the motion ; but out of both, the movableness and the movement, proceeds the rest, or end of the motion. In this process, the same thing is in motion with regard to the goal to be attained, and at the same time in rest with regard to that which has already been attained : it is itself, therefore, always both in motion and in rest. Precisely so is it with God. The Son goes forth in self-movement, the Holy Ghost in rest. Out of the Father is always flowing motion, *i. e.*, the Son ; out of both is ever proceeding rest, in which the movable and the motion are at their goal : motion and rest are here eternal. " See," says Luther at the close of this argument, " how ably Aristotle serves theology with his philosophy, if we understand and apply it, not as he himself desired, but better." It is his opinion, that Aristotle probably stole from some other source the tenable propositions which he pompously presents.

With such deep interest did Luther labor to comprehend philosophically the inner and eternal relations of the Trinity. It is only the definitions touching the immanent Trinity in itself that he has in view in this entire section. He speaks here only of the Word in its proper sense, only of an inner outpouring of self, not of a pouring of self out beyond self (*effundi foras*), not of the sending forth (*emitti*) of the Word in the incarnation of Christ, although he had already mentioned this in the preceding paragraph.[1] To the latter he here makes no further direct reference.

Luther's treatment of this subject is marked by a labored and cumbersome movement, which his later sermons, thoroughly penetrated by the spirit of religious life, never display even in the presentation of their deepest thoughts. But, none the less, this same life may here already be detected as the deepest inner source prompting his effort, even while it wearies itself upon such apparently abstract and theoretical problems ; and the interests of this life constitute the final and supreme goal aimed at in the sermon before us. His utterances in regard to the Divine Being are strongly characterized by the effort to apprehend the subject as vividly as possible. The danger was that he should go too far in the application to the Godhead of analogies derived from the processes of natural life. We are often reminded thus of the dar-

[1] We cannot therefore find that he here wishes to trace a tendency of divinity toward humanity similar to that of humanity toward divinity of which he afterwards spoke. (Thus Dorner, Entwicklungsgeschichte der Lehre von der Person Christi, Part II., p. 532.)

ing attempts of the Mystics; as, for example, in the oft-recurring
expression, "pouring out of self (*profundi*)." He himself,
moreover, prays God to forgive him for speaking so disrespect-
fully of the hidden divine nature; but yet, he pleads, he is only
seeking to climb up upon the ascending steps which God Himself has arranged. It is to be observed, further, that his inmost
effort is to penetrate with his own life into the living depths of
the divine nature. His hope is directed to the consummation in
which God shall open His own heart without reserve and lead us
into His heart, where we shall see the goodness of the Lord in
the land of the living (comp. Ps. xxvii. 13), and behold the pure
truth and wisdom. However earnestly, therefore, he strives to
apprehend the nature of the Father or the Son in itself, yet his
glance is from the very outset directed upon the Incarnate
One, the Redeemer. All his definitions touching the divine
nature are designed to assist in clearly presenting what has
appeared and is communicated in Him. He therefore proceeds
immediately to speak of the diffusion and activity of the "Word"
in the proclamation of salvation, and comes thus to the proposition so prominent in his teaching, that the grace of Christ descends upon us without our merit. The end and goal of the
sermon is finally reached in the application, in which he announces
that he will now draw the moral ("*mores*"), *i. e.*, he will show
what shall come to pass in us, and what we shall become through
the Word. This he then embraces in the one brief sentence:
"The Word has become flesh, in order that flesh might become
Word; therefore God becomes man, that man may become
God." But we become, says he, the Word, or like the Word—we
do not become God Himself nor truth, but godlike and truthful,
or partakers of the divine nature, since we accept (*assumimus—
annehmen*) the Word and by faith cling to it. For the Word
did not become flesh in such a way as to have forsaken itself and
been transformed into flesh, but in such a way that it assumed
flesh and united the latter with itself. Thus we are also not substantially transformed into the Word, but we unite it with ourselves through faith. In like manner the apostle declares: "The
Lord is the Spirit, and he who clings to Him is one spirit with
Him" (2 Cor. iii. 17; 1 Cor. vi. 17); and again, "in order
that we may be in Him the righteousness of God." But when
we accept the Word, we must forsake ourselves, divest or empty

ourselves of self (*exinanire*), retaining nothing of our own disposition, but renouncing it entirely.

At this point, again, Luther thinks it allowable to introduce Aristotelian propositions.[1] It is no matter for surprise, says he, that we are to become the Word; for even the philosophers declare, that the power of knowing (*intellectus*) becomes the thing that may be known itself through the act of attaining knowledge, and that the power of receiving sensations becomes the sensuous object itself through actual sensuous perception. How much more must this be true of the Spirit and the Word. Thus Aristotle says that knowledge is not possible except in relation to the objects of the act of knowing, but that, in possibility or potency, knowledge is itself to a certain extent everything. In precisely the same manner, desire and that which may be desired are one, as also love and the thing loved, although all this, if understood *substantially*, would be altogether false. Knowledge and feeling, in so far as they direct themselves with desire toward objects, are like matter striving to attain form; and in so far as they cherish desire, though not in so far as they subsist, are they a bare potentiality—to a certain extent, indeed, a nothing—and become a something only when they secure their objects: thus the objects are to a certain extent their essence and actualization, without which they would be nothing. Luther here remarks that this " philosophy, beautiful but understood by few," is useful for the highest theology. He further adds, that thus for example, God, as the object of eternal blessedness, is the essence of the blessed themselves, without which they would be nothing at all; attaining Him, however, they are transformed from a potentiality into a something: therefore, God is their actualization. With the words, " but of this more hereafter," the remarkable sermon is brought to a close.

b. *Relation to Aristotle and the Scholastics, and to Mysticism.*

The above references to Aristotle are, as already remarked, characteristic of the present work of Luther, in contrast with all his later writings. At the same time we note, especially in this last extract, ideas borrowed from Mysticism, such as never appear

[1] In what follows I think I have presented more correctly the meaning of the extracts, which are in Walch very obscurely and inaccurately translated.

in his earlier work, the *Exposition of the Psalms :* for example, the idea of becoming one with the Word and with the nature of God, with which is connected the reference to that which has been up to this time the fundamental conception of Luther, *i. e.,* the communicated righteousness of God ; also that " emptying of self " which is to be consummated in faith.   It is the *mystical* elements which from this time forth particularly characterize the labors of Luther.

It is the combination of these two tendencies, the philosophical, still clinging to Aristotle, and the practical, religious and mystical, giving to this sermon so peculiar a significance, which has induced us to dwell expressly and at such length upon it.   Entirely too little notice has been taken of it by the majority of those who have written upon the subject of Luther's theological develop-ment.[1]   The dominant influence is here already decidedly that of Mysticism, and we shall find the same to be true to a still greater extent of the labors and public utterances of Luther to which we now turn our attention.

It seems, indeed, as though Luther in this sermon had made the last attempt to grant some recognition in his own way to the acknowledged master of the scholastic theology.   He sought to understand and apply the philosophy of the latter, however, as we have seen, not according to the wish of its author, but in a better way.   Already in the *Exposition of the Psalms* he had opposed the evangelical doctrine of righteousness to that of Aristotle.   He now seeks to make what is true in the philosophy in question con-tribute directly to the establishment of the evangelical doctrine concerning the appropriation of salvation.   But from this time forward he refers to the principles of Aristotle only to reject them. He is led to this course by his desire to discredit openly and in the most effectual way the pupils of the latter, the Scholastics, whom he had in the *Exposition of the Psalms* simply ignored.

But a few weeks after the delivery of this sermon (on February 8th, 1516),[2] he sends to Joachim Lange a letter for his former teacher, Truttvetter, which, as he says, " is full of controversial questions in logic, philosophy and theology, *i. e.,* of slanders

---

[1] Cf., on the other hand, the thorough examination of the sermon by Dorner in the passage referred to.

[2] Briefe, i, 15.

against Aristotle, Porphyry and the authors of the Sentences, those unprofitable studies of our time :" for thus will it be interpreted, says he, by those who are always as silent as the dead, who believe everything, and will not even whimper in the least against Aristotle. What is there that *they* will not believe who have once believed Aristotle in what he, the most calumnious calumniator, has falsely charged upon others? To Lange he further declares, that he is burning with desire to expose the shameful character of that comedian, who deluded the Church with his Greek mask, and that he has at present in preparation a treatise against the physics of the latter (which appears never to have been completed). If Aristotle had not been clothed in flesh he would pronounce him a real devil. It is his own greatest cross, he declares, to look on quietly while the best heads among the brethren are wasting their time with such dung. A long array of similar declarations of hostility against Aristotle and the Scholastics might be collected from the writings of Luther during the period immediately following. Of the Scholastics in general he declares, that they never even understood their master—that Thomas and the Thomists did not understand a single chapter of Aristotle. The latter himself he regards with an unvarying feeling of hostility chiefly on account of his doctrine touching grace, pronouncing almost his entire system of ethics as constituting the worst enemy of grace. He gives it as his opinion, that if one should read Aristotle according to the counsel of the latter himself, an ordinary head would be done with him in half a year. It would then be no longer necessary to read him with faith and religious reverence, but only as one would read any other trivial and external matter, *i. e.*, not to defend him, but only to know about him. Against the common proverb : "Without Aristotle no one can become a theologian," he proposes : " No one can become a theologian unless he becomes such without Aristotle " (*theologus non fit, nisi id fiat sine Aristotle*).[1] He was permitted before long, to his great joy, to see his own theology and that of Augustine making marked progress and becoming dominant at Wittenberg, whilst that of Aristotle correspondingly declined and hastened to its fall.[2]

[1] Cf. Briefe, 59, 84. Thesen bei der Disput. v. J., 1517, Löscher, i, 543. Decem Praec., Op. Ex. Erl., xii, 196 sq.

[2] Briefe, i, 57.

In his own theology, he seeks to cling ever more closely to the *Scriptures*, although he well knows that a " thorough teaching of the Sacred Scriptures must make fools," according to 1 Cor. i.23.[1] We have just seen what a high estimate he continues to place upon Augustine. He engages in full earnest in the controversy of the latter with Pelagianism. The first thesis of his disputation in the year 1517 maintains (" against the common saying ") : that if any one says that Augustine went too far in his declarations against the heretics, he thereby charges him with having lied almost everywhere. The treatise, *De vera et falsa poenitentia*, attributed to Augustine, he now already pronounces unreliable, although he thereby takes issue with the hitherto prevailing authorities and offends especially his colleague, Carlstadt.[2]

Meanwhile, our attention has already been directed, especially by the Christmas sermon alluded to, to the influence exerted upon Luther by a Mysticism breathing the spirit of Tauler. Religious mysticism had already deeply affected him through his intercourse with Staupitz. In his work upon the Psalms, we have observed his references to Bernhard and Hugo. His familiarity with Tauler does not appear to have begun until a later date, as he is as yet not even named. In 1516, however, he urges Lange to devote himself to Tauler, and commends the sermons of the latter to Spalatin. In a sermon upon the parable of the sower (Matt. xiii. 18 sqq.), when treating of the seed sown among thorns, he refers to him as one who, in nearly all his sermons, displays the most thorough knowledge of such hypocrites and bears the most abundant testimony against them. After the outbreak of the indulgence controversy, Luther declared that Tauler was indeed unknown in the schools of the theologians, but that he himself had found more genuine and sound theology in him than could be gathered from all the scholastic theologians and universities.[3] His acquaintance with him had already become very intimate at the time of the publication of the pamphlet, *Was der alte und der neue Mensch sei*. It was his own strong inclination to the general views of Tauler that attracted him to the " German Theology." He says in his preface : " The subject-matter of this little book is in the style of the enlightened Doctor Tauler." It is to it, no

---

[1] Erl. Ed., lxiii, 238.   [2] Briefe, i, 34.
[3] Ibid., i, 34, 46; Löscher, i, 794; Resolut., Löscher, ii, 217.

doubt, that he refers in the above-mentioned letter to Spalatin, when he says : " I send you herewith, as it were, an epitome of all the writings of Tauler." He declares, further, that he does not know of any theology in either the Greek or the Latin language which is sounder, or in fuller accord with the Gospel. He counsels Spalatin to taste and see how good the Lord is after having first tasted how bitter is everything that we are. In the preface to the edition of the " German Theology," published in 1518, he affirms that, next to the Bible and Augustine, no book his fallen under his notice from which he has learned more as to the real nature of God, Christ, man and all things.[1]

c. Outline of Doctrine as Exhibited in Further Sermons and Writings.

RELATION BETWEEN GOD AND MAN—SIN—RIGHTEOUSNESS—THE WORD —THE SACRAMENTS—ETERNAL DECREE—SAINT WORSHIP—PILGRIM- AGES—INDULGENCES—THE HIERARCHY—FASTS—RELATIONS WITH THE CHURCH AND WITH HUMANISM.

Turning now to the examination of the DOCTRINAL VIEWS expressed in the sermons and other writings of the present period, we shall in none of them find a scientifically developed or logically formulated system cf doctrine. Luther had no occasion to attempt the formation of such a system, and, more than this, the religious interest by which he was controlled did not lead him in that direction. He wishes to bear living testimony to the truth, as he had appropriated it directly from the Scriptures and his own inner life, and in such a way that it might also become a power in the lives of his readers and hearers. The same practical and religious fundamental ideas which we have found in the *Exposition of the Psalms* still maintain their central position. We have here more frequent direct references to the underlying conception of the nature of God Himself than there, and greater definiteness upon points connected with the way of salvation ; but the general character of the discussion remains unchanged. His academic lectures during this period must also have borne essentially the same character ; as is evident, for example, from

---

[1] Erl. Ed., lxiii, 238 sq. Briefe, i, 46.

the *Operationes in Psalmos* which were the outgrowth of his lectures after 1519. He expressed himself with peculiar severity in the *Theses for Disputations;* but yet even these are con-cerned only with the same fundamental doctrines of salvation. He rejects the scholastic method of syllogistic demonstration. The common saying, that " a theologian who is not also a logician is a monstrous heretic," he declares to be a " monstrous and heretical maxim." He especially opposes the application of the syllogistic method to the definitions of God, as implying that the article concerning the Trinity is an article to be known, not one to be believed. Yet the truth of this article is not in contradic-tion of the syllogistic forms.[1] But his teaching was discriminated also, by the peculiar features which we have noted, from the mys-ticism of a Tauler and of the " German Theology." Its simple, practical religious tendency restrained it from entering to any-thing like an equal extent upon idle speculations, particularly in regard to the nature of God. In this respect, his relation to the so-called Areopagite, Dionysius, should be especially noted. The latter is often quoted by Tauler, and once, also, in the " German Theology " (Chap. VIII.). Luther must have studied this author also with care (as we shall presently see), and must have sought to profit by his writings. But he never, in the period before us, makes appeal to him; and immediately after-ward, he announces his utter rejection of the latter's teachings, declaring that there is to be found in them " nothing but irritating utterances of a science seeking to inflate and display itself," and that it were vain for any one to think of becoming a mystic theo-logian by his help. Luther for himself proposes, on the contrary, the following maxim : " One becomes a theologian through life and through the dying out of self, not through speculation." [2] In his pamphlet, *Of the Babylonian Captivity*, he further declares, that the mystical theology of Dionysius is very destructive, more Platonic than Christian ; that he would not have a believer pay the least attention to him ; that, instead of learning Christ there, the reader will be much more likely to lose Him. He adds the remark : " I speak as an expert," [3] indicating thus his own pre-vious study of Dionysius.

[1] Disput., A. D. 1517, Löscher, 542.   [2] Op. Ex. Erl., xiv, 239.

[3] Luth. Opera, Jena, 1560, Tom. II., Fol. 282.

It is a peculiarity of the writings of Luther now under consideration, that his utterances touching the RELATION OF MAN TO GOD, although revealing, as their starting-point and central idea, the consciousness of sin and grace, yet at the same time rest upon a peculiar conception of that relation, as existing universally by virtue of the original nature of man. In this we see the direct influence of the fundamental idea of Tauler's mysticism.

At the basis of Luther's entire teaching lay the deepest and most vivid consciousness of the truth, that the entire thinking and acting of man must, by virtue of his nature and calling, be directed purely and alone toward God and must be a surrender to Him, and that he must, without any claim to merit of his own, maintain a purely and simply receptive attitude toward God. The opposition of Luther to the conception of righteousness attaching to man as a sinner may be said to be here extended to embrace the further view, commonly expressed in the " German Theology," that man, even as a creature, dare attribute to himself absolutely no good, life, knowledge or ability. At the same time, a sharp discrimination is made between God and all that is not God Himself. He is represented not only as the contrary of that which is sensuous, or of creature-nature, but, already in the *Sermon on St. Stephen's Day* (December 26), *1515*, wisdom, virtues and the gifts of grace are described as something which is not God Himself, and, in so far, as belonging to the category of the sensuous and carnal, since they are also something which comes to view and may be seen. That which is in God Himself Luther then calls, upon the contrary, the invisible. Similarly, he maintains, in the *Theses of 1516*, that all good outside of God belongs to the *flesh*, and that only the uncreated good is spirit.[1] Now for him, says Luther, to whom this one God is anything, it is impossible for all things else combined to be anything.[2] Hereupon follow at once, in immediate connection, the two principles : first, that man should acknowledge all things to have been received from God alone, and trust Him unconditionally ; and, secondly, that he should be controlled, in all that he desires to do, by the will of God. Good deeds are such only as " come to pass from God and for God's sake, *i. e* which are acknowledged

---

[1] Löscher, 250, 331.   [2] Ibid., 753.

and traced back to God, as flowing only from Him." This entire right relation of man to God is in principle already embraced in the conception of *faith*, in so far as this is in general defined as a reference to the invisible, as a transporting of self into the invisible, even (according to Heb. xi. 1. Cf. already in the *Exposition of the Psalms*) as the substance (*substantia*) of things not seen. By such faith the spirit is said to be drawn away from all that is visible, and that kindles the lusts; it casts itself (*projicitur*) upon the invisible, and there it may stand firmly. The nature of good works, as above indicated, may in the view of Luther be accurately expressed by the declaration, that they spring " out of faith." [1] He employs these expressions in regard to faith in passages in which the subject of treatment is the present condition of man, but it is easily seen that they are in his mind founded mainly upon the idea of relation to God. We may compare also the similar expressions touching *love to God*. It is purely and only God Himself who is to be the object of such love. As virtues and the gifts of God are discriminated from God Himself, we may therefore not imagine that we love God merely because we love these. This, says Luther, is the most destructive error of heretics and haughty men. He makes the most profound attempt to comprehend the nature of this love, together with that of faith, in an interpretation of the frankincense and myrrh which the Magi brought to the infant Saviour. Faith is the frankincense. It recognizes good and evil (*i. e.*, suffering, misfortune, etc.) as coming from God, takes from us ourselves (*tollit nobis nos ipsos*) and leads all that we have back to God with praise and thanksgiving. Love is the myrrh. It takes from us also God and all that we are, and makes us a pure nothing. This is the pure myrrh : to regard ourselves a pure nothing, as we were before our existence, and to desire neither God nor anything outside of God, but only willingly to allow ourselves to be led back, according to God's will, to our beginning, *i. e.*, to nothing. As we before our creation were nothing and desired nothing, save only in the divine knowledge of us, so must we return to the condition in which we shall know nothing, desire nothing, be nothing.[2] We have here the boldest assertions of

---

[1] Dec. Praec., Op. Ex. Erl., xii, 57.   Löscher, 230; cf. 289 and 758.

[2] Löscher, 251, 782.

Mysticism in regard to the complete renunciation of self as de-manded by our very nature and origin. We hear again the echoes of Tauler's utterances in regard to the " sinking into our Not." [1]

Luther's declarations touching the perfect *Fear of God* must be regarded as likewise embraced under his conception of the relation to God which is supposed to have existed from the very beginning. He discriminates between this fear, which he regards as holy and filial, equivalent to reverence, and fear as dread (horror). The former is mingled, even in the case of the right-eous in so far as they are not perfect, with servile fear. It is further, in the true fear, purely God Himself for His own sake who is feared. We do not fear Him at the same time on account of something else, on account of impending retribution, or hell. He that has this fear has that which is good ; and only that is good which is done in it.

We recall that Luther in the *Christmas Sermon* already declared, that we ourselves are to a certain extent nothing ; that we are related to the divine, which should enter into us, as *bare material.* Now, all the commandments touching our relation to God appear to him to be embraced in the requirement, that we become *pure matter* for Him from whom alone we have our being and all things. The first commandments place man in relation to God as pure matter. Man is commanded to observe the Sabbath. He is to rest with his inner and outer nature, with his senses and spirit. He is to be pure rest.[2] With this correspond the very sweeping assertions touching God Himself and His working made in a sermon preached upon the *Day of the Assumption of Mary* (August 15), *1516.* Referring to Luke i. 49, he declares that Mary, in calling God the " Mighty," means to designate Him as the One who works *all in all.* His are all things. He alone does all things. Therefore, this name belongs to Him alone. His name is holy, and it is defiled whenever man attributes to himself any portion of the work of God.[3]

These utterances sprang from the profoundest depths of Luther's religious consciousness. Their peculiar character reveals, as we have said, an intimate relation to the form of Mysticism

[1] Cf., e. g., Tauler's Sermon on 13 Trinit.

[2] Dec. Praec., xii, 70.   [3] Löscher, 287.

with which he was brought into closest contact.   But it is for us to inquire in how far he had really, particularly in his underlying conception of the divine nature itself, adopted the position of this Mysticism.   What are really, in his case, the peculiar controlling principles?

In the passages quoted, God appears as absolute power.   We are here reminded of Mysticism, before which all independence of created things as related to God vanishes.   With this, the doctrine of grace, as taught by Augustine, was easily connected. In fact, we must always keep in view the peculiar character of the mystical, as well as that of the Augustinian view, if we would understand the decisive steps by which Luther now and afterwards developed his doctrine of grace to the definite view of predestination already hinted at in the *Exposition of the Psalms.* By the Mysticism in question the world is regarded as absolutely nothing more than a mere appearance,[1] whereas true existence is to be ascribed only to God.   The view of the existence and activity of God in the world, which has an existence only as existing in Him, threatens to run into Pantheism.   But the rich significance hereby attributed to the divine nature is again lost by this system, since it feels itself driven to conceive of this nature as in abstraction and estrangement from all that is concrete. The lingering influence of Neo-platonism, perpetuated especially in the Pseudo-dionysian writings, makes itself here powerfully felt.   Tauler, for example, says that God is " the Not " of which Dionysius speaks, and he brings into direct connection with this that sinking into the Not which he demands of man.   Man must " become Not " from love to this Not, and in order to become one with that into which he has sunk.[2]

But just at this point we must be on our guard lest we wrongly apprehend the position of Luther.   Above all, we must not imagine that he first established for himself certain metaphysical propositions touching the nature of God, and then, starting from these, proceeded to define the relation between God and the creature, or man.   On the contrary, his starting-point is invariably the living religious experience.   From this flow his

[1] Cf. also Die Deutsche Theol., Cap. I.: " It is a glitter and an appearance," etc.

[2] Vid. Sermon above cited.

propositions concerning God ; and he never in any of his writings
directly undertakes to lay down with scientific accuracy propositions concerning the nature of God in itself considered.   It is to
be observed, further, that, however certainly God is revealed to
his religious consciousness as the mighty and all-governing One,
yet the final ground of his utterances and the deepest interest in
connection with his presentation of doctrine must always be
sought in that consciousness of sin, of the absolute need of deliverance, and of redeeming grace, by which we found him so
strongly characterized at the beginning of his religious development.   It is just from the point of view of this inner consciousness that he is led to consider further the relation in general
between man and God.   He himself nowhere furnishes any
lengthy presentation of his own view of this relation as distinct
from that in which men stand as creatures in need of deliverance.
His consciousness of sin was from the beginning, and is still,
characterized by the decisive way in which he conceives of sin
as something positive.   This will be manifest to us especially in
his strict apprehension of the need of deliverance.   With the
conception of sin as a positive thing in direct opposition to God
is intimately connected the thought, that between the alienation
of man from God and life in communion with God there can be
no mediate position, and hence, that the transition from the one
condition to the other can be accomplished only by means of
a new divine act of deliverance.   Still further, we must not over-
look the significance of the emphasis constantly laid upon the
guilt of man and the condemnation resting upon him.   But this
leads us back to observe that man is, above all and essentially,
regarded as a *moral personality*.   It is as such essentially that he
stands related to God, and God to him, as a Being making moral
demands and pronouncing judgment.   Thus the chief question
for Luther still is, how man may be or become righteous before
God.   With this general view, which we shall presently be called
upon to examine more closely in detail, and in which Luther
merely remained true to the entire previous course of his religious
convictions, it was now necessary to guard against the possible
vagaries of Mysticism, both the relative *independence of man* as a
moral personality, and, as well, the pre-eminent *ethical conception
of the divine nature*.   God is the all-working One, or absolute
power.   But the chief stress is yet always laid, for Luther's own

religious consciousness and life and in his teaching, upon the *moral attributes* of God, as a revelation of which all exercise of His absolute power is presented to our view, through the apprehension of which the entire conduct of man is to be determined, and from the activity of which all life for man must flow. It is with the commandments of His holiness that the Almighty approaches man ; He is the object of *holy fear*. And, pre-eminent above everything else, is revealed at length His *love*. As Luther knows himself to have been lifted out of the consciousness of sin, guilt and misery, into the possession of salvation, and to have found therein the goal of the paths through which God had hitherto led him, the " peculiar work " of God consists, in his view, chiefly in the effecting and bestowing of salvation and life. He declares this expressly, maintaining that " God makes [men] sinners, unrighteous men and fools," *i. e.*, He leads them to become to their own view what they are before Him ; He wants to kill— that is, the old Adam. To this work of God belong also the sufferings and death of Christ, and the sufferings that are in Christ. But this is nevertheless, says he, only the " strange work (*opus alienum*) of God. His own work (*opus proprium*) is the raising of Christ from the dead, justification in the spirit, making alive—in a word, the working of peace, mercy, truth, joy and salvation.[1] We are reminded here of the expression in the *Exposition of the Psalms* concerning God's hatred of wrath. Thus, also, in that prominent passage in which Luther speaks of the *all-efficacious working* of the mighty God he has already in view His *gracious* working, and speaks directly of the latter in the following context. His object is to exhort men not to attribute any good to themselves, but to acknowledge all good as to be secured only as a gift from God. Among worldly men, he declares, he who has done much receives praise, but before God he who has received much.[2] Thus, also, in Luther's declarations in regard to the nature of man, or the creature, whilst a return of the latter to its nothingness is demanded, yet the created man himself is never depicted as non-existent, or as a mere appearance. The discussion is only in regard to a nothing which he was before he was created. Yet much less was Luther ever led into the abstract descriptions of the divine nature which were charac-

---

[1] Löscher, 769 sq.   [2] Ibid., 281.

teristic of Mysticism. Of especial significance, in determining
what was for him the chief thing in his entire teaching, is also the
abbreviation of the " German Theology " in his first publication
of it, inasmuch as the sections then left out can have contained
only matters which he considered of minor importance.   The
first six chapters are wanting.   These contain the prominent and
distinctive declarations concerning God as the perfect Being, and
concerning creature life as incomplete—as a mere accident, glitter
or semblance ; as, also, general definitions in regard to the nature
of sin and the fall of man, with, however, no more definite examination of the present attitude of the Christian in view of the
salvation revealed in Christ.   Luther's edition began with the
discussion of the proposition, that in the soul of Christ the right
eye was turned upon God and eternity and the left upon created
things, and that this should be the case with Christians now.
For the practical unfolding of the believer's life in Christ, of the
awakening of the new man and the new Christian course of conduct, Luther found Chapters VII.–XXVI. sufficient.   In the
omitted closing chapters, which treated further of the same subjects, are found again characteristic expressions of Mysticism in
regard to God, such as do not occur anywhere in the chapters
selected for publication : for example, that God, as God, belongs
neither to will nor to knowledge, nor to this, nor to that, nor to
anything which we can name or think of (Cap. XXIX., XXX.).

It must be admitted that, although Luther did not himself embrace the characteristic premises of Mysticism, yet he nowhere
expressly disclaimed them, nor attempted, in accordance with the
dominant central point of his own apprehension of truth, to
restrain them within their proper limits or guard them against
error.   As we dare not, on the one hand, without further ceremony conclude that his mode of apprehension was the same as
that which prevails in the mystical writings which he commends,
neither, on the other hand, have we any evidence of a *definite
consciousness* upon his part of the difference between the two.

Luther everywhere, as we have seen, sets out from the PRESENT
CONDITION OF MAN, as immediately revealed to the inner experience.   Everywhere he has in view the one practical and religious
aim, *i. e.*, to testify of the way of salvation, by pursuing which
man may be delivered from this condition.   It is for us, therefore, to trace more carefully the contents of his views and teachings in this particular.

Luther was compelled, as a necessary consequence of his view of the nature of sin and of the relation of God as a holy Being to the human personality, to firmly maintain that *sinning is not innate* in man.   Everything which God has created is good, and can, in accordance with its original nature, be inclined only to good.[1]   Luther, however, but seldom finds it necessary to state this expressly.   None the less stoutly does he insist upon it, that every man is now a sinner, and that even from the day of his birth.[2]   How comprehensive is Luther's idea of sin, and how profound his apprehension of it, may be inferred already from his demand that everything in our lives should come to pass " from God and on account of God."   With reference to the condition of man as a sinner, he then defines " as briefly as possible " the will of God as requiring us to slay the entire old Adam, to which belongs every evil inclination.   The Scholastics, he declares, do not know what it means to keep the commandments of God ; no Thomist understands how to define this.[3]   Luther then attributes sin to the " sensual man " (*sensualis homo*), and sensuality is to him identical with " flesh."   But under these terms he includes by no means only the multitude of sins which we are accustomed to call sins of the flesh in contradistinction from the higher forms of sin.   Spiritual evils (*spiritualia mala*) fall under these designations for him as well as sensuous evils (*sensibilia mala*).   The spiritual self-exaltation and pride of false, self-righteous saints are specially noted as exhibitions of the sensual man.   He regards it as wisdom of the flesh, or sensuality, when the reason itself undertakes to determine what is good and right.   We recall his definition of the " visible " as opposed to the " invisible," *i. e.*, to that which is God and in God.   In a thesis of his own he defines as follows : Flesh is the old man, not only in so far as he is impelled by sensual lust, but in so far as he, even though he be righteous, pure and wise, is not born of God through the Spirit : everything good outside of God is an affair of the flesh ; only the uncreated good is spirit (*vid. supra*).   Of a peculiar relation of this sinfulness to corporeality he does not speak.   Alienation from God is always for him an affair of the will.   The reference of

[1] Dec. Praec., p. 14.   [2] Ibid., p. 13.
[3] Erl. Ed., xxi, 187 (" Auslegung des Vaterunsers," delivered during Lent, 1517, published by Luther in 1518.   Cf. the edition published by Luther's hearer, Schneider, in 1517, in Walch, vii, 1049).

10

everything to God, which is represented as the fundamental divine demand, is set in opposition to man's own will.   In heaven there is no self-will, and, according to the third petition of the Lord's Prayer, it should be so on earth.   Our own will is the very greatest and profoundest evil in us, and nothing is dearer to us than our own will.[1]   We call especial attention to the above declarations in regard to the nature of the " flesh."   So clearly and distinctly did Luther at this time already comprehend the nature of sin.   Upon this point he purposely places himself in opposition to the entire prevalent view, as the latter was manifested especially in the value and honor accorded to the bodily exercise of asceticism and the holiness to which the latter laid claim.   The expressions concerning man's " own will " remind us again of Mysticism.[2]

With the above-noted conception of sin, it at once becomes evident to what an extent all men have actually fallen under its dominion, how often and grievously they transgress especially the First Commandment, which is the fundamental commandment of the Decalogue.   Luther points out how seriously—to say nothing of great and grievous sins, into which all but a very small minority have fallen—all men, even the Christian after entering the state of grace, fail, especially in the rendering of any worthy thanksgiving for all the benefits received, even for the daily external gifts of God[3].

This sinning is now, as has been said, inborn in man.   Luther discriminates in the usual way between original and actual sin, and represents the former as perpetuated through the carnal propagation of the race.   The Mosaic Law, says he, gave commandment to circumcise that member of the body from which the original evil (*originale malum*) comes.[4]

The question, how the inheriting of moral qualities can be possible, and how the first human beings, originally created good, could fall into sin, finds no place for fuller discussion in the writings of Luther, which maintain everywhere their practical character. To the first, he gives no further attention whatever.   In regard to

---

[1] Löscher, 751 sq., 247 sq.   Disp., A. D. 1516, Löscher, 330.   Erl. Ed., xxi, 193 sq.   Cf. Walch, vii, 1048–54.

[2] Cf., for distinction between "free will" and "own will," Deutsche Theol. Cap. L.

[3] Erl. Ed., xxi, 218.   Cf. Walch, vii, 1080.

[4] Löscher, 290, 780.

the second, he views the first sin simply as the deed of Adam, corresponding to the sinning of Satan. When speaking of the "own will," he declares that it comes from the devil and Adam; and that these made their own (transformed for themselves into an own will) the free will which they received from God.[1]

Upon the other hand, he is all the more particular to depict the state of sin, inherited even from the womb, as one in which man not only actually finds himself, but to which (leaving out of view redeeming grace) he is *unconditionally bound*. The original evil (*malum*) is a universal corruption of the nature (*universa corruptio naturae*).[2] The wisdom of the flesh is not able to fulfil the Law, which is spiritual; and yet the entire man has become fleshly. Already in the *Sermon on St. Stephen's Day* we read of an incapacity of the entire will for love of the good as well as of an incapacity of the reason for knowledge of the right and true. The *Theses for Disputations* then employ especially severe language, following Augustine. Man, they declare, independently of grace, can in no wise fulfil the commandments of God. He sins continually, since he does not spiritually fulfil them. He can of himself neither desire nor think that which is good. Thus Luther leads us back again to the fundamental tendency now dominating man, and to that which should control him. Even all apparently good works, he declares, are sin, since they are done without faith (in the sense of the word above indicated). Even in the case of an outwardly good work, nature cannot avoid the cherishing of pride. No moral virtue is without pride or chagrin, and therefore no such virtue is without sin. Man, created in the image of God, seeks now with his natural powers only that which is his, and that which is of the flesh. Why man cannot now in some way give himself another fundamental tendency, is sufficiently evident from the above-quoted utterance of Luther touching the original fall of man. He there sets in absolute opposition to one another the will which pursues its own ends and the free will. The will remains free only by gazing upon the will of God; only thus does it not hang nor cling fast to anything. When man turned away from God, it was an immediate result that he no longer had any free will at all, but a dependent and bound will. Hence Luther pronounces as

[1] Erl. Ed., xxi, 193.   [2] Löscher, 290.

in the highest degree absurd the conclusion that, as man can love
the creature above all things, he can therefore thus love God
also. He declares the proper inference to be, on the contrary,
that as man can love the creature above all things, it is therefore
impossible for him to love God. He puts the matter very point-
edly in the thesis : " The will of man without grace is not free,
but in slavery, and that not unwillingly ; appetite is not free, but
captive." Without grace, he regards man as ever remaining an
evil tree, which can hence bring forth only evil fruit. He is
able, therefore, in no way to prepare himself for grace, either in
fitness (*de congruo*) or in worthiness (*de condigno*) ; upon the
part of man nothing but indisposition—yea, rebellion—precedes
grace.[1]

In the *Sermon on St. Stephen's Day* (1515),[2] Luther speaks at
some length of a *remnant of the original human nature*, which
is preserved even in the fallen state, *i. e.*, a certain longing to be
saved, or to attain a state of blessedness ; and, on the other hand,
a shrinking from condemnation. This he calls *synteresis*. He
speaks likewise of a *synteresis* of the reason, which aims at what
is true and right, and is in conformity with the divine wisdom.
Man is by virtue of this *synteresis* inclined toward the knowledge
and love of the invisible. It is like tinder, seed or material, for
the arousing again and re-establishment of nature which is to be
effected by grace, as when it is said in Isa. i. 9 : " Had God not
left a seed remaining to us, we would have been as Sodom"—that
is, morally interpreted, nature would have been utterly destroyed.
Man is like the tree which has been cut down (Job xiv. 7 sqq.),
whose root waxeth old in the earth and whose stock dieth in the
ground, but which still has hope and becomes green again through
the scent of water. Nature is, therefore, capable of revival, if no
hindrance be placed in the way and no opposition offered to
grace. On the other hand, this element (*portio*) of the will is
the cause of the misery of the lost in hell, since they do not desire
hell, but with an inestimable ardor desire the very opposite, *i. e.*,
salvation. This will alone, in which they are in harmony with the
God who desires the salvation of men, will be the means of inflict-
ing severe punishment upon them. So ineradicable is " this good

---

[1] Löscher, 249, 250, 328 sqq., 541 sqq.   Erl. Ed., xxi, 193.

[2] Ibid., 245 sq., 250.

will" implanted in man. Luther has here accepted an idea which he found expressed, not only in the writings of the Scholastics, but also in Tauler. The latter describes the *synteresis* as the supreme power of the spirit, which before the fall enabled man to enjoy God without means. Luther's figure of the " tinder " is recalled to us by Tauler's " spark of the soul," which rises aloft and rests not until it returns into the divine source whence it sprung.[1] After this, even in the further writings of the present period, we no longer find, however, such sweeping utterances in regard to this " remnant;" and even in the immediate context in this sermon, his view of the perverted tendency and inner corruption of the *human personality* itself is vigorously presented in opposition to the view of the very theologians who were accustomed to employ the term in question. Even here already, as we have seen, he speaks of the inability of the will and of the reason. This exists, he declares, despite the inclination awakened by the *synteresis*. It is to be ascribed to the *entire* will. The *entire* reason, despite the harmony of its *synteresis* with the divine wisdom, is yet entirely arrayed in conflict against the latter, and cannot comprehend the invisible. There is great significance, too, in the difference between Luther's illustrations of the tinder and the seed, and that of the spark, or of the umbel, which Tauler employs. The former point to something which, as Luther says, needs a power from above to call them into life ; the latter, to something which is already in active motion and needs yet only further disclosure and unfolding. Luther has in view, so far as we can see, only what we would call the general testimony and impulses of conscience, and he evidently thinks of these as utterly unable in man's fallen state to make themselves effectually felt in the central point of the personality. At all events, he speaks of this yearning to be saved and desire to escape perdition only in such a way that we can never recognize in it any *ethical* character whatever. It may, however, be maintained that Luther has here called attention to elements of truth which it is very important to emphasize even in connection with a rigid view of the sole agency of grace, and in which, as Luther says, grace must find a point of attachment, but which in the

---

[1] Tauler, Nachfolge des armen Lebens Christi, Th. II., § 59. (Frankfort Edition, 1692, p. 95), zweite Pred. auf 13. Trinit.

later ecclesiastical formulation of the Lutheran confession are not sufficiently recognized. But, however little we may be disposed to dispute such an assertion, and however deep an interest we may ourselves feel in the utterances referred to, a strictly historical presentation of the matter must, upon the other hand, give prominence to the fact, that Luther, even in the present period, and likewise, as we shall see, throughout the remainder of his life, did not further emphasize these elements, but lays all the stress upon the other side, *i. e.*, upon the actual, general inability of the will and reason.   He acknowledges, further, indeed, that there must yet be something in fallen man which may serve as a point of attachment for grace.   Thus, in the *Theses of the year 1516*, man is described, despite his present condition, as not only originally created in the image of God, but as also being even yet in certain respects such an image : " Man, by reason of his (possession of a) soul, is an image of God, and thus *adapted to receive the grace of God*" (*ad gratiam Dei aptus*).[1]   But Luther even here simply makes this statement without dwelling further upon it, and only to oppose to it at once the declaration that man, despite of this, with his natural powers is entirely taken captive in selfish, carnal living.

Very important, however—and in its relation as well to the entire future doctrinal position of Luther—is a further definition which he appends to the above sweeping declaration concerning the slavery of the natural will.   He proposes, as he declares in the thesis upon the enslaved will, to speak only of freedom "with respect to merit and demerit ;" "*with respect to inferior things*" (*respectu inferiorum*), *he will not deny it.*   Unquestionably his meaning here is, that man is no longer free with respect to his relation to God or the " invisible," as though he could either turn to God or persist in alienation from Him, and not free, therefore, in respect to the services demanded by God and to be rendered to Him, as though he could himself perform or not perform them : he is, in so far, not free to choose contrary or contradictory things ("*ad contraria oder contradictoria*"), nor to choose either of two opposites ("*in utrumque oppositorum*").   Nevertheless, within this lower sphere, separate acts are committed to the arbitrary disposition of the will, which is, however, itself

[1] Löscher, 328 sq.

bound to that which is visible and creaturely. To this category then belong also, in Luther's view, services which are outwardly in conformity with the demands of God (thus even righteousness, chastity, etc., in the lower, human sense, as in the above quotation : " Even though he be righteous," etc.), but which nevertheless have their deepest source in the carnal nature and bear a sinful character.[1] We have here already the same distinction which is made, for example, in the Augsburg Confession (Art. XVIII.) between the free will " to work a civil righteousness, and to choose such things as reason can reach unto," and the ability by one's own strength to become pleasing to God, to believe, to cast out the inborn evil lust. Into the questions, whether the God who " works all in all " (cf. *supra*, p. 140) be not, after all, in the last analysis, the efficient agent even in the self-determination of the will within the lower sphere, or what is, in general terms, the relation of this human self-determination to the divine omnipotence, Luther does not at this time enter. It is enough for him, that what man thus chooses is not chosen by virtue of a truly good will—that he does not do what is pleasing to God. We see in this another confirmation of that which has been previously observed in regard to the peculiar central point of his religious consciousness and the relation of the metaphysical to the religious in his teaching. That the question referred to did not lie far from his path, and that he, when driven to a full presentation of his doctrine of the will, did actually at length draw the inferences indicated from his consciousness of God as the All-working One, will be manifest especially from an examination of his later treatise, *De sevo arbitrio*. It will be observed that he there also maintains in its integrity the difference between the higher and lower spheres of voluntary activity. But it is on this account all the more significant, that he has in his other writings never presented these inferences as a constituent element of religious truth. We recall, as pertinent here, the distinction drawn in the *Christmas Sermon of the year 1515* between *intellectus* and *ratio* (p. 127). By the former, he understands the faculty of apprehending the invisible and eternal, *i. e.*, the higher sphere above referred to. In the use of the two words he does not, indeed, afterwards strictly preserve the dis-

[1] Löscher, 343. Cf. passages already cited.

tinction, but uses the term *ratio*, according to the prevailing custom, in a general sense, as when he describes the *synteresis* simply as a *synteresis rationis*. Yet the distinction is essentially maintained in his apprehension of the spiritual nature of man, in so far as this is represented as fallen under ruin and death in its faculty for the higher sphere, whilst in its faculty for the lower sphere left free to act. Moreover, the severance between these two general spheres, namely, of the *temporal* and the *eternal* life, or, which is the same thing, between the *secular* and the *spiritual* spheres, will in our further investigations be found to be a fundamental mode of thought of the very highest significance for Luther's theology, and especially for his ethical system. This severance itself is also to be traced to the clearness and depth of his own personal relation to God; for, where such a relation asserts itself so clearly and deeply as we have seen in Luther's consciousness of sin and grace, there, upon the other hand, whatever does not belong to life in its direct relation to God will also be set apart by itself, and recognized, partly in its merely relatively inferior significance, partly also in its relatively independent position and in its own relative value.

Luther thus ascribes to the natural man a complete subjection under sin and a complete incapacity to contribute anything to his own deliverance from its power. But we know what a terrible feeling of *guilt* was in his case, from the beginning, combined with the consciousness of sin, even before he had recognized the power of sin over man in its entire extent. All his utterances now concerning the state of sin are designed to impress the truth, that man has fallen under judgment, wrath and perdition. From this point of view his doctrine of salvation also receives its peculiar character and its reformatory power: the first blessing which grace bestows—and that, too, at once in full measure—upon the believer is reconciliation, the forgiveness of sins. But for the present we must give due attention to the decisive way in which he represents the will, despite the fact that it no longer has its freedom, as under judgment and perdition. He does this without deeming it at all necessary to first meet the objections of reason against the accountability of such a will. Thus, he already in the *Sermon on St. Stephen's Day* declares expressly and bluntly that, since God has laid the impossible upon us, no one can escape condemnation. In the *Theses of the year 1517* he maintains, even "against all the Scholastics combined," that even invincible ignorance does not fully exculpate ; for, he adds, ignorance in regard to God and in regard to man's own works and good works is always by its very nature invincible.   Even upon original sin, independently of all actual sins, rest, in his view, wrath and perdition.   When disputing with those theologians who represent Christ's work as consisting merely in enabling man to lead a meritoriously good life and thus win heaven, he argues, that if this were so, by a child without actual sin Christ would not be needed as a deliverer from the power of the devil, but only as a helper in attaining heaven, since, if it should die without Christ, it would go neither to hell nor to heaven.   Luther affirms, on the other hand, that we are born as children of wrath and the devil, and that this does not mean merely that we are without merit.   In support of this position he appeals to the fact, that even the baptism of children is a baptism for the forgiveness of sins ; and this, he claims, is to be understood of condemning sins, and not only of such as consist merely in a lack of merit.[1]   This seems to open the way for the stern inference, that unbaptized children incur punishment in hell.   Upon this point the discussion of Luther does not now enter, but we shall see how he afterwards avoided the conclusion.

With such vigor did Luther even now carry out the principle embodied in the proposition, that man *cannot become righteous by his own works*.   He does so, as his theses testify, in open and direct opposition to the doctrine of the dominant schools.   He expressly denounces, also, that conception of St. Paul's declarations in regard to the works of the Law, which would apply those declarations only to the observance of the ceremonial law.   He does not hesitate in this to openly oppose Erasmus, whom he regarded in general as worthy of the highest honor.[2]   We find him at this time on friendly terms with the Humanists ; but he yet stringently denies all righteousness to even the relatively best men among the heroes of the ancient world.   Works of the Law, not only those conforming to the ceremonial commandments, but those meeting the requirements of the Decalogue as well, so long as they are performed without faith in Christ, though they may,

[1] Dec. Praec. 54 sq.

[2] Briefe, i, 39 sq.

indeed, make a Fabricius or Regulus, no more bear the flavor of righteousness than service-berries taste like figs.[1]

But this severe conception of the character of the natural man places Luther in actual, even though not in outspoken, opposition to Mysticism also, for in the latter we fail to find this sharp contrasting of the state of man as uninfluenced by the deliverance wrought through the personal Christ and life in the grace revealed only through Him. This is to be accounted for by the facts, that Mysticism is disposed to regard sin only as negative, and in its very nature temporary; and that it is precisely the ethical character of God which here fails to receive proper recognition, His holiness and righteousness, with their absolute claims upon man, retreating into the background, whereas they form the fundamental premises of Luther's doctrine of salvation (cf. what has been said of Luther, p. 142). Thus, for example, Tauler unhesitatingly speaks of heathen " who with a right nature forsake vice and practice virtue." [2]   In their case, to use his own conceptions above cited, the divine spark may flame up and the umbel unfold, without any necessity for the intervention of the message of the incarnate Christ. Yet even more marked in the Mystics than the absence of a deep and comprehensive view of the bondage of man under sin, is the lack of an overpowering sense of guilt. They thought to press forward with all energy to union with God and enjoyment of Him without having first of all approached Him as a holy God and obtained a positive assurance of the forgiveness of their sins upon His part. Tauler, indeed, bears vivid testimony to a sense of the wrath of God [3]— the feeling which was always so remarkably powerful in Luther. But instead of an objective attitude of the righteous God toward man as a sinner, this wrath is by him conceived to be a mere recognition on the part of men of their subjective alienation from God (which he accordingly describes as an "incident of infirmity"), or of the fact that the image imprinted upon their souls by God had been neglected, or not properly "perfected." This alienation itself, or the disorder of man as opposed to the order of God, he calls wrath.[4]

---

[1] Briefe, i, 40.   [2] Nachfolg. d. arm. Leb. Christi, Th. I., § 66.

[3] Cf. Sermon on St. Augustine's Day.

[4] Nachf. d. arm. Christi, Th. I.. § 106.

In Luther, we find ourselves now brought to face the further proposition, that RIGHTEOUSNESS COMES ONLY FROM GRACE, IN CHRIST, AND THAT THROUGH FAITH. Only after we have become righteous persons can we perform righteous works. This declaration he here again, as in the *Exposition of the Psalms*, opposes to the Aristotelian maxim, that man becomes righteous by doing that which is righteous.[1]

But the fuller elaboration of Luther's views upon this attributing of righteousness to faith now displays, especially in his utterances concerning faith itself, an evident lack of clearness in the doctrinal conception and definition of the component elements. Of the different elements which come into consideration in various passages, now one, now another, is placed in the foreground, and they are nowhere expressly, sharply and comprehensively defined in their relations to one another. This is evidently in some measure to be attributed to the varying circumstances which gave occasion for the different discussions and to the object in view in each case, especially to the particular texts or topics of the separate sermons. The real explanation, however, must be sought chiefly in the stage of inner development which had at this time been reached in the advancing knowledge of Luther himself, as may be clearly seen by a comparison with his later presentations of doctrine. Yet, on the other hand, there is even here already one all-pervasive mode of apprehension, which lacks only sharp definition and clearness of outline in its necessary development in some directions. It is our present task, while collecting the separate elements from the various discussions of Luther during this period, to depict the relations of these elements to one another, by virtue of which they were really already combined in one whole, and to note particularly those among them upon which Luther now already actually laid the greatest stress.

At first it might even appear as though Luther in this period still attributed to works performed by man himself, before justification by grace, some significance for the attainment of righteousness. In his *Sermon upon the Day of the Circumcision* (January 1), he declares that grace alone justifies, not works, although *grace must be sought through works ;* we can through works prepare ourselves for grace, but yet cannot receive grace through

works.[1]   But we are already familiar with the thesis which maintains that, without the grace of God, man cannot even prepare
himself in fitness (*de congruo*) for grace, but must remain entirely
under sin; and that other one, according to which there is in
man before grace nothing but rebellion.   The sermon in question
stands chronologically between these two theses.   In fact, Luther
had already declared, as in his *Sermon upon St. Bartholomew's
Day* (August 24), that, as Adam made us sinners without our
work, so Christ without our work makes us righteous.   He refers
to, but is not moved by, the objection that man may then say :
" Let us therefore do evil." [2]   Even the sermon before us itself
declares, that if man were not first already righteous and pure,
nothing could be accomplished by all his working; that no man
can become good without the righteousness which goes before
any work ; that righteousness is given through faith, without any
work, and it is from this righteousness that works must follow ;
that, before any work, the person himself must be graciously visited
(*gratificari*) by the grace which justifies through faith.

How shall we reconcile this apparent contradiction?   The
elaboration of another subject by Luther, in which, at first sight, a
similar difficulty seems to be presented, will furnish us a clue to
the solution of the problem.   During the years now under review,
he often expresses his disapproval of Peter Lombard's definition
of hope, as " a confident expectation of eternal happiness arising
from meritorious deeds " (*aus Verdiensten hervorgehende*).[3]   Now,
on the other hand, he declares, in the *Sermons on the 11th and
14th Sundays after Trinity*,[4] that one dare not entertain hope on
the ground that he has performed meritorious deeds.   Hope, he
maintains, must press on toward that which is before it, namely,
toward God ; it dare not look back upon that which is behind,
namely, antecedent meritorious deeds.   We hope, when we trust
in God as the Unseen (" *in nudum Deum*," etc.) ; whereas,
meritorious deeds are something which can be seen.   Only
through hoping and believing, says he (combining thus the two
in one conception), not through working, does one become righteous—and hope is for him a virtue imparted to us (" *eingegossene* ")
in advance of all merit upon our part, which then itself becomes

---

[1] Löscher, 776.   [2] Ibid., 284.   [3] Cf. also Thesis XXV. of the Disput., A. D. 1517.
[4] Löscher, 748 sqq., 288 sqq.

the source from which meritorious works originate. Yet he is willing to allow the above definition of Lombard to stand, if it is only properly explained, *i. e.*, if we observe the distinction between the two conceptions, whence this virtue arises and wherein its exercise consists—its source and its use (*principium et usus*). The latter is just that trust in God, as the Unseen, which has been advocated. Yet hope may also be said to arise from meritorious deeds, *i. e.*, from works and sufferings (*operibus et passionibus*)—as the material from which it is formed (*velut ex materia*), as we are taught in Rom. v. 3, 4. The case may be illustrated by a cup, which comes out of the fire, but is intended to hold, not fire, but wine. How it was possible for Luther to speak in this way of human efforts preceding hope may be seen from his still more definite explanation, *i. e.*, that he was willing to exonerate Lombard on the ground that he speaks of that *hope of future reward*, which is tested by many trials, and which, although the subject of the trials does not himself esteem his works meritorious, is yet by God, who does so esteem them, strengthened by means of these very works : for to the *hope of the forgiveness* of sins, which is the original and imparted hope, the definition in question cannot be applied.

In a manner similar to the above must we discriminate, in Luther's utterances during this period, between the first impartation of righteousness, which embraces, first of all, the forgiveness of sins, and by which alone such efforts on man's part as are certainly acceptable to God become possible, and a significance which he then allows to these efforts, at least for the constantly renewed enjoyment of grace, the enduring assurance of salvation, and the certain prospect of eternal happiness. We must constantly keep in view and apply the principle underlying the two exclusive conceptions of faith and hope, although we fail to find in the discussions of Luther himself in the *Sermons upon the Day of the Circumcision and the 14th Sunday after Trinity* any express and clear marking of the difference between the two. We are left in equal uncertainty, also, in the *Sermon on the 11th Sunday after Trinity*, in which, after explaining how Lombard may be exonerated, he teaches that beginners must therefore at first exercise themselves in many good works, and restrain themselves from evil works according to the sensual man (*secundum sensibilem hominem*), as by fasting, watching, praying, laboring, exercising mercy, serving, obeying, etc. But then they must be on their guard lest, in forsaking outward evils (*sensibilia mala*), they fall into spiritual evils, as do proud and self-righteous saints. The sensual man, when he has once learned to practice these exercises, never suffers himself to be led any further. But such as are led by the Spirit of God, having once learned to exercise this discipline of the outward man, do not trouble themselves much more about it, considering it as but a preparatory exercise. They now apply themselves entirely to every work to which they are called, allow themselves to be led entirely and alone by God through many sufferings and humiliations, and depend no longer upon any work. But the question may here be asked: Have these exercises of beginners already a value in the sight of God, and does hope or faith arise from them? If the answer is in the affirmative, is it not thereby granted that human efforts may then, after all, precede hope? If in the negative, how then can Luther recommend such efforts as morally good? There is here, as we have said, a lack of clear discrimination on the part of Luther. It was undoubtedly his meaning, as we may infer from all his teaching in other writings, that such exercises may be performed by a person who is yet entirely sensual, and they are then without any value in the sight of God, and are therefore not to be commended.[1] They may and should, however, also be observed in the first awakening of the impulses to a spiritual disposition of mind, and in that case, in so far as there is yet any positive good in them, they may have already, as a presupposition, a beginning of that moral character from which Luther elsewhere derives righteousness. Predominantly, however, they are to be thought of as contributing in the main only to the restraining and quenching of fleshly lusts, and, *in so far*, to the *negative* preparation of man for the reception of grace.

It still remains, accordingly, a principle universally applicable in the study of Luther's doctrine concerning the application of salvation to the sinner, that to this nothing can be contributed by any work of the sinner's own. For Luther's conception of *faith* we must now recur to the definitions in regard to its essential nature which have already been adduced (p. 139), in the pre-

---

[1] Cf. Löscher, 252: Prayer, fasting, watching, without true fear of God are themselves sin.

sentation of which Luther had in view particularly that faith
which justifies the sinner.

In opposition to the validity of works of an external nature,
Luther maintains that righteousness is to be sought inwardly, in
the heart, through faith.[1] But what is the precise nature of that
inward disposition which is called faith?

In the idea of *inwardness* we may already detect, in view of
what has been noted above, an opposition to all man's own
virtues, which Luther counts as belonging in a certain sense
to things visible and outwardly manifest, and, at the same time,
a demand for a turning to the invisible, as being that which is in
God.

It is distinctly characteristic of Luther's expositions during this
period, that he presents especially the negative side, *i. e.*, the
required turning away from. all that savors of self or of created
things, even at times appearing to base righteousness itself upon
this, and that, in his conception of this turning away, he unites
the renunciation of all outward goods directly with that of all
personal claim to moral desert (cf. *e. g.*, the above description of
" the visible," p. 138). The influence of Mysticism is here again
very clearly displayed, this aspect of the subject being much more
strongly emphasized than in the *Exposition of the Psalms*.

In a sermon on *St. Andrew's Day* (*November 30*), upon the
text, Mark i. 18 : " They left their nets," [2] Luther declares that
the heart cannot live in faith so long as it lives in that which is
bodily and visible, since faith is the substance of things to be
hoped for and not appearing. *Righteousness comes from faith,
since the latter forsakes all, and renounces all earthly goods*. In
describing what is to be forsaken, he mentions, first of all, all
things and all arts by which gain is sought, riches, pleasures, etc. ;
and he explains, that he is speaking of a " leaving with the heart,
not with the body," declaring that God accepts the man who is
in this sense " poor." Yet here already he, like Tauler, lays the
chief stress upon the " nets of wisdom, righteousness and good
works." In general, throughout his sermons, it is the pharisaical
and self-righteous against whom his zealous invectives, like those
of Tauler, are chiefly directed. In opposition to the idea that
the believer should strive in his own life to perform still further

---

[1] Löscher, 761.   [2] Ibid., 758 sqq.

works of merit, he, like Tauler, demands a complete dying on the part of self (*perfecte mortificatum esse*). If any one should fail to reach the highest stage, in which there is no more thought of works of merit, it would have been better for him never to have attained the lower stage. This is the " resignation and abnegation of self " which Luther demands—a returning to nothing ("*redigi in nihilum*"), in order that " grace alone may have room " and " God remain all in all." [1] To this, man is to be brought chiefly through crosses and sufferings. Sufferings destroy works of merit; and hence Luther says of hope, that it arises not from works of merit, but from sufferings, which destroy the works of merit. God interferes in many ways with the counsel of man, until the latter learns to despair of himself.[2] In this respect also, and especially, we must attribute a significance to outward discipline and ascetic practices of fasting, obedience, etc. Luther expressed his views upon this point more fully, at the time of which we are speaking, in his lectures upon the Decalogue, in which he declared that the weak, who are not yet slain according to the old man, need such discipline, in order by this means to make progress in the inner man ; the body must be chastened and brought into subjection.[3] Exercises of this kind had actually fulfilled precisely this office in Luther's own personal development; they had done their part in leading him to self-renunciation. In the same spirit in which he now still recommends them as a " *praeludium*," Tauler also represents similar outward exercises as a path and preparation, in which, however, we do not yet have the " marriage-feast " itself. He had compared them to the works and painful exercises of the Old Testament Law, declaring it to be their aim to lead us to renounce ourselves and all created things.[4] There is, however, only this one passage in Luther's writings in which he still recommends such exercises as a preliminary step ; and the regulations of the monastic orders for such discipline, which Tauler has here in view, are by Luther, on the contrary, left entirely out of consideration. The self-

---

[1] Löscher, 288, 767. Dec. Praec., 53 sq.

[2] Ibid., 758. Disput. of A. D., 1517. Löscher, 292.

[3] Dec. Praec., 71.

[4] Sermon on the Tuesday before Palm Sunday (in the Frankfort Edition, the second sermon on the Fourth Sunday in Lent).

renunciation so frequently commended is, therefore, essentially identical with faith.   It is just in view of this identity that Luther has, in the sentence above quoted, derived righteousness itself from the former.   At another time, he declares directly that only he can do good, who humbles himself in pain on account of his impurity, and in his works of merit recognizes rather sins. To this sorrow God grants forgiveness of what is sinful, and thus, says Luther, " *no good thing comes to pass without self-humiliation (humilitas), i. e., without righteousness preceding every work.*" [1] He speaks here, it will be observed, as though with the very act of self-humiliation, as such, were already given that righteousness which must precede every work.   Indeed, although habitually, as in the present passage, rejecting all claim to merit, and representing all works of merit, on the contrary, as sins, yet he in one place, when speaking of this mortification of self, employs (only, it is true, with the evident purpose of opposing to the common glorying in works of merit a counter proposition couched in the language of the prevailing terminology) the expression : Death, by suffering, merits sufficiently (*mors patiens meretur sufficienter*).[2]

But every more general and complete representation of the significance of faith which we now find in the writings of Luther plainly reveals the fact that for him its practical significance lies far more in the *positive relation to God* which it implies.   As a further characteristic of his present mode of expression, we must here observe, that this relation to God appears in the first instance as a very comprehensive one, embracing entire devotion of the will, obedience, and love.   But to this statement we must hasten to add, that wherever he had occasion to lay special emphasis upon that which actually secures grace for the sinner, especially where it is not his aim to humiliate the pride of the self-righteous but to point out to the humble the way of salvation, he already very definitely places the essence of faith in confidence in God, or a confident reposing upon the mercy of God, and in the very centre of his conception stands the One Christ, as the Saviour. Luther knows nothing of any true " resignation," except where there already exists also complete confidence in God.[3]   How clearly he has in view as the most important elements those just

[1] Löcher, 777.   [2] Ibid., 760.
[3] Ibid., 288: nemo sese resignat nisi qui—totum in Deum confidit.

11

indicated, even when starting with the negative aspects and when presenting, in the first instance, the most general definition of the positive aspect of faith, may be plainly seen, for example, in the above-cited *Sermon on St. Andrew's Day*. The turning away from the visible there commended is necessarily involved in the positive nature of faith, as a turning toward the invisible; and, since the entire affections are to be turned away from that which is visible to God, the invisible thus at once becomes more definitely the object of faith, in so far as it is the source whence something is communicated to man. The invisible is that which is to be hoped for, and, already in the present life, " by means of the invisible faith keeps the mortified from falling." More definitely still, that which is to be received is described as the righteousness which is in God; and faith, as confidence in this righteousness. Finally, Christ is mentioned as the One through whom we become righteous; and of Christ it is said, that we have Him through faith; that we should also live and suffer for Him; and that there should be a complete marriage with Him.

Further passages, in which Luther depicts the invisible in general as the object of faith, and in which he defines the latter in general terms as a turning toward or devotion to the invisible, have already been adduced when treating of the relation between God and man. He uses the word in this general sense also when describing various stages or " steps " of faith.[1] He represents the first step as that in which faith itself yet clings to signs or outward miracles, and thus to that which is visible; the second, as that in which we trust in the bare Word, without any attesting work (*nudo verbo sine opere*); the third, as that in which there is a complete surrender of self to the will of Him in whom we trust, even without any word and beyond words. Faith, in this last stage, is said to give itself away entirely and without reserve, to receive all things as coming from God, and to refer them all back again to Him, prepared to do everything which He desires. It is very evident that faith is here conceived of as a relation to the invisible, and as embracing the entire surrender of the will to God. We have already seen how he speaks of *love* in the *Exposition of the Psalms*, placing it in one passage at the beginning of Christian life. He now presents the same conception still more

---

[1] Löscher, 291–93.

definitely, declaring, in his *Explanation of the Third Command-ment*, that even sorrow for sin, by which man attains reconcilia-tion before God, must proceed from love [1]—a statement for which he is, by his own acknowledgement (*vid. supra*, p. 68), indebted to Staupitz ; [2] and in one place he briefly represents that in which righteousness consists to be (as opposed to works) : faith, hope and love.[3] But we have already cited the important passage which presents love as essentially the same thing as the return to nothing (*redigi in nihilum*) ; [4] and, as has been said, wherever the attempt is made to point out the special means for the actual attainment of righteousness, this office is assigned to faith, in the sense of trust (*confidere, fiducia*)—hope, however, being frequently (doubtless in view of the definition of faith in Heb. xi. 1) spoken of as identical with faith.[5] The simple faith, therefore, which looks only to the invisible and to God, is a *trusting* in God as the invisible (*confidere in nudum Deum*, etc.).[6] This relation to God is, however, so essentially mediated through Christ that faith, which is the direct opposite of confidence in man's own wisdom and righteousness, is without further ceremony said to be faith in Christ (*fides Christi*).[7] Luther frequently, as in the *Sermon upon St. Andrew's Day*, passes from the broadest definition of faith, as the turning to the invisible,[8] to the positive declaration that it is Christ upon whom, in this faith, we trust. There remains for us, he declares, no comfort and no salvation, except that Christ has been given to us by God, in Whom we may trust and Whom we may enjoy in such manner, that His righteousness alone shall sustain us. Faith is nothing else than the eating of this bread. The " real, thoroughly good righteousness " is *faith in Christ* (*der Glaube Christi*). Since faith is in the heart, Christ, in Whom we believe, is Himself also present. The entire counsel to be given to those who would secure eternal happiness is briefly given by Luther in a letter to his Augustinian brother, Spenlein, as follows : " Learn Christ and Him crucified ; learn to say : *Thou, Lord Jesus, art my righteousness, but I am Thy sin ; Thou hast taken upon Thee what was mine and hast given to me*

[1] Dec. Praec., 86 sq.

[2] Briefe, i, 116.

[3] Löscher, 288 sq.

[4] Ibid., 782.

[5] Cf. Löscher, 288, 756, 782.   [6] Ibid., 289.   [7] Dec. Praec., 5.

[8] Thus especially in the passage, Löscher, 230.

what was Thine,—for Christ dwells only in sinners."[1]   The origin
of the faith which thus looks to Christ is depicted in such a way
that faith, as a trustful reception of the offered grace, is placed
clearly before love, and that even the negative turning away from
created things appears to spring only from faith as such.   He
says : " When thou hearest that Christ suffered for thee, and
believest it, then arises trust in Him and sweet love, and vanished
is thus all desire for created things, and there is nothing left for
thee but Christ alone, so that thou, despairing of all else, settest
all thy hope upon Him alone, and therefore lovest Him above
all things." [2]   In fact, even in the passage cited from the *Explanation of the Third Commandment,* according to which contrition is
made to spring from antecedent love, the relation of the separate
elements will upon closer examination be seen to be the same as
that just indicated.   Contrition, as Luther adds, springs from
love, when man meditates—and it is, of course, a *believing* consideration that he has in view—again and again (ruminates)
upon : first, the natural gifts and works of the divine goodness ;
then, that which is spiritual, *i. e.,* the incarnation and death
of the Son ; and, finally, the promised eternal possessions.   Meditating upon these and contrasting with them his own ingratitude
and sin, he is aroused to hatred of himself and to love and praise
of God.   Only this is true, living, effectual contrition, whereas
that which grows out of the mere fear of punishment lasts but for
a little time.   Even in that prominent passage in which Luther
defines faith first, in general, as a turning away from the visible,
and, consequently, as a turning toward (*projici*) the invisible,[3] he
regards the turning away as fully effected only when faith abides
firmly in the invisible, or—what is there regarded as identical with
this—when Christ Himself is present in the heart.   " If faith
remains firmly settled there, it will with certainty tread under foot
all the desires excited by things visible."   Thus the different
utterances of Luther complete and explain one another.   It
remains, however, none the less a peculiarity of the works now
under consideration, that they contain no passage in which he has
himself given a precise and complete definition of the separate

---

[1] Erl. Ed., xxi, 206 sq.; xxxvii, 431.   Löscher, 230.   Briefe, i, 17 (April,
1516).

[2] Dec. Praec., 5.   [3] Löscher, 230.

elements of faith with regard to the entire scope of their mutual relations. He employs the separate conceptions, now with wider, now with narrower, range of meaning. For example, the term "*contritio*" indicates sometimes a sorrow for sin which impels to a believing trust, the latter already quite mature ; and sometimes, a sorrow for sin which itself presupposes the existence of a certain measure of faith. He often neglects to make special mention of elements which, according to his declarations in other places, really belong to the process which he proposes to describe ; as, for example, the element of trust in that meditation (*ruminatio*) out of which love is said to spring.

We now find ourselves driven, by the entire doctrine of repentance and faith as thus far unfolded, to the consideration of the *significance which the One Christ has for us*. But the conception of this significance stands in the most intimate mutual relationship with the conception of our own inwardly-experienced need of salvation ; and also, further, with the conception of what is now *actually through Christ and in Him imparted to the believer*, and, in turn, inwardly received and recognized in the experience of the latter. We do not by this mean that Luther conceived of the subject of the experiences in question as, in the first instance, by his own motion comprehending the need of salvation, or even already receiving the imparted gifts, and thus led to discover the objective Christ and His nature and work. Upon the contrary, we have just seen that not until Christ is held up before him, and the message of grace penetrates his soul, does man reach even a genuine or full consciousness of his own misery. But we, nevertheless, find Luther's true and spiritual apprehension of this Christ and his entire view of the latter's significance basing themselves upon, and taking shape in accordance with, the inner impressions which the proclamation of grace had produced upon him. We can present that view also only in direct connection with that which the believing, divinely-blessed Luther knows and has experienced as something which has been already imparted to himself. That which is in Christ imparted to us corresponds exactly with that which without grace we have lacked, and the lack of which has been most keenly felt.

Let us here first fix our attention upon the positive blessings of salvation as conceived by Luther.

Upon the basis of St. Paul's teachings, and with reference also

to the principles of Augustine, he in the *Exposition of the Psalms*
defined it chiefly as *righteousness*, or the *righteousness of God*,
and this in the comprehensive sense above indicated. Here
again we have seen this idea given the place of chief prominence.
Faith aims to secure " the attainable righteousness which is in
God," and it is precisely this which is imparted to it.[1] It is
called the righteousness of God, inasmuch as it is graciously
granted by God ; it is even defined as grace itself, by which we
are made righteous through Christ.[2] The idea embraces in its
scope all that is involved in a full contrast to the thought that we
were beforehand sinners. The guilt for which we could not atone
by our own works has now been removed from us; we are accepted by God as righteous ; and the *consciousness* of forgiveness
and grace is granted us. When Luther, in the passage above
cited (p. 161), declares that God grants to our sorrow for sin *the
forgiveness* of the latter, and thus presents the entrance of *righteousness* as in immediate connection with sorrow or self-humiliation, it is evident that he thinks of the former as consisting
essentially in the forgiveness of sins. In the *Disputation of the
Year 1516*, he declares that we become righteous persons when
God in grace looks upon and accepts us as such, *i. e.*, righteousness comes solely from the imputation of God. He speaks in
other places also of such an "*imputatio*." [3] He further affirms,
that God gives us a good conscience when He permits us to hear
His secret whisper : " Thy sins are forgiven thee ;" he thus fills us
with joy and rapture.[4] But the imparted righteousness is also a
new, right and divine inner life, acceptable to God. Luther,
when speaking of justification by grace as opposed to a justification by works, combines directly in one the two conceptions,
" to be righteous " and " to be pure, or purified," *i. e.*, " righteousness " and " holiness." Purification and the " infusing of
grace " are for him identical with the " justification without our
works" (*sine nobis*). The righteousness secured by man is called
an " infused " righteousness.[5] When Luther says that we become
righteous " *ex Deo justificante et imputante*," [6] he evidently, in this
combination of the two expressions, employs the first, *i. e.*, justifi-

[1] Löscher, 761.   [2] Erl. Ed., xxxvii, 430.

[3] Löscher, 335, 288.   [4] Erl. Ed., xxxvii, 393.

[5] Löscher, 776, 761.   [6] Ibid., 288.

cation, in distinction from the second, as designating the infusion of which he has spoken. But it is the entire nature of righteousness and the manner of its appropriation which he has in view when he describes it as an " inner " righteousness in opposition to work-righteousness.[1] With the apprehension of justification, or the making of men righteous, as we have now traced it, we find also constantly combined in Luther's utterances the conception of it as a continuous and progressive divine act. He speaks of the beginning of the experience defined as " becoming righteous " as the beginning of a new life. He declares that the term righteous is to be applied, not to the man who is righteous, but to him who is becoming so, according to the scriptural announcement: " He that is righteous, let him be righteous still " (Rev. xxii. 11) ; for grace is not infused all at once in its entirety, nor sin all at once driven out.[2] This entire righteousness of God, finally, comes to us as righteousness of Christ.[3]

Thus far, we have not passed beyond the subjects discussed at length in the *Annotations of the Psalms.* We note an advance upon the views there presented in but two points, *i. e.,* that justification is now so expressly described as *progressive,* and that the idea of *imputation* is so distinctly introduced. But the characteristic difference between the earlier and the present documents is found in the presentation here of that in which the believer finds his salvation as being nothing less than *full inner union and living fellowship with Christ Himself.* We have righteousness, just because we have Christ Himself; and to have Him present in the heart is, as we have seen, an essential feature of Christian faith itself. There is now thus revealed the entire depth of the expressions : " Christ is our righteousness ;" [4] " in Him are we the righteousness of God." The *Sermon on Christmas, 1515,* already grandly proclaimed this union, even quoting the above expression touching the righteousness of God. It is for him the goal of man, in faith, to have and to be that divine Word, which is itself essentially one with God. We recall, further, the propositions concerning faith as a faith upon Christ, in which we

---

[1] Löscher, 776 sq.　Cf. 761 : justitia quaerenda intus in corde per fidem.

[2] Löscher, 774, 258.

[3] Cf. the passages already cited touching the relation of faith to Christ.

[4] Löscher, 285.

are said to enjoy Him, to eat Him as the heavenly bread. He is elsewhere also called our food.[1] He dwells in us, and has given to us what is His. Luther expresses himself most fully in the *Commentary upon the Penitential Psalms*, as follows : " Christ is the grace of God, mercy, righteousness, truth, wisdom, strength, comfort and blessedness, given to us by God without any merit on our part. Christ, I say, not, as some in blind language declare, *causaliter*, giving us righteousness and Himself remaining without ; for righteousness is dead—rather, it is never given at all—unless Christ Himself is also present, just as there can be no rays of the sun nor warmth of fire where there is neither sun nor fire." [2] The entire subsequent life must then assume the character of " perfect marriage " with Christ, since we have Him through faith, and He has us and our works, so that we labor and suffer no longer for ourselves, but for Him.[3]

The richest and most profound views of Mysticism concerning oneness with Christ and life in Him thus re-appear in Luther with living power ; and the ideas of this character which his later writings, as especially the treatise *Von der Freiheit eines Christenmenschen*, contain in yet more copious and vital measure are here already clearly presented, as, *e. g.*, in the letter to Spenlein (*supra*, p. 163).

From this point of view, we may understand also the very intimate connection in which the doctrine of the *Nature of Christ* now stands with the doctrine of salvation. Luther presents no new dogmas in relation to the former ; but he now fully and clearly apprehends the connection itself, as he had not done when preparing the *Exposition of the Psalms*, and he, therefore penetrates also with genuine religious interest more deeply into the mysteries of that nature itself. We have already noted, that the real inward impulse leading to the preparation of the remarkable *Christmas Sermon*, venturing though it does so largely upon abstract philosophizing, was furnished by such religious interest. The theme is the divine nature of that Word, which became man, in order that man might become God. In the elaboration of this

---

[1] Löscher, 276 sq., with reference to the riddle of Samson : " Food came out of the eater." Cf. further references below.

[2] Erl. Ed., xxxvii, 441. Cf. Staupitz, supra, p. 67.

[3] Löscher, 761.

theme, that which in Christ is to become our portion is represented as consisting in His own nature, His own personality.   He
Himself is essentially the righteousness, truth, etc., which He is
to become for us and in us.   In Him God essentially and originally deposited His wisdom, righteousness and virtue, in order
that these might thus become ours.[1]

But, in the very sermon of which we are now speaking, the closer
definitions in regard to the union of man with the Word again reveal
the divergence from the Mystical view.   We have reference to the
decisive way in which Luther here guards himself against such
a misunderstanding of his language as should infer from it that
man is actually made God or substantially transformed into Christ.
Despite all that is said about returning into one's nothingness,
and about striving toward God, the " I " always maintains its
relatively independent existence (cf. especially the portrayal of
the relation between God and man, p. 142).   At the same time,
also, there is preserved for the Word, or Christ, His continued
objective significance for man, as opposed to the view according
to which the significance of Christ for us is at last resolved
entirely into the mere fact of His dwelling within us as a subjective principle.   It is, further, a significant indication of the divergence in question, that the relation to Christ is always apprehended
as " faith," and faith as essentially trust (*fiducia*).   While desiring to enter into union with us, Christ is yet always primarily
the object of our faith, *i. e.*, He always stands before our vision
primarily as an objective reality and personality.   The references
to *faith in Christ,* or the " faith of Christ," are as infrequent in
the mysticism even of a Tauler as they are constant and characteristic in the writings of Luther.

But the broad distinction between Luther's apprehension of
Christ and that of Mysticism becomes especially marked when
we turn to the examination of his fundamental views touching the
sinner's condition and need of salvation.   To the Mystic, the
objective, historical activity and the sufferings of the personal
Redeemer appear as essentially but a type of that which should
occur to and within the believer who joins himself to Christ.   For
him the significance of the work of Christ, and even of His
nature itself, is made to consist merely in the fact, that there is

---

[1] Löscher, 742.

therein presented to our vision and in an affecting way impressed
upon our hearts what we ourselves should become and be.   Luther,
on the other hand, felt that man, subject to the divine requirements, guilty and condemned to everlasting death, needs first of
all, in order to become one with God, a Redeemer who has
objectively interposed in his behalf, met the requirements of the
Law, and removed the sentence of guilt and judgment.   For
him, Christ can become Christ *in us* only as He shall have first
become, in this sense, Christ *for us*.   This is in entire keeping
with the general mode of apprehension pervading the writings of
Luther, and does not at all conflict with his above-cited criticism
of those who say that Christ is *causaliter* our righteousness.   He
there only means to say that Christ, in order to become our righteousness, must enter into us, and not that such an entrance can
occur independently of the objective significance of Christ for us.

We must here again recall the general conception of the *confidence* which is to be placed in the objective Christ, more definitely defined as a confidence which man as a sinner should cherish
toward the objective Redeemer and Deliverer from guilt.   In
illustration of this, we have the express utterances of Luther in
regard to the *activity and sufferings* of Christ.   We may range
the various deliverances upon this subject scattered throughout
his writings under the single sentence of his letter to Spenlein :
" *Thou, Jesus, hast taken upon Thee that which was mine.*"
Christ is represented as taking upon Him that which was ours,
as well in His *doing* as in His *suffering*.   These two elements
appear already with distinctness, although we find as yet no more
definite presentation of their mutual relations.   It is especially
important to observe the prominence already given by Luther to
the former of these elements, since we shall find it distinctly
recurring from time to time in his own writings, although not
until a quite late day securing formal recognition.   As early as
the year 1515, Luther, in his *Sermon on St. Stephen's Day*, declared that Christ came to *fulfil the Law*, which we could not
fulfil, but only violate ; that we must take refuge in Him, as a
brood under the wings of the hen, and receive out of His fulness ;
that He imparts to us His fulfilment of the Law ; and that
through this impartation we too may fulfil the Law.[1]   It is plain

[1] Löscher, 244, 249 sq.

that he here means an actual fulfilment of the Law by Christ, an active obedience of Christ in our stead. The impartation spoken of must, in accordance with what we have learned as to his views touching the impartation of the righteousness of God, or of Christ, be understood in a comprehensive sense, as signifying both that we are now for Christ's sake regarded by God as fulfillers of the Law, and that He, by an inward infusion (of grace) enables us to walk according to the will of God. Touching the *sufferings of Christ* we find again, especially in the interpretation of the third penitential Psalm (xxxviii) the same general conception as that prevailing in the *First Exposition of the Psalms*, *i. e.*, he puts this Psalm directly into the mouth of Christ, and we are to pray it after Christ. But Christ is said thus to pray " in the suffering and penitence, which He accomplished for our sin." [1] Christ therefore utters as His own experience what this Psalm in its opening verses declares concerning the punitive wrath of God and the burden of guilt. At various points in his comments upon it, Luther returns to this direct application to the experience of Christ Himself; as, for example, under verse 7, and still more notably under verse 10, which speaks of the distress and fainting of the heart under the terrors of divine wrath, and in connection with which he quotes also Ps. xxii. 14, 15, as words of Christ. We already meet here also in one passage with expressions setting forth a peculiar view of the relation of the death of Christ to the Law and to the devil—a view which occupies a large and important place in the later writings of Luther. It appears here in an undeveloped form, without dialectic analysis or accommodation, and we shall discover hereafter that a lack of dialectic development at this point remains a characteristic of Luther's teaching. This view is set forth in the peculiar allegorical interpretation of Judges xiv. 14 : " Out of the eater came forth meat, and out of the strong came forth sweetness." [2] Luther sees in the lion, the Jewish nation ; and in the mouth of the lion, the Law. But in the written Law lay the sweet honey, *i. e.*, the Gospel ; and since the eater has now been slain by the killing of the Letter, meat comes forth from the eater. Thus the Law has been fulfilled and the Letter killed. This is therefore " the strong one," since

---

[1] Erl. Ed., xxxvii, 370.

[2] Löscher, 275 sqq., Second sermon on Easter, 1516.

it is harsh and grievous, and its demands are such as we cannot fulfil; but now even its very Letter has become sweet to us. To this Luther adds, without any attempt to explain the connection: " And this all comes to pass through the *death of Christ.*" He then proceeds : " Let us now search out these mysteries. *Christ* came forth out of the mouth of the devil, who had eaten Him. He is our meat, our passover, our bread of heaven. Had the lion not eaten Him, and had He not killed the lion, the meat could not have come forth from Him. It was necessary that Christ should suffer and arise from the dead, and thus prepare the way for the preaching of repentance and the forgiveness of sins, *i. e.,* of the Gospel." It is here evident that Luther regards this reference to the devil as essential to a complete understanding of the mystery of scriptural teaching in regard to the death of Christ. As to the relation of the sufferings of Christ to the impartation of " righteousness," we must recall the remark above made touching the relation of His obedience to such impartation. The one element, *i. e.,* the effecting of inward righteousness in man, evidently preponderates, for example, in the *Sermon on the Day of St. Laurentius* (1516), in which Luther attributes it directly to the sufferings of Christ that the inner man " is justified and made new." [1] The other, or forensic, element is given the chief prominence when it is said, evidently with reference both to the sufferings of Christ and to His active life, that His *merits* are *imputed* to us.[2]

The objective endurance and activity of Christ, or, in general, all that He has objectively contributed to the work of salvation, are singled out for separate mention in this utterance concerning the " *Merita Christi.*" It is, however, to be borne in mind that it is a characteristic of Luther's teaching that he always regards what Christ has thus accomplished as standing in immediate connection with Christ Himself, with the entire content of His personality, and, at the same time, with Himself as the ever-living One. Moreover, for man as a sinner, this ever-living and ever-working One appears, not only as ready to enter into union with him, but, above all, as standing objectively

[1] Löscher, 756: (Christus) justificat sacramento (cf. seq.) hominem interiorem et facit novum.

[2] Löscher, 743.

before him in the capacity of a mediator of salvation, primarily
of reconciliation. Thus Luther describes, in a general way, all
that Christ has accomplished for us in the statement, that He has
bought us with Himself.[1] Thus Christ is for him a *propitiatorium*,
or throne of grace, inasmuch as He is the temple of God, in
whom the eternal God dwells bodily and wholly; and when we
bow before Him as such we receive the forgiveness of all sins
and all the blessings of grace—the connection with the once
completed atoning sufferings of Christ being here indicated by
Luther's reference to Rom. iii. 25.[2]

Finally, it is only as Christ has done and suffered thus for us
that He can become our pattern. Thus Luther remarks again,
when treating of Psalm xxxviii., as in his *First Exposition*, that
only he who has become conformed to the image of Christ in
penitence and suffering can rightly repeat this prayer after Him.
In the *Sermon upon St. Laurentius' Day*, he expressly maintains
that everything in Christ benefits us in two ways, *i. e.*, according
to a definition of Augustine, *sacramentaliter* and *exemplariter*.
He here designates the sufferings of Christ, according to their
sacred mysterious significance, a sacrament, inasmuch as in them
our deliverance is set forth. Christ has been bound for us, in
order that we who are in bondage may be eternally set free. He
was willing to be forsaken to the uttermost, bereft of everything
upon which He might place His confidence and trusting only
in God, in order that we might not be forsaken and left without
trust or hope. But we should then also suffer ourselves to be
bound by men, or by ourselves, with the chains of penitence for
the sins of the old man; and we should be willing, also, to be
forsaken in the outward man, without any trust or hope but in
God alone. Christ by His example turns our attention especially upon the outward and the old man, whereas by His sacrament He justifies and renews the inward man.

We have thus endeavored to collect and set forth in their inner
mutual connections all the more important declarations of Luther
concerning the *objective work of Christ* for the salvation of men
contained in the writings of the present period which are still
within our reach. Though they are few in number, yet they
display a decided advance in true richness and depth and in vital

---

[1] Erl. Ed., xxi, 183.   [2] Ibid., xxvii, 415 sq.

relation to the experiences and needs of the inner Christian life as these were now apprehended by Luther, beyond the standpoint and explanations of the prevalent scholastic theology. The living germs also of a new formulation of evangelical doctrine are here rapidly developing in Luther; and it may be said that the fundamental elements of his doctrine, as later developed, may all be found here already indicated. But, none the less, it is to be observed, on the other hand, that all these utterances appear as yet only in separate and unconnected passages. It is very seldom indeed that Luther enters upon any more minute explanations touching the work of Christ. It must be remembered, too, that it was always his first endeavor to announce to his hearers and readers the way in which the salvation, which for him rested upon the objective premises indicated, was to be appropriated. Inasmuch now as Christ and His righteousness, as involved in the conception of faith, and without which faith would be nothing, constitute the central point of his discourses, we find that those passages in which he enters more minutely into the discussion of the special particulars indicated above fall strikingly into the background in comparison with those in which he presents Christ and His salvation only in general and comprehensive terms. This is, beyond question, to be attributed in large measure to the fact that it was especially at this very point, *i. e.*, in regard to the way in which salvation is to be appropriated, that the people committed to his care were in special danger of being led into error by false teachers. What grave peril to the spiritual life was involved in such error, he had himself most fully experienced. Yet it is evident also that even in the midst of his earnest endeavors to deliver himself and others from the bondage of these errors, and to guard against their recurrence, Luther, in his public testimonies, as well as in his own apprehension of truth, was nevertheless comparatively tardy in the further unfolding and definition of the objective realities which then already lay at the basis of his theology. His affiliation with Tauler and the mystical tendency of his own disposition may also help to account for the fact that he manifested so little interest in the analysis and discrimination of elements which he yet regarded as in themselves so highly significant. This, again, is characteristic of the stage of development which his general religious views had at that time attained.

We are now, having given due attention to Luther's utterances concerning the object of faith, in a position to define more intelligently his views upon the question, in how far the *path to salvation* consists in the *"faith of Christ"*—or in how far *such faith assures the attainment of salvation.*

First of all, we meet with numerous passages in which *faith itself* appears to be regarded as a *service* rendered to God. Luther describes self-righteousness as a transgression of the First Commandment of the Decalogue, in which all the others are included, and in contrast represents faith as its proper *fulfilment.*[1] In another place, he declares that the Second Commandment is faith itself, the First Commandment being in the same connection described as love, and the Third as hope. In explanation of this, he adds that the name of God is polluted by reliance upon our own holiness, and, on the other hand, hallowed by faith as a renunciation of the latter.[2] He even traces righteousness itself to humility, despairing of itself and praying in faith, inasmuch as such humility *glorifies* God. The humble man, he declares, " glorifies God and is righteous." [3] But yet, on the other hand, we must keep steadily in view what for Luther is the really decisive aspect of the truth before us, namely, that faith, apart from its object, in the presence of which it renounces all confidence in itself, is nothing at all and has nothing whatsoever—that the first three Commandments aim to make man a mere material for God to work upon—that we become righteous through faith, not because the latter renders the service which God requires, but because it renounces all things—that God commends men, not when they do this or that, but when they receive from Him that which He offers to them.[4] Bearing this in mind, we may and should nevertheless allow to the above-cited declarations the full weight which they had in Luther's conception. They reveal the moral significance which he attributes to the nature of faith, and the authority which, despite all the emphasis laid upon the pure grace of God and our simple reception of it, he yet maintains for the claims of God as the Holy One and as the One Lord. But a closer analysis of the relation between these two important elements he has nowhere attempted to present.

[1] Löscher, 747, 748, 752 sq.　Dec. Praec., 53 sqq.

[2] Dec. Praec., 129.　Löscher, 295.

[3] Löscher, 746.　　　　[4] Ibid., 281.　Cf. supra, pp. 140, 143.

The faith of Christ, further, brings righteousness, since it *brings Christ Himself into the heart*, and holds Him in the heart as an *indwelling righteousness* and as the source and root of our own subsequent right conduct. What is now, under these circumstances, the relation of the act of God in which He, to speak negatively, forgives our sins, or, speaking positively, counts us as righteous, to the act of actual infusion and to the fact of such indwelling as has been indicated? Does not the former perhaps depend upon the latter in such a sense that the new practical righteousness dwelling within us is as such imputed to us, and we are just on account of it acceptable to God? Or, are we to understand that the forensic act, though always accompanied by an actual infusion and indwelling, yet stands with the latter in no such relation of cause and effect, but takes into consideration only the Christ *for us*, with His work and His righteousness? We might quote, in support of the first supposition, such passages as that in which Christ is said to be the righteousness of God for us, not as though He remained without, but because He is Himself present with us; and, for the second, the references to His merits as constituting that which is imputed to us (*vid. supra*). We must, it is true, at this point also carefully refrain from the attempt to extort keen logical and scholastic distinctions from the utterances of Luther. He was accustomed, as is evident from what has been above presented, to speak freely and without discrimination of both divine acts as though combined in one; and we have in this fact a distinctly characteristic trait of his mode of apprehending and presenting the process of salvation. Nevertheless, his uncompromising opposition to all claims of human righteousness leads him even at this time to expressly reject all attempts to ascribe an efficacious value to the new inwardly-imparted righteousness. It is precisely such as rest and trust in a righteousness already received from on high, instead of that yet to be attained, which is in God, whom he regards as self-righteous. In such case, says he, there is not faith (as a faith in the invisible) but experience (*experimentum;* cf. also Luther's designation of even the gifts of grace as things visible). The righteous man, on the other hand, lifted entirely out of himself, lives in God and His righteousness. And thus, adds Luther, he is righteous, not through his righteousness which he has attained in God, nor through that which has been infused into him, but in the divine righteousness itself, in the presence of which and in which he has lost his own, which has now become sin to him.[1]

Another distinction to be here observed is that, already hinted at, between the original impartation of righteousness and its *continuous possession culminating* finally in the *attainment of eternal happiness*. As conditioning the latter, Luther, in earnest warning, presents distinctly the conduct of man himself, which must now be marked by positive fruits and the rendering of becoming service to God. In a *Sermon upon Sirach*, xv. *1, 2*, he declares in a very general way that we must cling inseparably to righteousness. (which he here again identifies with Christ as the hen spreading out her wings—in Sirach, the " mother "), in order to attain it, or even to secure so much as the grace needed for our perfecting. Steadfastness is said to spring from the love and fear of God ; and the labor, which is difficult in the beginning of the new life, or of the process of making righteous, becomes light as it progresses.[2] Special points we have already found emphasized in the comments of Luther upon the saying of Peter the Lombard, as, *e. g.*, that hope should spring from meritorious works. It is there further maintained that God Himself attaches·value to the testing of believers in toil and suffering ; and, as a result of a course of life thus highly esteemed by God, we have, as a divine gift, the consequent strengthening of the hope of eternal happiness. But Luther in other passages goes even further than this. In one place he affirms :[3] It is a sin that man is not perfect, as he ought to be. This sin, however, is not imputed to those who with persistent earnestness struggle against it. It is not imputed to them just *in view of this zeal and advancement* (toward perfection), although it is in them ; because, although it is in them, it is yet not in their will, but against their will—in their flesh. Therefore what is in them is yet not in them. According to this, it is directly on account of the disposition of the regenerate themselves and their own efforts that the sin yet cleaving to them is forgiven.

Nevertheless, Luther even here again emphasizes, out of all proportion, the other side, namely, the inability and unworthiness of man even when regenerate and become one with Christ. He not only constantly warns against the making of the services ren-

---

[1] Löscher, 761.   [2] Ibid., 773.   [3] Dec. Praec., 124.

12

dered to God by the new man a basis of our confidence—declaring that faith and confidence, although to a certain extent and in a certain sense arising from such services, must yet be directed solely and entirely upon God and His grace ; and that the services in question are pleasing to God only in so far as they are performed without any thought of trusting in them or of taking them at all into account,[1]—but it is precisely to the continuous right conduct of those already made righteous that we are to apply the positive declaration, that the righteous man is not righteous (in the sight of God) by virtue of the righteousness which he has himself obtained through Christ. Luther himself does not explain to us how this is to be harmonized with the other statement, that man's own effort is the basis of the non-imputation of present sin. The two propositions may, however, be reconciled as follows : It is only by the free grace of God that man's own effort may form such a basis, and it is only by virtue of that faith in which the believer puts himself " entirely outside of himself " that God so accepts it. In general, the underlying tendency everywhere manifest in the positive utterances of Luther and in his polemical writings against the errors which imperil salvation is to reduce even the Christian to absolute humility, to represent him, even in view of his present personal walk and conversation, as simply a sinner. The view is presented with especial vigor in the *Theses of the year 1516*, in which Luther adduces the passage in Prov. vii. 21, afterwards repeated and applied with greater detail in the same sense, viz. : " There is none upon earth that doeth good and sinneth not." He understands this as affirming that every righteous man sins even in the very act of doing good. The words of St. Paul: " The evil which I would not, that I do," etc., he applies likewise to the Christian who has been made righteous. He finds a full justification of these scriptural statements in the reflections, that everything in which man fails to meet the obligation resting upon him is sin, and that man is under obligation to love God above all things, and to fulfil every iota of the Law. He meets the objection that, according to St. John, " whosoever is born of God doth not commit sin," by declaring, with appeal to St. Augustine, that we fulfil the commandments of God, inasmuch as all that fails of

[1] Löscher, 748.

accomplishment upon our part is forgiven us, and that these are more truly fulfilled when God in mercy pardons than when man by his (imparted) righteousness does what they require. He would have us attribute solely and alone to divine " imputation " the righteousness of believers, *i. e.*, the fact that they are accounted as righteous, and their sins, according to Ps. xxxii. 2, not imputed to them by God. Their righteousness remains a righteousness " hidden in God " (cf. *supra :* faith in the invisible, as opposed to the " *experimentum* "). Every saint remains in his own consciousness a sinner (*conscienter peccator*). Yes, adds Luther, he is a righteous man without knowing it (*ignoranter*). He is a sinner in fact, a righteous man in hope ; a sinner in reality, yet nevertheless a righteous man in the esteem of a pitying God.[1] With this apprehension of the essential character and condition of the righteous, we find Luther occupying precisely the position which he afterwards, as a Reformer, faithfully maintained.

But let us now turn our attention to the *present state* of the man who has *become righteous* through faith, regarding it in the light of its own actual character and content, apart from the question in how far it may involve the conditions requisite to the attainment of eternal happiness. It remains ever true, that the righteous man finds himself constantly referred to the invisible grace of God. He always remains a sinner. But what a revolution has been effected for him with the entrance of faith and with the very first impartation of righteousness ! He is *righteous*, though only, indeed, as we have seen, as one who is now just about to *become* so. He is not to be righteousness, but to hunger after it.[2] He must continually contend with lust (which yet constantly strives to hold the mastery over him), with the flesh, the world and the devil.[3] He is like the sparrow alone upon the house-top (Ps. cii. 7). The world beneath and the heavens above him, he soars alone in faith between the world and this present life and the life that is eternal.[4] Even in his fear of God are yet ever commingled the holy and the servile ;[5] and even the con-

[1] Peccator secundum rem, justus secundum spem, peccator revera, justus vero per reputationem Dei miserentis.—Löscher, 344 sqq., 335.

[2] Löscher, 296.   [3] Erl. Ed., xxi, 181.   [4] Ibid., xxxvii, 406 sq.

[5] Löscher, 257.   Cf. Erl. Ed., xxxvii, 421 sqq. : A man in the proper spiritual state always, on account of the old man, retains fear in view of the judgment of God.   Fear and hope dwell together.   The old man must fear and tremble.

sciousness of the forgiving grace of God, described as a "*whis-pering" of forgiveness* (*supra*, p. 166), is not by any means always realized at once upon the exercise of faith. To many believers God says nothing about forgiveness, but deals with them both outwardly and inwardly in such a way that He appears to them to be an ungracious God, who desires to give them over to destruction in time and in eternity. This is designed to prevent men from forgetting the fear of God even in the time of joy.[1]   Nevertheless, Christ is now already *present in our inward nature*, if we only believe. Now already it may be said of us, not only that we seek God, but also that we have Him, however far we may yet be from being ourselves God.[2]   Righteousness, as infused, is ever full of life, and cannot be idle ; the grace of God is a living, active spirit.[3]   Above all is the *forgiveness of sins*, just as soon as it is simply believed, fully and truly granted by God. Luther, when speaking of a growth of righteousness, or of an ad-vance in the process of becoming justified, nowhere refers in this language to forgiveness or acceptance as righteous, *i. e.*, to that which was afterwards, in Lutheran dogmatic theology, technically designated " justification ;" but it is only the inner moral life of the Christian which he regards as so imperfect in its beginning and in such constant need of improvement. Wherever, on the other hand, he attributes to faith the forgiveness of sins, all ante-cedent and present sins appear as at once forgiven ; and wherever he speaks of the divine imputation, the man who has just become enlisted in the process of becoming righteous, and who is still in view of his own character to be called a sinner, is yet, without any hesitation, represented as already a " righteous man." The very fact that we do not need, so to speak, a complete infusion of grace in order to attain peace and rest of conscience, is now regarded by Luther as a source of great comfort. He used to think, says he, that grace must be infused all at once, and hence despaired of God and all divine things.[4]   We should therefore not suffer ourselves to be misled if God, even while we continue to believe, should yet maintain entire silence concerning His forgiveness—if the sense of forgiveness, as received at His hand,

---

[1] Erl. Ed., xxi, 210. (This discussion, however, is not found in the Schneider Edition of the Lord's Prayer, A. D., 1517, vol. vii, pp. 1079, sq.)

[2] Cf. Löscher, 296.

[3] Löscher, 778. Disput., A. D. 1517, Thesis lv.   [4] Löscher, 258.

should not be immediately and at all times realized. On the contrary, Luther further maintains in the same connection that God does not always openly forgive guilt, or in such a way that we realize His forgiveness, but also sometimes secretly, without allowing us to realize it—just as He, on the other hand, imputes guilt to many who do not realize it nor care anything about it. This second forgiveness is said to be only " sometimes necessary, in order that man may not give way to despair." God is, therefore, still kindly disposed toward believers, and cordially forgives *all their guilt*, even while apparently dealing ungraciously with them. This forgiveness makes its subject pure (free from guilt in the sight of God) ; the second gives him peace (in his own heart). The former works and brings ; the latter rests and receives. The former exists only in faith, and merits much ; the latter exists in realization, and enjoys the reward. The former, says Luther, is indeed bitter and hard to bear, but it is also the noblest and best, and is employed in the dealings of God with men of lofty character, whereas the latter is employed by Him when dealing with weaklings and beginners. Vividly, however, does the Reformer portray the peace which the believer, after passing through such trials, shall certainly be permitted to attain. This, he declares, is a peace which is beyond all our feeling, thinking and wishing, incomparably better than all. It shall at length be experienced by every one who, in all that he feels, thinks and knows, willingly endures the cross.[1]

This is the state to which Luther knows himself as a believer to have been exalted in Christ—this the blissful consciousness of grace to which from the deepest sense of sin and guilt the Gospel has conducted him. We may add, that it is just in the position thus attained, and in the mature form which the consciousness of grace has here assumed, that we may most clearly see the lines of demarcation between his views and those both of Augustine and of the Mystics. In this lay also the power, peculiar to himself, with which his testimony to gospel truth now assumed a reformatory character. With Augustine he held in common the conception of the term "*justificatio*" noted above. But he presents the grace of God in a new and peculiar light when he maintains, that it " cordially forgives all guilt " in the very beginning of this

[1] Briefe, i. 27.

" justification ;" that the believer may be *perfectly* sure of its possession just as soon as he really believes ; and that it is not to be merited even in the progress of the advancing Christian life by human efforts and expiations, but always continues to be essentially a free gift bestowed upon faith alone. With Mysticism, Luther now accepts and teaches—differing thus again from Augustine and, as well, from his own former position as presented in the *First Exposition of the Psalms*—the duty of penetrating most profoundly into the fellowship of Christ, and even the actual unity of the Christian with his Saviour. With Luther's utterances touching the inward experience of grace and peace we may further compare the representations of Tauler, *i. e.*, that God visits, sorely presses and pursues His children with grievous assailments ; that He then grants them consolation in comparison with which all suffering seems trifling—permits them to become intoxicated in His love with jubilant joy ; and that He afterwards, lest they be injured by this delicious wine, withdraws again these sweet experiences, casting them again into sorrow—and that it is just upon the stronger and elect among His children that such trials are permitted to come.[1] But we have already called attention to the essential distinction between his views and those of the Mystics touching the positive blessings of salvation and their appropriation by the believer. Similarly, he now knows nothing of a long series of steps, or stages, in the process of going out of self and becoming one with God, such as the Mystics were accustomed to prescribe as means for the actual attainment of salvation. Instead of this, he presents what we have already heard him designate the " short path " of faith. This in itself constitutes the great, decisive, all-comprehensive line of demarcation between life beyond the pale of salvation and that within it. This is the source, likewise, whence proceeds the inner unfolding of the renewed life, which may from this point onward be distinctly traced. Thus even the attitude of the Christian in view of the great change from spiritual temptation and sorrow to peace and joy is essentially different from that under the teaching of the Mystics. Luther nowhere indulges in such extravagant expressions touching joy in God as does Tauler. This is fully explained by the fact, that in his seeking for salvation, and in his conscious-

[1] Cf., e. g., the Sermon preached on the Monday preceding Palm Sunday.

ness of its attainment, he does not attach the chief importance to the enjoyment of the Son of God, or of God as dwelling within us. Side by side with the blissful consciousness of this, there always remains for him the vivid sense of our own persistent sinfulness. Earnestly as he advocates the effort to attain oneness with God, the matter of chief importance yet ever remains for him the accepting and reconciling grace, the certainty of which faith realizes as it holds in view the objective Christ. Just in this the believer possesses, amid all possible variations in his own moods and inward experiences, a secure and changeless footing. He stands firmly supported by his faith in an objective Saviour. In this may—yea, must and shall—for him stand immovably secure, despite all appearance to the contrary, the grace or " favorable disposition " (*Holdsein*) of God.

Upon the basis thus laid, the CONCEPTION OF THE MORAL LIFE which should, and naturally will, distinguish man in the state of grace now assumes, as was to be expected, a new and peculiar form.

The natural inferences in this sphere from the new point of view attained by Luther are not developed to any large extent during this period. On the contrary, his attention is now (especially in his polemical and monitory writings) devoted to questions of moral conduct, and of works only in so far as this is necessary in emphasizing, on the one hand, his rejection of all meritorious character as inhering in the latter, and in revealing, on the other hand, the source from which they naturally flow. He does not enter upon any independent and more definite discussion of their character nor of the various degrees of worthiness to be attributed to them.

Yet even here we may detect already some general features at least which are new. The new life is in general terms, indeed, presented as simply a life *in love ;* more particularly a life in *humble love*, devoted to the well-being of others. This is for the righteous man the significance of his own works, *i. e.*, not that they bring him righteousness, but that through them he serves God and his fellowmen.[1] The discussions of this subject remind us again of the exhortations of the Mystics. Luther himself commends to a friend the statement, which he attributes to Tauler,

[1] Löscher, 776.

that the Christian must meet on a common level, without partiality, every one of his fellowmen as being a son of the one common God and of the one common Church.[1] Luther employs the commandment of love in a polemical way in assailing the opinion of certain erring scholastic theologians, who taught that this commandment is to become operative only in the case of extreme distress, and who recognized a mortal sin only in such a flagrant transgression of it as, for example, the denying of food to a starving man. This, says he, is a sluggish love, or, rather, no love at all.[2] The position here assumed is a natural outgrowth of a deeper conception of goodness, such as distinguishes also in like manner the teaching of the Mystics. We still meet, too, in Luther, as in the Mystics and in the general teachings of the Church of that age, a mainly *negative* conception of morality, as in the expressions already quoted touching the renunciation of all that belongs to self, and touching love as consisting just in such renunciation. We have seen that he still enumerates fasting and similar exercises as at least a good discipline for beginners. In one passage, he finds the chastity of *virginity* indicated by the seed bearing fruit an hundred-fold (Matt. xiii. 23), whereas the chastity of married life produces but thirty-fold.[3] In the counsels which he had occasion to give in his capacity as presiding officer in the affairs of the Augustinian monastery, he falls in entirely with the existing outward ordinances and customs, and gives his decisions in accordance with their requirements.[4]

But he no longer anywhere in his own writings or explanations of the Scripture commends to Christians the monastic exercises, or even thinks them worthy of mention ; not even, as we have observed, when speaking directly of works of external discipline. In this he differs in marked degree from Tauler. When he urges the forsaking of all visible possessions, he adds expressly : " with the heart, not with the body." He never urges such a leading of the " poor life of Christ " as he found inculcated in his favorite author, Tauler. Even when acknowledging, as above, the value of virgin chastity, he adds that we dare not, however, on this account deny that a married woman may be better than

[1] Briefe, i, 34.
[2] Disput., A D. 1516. Löscher, 336. Briefe, i, 35.
[3] Löscher, 795. Cf. supra.,p, 122. [4] Cf., e. g., Briefe, i, 35.

a virgin, since the preëminence of the hundred-fold fruit does not imply that the thirty-fold is the less extraordinary (*nec ideo— praestat—quia minus excedit*), inasmuch as these words are intended to express, not the measure of merit, but the honor attaching to degree. Precisely wherein the difference of valuation in this case consists he does not now attempt to explain. We find one more passage of special interest, occurring in the *Sermon upon the Fear of God*, preached toward the close of the year 1515. Having asserted here that prayer, fasting, etc., are well-pleasing to God, and good only when combined with the fear of God, he adds : " just as, likewise, the work of a tailor, shoemaker, councilor, prince, or that of any other art or calling." Thus, in penetrating to the very root of human actions, *i. e.*, the motives which alone give them moral character, Luther is led even at this early period to recognize the fact that a godly disposition may find exercise even in that sphere of activity which the supposed more perfect Christians of the day despised as common and profane, and may hallow even the apparently most trivial deeds performed in the pursuit of an earthly calling. We thus recognize already in the Luther of this period the germs of an entirely new and free moral theory of life, in direct opposition to the monastic theory, and to that of the entire mediæval Church as well ; and, as the root from which these germs have been developed, we cannot fail to note that consciousness of reconciliation and grace which had delivered him from the vain effort to render the meritorious services of a supposed higher morality, and, at the same time, from a false and contracted conscientiousness in the use of temporal things.

Of special interest, finally, in determining the conception of moral life entertained at this time by Luther, is a discussion of the New Testament injunction concerning the endurance of wrong.[1] It furnishes, at once, another striking illustration of the more profound conception of duty which was characteristic of his view in general, and illustrates, on the other hand, how gradually he advanced to perfectly clear apprehensions of the truth, especially, as in this case, in respect to the relation of the Christian to the sphere of secular life. He seeks in the passage referred to, appealing to 1 Cor. v. 7 and Matt. v. 39, to restrain Christians

---

[1] Dec. Praec., 196, 203 sqq.

from instituting legal proceedings on account of earthly things and from actual resistance of any violence which they may be called upon to endure. It is customary, he acknowledges, to regard these scriptural injunctions as merely counsels, and not commandments, and as such counsels, moreover, as are merely intended to aid in inducing a proper state of mind. But he does not understand what a state of mind can be that never leads to action. He appeals, further, to Matt. vii. 12, declaring that every one certainly wishes that his neighbor should not bring suit against him, and that Jesus pronounces this to be the law and the prophets. We are therefore not at liberty to interpret it as a mere word of counsel. To the objection, that if we did not resist wrong we would soon be trampled under foot, he replies that this is just what the Scriptures would have us endure; we are to be poor and oppressed on account of the Gospel. It is only to the " weak " that he yet allows the privilege of applying to the civil authorities for the avenging of wrong. " To Christians," he declares, " it is forbidden." Thus the requirement of the renunciation of self and the world appears to be carried to the utmost extreme. But just here the new evangelical view of Luther again asserts its power most distinctly, in leading him to ignore within the sphere of Christian morality all supposed distinctions between a higher and a lower stage, or such as is merely commended and such as is commanded. The Commandments are represented as addressed alike to all " Christians," and not merely to such as are supposed to be perfect. The " weak " are not recognized at all as genuine Christians. Yet Luther acknowledges the right and duty of civil government in the midst of the Christian world, to prevent the doing of wrong, and to punish that which has been perpetrated. The prohibitions above mentioned are to be applied only to private persons, and not to those in public office, whose duty it is to give attention to such things. The latter, he declares, " *ought to* " give such attention, implying that he regards the right and the office to which it has been assigned as ordained from on high. He, of course, in this assumes that true Christians may very properly discharge the duties of such positions. His later conception in this matter differs from that which is here dominant, in that he has there learned to regard not only the civil authorities, but also other Christians, as at the same time also secular (*weltliche*) personages, such as lords, servants, husbands,

wives, parents, children, neighbors, subjects, etc., and as under
obligation to conduct themselves among one another in the world
according to the requirements of civil law and government.[1]

We have now noted the leading principles which had up to this
time found definite expression under the impulse of Luther's new
evangelical apprehension of the truth and his official proclamation of the doctrines of salvation.   It only remains for us to define
yet more precisely the agency which the *Divine Word* is to exert
in the initiation of the saving process in the individual, and,
finally, to inquire as to the relation of the entire process to the
original divine decree.

That it is the WORD OF GOD, by which divine truth and the
blessings of salvation are to be imparted to men, by which faith
is to be awakened and the new life cultivated, Luther everywhere
assumes as beyond all question.   He always, too, in such connections, thinks of the Word as it is presented in the Sacred Scriptures and proclaimed by the mouth of the Church.   As yet he has
no suspicion that the teaching prevalent in the Church can be
otherwise than identical with the doctrines of the Scriptures.
The theories touching the way of salvation which he now combats,
he does not by any means regard as supported by the official
endorsement of the Church.   He does not as yet expressly assail
the position of such as would place their own subjective spirit
upon a level with, or above, the word of Scripture.   The claims of
the natural spirit and of natural wisdom he has already rejected,
along with those of man's own righteousness, in his doctrine of
human depravity.   The opinion that the Spirit of grace which is
granted to believers may also be imparted to them otherwise
than through the divine Word, or may by its light lead them to
fuller knowledge than that imparted by the Word, has not as yet
arrested his attention.   We have already seen the intimate connection which the *Christmas Sermon of the year 1515* traces
between the proclamation of the Word and the nature and incarnation of Christ as the eternal Word.   The incarnation of the
Word in Christ is there described as the assuming of a voice
(*induere vocem*).   This Word then is carried abroad (*dispergitur*)
to the multitude, working instruction and salvation.   Those who
receive it in faith are thereby attached to Christ and God, and

[1] Cf., e. g., under Matt., v. 39.   Erl. Ed., 43, 135 sqq.

thus themselves become entirely "Word." [1] Finally, Luther there declares, in the future, *i. e.*, in the perfect life beyond, the Lord will uphold us by His Word; but this will then be the indivisible Word (as opposed to the present " *dispergi* "), or the incarnate Word as then at length without outward sound or letter. Meanwhile, the present inner word is enveloped in sound and letter as honey in the comb, grain in the hull, life in the body, the Word (Christ) in flesh.[2]

But we must yet, in seeking to determine the significance of the Word in its relation to the process of salvation, recalling the ideas dominant in the *Exposition of the Psalms*, give especial attention to the relation of LAW and GOSPEL.

Luther still frequently employs the term Gospel in the general sense, which embraces also the clear revelation of the prescriptive and punitive will of God.   In a *Sermon on the Second Sunday in Advent, 1516*, he speaks expressly of a two-fold office of the Gospel.   The first expounds the Law, *i. e.*, its spiritual sense, and it is just this sense of the Law which really slays men, since it makes the fulfilment of the Law an impossibility; it then, in the second place, announces the forgiveness of sins, peace and grace. He even directly calls the spiritual interpretation of the Law "Gospel," declaring that the latter is a " revelation and interpretation of the Old Law."   He understands Rom. i. 18 as teaching that even in the Gospel itself the wrath of God is revealed in order to humiliate us; [3] and the above-cited extracts from the *Easter Sermon of the Year 1516*, expounding the riddle of Samson, plainly carry us back to the conception of the relation between God and the Gospel, and that of the significance of the letter of the Law, which we have found pervading the entire *First Exposition of the Psalms*.

Nevertheless, in this very *Advent Sermon*, and in the further contemporaneous utterances of Luther, we find the ambiguity formerly attaching to his delineation of the distinction between Law and Gospel already essentially overcome.   In the sermon in question, he already distinctly affirms that it is only the second-named which is the " peculiar and true office of the Gospel."

---

[1] Löscher, 238.

[2] This is, indeed, the sense of the propositions, p. 242.

[3] Löscher, 762, 765, 785.   Erl. Ed., xxxvii, 410.

Thus again, on the following St. Thomas' Day, when speaking of God's *own work* and His *strange work* (*opus proprium, opus alienum—supra*, p. 115), he in a similar strain describes the first office of the Gospel, in which it extends the scope of the Commandments and thus makes sin appear the greater, as only its " strange work." [1] He now, on the other hand, employs the term " Law " only as expressing the positive requirements of the divine will, no longer as including the message of salvation. Nor do the writings of the present period ever give the impression that the inability of the Old Testament Law to effect salvation finds its real explanation in the ceremonial character of the latter. On the contrary, the fulfilment of the Law, as now understood in its deeper sense, is seen to be beyond the power of man; and the reason of this is located simply in the carnal, depraved nature of man himself. The " spiritual understanding " (*spiritualis intelligentia*) of the Law, to which the Gospel (by virtue of its first office) seeks to lead us, is so designated because it teaches us to advance from a barely literal fulfilment to a fulfilment with the heart or spirit, as, *e. g.*, from a literal observance of the Commandment against murder to the Commandment not to become angry, but to maintain a spirit of meekness under provocations. Actual fulfilment of the Commandments can, however, never be produced by the Law, but only by the grace which the Gospel by virtue of its own peculiar office proclaims. After the Gospel has humiliated and slain by expounding the Law, it must rejoice and quicken by the announcement of grace, as it would otherwise become a greater burden than the Law had been. The Gospel message therefore proclaims that Christ has already fulfilled the Law, and that, since He has become our righteousness, we have only to cling to the already-fulfilled Law and become conformed to it. Whoever, then, has the spirit and grace (attained in the Gospel way of salvation) has that which the Law commands.[2]

Although Luther still continues to employ the word " Gospel " in the sense above indicated, he yet, with perfect clearness of thought, assigns to the Law and the proclamation of grace, *i. e.*, the Gospel in the proper sense of the term, essentially the same relation to one another and the same position in the order of

---

[1] Löscher, 770–772.

[2] In above-cited Sermon on Second Sunday in Advent.

salvation as afterwards in the full maturity of his theological views. The object of the Law is essentially, as we have seen, the separation of man from his sin,[1] in order that he may in humiliation and self-mortification be prepared for the reception of grace. With this agency of the Law God associates also the afflictions, calculated to humiliate and assist in the crucifixion of the old man, which He suffers to befall us both in our inner and in our outer life, chiefly through the agency of our fellowmen, in the midst of which He awakens in us a hunger and thirst for His grace.[2] More exact, express definitions touching the significance of the Law in bringing men to repentance we fail to find in the above-quoted saying of Luther (p. 164), that true repentance springs from love, and that man must be incited to true hatred of self and true love for God by the contemplation of the acts of divine love.[3] In our former study of the passage, we sought to discover the relation which it implied as existing between faith and love. The question now arises: What position is then to be assigned to the preaching of the Law, if penitence is to be effected essentially through the impression made upon the heart by the divine benefits conferred upon us? The various utterances of Luther upon this subject may be very readily harmonized. Penitence, says he, is produced when we contrast our own sins with the divine benefits. Applying now the significance of the Law upon which he elsewhere lays so much stress, it will be easily seen how the contrast between our sins and the divine benefits must be vividly revealed to us in the light which the Law casts upon our deeds as offences against the divine will and against this benevolent God. Luther himself, however, never gave any such solution of the apparent difficulty. We shall hereafter have occasion to speak of the discussions occasioned at a later day by the question as to the justification and the proper office of the preaching of the Law in connection with the preaching of the goodness and love of God.

It is the Gospel, therefore, in the proper sense of the word, by

[1] Cf., e. g., also Dec. Praec., I : Every commandment has been given rather with the design of making manifest the sin already committed and that now cherished, than for the purpose of restraining us from future sin. Luther refers in this connection to Rom. iii. 20; xi. 32; v. 20.

[2] Cf., e. g., Erl. Ed., xxi, 189, 195.

[3] Dec. Praec., 86 sq.

which righteousness, salvation and life are brought to those who have been smitten by the Law. When Luther speaks of becoming one with Christ, the Logos, through a reception of the preached Word, he can refer only to the preaching of the Gospel in the proper sense of the term. It is the word of grace which he has in mind, when in the *Exposition of the Lord's Prayer* he speaks of the divine Word as the daily bread by which God must strengthen and comfort us. Of . this he declares, that it nourishes unto eternal life. Indeed, this bread, or Word, is none other than Christ Himself, as represented in John vi. 35, 51. The bread is distributed when Christ is preached. Christ Himself must be divided, prepared and transformed into words (as in the *Christmas Sermon*). This bread must then be eaten in faith; faith is called eating.[1] But the question still remains : whether and in how far the Law yet retains its validity for the man who already believes and lives in God. From the utterances already adduced as bearing upon the subject of salvation we may easily glean the reply : In so far as man still carries sin continually within his bosom, he yet also stands in continual need of humiliation and mortification ; and it is to this repentance of the regenerate that Luther applies what he has said of the continued efficacy of the Law. But what is to be said, on the other hand, of the uses of the Law for the new man in so far as he is now willing to do right and already inwardly impelled by the spirit of a new life? Upon this point we find no such definite expressions, and indeed very few hints of any kind. In the *Sermon on the Second Sunday in Advent*, Luther asserts that he who has the spirit, has already what the Law commands. In another passage in the same sermon, he declares that the anointing then teaches man what he shall do ; that what the Law commands now comes to pass ; that words now cease, since works (of Christ and His Spirit in us) are come, and thus there is no more Law where there is the fulfilment of Law. Luther here appears to assume that instruction through specific-objective commandments is no longer needful for the man who has the Spirit within, save in so far as the Spirit, or efficacious working, of Christ does not as yet assert its power. Yet he still elsewhere maintains in general terms that the Commandments are given for the instruction of our wills and *afterwards also for their exercise,*

[1] Erl. Ed., xxi, 197, 200-207.   Cf. Walch, vii, 1058 sqq.

without stopping to explain that the will, in so far as it already truly has in itself the impulse of the Spirit, no longer stands in need of such assistance.[1]   The attitude of Luther in regard to the question before us is, however, substantially the same as that which he afterwards maintained.   We shall hereafter have further occasion to observe his tendency toward the assumption above noted, combined with expressions of different import, and to recognize, in general, the absence of any careful analysis or satisfactory disposition of the question.

Having now carefully observed the significance which, according to Luther, the Word of God in its two principal constituent elements possesses for the work of grace, we are prepared to appreciate a progressive tendency which now begins to assert itself in his view of the proper INTERPRETATION OF THE SCRIPTURES.   He had at first simply adopted in its traditional form the theory of the manifold sense of Scripture.   How far he could even yet go in allegorizing we have seen in the *Sermon upon the Riddle of Samson*, although that is the most extreme instance occurring in his writings.   He prefers Augustine to Jerome, because the latter is disposed to cling so closely to the bare historical sense of the sacred writings.[2] Yet, so early as the first Sunday in the year 1517, in explaining the Ten Commandments, he speaks in vigorous denunciation of the way in which the Scholastics carried out that theory, and quite contemptuously of the theory itself.   He declares the scholastic doctors, sporting with their four-fold sense, to be silly dreamers.   They understand neither what letter is nor what spirit is.   It is their fault that it has already become a proverb that the Scriptures have a wax nose.   He even now quotes Jerome himself against such a treatment of the Scriptures.   He approves of the study of the four-fold interpretation only as an exercise for beginners.[3]   In the *Advent Sermon of 1516*, he had said of the spiritual sense of the Law, that many regard it as the allegorical, tropological, anagogical, but had at once added : " which indeed is true, but let me state the matter more correctly," and then proceeds to present his own explanation of the spiritual sense, as

[1] Dec. Praec., 73.

[2] Briefe, i, 40.   Cf. also utterance in the same connection against Nikolaus of Lyra.

[3] Dec. Praec., 194–5 : ferendum erat tale studium—si modo tanquem rudimenta haberentur pro incipientibus.

given above, and defines tropology as looking not upon external works, but upon the heart and spirit, and allegory as a regarding of the Church as having its being in the spirit, and from its own choice living in the Law of God. In this manner he himself now continues to allegorize. In the *Commentary upon the Penitential Psalms*, for example, he always promptly applies expressions concerning the people of God under the old covenant, and concerning Zion, the temple, etc., directly to the spiritual Christian Church (*Gemeinde*).[1] But he seeks to avoid every intrusion of arbitrary thoughts and speculations, invented by the commentator himself or imported from the sphere of philosophy. To state his method briefly, it may be said, that he finds in the deeper sense of the letter in the Old Testament only such ideas and facts bearing upon the theme of salvation as belong really and clearly to the essential content of the Gospel, and the disclosing and actualizing of which has been from the beginning the aim of the divine revelation itself. His whole effort in dealing with the Scriptures was directed, not to discover artificial and supposed spiritual meanings by the allegorical interpretation of separate passages, but to present with the greatest possible directness the two elements of preaching, the Law and the message of grace, by means of which salvation is applied to the souls of men, and in which he found the entire content and purpose of the divine Word grandly comprehended. The natural sense to which the separate external incidents of history and the outward forms and ordinances of the old covenant could, in themselves and in their original place within the limits of the historical development of divine revelation, lay claim was not sufficient to satisfy him. Without stopping long to examine this, he always hastens on to the spiritual application. He afterwards became much more moderate in his use of the allegorizing method; but the change was only gradual, and the dogmatic and practical interest, aiming directly at the presentation of the gospel message as such, ever remains by far the controlling one. In this, again, we find the fundamental character of his theology already firmly settled.

The consideration of the Word as a means of grace leads us

[1] Cf., e. g., his discussion of the stones for the building of Zion. Erl. Ed., xxxvii, 410.

naturally to inquire as to Luther's attitude toward the OTHER
MEANS OF GRACE. But his writings of this period furnish us no
thorough discussion of the sacraments; he does not even mention
any but Baptism and the Lord's Supper. His independent search
for evangelical truth had not yet led him to serious reflection
upon the sacraments. This fact is itself a striking evidence of
the profound and comprehensive significance which he attached
to the Word. It is, in his conception, essentially the Word by
which faith, righteousness and the indwelling of Christ are
effected. The statement occurring in his *Thesis upon Baptism*
must evidently be interpreted in consonance with his general
view of the plan of salvation, although he does not himself define
more definitely the meaning and object of the declaration.[1] He
there maintains that the grace of baptism is everywhere one and
the same upon the part of God and the sacrament, but different
so far as the minister of the Church imparting and the subject
receiving it are concerned; and that we must discriminate between the effect of the sacrament as such (in itself) and its effect
in view of the " disposition " of the administrant and that of the
recipient. The first position of this thesis is in harmony as well
with his own later view of the objective content of the sacrament
as with the fundamental teaching of the Roman Catholic church.
We cannot positively determine what he here means by the " disposition " of the administrant. If we understand him as teaching
that the efficacy of the sacrament depends upon the moral character of him who administers it, we place him in direct conflict
with the view which he always afterward maintained when
speaking more definitely upon the subject. It is much more
probable that he has in mind the " intention " of the administrant, in this respect still clinging to the doctrine of the then
dominant theology. It would, however, harmonize entirely, not
only with the express teaching of his later years, but also with the
emphasis which he at this time constantly laid upon faith as the
necessary condition for any bestowal of salvation, if, while regarding grace as objectively offered to every one in the sacrament, he
yet meant to indicate, by his reference to the " disposition of the
recipient," that the subjective appropriation could not be made
without faith.

[1] A. D. 1516. Löscher, 339.

It is only in relation to the *Sacrament of the Altar* that we find as yet any more definite statements, and in these we can already, as in other cases, trace the course followed consistently in his later teachings.   It is, moreover, particularly the relation of the sacrament to the Word as means of grace, and, still further, to faith as, according to Luther's universal premise, the organ for the reception of the Word, that here forms the subject of discussion. Even as early as 1516, Luther declares the hearing of the Word to be far more necessary than the hearing of the mass.   The latter was to be held, indeed, only for the sake of the Word, according to the saying of Christ, " Do this, as oft as ye do it, in remembrance of me "—as though He would say, Ye shall not celebrate mass without preaching the Gospel; and, according to the teaching of St. Paul, " as often as ye eat * * * ye do show forth the Lord's death." [1]   In the *Exposition of the Lord's Prayer*, he expresses himself still further, speaking now more definitely of the mass, not only of the " hearing " of it, but of the enjoyment in it of the Lord's Supper.   Christ, our Bread, says he, is given to us, first through the Word, and, secondly, in the sacrament of the altar.   But the reception of Christ in the sacrament would be in vain if He were not at the same time distributed and applied through the Word.   It is this which first makes Christ known in the hearts of the people.   Unfortunately, indeed, it is now the custom to leave the most important thing, for the sake of which masses (again according to the declarations of Christ and Paul quoted above) are appointed, namely, preaching, in the background; and thus, at last, the sacrament degenerates into vain and barren formality and falls into contempt.[2]   We have already observed how earnestly he maintains that the Word in itself, not merely the sacrament, is the bread, or Christ Himself, and how he regards faith as the eating of the Word, or bread. Nor have we any reason to suppose that the expressions now under review did not belong to the original draft of his *Exposition*, but were inserted as the latter was being prepared for publication (A. D. 1518) ; for we find here only the same view of the becom-

[1] Dec. Praec., 84.

[2] Erl. Ed., xxi, 204.   (Schneider's edition of the Lord's Prayer does not, indeed, contain the precise language above quoted, but urges none the less strongly the reception and contemplation of the Word in the mass.)

ing one with Christ through the Word accepted in faith which
has been seen in the *Christmas Sermon,* and the same conception of the character of the mass which we have already noted
in the extract treating of the Decalogue.

But how far, we naturally inquire, in the employment of these
means, especially of the Word, does the AGENCY OF GOD HIMSELF,
who employs such means, extend? We have been told that the
Word awakens men to repentance and faith. But what is, in this
process, the relation between the conduct of the man who accepts
the Word on the one hand, and the will and effective agency
of God upon the other?

The mention of the agency of God brings us back again to the
consideration of the *eternal decree.* Upon this topic, the writings
of the period yield the same results as those which we have
already noted when speaking of the *Annotations of the Psalms.*
The pious themselves, as well as their repentance and faith, are
spoken of directly as works of God. He begets and creates
them out of pure grace, without any co-operation on their part.
Then, having so created them, He works through them, and they
become His co-workers.[1] This working of God is accomplished,
moreover, by means of the Word, since He Himself must first of
all inwardly impart and make effectual that which is outwardly
preached (cf. here also the *Exposition of the Psalms*). Similarly,
in the *Sermon on Epiphany Sunday, 1517,* occurs the statement,
that the word of the preacher reaches only the ears, but God
causes the sound of it to find its way inwardly to the heart, and
thus imparts instruction.[2] We find the same idea still more fully
developed in the *Explanation of the Lord's Prayer.* The Word
of God, it is there said, has not power to speak in man, nor to
reach him in any effectual way, save only when wielded by the
hand of God. Not of ourselves, by studying or hearing, can we
obtain the Bread, or Christ; but the Father Himself must reveal
and give Him, as is taught in John vi. 44 sq., 65. If the inward

---

[1] Thus in the passage, Erl. Ed., xxxvii, 434–5.—Ibid., 430, we find, in the
Exposition of the Penitential Psalms, further statements concerning faith as
a gift of God and a work accomplished by Him (cf. also in the *First Exposition of the Psalms*). The words in question are found, however, only in
the later edition, inasmuch as Luther, in 1517, employed the word "truth" in
his translation of the text instead of "faith."

[2] Löscher, 753.

teaching of God do not accompany the outward, the latter is in vain.[1] The expressions now occurring, in which the inner trans-formation of man in faith and through faith is described simply as a work of God, remind us again of the general statement in the *Sermon on Assumption Day:* " God works all in all things; He alone works all, as the only Mighty One;" and the *Theses of 1517* carry us back to the earlier statements concerning the eternal decree, in which alone conversion is said to have its origin. The proposition in the *Theses,* that upon the part of man nothing but indisposition and actual rebellion precedes grace (*vid. supra*), is preceded by the statement : " The best and infallible prepara-tion for, and the only disposition (inclining) toward, grace is the eternal election and preparation of God." We find ourselves thus again upon the basis of strict Augustinianism. Even the conquest of the " rebellion " by grace appears entirely as an act of God, based upon the eternal decree.

It must, however, have been very seldom indeed that Luther now appealed expressly to these, his ultimate premises, for in his sermons and exegetical writings of the period we find no discus-sion of them whatever. Moreover, the point of view from which he, at least in his practical expositions of saving truth, regarded the doctrine of fore-ordination, is revealed to us through the report of a *Sermon preached at Dresden* on St. James' Day (July 25), 1517, but unfortunately not preserved. Its argument is summarized as follows : No man dare cast away his assurance of salvation ; for those who attentively hear the Word of God are true pupils of Christ, elected and predestinated to eternal life. The entire doctrine of predestination has, when viewed in the light of our knowledge of Christ, a peculiar power to deliver us from such anxiety on account of our unworthiness as would drive us away from God, when we need above all else to draw near to Him.[2] It is evident that he must in this case have preached predestination as Staupitz had taught him to regard it, and as he himself afterward in many instances explained it to persons in spiritual distress. Instead of encouraging speculations upon the questions, whether God's gracious decree may not have left out

[1] Erl. Ed., xxi, 198 sq., 203-5.

[2] Seckendorf, Hist. Luth., Lib. I., § viii., Add. 7. Cf., touching Luther's visit to Dresden, Briefe, i, 84.

many persons; whether, in consequence of this, it is not impossible that Christ should be an actual Saviour for all men; and whether the proper hearing of the message of grace is possible to all—he simply exhorts all to such a hearing and to the contemplation of Christ as the central object in all divine revelation. But the *Expositions of the Lord's Prayer* appear to lead us farther than this. To the closing declaration in the passage last cited from that work Luther adds: " But if the outward teaching be rightly conducted, the inward will not be lacking; for God never suffers His Word to go forth upon a fruitless errand; He accompanies it and Himself teaches inwardly, as He declares in Isa. lv. (cf. vv. 10, 11)." According to this, it would appear that when the Word outwardly preached remains without results, we are nevertheless to think of God as doing His part, and to find the cause of the failure entirely upon the side of man—that, accordingly, the inward rejection or acceptance of the message of grace is, in the last analysis, a matter of man's determination, inasmuch as he may either repulse or welcome the God who is ready to exert or already actually exerting His energy. We must bear in mind, however, that Luther himself does not carry out the discussion to this conclusion. He does not, in the passage before us, enter at all upon the question, how it is possible for the Word ever to remain without results.

Finally, we may adduce, as bearing at least upon the subject of the original entrance of sin into the world, the statements in the *Sermon upon the Decalogue*, which represent everything created by God as good, and hence, according to its own nature, inclined only to that which is good.[1] Applying this to man, the immediate inference must be that the first sin, at least, cannot have been caused by an act of God originating in His eternal decree, whether such act be conceived of as a positive exertion of energy or as a forbearance or passive attitude on His part, but must have been the result of a decision of man's own will. Luther is speaking, it must, however, be remembered, in opposition to the claims of astrology, only of an inclination to evil supposed to be produced in man by other created things, especially by the stars. They, says he, must, on the contrary, work together for man's good; otherwise we could not explain why the stars did not exert

[1] Dec. Praec., 13–14.

such an evil influence upon man before the temptation by the
serpent. Of man, upon the other hand, he simply asserts, that
no one sins against his will, or by compulsion, meaning by this
that the evil inclination (according to Matt. xv. 19 and James
i. 14) is not outside of us, but within us. Whence such inclination originally came, is a question which he does not here attempt
to answer (cf. observations already made touching Luther's doctrine of sin). We must be particularly careful, when selecting
separate sentences from Luther's writings which appear to oppose
a strict theory of predestination, not to imagine that the consequences which may be naturally involved in them were already
clearly developed in the mind of Luther; for it is just the question, how much weight should be attached to such sporadic utterances when compared with the other aspect of his religious views,
i. e., with the stress which he habitually laid upon the absolute
nature of grace, and his consequent deep conviction of the efficient agency of God in all things.[1] We must always be content
to discover the ideas upon which the chief stress was laid in the
religious consciousness of Luther and the real central point in his
preaching, as has been already remarked when tracing his conception of God Himself. If we then observe a lack of careful-
ness in adjusting the relations of concomitant ideas, this must be
set down as a characteristic trait of the Reformer.

All the ideas which we have thus far traced in the writings of
Luther constitute but one general theory of salvation and the way
to its attainment, already richly developed and, in its leading
features, definitely fixed. But he does not even yet realize that
he is by the adoption of these principles placed in antagonism to
the Church. Was it not the authority of an Augustine which, as
he fully believed, supported him in the maintenance of his views?
He regards himself as in conflict only with errors, widely spread
indeed, and advocated by the more recent theologians, but not
on that account to be acknowledged as sanctioned by the Church.
He knows that the theologians in question are held in high
esteem by the multitude, but he does not recognize them as truly
Catholic teachers. Thus, he declares in the conclusion of the
Theses of 1517, that he hopes and believes that he has said
nothing which is not in harmony with the Catholic Church and

[1] Cf. the Fifteen Theses of the Heidelberg Disputation, A. D. 1518; also
Book II., Chap. 2.

Catholic teachers. His theses may be regarded by others as *paradoxa* and by his opponents as *kakodoxa*, but they are, according to his own conviction, *orthodoxa*.[1]

Luther, therefore, leaves as yet untouched all the articles of faith commonly accepted in the Church, except those to which reference has been made in the preceding pages. The inner impulse of his new apprehensions of evangelical truth had not yet advanced to the independent examination of doctrines which were entrenched in the traditional teaching of the Church, and in connection with which it was still possible for the pregnant germ of a new system of saving truth to expand. He even still adhered with unquestioning confidence to those prevalent views concerning the Church which closed the way against any such examination. He says bluntly (when speaking of an outward order of service in connection with the hearing of the mass) : " *The Church cannot err*," whereas any single man, however devoted in spirit, may err.[2] In a *Sermon preached on the Day of St. Peter's Chains* (August 1), *1516*, the very continued existence of the Church is made to depend upon the plenary authority bestowed upon its leaders, and the plain duty of every individual appears to be simple submission. Had Christ, says he, not given all His power to man, there could have been no complete Church, since there could have been no order, as every man could then have said that he was moved by the Holy Spirit.[3]

Yet, in regard to the articles now in question, we must repeat the statement made when reviewing the *Exposition of the Psalms*, that, although he does not assail them, nor even appear to cherish any doubt as to their validity, it is none the less remarkable how entirely they have retreated into the background ; and his manner of treatment, when he has occasion to refer to them, is exceedingly significant.

His faith in the INTERCESSION OF THE SAINTS remains unshaken. He regarded the Virgin Mary as especially an object of veneration. Yet, when he undertakes to point out the way of salvation, he always directs faith simply and alone to Christ. Referring to the interpretation of her name adopted by some writers (Marjam—drop of the ocean) he says that she was really preserved as a single drop out of the ocean of the entire human race.

---

[1] Briefe, 1, 60.   [2] Dec. Praec., 85.   [3] Löscher, 280.

In one place, he addresses her as the blessed Mother, the most worthy Virgin, imploring her to remember us and to influence the Lord to do for us also the great things which He has done for her. But the praise bestowed upon her even here is based upon the fact that she makes no boast of any merit or work of her own, presenting herself before the God who doeth all things, not as herself doing anything, but simply as a recipient of His good works. She has nothing now, he declares, which we do not also have. We, too, may carry the Son in our hearts, may with pious thoughts nourish Him at our breasts, and may embrace Him with the arms of our love. Jesus Himself calls those who do His Father's will His mother, His sisters and His brethren. Luther even now expresses his disapproval of those who " think of the mother of the Lord in altogether too carnal and human a manner, and suffer themselves to be controlled by emotions of carnal piety." It was to avoid this, he explains in a *Sermon upon the Narrative of the Resurrection*, preached in 1516, that the Scriptures tell us nothing of an appearance of the Lord first of all to Mary, but rather relate how harshly He treated her.[1] The *Lectures upon the Decalogue* contain a lengthy discussion of the worship of saints.[2] It is very remarkable that Luther in this passage, while, on the one hand, remaining true to the common faith in the activity of the saints in response to prayers addressed to them, and, on the other, seeking to guard against arbitrary human inventions concerning them, yet himself appears to give even a wider scope to the worship of saints than that assigned in the traditional opinions upon the subject. He regards it as a mere human notion, and a modern one at that, to attribute to the saints in heaven various special talents for particular forms of service in behalf of men, after the analogy of the diverse talents possessed by them in their lives on earth. He teaches, on the contrary, that each of the saints has the ability to do all things, and that they, accordingly, always give to us as much as we expect to receive from them. In one of the *Theses of A. D. 1516* it is declared that, inasmuch as everything is through Christ possible to the believer, it is superstition to attribute to one believer the ability to render assistance in one way while another can help only in a different way.[3] In these lectures Luther does not for-

---

[1] Löscher, 764, 281 sqq., 275.   [2] Dec. Praec., 26–53.   [3] Löscher, 337.

bid appeal to the saints for *bodily* assistance and gifts, although
condemning the prevalent method of doing so, but he only urges
that petitions for spiritual blessings should always have the pre-
eminence.   But he asserts further, in the same passage, that the
only " *true and inner* " worship of the saints is the extolling of
God in them and of them in God, the contemplation of the grace
of God in them, and especially the uplifting of our hearts to God
and His works, just as the saints themselves in their whole lives
on earth sought the things of God ; and that such has certainly
been the object of the Holy Spirit and the Church in all the worship and festivals of the saints.   He disclaims, finally, with great
emphasis, all sympathy with the miserable heretics, the Picards,
in their denunciation of the worship of saints as idolatry.   He
maintains, on the contrary, that we should by all means (*omni
mode*) hold fast to our faith in the intercession of the saints.   Is
it not written that David and Solomon and many others were
adored?   Even in modern times the attendants at royal courts
are honored, and in a measure adored, in order that a readier
access to the presence of the king may thereby be secured.   Yet
it is noticeable that Luther is already suspicious at least in regard
to very many of the traditions concerning the saints.   He grows
warm in his denunciation of a host of false miracles, lying legends
and counterfeit relics, which he asserts to be then in circulation.[1]
He speaks from the pulpit most contemptuously of the legends
concerning Saint Bartholomew.[2]   Finally, in his *Comments upon
the Decalogue,* he openly assails a number of further abuses frequently connected with the worship of the saints, such as new
festivals of saints, church dedications, etc., designed merely to
secure honor for those who appointed them ; pilgrimages to
shrines of saints, leading many to neglect their primary domestic
duties ; and the indulgences which were distributed upon such
occasions.

The mention of PILGRIMAGES calls to mind the deliverance
already quoted touching the good works which may and should
be performed in the pursuit of one's *ordinary secular calling* as
contrasted with the supposed *specially meritorious services* so
highy commended by the dominant opinion in the Church of the
day.   Luther now declares that, if any one thinks of undertaking

---

[1] Dec. Praec., 197 sq.   [2] Löscher, 283.

such pilgrimages, he should at least remember that it would be an incomparably better service of God for him to remain at home, there ministering to the poor and the members of his own family and serving the Lord.   He even advises the head of the household, whose wife or servant has caught the pilgrimage fever, to hallow the back of the latter right well with a few lashes.   But here, as before, he disclaims all intention of opposing any requirement of the Church ; for these pilgrimages, he maintains, are not required, but voluntarily undertaken.

In concluding the section referred to in the *Comments upon the Decalogue*, he remarks that he might here treat of the confidence placed in INDULGENCES, but that he has already expressed his opinion far more than sufficiently upon that subject.   We have, in fact, a sermon of his, preached on the *Tenth Sunday after Trinity, 1516*, which treats particularly of indulgences.[1]   Luther had originally (according to the Latin manuscript, cited in Löscher) bound this sermon in connection with the *Lectures upon the First Commandment*, to which the above comments belonged. The remark just quoted was doubtless not inserted until the publication of the lectures, which did not occur until after his later vigorous assaults upon the practice of indulgences.   The discussion in this sermon is intimately connected, first of all, as was to be expected from the nature of the subject, with Luther's doctrine concerning the appropriation of grace, the leading features of which we have already noted ; secondly, with the doctrine of purgatory, inasmuch as Luther treats mainly of the employment of indulgences in behalf of the dead ; and, finally and most strikingly, with the doctrine concerning the Church, since special effort is made to present a true conception of the papal power which granted the indulgences.   But a careful elucidation of the material contained in this sermon would require us to take into consideration specifications and utterances which appear more distinctly in two sermons preached toward the close of the period which we are now studying; and these sermons, in turn, lead us directly up to the propositions involved in the indulgence controversy itself.   It seems more appropriate, therefore, to postpone the further consideration of this single discourse until the beginning of the following chapter.   For the present, let it suffice to

[1] Löscher, 729 sqq.

say that, as a result of Luther's positive apprehension of the way
of salvation, and, still more directly, in consequence of his deeper
apprehension of repentance, the significance of indulgences has
already come to be regarded as at least very questionable, but
that Luther nevertheless still strives to retain a place for them
as remitting outward penalties prescribed by the Church, confessing, however, his ignorance in regard to the difficulties connected
with this view—that, furthermore, he endeavors to maintain the
validity of indulgences for the dead with certain restrictive conditions, but here, too, confesses himself to be yet involved in
doubt—that, finally, whilst he endeavors still, under the conditions stated by him, to ascribe some benefit to indulgences, the
real aim of the sermon is earnestly to warn against misuse of the
latter and against false security and indolence.

In regard to the sacraments, we refer to what has been already
said.   That the character of the OFFERING IN THE MASS dare
itself be assailed, was a thought that had never as yet occurred to
him—even when subordinating the former, as we have seen, to
the preaching of the Word.   In the *Lectures upon the Decalogue*
he cherishes not the least suspicion of the propriety of the canon
of the mass, declaring that this alone is properly the mass.   He
refuses even to concede the demand that the canon be read
aloud.   The Commandment in regard to the divine Word and
that concerning the mass are, he affirms, quite different.   He
even finds a sacred mystery in the inaudible reading of the
canon, as even Christ, the true priest, does for us before God
much which the people and the congregation can neither see nor
understand.[1]

No doubts are entertained as yet in regard to the teachings of
the Church upon the subject of CONFESSION and the necessity of
auricular confession.   Luther protests only against such a minute
analysis and classification of sins as to burden the memory of the
people and weary the confessor.   He does not consider it necessary, for example, to make exactly seven classes of mortal sins ;
the number might as well be made greater or less.   Especially
noteworthy is his declaration that it is not necessary to confess
an inclination to pride unless one has yielded to it, since we are
all constantly inclined in that direction ; we ought therefore to

[1] Dec. Praec., 81,

mourn over it in secret and confess it before God. He maintains, moreover, that *acedia* (disinclination to that which is good—indolence) being a spiritual infirmity, is not a proper subject for the confessional, but is to be made known to God alone, who is the only one who can provide a remedy. Thus Luther already assumes that there is at least a certain sphere of the inner life which may be exempt from the supervision of the confessional, and that within this sphere the sinner may himself deal directly with his God.[1]

The sermons of Luther contain no more specific discussion of the general proposition already quoted touching the power conferred upon the CHURCH. In the *Sermon upon Indulgences* he acknowledges the plenary power of the Pope, inasmuch as he has in his hands, and can apply, all the works and merits of Christ and the Church. He calls the bishops and prelates (with reference to Luke xi. 34) the " eye of the body," which is to be found in us, *i. e.*, not among heretics, but in the Church, and also outside of us, since governments and kingdoms are established by God. The entire power lies in the prelates. When they see, the people see also.[2] Priests, especially, he regards as men appointed for the purpose of furnishing to the Christian world its bread, the Word.[3] It is beyond question that Luther still clung with entire simplicity to the external, hierarchical order of the Church. His view of the priestly office is plainly enough revealed in the comparison of the priest officiating at the mass with Christ Himself. Yet he was able to proceed in the development of his own peculiar theory of salvation without ever referring to the specific outward ordinances of the Church as necessary conditions. He now emphasizes still more strongly than in the *Exposition of the Psalms*, as the peculiar office of the clergy, not any exercise of outward power, but simply and alone the preaching of the Word. In a similar spirit, when speaking as above of the prelates, he adds the remark that a bishop must therefore be pre-eminently a preacher, although, indeed, at the present time nothing is so little esteemed as the preaching office. The provost of Litzka is instructed to represent to the council that " the greatest and very

---

[1] Dec. Praec., 210, 212, 218.

[2] Löscher, 757.

[3] Cf., e. g., Erl. Ed., xxi, 205, 207.

first thing to be secured is that the priests may be full to over-
flowing of the Word of truth." The proclamation of the Word is
the most important thing, because through it by means of faith
Christ is to be brought into the hearts of men.[1]

Bitterly does Luther now lament the moral corruption prevalent
in the Church, and especially among the clergy everywhere.
One is compelled, he declares, to behold the careless, indifferent
and utterly indolent life of the monks, the priests, the Pope and
others. The second duty of the council (next to providing for
the preaching of the Word) must be the adoption of laws for the
suppression of the immorality so widely prevalent, especially
among the clergy. As means to this end, he again emphasizes
the faith which is produced by the Word, inasmuch as by it the
attention of men is directed to heavenly things, and as all things
may be overcome by the presence of Christ in faith.[2] So great
appear to him the temptations inseparable at that day from the
position of a bishop, that he fears it may prove perilous even for
such a man as Staupitz, far removed as he knows the latter to be
from any taint of the prevailing vices. "To be a prelate"
(*praesulari*), he declares, "means in our day to live like the
Greeks, Sodomites or Romans" (*pergraecari, sodomitari, ro-
manari*). The best ecclesiastical princes, in the common esteem,
are those who resort to the most cunning artifices in the conduct
of judicial business and toil to drag everything into the bottomless pit of avarice.[3] Yet with all these bitter laments, the thought
seems never to have occurred to Luther that any change should
be necessary or possible in the hierarchical polity of the Church
itself.

The complaint in regard to the neglect of the Word is based
not only upon the actual omission of preaching in many places,
but more particularly upon the character of the sermons delivered
where preaching was still in vogue. Everything is full of human
ordinances, human opinions, superstitions, etc., and the attention
of a council should be called to this abuse.[4]

Under this condemnation he includes fables and relics of the

[1] Löscher, 225, 231.
[2] Ibid., 792, 229 sq.
[3] Briefe, i, 25 (June 8, 1516).
[4] Löscher, 225.

saints. He maintains expressly that there is need here of a great reform in the Church, not indeed to exclude from preaching altogether the legends of the saints, but only to arrest the tendency to arbitrary and inappropriate tales. That only, he maintains, should be allowed, which is " authentic and canonically approved." [1]

But his indignation rose to the highest pitch when the true evangelical way of salvation was misrepresented or denied from the pulpit. Among those who violate the Eighth Commandment, he mentions particularly such as, while indeed teaching faith in Christ, at the same time commend work-righteousness, dwelling, of course, in their sermons but seldom on the former and far oftener upon the latter. It is these, he thinks, who are in the ninth chapter of Revelation described as locusts which cannot kill, but torment men. He then pays his respects to the Scholastics with their perversion of the plain sense of Scripture. [2] Yet he still proceeds upon the supposition that the authority of the Church, at least, has not yet been enlisted upon the side of these errorists. He is convinced that not only Christ and the Sacred Scriptures are upon his side, but also, as well, the great teacher of the Catholic church, Augustine. [3]

In regard to ECCLESIASTICAL ORDINANCES for the culture of the Christian life, the question already arose in Luther's mind, whether such external legal appointments and exercises as fasting, the keeping of holy days, and the like, have any value in view of the evangelical order of salvation, whether indeed they are even allowable, especially for those who live in faith and grace. We recall the denunciation of the multiplicity of legal enactments found already in the *Exposition of the Psalms*. Luther now employs most effectively the declaration of St. Paul, that no law is given for the righteous. He affirms that the Old Testament law in regard to the Sabbath and other days has really terminated, and, in general, everything of that kind, so far as perfect Christians are concerned. The Church, he then says, has preserved the festival-days for the proclamation of the divine Word for the imperfect. The righteous man, like God, is not

[1] Dec. Praec., 85, 198.

[2] Ibid., 194.

[3] Cf., e. g., Briefe, i, 55, 57.

concerned about days or places; every day is for him a festival-
day. But the weak, who are not yet mortified, require such
things for the sake of the old man. He then enumerates further,
as in the same category, watching and fasting, with other similar
exercises of discipline and bodily mortifications, concluding with
the declaration that the Church continues to observe the commandment concerning the Sabbath, and many other things of a
figurative nature, for the training of the weak.[1] He always, however, assumes that, at all events, when the Church establishes
anything of the kind, all individuals are under obligation to submit to her authority.

Thus Luther continued to acknowledge the *authority* of the
Church in external appointments and its *infallibility* in doctrine,
although the statutes enacted were out of harmony with the position which he had now through inward conflicts securely attained,
and the conception of evangelical truth which he had derived
from the study of the Sacred Scriptures was seriously at variance
with the doctrines openly and universally taught in the Church.
Honestly believing that his own convictions, according as they
did with the Sacred Scriptures, could not be in conflict with any
doctrine that was entitled to be regarded as really catholic and
sanctioned by the Church, it does not even occur to him as a
possibility, that the divinely ordained leaders and representatives
of the Church on earth should actually reject that which the
Scriptures taught and to which they had for him borne such im-
pregnable testimony. That which we designate the *material
principle of evangelical faith*, or of Protestantism, he has already
accepted in its full force as the central position of his theology
and most positively and clearly maintained in his public utterances. The *formal principle*, the exclusively normative authority of the Sacred Scriptures, does not as yet secure expression in that definite statement opposing the prevailing view, by
which alone it could be clearly brought to general recognition,
only because Luther himself does not yet recognize the actual
existence of such opposition. As a matter of fact, Luther's
doctrine of faith and righteousness not only placed him in a
position directly in conflict with the prevailing doctrinal views,
but constituted also an essential advance upon the teachings of

[1] Dec. Praec., 70–72.

the Mystics and of Augustine, the Sacred Scriptures, meanwhile, really constituting the only rule and authority by which he was constantly controlled in the maintaining of his position. That he did not himself more fully *realize* the peculiarity of his situation, can only be accounted for by his deep and humble desire to maintain unity with all previous teachers of divine truth, and also with the entire polity and life of the Church as hitherto appointed and preserved by God. His entire doctrinal position thus reveals the fact, that his development, proceeding originally from an inward principle, advanced toward maturity upon a positive path, and yet always in a conservative spirit. But how firmly fixed the results of this development had already become for him, and how little they could be disturbed even by the discovery of the profound contradiction of prevailing sentiment which they involved, was plainly manifest the moment he was compelled to decide between the authority of Scripture and that of an external ecclesiastical organization, or even that of any human teachers whatsoever, however highly honored in the Church.

Such, then, were the character and tendency of Luther's religious convictions and theology, as gleaned from those of his writings which appeared during the years immediately preceding the Indulgence Controversy.

As was to be anticipated, hostility and suspicion were aroused in various forms against his teaching. When condemning the self-righteous and denouncing the proud saints, he well knew that they would not be pleased with his candor. Yea, says he already in the *Sermon on St. Stephen's Day* (December 26, 1515), they persecute the chickens which seek their salvation in the mercy of the Hen, and kill those who speak the truth; and thus, when he himself preaches of Christ, the Hen, they charge him with error and false teaching. He is accused of giving offence to the weak by his sermons, to which he replies, that the crucified Christ must of course be an occasion of offence. He makes reference to similar accusations also in his criticism of the legends concerning St. Bartholomew.[1]

He is surrounded, upon the other hand, as we learn from his letters, by a circle of friends and acquaintances who labor in

[1] Löscher, 244, 284.

sympathy with him for the fuller apprehension of saving truth, and who welcome the refreshing message of grace received chiefly at his hands. They have as little thought of being thus brought into an attitude of opposition to the Church as had he himself.

He joyfully recognizes, also, the services rendered by Humanism, in the help which it promised to afford in developing scriptural truth, and in the conflict which it waged in the name of an independent search for truth against the unscientific methods and suspicious temper of the professed defenders of orthodoxy. This is the spirit of the first of his utterances preserved to us in regard to the Reuchlin controversy, which is to be dated some time before the year 1515,[1] and also of the second, occurring in August, 1514.[2] He urges full confidence in the protestations of Reuchlin. Otherwise, he declares, one might fear that the inquisitors who were assailing him might take to straining out gnats and make heretics out of orthodox teachers. Referring to Ortuin, of Cologne, he gruffly says that when the ass sought to clothe itself in the majesty of the lion, it became a dog, wolf or crocodile. He confesses that he himself may be thought to be captivated by Reuchlin and partial in his judgment, since he does really esteem him most highly and truly love him. In his *Exposition of the Penitential Psalms* he quotes from Reuchlin's translation.[3] He held Erasmus in peculiarly high esteem. We have already noted (p. 153) that, even when compelled to differ with him, he yet expresses the desire and hope that he may attain the widest fame and enjoy the largest measure of respect.[4] We have observed, too, the friendly attitude which he assumed toward Mutianus in the year 1516, as manifested by the personal letter then addressed to the latter.

As to any influence, however, which Humanism may or may not have exercised upon the positive formation of Luther's theology, we can only repeat what has before been said. Wherever any contradiction appeared between convictions arising from the basis of his own faith and life and the Humanistic mode of thought, he stood up in defence of the former against an Erasmus just as resolutely as against the Scholastics. How utterly

[1] Briefe, i, 7 sqq. As to the date of this letter, cf. supra, p. 84.
[2] Ibid., i, 13 sq.
[3] Erl. Ed., xxxvii, 344.   [4] Briefe, i, 40.

opposed to the ruling tendency of Humanism was also his entire theory as to the moral and religious character of the heathen world ! Still further, he manifests no sympathy whatever with the mode of warfare commonly adopted by the Humanists, a striking example of which is seen in the *Epistolæ obscurorum virorum*. He is led to speak of these when referring to another book sent to him, which, as he declared, tasted of the same pot. He expresses his disapproval of the abusive and insulting language in which such writers indulge. But he especially deplores the absence, both in the writing under review and in the *Letters* referred to, of positive testimony to the truth. He describes their contents as impertinences (*ineptiae*) and their authors as stage-actors.[1]

As often as occasion is afforded, he contends with the greatest possible earnestness against those in the Church who oppose the doctrine of grace which he has espoused. It is evident that he recognizes in this the chief point in the public testimony which he has been called to bear before his fellowmen. But we can never discover the slightest trace of haughty self-conceit in the consciousness of this calling, nor of any large ideas or plans for the extension and prosecution of the conflict, his own conception as to the scope and the profound nature of the opposition which he would be called upon to wage being yet so incomplete. This feature of his public utterances becomes especially striking when compared with the trumpet-blasts with which other advocates of reform, as, for example, an Ulrich von Hutten, thought it necessary to inaugurate their work. This is in perfect keeping, how-

---

[1] In a letter to Johann Lange, under date of October 5, 1816 (Briefe, i, 37), he writes: "Ineptias illas, quas ad me misisti, de supplicationibus ad S. Pontificem contra theologastros (a satirical pamphlet, entitled, *Tenor suppli cationibus Pasquillianae*, to be found in Vol. xi, Pasquillorum, pp. 196 sq.) nimis apparet, a non modesto ingenio effictas, prorsusque eandem olentes testam, quam Epistolae obscurorum virorum."

To Spalatin he writes, at about the same time (Briefe, i, 38): "Accepi et literas et fl. heri a te ad me missos. Fiet, quod faciendum est. Porro misit ad me Prior Erfordiensis Johann Langus supplicationem contra theologastros, quae cum nihil gestae veritatis contineant, eundem vel similem histrionem sui testantur autorem, quem et Epistolae obscurorum virorum. Votum ejus probo, sed opus non probo, quod nec a conviciis et contumelis sibi temperat. Denique statim deridebatur ab omnibus, quibus ego nuper cognitum feci, quicquid illud sit. Vide ergo et lege cum solita modestia tua."

ever, with the calm security and positive fullness of the faith
which he cherished within, and by virtue of which he was already
so well prepared in advance for conflicts which were to extend
far beyond the circle of his present vision. It was while maintaining this attitude that he heard the call to the decisive and
far-reaching controversy in regard to papal indulgences.

BOOK II.

THE GREAT REFORMATORY TESTIMONY OF
LUTHER, FROM THE PROMULGATION OF
THE NINETY-FIVE THESES UNTIL THE
DIET AT WORMS. A. D. 1517 TO A. D. 1521.

INTRODUCTORY.

FUNDAMENTAL PRINCIPLES INVOLVED IN THE THEORY OF INDULGENCES.

THE question in regard to Indulgences, what their nature and value, and whether they are at all allowable, is presented to us in the history of the Reformation and of Luther himself as a subject of the profoundest significance. As we review the course of history, we can entertain no doubt as to the importance once attaching to the question. The results to which the controversy upon this subject led by an inner necessity are still plainly visible. They must be traceable to some profound cause in the nature of indulgences upon the one hand, and in that of the evangelical theory of saving truth upon the other.

It does not follow, however, that the significance of the question must appear at the first glance to any one who merely passes in direct review the doctrinal statements upon the subject which are to be regarded as officially endorsed by the Church of that day and even of the present. Exceedingly offensive, indeed, to an evangelically enlightened mind, and especially to one religiously and morally inclined, must have been the invitation, then heard echoing far and wide, to come and buy for one's self the forgiveness of sins. But even those teachers of the Church who most highly lauded the indulgences, when called upon to define dogmatically their nature and to justify their use, did not by any means venture to ascribe to them such a broad significance.

We must recollect precisely what the indulgences were supposed to be. Forgiveness of sins, it was taught, is to be secured in penance (*poenitentia*), which consists of three parts, *i. e.*, contrition, confession, satisfaction. This terminology had been sanctioned by the Church, especially at the Council of Florence, A. D. 1439. The contrite one, having made formal confession, is absolved from the guilt of his sins by virtue of the power which the Lord conferred upon Peter and the Church. With this guilt, the eternal punishment is also remitted; and this is done through the grace of Christ upon the ground of the atonement made by Him. But this does not yet bring release from every punishment; entrance to heaven has not yet by this means been secured. The one undergoing penance must first himself render whatever satisfaction the priest may impose upon him as ordained by divine righteousness. Among such works of satisfaction are counted prayer, fasting and the giving of alms. It is not, therefore, guilt which is supposed to be thus remitted, but the temporal punishment of sin. For this purpose only can indulgences be granted. It is for such penalty, or punishment, and the corresponding works of satisfaction that the latter may be substituted. For the establishment of reconciliation itself, or the actual removal of guilt, they have no efficacy. It is this same penalty, or the satisfaction to be rendered in view of it, that is had in mind in the doctrine of purgatory. The souls that have been sent, not to hell, but to purgatory, must have been already during their earthly life released from eternal punishment. They have, however, failed to fully meet while living the third requirement of penance, i. e., satisfaction. It is for this neglect that they are now atoning; and they may still be benefited by the indulgences which the living secure for them.

Luther was himself perfectly familiar with the position and limitations of the doctrine of indulgences within the ecclesiastical system of the day. Several questions naturally arise in view of the severity which he employed in dealing with the subject. In the first place, when the preachers of indulgences so shamelessly urged the people to the purchase of " the forgiveness of sins," was not this to be regarded from the strict churchly point of view as merely a gross abuse? We shall find that even Tetzel, in his justification of indulgences, does not venture to defend the interpretation thus put upon them. Again, did not the official theory of indulgences still acknowledge all that was essential in the institution and application of salvation as a work of divine grace, and as attainable only through inward penitence and faith? It was only upon the basis of contrition, and of a remission of guilt conditioned upon it, that there could be any thought at all of outward penances and satisfactions, or, consequently, of any substitute for the latter. Was it not at least possible to give to the accepted statements of the Church upon the subject such an interpretation as would dispel the gathering suspicions? Finally, if, indeed, the practice of indulgences should be found utterly incompatible with a profounder conception of the way of salvation, must the opposition to them lead to an assault upon the fundamental doctrines of the Church upon the subject of salvation, and even to an open rupture with the existing ecclesiastical system? Luther believed that, with all his opposition to certain individual doctors of the Church, he had hitherto, in the presentation of his own fundamental doctrine of salvation, by no means contradicted the teachings of the Church itself, but that he was, on the contrary, in full accord with so eminent an authority in her bounds as Augustine. Might not the Church now, on the basis of the principles which she had herself adopted and never yet renounced, remove again the offences which she had, as it were, in an unguarded moment allowed to arise in connection with indulgences? They had never been accepted by general resolution at any council. Luther actually began his conflict against these offences under the influence of such presumptions in their favor, and with a disposition to put upon them the most charitable construction possible. He did not himself as yet detect the consequences which were involved in them. It will be our task to follow step by step the gradual process by which the latter were brought into clear view.

There was reason, indeed, whatever might be the real inner relation of indulgences to the fundamental doctrines of the Church, to fear the effect of the great external, temporal interest involved in the indulgence theory as a rich source of pecuniary profit for the Pope and the ecclesiastical princes. But Luther would most gladly, in the goodness of his heart, have refused to entertain a fear that such base influences could prove decisive in a matter of such lofty character.

It was very fortunate, at this juncture, that Luther had not yet become acquainted with the polemical writings of earlier teachers, especially Johann of Wesel, against indulgences. Had it been otherwise, he would have been led to realize from the outset the wide scope of the conflict which he was instituting, and compelled to advance much more rapidly in its prosecution. All the more clearly, in view of his ignorance of these earlier assaults, do we now recognize the entire course of his opposition to indul-

gences as an independent product of that apprehension of the
truth which had already before the conflict become his sure
possession, and which now, from its very nature, must inevitably
carry him still farther.

We shall treat, first of all, of Luther's first great utterances in
condemnation of indulgences, *i. e.*, of those which preceded the
Ninety-five Theses of October 31, 1517, of the contents of these
theses themselves, and of the documents immediately connected
with the latter. In the defence of his Theses, he is then led to
an extensive presentation of the grounds of his opposition to the
indulgence theory, which involves, at the same time, a statement
of the entire doctrine of salvation. The next great decisive step
in the process thus instituted is the open breach with the authority
of the Romish Church, which naturally followed. Finally, in the
voluminous writings which he published after the decisive rupture
had occurred, we have an elaborate presentation of the comprehensive and evangelically reformatory views, which he refused to
revoke when arraigned before the Diet at Worms. We know how
securely at the very beginning of this period he had grasped the
central principle of the evangelical doctrine of salvation. As he
was now called upon to defend this principle in the conflict which
began with the discussion of indulgences, he defined it still more
accurately, established it more firmly, and developed from it with
ever-increasing fullness the natural consequences which it involved,
impelled in the important work by the opposition of his enemies
and by his own zealous study of the subject. But the most important new direction which now becomes manifest in his apprehension and public testimony touching the plan of salvation may
be thus briefly stated : As he had up to this time proclaimed
salvation in Christ through faith, in opposition to all human merit,
so he now proclaims it also in opposition to an external human
ecclesiasticism and priesthood, whose acts are represented as
conditioning the imparting of salvation itself, and as in and of
themselves, even without faith, effecting salvation for those in
whose interest they are performed. In the opposition thus
developed, we find the explanation of the positive energy with
which he now announces the so-called formal principle of the
Reformation, *i. e.*, the exclusive, normative authority of the
Sacred Scriptures.

CHAPTER I.

LUTHER'S FIRST GREAT UTTERANCES IN CONDEMNATION
OF INDULGENCES.

1. TESTIMONY BEFORE THE PROMULGATION OF THE NINETY-FIVE
THESES.

DOCUMENTS—TRADITIONAL THEORY—TETZEL—APPEAL TO THE ARCH-
BISHOP—RESORT TO PUBLIC DISCUSSION.

LUTHER had often had occasion to witness the liberal distribution of indulgences in his own immediate neighborhood. The
Popes had given a standing promise of indulgence to all who
should at certain times visit the castle-church at Wittenberg.
This distinction had been granted on account of the relics which
the Elector had with great diligence and at large expense collected there. In the year 1516, a new indulgence was granted
by the Pope for All Saints' Day, when the church was to be re-
dedicated. It was thus that Luther was led, in his *Lectures upon
the Ten Commandments* in the summer of 1516, to assail the
indulgence-abomination in its direct connection with relics and
dedication-days.[1] It is reported that Luther had his attention
for the first time called to the transactions of Tetzel in the
spring of 1516, while making a visitation as Vicar of the Order.
He is said to have been in company with Staupitz, in the monastery of Grimma, when the latter received word of Tetzel's
scandalous traffic in indulgences in the neighboring village
of Wurzen, and to have at once declared : " Now I'll make a
hole in his drum, please God," and immediately undertaken
to write against Tetzel.[2] It is certain, however, that no document of this kind was then prepared, and it is doubtful whether

---

[1] Cf. the displeasure which Luther's attack upon indulgences at first awakened for this reason in the mind of the Elector Frederick.—Erl. Ed., xxvi, 51.

[2] Cf. Jürgens, ii, 642 sqq., and the MS. cited by him upon page 644.

there was any real foundation for the report that he then already had one in contemplation. But that he was deeply agitated upon the question as to the proper conception and the permissibility of the indulgence business, so early as the summer of 1516, is distinctly evident from the *Sermon on the Tenth Sunday after Trinity*, to which reference has already been made.[1] The point of view from which he regards the subject in this discourse is precisely the same as that revealed in the writings published after October 31, 1517. His next utterance upon the subject which has been preserved is that contained in his *Lectures upon the Decalogue*, and was made immediately afterward (according to the report preserved by Löscher, on the same Sunday), with special reference to indulgences granted at the dedication of churches. A sermon preached on *St. Matthias' Day* (February 24), *1517*, also treats of indulgences.[2]

The anxiety of Luther, despite all his suspicions upon the subject of indulgences, yet to remain in accord with the Church finds expression in the very introduction to his remarks on the Tenth Sunday after Trinity. He then acknowledges that indulgences are the merits of Christ and of His saints, and must therefore be accepted with all reverence ; yet, at the present time, he laments, they are horribly perverted to the service of avarice. He then, further, grants that all the works and merits of Christ and of the Church are in the hand of the Pope. But what is it precisely that is supposed to be, or may be, by virtue of this plenary power of the Pope, dispensed in the indulgences? In the discussion of the question, Luther has throughout the entire sermon chiefly in view the indulgences granted for souls in purgatory. He is led to dwell upon the latter in presenting the difference between grace, as inwardly imparted or infused (*gratia intrinsica ;* cf. the "*infusio*," p. 166), and as remitting or relaxing the temporal penalties which are laid upon the believer in this life and for which he must afterwards atone in purgatory (*gratia extrinsica*). He does not doubt the right of the priest to impose such penalties. Nor does he take exception to the view that these penalties may rest upon the soul after death. He even agrees that the Pope may release a soul in purgatory from the penance which he himself has imposed upon it. But suspicions now arise in his mind

---

[1] Löscher, i, 729 sqq.   [2] Ibid., 744.

in consequence of a deeper moral apprehension of the conditions upon which actual entrance to heaven must be dependent.   By the remission of penalty, as supposed, the lusts and moral failings of the soul in purgatory are certainly not made less, nor their virtue, love, etc., made greater; and yet they cannot attain to the kingdom of God before this occurs, for nothing impure can enter there.   Who knows when the soul in purgatory reaches such a stage?   Even the Pope, says he, cannot in this sense release by the authority of the keys, but only by applying the intercession of the Church; and it must then still remain uncertain to what extent God may be willing to accept this in lieu of the services yet to be rendered.   We dare not, therefore, preach that the souls of men are released from purgatory by means of indulgences.   All that we could assert in matters of this kind would be, that a soul of whose perfect contrition we were absolutely certain should immediately escape from purgatory.   He confesses that the subject is not yet clear in his own mind.   At all events, he adds, it is uncertain whether God pardons the imperfect contrition of souls in purgatory by means of indulgences.   But suppose some one should say, that perfect contrition in itself frees from all punishment, and there is therefore no longer any need of indulgences? " I confess my ignorance."   He then comes back again to the application of the intercession of the Church.   The Pope, he declares, does not apply the treasure of the merits of Christ in behalf of the dead as a satisfaction, but only in the way of intercession (*suffragium*).   This, says he, is not strictly an indulgence, but the Pope here merely intercedes with God to grant indulgence and remission for actual sins and for the yet uncanceled original sin, and this occurs by an inward impartation of grace to such souls.   The Pope, he adds, thus appears to do more for the dead than for the living, inasmuch as he does not secure such grace for the latter through the indulgences granted to them. But then, again, the question forces itself upon him, whether the liberation of souls by this means is at all certain, inasmuch as it depends altogether upon the will of God how far the prayers of His Church shall be answered.   He himself, however, then reminds his hearers that Christ unites His own prayers with those of the Church, and that He has given the promise : " Ask, and ye shall receive."   In view of this, he after all reaches the conclusion that the indulgences in question are very useful, notwithstanding the fact that there is great danger of an avaricious spirit in the distribution of them. He adds the peculiar suggestion, that God may perhaps exercise His mercy all the more abundantly in behalf of the dead when He sees that they are despised by the living. It is only incidentally that reference is here made to indulgences for the living, in whose behalf they are accepted as satisfying demands which the recipient has failed to meet (*ad satisfactionem*). He who, with contrition of heart, applies for these receives the benefit of all the fasting and good works of the Church, so that he is spared the labor of penance and satisfaction. So completely does Luther here still accept the theory of the Church. But he is careful to add, that this should not be regarded by the penitent as sufficient, since he does not yet have all the inward grace that he needs : he must now, on the contrary, all the more constantly crucify the sin within. The sermon reaches its aim and conclusion in a warning not to be misled by indulgences to carnal security and indolence.

It is evident, therefore, that what constantly disturbed Luther, in the midst of all his efforts to find a satisfactory explanation of this indulgence business, was the conflict between the demands of divine holiness upon the inner moral disposition of all who desire to attain eternal happiness and a theory, upon the other hand, which looks only to the performance of tasks imposed by the Church. In view of these direct divine demands upon the individual, he cannot rest even in the plenary authority claimed by Church and Pope. The question does not yet occur to him here (nor, as we shall see, in the subsequent writings of this period), whether the grace of God, truly accepted in faith, might not in itself involve the assurance that it would itself at the death of the believer complete the inward purification hitherto imperfectly attained. This question would at once have raised doubts in regard to the whole doctrine of purgatory, and of these there is as yet not the slightest trace in his writings.

In the *Sermon on St. Matthias' Day* (February 24), *1517*, he speaks of Christ as our righteousness, of the imputation of His merits, and of the fact that He is not idle in His followers. It is thus that he is led to speak again of indulgences. They promote, he declares, a miserable, servile righteousness, and the people learn to fear, not sin, but only its punishment. The indulgences are interpreted as a permission to sin with impunity

and to forsake the cross of Christ. They cannot give rest to
the soul. This is to be attained only through meekness and
humility, and these, in turn, require for their cultivation the punishments and the cross from which indulgences promise to exempt.
Here, too, it will be observed, the decisive element is for Luther,
not, in the first instance, his doctrine of the bestowal of eternal
happiness upon faith by grace, nor, much less, any dread of personal suffering or labor which might have been associated with the
theory of free grace ; but, evidently, the strictest moral earnestness in the conception of that suffering and inward dying to sin,
which, according to his own doctrine, must be associated with
faith and must continue, even in the accepted believer, for the
promotion of more complete purification and sanctification. He
remarks, further, that indulgences may be granted to weak Christians, *i. e.*, such as are morally too weak to endure the wholesome
burden of punishment ; but that those who, as genuine Christians,
are striving by means of the cross to attain meekness and humility
should not be annoyed with such things.

Meanwhile Tetzel was drawing nearer to Wittenberg with his
indulgence-traffic. The people of Wittenberg went out to the
neighboring towns of Jüterbog, Zerbst, etc., to hear him.[1] He
himself now posed as a herald of the doctrine of grace. In his
published sermons, he at first strikes a tone like that of Luther
himself when inveighing against self-righteousness and work-
righteousness. We have been conceived, he declares, in sin and
wrapped in bands of sin. It is hard—yea, impossible—to attain
salvation without divine help. Not by works of righteousness
which we have done, but of His mercy, has God saved us. Therefore, says he, put on the armor of God. Take the letters of safe-
conduct from the Vicar of Christ, by which you can deliver your
souls from the hand of your enemies and carry them safely
through, by the way of contrition and confession, to the kingdom
of eternal bliss. He constantly repeats the assurance that whoever, having made confession and experienced sorrow for sin,
drops his alms into the chest shall receive full forgiveness of all
his sins. He professes to furnish plenary indulgences for all the
punishments of purgatory.[2] He includes thus, it will be seen,
in these announcements the demand of penance (in the wide

---

[1] Erl. Ed., xxvi, 50.   [2] Löscher, i, 418 sqq., 416.

sense of the term) according to the prevalent teaching of the Church. Nor does he assert that indulgences are themselves the ground upon which is based forgiveness of sins to the contrite and confessing. But such ideas could scarcely have been more forcibly suggested to the people than by the manner in which the grace of the indulgences was announced. When " full forgiveness of sins " was, as we have seen, promised upon the payment of the price of the indulgence, the preacher did not stop to explain that the indulgence could have no effect whatever in the remission of guilt, nor of eternal punishment, but availed only to release from such additional works of satisfaction as had been imposed but not yet perfectly performed. The archiepiscopal instructions for indulgence commissaries displayed no greater conscientiousness, extolling, as the first chief grace of the indulgences, a " *plenaria remissio omnium peccatorum*." When speaking of the conditions required upon the part of man, sorrow for sin is not indeed ignored in this document, but most artfully allowed only incidental mention, while, on the contrary, with equal artfulness, great stress is laid upon the advantages to be secured by the payment of the money. Tetzel, indeed, in the sermons referred to, blows his trumpet as loudly as though the morning-light of real and sure salvation were just beginning to dawn—now that grace could be had for money. He cries aloud in the words of Christ, " Blessed are they that see what these see," *i. e.*, those who are receiving letters of safe-conduct to heaven.

Luther was thus compelled to bring before Archbishop Albrecht the charge that, according to the instructions issued under his name, one of the chief graces of indulgences is the inestimable gift of reconciliation itself.[1] Thus, too, it may have reached his ears that, according to Tetzel's teaching, it is not at all necessary to have contrition and sorrow for sin, if only the indugences are purchased.[2] In the former chapter we have spoken of the scriptural conception of repentance as a change of heart, to which he confesses himself to have been led by Staupitz.[3] He recognized, accordingly, the perversity of such as, without understanding the meaning of μετανοια, as a change of mind or heart, left nothing remain in repentance except certain cold external works of satisfaction and a painful enumeration of sins in the confessional.

[1] Briefe, i, 69.   [2] Erl. Ed., xxvi, 51.   [3] Briefe, i, 116 sqq.

Now that the indulgence-trumpet was being sounded, he no longer heard laudations of even that least part of repentance, satisfaction, but even this remnant must now, too, be done away with.[1]

This compelled him to take a stand publicly against the scandal. He proposed to claim in his support the view of "all the doctors and the entire Church." His attack assumed the immediate form of a defence of the traditional "satisfaction," as against the remission of it. He quotes the opinion of the teachers of the Church, that satisfaction is better than the remission of satisfaction.[2] What he undertook to assail was simply avarice, leading to the rejection of this view of the fathers. But that which, in the development of the conflict, proved to be the point of controversy was the difference between his view and that which had become dominant in the Church touching the nature and significance of satisfaction; and this led to a review of the entire doctrine of the appropriation of salvation.

It is to be borne in mind, as we turn to an examination of the *Theses* which Luther now presented for discussion, that he did not mean to maintain them as containing only truth which was perfectly clear and certain to his own mind. On the contrary, he still felt uncertain upon many points, as he had so frankly confessed in his *Sermon on the Tenth Sunday after Trinity*. The lack of clearness appeared to him, however, to lie in the doctrine and practice of the Church itself. A conscientious discussion upon the points which seemed open to question in connection with the theory and practice of indulgences ought to help, he argued, in placing the truth and the truth-loving spirit of the Church in a clearer light.

As Luther now wished, by means of his *Ninety-five Theses*, to open a controversy upon the entire question of indulgences, he published at the same time a *Sermon vom Ablass und Gnade* in order to warn the Christian people of Germany of that danger in the indulgence business of which he had already in 1516 publicly spoken at Wittenberg.[3] There has also been preserved a *Sermon in Latin*, which he delivered at Wittenberg at the time when the *Theses* were published, in connection with the dedica-

---

[1] Vid. l. c.   [2] Ibid.

[3] Erl. Ed., xxvii, 1 sqq. Cf. Briefe, i, 71, and De Wette's annotation in loco.

tion of the church at that place.[1] The great prominence which
the *Theses* have attained requires that we, first of all, consider their
actual contents independently. In order to set in a clear light
in its inner consistency the entire doctrinal view which finds
expression in them, we may be permitted to depart, if need be,
from the original numerical arrangement.

2. The Ninety-five Theses of October 31, 1517.

ANALYSIS OF THE NINETY-FIVE THESES—THE NATURE AND FRUITS
OF REPENTANCE—THE POPE AND THE PENITENT—RELIANCE UPON
SCRIPTURE.

The key to the entire theory of Luther is found in that which
he presents in the very first thesis, *i. e.*, his biblical conception of Repentance. When Christ gave commandment to
repent, it was His desire that the whole life of believers should
be a repentance. This word dare not, therefore, be understood as
indicating merely sacramental penance, *i. e.*, confession and satisfaction, with which the office of the priest has to do. But neither
is it merely the inward repentance (the change of the disposition
as such, "μετανοια") which is meant. This latter is not possible
at all without effecting also in the outward life all manner of crucifixion of the flesh. Punitive expiation (*poena*) remains, therefore, as long as hatred of self or true inward repentance remains,
i. e., until our entrance into heaven (Thes. i.–iv.).

The proper expiation (*poena*) which belongs to repentance
(*poenitentia*) is, therefore, that moral act of self-crucifixion which
necessarily results from the inward transformation, even without
regard to any penalties imposed by the priest, just so long and in
so far as our nature (self) remains prone to sin and carnal.
Side by side with this act are now seen to appear the positive
efforts of the new disposition, to which belong especially works
of love and mercy. It was for Luther the great abomination of
the indulgence business that people were thereby induced to
neglect these constituent elements of repentance. In his view
they are absolute divine requirements and necessary manifesta-
tions of repentance, in the true sense of the word, which cannot

[1] Löscher, i, 734 sqq. Jürgens, iii, 580 sqq.

therefore be remitted by any ecclesiastical ordinance whatever, and which take precedence of all payments of indulgence-money which the Church may choose to recognize as good works. These principles find expression in the following theses, namely, that true contrition demands and loves the punishments imposed, whereas the frequent offering of indulgences awakens a dislike for these (xl.) ; that a perfect exemption from punishment could be granted only to the most perfect persons, *i. e.*, to very few (xxiii.) ; and that great care should be exercised in the announcement of indulgences, lest the people be led to think that the latter are preferred to other good works of love (xli.).

Luther felt it necessary to guard most carefully against the impression that the guilt of sin might be removed by indulgences, or even the actual grace of salvation thereby bestowed. Indulgences, he declared, are not that inestimable gift by which man is reconciled to God (xxxiii.). The appropriation of the forgiveness of sins (as the objective ground of which Luther recognizes only Christ and His work) results, on the contrary, directly through true contrition, and that, too, without indulgences (xxxvi.). Indulgences themselves, on the other hand, are not even able to take away the smallest pardonable sin, in the sense of removing its guilt (lxxvi.). Finally, he declares in general, that the remission of guilt can in no wise proceed from man, not even from the Pope, but alone from God. In *Thesis vi.* already, he declares that the Pope can remit no guilt, except in the sense of declaring and confirming the fact that it has been remitted by God.

Indulgences now retain for Luther a relation only to the penalties of sacramental satisfaction imposed by men (xxxiv.) ; and his fundamental premise in regard to them, as revealed in the very first thesis, is that these humanly-imposed penalties can by no means take the place of those penitential exercises which are required by God, and which have their origin in the repentant disposition itself, but that they are, on the contrary, merely additional to the latter and entirely subordinate. God has not, forsooth, placed the proper exercises of penitence under the control of the Church in such a way that the latter may impose them upon men in definite form and measure, and then, again, substitute something else as an equivalent for that which it has so imposed.

In all of this, however, Luther still claims to be speaking in the spirit of the Pope himself. It is beyond question that he really and confidently believed his views to be in full accord, at least, with the genuine doctrine of the Church as maintained by her acknowledged teachers. He hence declares in regard to penalties, that the Pope himself would not undertake to remit any others than those which he had imposed in accordance with his own judgment or the prescriptions of the canon law (v.). In the perfect remission of all penalties the Pope understands only those to be included which he has himself imposed. The indulgence preachers err, therefore, when they say that a man may be freed from all penalties by papal indulgences (xx., xxi.).

A plenary authority of the Pope is also acknowledged, to which the penitent must submit in order to receive the forgiveness of sins and to meet all the demands which should then further be made upon him in the completing of his " penance." It is the Pope who (through the confessor) announces the remission of guilt by God. Hence the " papal remission " and the impartation of the treasures of Christ and the Church by the Pope are by no means to be despised (xxxviii.). Further, God Himself brings every one whose sins He remits at the same time into humble submission in all things to His representative, the priest (vii.). It is especially a subjection to punishments and exercises, as prescribed by the Pope and the Church, which is here had in mind. Granting thus to the Pope the authority to make such regulations, he acknowledges also his authority to recall them by means of indulgences. In this their " relation to the penalties of sacramental satisfaction imposed by man" he is yet willing to recognize indulgences. The indulgence-commissioners should therefore be received with all reverence—only they should not be permitted to proclaim their own dreams instead of the papal commission entrusted to them (lxix.). Cursed be he who speaks against the truth which the indulgence proclaims ; but blessed be he who is on his guard against the reckless words of the indulgence-preachers (lxxi., lxxii.).

Luther still holds also to the view that the treasures of the Church are the source whence the Pope derives the indulgences which he grants. He, however, sought to explain this in a way different from that which was then customary. These treasures, says he, are not sufficiently spoken of or known among Christian people (lvi.). He denies that they consist of the merits of

Christ and His saints; for these constantly, and without any assistance from the Pope, effect grace in the inward man and cross, death, and hell in the outward man (lviii.). With cutting reference to that which it was then customary to speak of as the "treasures of the Church," he quotes (lix.) the saying of St. Laurentius, which applied this designation to the poor of the Church. He himself finally declares that the mild Gospel of the glory and grace of God is the true treasure of the Church (lxii.). Yet he acknowledges also a further treasure, which is the source whence indulgences are derived. He would deliberately designate in this way the keys of the Church, which are granted to her through the merit of Christ; since it is clear that the plenary authority of the Pope (*i. e.*, the power of the keys committed to him) is in itself sufficient (lx., lxi.) for the remission of penalties (*i. e.*, such as have been imposed by the Church).

Although he in the course of the *Theses* greatly depreciates the value of the indulgence-grace which the Pope dispenses, yet he does not hesitate to attribute to the Pope directly the dispensation of the far richer gifts of grace which he so earnestly strives to exalt above the former. We have seen how plainly he pronounces the remission of guilt a "remission of the Pope," and exhorts all accordingly to honor the latter. The claim of the indulgence-venders, that not even Peter himself, if he were now the Pope, could dispense greater gifts of grace than those which they had to offer, he denounces as a slander, not only against Peter, but against the Pope as well. Peter and the Pope, he declares, have both greater gifts of grace, namely, the Gospel, powers, gifts of healing, etc., as enumerated in the twelfth chapter of 1 Corinthians (lxxvii., lxxviii.).

We have in the above paragraphs collected the principal theses which deal with the general doctrine of indulgences, and thus, primarily, with indulgences granted in favor of the living. Luther himself was chiefly exercised in regard to those sold for the benefit of souls in purgatory. That a shameful traffic was carried on, especially in the latter, and that Luther's indignation was excited by it, is evident from the predominant reference of the *Sermon of the Year 1516* to indulgences for the dead.

At this point Luther's apprehension of the penitential exercises appointed by the Church asserted itself at once in its full significance. As he discriminates so positively between these duties imposed by the Church and that which God and the inner nature of repentance always and plainly demand, so, too, the sphere of the former does not for him extend beyond the present life. Hence we have in the *Theses* the declarations : that the penitential canons are imposed only upon the living, and, according to these very canons, nothing should be imposed upon the dying; that those priests act stupidly and wickedly who represent to the dying that the canonical penances are reserved for purgatory; that the theory of a transformation of canonical penalty into the penalty of purgatory seems to have been sown broadcast like tares whilst the bishops slept; that the dying are, upon the contrary, released by death from everything, and are dead, as far as the canonical laws are concerned, inasmuch as they are legally justly entitled to exemption from the latter (viii., x., xi., xiii.). The Pope can, therefore, no longer by virtue of the canonical laws remit such penalties for souls in purgatory (xxii.). Even purgatory itself, although Luther does not question the reality of its existence, has attained for him a quite different significance. Spiritual advancement, inward purification, and sanctification of the soul are the ends in view; hence there is to be a continued exercise of repentance, not with reference to works of penance imposed by the Church, but with reference to that inward state which, in the scriptural conception, is the essential thing in repentance (cf. the above-mentioned sermon). Luther says, further (xiii.–xvi.), that the imperfect (mental or spiritual) health and love (which is the fundamental requisite in the character of the new man) of the dying brings with it great fear, in proportion to the degree of their remaining imperfection (xiv.). In this he sees the real pangs of purgatory, which are not therefore the consequences of ecclesiastical penalties not yet fully discharged. This fear and these terrors are in themselves sufficient, to say nothing of anything else, to constitute the pangs of purgatory, since they are the next thing to the terror of despair. Hell, purgatory and heaven may be distinguished from one another in the same way as despair, almost-despair, and security (complete, blissful peace of soul) (xv., xvi.). It appears to him to follow of necessity that the terrors of purgatory will diminish as love increases; and he knows no reason nor scriptural basis for the belief that souls in purgatory will find themselves beyond the sphere of meritorious conduct or of the possible increase of love (xvii., xviii.).

As in the *Sermon*, however, he here speaks of an influence which the Pope is yet able to exert, at least through the agency of the prayers of the Church, upon souls in purgatory. He commends the Pope for granting remission, not by virtue of the power of the keys, which (with reference to purgatory) he does not possess, but " by means of intercession " (*per modum suffragii,* xxvi.) But then, again, he declares that the intercession of the Church is entirely subject to God's own good pleasure (xxviii.). Hence, it is mere man-preaching to declare that as the groschen rings in the chest the soul escapes from purgatory. The only certainty in the case is that when the groschen rings in the chest, there is a growth of gain and greed (xxvii., xxviii.). He is not even sure that the souls in purgatory themselves commonly entertain a desire to be delivered from it, referring for illustration to the traditions concerning Severin and Paschalis, who are said to have preferred to remain longer in purgatory, in order that they might afterwards be accounted worthy of a higher measure of glory. This view of the influence of the prayers of the Church upon souls in purgatory prompts the declaration, that every bishop or pastor possesses just as much power within his own diocese or parish in matters pertaining to purgatory as the Pope enjoys in his relation to the whole Church (xxv.) ; and leads, also, to the rejection of the proposition, that those who desire to deliver the souls of others (by means of indulgences) from purgatory, do not need to manifest contrition themselves (xxxv.). A child of the devil, Luther at a later date, in the *Resolutiones* (*Elucidations of the Theses*), explains, can as little secure from God the deliverance of a yet imperfect child of God as an enemy of a king could make intercession for the king's friend.

Such are the most important leading propositions presented by the *Theses* in regard to the doctrine of indulgences. A superficial review of them must awaken a sense of great astonishment that Luther, in view of the evangelical position which he had occupied for several years previous, did not take much more advanced ground, and equally great surprise that they should, nevertheless, have occasioned such far-reaching conflicts and divisions. The validity of the indulgences in general was not even called in question. They had long before been much more vigorously assailed by others, as, for example, Johann of Wesel. It could not, moreover, but appear very questionable, how far the views opposed by Luther could really appeal to formal ecclesiastical sanction. Finally, even Luther's own *Theses* still confined themselves to the conceptions and terminology of the dominant ecclesiastical and scholastic system, however conscious he must have been of the difference between the biblical and the ecclesiastical usage of the fundamental term, *poenitentia* (cf. his application of the terms, *poena*, *meritum*, etc.).

But how much authority could the indulgences still really claim, according to the *Theses?* The Pope was authorized, it was granted, to issue them, and the indulgence-commissioners were to be received with great respect. But how much value could still attach to the benefit supposed to be conferred, when this had been expressly confined to the remission simply of the penitential exercises imposed by the Church, a remission which could contribute nothing toward the removal of the guilt of sin, and which could not diminish in the least the requirements growing out of the essential nature of contrition. The benefits of indulgences are, as Luther now expressly declares, the most insignificant when compared with the grace of God and the piety of the cross (lxviii.). The hope of being saved by letters of indulgence is a vain notion, even though the Pope himself should pledge his soul as security for its realization (lii.). The preaching of indulgences, which is a thing of the least importance, is far excelled by the preaching of the Gospel, which is a matter of the highest importance. He is an enemy of Christ who would subordinate the latter to the former (liii.–lv.). So, also, the exercise of love is far more important than the purchase of indulgences. In the opinion of the Pope himself, the latter is by no means to be compared with works of mercy. By the performance of works of love, love grows and a man is made better; by indulgences, he is not made better, but only more free from punishment. He who sees his neighbor in want, and, instead of helping him, buys letters of indulgence, buys for himself, not the indulgence of the Pope, but the wrath of God (xli.–xlv.). Even one's duties to his own family take precedence of indulgences. He who has no superabundance of this world's goods should keep what he needs for household expenses, and not squander it upon indulgences (xlvi.).

It is declared (xlix.) that Christians should be taught that indulgences are indeed useful, if one do not place his confidence

in them, but very injurious, if one be led by them to lose the
fear of God. But there is no attempt in this connection to explain wherein their usefulness consists. We have been told
(xliv.) that indulgences make more free from punishment; but
also (xl.; cf. *supra*) that true contrition seeks and loves punishment. It has been declared, further (xlvii.), that Christians
should be taught that the purchase of indulgences is a voluntary
matter, and not commanded. Still further, in *Thesis xxxvi.*,
already quoted, it is declared, not only that true contrition ap-
propriates the forgiveness of sins even without any indulgence,
but that the truly contrite man is entitled to a full remission of
penalty even without any indulgence. Every true Christian,
Luther then proceeds to say (xxxvii.), has already a share in all
the possessions of Christ and the Church even without any indulgence. It will be inquired, says he (lxxxvii.) : What does
the Pope remit, or grant, to those who by virtue of perfect contrition already have a claim to a full participation in these possessions?

While thus the benefits and significance of indulgences appear
to vanish before our eyes, we are, throughout the entire series of
the *Theses*, impressively reminded of the great danger connected
with the public proclamation of them. It is, says Luther, exceedingly difficult for even the keenest theologians to present to
the common people at the same time the wealth of indulgences
and the truth of contrition (xxxix.). Indulgences lead to a
hatred of the penalty which the contrite loves (xl.; cf. *supra*).
The true treasure of the Church, *i. e.*, the Gospel (cf. *supra*),
comes to be hated, since it makes the first last, whereas the
treasures of the indulgences, which make the last first, are eagerly
accepted (lxii., lxiii.). The treasures of the Gospel are nets with
which in former times a wealth of people were caught; the in-
dulgence-treasures are nets with which now-a-days the wealth of
the people is caught (lxiv., lxv.).

Very earnestly does Luther, in the last section of the *Theses*,
urge upon the attention of the Church the suspicions which must
be aroused in the minds of the people by the traffic in indulgences, as then conducted, and the jeopardy in which the reputation of the Pope himself was thereby placed (lxxxi.–xc.). Why,
it might be asked, does not the Pope, for the sake of holy love,
and in view of the distress of suffering souls, which certainly

furnish a most righteous motive, empty out purgatory entirely, seeing that he now, for the sake of unhallowed lucre for the building of St. Peter's church, which is a motive of such trifling weight, is releasing innumerable souls? What new sort of piety is this, that permits a wicked man and enemy of God, for the sake of money, to deliver a pious and godly soul, and yet will not out of pure love, in view of the great distress of such pious soul, gratuitously deliver it? Why does not the Pope, who is to-day richer than the richest Crœsus, rather build the One Peter's church with his own money than with that of poor believers? What has the Pope to remit, in any event, for those who are perfectly contrite? What better donation could be made to the Church than for the Pope to grant a hundred times daily to every believer the indulgences and benefits which he now distributes only at one fixed time? etc. Such keen arguments, when employed by the laity, dare not, says Luther, be overwhelmed by sheer force, but must be met in turn by solid arguments; otherwise Church and Pope will be made objects for the ridicule of their enemies and Christians will be brought to grief. He himself had, as we have seen, constantly endeavored to place upon the papal ordinances concerning indulgences such an interpretation as would leave them free from reasonable objections. Christian people should be taught, says he, that the Pope himself is zealously striving to reform the abuses complained of. The Pope, in granting indulgences, is more anxious to secure a devout prayer than the money (xlviii.). If he knew of the extortion practiced by the indulgence-preachers, he would be incensed, and would rather see St. Peter's church burnt to ashes than that it should be built with the skin, flesh and bones of his flock (l.) If he hurls thunderbolts against those who engage in wicked machinations against the indulgence business, it is his purpose to deal yet much more severely with those who, under the pretext of indulgences, work in opposition to holy love and truth (lxxiii., lxxiv.). Thus, declares Luther finally (xci.), if indulgences were proclaimed according to the spirit and intention of the Pope, the sharp criticisms might all be easily answered, or, rather, would never be heard at all. But are there not still many suspicious features connected with the theory of indulgences, even under Luther's interpretation? Do they not even thus appear perilous far more than commendable?

We must endeavor to discover the fundamental basis upon which rested Luther's polemical attitude towards the prevailing abuse of indulgences and his own theory of their proper use. Is not his conception of the penalties and services demanded by the nature of repentance quite different from that upon which the entire structure of the indulgence theory depended? Was not the latter conception really repudiated in his clear discrimination between the exercises appointed by the Church and those essentially involved in the nature of repentance? The fundamental characteristic of his conception lies in his persistent refusal to consider the outward exercises of penitence, except as these are found in most intimate connection with a penitent frame of mind. Hence, these exercises cannot be subjected to an external valuation, nor can they be transmuted into an outward equivalent in money or in personal sacrifice of any kind. But according to the prevalent ecclesiastical system, such an external valuation was possible, and was under certain circumstances to be made ; and, accordingly, these exercises could and should be fixed and assigned by the confessor and the regulations of the Church, the obligations thus laid upon the individual being supposed, if unmet in the present life, to extend to purgatory. It followed, likewise, from Luther's conception of the intimate connection between true repentance and the outward exercises naturally attending it, that the latter could never, under any circumstances, be considered otherwise than as obligatory upon the Christian ; and the unlimited motives and demands of such an inward disposition must so entirely claim the attention of the believer, and he must find himself so utterly unable to meet them, that there can be no room for the rendering of any service whatsoever beyond that which he is already bound to render. Thus the ecclesiastical doctrine concerning works of merit, by which the penitent might afterward make good, or in this sense " render satisfaction " for, transgressions committed for which he upon contrition had received absolution, was already made untenable. But it was precisely exercises of this character which the teachers of the Church had in mind when speaking of the satisfactions which should be required of the penitent. Tetzel was able, in opposing Luther, to appeal to an Anselm of Canterbury as declaring, that man can render satisfaction for his sins only by means of such good works as could not be demanded of

man had he not sinned, and not, therefore, by means of the good
works of the commandments of God, which man is already by
virtue of his creation under obligation to perform. He thus,
then, represents himself as inciting to the general practice of what
is good, especially of love, and maintains that the indulgences are
directly calculated to promote such exercises ; persisting, however,
in his declaration, that it is much better for a man to buy the indulgence which he needs in order to escape the penalty of his
sins than to give his money in alms to a pauper not in the greatest possible distress.[1]

The peculiarity of Luther's theory which was calculated to give
the most serious offence to his opponents was the limitation which
it involved in the authority which the Church claimed the right
to exercise over the souls of men. We have seen that he utterly
refuses to grant to the Pope any real power over souls in purgatory. His opponents, even Tetzel, did not, to be sure, venture
to ascribe to the Pope in this sphere any further influence than
" by means of supplication " (*per modum suffragii*). But they
inferred from the preëminence of the papal authority that such
intercession is certain to attain its end. It was even considered,
therefore, as an exercise of the power of the keys, and thus
Tetzel was still enabled to insist that the soul does really escape
from purgatory as soon as the groschen rings in the chest.[2]

In regard to penitential exercises in the present life, Luther
maintained that, in that which is first and most essential, the believer is responsible only to God. The additional requirements
of the Church did not appear to him to further define the relation
of the believer to God in such a way as though they were a direct
revelation of the unchangeable divine will, but only in so far as
the believer is under obligation to submit humbly to the outward
ordinances of the Church for God's sake. Already in *Thesis
vi*. he trenches very seriously upon the claim of the Church to
a mediating office in the dispensing of the chief blessing of
salvation, the forgiveness of sins. It is evident that at this point
also he is unwilling to concede to the Church any real authority.
We shall find that his conception, which in this particular still
lacks positive and clear conviction, assumed at the next stage of

---

[1] Tetzel, Vorlegung, etc.   Löscher, i, 494 sqq.

[2] First disputation of Tetzel, as candidate for the degree of licentiate.   Löscher, 503 sqq.   Thesis liii, sqq.

the conflict a definite form, granting that a real impartation of the forgiveness of sins through the agencies of the Church should indeed be maintained, but in such a way that the Church should no longer be conceived of as exercising a directive, mediating authority, but that the attainment of salvation should be made to depend entirely upon the divine promise of grace, on the one hand, and, on the other, upon the appropriating faith of the individual.

But upon what support did Luther rely in advancing his views? He confidently believed that he was speaking in accordance with the spirit of the " Catholic Church." Yet it must not only have been very difficult for him to adduce any acknowledged authorities in the Church in support of the definite propositions which he advanced ; but he could not but be aware of the fact that he was opposing at least the current of sentiment then prevailing among the leading representatives of the ecclesiastical affairs. By what authority did he undertake to arrest and turn back this current, in order to gain recognition for the opposite principles, which had, indeed, not as yet been condemned by formal ecclesiastical decrees? How would he prevent the establishment by formal decree, in opposition to his own position, of that which lay embedded in this popular current? The Word of Sacred Scripture was the only weapon with which he entered upon the conflict. That which our Lord Jesus Christ has said in the Sacred Scriptures concerning repentance (*Thesis i.*) was the basis upon which he proceeded in the construction of his *Theses*.

It may occasion surprise that the *Theses*, so significant in the general character of their contents, should yet make so little reference to that particular doctrine upon which Luther had previously laid the greatest stress, namely, that of grace and faith. How could he in *Thesis xxxvi.*, when assuring to penitents the forgiveness of sins, fail to speak of the significance of faith? Why does he appear, in general, to take so little account of the need of the soul for a repose which is the pure gift of grace? In fact, we see him here also, as we have observed before in opposing indulgences, emphasize all the more the duty of personal integrity in opposition to false security. It is works of atonement upon the part of man which he now urges. He presents the cross of Christ as one which we must ourselves bear, and it is thus that we are to attain to the blessedness of heaven.

That such was the spirit and aim of the entire discussion is clearly manifest, finally, from the concluding *Theses* (xcii.–xcv.). Away, he cries, with the prophets who say, " Peace, Peace," when there is yet no peace (cf. Jer. v. 14) ; but prosperity attend those who say, " Cross, Cross," when there is yet no cross. Christians should be exhorted to endeavor to follow their Head through punishments, death and hell, and thus, through great tribulations rather than through peaceful security, find comfort in the thought of entering heaven at last. We can easily see how the occasion which led to the preparation of the *Theses* gave them also this earnestly practical direction. It was exceedingly significant that, at the very beginning of the conflict which he was compelled to maintain chiefly for the defence of his doctrine of free grace, it should be so apparent upon which side was to be found strict moral earnestness and where was cherished the tendency to in-dolent repose in ineffectual grace. All the endurance and all the personal activity which he now demands of the penitent presuppose the acceptance in advance of the reconciling, sin-pardoning grace of God. There is now no longer any thought of services by which, according to the demands of divine righteousness, an expiation should be rendered for the canceling of guilt; but attention is fixed solely upon the course of conduct which should, by an inward necessity, distinguish the life of those whose hearts have been reached by grace and by it reconciled, inspired and impelled to appropriate action. For the appropriation of this grace upon the part of man, the only condition is genuine con-trition. In this contrition, however (as is manifest, not indeed from the *Theses* themselves, but from the utterances of Luther immediately following their promulgation), he now, as before, lays the chief stress entirely upon faith. It does not lie within the scope of the *Theses* to enter more fully upon the discussion of the separate elements of contrition, the first of the three prin-cipal articles in the traditional conception of " penance." In their opposition to indulgences they, as well as the *Sermon of A. D. 1516*, have to do with the third article, or " satisfaction." It is to be remembered, finally, that the trials to be endured were no longer regarded as " penalties," nor the moral requirements as an oppressive burden. The " cross, death and hell " of the outward man goes hand in hand with the grace bestowed upon the inward man, and is, like the latter, a fruit of the merits of

Christ Himself (lviii.). The "piety (*Gottseligkeit*) of the cross" is conceived of as in intimate connection with the "grace of God," is regarded as infinitely more to be desired than indulgences (lxviii.). This is the spirit of the thesis above quoted : "Prosperity attend those who say to the people of Christ, 'Cross, Cross,' when there is yet no cross." It is a cross which is no longer really a cross.[1]

The entire spirit and scope of the *Theses*, which we have thus endeavored briefly to indicate, find confirmation and further elucidation in the contemporaneous *Sermon preached at Wittenberg* and in that originally printed in connection with the *Theses* themselves. With these we must examine also the *Latin Dissertation upon Repentance* which appeared in the same year (1517).[2] In the latter, Luther treats specifically of that which is for him the principal part of repentance, *i. e.*, the *contrition* referred to in the *Theses*.

3. CONTEMPORANEOUS DELIVERANCES.

a. Dissertation upon Indulgences and Grace.

THREE-FOLD DIVISION OF REPENTANCE—PROVINCE OF INDULGENCES — SATISFACTION—RELIANCE ONLY UPON SCRIPTURE.

We assign the first place in our investigation to this document,[2] *Sermon vom Ablass und Gnade*, because its contents stand in the most intimate relation to the theme of the *Theses*, and because Luther himself desired it to be published in immediate connection with them.

As he wishes to speak, as far as possible, in the traditional way, he here starts out with the declaration, that it is customary to recognize three elements in repentance (or penance), and to attribute to indulgences the power to remit the third part, namely, the works of satisfaction, consisting of prayer, fasting and alms-giving, in so far as these have been required of any one on account of his sin. He declares it to be, however, a question as yet left undecided in the official declarations of the Church,

---

[1] The special occasion for the Theses, and their special subject, appear to me to receive too little attention even from Dieckhoff in his Theol. Zeitschrift, II., pp. 2 sqq.

[2] Löscher, 567 sqq. Jena i, 13 sqq.

whether indulgences can also remit the penalties (*poenae*) which divine justice demands for sin. He himself maintains that divine justice demands from the sinner no other penalty in the way of satisfaction than true contrition, together with the resolution thenceforth to bear the cross of Christ and to perform the appropriate works (even though the latter be not required by any human authority). He adds the remark, that we find, indeed, that God punishes even His children, as declared in Ps. lxxxix. 30–33, and through punitive suffering (penalty) brings them to contrition, but to remit *this* penalty stands in the power of none but God. But if the " imaginary penalty " (*i. e.*, the punitive suffering demanded by divine justice, which the indulgences are supposed to remit) be not the actual punishment just mentioned, nor the performance of the good works referred to, then, says Luther, we can find no name for it, and no one knows what it is. But, even in case the Church should really decide that indulgences could remit more than the works of satisfaction, he would still, he declares, be unable to see anything commendable in them. He now expresses his opinion much more decidedly than in the *Theses* as to the value, or rather worthlessness, to be in any case attributed to them. He still admits that the Church may remit what she herself (not God) has required, and he still counts the sale of indulgences among the things tolerated and allowed ; but he no longer ascribes any " usefulness " to them. He declares bluntly that it would be a thousand times better if no Christian should purchase any indulgence, but if, instead, every one should perform the works required and endure the penalties assigned. He attaches no weight whatever to the objection, that the penalty and works are too much for man to endure, and that indulgences are therefore necessary ; for God and the Church lay no burden upon any one which it is impossible for him to bear, and the charge that they do so brings no little reproach upon both. Although the purchase of indulgences is therefore not to be prohibited, yet we should endeavor to dissuade Christians from the practice. He would have indulgences looked upon as tolerated (cf. the *Sermon on St. Matthias' Day*, September 21, 1517) only " for the sake of imperfect and indolent Christians, who are unwilling to exercise themselves courageously in good works, or who are incapable of endurance." Indulgences do not help any one to live better, but they tolerate the imperfection of professing Christians.

In regard to the efficacy of indulgences for the dead, he now merely takes occasion to declare, that he does not know whether souls can be delivered from purgatory by means of indulgences, nor does he believe it. Some recent doctors maintain that they can be so delivered, but they are not able to prove it, and the Church has never yet asserted it. It is, therefore, safer and better simply to pray and work in behalf of such souls. He thus, it will be observed, still recognizes a vicarious working in behalf of the dead as well as intercession for them (cf. also the significance attached in *Thesis xxxv.* to the contrition of the interceding party).

It is now very evident how little remains for Luther of the third part of repentance (penance), the so-called " satisfaction." Every attempt to render satisfaction for sin he now declares to be a great error, since God always pardons sins gratuitously, out of pure inestimable grace, and requires further of the pardoned sinner only that he " thereafter live aright." In regard to the proper conception of the penalty, or punitive suffering (*poena*), so frequently referred to in the religious discussions of the day, Luther mentions a distinction drawn by some modern teachers between *medicative* penalties and *satisfactorial* penalties. This he rejects with contempt as vain babbling, asserting that all punitive suffering, and indeed everything which God calls upon men to endure, is " improving and helpful " for Christians. Even punishment itself is no longer for him, as in the traditional conception of it, a satisfaction rendered to a sin-avenging God, but, as indicated in the above quotation from Ps. lxxxix., a wholesome discipline imposed by a God of paternal disposition.

But even with the fundamental analysis of penance (repentance) as consisting of three principal parts, and hence with the entire prevalent conception of the subject, Luther now openly expresses his dissatisfaction. In the very introduction of the dissertation, while following the common method of division, he declares that he does so with hesitation, as the latter can hardly, or not at all, be established from the Scriptures, nor from the ancient holy Christian teachers.

It is worthy of special remark how confidently he still feels authorized to quote in his defence, not only the authority of Scripture, but that of the " ancient teachers " as well. He regards the Scholastics as furnishing a direct contrast to the latter.

16

In the conclusion of the "*Sermon*," he bases the propositions advanced simply upon the Sacred Scriptures, declaring that he entertains no doubt whatever in regard to the points which he has presented, and that they are abundantly sustained by the Scriptures. He charges upon those who seek to denounce him as a heretic, not only that they are totally ignorant of the Bible, but that they have not even read the writings of the teachers of the Church.

The declaration that he " entertains no doubt " reveals for us a marked difference between the contents of this document and certain parts of the *Ninety-five Theses*, in regard to which he confessed that he himself was not fully satisfied, or which he even regarded as open to serious dispute. Such points he does not here introduce at all.

b. Sermon Preached at Wittenberg on the Day before the Dedication of the Church, October 31, 1517.

REPENTANCE HAS BUT TWO PARTS—CROSS WILLINGLY BORNE—SALVA-
TION IN RESPONSE TO PENITENCE AND FAITH.

This sermon (*pridie dedicationis*) is important, as compared with the two original documents already analyzed, chiefly in view of the fact that a new and better analysis of repentance is here opposed to the traditional three-fold division. It is made to consist of but two principal parts, namely, actual repentance (*poenitentia rei*) and displayed repentance (*poenitentia signi*). The former is that of the heart, and is the only true repentance ; the latter is the external manifestation, and is very frequently feigned. By the former he means that which he in the first and second *Theses* described as commanded by Christ, the real change of heart and mind (μετανοια) ; by the latter that which he there designates " sacramental." This division he therefore now formally adopts, and employs it in opposition to the traditional theory. When he then proceeds to mention, as the constituent elements of the second part of repentance (cf. *Thesis ii.*), confession and satisfaction, he openly declares that he does not know where the Sacred Scriptures have anything to say about private confession. He finds only a public confession justified by James v. 16. In regard to the entire method of exercising the second part of repentance, as at present pursued in the Church, namely, the private confession referred to and satisfaction, he declares that he leaves it to the jurists to adduce the divine warrant for this, inasmuch as the satisfaction which John the Baptist requires is a matter of the entire life, and is public and general.   Thus he has here also gone beyond the positions maintained in the *Theses*. He not only denies that the traditional second and third parts of repentance are referred to in the preaching of Christ or of John the Baptist, but he raises the question whether there be any foundation at all for them in the Word of God.   The views upon the subject of indulgences are the same as those which we have noted elsewhere.   They are said to remove nothing more than the special outward penalties imposed upon individuals (*impositiones privatae significationis*; cf. the expression, "*poenitentia signi*").   But the truly penitent, in disgust with himself, inflicts penalty (torture) upon himself, and this is the satisfaction which he renders to God.   He is even willing to allow himself to be trodden upon by all men.   He seeks, not remission of the penalty, but its full endurance ; not indulgence, but the cross.

It is further very significant, especially when viewed in connection with the discussion of repentance which immediately follows, that Luther, in the first division of the sermon, directs the attention entirely away from satisfaction and indulgences, dwelling, in illustration of the narrative of Zacchæus, which furnishes his text, upon the search of man, in his need of salvation, after God and Christ.   We can here see upon what basis the certainty of salvation rests for him, *i. e.*, upon the gracious acceptance of the heartfelt prayer which implores grace, which knows nothing of any worthiness of its own, which never brings its own works of satisfaction into the account, and in which the petitioner dare not in peaceful consciousness extol even the deepest feature of his prayer, in view of which it proves acceptable to God.   Luther has in view especially such as on account of their own conscious unworthiness do not even venture to long for fellowship with God or Christ.   Thus, says he, God is sought after when he is not sought after ; and true prayer is therefore heard by none but God alone, not even by the praying man himself.   He endeavors to explain the process by means of an illustration.   What we bring to God in prayer may be compared to a circle.   The circumference, *i. e.*, our outward acts, our words and thoughts, we indeed

recognize and feel; but God responds to the central and fundamental desires of our inmost hearts, which far exceed all our
thoughts. Thus we see in Zacchæus the depths of the heart
(deeply and in faith longing for God). The real content of such
a heart is such a profound and secret longing that the longing
one himself is not conscious of it, and does not rejoice in it. It
is to be observed that we do not here find the definite conception of saving faith which was afterwards so constantly dominant
in Luther's teaching. He here still speaks of faith as longing
and imploring, rather than as reposing upon the assurance of
grace already granted and cordially accepting it. Even a church
dedication, such as that to be celebrated on the day when this
sermon was preached, appeals to the deepest feelings of his heart.
Church dedications are designed to indicate, through the ceremonies then observed, how we should dedicate our hearts to God.
Condemning, by way of contrast, a merely outward carnal celebration of such occasions, he turns his invectives against the fable-
mongers (*fabulatores*) who mislead the people, and thus against
the indulgence-preachers.

c. Latin Sermon upon Repentance.

EVANGELICAL VIEWS OF CONTRITION AND CONFESSION.

Finally, the Latin sermon, " *De Poenitentia*," professes to give
complete evangelical instruction as to the true interpretation of
that which is commonly included in the first two principal parts
of repentance.

The name " contrition," says Luther, has been given to the
" true inward repentance ;" and we at once observe that he has
in view, not merely the sorrow for sin which marks the original
entrance upon the new life, but, on the contrary, the repentance
which the true Christian must continually cultivate (cf. *Thesis i.*)
He himself here again repeats the statement that contrition does
not cease while life endures. He opens the discussion with the
leading thought, already grown familiar to us, that contrition must
be awakened by the love of righteousness. The mere contemplation of sins, perdition, and penalties makes hypocrites. Man
must therefore first be persuaded to love righteousness and
Christ ; only then will he hate himself. It is a true proverb, and

better than all the doctrine hitherto prevalent concerning the varied forms of contrition: " Never to do is the highest kind of repentance." The best repentance is a new life—to become a new creature in Christ. But how can man attain to this—even though he have already become a Christian? This brings us, at length, to the foundation upon which rests Luther's doctrine of salvation, now again plainly revealed. We should examine ourselves, says he, and discover whether we really cherish contrition simply out of love for a new life. We shall then discover that we are not yet such new men in Christ, since we are still constantly and in many ways sensible of an inclination to the former life. We shall be compelled to confess that, were it not for God and hell, we would certainly have little thought of repentance. What is then to be done? We *ought to*, and yet we *cannot*. Shall we, accordingly, all be lost forever? No! we are to confess, to go into some corner and, according to Christ's counsel, ask God for the sake of His grace and mercy to grant us a new heart. God will then regard us (*reputet*) as truly penitent. We should firmly *believe*. God, who without any petition from us has aroused in us such a consciousness of sin, will also grant grace in answer to our prayer. The true and good God will not allow prayer to Him and trust in Him to be in vain. True contrition comes not from within our own hearts, but from the grace of God. To this we must appeal. We ourselves do not even know whether we are really contrite, but we pray to God and trust that by His favor we are contrite and shall constantly become more so.

That phenomenon, therefore, in the inward nature of man, which is to be embraced in the conception of contrition, or, as Luther calls it, of " inward repentance," is a work of divine grace. But we reach the chief point of saving truth only when the question is raised, by what means the penitent may actually obtain the *forgiveness of sins* for which he in his contrition longs. The impartation of this, according to the current analysis of repentance, belonged to the second part, or confession. Luther speaks also of the *absolution* associated with confession. The Church declared that the former should be granted to the contrite upon confession. But Luther now teaches: Do not cherish the confidence that you will be absolved on account of your contrition, but on account of the promise of Christ to Peter, Matt. xvi. 19. Trust to this. Believe firmly and boldly that you are absolved, and you will truly be absolved. Contrition is never as complete as it should be ; but faith and the Word of Christ are sure and amply sufficient. Hence, says he, there is nothing else upon which we should so strongly insist as that the penitent be not lacking in faith. He even supposes the impossible case, that a person confessing should not be contrite but yet should believe, or a case in which the priest should not be in earnest but should speak the words of absolution merely in sport, and even in these cases he gives the counsel : Let such a person only believe that he is absolved, and he is in veriest truth absolved. So great a thing is faith, so mighty a thing the Word of God.[1] This is the first time that we find Luther asserting his doctrine of salvation with special reference to the absolution of the confessional. Hitherto he has never, perhaps, so sharply as he is here led to do opposed faith, as a simple confidence in that which a gracious God objectively offers, to every moral exercise of man himself and every merit attaching to man's own efforts. Further, he now emphasizes, as we have never before observed, faith itself as distinguished even from the objective divine offer of salvation, as the condition without which the latter, despite all its inherent power, cannot and will not become effective in the individual nor impart to him its blessings. His utterances in this connection extend already, while applied immediately to the sacrament of penance, to the relation of faith to the sacraments in general. He opposes those teachers who declare that the sacraments of the New Testament *are efficacious signs* in the sense that through them every one who does *not oppose any obstacle*, by means of mortal sin or an evil purpose (even though he be not *contritus*, but only *attritus*), receives the offered grace. He maintains, upon the contrary, that without faith the sacrament serves only for condemnation, and that, too, despite contrition. It is only the believer who opposes no obstacle, since *only faith justifies*.

[1] Löscher observes, i, p. 756, that Luther here seems to forget the office of justifying faith as a confidence in the merit of Christ, and to ascribe too much to confidence in the spoken word of absolution. But it is to be presumed, upon the basis of all his previous and succeeding declarations, that the significance of this word rests for him upon the entire saving work of Christ. We shall, moreover, find him in later years still, whenever occasion called for it, insisting in the same way upon this word and the confidence which should be placed in it.

There is perfect truth in the proposition : "*Not the sacrament, but faith in the sacrament, justifies.*" [1]

In connection with the importance which Luther here attaches to the simple Word of promise in absolution, the question might very naturally arise, what is the authority of the priest who announces this Word to the person confessing, and in how far is the Word bound to this authority? Upon this question Luther does not enter at all in the sermon before us.

He admits, in a general way, the obligation to confess sins to the priest before absolution, without stopping to raise the question, as he had already done in the *Wittenberg Sermon*, as to the scriptural warrant for the practice. But, as he had already before the outbreak of the indulgence controversy suggested various limitations of this supposed duty, he now proceeds still further in the same direction. We are not to think, says he, that we must *confess everything* to the priest. That would be impossible. We cannot even confess all mortal sins, which are, in any event, hard to distinguish from those which are venial. It is only mortal sins that we have to confess to the priest; everything else, to God only. The fundamental idea which controls the entire discussion of the subject, and which prompts the above utterances, is, that otherwise the whole aim of the person confessing will be to leave nothing for the divine mercy to pardon, and to place his trust, not in God, but in his own confession.

In regard to the third part of penance, Luther here simply asserts that nothing is said about it in the Sacred Scriptures. For further discussion of it, he refers to his *German Sermon* then recently printed.

[1] Cf. in regard to Baptism, supra, i, p. 163.

CHAPTER II.

CONTINUED OPPOSITION TO THE THEORY OF INDULGENCES,
IN CONNECTION WITH THE ENTIRE DOCTRINE
OF SALVATION.—A. D. 1518.

1. DOCUMENTS OF THE PERIOD.

THE opinions and teachings of Luther which we have thus far gathered from various publications of the Reformer belong, as the occasions which called them forth sufficiently testify, to the general view of one and the same period in his doctrinal development. Although they do not all find a place in the *Ninety-five Theses*, yet they are certainly all constituent elements in that doctrinal view and conviction which originally impelled him to undertake the assault upon indulgences. But he had not, up to this time, embraced them all with equal certitude and clearness of conviction, and the conflict which he had now precipitated impelled him to further labor upon them. Inasmuch as he, in spite of the attacks made upon his *Theses*, or, rather, on account of the manner in which these attacks were conducted by his opponents, maintained them all, even those which had appeared to him still open to question, in their essential contents and for the most part to the very letter, he was compelled not only to defend them, but also to define yet more accurately the principles presented in them and to justify them more completely by displaying their intimate connection with the fundamental doctrine of salvation. In this process, the natural consequences of the views in question were still further developed.

Luther had, indeed, anticipated that the publication of his *Theses* would occasion a great sensation and tumult. But the impression which they really produced far exceeded his expectation. He was amazed to note how quickly they were scattered far and wide. This had not been his design, and did not greatly please him. Had he foreseen it, he declares, he would not have expressed himself so darkly and enigmatically upon many points. Nevertheless, he spoke only because circumstances would no longer permit him to be silent; perhaps it was God's will that it should be so.[1] He now openly proclaims his conviction that a reformation of the Church will not be possible unless the canons and decretals, the scholastic theology and the accepted philosophy and logic of the day, be thoroughly repudiated, and other studies substituted for them. Daily, he declares, does he pray to God that He may again revive the pure study of the Bible and the holy Fathers.[2]

It is not for us here to enter in detail upon the history of the controversial writings exchanged with the ecclesiastical opponents of the *Theses*, nor of the measures adopted by the Pope and his defenders in dealing with Luther. Tetzel, in the same year, 1517, published two series of *Theses*, securing thereby the degrees of Licentiate and Doctor; also, a refutation in German of Luther's *Sermon vom Ablass und Gnade*. It was Luther's conviction that the suspicion was well founded which attributed the authorship of these documents to Conrad Wimpina, of the University at Frankfort on the Oder.[3] In the same year appeared also the *"Dialogus,"* etc., of the Dominican, Sylvester Prierias, *Magister Sancti Palatii* at Rome. In the spring of 1518, the *"Obelisci"* of Johann Eck saw the light. Luther wrote in reply to Tetzel his *Freiheit des Sermons*, etc.[4]; in reply to Eck's *Obelisci*, his *Asterisci;*[5] in reply to Prierias, a *Responsio*.[6] But it was chiefly in the elucidation of his *Theses*, entitled *Resolutiones disputationum de virtute indulgentiarum*, that he presented his conception of the doctrines in dispute and his reasons for it. As early as November, 1517, he had thought of publishing these (he then calls them *"probationes"*). This purpose was not, however, carried out until the summer of 1518. The letter to the Pope, with which they appeared, is dated May 30; they were under the press in

---

[1] Briefe, i, 108, 114, 121.   Respons. ad—Prier. dialog., Löscher, ii, 427.

[2] Briefe, i, 108.

[3] Ibid., i, 99.   Resolut. disput. de virt. indulg.   Löscher, ii, 187.

[4] Cf., in Briefe, i, 123 sq., the letters of June 4, 1518, at which time Luther was still engaged in the preparation of this document.

[5] Cf. Briefe, i, 100.   The date of the writing is August 10, 1518.

[6] Also appearing in August.   Cf. Briefe, i, 83, 86, 131, 135.

June,[1] but it was not until August 21 that he was able to send a copy to Spalatin.[2] All these writings are hence, as their contents also testify, to be regarded as products of one and the same period in the development of the controversy which had arisen. In addition to them, we must here call special attention to the *Sermon vom Sacrament der Busse*, which Luther dedicated to the Duchess Margarethe of Brunswick and Lüneberg.[3] In October, 1518, Luther was summoned to appear before the cardinal-legate Cajetan, at Augsburg. We must give due attention to the important theses which he there maintained against the latter. A series of shorter writings, theses, sermons, etc., will also demand casual notice.

As the controversy proceeded, increasing prominence was given to the question as to the authorities which were to be regarded as decisive in all doctrinal conflicts within the Church— the effort to determine what is the highest norm of Christian doctrine, the formal principle of evangelical faith. This did not, however, as yet become an actual subject of dispute. Luther himself did not yet realize the wide divergence between his position and the views prevailing in the Church upon this point. We have seen that it was his desire to see, in opposition to the existing mode of teaching, a revival of the study, not only of the Scriptures, but of the Fathers as well. He still endeavored, little as was the importance which he attached to the study of the papal decretals and canons, to maintain stoutly the consistency of his views even with the latter. He constantly found support also, for the doctrine which he advanced, against recent errorists, especially in the mysticism of Tauler. He writes to Staupitz,[4] under date of March 31, 1518, that he was merely following the theology of Tauler and of the little volume which Staupitz himself had recently given to the press (meaning evidently the latter's tract, *Von der holdseligen Liebe Gottes*, which appeared in 1518 [5]) ; that he teaches, in accordance with these models, to place con-

---

[1] Briefe, i, 122; cf. ibid., p. 129.   [2] Briefe, i, 133.

[3] Erl. Ed., xx, 179 sqq. According to Löscher, ii, 512 sqq., it was printed about November, 1518.

[4] Briefe, i, 102.

[5] De Wette's annotation, l. c., that Luther means the " German Theology," evidently rests upon a misunderstanding. Luther certainly means a writing given to the press by Staupitz himself.

fidence in Christ alone, and not in one's own work and merit; and that he incurs hostility because of his preference of the Mystics and the Bible to the scholastic doctors. It was at this time that he published his complete edition of the *German Theology*. He declares in the preface, that he has met with no other book except the Bible and Augustine from which he has more clearly learned what God, Christ and all things are; and that from it he clearly sees how slanderous is the charge made against himself and the other Wittenbergers, that they were attempting to introduce new things, as though there had been none before them nor in other places. Yea, verily, says he, there have indeed been others before them, but the wrath of God has not permitted sinful Christians to see and hear these. Let people read this little book, and then say whether this Wittenberg theology is a new thing.[1] It is only gradually, step by step, that Luther is driven to sharper discrimination in the questions concerning the supreme rule of faith and doctrine, and the advancement manifested in the expression of his views from time to time stands in intimate connection with the attitude which he assumed toward the Church and her authority in general. We shall, therefore, before attempting to exhibit and epitomize what is to be said upon this subject, examine those material articles of faith which had become the immediate and special objects of controversy; and we shall then, furthermore, consider the subject in connection with Luther's conception of the Church and her activities. We shall thus, at the same time, reach the point of transition which marks the next important step in the development of the Reformer.

2. Doctrines Bearing Immediate Relation to the Indulgence Controversy.

REPENTANCE—PENALTY—GRACE AND FAITH IN SACRAMENTS—TREASURE OF THE CHURCH—PURGATORY—THE CHURCH AND THE SCRIPTURES.

The doctrine of REPENTANCE, or penance, constituted the central point in the controversy, and it must be borne constantly in mind that the discussion was in regard essentially to that repent-

[1] Erl. Ed., xliii, 239.

ance which must, on account of the sins which they still constantly
commit, be renewedly exercised by those who have already entered
upon the Christian life and been received under the covenant of
grace. It was the repentance of such persons which came into
consideration in the granting of indulgences—not that of persons
just entering upon Christian life and becoming partakers of the
blessings of salvation.

Luther here, first of all, insists upon the position taken in the
First Thesis, *i. e.*, that the whole life must be a repentance—a
change of the inner disposition ($\nu o\tilde{v}\varsigma$), a crucifying of the old man,
etc. Inward repentance always remains, with mourning (Matt. v.),
and the crucifying of the flesh (Rom. vi. and viii.), because sin and
the body of sin still remain. Thus the fear of death also remains,
which is the penalty of all penalties.[1] The external experiences,
also, which correspond to these inward exercises must continue ;
the outward cross must be willingly borne, as a means of effecting
such spiritual mortification. He proceeds to explain at length
how this fundamental attitude of repentance, this mourning and
the corresponding general disposition of the heart toward God,
may and must be maintained through every moment of the
Christian life. Prierias objected to this view that the Christian
is commanded also to rejoice. To this Luther replied, that Paul
does indeed exhort us to " rejoice always in the Lord," *i. e.*, we
are always to have joy *in Him*, but in ourselves mourning and
lamenting—joy in grief and grief in joy. Prierias ventured to
suggest that repentance may be interrupted at least during sleep ;
but Luther appealed in response to the apostolic injunction to let
all things, even eating and drinking, be done to the Lord and in
His name.[2]

He now presents also a more detailed and definite statement
of his view upon the subject of PENALTY. Tetzel had maintained,
in harmony with all the other opponents of Luther, that the
Church had by her own practice decided that plenary indulgence
remits also those satisfactions and punishments which divine
righteousness demands for sins repented of and confessed, and
which the priest, on his part, may not have imposed with sufficient
rigor. It remits the penalty, he claimed, whether imposed by the
priest or by God. It is only the " medicative " and " preserva-

---

[1] Resol., Löscher, ii, 185, 189.   [2] Respons. ad. Prier. dial., Löscher, ii. 395.

tive " penalty that is not canceled. The penalty still needful to
drive to repentance is not remitted, but only that which attaches
to the sins repented of.[1] Luther now designates five kinds of
penalty, viz.: 1. Those of hell. 2. Those of purgatory. 3. The
evangelical, voluntary inflictions of spiritual penitence, the mortification of the fleshly passions, etc. 4. Divine chastisements by
visitations of war, earthquake, the Turks, etc., such as are referred
to in Ps. lxxxix. 30–33.[2] 5. The canonical penalties imposed by
the Church. Now, we nowhere read, he declares, that God Himself has demanded any penalties save those of the third and fourth
kinds here mentioned.[3] Moreover, these depend entirely and
alone upon the will of God, and are not subject to the authority of
the priest; they cannot, therefore, as the *Ninety-five Theses* had
already maintained, be in any way remitted by the Church.[4] At
this point, Luther makes a correction in the *Twenty-third Thesis*.
He had there originally held that complete remission of penalty
could be granted only to the most perfect. He now declares
that to no one, however perfect he may be, can all penalty be
remitted, since there must always remain for every one at least
the third form of penalty.[5]

It now, finally, becomes perfectly clear that for Luther nothing
which God suffers to befall the truly repentant can longer be
called penalty. He declares that God appoints no penalty to
follow repentance, but is content to have brought man to the
state of mind in which he judges, condemns, etc., himself.
When He forgives sin, He remits at once both guilt and penalty,
since He knows that the sinner will have penalty enough if he lives
aright and contends against the evil that is yet within. Those
punishments, moreover, which God suffers to befall man before
his repentance are not at all to be considered in the light of the
penalty which is, in the practice of the Church, imposed upon the
penitent after his confession—as though man were to make satisfaction to the divine righteousness by his own deeds or endurance, but even these are designed to " drive to repentance " (cf.
Tetzel) : " God smites His children, in order to humiliate them
and thus lead them to repentance." Eck had taken occasion, in

<hr>

[1] Löscher, i, 488–491, 504 (I. Disput., Thes. xiv).

[2] Cf. the Sermon Vom Ablass und Gnade.   Resol. 189.

[4] Ibid., Erl. Ed.. xxvii, 11, 15,   Asterisci, Löscher, ii, 338.   [5] Resol. 235.

discussing *Thesis xlii.*, to emphasize the prevalent distinction between conduct, or suffering, as serving for the attaining of merit (*ad merendum*), on the one hand, or, on the other hand, for the rendering of satisfaction (*ad satisfaciendum*). Luther, in his reply, declares that even penalties are meritorious, according to the assurance of St. Paul, that to the elect all things must work together for good; and he utterly refuses to accept the validity of the distinction quoted by Eck. From other utterances of the Reformer, and from the above scriptural citation, we may gather in what sense he employs the predicate "meritorious," *i. e.*, not that the enduring of penalties affords man a legal claim before the bar of God, but only that it assists him in the attaining of some good.[1] A flood of light is thus cast upon the significance of one of the *Theses* (No. xii.), which stood originally in apparent isolation, and which we have in the above review been unable to place in close connection with any other. It reads: "The canonical penalties were at one time imposed, not before, but after, absolution, as a test of true contrition." In its original connection, this was intended to assist in justifying opposition to the transfer of penalties to the souls of such in Purgatory as had received absolution before their death. Luther now appeals to the same ancient custom as an evidence that, according to the view of the Church, even the penalties which she herself imposes are not designed to follow the forgiveness of sins and serve as means for the rendering of satisfaction. In this, he declares, the Church has followed the example of God Himself. He wishes to regard this as still, in the current usage, the view of the Church. The Church assumes that the penalty has been already endured—if not actually, yet essentially, through the vow of the confessing penitent.[2]

Yet with all this, Luther still concedes the general authority of the Church to impose her own penalties upon the penitent and confessing. But he has made it very clear that these penalties are not demanded by God. To state the case more precisely, the subjection to this outward discipline is only in so far the Christian's duty, as authority has been given to the Church to make proper regulations in regard to such external things. The remission of these penalties he utterly refuses to make dependent

---

[1] Asterisci. Löscher, ii, 337 sq., 359.   [2] Ibid., 338.

upon the contrition of the penitent, referring it entirely to the will of the Pope. In regard to them even he attributes to the Pope unlimited authority for the granting of indulgences. In *Thesis xxx. and xxxi.*, he had asserted, that, since no one can be perfectly sure of the reality of his contrition, neither can he be perfectly sure of the complete remission of penalties, and that a genuine purchase of indulgence was as rare a thing as genuine repentance. He now declares, that he was there speaking from the point of view of those who regard contrition as the necessary condition for the securing of such remission. He announces it as his own conviction, that the remission of canonical penalties may be secured with absolute certainty even by those whose lives are unworthy and who know nothing of contrition ; for such remission is valid itself, inasmuch as it lies entirely within the power of the Pope.[1] He acknowledges this, however, not because of any lofty conception of the papal authority, but on account of the extremely trifling importance which he had learned to attach to the whole subject under discussion. Whereas his opponents maintained that the penalties imposed by the Church determine absolutely the relation of man to God, and thus, also, that indulgences effect reconciliation between man and God,[2] there was for Luther no longer any thought of such an efficacy. Under these circumstances, the exceedingly important distinction between the relation of man to the Church and his relation to God was brought out in clear light and with great prominence in the utterances of Luther. The forgiveness of the (ecclesiastical) penalty, he argued, reconciles only with the Church ; the forgiveness of guilt, or the " heavenly absolution," makes the heart fearless and joyous before God, or, in other words, reconciles with God. The former reconciliation he designates a merely external one, a reconciliation merely with men.[3]

As the third element in penance the traditional theory presented satisfaction, *i. e.*, the endurance of punishment and the performance of good works, to the rendering of which the penitent was supposed to be still in duty bound after the reception of abso-

---

[1] Resol., 194, 189. Ad. Prier., 411. Resol., 252 sq. Asterisci, 355.

[2] Disput., i., Thes., xii.

[3] " Remissio poenae reconciliat homini, id est ecclesiae ": Erl. Ed., xx, 180 : Luther's Circular " Disputation " of A. D. 1518, in Löscher, ii, 580.

lution. We have seen what position and significance the penalties inflicted by God had come to occupy in the mind of Luther.
The positive acts which God Himself requires of the repentant
can, in his view, have significance only when we presuppose forgiveness as already granted by God. How THEN, according to his
theory, IS THE FORGIVENESS OF SINS TO BE ATTAINED?

This question now led the Reformer to profound and fruitful
investigations. He was especially concerned to determine what
significance is to be attributed to the *words of absolution uttered
by the priest* as the official intermediary. Even the *Sermo de
Poenitentia* had not advanced to clearer definitions upon this
point. We must have recourse mainly to the *Resolutiones* of
Theses vi., vii., xxxvii. and xxxviii. With these the *Sermon vom
Sacrament der Busse* will be found also, in its main positions,
closely allied.

Luther affirms that the position maintained in his Thesis vi.
(that the Pope can forgive guilt only in the sense of announcing
the divine forgiveness) is granted by all. Even Prierias had
admitted it in the case of *such* penitents as, with sorrow for their
sins, submit to the keys of the Church and are, *in consequence of
such submission,* justified from guilt; but in regard to such as
have not as yet experienced full *contritio,* but only *attritio* or
incomplete sorrow for sin, he maintained, in accord with the
scholastic theory, that they become contrite through the power of
the keys, and that it is, therefore, the priest who remits their
sins, viz., influentially and ministerially (*dispositive et ministerialiter*), by the application of the keys and the sacraments.[1]
Luther, however, confesses, in the discussion of this, as well as
the following thesis, that he has not yet attained a clear apprehension of the subject, and should be glad to receive proper instruction upon it. We do not read, says he, in Matt. xvi. :
" Whatsoever *I* shall have loosed in heaven shall be loosed on

---

[1] Diologus, Löscher, ii, 18. Cf. Thom. von Aquino Summa Suppl. P. viii,
Qu. 18, Art. 1 (Cited in Gieseler's Kirchengesehichte, Vol. II., Chap. ii, p. 81,
note 9) : God only by his own power remits guilt ; by his power baptism works
instrumentally in the person baptized, and the priest instrumentally in the repentant. " Thus it is evident that the power of the keys is appointed in some
way for the remission of guilt, not as effecting it, but as disposing to it.
Whence, *if any one before absolution had not been perfectly disposed* to the
reception of grace, in the very act of confession and sacramental absolution he
would attain grace, *if he should place no obstacle* in the way."

earth," but : " Whatsoever *thou* shalt loose on earth," etc.   According to this, God *confirms the forgiveness granted by the priest,* and not the reverse.   God appears to remit the guilt after the remission by the priest has been already accomplished.   But how can this occur before the infusion of grace, *i. e.,* before the divine remission, since without the grace of God, which remits our sins, we could not even cherish the desire for remission?   It is a question, too, whether every one who is reconciled to the Church (through her representative, who pronounces the absolution) is thereby also really reconciled likewise to God.[1]

As his own view, Luther now offers the following : [2]   God has before absolution already begun to justify the man, or make him righteous (*justificare* in the sense above indicated).   He condemns him beforehand, crushes him, slays him, etc., and in these very acts begins the work of His salvation ; he performs His " strange work " (*opus alienum*) in order to perform His own peculiar work (*opus suum*).   Hence there occurs already, before the priestly forgiveness of sins, a divine infusion of grace.   Thus David, for example, even before his absolution by Nathan, while he could as yet only cry, " I have sinned," stood already under the influence of the grace of justification.   The heart of man is already " made righteous by grace."   Especially is participation in the blessings of salvation already bestowed by God.   But man himself does not as yet know that he is justified, but, on the contrary, regards himself as upon the verge of perdition ; he thinks that what God is doing for him is not an infusion of grace, but rather an effusion of wrath ; he is more uncertain of grace when it is actually present than when it was yet far from him.   Thus, the sins of the woman who washed the Saviour's feet with her tears were forgiven already before the cheering word of the Lord was spoken, but she knew it not.   Thus, too, David would have died in the remorse for his sin which he experienced under the operation of grace upon his conscience, if Nathan had not absolved him.   Man attains peace and comfort under the lashings of conscience only when he takes refuge in the Church and there seeks the remedy ; for he can never attain rest by his own

[1] Resol., 195, 196.

[2] Cf. for the summary here presented, where other references are not given, Resol., 196–202, 260–265.

counsel or help. The priest should then, with the utmost confidence in the power which he has received for the exercise of mercy, loose (λύειν, Matt. xvi.) the broken hearted and declare him loosed, and thus bestow upon him peace of conscience. God knew that the conscience, although already made righteous by grace, would yet, in its distress, reject grace unless He should come to its assistance and lead it to believe in the grace which is present in the ministration of the priest. Thus the believer now attains the certainty of forgiveness—*the certainty, not of the fact, but of faith*. But even the divine forgiveness can only now be truly said to have become actualized ; for although the forgiveness of guilt has already occurred before the remission by the priest, yet the forgiveness is still not yet actual forgiveness, inasmuch as it has not yet become such for us. Sin, without faith in the fact of its forgiveness, would yet, in great part, rest upon man.

It is evident that Luther understands by the forgiveness which the believer receives from the priest the *application* to the *consciousness of the penitent* of that forgiving grace of God which had in truth before already addressed itself to him, wrought upon his heart, and awakened especially that very longing for the inner attestation of its own presence to the conscience. It is in this sense that Luther speaks of a forgiveness before forgiveness, of an absolution before absolution, and of a participation in the blessings of salvation before such participation.

Now the *priest* has full authority, it is maintained, to *impart this certainty* to the repentant. The conscience of the penitent himself, says Luther, will generally, if he be truly humbled on account of his sin, make him feel uncertain in regard to grace. It is so hard to trust in mercy. The experience of the soul is like that of the disciples, to whom the first announcement of the resurrection appeared scarcely credible. It is exceedingly hard to believe that we may have a part in all the blessings of Christ, that not only is the forgiveness of sins bestowed upon the believer, but with this, also, sonship with God, heirship, brotherhood with Christ, companionship with angels, dominion over the world. Now man is not required to accept the assurance of all this from himself, but rather from the office of the keys, *i. e.*, from the priest. He is exhorted to repose confidence in the judgment of another.

But it is to be observed, in the first place, Luther now declares

very emphatically—touching the *objective* impartation of grace by
the priest, that he who receives absolution should depend upon
the judgment of another, not at all on account of the dignity of
the ecclesiastical person pronouncing it, or on account of the
power with which the latter is clothed, but only on account of
Christ's Word of promise, upon which faith should firmly rest;
for the Word of Christ stands secure : " Whatsoever ye shall loose
on earth shall be loosed also in heaven." Nor should any one
here stop to think : " What if the priest should be mistaken?"
For the forgiveness rests, not upon the priest, but upon the Word
of Christ, and faith in this would secure peace to the heart even
though the priest had pronounced the absolution with the utmost
levity. The keys do not err, even though he who bears them
be a trifler.[1] On the other hand—touching the impartation of
the blessings of salvation to the individual, Luther finds this
possible only through the channel of *faith*. If this be lacking,
the divine Word of grace from the lips of the priest is unable to
bestow any gift whatsoever upon the person to whom it is addressed. Wherever Luther emphasizes the sure objective Word
of promise, he emphasizes none the less this condition, faith.
" Thou hast," says he, " just as much as thou believest." [2]

But in how far is that special Word upon which faith is firmly
to rest, viz., the declaration : " Whatsoever ye shall loose," etc.,
to be regarded as addressed by Christ Himself to certain particular individuals, to a special definite class of persons, *i. e., priests*
and *confessors ?* In how far, consequently, is the believer who
desires to receive the consolation of this Word of Christ referred
to particular men, who have been empowered by Christ to impart
it? In how far are his peace and salvation dependent upon the
agency of these particular persons in assuring him of forgiveness
by virtue of the authority thus given them? There is no question
that Luther would direct the inquirer immediately to the spiritual
office, the confessor duly appointed in the Church. As we have
already seen, the awakened soul is to receive help through faith
in the presence of the grace which offers itself in the *ministra-
tions of the priests ;* it is to " believe the key, *i. e.,* the priest."

[1] Cf. also Erl. Ed., xx, 187, and citations above from the *Sermo de poenitentia.*

[2] Resol., 263.

"Nothing justifies, save alone faith in Christ, and to this is necessary the presentation of the Word by the priest."[1] Such is the language of the Reformer when speaking of ecclesiastical confession. But he does not mean to thereby grant to the priest any lordship over the souls of men, nor dare the Pope be exalted and looked upon as a terrible man by virtue of his possession of the power of the keys. "For," says he, "the keys do not belong to him, but much rather to me. To me have they been given, for my salvation, my comfort and peace. In the (use of the) keys, the Pope is my minister and servant."

But Luther goes still farther, even at this period of his development, rejecting already in clear and positive expressions all dependence of the soul for its salvation upon the arbitrary decision of those holding official positions in the Church. If he always assumes that the regular and proper place for the reception of forgiveness is the confessional of the Church, and that the general and regular administrators of the power of the keys are the priests, it is equally clear that he yet does not regard the dispensation of the divine forgiveness as a matter committed to the priest *alone*. Already in the German *Sermon vom Sacrament der Busse* (which is not to be confounded with the Latin *Sermo de Poenitentia*), he places upon the same plane as that assigned to the official announcement by the priest the declaration made by *any Christian brother* who assures us of the divine grace. So fully does he lay all the stress upon the Word of grace itself, not upon any particular human administrator, and, on the other hand, upon the faith which receives it wherever and however it be offered. He declares:[2] It follows, that in the sacrament of repentance and forgiveness of guilt a Pope or bishop does no more than the most obscure priest. Yea, where there is no priest, *any Christian person*, even a woman or child, may do just as much; for when any Christian person can say to thee: "God forgives thy sins in the name of Christ," etc., and thou canst receive the Word with an unwavering faith, as though God spake it to thee, thou art certainly absolved in this thy faith: so utterly and entirely does everything depend upon *faith in the Word of God*. * * * Yet the ordinances of the proper authorities are to be observed, and not despised; but we must be upon our

[1] Circ. Disp., Löscher, ii, 582.   [2] Erl. Ed., xx, 183–184, 191 sq., 185.

guard lest we fall into error in regard to this sacrament and its efficacy, imagining it to be any better when administered by a bishop or Pope than when received at the hands of a priest or layman. " This power to forgive sins (as Christ forgives, Matt. ix. 6 sqq.) is nothing else than that a priest, or in case of necessity any Christian person, may speak to a fellowman, and, if he observe the latter to be grieved and distressed on account of his sins, may joyfully pronounce the judgment : ' Be of good cheer ; thy sins are forgiven thee.' * * * Thou seest that the whole Church is thus full of the forgiveness of sins." Luther combines this " comforting " of those under conviction of sin by the Word of grace from the lips of any brother with the formal absolution, in the statement : " And when thou art absolved from (thy) sins, yea, when in thy sense of sin a pious Christian comforts thee, thou shouldst accept this with such faith that thou wouldst rather suffer thyself to be torn to pieces than have any doubt that it is really so before God."

What peculiar value attaches to the Word of forgiveness when it is not only taken by the individual believer for himself out of the Scriptures, but addressed to him by others, whether by the priest or by any sympathizing brother, Luther does not now further explain. We can, however, comprehend at least this much : Such an application of the promises of grace is supposed to serve in a peculiar manner for the awakening and strengthening of faith. The priests and comforting brethren appear in the transaction as sent to the distressed one by God, who designs thus to give the latter a further testimony and evidence of His grace. If, says Luther, we have been, even without this, commanded to believe in the grace of God and to hope that our sins are forgiven —" how much more shouldst thou then believe it when He gives thee an evidence of it through a fellowman." [1] He declares, in general, that the confessor *exercises* (*exercet*) *faith*, inasmuch as he presents the Word of Christ.[2] We shall hereafter, in our systematic summary of the doctrinal views of Luther, have occasion to estimate more carefully the significance which he always continued to attach to the ministry of the priest or brother. But in the present connection the declarations which have been adduced are important chiefly as testifying how positively and clearly his

[1] Erl. Ed., xx, 185.   [2] Löscher, ii, 581.

view had already advanced beyond the theory of a dependence of the forgiveness of sins, and thus of all salvation, upon particular human ecclesiastical organs of divine grace. He is thus able to maintain in all earnestness the position which he now assumes in the proposition : *That Christ did not wish to have the salvation of men depend upon the power and will of a man.*[1]

As Luther was led through the discussions concerning the sacrament of penance to sharp discrimination in regard to the forgiveness of sins and absolution, the central point of his whole doctrine of salvation, and thus of his entire reformatory teaching, already came into view. We must, therefore, direct our attention still further to the leading principles here involved. These are, as already remarked,—on the one hand, the certain objective offer of grace through *the Word of God*, which approaches us, indeed, through the mediation of human ecclesiastical administrators, but refuses to be subject to the power of any administrator ; and on the other hand, *faith*, by means of which the offered grace is to be transferred to our hearts. In respect to the first principle, Luther now, in his effort to express the full *objective reality and certainty* of the offer, presses on to the proposition : The forgiveness which, in accordance with Christ's promise of " loosing," is declared in absolution is as certainly true, *whether it become effective through faith or not*, as though God Himself uttered it ; but, of course, it cannot without faith become the actual possession of man, since God can give to no one who is unwilling to receive.[2] We shall hereafter have occasion to recall the above proposition, which Luther himself also repeated in later years. In respect to the second principle, *faith*, it is even more distinctly noticeable how absolutely Luther makes salvation dependent upon it alone, and not upon other subjective conditions, which are nevertheless to be associated with it.[3] In the prevailing usages of the Church in connection with confession, the entire stress, so far as the attitude of the individual himself was concerned, was laid upon his penitence, or contrition. By virtue of his penitence he was to secure grace. Any doubt as to the completeness of this made doubtful again the reality of the attested forgiveness. In opposition to this, Luther now gives even more impressive

---

[1] Löscher, ii, 581. [2] Erl. Ed., xx, 192.

[3] Cf. for the following, the *Sermo de poenitentia.*

warning than in the *Sermo de Poenitentia*, that no one should ever place his confidence in the depth of his own sorrow for sin, and he comforts, at the same time, those who in faith apprehend the offered grace, but yet mourn that their sorrow is so incomplete. Faith, in which man turns away entirely from himself to the Saviour, should nevertheless be sure of salvation. Hope is to be founded, not on our own contrition, but upon the Word of grace (which faith alone apprehends). If men are taught to build their confidence of the forgiveness of sin upon their own feeling of perfect contrition, they can never be brought to such confidence, but will only be led to wear themselves out to the point of despair. But whereas our own hearts may deceive us with such feeling, the Saviour, Jesus Christ, will never deceive us if we have or desire Him (*vel habitus vel desideratus*). Moreover, sorrow for sin is never in truth sufficiently deep.[1] Again, he boldly declares : Even supposing the impossible case, that a person were not contrite, or that he himself at least did not consider himself sufficiently contrite, and that he should yet with full confidence, upon the testimony of the one pronouncing absolution, believe that he is absolved, this very faith in Him who says : " whatsoever ye shall loose," etc., would make him a most thoroughly absolved person.[2] We may argue thus, he further remarks, from the impossible ; but he himself fully recognizes that faith from its very nature cannot exist without contrition, as he elsewhere declares all approach to the sacrament unworthy that is not accompanied with true contrition, affirming at the same time that faith itself makes contrite.[3] Thus God not only permits, but, according to Luther, He desires the penitent and confessing to be in his faith certain of forgiveness. He miserably errs who would make forgiveness uncertain on account of the uncertainty of the penitence.[4] But none the less strongly does he maintain, on the other hand, that nothing less than faith can meet the divine requirement— that the man who does not have faith can receive nothing from the salvation objectively offered. He insists upon this again in opposition to the doctrine that, in order to receive saving grace from the sacrament, it is sufficient that one interpose no obstacle.[5]

[1] Resol., 199, 264. Erl. Ed., xx, 183, 186. Circ. Disp., Löscher, ii, 581.
[2] Resol., 263.   [3] Respons. ad Prier., Löscher, ii, 403.
[4] Circ. Disp., Löscher, ii, 580.   [5] Cf. Sermo de poenitentia.

He declares this to be " most horrifying heresy."[1]   In a similar
way he confronts also the accepted doctrine, that mere *attritio*,
as distinguished from *contritio*, that is, a penitence which is yet
essentially defective because still without the love of God, may
nevertheless attain grace ; or, as Prierias maintained, that the
attritio may through the power of the keys become *contritio*.
Luther, denying this, maintains, upon the one hand, that only
faith can receive salvation from the keys, and, upon the other
hand, as already observed, he recognizes nothing as true faith
which does not already imply and itself produce actual contrition.
In response to the definition of *attritio* as a willingness to entertain a painful sense of sin and the grace of God, he declares that
such a willingness would be either hypocrisy, or itself already
a real beginning of grace even before the supposed efficacious
agency of the keys.[2]   With such a conception of the way to the
attainment of forgiveness, it became evident to Luther that it
must be wrong to commend in the confessional an *enumeration
of all separate sins*.   At the very best, penitence could only be
thus incited to violence of grief, feigned from fear of punishment.
Penitence should, upon the contrary, be awakened by the contemplation of the mercies of God, especially the wounds of
Christ.   It is thus that man is to be brought to hatred of himself
as an ingrate and to love of the divine goodness.[3]   We see here
again how intimately penitence is associated with faith.   We are
reminded of the insistence of Luther upon this point in his
Exposition of the Decalogue (*supra*, p. 164).   What, then, in
view of all that has been said, shall the confessor be authorized to
accept as a genuine evidence of penitence, such as will justify
him in imparting absolution?   Luther answers briefly : That he
observes that *the sinner demands and believes the absolution itself*.[4]

    This entire conception as to the appropriation of salvation ex-
tends also, as observed when analyzing the *Sermo de Poenitentia*,
to the doctrine of the *sacraments in general*.   Luther there, as
afterwards, describes repentance itself as a sacrament, without
instituting any original investigations as to the significance of the
term.   And, in treating of that particular element in the doctrine

[1] Resol., 202.   Asterisci, Löscher, i, 339.
[2] Prierias, Löscher, ii, 18.—Luther, ibid., 403, 410 sqq.
[3] Resol., 340.   [4] Circ. Disp., 581.

of repentance which we are now considering, the interest actually centered in a leading question, which no less pressed for decision in the doctrines of baptism and the Lord's Supper, namely, the question how the blessings of salvation objectively offered in absolution, as well as in the other sacraments mentioned, can be truly passed over to and into the individual. Hence, to the proposition that the absolution of the confessor, in order to become effective, must be received in faith, Luther expressly adds the remark, that this is likewise the case in baptism and the Lord's Supper and in all the sacraments. It is impossible, he affirms, for a sacrament to be savingly administered to a person unless he already believes, and by virtue of his faith is justified and worthy (in opposition to the "heretical" theory that the sacraments bestow justifying grace upon every one who interposes no obstacle). Luther repeats the axiom : " *Not the sacrament, but faith in the sacrament justifies ;*" that is, he who comes to the sacrament must believe that he there receives grace.[1] It naturally follows that what Luther says of absolution may be applied also to baptism and the Lord's Supper, namely, that the reality of the *offer* of the bessings of salvation, or, in other words, the reality of the offer of grace, is not determined by the existence of faith.

Upon the basis of the principle that the appropriation of that which is offered in the sacrament cannot be effected without faith, Luther now defines more carefully, in opposition to the prevailing theory, his view of the difference between the sacraments of the *Old* and those of the *New Testament*, between the forgiveness of sins under the old covenant and under the new, between priesthood there and here. The difference had been held to be,[2] that grace was there only announced, whereas under the new covenant it was actually imparted by the priest to men, in so far as they merely interpose no obstacle. This Luther no longer concedes, inasmuch as he claims that even under the old covenant the reception of grace was conditioned, as now, upon something in the individual, namely, his faith. Yet he, too, marks a difference between the economy of the Old Testament and that of the New. In matters touching the forgiveness of sin and justification, he denies in general that those figures and sacraments of the Jewish

---

[1] Resol., 201, 263.—Circ. Disp., 581.—Briefe, i, 154 sq.

[2] As Eck in his Obelisci still maintained.

priesthood with which it was customary to compare the sacraments of the New Testament really had anything to do with the latter. It was the peculiarity of those ancient ordinances, on the contrary, that they had in view only the justification and purifications of the flesh, carnal washings and justifications in food, drink, etc. (cf. Heb. ix. and x.), which were merely figures of the *one* baptism and the *one* spiritual justification of faith. He acknowledges further, indeed, that in connection with these there was also for the pious under the Old Testament dispensation an actual forgiveness of sins; as, for example, the sins of David were forgiven through Nathan. But then, he declares, God announced His grace only through special inspiration or through miraculous signs, and the authority to forgive sins was imparted to no one except to such men as, like Nathan, received special commandment from God for its exercise. Under the New Testament, on the contrary, God desires that such announcement and offer be constantly made through the Word of the confessor; yea, the power to forgive sins is now, according to Matt. xviii. 18, committed to every Christian believer.[1]

This claim of Luther, that *faith is necessary for an approach to the sacrament*, was one of the leading subjects of dispute in the controversy with the papal commissary, Cajetan. Luther here again maintained with unswerving steadfastness the proposition, that only faith justifies, that is, that one must believe with certainty in justification, and dare in no wise doubt that he receives grace. But Word and faith must in this case be together; without the Word, no faith would be possible. Thus Luther at Augsburg also maintained: Only the belief (*fides*) of Christ's Word justifies, makes worthy, quickens, prepares, without which all other things are schools of presumption or despair; for the just * * * lives by faith. In vain did the Cardinal demand an immediate recantation, threatening otherwise on account of this one point to condemn all the *Theses* of Luther. The latter declared at Augsburg, and also afterwards in a report to the Elector, in which he justified his course, that he would now and forever refuse to yield at this point.[2]

---

[1] Resol., 198, 202.—Asterisci, 340. Erl. Ed., xx, 192.—For the Roman Catholic doctrine, cf. the theses of Tetzel in his Disput. I, Theses xvii to xxii, Löscher, i, 504 sq.

[2] Löscher, ii, 468 sq.—Briefe, i, 155 sq., 176.

We have now discussed in detail that principle which Luther had come to regard as the most important in the sacrament of penance and the doctrine involved in the latter, and in which the essential peculiarity of his conception of salvation was revealed, namely, the forgiveness of sins and impartation of grace in view of faith alone.

In what relation to this, we must now inquire, stand those *positive human exercises* which the penitent are said to be under obligation to perform, and which, in the traditional teaching and prevailing customs of the Church, were regarded as rendering " satisfaction"? With reference to these Luther, in his *Sermon vom Sacrament der Busse*, retaining the name, declares : " As to satisfaction, it will suffice to say that the best is never to sin [1] and to do all that is good to one's neighbor, be he friend or enemy." [2] It is evident, however, from the entire harmonious development of Luther's doctrine as we have thus far traced it, that this satisfaction, which he here substitutes for the special exercises imposed by a confessor, is no longer in any sense a provision by which one may, after release from guilt, still make restitution or atonement.   These are rather fruits of the new life, borne by the believer after he has already, in his faith, attained to the full forgiveness of his sins.   One's sins, says he in the same discourse, must first be forgiven before good works can be performed. Works do not drive out sin, but the driving out of sin performs good works ; for good works must be performed with a cheerful heart and a good conscience toward God, that is, in the forgiveness of sins.[3]   And this, we know, comes through faith : " The heavenly indulgence is granted to no one on account of works of satisfaction, but only on account of faith in the promise of God." [4]

Before this, indeed, in his *Freiheit des Sermons*, Luther lays down a proposition, which attributes also to works themselves, *i. e.*, those of love, a significance for the attainment of remission of sins.   He there quotes the scriptural declarations : " Love covereth a multitude of sins " (1 Pet. iv. 8 ; Prov. x. 12) ; give alms, and all things will then be " clean or forgiven " (Luke xi. 41) ; " free thyself from thy sins by almsgiving " (Dan. iv. 24). But in the light of the general views which Luther had at that

---

[1] Cf. Sermo de Poenitentia.

[2] Erl. Ed., xx, 191.

[3] Ibid., 181.

[4] Ibid., 183.

time already attained, and had expressed even before the indulgence controversy, we cannot believe that he here really means
to find in the conduct and activity commended the actual ground
of the impartation of forgiveness. We must rather assume that,
in the discussion in which the above expressions occur, he was
not at all attempting to present accurate definitions either of faith
and its significance, separately considered, or of the disposition
and conduct resulting from justifying faith. We must bear in
mind, too, the occasion which led him to make the above declarations. It was in his refutation of Tetzel's position, that he who
purchases indulgence does better than he who gives alms to the
poor, unless the latter be in the utmost possible distress. He is
not, therefore, treating of the comparative value of faith and works,
but of the relation between the value of the purchase of indulgences and that of works of love.[1]

Thus fully and definitely do we find in the writings of Luther
in the present period that doctrine of repentance unfolded which
alone he recognized as in accord with the teachings of the Gospel.
With this in mind, we turn again to the original occasion of
Luther's entire polemic activity, the question concerning indulgences.

In regard to the SIGNIFICANCE AND VALUE OF INDULGENCES, we find
only a substantial repetition of the principles previously announced
by the Reformer. He continues to hold that the Pope understands by that from which he grants immunity in the indulgence
only the penalties imposed by himself. In the *Resolutiones* he
observes, further, that he holds this view not stubbornly, but as
open to dispute, and demands that, not the Pope by his own
authority, but a general council, give final decision in the matter.[2]
He grants, therefore, as we have seen, the validity of an indul-
ence for *this class* of penalties, even without inward contrition or
repentance. But he still, at the same time, maintains that a work
without indulgence is purer than when remitted by indulgence.
In indulgences man always seeks something for himself, whereas
he should do everything for God's sake. We must be upon our
guard, lest the people be led by indulgences to fix their aims, not
upon God, but upon creature good instead, namely, upon the

---

[1] Erl. Ed., xxvii, 16–19.

[2] *Resol.*, 230 sq.

remission of their own punishment.[1] The *Thesis*, that works of love and mercy toward one's fellowmen are better than the purchase of indulgences, Luther was compelled to maintain especially against Prierias and Eck. Even the latter had affirmed that it was only *in extremis*, in the case of the utmost distress, that it was allowable to assist the needy at the expense of at least subordinating the purchase of indulgences.[2] Prierias thought that the denying of alms to the poor might be only a venial, not necessarily a mortal sin; to which Luther replied by inquiring whether the want of love does not always bring with it mortal sin.[3] He comments upon the exception allowed in case of utmost distress, by quoting 1 John iii. 17; " distress," says he, is everywhere where a brother stands in need of anything.[4] Here occur then the utterances concerning the love which hides a multitude of sins, etc. Luther still speaks, indeed, of a use, or benefit, of indulgences; but he very distinctly depicts them also as useful only for indolent Christians; for others they are entirely useless.[5]

Very peculiar prominence was now given to the investigation and discussion of the question, upon what resources the Pope drew when dispensing indulgences. The controversy was centred about the *Theses vii.* and *xcv.*, in which Luther denied that the treasure of the Church, out of which the Pope dispenses indulgences, consists of the merits of Christ and the saints.

Luther makes use of the traditional expression " merits (*merita, Verdienste*) of Christ." But from the very way in which he employs it, it is manifest that he could not acquiesce in the traditional reference of indulgences to the merit of Christ; for he is far from conceiving it as something external, the disposal of which might be committed to the power of a Pope. He includes under the term all that Christ has accomplished and secured for our salvation by His doing, His suffering, and His entire disposition and manner of life; and he even refers it back to the moral perfection found in Christ, and embraces under it the grace and truth that have come by Him. He thus places the " merits of Christ " side by side with His justice, virtue, patience and humility, and

---

[1] Resol., 268.—Resp. ad Prier., 412.   [2] Cf. Asterisci, 360.

[3] Prier. Dialog., Löscher, ii, 28; Luther's Respons., 422.

[4] Erl. Ed., xxvii, 16.

[5] Resol., 272.—Briefe, i, 92.

even uses it as a comprehensive term embracing them all.[1] In a similar way he, at the Leipzig disputation, speaks of the grace and truth which, according to John i. 17, have come by Christ as His " merits." To give grace and truth is to dispense the merits of Christ. He says again : Christ's merits are spirit and life, grace and truth.[2] He even directly calls Christ Himself the true and only treasure of the Church.[3] Accursed now, says he, be the man who does not trust with his whole heart in the treasure of these merits of Christ. And they are dispensed to us in a two-fold sense. In the first place, He is to be to us the embodiment of our assurance of faith, and our righteousness—Christ of God made to us righteousness, having made His righteousness ours, as He has made our sins His own. In the second place, this becomes to us an incitement to do the same, and the works thus done are the "*opera operata*" of the merits of Christ. Augustine refers to both of these when he says that the life of Christ is at the same time a sacrament and an example.[4] It is the former, in so far as Christ justifies us in the spirit without our aid ; it is the latter, in so far as He exhorts us to do the same things in the flesh, and Himself works with us for their accomplishment. In regard to a third method of dispensing this treasure, namely, for the remission of " satisfactions," that is, for indulgences, the ac-ceptance of such a theory is without any foundation, without reason or authority, without scriptural warrant or churchly sanc-tion. By being placed in such a relation to indulgences, the merits of Christ would moreover be depreciated. The latter are not designed to serve the indolent, but, on the contrary, Christ Himself desires us to bear and endure our part. His merits are not intended to furnish us a pillow to rest upon, but rather to arm us and incite us to the works and the endurance of repent-ance.[5] Moreover, indulgences afford nothing at all that is posi-tive, but only allow a neglect of positive effort ; and on this ac-count, if on no other, we cannot, when treating of them, properly speak of the dispensing of a treasure.[6] But, in order to be actually effective, the merits of Christ need neither Pope nor keys. They are, by virtue of their own nature, never idle. They

[1] Resol., 260; justitia, virtus, patientia, humilitas, omnia merita Christi.

[2] Löscher, iii, 453, 775 sq. [3] Resol., 278. [4] Cf. supra, p. 179.

[5] Asterisci, 365.—Resol., 279.—Briefe. i, 179. [6] Briefe, i, 152.

perform, too, without the Pope, their own peculiar work, namely, grace, righteousness, truth, etc., in the spirit of the elect, and also their strange work (*supra : opus alienum*), namely, cross, manifold chastisements, etc., in which the theology of the cross recognizes the most precious treasure.[1]

It is already manifest that the traditional doctrine as to the merits of the saints can no longer be entertained in connection with Luther's view of the condition of man, with his obligations and possible exertions in his own behalf. The entire assumption of " works of supererogation " is already in the *Resolutiones* most positively rejected. It is taught, says he, that the saints have done many things which they were not in duty bound to do, and that they are not themselves rewarded for these works, but the just compensation of the latter has been deposited in the treasury of the Church, whence the indulgences are now derived. Against this he vigorously urges, that no one of the saints ever completely fulfilled the commandments of God in this life, much less performed any superfluous work, and that no one of them can therefore have left anything to be distributed for indulgences. We must always acknowledge ourselves unprofitable servants. Yea, even in their most perfect work, their suffering and death, the saints do no more than it is their duty to do, and, indeed, scarcely do even that. Luther declares that he has not the slightest doubt upon this point, and that he is willing to endure fire and death for this conviction. This position he maintains against Cajetan. He is willing to allow the statement, that the merits of the saints are a treasure for us, only in so far as there exists a " communion of saints," in which every Christian labors for every other, just as one member of the body for every other. But this, he adds, these saints of olden time have already done during their earthly life ; and if they were still to do so, it would be much rather by means of their supplications than a matter committed to the power of the keys. He grants also, in his discussion with Cajetan, that the merits of the saints may be called a treasure in so far as they have been through faith in Christ merged in *His* merits, and have become one with the latter, and thus have now the same effect,—in accordance with the declaration of the apostle, that the believer no longer liveth unto himself, but Christ liveth in him.

[1] Resol., 279, 284.

Yet, in this case, the language is used merely in a figurative sense.[1] But, however much might be granted in this direction, it would ever remain an unbecoming thing to employ such costly merits for the purchase of so trifling a benefit as the remission of punishments. Much rather should the very punishments which the martyrs and saints have endured be regarded as a pattern for our own endurance.[2]

Thus Luther firmly maintained his *Thesis*, that the remission of canonical penalties is accomplished simply by the power of the Pope, and not at all by a dispensation of the merits of Christ and the saints.[3] Eck quoted, in opposition to this, the expression employed by the priest in reference to the penalties and satisfactions imposed: "What I have too lightly imposed, may the bitter sufferings of Christ [not, forsooth, the will of the Pope] supplement." But Luther does not hesitate to express his disapproval even of this formula, declaring that the sufferings of Christ are shamefully depreciated when they are thus hung on as a supplement, or tail, to our own efforts.[4] He found it much more difficult to meet the objection, that the doctrine which represents the treasure of indulgence as consisting of the treasure of the merits of Christ rests upon an express papal deliverance, *i. e.*, the bull *Unigenitus*, of Clement VI. It is there asserted,[5] that Christ has by His blood won a treasure for the Church, which has been entrusted to Peter and his successors for distribution to believers, and which is to be applied to the penitent and confessing for the remission of the temporal penalties of sin. Upon the ground that Luther's thesis thus contradicts an authorized statement of the Church, this became the first chief point in the indictment and discussion at Augsburg (the second being his assertion of the necessity of faith in approach to the sacrament). We shall hereafter observe to what deliverances as to the validity of papal utterances Luther was thus driven. For the present, we shall only note his endeavor, by placing his own private interpretation upon the papal language, to harmonize his view with these official deliverances. In a certain figurative sense he still manages to find room for a designation of the treasure of indulgences

---

[1] Resol., 275 sqq. Briefe, i, 151, 153.   [2] Resol., 278.
[3] Resol., 287.   [4] Asterisci, 356.
[5] Extravagg. Comm., Lib. V., Tit. ix, Cap. ii.

as the treasure of the merits of Christ. The Pope, says he, dispenses indulgences out of the merits of Christ, at least in so far as he does so by means of the keys, which have been won for the Church by the merits of Christ. The " merits of Christ " are in this case to be understood " effectively," *i. e.*, as equivalent to that *which has been effected* by the merits of Christ. He even attempts to derive this interpretation from the very language of the Bull itself, which speaks of an " acquiring " of the treasure. The word *acquisivit*, he declares, shows plainly that the merits of Christ, by which he has acquired the treasure, are something different from the treasure thereby acquired, which is the power of the keys applied by the Popes to indulgences.[1]

The question as to the treasure of the Church from which the indulgences were derived was important enough to furnish appropriate occasion for such careful definitions on the part of Luther. It was not only the value of indulgences (which, of course, depended upon the opinion entertained as to their source) which here became the subject of discussion, but, especially, the proper conception of the power of the Pope and of the Church. And here, again, it was to be considered, not only whether the view as to this treasure which Luther rejected had been finally sanctioned by a papal deliverance, and, consequently, what authority attached to such papal deliverances ; but, especially, whether the Pope himself, as appeared from the deliverance in question, had really received from God full authority to preside over the dispensation of the merits of Christ.

In immediate connection with the questions concerning indulgences stood also, as we have seen, Luther's theses upon PURGATORY. First of all, he now endeavored, in entire harmony with his earlier attempts in the same direction, to define more reliably what is the real condition of souls in purgatory, without, however, even yet attaining results satisfactory to his own mind. The further question also remained, in how far the living can exert any influence upon the condition of the departed.

The place where undischarged penalties were yet to be paid was supposed to be purgatory. But what sort of penalties are these? Luther continued to deny positively that the canonical penances extended to the future life. The penitential canons he

[1] Briefe, i, 152, 153 sq. (Löscher, ii, 466 sqq. Jena, i, 197.)

regarded as on the same plane as the civil laws. They, as well
as the latter, he maintains, lose their authority at the death of
the individual. He cites as a parallel the fact, that it is customary
to exempt the sick from punishment, because the hand of God
has been laid upon them. But then he finds himself unable to
discover any penalties whatever which the soul preserved from
perdition might yet be called upon to endure in the other world.
If I knew of any such, says he, I would not now be disputing and
inquiring about them. He thus candidly acknowledges that the
whole subject is yet obscure to him. Meanwhile, his own view
gradually took shape in the theory, that what the souls of men are
called upon to endure in purgatory is not an atonement, or expiation, instead of actual satisfaction, but that it is designed to assist
in preparing and advancing such souls still farther in their inner
life by means of suffering in a way entirely analogous to the purpose of the spiritual trials appointed for the pious in their earthly
life. The suffering in question consists of hellish distress and
temptation, such as many even during their earthly life are called
upon to endure.[1] But God seeks by these means to lead to more
perfect love. Man is to be thus impelled to present himself entirely to God; he must learn to love the will of God even in such
punishment, and to love it more than he fears the punishment.
Thus Luther develops the thought expressed in *Thesis xvii.:*
It appears to be without proof, that the souls in purgatory are
beyond the state of increasing love.[2] The meaning of *Thesis
xix.* also becomes thus manifest : We are not justified in assuming that the souls in purgatory are certain of their own eternal
happiness. Uncertainty as to their own salvation, however sure
others might be of the salvation of the souls in question, belonged
especially, according to Luther, to such spiritual temptations,
which serve likewise in this world as a discipline of the pious.
With the above train of thought *Thesis xxi.* is also closely connected, which pronounces it uncertain whether all souls will themselves desire to be delivered from purgatory. Luther quotes, in
illustration, Tauler's narrative of a pious woman, who, from love
for the divine will, voluntarily surrendered herself to the punish-

---

[1] Luther here (Resol., 217) appeals to Tauler and then to a certain man
whom he knows to have often suffered unutterable pangs of hell, evidently referring to himself. Cf. supra, p. 58.

[2] Resol., 203–224, 230.

ments of purgatory, and also the desire of a Moses and Paul to endure for their people punishment from God.[1]

In the general discussion, Luther was confronted with such passages as Gal. vi. 10, John ix. 4, and especially Eccl. xi. 3 : " Where the tree falleth, there it shall lie," which were supposed to prove that all progress of the soul after death is excluded. Instead of a positive attempt to reconcile the idea of such progress with the passages cited, he merely replied to these objections, that all such declarations of Scripture would militate as well against the whole idea of purgatory, inasmuch as they leave no place at all for any intermediate condition. If they are not irreconcilable with the general conception of purgatory, neither do they exclude the idea that there may still be a development of good and evil. But in regard to purgatory itself, he still gives the assurance, in opposition to the teaching of the Picards, that its existence appears to him to be perfectly certain.[2] So firmly did he yet cling to the notion of purgatory, while yet attributing to it a significance essentially different from that of the Church, and notwithstanding the fact, that he already had before his eyes scriptural passages the natural interpretation of which, he himself suggests, would apparently nullify the whole conception. We can only, says he, avoid drawing such a conclusion from these passages by asserting that they do not oppose the theory of an intermediate state, inasmuch as they do not treat of the subject. How they can avoid treating of it, he does not further explain.[3]

As to the influence of the living upon the condition of departed fellowchristians, it need scarcely be said that Luther persisted in his opposition to the supposed deliverance of souls from purgatory for a money consideration. On the other hand, he still concedes an influence exerted through the intercession of the Church, but in regard to such as desire to contribute in any way to the release of the departed, he maintains also the position of his *Thesis xxxv.*, that they must themselves be contrite on account of their own sins.[4] In regard to works for the dead in general, he says : " It is ours to work ; it is God's to apply and grant." [5]

We have thus gleaned the most important declarations touching

[1] Asterisci, 348, 353.   [2] Resol., 225 sq.   Asterisci, 346.   Resol., 215.

[3] Resol., 226.   [4] Resol., 258.   [5] Briefe, i, 86.

the way of salvation and its appropriation by the individual soul to which Luther was led during this period by the controversy concerning indulgences.

But our attention has also long since been called to the advance in his relation to the entire ECCLESIASTICISM of the day and to the prevailing doctrine concerning THE CHURCH to which he was impelled by the course of the controversy.

Luther still, indeed, continued to regard the life of those who personally participate in the actual blessing of salvation as a life in the fellowship of the Church, and even as a life originated and sustained through the mediation of the Church as an institution. It is especially, in his conception, the Church in and through which the dispensation of grace is effected. Still more definitely, he attributes the dispensation of the gifts of divine grace to the Pope, re-affirming his own *Theses lxxvii.* and *lxxviii.*, according to which the Pope has much greater things than indulgences to bestow. Prierias had supposed that Luther said this merely in scornful irony ; but the latter justifies the statement by acknowledging that all gifts and offices, or ministries, in the Church are in the hand of the Pope, inasmuch as he ordains, installs, etc.[1] How far the Reformer would at this time yet go in acknowledging a mediation of the Church before God in behalf of the individual, is manifest especially from an utterance in his *Sermon on Maunday Thursday, 1518,* upon the worthy preparation for the sacrament. If any one, says he, be altogether too weak in faith, let him suffer himself to be borne (as the paralytic in Matt. ix.) in the arms of the holy Mother, the Church, that the Lord may at least be induced to regard *her* faith. He should go to the sacrament in faith, either that of the entire Christian Church, or, at least, that of some pious individual Christian of his acquaintance. He should say : " Lord, accept me in the faith of the whole Christian Church, or of this or that man ; for, however it may be with me, I must be obedient to thy Church, which bids me come to the sacrament." No doubt God will accept the obedience rendered to the Church as rendered to Himself ; and it is impossible that any one should perish when thus supported by the faith of the Church, just as a little child is baptized and saved by the merit of the faith of another person.[2]

[1] Asterisci, 368.   Ad Prier., 430.   [2] Erl. Ed., xvii, 62.   Latin, Jena, i, 175 b.

Yet we have also observed how little, at the present stage of Luther's advancement, he regarded the grace of God as dependent upon the power and caprice of the clerical dispenser. It is not the ecclesiastical office, but the divine Word of grace itself, which is for him the real source and the real bearer of salvation. Forgiveness may be announced not only by those in official position, but with equal efficacy also by any plain Christian brother. In the very passage just cited, side by side with the whole Church is placed the pious individual believer, upon whom the weaker Christian may lean for support. It now at length also became perfectly clear, as the danger of expulsion from the fellowship of the external Romish ecclesiastical organization began to threaten him and those who shared his views, how far he was from regarding salvation as dependent upon fellowship with the latter. Already before the middle of July, 1518, he delivered a sermon upon the *Efficacy of Excommunication*, in condemnation of the " tyranny and ignorance " of the papal commissioners.[1] He there discriminates between two forms of *communio fidelium*. The one is the inner and spiritual—one faith, one hope, one love to God ; the other is the outward and bodily—participation in the same sacraments, which are the signs of faith, hope, etc., and also in common intercourse, conversation, and the like. He therefore proceeds to declare that, as no being except God alone can give to a soul participation in such spiritual fellowship, or restore again to it a soul once excluded therefrom, so, likewise, can no creature exclude any man from it, save the man himself by his own sin. Ecclesiastical excommunication deprives only of the external fellowship ; the soul is not thereby given over to the devil, nor deprived of the blessings of the Church. When righteously administered, it is the outward sign that the soul itself has already, by its own sin, forfeited the inner fellowship and given itself over to the devil. When it is administered as an instrument of violent tyranny, it must, indeed, be treated with all due respect, since the power of the Church is the power of Christ ; but in such a case it is sweet to bear, is a noble work of merit, and dare not affright any one from the truth, for the sake of which it has been inflicted upon

---

[1] Sermo de virtute excommunicationis, Löscher, ii, 378 sqq. Cf. Briefe, i, 130 (July 15, 1518), 138. Cf. also passages quoted below from Resol., 291.

him. If but faith, hope and love abide, there abides also for the
excommunicated the inner fellowship above described and participation in all the blessings of the Church.

Luther was now driven to most important conclusions in regard
to the *doctrinal authority* of the Church and the Pope. As, in
discussing the question of penance, the material principle of the
Reformation has already been distinctly presented to us, so now,
gradually indeed, but with the force of inner necessity, the
formal principle also comes into view.

In the introduction to the *Resolutiones*, Luther declares that he
proposes to advance nothing which is not contained, first of all,
in the Sacred Scriptures, and also in the writings of the Church
Fathers and in the papal canons and decretals; but bare, unproved statements of Thomas Aquinas and others he shall count
himself at liberty to accept or reject at his own option. He
fully coincides with Prierias in maintaining that the faith of all
believers must keep itself in harmony with the rule of faith existing in the Romish Church ; for he thanks Christ that He in
the most wonderful manner preserves *one* Church upon earth, that
it has never in any doctrinal definition departed from the true
faith, and that, in defiance of the devil, the Bible and, with it, the
authority of the Church Fathers and interpreters, has remained
undisturbed. The points which he had been led to dispute he
regarded as not yet positively defined by the Church at large ; as,
for example, the principles combated in his thesis declaring
that the Pope neither desires nor is able to remit all penalties,
but only those imposed by himself,—in his conception of the
treasure of the Church, of the influence of the living upon souls
in purgatory, etc. He was not convinced by those who rose up
to oppose his views upon these points, because their arguments
rested, not upon the authorities referred to, but upon mere scholastic opinions. They speak, said he, without a text—not only
without citations from Aristotle, but without even a text from
Scripture, the canons, or the Fathers. He himself, he declares,
is still waiting submissively for a decision by the Church, for the
deliverance of a council. He will be a heretic, should he refuse
to accommodate himself to such a deliverance.[1] In the dedica-

[1] Resol., 184; Jena, i, 195–196. Resp. ad Prier., 407.—Resol., 230–233;
ad Prier., 400.—Asterisci, 334; Briefe, i, 113.—Resp. ad Prier., 427; Briefe, i,
113.

tion of his *Resolutiones* to the Pope, he yet casts himself down in complete humility at the feet of the latter : " Thy voice," says he, " I shall acknowledge as the voice of the Christ speaking in thee." [1]

Yet, in these very *Resolutiones*, he declares that papal decisions are not in themselves sufficient. Final decision touching the questions in dispute is a matter, not for the Pope as such, but for a general council alone. He himself is willing to hear the Pope as Pope, that is, when speaking in the canons, and according to the canons, and when coinciding with a council; but he does not care to hear him when he speaks out of his own head. The relation of a council to the Pope became a subject of special discussion with Prierias, who laid down the propositions : " The Church Universal is practically (*virtualiter*) the Roman Church— the Roman Church, in a representative sense, is the college of cardinals, but practically it is the *pontifex maximus*, who is the head of the Church—the Roman Church is virtually included in the Roman pontifex." To this Luther replied : " I know no Church virtually except in Christ, none in a representative sense except in a council." That the Pope is a man, and, as such, may be deceived and fall into error, he maintained with special emphasis also against Eck. In his *Freiheit des Sermons* he says bluntly : " What the holy father proves from Scripture or reason I accept; the rest I let pass as a pious fancy." [2] He had already said in the *Resolutiones*, when speaking of unjust sentences pronounced upon individuals by the Pope, that they are to be feared and borne, but only as one should likewise bear what the Emperor should impose upon him. He declares still further, in the same connection, that such sentences are to be submitted to, not on account of the Saviour's declaration, " Whatsoever thou shalt bind," etc., but on account of the injunctions, " Agree with thine adversary," etc., and, " Whosoever shall smite thee on thy right cheek, turn to him the other also." Such sentences dare not therefore be approved, and no man is bound by them before God.[3] It was especially the bull of Clement VI. upon indulgences

[1] Briefe, i, 122.

[2] Resol., 231, 248. Prier. dial., 14 sq., 38; Respons. ad Prier., 401. Asterisci, 362. Erl. Ed., xxvii, 21.

[3] Resol., 290 sq. Cf. supra, sermo de virtute excommunicationis.

and the indulgence-treasure that compelled Luther to express his opinion as to the validity of official utterances of the Pope.   To Eck, who quoted this document against him, he replied that he recognized in it, indeed, a " saying " in regard to the treasure of merits as subject to dispensation by means of indulgences : but, he proceeds to say, it is one thing for a Pope to say, and another for him to decree ; and for a Pope to decree, and for a council to approve, are two very far different things.[1]   How gladly Luther would, nevertheless, have avoided the necessity of rejecting such a definite papal utterance is manifest from his attempt in the discussion with Cajetan to interpret in his own sense, if possible, these extravagant claims (cf. *supra*, p. 272).   Yet he does not shrink from asserting, even in the presence of Cajetan, that the Pope there employs Scripture language in an improper and forced way ; that even decretals may contain error ; that the axiom, that the latter are to be heard as the voice of Peter would be heard, is applicable only in case of those which are in harmony with the Holy Scriptures.   He appeals to the maxim of the famous canonist, Panormitanus (Nicolaus de Tudesco, Archbishop of Palermo), that, in matters of faith, every believer stands above the Pope, if he supports his position by better authorities and arguments.[2]

Luther had thus appealed to a council, refusing without such authority to surrender the theses assailed by his opponents.   But it was already to be foreseen that even the utterance of a council, in and of itself, would no longer receive unconditional recognition at his hands.   He had openly asserted, in argument with Prierias, that the Pope, *as well as a council,* may err, as Panormitanus has well shown.[3]   In general, he was never satisfied with bare assertions, but only with such as were supported by reasons (*ratio*). Otherwise, says he, the Church is made an object of ridicule for enemies and heretics ; and it must be remembered that St, Peter requires us to be ready to render an account of that which we believe and hope (1 Pet. iii. 15).[4]

Luther might, in fact, in assailing the infallibility of councils as well as of the Pope, have appealed not only to Panormitanus, but also to various other writers of the first half of the fifteenth

[1] Asterisci, 364.   [2] Briefe, i, 150 sq.

[3] Resp. ad Prier., 401.   [4] Resol., 279. Briefe, i, 113.

century, the time of the great councils and their conflict with the Papacy. But the entire ecclesiastical tendency of the age had for a long time been manifestly impelling toward the acceptance of some such supreme, external human authority for the decision of doctrinal questions; and the adherents of the councils, as against the Papacy, had claimed for the former such decisive authority. Just as decidedly, upon the contrary, was our Reformer impelled by the development of his own convictions and the progress of the controversy to withhold his assent from this theory. It is not to be denied that his utterances upon the subject have at first something of an uncertain, wavering, discordant character. He desires to remain in harmony with the ecclesiastical authorities of the day, and yet he can by no means longer bind himself to them unconditionally or in every instance. But there could no longer be any doubt whither his path was leading him, nor that he would unflinchingly pursue it.

Even upon the question as to what constitutes a sufficient confirmation of a decision of Pope or council, we find as yet no clear definition in the utterances of Luther. Yet here, too, it is already evident enough toward what conclusion his convictions are really bearing him. He criticises in his opponents the absence of proofs from the Church Fathers; but his own expositions, while seeking to remain in harmony with the latter, are not based upon them as the decisive authority. On the contrary, throughout all his discussions with his opponents, he draws positive support only from the Holy Scriptures and from inferences drawn from the saving truth there presented. He thus himself practices the account-rendering which he demands of others. This is his reason (*ratio*). He will not depart from clear testimonies of Holy Scripture on account of a papal, human decretal. The words of Scripture, he declares, are incomparably preferable to all the words of men. However many teachers, yea, though all the holy teachers of the Church, should hold this or that, they would yet all avail nothing against a single passage of Scripture. Apt quotation is here made of Gal. i. 8 : " Though we, or an angel from heaven, preach any other gospel," etc.[1] Inasmuch as Prierias has, in his publication against Luther, presented as fundamental principles the theses touching the Church, as included in the Pope,

---

[1] Briefe, i, 151. Erl. Ed., xxvii, 12.

and her infallibility, the latter, in his reply, proposes also to lay down two fundamental principles : first, the injunction of St. Paul, "Prove all things," and his assertion in Gal. i. 8 ; second, the saying of Augustine, that it is only of the holy canonical Scriptures that he believes that no one of its authors has erred.[1] It is evident from this that Luther no longer considered it impossible that error might be found even in the Church Fathers, although, as he refers his opponents to them, he still confidently assumes that their teaching is, in fact, in harmony with that of the Scriptures.

But what, it may be asked, does Luther mean when he demands that the Pope shall defend his positions by Scripture or *reason ?*[2] He never undertakes to explain the relation between proof from reason and that derived from Scripture. But it is evident, as well from his own manner of adducing proof as from his declarations concerning the perfect infallibility of the Holy Scriptures and the natural incompetency of sinful man to comprehend divine things, that he does not by this language mean an independent activity of the reason parallel with, or even above and against, the Scriptures. He can mean nothing more than a proper, reasonable inference drawn by the human spirit clinging to the Scriptures, submitting to, and enlightened by them. We shall recur to this matter at a later point, and shall then adduce further utterances of Luther in illustration (cf. especially his declaration at the Diet of Worms).

Dauntless and bold, relying with confidence upon his own fundamental principles, Luther, in his *Resolutiones*, replied to the taunting inquiry, whether he supposed that he alone was right in his opinions, though opposing Thomas and all others : "I am not alone, but the truth is with me."[3] He boldly declares when confronting Eck : "Let Christ be with me and His Word, and I will not fear what even the whole world may do to me."[4]

When the Pope, at length, actually placed under the ban all who refused to acknowledge his dispensation of indulgences out of the treasure of the merits of Christ and the saints, Luther, upon the ground that the Pope ranks, not above, but beneath the majesty of the Scriptures and the truth, made formal appeal to a

[1] Respons. ad Prier., 390.   [2] Erl. Ed., xxvii, 21 sq.—Cf. supra, p. 279.

[3] Resol., 282.   [4] Aster., 361 sq.

council.[1] It is evident, however, from what has been already said, that he can by no means have taken this step with the idea of pledging himself in advance to adopt every deliverance of such a council. We have observed, too, how calmly he could endure the thought of excommunication. The inner fellowship of which he had spoken would yet remain for him, even though the outward fellowship should be denied to him. Even though the Romish, papal Church should cast him out, he could yet repeat with confidence undisturbed : " I know no Church practically (*virtualiter*) except in Christ."

Meanwhile, independently of these dogmatic questions, there had arisen also in Luther's mind great difficulties in regard to the existing *church government*, to which he had already given candid expression in the *Resolutiones*. He complains of the burden of canonical ordinances (with regard to fasting, etc.), resting upon the once so free but now miserable Church of Christ, and of the tyranny of the heresy-hunters, selecting as its victims such men as a Picus of Mirandola, a Laurentius Valla, a Johann Wesel, etc.[2] He already takes offence, too, at the *temporal power* of the Pope. He wonders who invented the theory of the two swords of Peter, the spiritual and the temporal, by which the Pope has been transformed into a dreadful tyrant instead of an amiable father.[3] He ventures, further, when speaking of the widespread infliction of papal penalties, to recall the time *when the Romish Church had not yet been exalted above others*, at least not above the Greek Church, declaring that such had been the situation up to the time of Gregory the Great.[4]

Together with these difficulties, the urgent necessity for a great reformation of the Church was also confessed. We have already noted Luther's expression of his conviction, that such a reformation would not be possible until the accepted canons and decretals and the scholastic theology and philosophy should be thoroughly repudiated.[5] But such a reformation, he declares, is not a matter for one single man, the Pope, nor even for the many cardinals, but for the entire Christian world—yea, for God alone. The time for this is known alone to Him who has appointed the time for everything.[6]

---

[1] Löscher, ii, 500, 505 sqq. Briefe, i, 193, 198. [2] Resol., 203 sq, 238.
[3] Resol., 297. [4] Resol., 234. [5] Briefe, i, 108. [6] Resol., 301.

3. Doctrines not Directly Involved in the Indulgence Controversy.

FREE WILL—THE WORK OF CHRIST—TWO-FOLD RIGHTEOUSNESS—SACRAMENTS.

The relation in which Luther had now placed himself toward the Pope and the Romish Church determined largely the progress of the conflict between himself and his opponents.   Before entering upon the study of the latter, however, we must briefly notice some utterances of the Reformer, originating in this period, and bearing upon points of doctrine which did not enter directly into the discussions of the indulgence controversy, but which were yet closely connected with the general conception of Christian saving truth developed during the conflict, and in which, for the most part, may be noted a similar advance in his views and doctrinal attainments.

In the Disputation into which he was led at the Augustinian monastery at Heidelberg (April 26, 1518), he had very positively re-asserted his doctrine of the FREE WILL, or rather the *unfree will*, as he had presented it, with appeal to Augustine, before the outbreak of the indulgence controversy.[1]   The free will, he declares, has since the fall a real capacity only for evil.   Yea, he now asserts, even *in the state of innocence* the will had no actual, active ability to hold to the good, to say nothing of making progress in it.   The writer of the *Sententiae* maintains, indeed, that man received at the creation a good will, and help from above, by virtue of which he might have remained steadfast; but this contradicts the principle of Augustine : " he had received the ability to do if he should will, but he had not the will to do what he was able to do " (*aeceperat posse si vellet, sed non habuit velle quo posset*).   But this very will to do what one is able to do is the active ability in question.[2]   The opponents in the indulgence controversy did not as yet bring these questions into the discussion.

The *Theses* upon the treasure of the merits of Christ have

---

[1] Löscher, ii, 43 sqq.   Jena, i, 27 sqq.

[2] Theses xiv. and xv.   Cf. supra, p. 199.   In regard to the sense in which the language is employed in Augustine (de corrept. et grat., 11), cf. Dieckhoff, in his Theol. Zeitschrift, 1860, p. 723.

brought into view CHRIST'S WORK OF SALVATION completed once for all. Discriminating between *sacramentum* and *exemplum* (*supra*, p. 270), he lays all the stress, in the first instance, upon the former, as that through which the peculiar economy of salvation is produced. He thus more fully explains the term : " Sacrament—or significant sign—that Christ by His temporal, bodily sufferings has conquered and crucified our spiritual and eternal sufferings of the old man." In this he sees the old nature of man in so far slain that the might of sin is thus broken for us, and we arise with Christ to new life ; but also, at the same time, in so far as the transgressions which rise in accusation against us are swallowed up in Christ.[1] The experience of becoming one with Christ, in which all the sins of the believer become Christ's and are swallowed up in Him, while, on the other hand, all the possessions and merits of Christ become the property of the believer, is described in the *Resolutiones*[2] in a peculiarly full and vivid manner.

That it is everywhere only faith that justifies, was maintained by Luther throughout the controversy of this period, especially, as above described, when treating of the doctrine of the sacrament. But in the year 1518 he developed in the most comprehensive way his doctrine of JUSTIFICATION AND RIGHTEOUSNESS in two Latin sermons yet in our possession, treating "*Of the Three-fold*" and "*Of the Two-fold Righteousness*."[3] The one (kind of) righteousness, as he proceeds to explain, is that which is merely apparent. This is the righteousness of a man who is upright only before men, and refrains from the offences which are punished by the civil government. Such a man secures the temporal blessings promised in the Law, as did many of the kings of Israel, and likewise the Romans, who became lords of the world ; and he will also have less severe punishment to endure in the future life than a gross offender. But such righteous persons, after all, serve only themselves, and not God, and theirs is a righteousness of slaves, not of souls. True righteousness is two-fold. First, is the essential, original righteousness from without, which is the righteousness of Christ? It is imparted in baptism, and continuously appropriated by faith in true repentance. We are, in this case, born of

---

[1] Erl. Ed., xvii, 64. Jen., i, 176 ("saeramentum et mysterium"); sermo de passione Christi, Löscher, ii, 588–591; also, Comm. ad Gal., iii, 442 sq., where reference is made to Rom. iv. 25, as well as to Rom. vi. and Col. iii.

[2] Resol., 260 sq.   [3] Jena, i, 176 b, 181.

God, the entire Christ, with all His possessions, becomes ours, and we ourselves become free from sin. Christ then, as faith increases, drives the old Adam more and more completely out from day to day; for this righteousness is not all at once infused, but it advances from day to day. (It will be observed that Luther still, as at an earlier period, combines in this justification the acceptance of the believer as righteous and the initial inward renewal.) To this true righteousness belongs, secondly, our own actual righteousness, which must proceed from that essential righteousness which is from without. This consists of devotion to good works, mortification of the flesh, love to our neighbor, humility and the fear of God. The first righteousness becomes complete in the second, since the latter is constantly laboring for the mortification of the old Adam. But the first, meanwhile, always remains in the believer, whereas the second is subject to interruption.

But, in regard to the life and conduct of the believer, with which this second form of righteousness has to do, Luther now, on the other hand, declares that so much of evil ever yet clings to it from the old, selfish, natural heart of man, that every one of his own works still in itself remains sin. He thus explained the matter at the Heidelberg disputation by means of various theses in paradoxical form, in which he again appeals especially, as in the disputation of 1516, to Eccl vii. 20: "There is not a just man upon earth that doeth good and sinneth not." He then gave a peculiar exposition of this passage,[1] in which he also has recourse to leading propositions of the earlier disputation. With a reference to Rom. vii., he says: Willing the good and not-willing it are always commingled even in the pious, but there is everywhere as much sin as not-willing: but God accepts the acts of the pious as good, since He pardons us, accepts Christ for us, and allows our conduct to be supplemented out of Christ's fullness. He then speaks of "merits" of believers, in so far as their works are acceptable, and have worth, in the sight of God. But they are acceptable only in Christ, since he who performs them believes in Him, and they are good only in so far as God Himself is their author. Hence, Luther says in the *Sermon upon the Three-fold Righteousness* that faith is the entire merit—that Christ merited

[1] Op. Ex., E:l., xxi, 251 sqq.

for us—and that it is not the personal acts of the pious man (in his actual righteousness) that merit, but the merit is the essential righteousness from without, and can only be *promoted* by the act of actual righteousness which further mortifies sin. He declares, on the other hand, in the *Heidelberg Thesis vii.*, when speaking of the works of God accomplished in the righteous, that these works of God are not in such a sense merits, as not to be at the same time sin, as asserted in Eccl. vii. 21. Thus again, in every work of the pious, despair and the confidence of faith dwell together in his heart; despair on account of himself and his own work, confidence on account of God and His mercy.[1] It is self-evident that Luther, entertaining such views, must, as we have seen in the *Resolutiones*, reject the traditional doctrine concerning the merit of saints.

The doctrine of the SACRAMENTS became involved in the indulgence controversy in connection with that concerning the sacrament of penance. Luther's fundamental principle here was: Only faith secures the grace of the sacrament. He then at once, as notably in the above-mentioned sermon, *Von der Bereitung zum hochwürdigen Sacrament des Abendmahls*, assures the spiritually distressed that wherever there is but firm faith in the grace to be obtained, *there* is already also the worthy preparation. But faith must now cling to the *Word* of grace, the promise connected with the sacrament. This brings us back again to the essential significance which Luther, in treating of the sacrament, has up to this time attributed, and continues to attribute, to the *Word*. This is constantly represented as the universal means of grace, which, inasmuch as faith in it justifies, saves *wherever* it is dispensed and believed. This dispensation occurs everywhere in the proclamation of the Gospel, and not only in connection with the sacraments. Luther, in the *Resolutiones*, supports this position by appealing to the fact that the Church does not allow mass to be held without the reading of the Gospel, and adds: God lays more stress upon the Gospel than upon the mass, because man can have no spiritual life without the Gospel, though he may without the mass; for man liveth by every word that proceedeth out of the mouth of God, as the Lord Himself further teaches in John vi.[2] In the light of this, we may the better understand

[1] Briefe, i, 90.   [2] Resol., 27

the consolation which he, in the *Sermo de virtute excommunica-tionis*, administers to those who are thereby excluded from the external fellowship of the Church, and thus also from the sacraments. We need not dread, he there asserts, even the deprivation of the sacrament of the Eucharist.[1]

These utterances of Luther attest that a peculiar conception of the entire nature and efficacy of the means of grace had already been developed in his mind He himself does not yet realize the profound divergence of this conception from that which held sway in the Church ; nor do his opponents as yet make any intelligent attempt to bring it fully into view.

[1] Löscher, ii, 382.

CHAPTER III.

THE DECISIVE RUPTURE WITH THE AUTHORITY OF THE
ROMAN CHURCH IN THE FURTHER PROGRESS
OF THE CONTROVERSY.

INTRODUCTORY.

PEACE NEGOTIATIONS—LETTER TO THE POPE—CIRCULAR URGING
RESPECT FOR THE ROMAN CATHOLIC CHURCH.

THUS far had the convictions of Luther taken shape in his own
mind, and so definitely had he already publicly declared them,
when the course of events suggested the possibility that he might
even yet be induced to halt in his career. The papal chamber-
lain, Miltitz, now entered into negotiations with him, employing,
instead of the stern and threatening tone of Cajetan, which had
so signally failed to accomplish anything at Augsburg, a soothing
and even friendly manner of address. Miltitz recognized clearly
enough the perils which would attend any violent demonstration
against Luther in Germany. Moreover, it was necessary for the
Pope to act with caution in order not to offend the Elector,
under whose protection Luther was living. It now became again
most plainly manifest how hard it was for Luther to renounce the
prospect of reconciliation with the Pope and the Church of
Rome. Resolutely, boldly, even recklessly, did he maintain his
position, in defiance even of the Pope, when his opponents
attempted to overwhelm him by assaults and threatenings. They
thus but aroused in him most thoroughly the joyous consciousness
of his calling to press right on upon his way against them, and, with
this, a defiant and pugnacious spirit which they could not quell.
With all possible submissiveness to the existing powers, on the
other hand, does he again endeavor to open the way for reconciliation whenever the attitude of his opponents appears to make
possible the attainment of a result so much desired. It is not to

be denied that his course was somewhat wavering. His own heart was still wavering between the old submission to the papal authority and power and the most distressing convictions concerning the real character of the leaders of the Church, which forced themselves even more resistlessly upon him. In view of the facts in the case, cowardice is, however, the very last charge which could be brought against him.

He promised Miltitz[1] to allow the controversy to rest, provided the opposite party should also remain silent. He agreed, also, to write to his Holiness, the Pope, expressing humble submission, and confessing that he had been too severe and passionate in the controversy, although contending only for the honor of the Church. Further still, he agreed to publish a note in which he should openly make the same confession and exhort all to obey the Church of Rome and to interpret his own writings as intended to advance her honor. He, accordingly, wrote a letter to the Pope under date of March 3, 1519.[2] With the most profound humility, he writes : " Necessity compels me, the off-scouring of humanity and dust of the earth, to speak to your Blessedness and exalted Majesty." He laments that what he had undertaken for the honor of the Romish Church had been interpreted in just the contrary way. He acknowledges that the authority of the Roman Church is beyond all else ; there is nothing beyond it in heaven or on earth, save only Jesus Christ, the Lord of all. Although speaking thus, we know that the mind of Luther was at this very time seriously agitated by the question, whether the Pope was not really Antichrist himself, or the apostle of Antichrist. This suspicion was aroused, as he is said to have secretly confessed to Spalatin, by the study of the papal decretals in which he was then engaged.[3] With all the humility of his tone, he, even in this letter itself, most positively declines to recall anything that he has written. This, he declares, would be impossible, if for no other reason, on account of the wide circulation which the matters in dispute had already attained in Germany, and would only tend to bring yet more shame and reproach upon the Roman Church. Very far, indeed, from a recantation is the

[1] Cf. Luther's own report, Briefe, **i, 207** sqq.

[2] Ibid., 233 sqq.

[3] Ibid., 239 (March 13).

" note " which he published in pursuance of the above agreement. It was entitled : "*Instruction upon Certain Points*," which were attributed to him and charged upon him by his adversaries.[1]   In it, he re-asserts the positions formerly taken, or, at least, the suspicions which he has uttered against the prevailing type of doctrine.   Again he grants the existence of purgatory, and also that the souls there imprisoned may be succored by prayer, fasting, etc. ; but, says he, whether their suffering contributes anything toward satisfaction for their shortcomings, or even toward their own improvement, no one clearly knows.   That any one can by indulgences interfere with the judgment of God, he does not believe.   Indulgences are, indeed, to be allowed, but should be regarded as inferior in value to good works.   Good works which do not flow from grace are in vain : God grants, indeed, in view of them temporal reward, but not eternal life.   We must therefore despair of ourselves, and rely only upon grace.   For the Church of Rome, finally, Luther, as he had promised, exhorts all to cherish reverent regard.   But he supports this exhortation only on the ground that Peter and Paul, and many thousand other martyrs, have in this Church shed their blood and overcome hell and the world.   It may be seen from this, says he, that God has had His eye especially upon this Church.   There is no doubt that it " is honored by God above all others."   He expresses the hope that, despite all the charges which may rightfully be brought against the Church of the day, no one would sever his connection with it ; but the only argument adduced for such fidelity is the general duty of love and harmony.   Out of regard for these, men should refrain from resisting papal enactments.   In conclusion, he declares that the learned may be allowed to fight out the problem as to how far the power of the papal throne extends ; it has nothing to do with the eternal happiness of the souls of men. Christ has not founded His Church upon external power or temporal things, but upon inward love, humility and harmony.

If these were the utmost concessions which Luther felt himself at that time authorized to make, we can no longer wonder at the mighty step in advance which he took immediately afterwards, when challenged anew to the conflict.

[1] Erl. Ed., xxiv, 1-9.

1. Controversy with Eck.

PAPAL SUPREMACY—THE COMMUNION OF SAINTS—SECULAR GOVERN-
MENT—AUTHORITY IN MATTERS OF FAITH AND DOCTRINE.

Eck, who had invited Luther's colleague, Carlstadt, to a disputation at Leipzig, during the course of the latter presented also
thirteen theses against Luther. Of these, the last was by far the
most important in relation to the further development of the
controversy and the confirmation of Luther in the views already
attained.[1] It denies the charge that the Church of Rome had
not already before the time of Pope Sylvester stood above all
others. In connection with this, we at once recall the statement
of Luther in his *Resolutiones*, according to which the Church of
Rome, as late at least as in the time of Gregory I., was not
superior to the Greek Church.[2] Luther had meanwhile not
referred again to the subject. He regarded it, therefore, as an
evidence of malicious design, that Eck should now endeavor to
drag it into the controversy. In the introduction to the disputation which followed, he asserted that, if Eck had not urged him,
he would, out of reverence for the Pope and the Church of
Rome, gladly have left this question alone as an unnecessary and
peculiarly odious one.[3] We see, however, the ordering of a
higher Power in the fact that Luther, while at the beginning of
the conflict allowed to neglect this question for the study of the
fundamental theory of salvation, was now compelled to reach
definite conclusions in regard to it, and to proclaim them publicly to the world. Before the disputation, Luther prepared his
Resolutio super propositione xiii. de potestate Papae."[4] The
disputation at Leipzig lasted from June 27 to July 16.[5] During
this time, on the festival of Peter and Paul, Luther preached a
sermon, which immediately appeared in print.[6] After the disputation, Luther published *Resolutiones Lipsianae*, etc.

---

[1] Luther calls it the *twelfth*. Briefe, i, 254, 261, 262.

[2] Cf. supra, p. 283.   [3] Löscher, iii, 124, 330.

[4] Cf. Briefe, i, 282. It is generally supposed that this *Resolutio* was not
printed until after the disputation, but what else can the "little printed book"
have been which Luther, as Eck declares (Löscher, 336), already referred to
during the disputation?

[5] Acta, etc., Löscher, iii, 292 sqq.   [6] Erl. Ed., xv, 396 sqq.

The place of prominence, in this discussion with Eck, was given to the question above stated in regard to the Church of Rome. We shall, therefore, here give our attention first to that subject, after which a few other points will be brought to our notice. In this connection, we must examine also Luther's first publication against Emser, *Ad aegocerotem Emserianum responsio*, composed in August, which is of interest to us chiefly on account of its utterances in regard to ecclesiastical and papal power. Finally, among the writings of the period which prepared the way for the Leipzig disputation, special notice must be taken of a letter of Luther *To the Minorites at Jüterbog*,[1] some of whom had brought charge against him before the bishop of Brandenburg on the ground of false teaching. The conflict thus precipitated was continued after the disputation, Eck having espoused the cause of the monks. In a positive way, Luther at this time developed the fundamental doctrine of salvation in immediate connection with the Scriptures, in his smaller *Commentary upon the Epistle to the Galatians* (his most important exegetical work since his *First Exposition of the Psalms*, which he himself never published), which was under press already in May.[2]

We have quoted Eck's *Thesis* upon *Die Hoheit der Römischen Kirche*. Luther proposed in antithesis: " That the Roman Church is superior to all others is attested by utterly valueless decretals of Roman pontiffs, issued within the last four hundred years, against which stand the approved histories of eleven hundred years, the text of divine Scripture, and that of all the decrees of the most holy Nicene Council." In his *Resolutio* upon this *Thesis*, Luther remarks : The reader will observe that the dispute between Eck and himself relates not so much to the real matter in hand itself as to its ground and origin ; for he himself does not deny the primacy of the Pope, but only the force of the arguments which are commonly adduced in its support. It will be remembered that, in his letter to the Pope, he had distinctly acknowledged the Roman Church to be above all others. It is very apparent, indeed, that with the different conception of the ground and origin of the Church's exaltation, the conception of that exaltation itself and the rights involved becomes also an essentially different one. We cannot, therefore,

[1] Briefe, i, 264 sqq.   [2] Ibid., 280.

fail to recognize the great dogmatic significance of the discussions upon which Luther now enters, even when they appear to be confined entirely to the domain of history. The real issue at stake may be very briefly stated. It was nothing less than the DIVINE RIGHT OF THE PAPAL PRIMACY. Luther himself, in the *Resolutio* before us, touches distinctly upon this idea of divine right (*jus divinum*).

First of all, we shall endeavor to note the objections which Luther raises against the theory of his antagonists touching the origin of the divine right, which objections will be found to lie equally against the divine right itself. We must then inquire what right even he would still accord to the Papacy?

In order to prove that the arguments of his opponents were not tenable, he first examined the utterances of Christ to which they made appeal, especially Matt. xvi. 18, 19,[1] in which the Lord assigns to Peter the keys of the kingdom of heaven. But, says Luther, He at that time only promised them, and did not actually commit them to him; and when He afterwards (John xx. 22, 23) commits them, it is not only to Peter, but to all the apostles. Even the saying of Matt. xvi., he declares, was originally spoken, as the fathers, Jerome, Origen, etc., rightly observe, not only to Peter, but to the disciples in general; for Peter there spoke as the representative of them all, since, if they had not all answered through him, they would not have been disciples at all : the answer of Christ must therefore have been intended also for them. Still further, Peter here comes into view not at all as Peter, but only as the one to whom the Father reveals— as a hearer of the revealing Word of the Father : the keys are therefore given by Jesus, not to Peter—not to flesh and blood— but to the hearers of the Father's revelation. Hence it follows, that they are not given to any single man as such, but only to the Church : for we can never be certain, in regard to any single man, that he has the revelation of the Father—yea, no single man remains steadfast and secure in his confession, as even Peter wavered. But it is *the Church*, of whose fidelity we need have no fear, since it is the body of Christ, living in the same Spirit as Christ Himself. The Church is the Peter who understands the revelation and receives the keys. Thus, also, the Creed plainly

[1] Resol. sup. propos. xiii., Löscher, iii, 127–139.

declares: " I believe in a holy Church, the communion of saints "—not, as some fancy; I believe the holy Church is a prelate, or—some other invention of their own. The whole world confesses that the holy Catholic Church is nothing else than the *communion of saints*. This article in the Creed was in ancient times not recited with the others, as Rufinus has shown, but it was doubtless originally a gloss declaring that the Catholic Church is the communion of saints, and this was in the course of time taken up into the text. Such an insertion was necessary, and most desirable, on account of such as in our day would rather call the Church anything else than the communion of saints.

Such is the connection in which Luther is now led to present this as his definition of the nature of Church. The substance of the conception has, indeed, already appeared plainly enough in his previous utterances in relation to ecclesiastical fellowship, abso‧lution, excommunication, etc. His utterances at this time, in connection with the exegesis of Matt. xvi. 18, 19, did really, as he maintained, harmonize with explanations given by teachers of the ancient Church. But the definite and thoroughgoing emphasis laid upon this conception of the Church was new, and peculiar to himself.

He appeals also to Matt. xviii. 17, 18, declaring that Christ is there speaking of the whole Church when He says : " Whatsoever ye shall bind," etc. The passage in Matt. xvi., he affirms, is to be interpreted in harmony with this, and it is therefore clear that the keys have been given to the Church.

Inasmuch, then, as the keys do not belong to any single person, but to the Church and the " communion," it must be granted that the priest does not administer the keys of the Church by virtue of any right of his own (*suo jure*), but by virtue of a min‐istry (*ministerio*), he being a minister of the Church.

No more readily can Luther see in the " rock " upon which Christ proposes to build His Church the single personality of Peter. He here again has recourse to the ancient teachers of the Church. Like them, he discusses in detail and critically, as against the interpretation of the Romanists, only the conception of the " rock," while accepting without further investigation the remaining words of the passage, " built upon," etc., in the tradi‐tionally received sense and scope. As in the writings of the ancients, so in those of Luther, we find two parallel interpretations of this " rock." In the *Resolutio upon Thesis xiii.*, he maintains that the Church is built upon the *faith* which Peter in the name of the whole Church confessed. It is, therefore, the Church, or the *faith* there asserted by Peter, against which " the gates of hell shall not prevail, whereas against the person of Peter even the damsel who kept the door was able to prevail, leading him to deny Christ." At the Leipzig disputation also Luther insisted that by the rock we are to understand faith, and the faith, moreover, which is common to all churches and referred to in Paul's words : " One faith, one baptism." [1] Luther, then, in the course of the disputation, impelled by Eck's appeal to Augustine, who recognized Peter as the rock, introduces also another interpretation, which Augustine himself had more than once employed, namely, that the rock is the *object of faith*, Christ Himself. In support of this, he quotes 1 Cor. iii. 11 and 1 Pet. ii. 6, where Christ is represented as the only foundation and the living corner-stone.[2] Soon after the disputation, in a writing entitled *Contra malignum Eccii judicium*, he appeals also to the fact that the name, Rock, is elsewhere in the New Testament applied only to Christ.[3]

Not to Peter himself, therefore, but to the Church, that is, to the congregation (*Gemeinde*), have the keys been given. By it they are entrusted to the priests and to the Pope. As a further proof that Christ originally intended to grant them to the Church, Luther argues that otherwise the words could at best be applied to *Peter only*, so that the keys would then not only have come with Peter, but must also go with him again, for Jesus said nothing there about any successor of Peter. He inquires still further : Who then may be supposed to actually hold the keys in the Roman Church itself ? Does the Pope, when he is elected, bring the keys with him ? Then he would be Pope already before his election. But if he does not bring them with him, from whom does he receive them ? Through an angel from heaven, perhaps ? Or not, rather, from the Church ? Again, to whom does he leave them when he dies ? Does he, perhaps, take them with him ? If not, to whom else does he leave them than to the Church, from whom he received them ? It is only by acknowledging this, he maintains, that it is possible to withstand the error of the Donatists, who hold that a wicked bishop is no longer a

---

[1] Löscher, iii, 352.   [2] Ibid., 358, 369.   [3] Ibid., 860.

bishop at all.   If the impartation of the keys were in the power of the Pope alone, and not in that of the whole Church, then all Popes must, like Peter in the case before us, have the revelation of the Father, and be holy and no more flesh and blood, for otherwise they would then be no longer Popes nor possessors of the keys, since the latter are granted only to those who hear the heavenly Father.   We maintain, on the other hand, that the Gospel here refers to the communion of saints, which is the Church.   The Church may now entrust the keys to a worthy, or even to an unworthy, person.   She *ought*, indeed, to entrust them only to those who are worthy, but she does not always know who is worthy in the sight of God ; and even an ungodly man may be a servant of the holy and true Church.

The principal passage brought into the discussion, after Matt. xvi., was John xxi. 15–17 : " Lovest thou me?   Feed my sheep."[1] Those who from this infer the supremacy of the Pope over the entire Church are confronted by Luther, first of all, with the historical fact, that no one of the other apostles was sent out by Peter, each one having his own field assigned to him, Peter himself, according to Gal. ii., being sent only to those of the circumcision, as Paul to the uncircumcised.   Not all the Saviour's sheep were, therefore, entrusted to Peter, as Jesus is not, indeed, there speaking of them all.   Luther then proceeds to explain what it was that Jesus wished to accomplish by His command to " feed " the sheep.   It was not especially intended to be a commandment to the sheep to be submissive, for we might then logically infer that, inasmuch as Christ entrusted the feeding to Peter only on condition of his exercising love, if a shepherd should in any case not love, we would no longer be under any obligation to obey him—and who then should make us perfectly sure of the shepherd's love?   The commandment is much rather to be understood as an exhortation of the shepherd himself to the exercise of love and to a proper feeding of the sheep.   It is not the power to exercise the office which is conveyed in these words, but the duty of loving and teaching was thus impressed upon one who already has the power (as had Peter by virtue of his calling as an apostle).   Would the Popes, exclaims Luther, only at

[1] Cf. Resol. sup. prop , xiii., Löscher, iii, 136 sqq.; also Leipz. Disput., Löscher, iii, 386 sq.

length apply the words in this sense to themselves—the Popes, not one of whom has understood this feeding !

To this interpretation of the utterances of Christ in question, especially to that of Matt. xvi., Luther afterwards adhered.[1] As to the " Rock " upon which Christ would build His Church, he firmly maintains : " Upon the rock—not which thou art—but upon the confession of faith which makes thee a rock, and upon the preaching of this, I will build my Church : the Church is nowhere save where is found this rock, *i. e.*, this confession and faith, which Peter and the other disciples hold." [2] In the sermon preached at Leipzig he explained, however, how he would have this utterance of Christ presented to the common people.[3] It is not necessary, he says, for a plain man to dispute much about the power of St. Peter or of the Pope ; it is of much more moment that he should know how to make use of them for his own spiritual welfare. In this spirit, he then urges that the keys were given to Peter only as representing the Christian Church, and they are given to us for the comforting of our consciences, which ought in faith to lay hold upon the words of absolution. He who believes these words of forgiveness will highly esteem the power of the priest.

We now turn to notice the evidence upon the question of the papal supremacy which Luther gleaned in a thorough examination of *historical* sources. We are at first led back to the history of apostolic times. As against the supposition of a primacy of St. Peter handed down through the succession of Popes, he appeals, as we have already seen, to the fact that the other apostles labored with independent and equal authority upon their own territory,[4] as seen, notably, in the case of St. Paul. Christ Himself, he declares,[5] never conceded a primacy to any one of His disciples, although there was a strife among them for the ascendency even up to the close of His earthly life. They afterwards took the lesson well to heart, and Peter himself and John renounced all claim to a primacy when they made James the

---

[1] Cf., e. g., upon Matt. xvi., the sermon in the House Postils, Erl. Ed., vi, 283 sqq., and xxviii, 395 ; upon Jn. xxi, the Church Postils, Erl. Ed., x, 232 sqq.

[2] Erl. Ed., vi, 291 sq. [3] Ibid., xv, 401 sqq.

[4] Cf. also Briefe, i, 206 ; omnes apostoli fuerunt aequales.

[5] Löscher, iii, 192.

Younger bishop of Jerusalem.   Paul also, in Gal. ii., mentions
James before Paul among the pillars of the Church.   But soon
after the time of the apostles the struggle began again.   In the
disputation against Eck, he returns again and again to 1 Cor. iii.
22 (whether Paul, or Apollos, or Cephas).   He quotes also 1 Cor.
xii. 28, where " governments " are mentioned at the end of the
list and the primacy of Peter not at all.   The field assigned to
Paul, according to Gal. ii. 8, 9, was a wider one than that committed to Peter.   Neither Matthias (Acts i. 26) nor Paul and
Barnabas (Acts xiii. 2) were ordained by Peter.   In Rev. xxi. 14
no difference is made among the twelve foundations of the walls,
which represent the twelve apostles.[1]   So far as the original relations among the leading churches of early Christendom are concerned, he declares that, according to the testimony of Scripture,
if any one of them was the chief and the mother of them all, it
could be only that at Jerusalem.[2]

More than a thousand years, declares Luther in his *Thesis*,
after the time of the apostles continue to bear testimony against
that primacy which depends entirely for its support upon the
papal decretals of the last four hundred years.   He then proceeds
to explain at some length.   He knows very well, he acknowledges
at the start, that some will make very merry over this statement,
inasmuch as the Popes had been claiming such supremacy for
already more than a thousand years.   But the earlier decretals
had never been accepted by the Church at large.   They would
not have been even known at all in Germany had it not been for
the collection of decretals adopted only since the time of Gregory
IX.   It was only since the days of this Gregory, of Boniface and
Clement V., that the decretals of the Pope have been so widely
distributed, and the Roman tyranny thereby confirmed.[3]   It is
chiefly upon the Nicene Council that Luther relies for proof that
the Papacy did not originally possess the power claimed for it.
This council did not, he argues, derive its authority, in the first
instance, from the Pope.   The Pope did not there, either in person or by a substitute, occupy the chief place.   The council did
not concede to him the primacy, but only the care of the Italian
churches, and even this not by divine right, but only in deference

[1] Löscher, iii, 334, 341, 390 sq., 402.   [2] Ibid., 195, 335.
[3] Briefe, i, 262 sq.   Löscher, iii, 179.

to ancient tradition.[1]   From the time preceding the Council of
Nice, he cites Cyprian, whose language is also quoted by Augustine, as saying : " Let no bishop make himself a bishop of bishops
and endeavor to coerce the others into obedience to himself." [2]
He then mentions Jerome, Athanasius, Augustine, and even
Gregory the Great, declaring that he should have to pronounce
them all heretics, if he desired to maintain the sole dominion of
the Papacy.[3]   But it is to the *Eastern Church* especially that he
constantly calls attention, inquiring whether it is really supposed
that there are no Christians there : and yet their bishops are
neither appointed nor confirmed by the Pope ! Eck had the
effrontery to reply, that the Greeks had been for a long time such
schismatics and such great heretics that only very few, or none at
all of them, except some who submit to Rome, could be saved.
To this Luther responded, that he would never in the world approve any schism ; but that it was shameless impertinence to cast
out of the Church, and attempt to drive out of heaven, so many
thousands of martyrs and saints as had lived in the Greek Church
within the past fourteen hundred years.[4]   It is only we Germans,
he declares, who, since the kingdom has extended to us, have
done all that we could to bolster up the Roman pontificate ; and,
for our punishment, we must now endure these terrible tormentors,
the Popes.[5]

We are now prepared to inquire : What is for Luther the TOTAL
RESULT of all these discussions?   He had not in his *Thesis*, as he
himself said, given full expression to the conviction to which he
had then already been led, *i. e.*, that the Church of Rome did
not even at that day stand above all others, and that the history
of the Church down to his own day testified against Eck.[6]   But
the chief point in the case is the nature of the justification which,
in accordance with the above facts, may yet be accorded for the
existence of the papal primacy ; and this brings to view the great
dogmatic significance of the entire question.   The result, briefly
stated, is nothing less than the *absolute denial of the divine right
of this primacy*.   It is important that we, first of all, clearly

---

[1] Löscher, iii, 166, 195 sq.   Briefe, i, 206, 219.   [2] Ibid., 186, 335.

[3] Ibid., 335, 146.   Briefe, i, 219, 263, 269.

[4] Ibid., 143, 179, 193, 348, 351, 356.

[5] Briefe, i, 263.   [6] Ibid.

understand what is meant by the claim that the Papacy exists by virtue of divine right. The term is not intended to include such ordinances as have been established in the varying course of historical development, and which have therefore divine sanction as belonging to the existing order, but which may themselves be changed again by men in an orderly way. The idea of the term has occasionally, even in modern times, been thus imperfectly grasped, and the difference between human right sanctioned by God and actual divine right has, in consequence, been overlooked, and the very conception of divine right lost sight of. Luther, on the other hand, defines most clearly : " Divine right remains unalterable in its own character (*stat fixum in eo quod est*) ; whatever is of divine right is immutable, and cannot for any reason yield to anything else, nor endure an authority above its own, without injury of the divine right." He therefore infers that either all the ancient teachers of the Church and all the churches which have not at all times and everywhere acknowledged the supremacy of the Pope are to be condemned, and, where such acknowledgment has not been or is not now made, there can be no true churches nor Christianity ; or, upon the other hand, such supremacy is not a matter of divine right. He even maintains that, for the purposes of this argument, even a single case in which the Papacy had failed of recognition upon acknowledged territory of the Church would be sufficient, since divine right must be universally observed (*rotunde observari*). In no century, nor moment, nor case, dare that which is of divine right undergo change or interruption. Even the Pope could not under any circumstances surrender any part of his supremacy. At this point Luther then refers to certain letters of Gregory I. addressed to the Byzantine Emperor and the Patriarchs, in which the former protests that the primacy was offered to the Pope by the Council of Chalcedon, but never accepted. The canonists claim now, says Luther, that the exercise of this office was after that time abandoned by custom. He thanks them for the admission ; for it logically follows that the primacy in question rests not upon the Word of the Gospel and divine right, but upon human law and custom. Otherwise, Gregory would have committed a mortal sin in breaking a divine law.[1]

---

[1] Briefe, i, 206, 269, 299. Löscher, iii, 197, 146.

Yet Luther, while denying to Peter supreme authority, or a *primatus potestatis*, still concedes to him a certain *precedency in honor (primatus honoris)*. No one, says he in the *Elucidation of Thesis xiii.*, denies this. Peter is the foremost member of the Church, the head of the college of the apostles, just as also, in an assembly of bishops or princes, one must occupy the first place; but it does not follow that the others are therefore in subjection to such a one, nor that he is authorized to issue commands to them. Just so we find that the Popes have always been honored as successors of Peter. This is repeated at the disputation, and in the subsequent justification of his course on that occasion before the Elector he says: " I give St. Peter a primacy of honor, not of authority; for he had no power either to make, or send, or control, or ordain the apostles.[1] We remind the reader also of the special honor which, in his *Unterricht, etc.*, he confesses God to have given to the Roman Church.

But Luther's historical studies led him yet further than merely to the above Theses upon the papal authority. He found, through the writings of Jerome, that not only are the apostles and bishops all equal, but also that *elders* and *bishops* are, of divine right, the same.[1] It was only after the lapse of some time, and the establishment of positive laws, that one elder was exalted above another, and even then the elders in Alexandria elected one of their own number to the position. Bishops are greater than elders, not by a reality of divine appointment, but by a custom of the Church.[2]

Luther even already discusses, with appeal to Cyprian, the *right of congregations* in the appointment of bishops. He quotes from a letter of Cyprian (No. lxviii, according to the usual notation) certain utterances concerning the authority of congregations to elect their own bishops. In many other letters also, he asserts, Cyprian speaks of the voice of the people in the election of a bishop, and of the judgment of neighboring bishops as to the one who should be elected, which method he (Cyprian) confidently declares to be that divinely appointed. Luther now proposes to leave it to others to compare with this custom the course demanded by Rome, in which not only are the people excluded,

---

[1] Löscher, iii, 157, 408.—Briefe, i, 318.

[2] Ibid., 182–187, 198.—Briefe, i, 269.

but not even an election by the priests is regarded sufficient. He does not consider it necessary to show how much better it would be if this " divine custom " were still observed, whereas now so many poor priests hold office and are forced upon the people. He can only lament that this hallowed ancient custom, " in thorough conformity with divine right," is now, in the interest of the more recent custom, declared heretical. Whatever may be thought of the new custom, only let no one imagine that the Roman Pontifex holds authority by *divine* right.[1]

This entire demonstration against the divine right of the papal supremacy carries us back again to Luther's fundamental conception of the *nature of the Church*. He held the Church, as we have seen, to be nothing else than the " communion of saints," and the rock upon which it rests, faith. He thus recognizes Christendom and a Christian Church wherever he finds faith in Christ, the preaching of Christ, and holiness in Christ. Christianity and the Christian Church are not therefore dependent upon the mediation of the Roman ecclesiastical authority. The Church of Rome has no original superiority to others. Wherever there is faith, there is the same power of the keys, there are all things held in common, there applies the saying of the apostle : "All things are yours, and ye are Christ's." It would be indeed ridiculous, he proceeds to say, if all churches should have in common the same baptism, the same Eucharist, confirmation, the Word of God, the priesthood, the sacraments of penance, extreme unction and marriage, faith, hope, love, grace, death, life, glory—and if this divine power alone were reserved to be imparted to a single church by the Word of God, which is itself common to all. Therefore, wherever the Word of God is preached and believed, *there* is true faith, there the Church, there the bride of Christ, there all things that belong to the bridegroom. Faith carries with it the keys, the sacraments, the power, and everything else.[2] To the unity of the Church, likewise, no vow of obedience to the Roman throne is needful, such as the Popes require of the archbishops at the conferring of the pallium. The unity rests much rather in faith, hope, love, the sacraments, the Word, and whatever else the churches have in common—not

[1] Löscher, iii, 187.
[2] Ibid., 136, 155.

in something which can be attributed only to the single Church of Rome. Christ says, in John xvii. : " That they may be one in us," *i. e.*, one " in us," not " in the Roman Church." [1]

At the very opening of the disputation, Eck presented the following argument for the divine right of the papal primacy : The Church Militant has its type and pattern in the Church Triumphant. In the latter, however, there exists a *monarchy*, organized through ascending ranks until it culminates in the one head, God. It was therefore necessary that Christ, who did only those things which He had seen His Father do, should also establish such an economy on earth. If, now, the Church Militant cannot be without a head, who can this be but the Pope? After the death of a Pope, the cardinals hold the rights (of the office) until a new election. Luther, in reply, fully accepts the definition of the Church Militant as a monarchy, but declares that its head is now already Christ. He appeals to 1 Cor. xv. 25 (where Paul, according to Augustine, is speaking of a kingdom of Christ in the present world), to Matt. xxviii. 20, to Acts ix. 4 (where, as Augustine says, the head speaks for the members), and, with very special emphasis, to 1 Cor. iii. 22, in which passage, he declares, Paul refuses to acknowledge any head whatever, save Christ.[2] In the canons, Luther found the papal supremacy supported by that of Moses and Aaron in the Old Testament, which was claimed as a type. To this he replies,[3] that, in the first place, this, if at all applicable, would prove that not one, but two, must stand at the head ; and, in the second place, it is not the Pope who is prefigured in the high-priest of the Old Testament, but, as the Epistle to the Hebrews most clearly proves, only Christ. When Emser makes use of the same argument, he tells him [4] that he is not willing to go back and take Old Testament figures instead of New Testament truth. Here, he declares, rules the Spirit, who no longer needs those shadows of the olden time. In a letter previously written to the Elector, he asserts that Christ has committed His eternal priesthood to no other, not even to Peter, and it were better to say that Peter had received, not a priesthood, but only a service (ministry) of the priesthood, as also his fellow apostles : for the apostles, as sinners, had nothing to offer.[5]

---

[1] Löscher, iii, 166.   [2] Ibid., 331 sqq.   [3] Ibid., 160.
[4] Ibid., 680.   [5] Briefe, i, 178.

In concluding his *Resolutio upon Thesis xiii.*, Luther expresses a doubt whether the Christian faith itself could allow any other head of the Church Universal on earth except Christ : and he then, in noting the relations between priest and bishop and Pope, finally argues, that, as in cases of death, or in the last extremity, the priest has the authority of a bishop over the confessing soul, it follows, that neither does the Pope stand above the bishops, nor a bishop above the elders, by divine right ; for the divine right is unalterable in life and in death.[1]

The question inevitably forces itself already upon us : What conception did Luther still entertain of an ecclesiastical "power" (*Gewalt*) ? This question he has not as yet thoroughly discussed. It has, however, long been evident that he could by no means longer recognize within the Church of Christ the existence or exercise of any such power as his opponents maintained, *i. e.*, a dominion, and a competency to make arbitrary enactments. He had long since affirmed that, in the administration of the keys, only the reconciling, pardoning grace of God should be dispensed, and that the exercise of the power of the keys must be a ministry —the rendering of a service. It is thus that he, in discussing the command of Christ to Peter (John xxi.), interprets the "feeding" as essentially a dispensing of the Gospel message. Thus, too, in the Leipzig disputation, he points to the fact that Paul, in describing the body of the Church, mentions the "governments" almost last in the list, and after apostles, prophets and teachers. In the same spirit, he afterwards, in his publication against Emser, says that the latter will no doubt charge that he has left no power nor supremacy (*majoritas*) at all in the Church ; but he does not care, indeed, to deny the charge, since Christ has said : Let him that will be greater be your servant ; in the Church the power is not, as in the world, a power of reigning, but a service, a power of serving.[2] Governing, the *gubernatio*, had at any rate for Luther, in comparison with the actual feeding, only a subordinate significance in the Church. It might even be asked, whether and in how far, according to his view, the former should, or could, still find any place. In no case whatever could he longer regard participation in the blessings of salvation as de-

[1] Löscher, iii, 197 sq.
[2] Ibid., 691.

pendent upon submission to a definite church government, to the Roman or any other hierarchy.

Beneath all the principles thus developed lies already, in clear and complete form, that *conception of the Church* which may from this time forward be designated as the *churchly-reformatory*. The Church is essentially a communion of saints, resting upon faith in Christ. The relation which faith and holiness are to be regarded as holding to one another is determined in accordance with Luther's early teaching concerning the significance of faith. Luther presupposes, however, as self-evident, that the faith of the individual rests upon preaching (cf. *supra*, " where the Word is preached "), upon the Word objectively presented. In this communion, the blessings of salvation are now perpetually enjoyed, and, in the administration of the means of grace, dispensed, chiefly the forgiveness of sins by virtue of the power of the keys. For this purpose, shepherds and priests are appointed. In this is found the entire essential function and authority belonging, of divine right, to the latter; if they exercise any outward power, or are made subject to one another, that is, at least, no matter of divine right. Even as compared with the members of the congregation at large, no peculiar higher character is to be attributed to them. The keys which they administer are given to them for the sake of that faith in which the congregation itself lives, yea, are even derived from the congregation to be placed in their hands.

In his conception of the Church, Luther sees also all the characteristics preserved which, according to universal Christian belief, should belong to her. He maintains them as not dependent upon subjection to Rome and the Roman hierarchy. Thus we can now recognize the true *holiness* of the Church. It rests, as the communion of saints, upon faith in Christ, not upon the rock of the Roman pontificate. To the question here naturally arising, whether the existing churches are then to be regarded as holy and as real churches, we have a reply in the *Commentary upon the Galatians*. Quoting there the saying of Jerome, that not only faultless congregations are to be acknowledged as true churches, but also such as, though assembled in Christ's name, are yet imperfect in virtue, he adds : No one is perfect in this life, but there is a relative perfection in the case of such as daily begin anew and press forward. If there are yet evil persons in the

Church, we must do all in our power to make them better, but we dare not, by a display of ungodly conscientiousness, cause a schism.[1]   It will be observed that Luther does not as yet present that sharper definition, framed in accordance with his own principle, which afterwards appears constantly in his writings, *i. e.*, that the holiness of a Church, existing in connection with its imperfection, is involved already, objectively, on the one hand, in the effectual working of the means of grace committed to it, and, on the other hand, in the faith which, although still imperfect, yet unites with Christ.[2]   The character of *apostolicity* no longer, in Luther's view, depends upon subjection to regularly appointed successors of an apostolic head, nor even to bishops supposed to be by divine right successors of the apostles.   It was his special effort to bring to view a *unity* and *universality* of the Church, not dependent upon the Roman primacy nor upon any outward system of government whatsoever.   How he justified this conception we have already seen.

It was especially the last-mentioned point which claimed his attention in the discussion of certain propositions of Huss in regard to the Church which were brought into the disputation at Leipzig and defended by him against the condemnatory decree of the Council of Constance.   Huss maintained : " There is one holy universal Church, which is the totality (*universitas*) of the predestinated ; the universal holy Church is but one, just as the number of the predestinated is but one." [3]   The correctness and value of these propositions evidently lies, in Luther's opinion, in the fact that they do not make membership in the Church of Christ dependent upon outward ordinances of a worldly character, especially not upon subjection to the Roman primacy, but include all who inwardly belong to Christ as members of one universal Church.   He is brought to speak of them in connection with the discussion of the other proposition : " It is necessary to salvation to believe that the Roman Church is superior to all others," and with his protest against the condemnation of the Eastern Christians who do not acknowledge such a primacy.   He does not

---

[1] Comm. ad Gal., Erl., iii, 151 sq.

[2] Cf. the amended edition of the Commentary of the year 1523 ; quia verbum et baptismum habent, recte ecclesiae vocantur.

[3] Löscher, iii, 360, 371.

draw from the definition in question the inference on account of
which, as Eck declared,[1] the Council had rejected the propositions, *i. e.*, that those guilty of mortal sin do not belong to the
Church at all.   Upon the question of the relation of such to the
" communion of saints " he does not enter at all in his controversy with Eck.   Nor does he lay any stress upon the eternal
decree of election, or predestination, in distinction from the
present faith of the members of the Church and their present
holiness.   The significance which he attached to these propositions appears very clearly from certain expressions in the explanation of Psalms xv. (xvi.), published in the year 1521.[2]   He
there maintains that the Church is not bound to Rome, being
nothing else than the spiritual assembly of believers, wherever
they may live on earth, without distinction of person, place or
time ; and he is thus led to quote again the proposition of Huss :
" *Ecclesia universalis praedestinatorum universitas.*"   He undertook, says he, the defence of this definition at Leipzig, and now
again openly before heaven and earth affirms his adherence to it.

By Luther's entire conception of the nature of the Church and
of ecclesiastical authority, moreover, every extension of that
authority, as divinely ordained, to the sphere of *temporal, political*
or *civil* life was excluded.   In his *Resolutio* touching papal
primacy he cites an explanation of 1 Pet. ii. 13 (submit yourselves to every ordinance of man) by Pope Innocent III., in
which the latter maintains that subjection is not here imposed
upon the priests, and that, although the Emperor has supremacy
in temporal affairs, it extends only to such as receive temporal
things from him.   Luther, on the contrary, claims for the Emperor supremacy over all, even the clergy, and this, too, by *divine*
right, according to the words of Peter.   Yet the Emperor may
also by divine right, inasmuch as only human ordinances are involved, voluntarily relinquish something of his supremacy ; and the
Emperors have, accordingly, allowed some liberties to ecclesiastical persons and things, but may also recall these at pleasure.   In
the view of Luther, it would, in the present state of affairs among
the clergy, be really better if these exemptions were canceled and
the offenders held in restraint by fear of the temporal sword.[3]

---

[1] Löscher, iii, 380.   [2] Operat. in Psalm., Op. Ex., Erl., xv, 357–359.
[3] Löscher, iii, 167–177.

By the *divine right of the Emperor* Luther means here, as his further utterances show, the right of temporal dominion in general.   He proceeds to say : We are subject to the *potestas mundana*, according to Rom. xiii. 1 and Tit. iii. 1 ; in temporal affairs, duties and burdens, the Popes and clergy are subject to the civil authorities.   By *spiritual things*, as distinguished from temporal, he understands the administration of the Word and sacraments ; in these the Pope is above all.   He rejects the employment of the two great lights in the heavens to represent the papal and the civil authority, the latter being the less of the two.   The sun is much rather, he declares, an image of Christ ; the moon, of the Church ; the sky, of the apostles ; and the stars, of the saints : the imperial power has no place in the picture, as it has nothing to do with the Church.   We thus already find in Luther, along with the rejection of an ecclesiastical power modeled after that of the world, a clear recognition and acknowledgment of the divine right of the civil and political order as such.

If dominion over all were to be attributed to the Pope, Luther could foresee, as a result, nothing else than the undisputed sway of Anti-Christ (*Anti-christenthum*).   He was familiar, it is true, with the papal utterance which claimed that the Lord had entrusted to Peter the two-fold right of earthly and heavenly dominion.[1]   But he pronounces this " the most impious blasphemy."   He exclaims : " And we have all along been dreaming of the good state of the Church, and have not recognized Antichrist in the midst of the temple !"   In reality, the suspicion which we have heard him secretly express to Spalatin in regard to a papal Anti-christendom stood in intimate connection with his most profound conviction of the Lordship of Christ and the nature of His Church.

In the midst of the controversy, Luther had asserted that the question at issue was not so much the supremacy of the Roman Church, in itself considered, as the ground and origin of such supremacy.   We can now understand why the inquiry as to the " ground and origin " had such decisive significance for him.   He was investigating the divine right, and, with this, the entire essential character of that supremacy.

But how could Luther yet *continue to acknowledge a supremacy*

[1] Löscher, iii, 1507 .

of Rome? How could he, not only grant the "primacy of honor," but declare in general terms that the Roman Church is above all others?[1] How could he, while so zealously opposing the conditioning of the fellowship of salvation in the world at large upon subjection to Rome, yet, at the same time, so readily concede the supremacy of that Church at least over Western Christianity?[2] He has himself, in the *Resolutio*, presented the actual grounds upon which, according to his view, a papal primacy may be justified; whereas it was not until afterwards that he prepared the refutation of the arguments offered by his opponents which we have above reviewed. He presents the grounds upon which such primacy may be defended, as follows:[3] (1) The will of God is of itself a sufficient justification, and this may be inferred from the fact of the actual existence of the Roman monarchy; for the Pope could never without the will of God have attained such dominion. (2) If it is our duty, according to Christ's command, to agree with our adversary and with him who would compel us to take a thousand steps, much more should we yield to the Pope. His precedency is something of far too little importance to justify any one in disturbing merely on its account unity, love and humility. We dare not break the unity of the Church in order to escape from the temporal, earthly supremacy of the Pope, but must endure everything which is not actually sin. (3) We must, in pious submissiveness and godly fear, be content with the princes placed over us by God, whether He have appointed them in grace or whether, in anger on account of our sins, He desires thus to punish us. We should thus submit even to the hated Turk, if it should be God's will to place us under his power.[4] (4) Every power is, according to Rom. xiii., ordained of God, etc. This, says Luther, is the strongest argument of all for the duty of submission to the Pope; for the papal power is beyond question clearly and powerfully established: we dare not, therefore, resist this divine ordinance, and must commit its iniquities to the divine judgment. (5) The command in 1 Pet. ii. 13. By the "ordinance of man," to which we are to be subject, Peter

---

[1] Cf. Briefe, i, 206, 219. Löscher, iii, 173.

[2] Letter to Spatatin in Briefe, i, 263; ego nego Romanam ecclesiam omnibus ecclesiis superiorem, non nego eam nostris, ut nunc regnat, superiorem.

[3] Löscher, iii, 124–126.   [4] Cf. also Briefe, i, 236.

here means the government established by the will of man. The papal power has also been established by human decree, and is thus confirmed by an ordinance of God (*ordinante Deo roborata*). (6) To the above must be added the consent of all believers who to-day live under the dominion of the Pope; for, since the power in question is a temporal thing, and of far less significance than the unity of believers, it would be a shameful offence, for the sake of this temporal thing, to lightly esteem the consent of so many believers and thus deny Christ. If Christ be but with us, we must with Him and His followers retain, in every rank of society, whatever is not opposed to His commandment.

In this characteristic argument of Luther, the chief thing to be remarked in this connection is that he concedes to the papal power which he thus acknowledges merely a temporal character. He takes no account whatever of any such power as extending to the sphere of spiritual things—to the faith of Christians, the treasures of salvation, or salvation itself. We are thus enabled to understand, also, how he can speak, with appeal to Cyprian, of a *divine* right of the congregation in its relation to ecclesiastical power, and yet, at the same time, counsel submission to the present power —yea, tyranny—of the hierarchy. The question, in the latter case, relates to a sphere in which those who are divinely authorized to act may yet be allowed to yield and waive their rights, and in which it may even be their duty to do so. We have a parallel case in the statement already cited, that the civil power, or the Emperor, may allow exemptions in the discharge of the functions devolving upon it by divine right. There is here, then, a sphere in which there may arise a development of historical and positive " right," not " divine," as immediately, originally and absolutely established by God, but yet sanctioned for the time being through the historical ordering of divine providence. Luther's utterances upon this point have a further special interest for us, inasmuch as his view of the authority of the concrete political organization rests upon the same basis.

Luther, in accordance with these principles, very strenuously maintains that no one should of his own accord sever his relations with the Roman ecclesiasticism. He, at this time, denounces particularly the conduct of the Bohemian Brethren, who, as he declared, wantonly separated themselves from the unity of the Church, whereas the highest divine right is love and harmony of spirit.[1] At the Leipzig disputation, he declared that, if all believers in the whole world should agree to accept the bishop of Rome, or of Paris, or of Magdeburg, as the first and supreme pontifex, it would then become our duty, out of reverence for the entire unanimous congregation of believers, to accept such bishop as the supreme monarch. Only, he naively adds, it will never really come to that.[2]

In regard to *external ordinances imposed by the Pope*, such as rules for fasting, etc., he, in the *Commentary upon Galatians*, gives advice as follows : Let him who has the disposition to endure willingly the oppressive burdens do so, just as he would do if he were in the providence of God oppressed by the Turk or any other tyrant. He who is not willing to do this may purchase for himself with money the liberty which ought to have been granted him without money. He who is too poor for this should, to avoid offence, at least publicly observe the commandments, and meanwhile privately seek the advice of some Christian man.[3]

Luther's opinion in regard to all such matters is tersely and clearly expressed in a letter to Spalatin, in which he declares that he counts the papal power, like riches, health and other temporal concerns, among *neutral things ;* and that it greatly displeases him that such strife should be waged about them, and that men should attempt to employ in their support the Word of God, which teaches us to despise such things.[4]

In connection with the above argument for the papal primacy, it was maintained that the Orientals were not to be urged to subjection to such authority. In a similar spirit, with the exhortation to observe ecclesiastical ordinances was combined an exception of those cases in which their observance might involve a neglect of one's immediate duties toward God, his neighbor or his own wife. To the exhortation itself he adds, in his *Commentary upon Galatians*, the remark, that he refers only to those commandments whose observance will not interfere with the requirements of necessity or charity : commandments of the latter class may be broken without the purchase of indulgence or any qualms of con-

---

[1] Briefe, i, 298.   Löscher, iii, 386.   Comm. ad Gal., Erl., iii, 458.

[2] Löscher, iii, 335.

[3] Comm. ad Gal., iii, 242 sq.   [4] Briefe, i, 264.

science.[1] His argument left room, also, for the quite supposable case, that the Pope might, by the imposition of requirements not merely "neutral," but contrary to divine law, and by an insufferable oppression of the consciences of believers, compel the latter, despite all their humility, love and desire for harmony, to assert their independence. It was not long until Luther recognized such occasions as amply justifying the conduct of the Bohemian Brethren.[2] It was, moreover, already taken for granted, as Luther had asserted in his *Theses*, that when any one was excluded by the Pope from the external fellowship of the Church on account of the true faith and the divine Word, he might endure his punishment with a cheerful conscience.

Amid all the above discussions touching the papal primacy, we must regard as the most important element in the position of Luther his conviction that the *Pope and the hierarchical power in general do not belong to the essential structure nor to the fundamental divinely-appointed ordinances of the Church*, to say nothing of the claim that upon them rests the Church itself. The latter is for Luther essentially, as we have seen, a communion of saints, resting upon faith and upon the objectively-presented divine realities upon which faith lays hold. In so far as he recognizes the ecclesiastical power at all, he concedes it supremacy only in the sphere of external things.

But whence now, according to Luther's conception, is faith itself to derive divine truth? Who has the right to decide what is really God's will and divine revelation? Not only did this inquiry for the *authorities in matters of faith and doctrine* stand in close connection with the entire question as to the nature of the Church, but Luther was, in the controversy over the Roman primacy, driven directly to the most significant utterances in regard to this very point, since it became necessary for him to define with great accuracy his attitude toward the Church authorities appealed to by his adversaries. Hence, there now appears in the reformatory development of Luther, simultaneously with the decisive declarations touching the Roman ecclesiasticism and the nature of the Church, also, and particularly, the announcement

[1] In the later, revised edition the entire exhortation is omitted.

[2] The passage in the Comm. ad Gal., iii, 458, expressing disapproval of their course, is also omitted in the revised edition.

of the *formal principle* of a truly Christian Church. The most significant fact, however, in the discussions of this period, is that Luther was now led to express himself, not only in regard to the supreme authority of the Pope, but also, with great definiteness and logical consistency, in regard to that of a council as well. That he should be compelled to take this position, and had indeed already done so, was a necessary consequence of the convictions which he had already publicly maintained. But that he should now bear such positive and reckless testimony in this direction was a result of Eck's right artful urgency at the disputation.

Against the binding authority of the papal decretals Luther now declares himself everywhere with the greatest freedom. There is no longer any trace of that shrinking from direct contradiction of the latter which was still so plainly visible in his discussion of the treasure of indulgences with Cajetan. It had been banished entirely by his thorough investigation of the documents themselves. Without any hesitancy, he asserts in his *Resolutio* that they present, for the most part, untenable, unproved, and even offensive and wicked propositions. We have already heard him denounce the " blasphemy " found in a papal utterance. Although he acknowledges Pope Leo as a holy man, he yet ventures to say in reference to a declaration of the latter: A human experience has here befallen the holy man.[1]

Even those *ancient teachers* of the Church whom he most highly venerates he yet does not hesitate to contradict when they appear to him to depart from scriptural teaching or to misapply scriptural passages. He deals thus, for example, with Augustine and St. Bernhard. Yea, he declares at Leipzig, he would, upon the basis of an apostolic word, enter the lists alone against all the Fathers by virtue of a divine right.[2] At about this time, Luther, in dispute with the Leipzig professor, Hieronymus Düngersheim, gives adequate explanation of his relation to the Fathers. Eck and Düngersheim, he asserts, are accustomed to understand the words of Scripture in accordance with the words of the Fathers; but he proposes, with all reverence for the latter, to follow up the streams to the fountain: even the Fathers themselves would much rather lead us to the Scriptures than to themselves. He by no means wishes to bring the charge of heresy against the

[1] Löscher, iii, 141.   [2] Ibid., 341, 358.

Fathers, but he does mean to affirm that they, especially when opposing heretics, apply many passages of Scripture wrongfully ; that they err ; and even that they do violence to the Scriptures. In reference to all the utterances of the Fathers, he declares that, however strong they may be in their advocacy of any doctrine whatsoever, he yet does not hold anything to be true because it is their view ; he does not suffer himself to be deprived of the liberty given him by the apostolic admonition : " Prove all things ; hold fast that which is good." [1]

But what shall be said now when the representatives of the Church Universal, when *Councils*, have spoken? Eck, at Leipzig, appealed, in opposition to Luther's views concerning the Papacy, to the fact that the *Theses* of Wickliffe and Huss, according to which faith in the Roman supremacy is not a condition of salvation, Peter not the head of the Catholic Church, and a single ruler for the Church not necessary, had been condemned by the Church. It here became at once apparent that it was even yet not an easy thing for Luther to absolutely reject such decisions, which had been accepted as utterances of the entire Church. We have, indeed, at an earlier period, heard him appealing to the assertion of Panormitanus, that even a council may err. But now he was challenged to assert that a council has actually erred and done a wrong, and that in a most highly important case. He at once affirms plainly, that there are among the articles of Huss and the Bohemians condemned at Constance some which are thoroughly Christian and evangelical, such as the one treating of the Church Universal (cf. *supra*, p. 265), and that they were unrighteously condemned at the instigation of ungodly sycophants.[2] He persists, without the least wavering, in the defence of the condemned articles, and afterwards specifies four which have been unjustly stigmatized, viz. : the two above cited concerning the Church ; thirdly, the one which asserts that " the two natures, the divinity and the humanity, are one Christ " ; fourthly, that which maintains that every human action is either good and virtuous, or bad and vicious, and that there is no middle ground.[3] He asserts, further, that the Pope and the inquisitors

---

[1] Briefe, i, 220, 281.   [2] Löscher, iii, 360.

[3] Löscher, iii, 371 ; cf. also Briefe, i, 315. Upon the third proposition, cf. the reply of Eck, Löscher, iii, 380: In Athanasii symbolo aliter legimus ; Deus et homo unus est Christus.

dare not establish any new articles of faith, and that, in general, no article can be forced upon the believing Christian which *goes beyond the Holy Scriptures, which are themselves, in the proper sense, the divine right (non potest cogi ultra sacram scripturam,* etc.). By virtue of divine right we can believe nothing whatsoever which is not proved by the Holy Scriptures or by a clear revelation.[1] He repeatedly quotes, also, the saying of Panormitanus, that the view of a single man is to be preferred to that of the Pope and councils, if it rests upon better authorities and reasons. From this position he does not allow himself to be driven by Eck's response,[2] that it is genuine Bohemianism to profess to understand the Scriptures better than the Popes, councils, doctors, universities, etc., notwithstanding the fact that the Holy Spirit has never left His Church. Meanwhile, however, he does still waver with respect to the error which he was compelled to lay to the charge of the council for its condemnation of propositions so certainly true. He endeavored still to acknowledge the work of the council, in so far as it was at all possible to do so while maintaining the correctness of the condemned propositions. But, as Eck rightly observed, the entire authority of a council is undermined just as soon as any of its separate utterances are proved untenable. He might, Luther first of all declares, out of reverence for the council, pronounce the insertion of these articles in the decree of condemnation to be the work of a deceiver; but he prefers to justify himself from the language of the council itself. The council, he observes, did not describe the articles against which it expressed itself as heretical throughout, but as in part erroneous, in part presumptuous and offensive to pious ears—which last charge may be brought against the truth itself, and was actually employed against Christ. He afterwards refers to this in some of his letters, declaring that it does not worry him that he should be guilty of speaking presumptuously and offensively, provided what he says be only true, and adding: " It has always been the case that truth was presumptuous, biting, seditious and offensive." [3] It is evident enough that Luther has not at all succeeded in preserving the integrity and honor of the council. But he is yet anxious to save it, at least, from the odium of formal error in doctrine or the formal rejection of true doctrine. He

[1] Löscher, iii, 360.   [2] Ibid., 364.   [3] Ibid., 395 sq., 389.

therefore still challenges his opponent to first prove that a council cannot err, and maintains, upon his part, that a council has no authority to establish new articles of faith, nor any divine right. But whilst insisting that a council may err, and that some have already erred, he is at pains to add, " especially in that which is not matter of faith," and concedes that the decisions of councils in that which is not matter of faith are to be by all means accepted (*sunt omni modo amplectenda*).[1]

The question, in how far it is possible for the Church as a whole to err, recurred again at the disputation in the discussion as to indulgences. Eck insisted that the Church cannot err in matters of faith and the soul's salvation, *i. e.*, to the destruction of souls. This Luther conceded. He denied only that indulgences have anything to do with these things, and asserted that at least the *whole Church* had not erred. To the assertion of Eck, that a council cannot err, because it is controlled by the Holy Spirit, he merely adds : that is, in the things in which it is really controlled by the Holy Spirit, namely, in the things of faith. But, at the same time, he refused his assent to the proposition cited from Cyprian touching the clergy, viz., that God does not permit a majority of them to fall into error,—since in the days of Arius the majority of the bishops were in error upon so important an article.[2]

The question as to the *right of the Church*, upon its own authority, to *declare a writing canonical* also arose at the disputation. During the discussion of the subject of purgatory, a quotation was made from the Books of the Maccabees (2 Macc. xii. 45), in which prayer for the dead is commended. Luther did not wish to reject the teaching of the passage, but he pronounced it insufficient as evidence, since the books in question do not belong to the canon. In defence of their canonicity, Eck appealed to Augustine and to the Church at large, which had accepted them. To the authority of Augustine, Luther opposed that of Jerome, and declared that the Church can give to a book no more anthority than it has *in itself* (*non plus autoritatis et firmitatis, quam per se ipsum habeat*).

The discussion in regard to purgatory led, still further, to a

[1] Löscher, iii, 389.

[2] Ibid., 441–450.

consideration of the *authority of councils in the interpretation of Scripture*. Luther maintained that there are, in the entire Scriptures, no such proof-passages for the doctrine of purgatory as would be found tenable in controversy. Eck reminded him that the Council of Florence had found the doctrine taught in the Scriptures. Luther would tolerate such a reading of its own opinions into the Scriptures by a council just as little as the un-authorized reception of a book into the canon of Scripture. He declares : " A council cannot make that to be scriptural which is not of its own nature scriptural." Yet, even after this discussion of purgatory, he again repeats his acknowledgment that a council and the Church do not err in that which is matter of faith.[1]

At the conclusion of the entire disputation at Leipzig, he briefly reiterates his fundamental principle, in the declaration : " With all reverence for the Fathers, I prefer the authority of Scripture, commending my course to the judgment of the future." [2]

It is certainly most interesting to observe the bearing of Luther during the discussion of this question at Leipzig. We cannot fail to be impressed with the fact, that the answer finally given occasions him anxiety, and this, surely, not on account of any fear of his opponents, but because the importance of the decision and the significance of the subject itself had now been revealed to his own soul. Must he not, if accepting seriously the declaration of Panormitanus as to the fallibility of councils as well as of the Pope, despair of all secure identification and attestation of divine truth for the use of the Christian world? And how should he reconcile his view with the promises by which Eck sought to fortify his position, *i. e.*, that Christ would remain always with His Church, and that where two or three should assemble in His name, He would be in their midst? [3]

But from the writings of Luther published immediately after the disputation, it is clearly manifest with what decision and assurance he had then already risen above the doubts which there oppressed him. The more profoundly his soul was there agitated by them, the more certain is it that his present testimony arises from a clear consciousness and the most mature conviction.

In the *Resolutiones* which he prepared and published after the disputation, he first points again to the fact, that the Council of

---

[1] Löscher, iii, 411–432.   [2] Ibid., 482.   [3] Cf. ibid., 381.

Constance had not itself described all of the contested propositions of Huss as heretical.   But that councils in general may err,
and have already often erred, he now affirms without any hesitancy.   Even an African council, he declares, fell with Cyprian
into error, and that in a very important *article of faith, i. e.,* in
the question as to the power of baptism.   He then openly and
solemnly avows : " I believe that I am a Christian theologian,
and that I live in the kingdom of truth ; wherefore, I desire to be
free, and to be so made a captive by the authority of no council,
nor power, nor university, nor pontifex, that I may not confidently confess whatsoever I may see to be true, whether it be
asserted by a Catholic or a heretic, and whether it shall have
been approved or disapproved by any council whatsoever."   He
cites again the saying of Panormitanus, that a single Christian
deserves more confidence than Pope or council, if he have better
proofs, and boldly asks : " Why may not I dare to try whether I
alone may not be able to show better authority than a council?"
He appeals also to the fact that councils have contradicted
one another.[1]

But has the Church, then, if even councils have erred, *been
forsaken by Christ* and His Spirit?   Luther replies : We confess
that the Church has not been deserted by the Spirit of Christ,
but by the Church here is not meant the Pope and cardinals,
nor even a council.[2]   This is a discrimination which was involved
in that conception of the nature of the Church which we have
already found in his previous writings.   But the declaration now
meant, further, that for the Church, or communion of saints in
general, there exists no external tribunal which may, as such,
always be sure of the presence of the divine Spirit, and is therefore competent to bind individual believers absolutely by its
decisions.

What authority, then, the individual believer may and must
prefer even to a council, as supreme and as alone valid, is no
longer a question with Luther.   Every individual should, according to his conviction, *rely upon the Holy Scriptures,* as over against
any decisions of the so-called Universal Church.   We " should
rather believe a layman who has the Scriptures than Pope and
council without the Scriptures." [3]   He refuses, as we have seen,

[1] Löscher, iii, 747–750. Briefe, i, 302, 314 sq. [2] Ibid., 775. [3] Briefe, i, 315.

to concede the establishment of *any articles of faith beyond* those contained in the Scriptures. In the *Resolutiones*, he repeats this declaration, extends it expressly so as to include prescriptions for practical Christian life, and adds, in confirmation, that this is all contained in the Holy Scriptures. He grants, however, the appointment of ceremonies for the external institution of the Church, but in such a sense that they may be disregarded whenever the interests of piety may so require (in opposition to the claim of divine right for such external and really " neutral " forms. Cf. *supra*).[1]

It might be asked, in criticism of these views of the relation between the Scriptures and the Church (as has, in fact, since then been asked time and again), whether the validity of the Scriptures themselves does not rest originally upon the authority of the Church. Luther says that his antagonists hold up to him, as a saying of Augustine, the declaration : " I would not believe the Gospel unless I believed the Church " (*evangelio non crederem, nisi ecclesiae crederem*). The *Resolutiones* furnish also his response.[2] He asserts that the Church, upon the contrary, is begotten of the Gospel, and stands incomparably below it (*creatura est evangelii, incomparabiliter minor ipso*), for we (*i. e.*, those who compose the Church) are begotten, according to the declarations of James and Paul (Jas. i. 18 and 1 Cor. iv. 15), by the Word of truth, *i. e.*, the Gospel. The quotation from Augustine he traces back to its original form : " I would not believe the Gospel unless the authority of the Church had aroused me " (*nisi me ecclesiae commoveret autoritas*). He then attempts, as well he may, to deduce from it the idea, that the authority of the Church was not, after all, the really determining factor in producing Augustine's faith in the Gospel. In the word " *autoritas*," he declares, is not necessarily involved, and so not here, the conception of a determining power, but the expression is used also in speaking of anything attested by worthy or important witnesses ; and Augustine means to say that, as he would not have been brought to faith in the Gospel unless he had been impressed by the remarkably harmonious doctrine of Christianity throughout the whole world, so this same " authority " now impels him to refuse credence to the Manichæans. The chief point in Luther's

---

[1] Löscher, iii, 775.   [2] Ibid., 778–780.

exegesis of this saying of Augustine (which we do not deny to be somewhat forced) is that the latter wished to mention an authority which had really exerted an influence upon him, but which was not, on that account, the power that had won and still perpetually bound him in the depths of his inner nature. That he should here speak of the former, and not the latter, Luther finds explained in the fact that he was striving, not so much to give expression to his own personal faith, as to convince the heretics. He holds up to them, in order that they may believe, the whole Church scattered throughout the world; for by means of his own faith, however strong that might be, he could never have convinced them, if he had not also produced an example, and as strong a one as possible, of the faith of others. We have examined this explanation at such length because it shows us how reluctant Luther was to reject the saying of an Augustine, and because he himself repeats it at a later day. For us, however, the significant point at present is to discover how, in Luther's conception, the faith of the individual in the Gospel, whose off-spring is the Church, is to be actually brought about. Of personal faith he says: " It arises in the heart, not by the authority of any, but by the *sole Spirit of God*, although man may be moved thereto by word and example." He declares that the utterance of Augustine, if it had any other meaning than this, would be fundamentally false, since the *Holy Spirit alone awakens faith in any soul* (*faciat credere quemque*).

With this account of the origin of faith in the Gospel corres-ponds that *freedom in the interpretation of Scripture* which Luther claims for the individual believer, as over against an absolute ec-clesiastical authority. We have already seen that, in his own independent study of the Scriptures, Luther himself no longer hesitates to set aside the exegesis even of Augustine. We here observe, still further, that he now accords especially to philology its rightful place as against such exegesis, and thus does not hesitate to quote a Lyra against an Augustine.[1]

Finally, the free investigations of Luther had already, as we have seen in his attitude toward the Book of the Maccabees, extended to the accepted canon of Scripture. In the above instance, he relied mainly upon criticism of the outward authori-

---

[1] Briefe, i, 220.

ties adduced, although, even then, his reference to the authority which a writing has *in itself* must have directed attention to the *contents* of the document in dispute as requiring examination. In the Leipzig *Resolutiones*, he now ventures to employ purely internal criticism, and that against a book of the New Testament, the *Epistle of James*. This is the first time, as far as we know, that he assailed the authority of this book, upon which the opponents of his doctrine of justification so largely relied. He declares: "The style of that epistle is far beneath apostolic dignity, and by no means to be compared with that of Paul." At the same time, he casts up to his opponents, that they all hang on to this single authority, in opposition to all the rest of the Holy Scriptures; but that it is just their usual way to tear out one piece of the text of Scripture and then turn their horns against all the rest.[1]

What was now the ground of Luther's confidence that, nevertheless, even without that ecclesiastical authority upon which reliance had hitherto been placed, the divine truth and the contents of Scripture might yet be surely and harmoniously ascertained for believers? For this he had no other basis than the Scriptures themselves (in which each separate passage must be interpreted only in its connection with all the rest) and the Holy Spirit, by whose aid the Scriptures are attested to faith and also interpret themselves for every believer. Thus he had already, in January, 1518, written to Spalatin, in order to admonish him to humble, reverent study of the Scriptures in entire and sole dependence upon God: "There is no master of divine words except the very author of the Word itself, just as He says: 'They shall all be taught of God.'" (The language was here used by Luther as presenting the antithesis to confidence in one's own labors.)[2] In sending to the same friend, in February, 1519, an exposition of John vi. 37, he writes: "You see how the words of the Gospel explain themselves, and have their own glosses, so that it is not at all necessary that other and human words be mixed with them."[3]

This development of Luther's fundamental principles is, therefore, the great result of the conflict waged at Leipzig. We must now more briefly present what remains to be noted in the further

---

[1] Löscher, iii, 772.   [2] Briefe, i, 88.   [3] Ibid., i, 228.

unfolding and definition of other doctrinal points during the same period, and especially during the course of the same controversy.

2. FURTHER POINTS OF DOCTRINE DEVELOPED IN THE CONTROVERSY OR IN THE WRITINGS OF THE PERIOD.

PURGATORY—REPENTANCE—FREE WILL—JUSTIFICATION BY FAITH—PREDESTINATION.

The principal subjects of dispute at Leipzig were, in addition to the primacy of the Pope, the treasure of indulgences, repentance, and the penalties inflicted by God, together with the remission of penalty and guilt by the Church.

The existence of a PURGATORY [1] was again willingly conceded by Luther.   In regard to the question, whether progress and merit are there still possible, he replied to the objection of Eck that he could produce no authority for such an apinion, that he was himself seeking for further instruction upon the point, and that he knew really nothing about purgatory except that the souls there are in suffering, and may be assisted by our works and prayers.   But the most important point in this connection was the controversy concerning the scriptural testimony for the doctrine of purgatory itself, since Luther, as already observed, denied that any one of the proof-passages commonly adduced could with certainty be applied to purgatory.   When, in Matt. xii. 32, the Saviour speaks of sins which shall not be forgiven in this world nor in that which is to come, it does not follow that other sins shall be forgiven after this life, *i. e.*, in purgatory, but by the " neither—nor," etc., he may mean simply " not at all."   Ambrose, it is true, interprets Matt. v. 26 as referring to purgatory.   This should not be denied, but it is at least doubtful.   Augustine understands the word as indicating hell, from which there is no release.   In regard to 1 Cor. iii. 15, Luther confesses that the meaning of the apostle is not yet clear to him.   The opinions of interpreters vary greatly, but it seems to him most probable that the fire of the Judgment Day is meant, inasmuch as the day of the Lord is elsewhere spoken of in the context.   Upon Eccl. xi. 3 he again remarks, as in the *Resolutiones upon Indulgences* (*supra*, p. 235), that we

---

[1] Löscher, iii, 411–422.

should much rather infer from this an eternal continuation in the condition entered upon after death. It is now evident that the belief in a purgatory has no longer, to Luther's mind, any basis in Scripture. The Scriptures, however, still appear to him to allow liberty for the acceptance of the doctrine as in harmony with the belief of the Church. But there can be no doubt as to what he would have said to any one who should have refused assent to this article of faith on the ground that it was " beyond the Scriptures."

Of a *treasure of the Church applicable to indulgences* [1] Luther no longer speaks at all. The merits of Christ are the treasure of the Church. These merits are (cf. *supra*, p. 230) spirit and life, grace and truth. But grace and truth are in the hand of no man. A man may, indeed, dispense them *ministerialiter*, but not in indulgences. Indulgences are not a treasure for believers, but the destruction (*vitium*) of a good work. The papal utterances upon the subject are dismissed with the remark, already cited, that the Church is, indeed, not forsaken by the Spirit of Christ, but that by the Church we are not to understand the Pope, etc.

Under the doctrine of REPENTANCE, Eck now proposed, as a topic for discussion, the question, how, on the one hand, the mere *fear of punishment*, with the consequent abhorrence of sin, and, on the other hand, the *love of righteousness*, are related to repentance itself. We long since met with expressions of Luther indicating that repentance must begin with such love. [2] Eck now rejected the thesis : " That the proper beginning of repentance is not abhorrence of sin in reflection upon the gravity of sin and punishment, and that this makes one a still greater sinner." Luther rejected the statement, that repentance begins with this abhorrence of sin before the love of righteousness. What Luther regarded as the important point in this dispute is evident at once from his rejection of the above proposition as *Pelagian*, and, still further, from the statement made in writing to Spalatin : " That repentance begins with the love of righteousness * * * I assert to be necessary * * * since *before grace (which is caritas) there can be no good work*." The question was, whether

---

[1] Luther's Theses X. and XI., Löscher, iii, 213. Disput., ibid., 438 sqq. Resol., ibid., 776.

[2] Cf. supra, pp. 68, 162 sq.

anything which man of himself, independently of the working of grace (and, we may add, under the working of the bare Law), can experience within himself, or do, can have any quality of moral goodness; but that the love of righteousness arises only through the working of grace, both parties agreed. The declarations of Luther at the disputation itself were in entire harmony with the statements here noted. The Law, he there maintained, only increases sin, because the will hates the Law. The latter and the thought of sin and punishment may, indeed, terrify one, but they do not make him penitent. The lost son, in the parable, was converted because the father inwardly drew him and infused a love for the paternal home. The preacher of repentance may exhort and terrify, but this has no result, unless grace move the will. It is only with the entrance of love that repentance begins, *i. e.*, the love of righteousness and the (real) hatred of sin. Of the relation and office of the *faith* which accepts this love-awakening grace, nothing was here said—an omission which has been already explained in connection with earlier utterances of the Reformer. Nor is fear by any means wanting in repentance, according to Luther's conception. On the contrary, with love is combined the *fear of God*, and thus repentance begins with fear in love; but we are to repent, not from fear of punishment, or servile fear, but from the fear of God, or filial fear.[1]

The point last mentioned was only briefly discussed at the close of the disputation, and without developing anything new which requires our notice.

But the *Theses* which the two resolute disputants had prepared for the occasion, and in regard to which Luther afterwards expressed himself at length in his *Resolutiones*, extended to all the most important principles of Luther touching the appropriation of salvation.

Luther had to defend his doctrine, that the life of the believer, since the latter still sins daily, must be a *continual repentance* (*Thesis i.*) ; and, further, that man, *even in doing good, always sins* (*Thesis ii.*). In connection with the first *Thesis*,[2] he now presents the statement of Huss condemned at Constance : "Every act of man is either good or evil." To the second, he

---

[1] Thesis iii, Löscher, iii, 212. Briefe, i, 296. Löscher, iii, 455–461.

[2] Resol., 751.

now adds the proposition :[1] To deny that sin remains in a child after baptism, is to trample Paul and Christ under foot. In the *Resolutiones*, he defends this against the modern theologians who consider the " tinder " (*fomes peccati*) yet remaining after sin, not as sin, but as only infirmity. Sin, he contends, is remitted in baptism, but not in such a way as no longer to exist, but only in such a way that, since its rejection has already begun, it is no more imputed ; sin it still is, in very truth. He pronounces a mere human fancy the doctrine of these theologians, that the sin of the baptized person is forgiven in so far as its formal principle (by which only it is supposed to become sin), namely, the lack of (indwelling) grace, is concerned. The lack of grace continues, he declares, upon the contrary, just in so far as evil lust still remains. But the sin of the " tinder " is sin just as well as any other, inasmuch as it is just as truly contrary to the divine Law. At this point, Luther himself calls attention to the deeper ground of the difference between his general doctrinal conception and that of his opponents. It is the relation in which sin is supposed to stand to the actual personality of the individual still burdened with it. He describes the foundation of the error as lying in the fact, that grace is referred to the nobler element of the soul, as such, and that spirit and flesh are therefore spoken of as two substances, whereas in fact the entire man is spirit and flesh— spirit, in so far as he loves the Law of God, and flesh, in so far as he hates that Law.

Luther had, in his *Seventh Thesis*, in order to maintain justification by grace alone as against any righteousness supposed to inhere in the works of man himself, reiterated his DENIAL OF A FREE WILL, having power to do good or evil—without, however, touching the question of the original state of the human will before the fall. Among his strongest utterances upon this subject are to be accounted those now made in his *Resolutiones, e. g.*, that the free will is merely passive in every act of its own which is called willing (*in omni actu suo qui velle vocatur*) ; for the will is carried along and borne forward by grace. The case may be illustrated by a saw in the hand of a carpenter, which is entirely passive in its relation to him, and contributes nothing to its own motion across the fibres of the wood, but, when thus drawn by

[1] Resol., 758–761. Cf. Comm. ad Gal., Erl., iii, 415 sq.

the carpenter, cuts the wood. We are servants (*servi*), he further declares, at every stage of our life, whether it be the servants of lust or the servants of love; for one or the other of these rules the will.[1]

In Luther's defence of the doctrine of JUSTIFICATION BY FAITH ALONE against Eck, we are especially impressed by his earnestness in insisting that, as justification can come, not from works, but only from faith, so the man who has been justified will certainly do corresponding works, and the faith itself be destroyed by every transgression.   This last assertion Luther had embodied in his *Seventh Thesis*, and in the *Resolutio* he briefly states the argument in its support as follows : " Since faith is righteousness, an offence, or the contrary conception, must be unrighteousness." It is here again manifest how essentially his conception of the righteousness attained by faith embraced, not only the acknowledgment of the individual as righteous, but also inwardly-implanted rightness of character.   From this point he was led to the stricture upon the Epistle of James, already quoted, while commenting upon the declaration of the latter, that faith without works is dead. Luther says, upon the contrary : *"A dead faith is not faith, but opinion."* [2]

Luther has now already reached the conviction, that even Augustine has nowhere expressed the full scriptural truth upon the subject of justification. He says in his *Commentary upon Galatians*,[3] that no one of the church authorities is here satisfactory except Augustine, and *even he* not in all passages, but only when disputing against the Pelagians, who are the enemies of grace.

The *Commentary upon the Epistle to the Galatians* contains, as was to be expected, next to the Leipzig *Theses* and *Resolutiones*, the most important discussions of this period upon justification by faith, the Law, which can produce no good works, etc.   Luther now, here and elsewhere, expressly rejects the entire theory of a *merit of fitness* (*de congruo*), which, it was supposed, might precede the possession of grace.[4]

If we now inquire more particularly what it is that gives efficacy to the faith which, according to Luther, alone justifies, he points

---

[1] Löscher, iii, 213, 768, 771.   [2] Ibid., 213, 772.

[3] Erl., iii, 217.   [4] Ibid., 258 sq. Br., i, 306. Cf. supra, p. 148.

us, indeed, to the free mercy of God, to the Word of grace, to the name of the Saviour, in the confident apprehension of whom faith essentially consists. But he also—without defining more distinctly the relation between the two elements—refers to that inner personal quality, or higher endowment, of the individual, which is a product of his faith. He thus, in his *Commentary*, says directly : Faith justifies, because it procures the spirit of love. Nor are we to think of " justification " here merely in the sense in which it is, by its very nature, one with the implanting of the new moral life-principle, and also with the impartation of the spirit of love ; but in the sense, likewise, of the pardon of guilt. As the ground of the forgiveness of sins in the regenerate, he gives, therefore, along with the faith of the latter, the fact that he is led by the Spirit, and contends and toils in the Spirit against the sins yet remaining ; but, as he declared in the *Resolutiones* against Eck, " the remaining sin, because its expulsion has begun, is not imputed to him who is engaged in its expulsion." [1]

As we have been thus led to the subject of the moral life, we should observe also his utterances concerning the difference between *consilia* and *praecepta*. He everywhere and always assumes that the will and Law of God always, by their very nature, demand that which is perfect, and that every deficiency in the meeting of this demand is in itself sin.[2] There was, therefore, no room for such " counsels " as were supposed to go beyond the requirements of the Law, by the observance of which man might accomplish " works of supererogation." [3]   The monks of Jüterbog had charged him with maintaining that there are no counsels in the Gospel, but that its admonitions are all precepts. This charge, he responds, is a lie ; but the precepts are, nevertheless, superior to the counsels, for the latter are merely means to assist in the fulfilment of the former. Thus, for example, the unmarried may more easily than the married fulfil the commandment : " Thou shalt not lust." [4]   He employs the same illustration afterwards in controversy with Eck, when the latter had espoused the cause of the monks, maintaining then that the highest chastity consists, not in celibacy, but in the refraining from fleshly lust, to which,

[1] Cf. especially Comm. ad Gal., Erl., iii, 429 sq., 421.   Löscher, iii, 759.

[2] Vide, e. g., Resol., Löscher, iii, 766.

[3] Cf. supra, p. 186.   [4] Briefe, i, 267.

however, the former may be helpful.[1] Soon afterward, in view of
the extravagant laudation of the celibate vow, he expresses the
conviction, that in most cases the unmarried state much rather
excites the lusts than helps to control them. But his general
view as to the divine commandments and moral perfection
remained the same.

Finally, not in the controversy with Eck, but in the practical
writings of the Reformer, *i. e.*, in his *Operationes in Psalmos*, we
find a more lengthy presentation of his views upon the questions
touching PREDESTINATION, which were so unavoidably suggested
by his doctrines of the human will and grace.[2]

He here quotes again the saying of the Lombard, that " hope
springs from merits " (meritorious works),[3] and explains the
passage quoted in its support (Rom. v. 3 sq.) by saying that St.
Paul is there speaking, not so much of the attainment of hope
itself, as of that assurance of the heart in the exercise of hope,
which is attained through the endurance of temptations. Faith
and hope must be wrought by God, and are present at the very
beginning of good works and sufferings, but they only become
manifest as the latter progress ; it is only thus that the believer
himself comes to realize that he possesses them. The object of
faith must, therefore, be God Himself solely and alone. Solely
upon Him, and not upon his own merits, must man trust ; and
hence, in temptation he should wait upon the hand of God, who
will act in his behalf, and in the midst of suffering bestow grace
upon him. But, says Luther, further, some weak conscience may
say : What if I cannot hope, and am in consequence filled with
unconquerable despair? To this he would say : Although the
person is himself in this case filled with a sense of despair, yet
this is not truly despair, inasmuch as he does not wish to despair,
and is grieved because he has such a feeling ; but it is a temptation, and one, indeed, of the very gravest kind. He who thus
suffers should plead guilty to the charges of his own conscience,
and persevere in prayer for hope, while, at the same time, submitting, even unto death, to the divine will which has called him
to suffer from such an infirmity. But what, he asks still further,
if one be alarmed at the thought of predestination—that his hope

[1] Contra mal. Ecc. judic., Löscher, iii, 879.
[2] Op. Ex., Erl., xiv, 240–262.   [3] Cf. supra, p. 156 sq.

is all in vain, unless he has been predestinated? This he declares
to be by far the most perilous of all temptations, and his earnest
counsel to those assailed by it is to cast away the thought as displeasing to God. That it does not come from God may be clearly
recognized, because everything that comes from Him impels us
to fulfil His commandments and will, whereas these inquisitive
and anxious cares about predestination are forbidden by God,
who would have all care cast upon Himself. They come from
the devil, who wants to make us forget the divine commandment
that we should believe and hope. If we, on the other hand,
obey the will of God, predestination will find its own fulfilment
without our cares. Furthermore, the devil tries thus to lead us
to the two most heinous offences against God : first, to tempt
God, desiring a certification of our predestination, or a sign from
heaven, whereas we should not wish to know the secrets of God,
but should rejoice in His divine will, which He has commanded
us to obey ; secondly, to become guilty of a self-exaltation similar
to that by which the devil himself fell and brought Adam to his
fall, since the wish to know the divine counsel is nothing else
than the wish to be like God. We should meet such a temptation by hurling upon the devil the thunderbolt of the divine Word,
which declares : " As it is not good to eat much honey, so he
who searches majesty is oppressed by the glory " (Prov. xxv. 27,
Vulg.), and : " Inquire not into things too high for thee, etc., but
think always upon those things which God has commanded thee,"
etc. (Ecclesiasticus iii. 22). Men do not, he adds, in worldly
matters, as, for example, in the building of a house, first stop to
dispute about predestination—whether the house will burn down or
remain standing—but they confidently begin and finish the work.
Yet such things are not commanded by God, whereas we have here
to do with His commandments and works. We should lay to
heart the words of Solomon : " He that observeth the wind shall
not sow, etc. ; as thou knowest not the way of the spirit (wind)
* * *   even so thou knowest not the works of God who mak-
eth all " (Eccl. xi. 4, 5). We dare not do anything, because
God does all things ; and we do not know all, but, as Solomon
there teaches (v. 7) : " Sow thy seed, for thou knowest not whether
shall prosper either this or that," etc., so must we but work the
more because we do not know the future. Luther remarks, in
conclusion, that if God should reveal to us His secret counsels,

we would first tremble, and then become either despisers or despairing; if He had no secret thoughts concerning us, neither would He be feared, nor would there be any room for faith, hope or love upon our part. He then returns again to the relation of hope and " merits." The latter, he says, are a work of the former, and that is a work of the Word of promise. The object of both faith and hope is God, who promises gratuitously, or His given Word of promise. And it is not free will that is active in the work progressing in the heart of man; but that inner motion, or desire, which we call faith, or hope, is a moving, impelling, leading (*motus, raptus, ductus*), of the Word of God, and a divinely-wrought, continual purification and renewal, and is, therefore, only a passivity (*passio*) on the part of man, or such an activity as has the clay in the hand of the potter, which can be moulded according to the design of the latter only when itself in a state of pure passivity.

Hearing these exhortations of Luther to perseverance in faith and hope, as God has commanded, accompanied by the assurance that predestination will then secure its own fulfilment, we might easily infer that they are based upon the conviction that the power thus to persevere is certainly granted to every Christian, and that it depends only upon himself whether he will, by virtue of the power thus granted, obey the commandment, and submit himself to the always ready, moulding hand of God. We might thus be led to the idea, that our salvation cannot appear at all doubtful because dependent upon a counsel of God still hidden from us (that God, upon the contrary, certainly desires it), but only because a different decision is possible on our part. But this Luther does not by any means assert. Much rather does salvation appear to him uncertain because the work and counsel *of God* are concealed from us. It does appear certain to him, indeed, that, for him who fulfils that commandment, the counsel of God will prove to be a counsel of salvation; but by no means that to all to whom that will is proclaimed the power to fulfil it must, by the act of God and in accordance with His counsel, also be granted. On the contrary, whoever makes bold to ask of the Reformer whether he may be sure of such power in his own case receives, not such assurance, but, instead of it, a warning against such questions, and an admonition to strive after hope with prayer and patience. Only this can be here the idea of Luther:

In case God has predestinated any individual to salvation, He
will, by the very impression made upon such an one by such
admonition, and by His own commandment to hope, assist him
onward toward the attainment of salvation. In case the individual in question has not been predestinated, the admonition
will simply be lost upon him.

We shall find the conception here presented of Luther's doctrine of predestination absolutely confirmed in the writings of the
following years. He had, indeed, long since learned from Staupitz to seek comfort, when distressed by the terrors of the absolute
divine decree, not in the conviction that God has truly, so far
as the decision lies in His hands, prepared salvation for all, but
by casting such anxieties entirely aside as displeasing to God.[1]

It may strike us as remarkable, especially in view of what we
know of the method of Staupitz in administering consolation,
that Luther holds before such distressed souls, not so much the
objective content of the Gospel, the crucified Saviour and the
objective pledges of His grace, as the *command* to believe, appearing to warn and urge rather than really to comfort. This
really seems to give countenance to the view that his mode of
conceiving and presenting Gospel truth was then not yet so fully
developed as it afterwards became, nor as had been that of
Staupitz at an earlier period. We recall how the latter had held up
simply the wounds of Christ, because assured that the simple presentation of them would awaken the faith which Luther here
commands men to exercise. But we find also the same method
employed by Luther, not only in the documents above examined,
but also, at about the same time, in his *Sermon von Bereitung zum
Sterben*.[2] He there again declares, that it is the greatest wile of
the devil to lead us to search out the " divine counsel of
secrecy," and seek a sign of the divine will; and he now
points simply and directly to the picture of Christ (and, further,
to that of His saints, who have, in the grace of God, overcome death and sin). In Christ, and His sufferings and death,
we are to see our sins already overcome and death slain. Behold-
ing this, the uncertain predestination is made certain to us. That
we should thus cling to Christ, is the will of the Father. Of all
this, moreover, the outward words spoken by the priest and the

---

[1] Supra, p. 44.   [2] Erl. Ed., xxi, 259 sqq

sacraments are the signs and recorded testimonials. If any man take his stand upon these, and boast of them, his election and predestination will of themselves, without his care and toil, become manifest. We have here already, in outlines clear and definite, the course which Luther was ever afterward accustomed to pursue when dealing with those who were distressed upon the subject of predestination. The only question remaining is, whether he retained also at a later day his belief in a secret counsel of God as to the individuals in whom He would bring to pass such a looking upon Christ.

CHAPTER IV.

PRINCIPAL REFORMATORY WRITINGS AFTER THE RUPTURE WITH THE ROMAN CHURCH AND BEFORE THE DIET AT WORMS.

" I AM compelled, whether I will or no, to become daily more learned, having so many notable teachers diligently pushing me on and keeping me at work." Thus writes Luther in the introduction to his tract, *De captivitate Babylonica*, published in the year 1520, having in mind the steady advance in his views which had been occasioned, and to which he had been driven, and even forced, by the assaults of his opponents since the publication of the *Ninety-five Theses*. But it was the discussion with Eck that had exerted by far the most powerful influence upon the development and public avowal of his convictions. The clear, sure consciousness of his faith had now freed itself entirely from the limitations of the papal authority, or, indeed, of the authority with which any external ecclesiastical court might have sought to restrain him in his course of independent scriptural investigation. We now witness, between the Leipzig Disputation and the Diet at Worms, the unfolding, with extraordinary rapidity and fullness, of the evangelical and reformatory germs imbedded in the formal and material principles which formed the basis of his teaching.

SECTION I. PUBLICATIONS IN THE LATTER PART OF A. D. 1519 AND IN THE EARLY PART OF A. D. 1520, BEARING UPON THE LORD'S SUPPER AND THE CHURCH.

1. *Publications of the Year 1519 upon the Lord's Supper, Christian Communion and Excommunication.*

INNER SIGNIFICANCE OF THE LORD'S SUPPER—THE WORK OF THE SACRAMENT—ITS SIGN—ITS THIRD PART, FAITH—INCITES TO CHRISTIAN LOVE—NO " OPUS OPERATUM "—OUTWARD PARTICIPATION NOT ABSOLUTELY ESSENTIAL.

We shall first carefully examine two publications which appeared before the close of the year 1519, the *Sermon von dem hochwürdigen Sacrament des heiligen wahren Leichnams Christi und von den Brüderschaften,*[1] and the *Sermon vom Bann.*[2] We must especially endeavor to determine accurately the meaning of the former, no one of the more recent interpretations of which appears to me to be entirely correct.

We remark, in the first place, that there is nothing arbitrary in our consideration of the two documents in such close connection, inasmuch as Luther himself has represented them as most intimately related to one another. In the former, he has occasion to touch upon the conception of *excommunicare*, and, in doing so, refers to that which he intends to explain more fully in the latter;[3] and in the very introduction to the latter, he notes the immediate connection of the contents of the two as follows: " Inasmuch as we have heard that the sacrament of the holy human body (*Leichnams*) of Christ is a sign of communion of all saints, it is now necessary also to know what excommunication, or the ban, is; for the especial office of the latter * * * is to forbid the holy sacrament * * * to a Christian guilty of some offence. The word *communio* means fellowship (communion), and hence learned men give this name to the holy sacrament; the word *excommunicatio*, on the other hand, means the suspension (deprivation) of this fellowship, and hence learned men give this name to the ban." The further statements, likewise, with which the second *Sermon* sets out refer back directly to the contents of the first. The real subject of which the first proposes to treat is precisely participation in the fellowship (communion) of the saints and of salvation—which is regarded as the meaning, work and fruit of the sacrament. This is the inner blessing of salvation, which is indicated, and at the same time offered, through the external element of the sacrament. And it is the chief aim of Luther to lead the thought away from the outward to the inward, in opposition to a tendency which rested content with the outward. As he, accordingly, lays special stress upon the peculiar fruit of the sacrament, and, in doing so, empha-

---

[1] Erl. Ed., xxvii, 25 sqq. Cf. Briefe, i, 369.

[2] Ibid., 50 sqq.—Not to be confused with the " Sermo de virtute excommunicationis," 1518.

[3] Ibid., xxvii, 29.

sizes faith as the only necessary condition for its appropriation, he points out that participation in the outward sacramental administration is not even absolutely necessary, but that, upon the other hand, even without the latter, faith may rejoice in possession of the blessings of salvation. It is precisely this idea which furnishes the point of attachment for the underlying thought of the second *Sermon*.

Participation in the communion of saints is here for Luther precisely the same thing as participation in salvation itself; for such communion itself rests in Christ, the Saviour; no one can participate in it except as he is united with Christ; and whoever participates in it enjoys all the blessings which are in Christ. At the same time, it is to be further observed that, whilst the first-named dissertation treats with great fervor and fullness of this union *with Christ*, yet, immediately and repeatedly, with evident and very special interest, reference is made also to the communion, or fellowship, *of the saints who are united with Him :* and, inasmuch as the former relation does not in itself come separately into view unassociated with the latter, so also the peculiar benefit to be derived from that relation is not more accurately defined in its separate character, nor, especially, do we find the forgiveness to be attained in Christ so distinctly emphasized, separately and above all, else as we might have expected. But this, too, is to be explained largely by recalling the peculiar circumstances which led to the preparation of the *Sermon* and to the objects which it has in view. In the first place, we must here again recall its relation to the *Sermon vom Bann*. It might have been naturally supposed that excommunication would at least exclude from the communion of true Christendom, or, in other words, from the communion of saints, as the very name seemed to imply. Against such a view Luther contends in the second *Sermon*, affirming that the communion of love, of intercession and of good works is not necessarily forfeited, and he, therefore, in the first *Sermon*, undertakes to explain wherein exactly this communion, as one indicated by the sacrament (the communion), consists, and upon what it rests. But we note further, as a prominent feature in the present dissertation, that which is expressly suggested in the very title itself, and which modern theologians have in their discussions of the *Sermon* so largely overlooked. We there read : " And upon the Brotherhoods." To these he actually devotes one whole division of the *Sermon*, namely, the last. He had in view, no doubt, especially the " Brotherhood of the Holy Body of Christ " (*corporis Christi*), which was at that time one of the most prominent. To these brotherhoods he would now oppose the true *Christian brotherhood*, the communion of saints, and he would present it as one indicated and wrought by the sacrament of the body of Christ. Luther would have men honor that general Christian brotherhood alone, and not imagine that any one could " secure something special " in the others. While making this distinction, he always, in treating of the true communion, laid special emphasis upon the duty of individual Christians, as they are permitted to lay all their sorrows upon Christ and the congregation of the saints, so also to bear one another's burdens and to minister to one another in love. This he holds up in contrast with those brotherhoods which, with their especial good works, " run in advance " of the rest of Christendom, and would seek advantage and reward for themselves, instead of endeavoring " as free servants to serve the whole congregation of Christendom."

What is the precise objective reality which is offered in the external sacrament as such, does not here as yet become the subject of personal examination upon the part of Luther. He simply follows the mode of presentation prevalent in the Church. His principal object in the publication of this *Sermon* did not require independent investigations or discussions of this point.

By thus pointing out the special motives which led to the preparation of this dissertation, as manifest from its form and contents, we have by no means meant to intimate that the truths and modes of thought which here prevail did not at that time influence and dominate the Reformer in his general work. We shall find them also in some of his other writings of the period. And what an intimate relation we may trace between the deep interest which he now displays in this subject and the very significant crisis which he has now reached in his life and activity. This consoling communion of the saints, of which the believer can be robbed by no utterance of authority, is revealed the more profoundly and richly to his own consciousness, and he discourses upon it the more impressively to his readers, the more certain it becomes that he and they will soon be ejected from the external communion (fellowship) of the Church. But the caution must here be given in advance, that we are not to regard the entire view and doctrine of the Lord's Supper then entertained by him as included and exhausted in these discussions, and then find ourselves compelled, in the writings immediately subsequent, to discover a sudden and unaccountable vaulting to an entirely different position.

But the very significant statements, especially of the first *Sermon*, demand a more detailed presentation.

Luther here discriminates, first of all, in the *Sacrament of the Altar* between the " sacrament, or sign," in and of itself, which must be outward and visible, and the significance, which must be inward and spiritual—in the spirit of man. It is to the exposition of the latter, which he calls also the " work " and the " fruit " of the sacrament, that he chiefly addresses himself in the document before us. His only direct statement concerning the former is that the outward sign consists in the shape and form of the bread and wine, which we are to desire and enjoy—to which he adds a plea for the granting of the cup to the laity.

The " *Import, or Work, of the Sacrament*," he now declares to be the communion of saints, appealing to the name συναξις, or *communio*. The saints are members of Christ and of the Church, and, just in the sacrament, the participant receives a certain sign of an incarnation with Christ and all saints, according to 1 Cor. x. 17. All the spiritual possessions of Christ and His saints are imparted to, and become the common possession of, him who receives the sacrament, and, upon the other hand, all sufferings and sins become a common possession. The individual receives, in the sacrament, a sign of such union with Christ and the saints as makes the sufferings and life of Christ, as well as the lives and sufferings of all the saints, his own. The assurance is thus given to him in the sacrament that the sin by which he feels himself assailed assails not him alone, but the Son of God and all the saints in heaven and on earth ; and that Christ and the saints intercede before God for us, that our sins may not be charged against us according to the strict judgment of God. Let the faint-hearted, therefore, come joyfully to the sacrament of the altar ; let him come, seeking help, to the whole company of the spiritual body ; let him lay all his grief upon the congregation, and especially upon Christ, and say : I receive a sign from God that Christ's righteousness, His life and sufferings, are arrayed in my behalf, together with all the holy angels and redeemed in heaven and all pious men on earth. With this representation is associated also the admonition to a corresponding disposition and bearing upon the part of the recipient of the sacrament in his intercourse with others: " Love is enkindled by contact with love." The recipient must also, upon his part, bear the misfortunes and adversities of Christ and His saints; we must make the sorrows of all others our own. This exhortation is enforced by the citation of the words of institution in Lk. xxii. 19 : " This is my body which is given for you * * *; do this in remembrance of me." It is, says Luther, as though Christ said : I am the Head; I will be the first to give myself for you, will make your sorrow my own, in order that you again may do the same for me and among yourselves; and, as a sure testimonial of all this, I leave you this sacrament." Luther recalls also the ancient custom of bringing the outward elements and provisions for bodily needs to the Church, and there distributing them to the poor, to which Paul refers in 1 Cor.; and he explains that this was the origin of the word " collect," or general gathering, still retained in the celebration of the mass. He there further employs the figure, derived also from the Ancient Church, and already applied by himself in his dissertation, *De digna preparatione, etc.*, of bread as composed of many grains. Just as each separate grain loses its form and takes upon itself the common body of the bread, and, similarly, the drops of wine become the body of one beverage, so Christ, with all saints, takes upon Himself our form, and we, enkindled thereby to love, take upon ourselves His form, rely upon His righteousness, life and eternal blessedness, and are in consequence one loaf, one bread, one body, one beverage—and everything is in common. We, on the other hand, should also be transformed by this love, and let the infirmities of all other Christians become our own. Even the bodily reception of bread and wine is considered as setting forth the communion which is realized in this sacrament, since there is no more intimate combination than that of the food with the individual who is nourished by it. We are thus made conformable to Christ, as St. John says (1 John iii. 2). Then, finally, Luther declares : Beyond all this, He has not appointed these two elements as bare and empty forms, but has given His *true, natural flesh in the bread, and His natural, true blood in the wine,* that He might thereby give a complete sacrament, or sign : for, just as the bread is *transformed* into His true, natural body, and the wine into His natural, true blood, so also are we taken up and transformed into the spiritual body, that is, into the communion of Christ and all the saints. He regards the sufferings of Christ for us as especially represented by the blood. Christ, says he, has not appointed but one form, but separately, His flesh under the bread and His blood under the wine, in order to indicate that not alone are His life, indicated by the flesh, and His good works, done in the flesh, ours, but also His bitter sufferings, indicated by His blood—yea, all is ours. He concludes this section of the discourse with the comprehensive words : From all of this it is clear that this sacrament is nothing else than a divine sign, in which Christ and all the saints, with all their works, sufferings, possessions, etc., are *pledged, given* and *appropriated* for the consolation of all who are in distress, etc. ; and to receive the sacrament is nothing else than to desire all this and firmly to believe that it takes place.

It is only after having noted the final point in the above discussion, which Luther seeks to exalt beyond all else, that we are in a position to entirely comprehend his meaning when he speaks of the difference between the *sign*, or *thing signifying,* and the *signification*, or *thing signified*. He regards as a sign of that inner communion with Christ and the saints, we thus see, not only that which is visible in the sacrament, the " shape and form " of the bread and wine, but also the body and the blood themselves, into which he, according to the prevalent theory, supposes the bread and wine to be transformed. The real value of the sacrament does not lie even in the partaking of the body of Christ itself, but in a good, or blessing, which is, strictly speaking, only signified by the body of Christ, and which alone is truly an inward spiritual good, whereas the partaking of the body of Christ may remain a merely external and material exercise. This is a conception which was not peculiar to Luther, but which is to be met with also in scholastic authors. As they also discriminate between the sacrament, as a sign, and the gracious effect which should be wrought in the individual receiving it, we find in their writings also the body of Christ included, in a certain sense, under the conception of the sign, and, still further, we find the " mystical body of Christ " (cf. Luther's conception of the communion of saints) represented as being that which is signified by the natural body dispensed in the sacrament. We even find also *unitas* and *caritas* described in these writers as the fruit of the sacrament.[1] What is to be regarded here as peculiar, and characteristic of Luther, is the great importance which he attaches to the significance and fruit, in contrast with a merely external use of the sign, and his profound and fervent exposition of the former.

But how, it must still be asked, does the recipient of the sign, *i. e.*, of the form of bread and wine, and the body and blood of Christ offered under this form, really become also a partaker of that which is thereby signified? This brings us, at length, face to face with the point of chief importance characterizing the theory of Luther. The reply to the inquiry presents us a conception long since grown familiar to us in the study of his writings, and now again laid to our hand in the above-cited closing words of the final division of his *Sermon*. It is *faith* which, as he had stated in the very introduction of his discourse, must bring both the sign and the thing signified together " into practice and use." [2] He therefore proceeds, after the conclusion of the division referred to, to say : " Here belongs the third part of the sacrament, namely, faith, in which the power lies," repeating the assertion : Thou must also desire and firmly believe that thou hast received it (the communion, etc.). If, therefore, Luther describes such communion as a result and fruit of the sacrament, it can yet only become such, according to his view, through faith. But faith, says he, is to be constantly exercised by approaching the sacrament and in attending mass—by looking upon the divinely-ordained sign : " It is necessary and good to go often to the sacrament, or to exercise and strengthen such faith even daily in the mass."

From the section of the *Sermon* treating of this " third part," we note the following particulars :

Luther warns against subtle questions, which are detrimental to faith, such as, what becomes of the bread in the transubstantia-

---

[1] Cf. Dieckhoff: Die evangelische Abendmahlslehre im Reformationszeitalter, i, 95 sq.

[2] Cf. statement in regard to Baptism, Erl. Ed., xxi, 230, 236: To the sign and significance belongs, as a third element, faith.

tion, how the entire Christ can be included in so small a piece of bread, etc. There is no benefit, he declares, in such investigations. "It is enough that thou knowest it is a divine sign wherein Christ's flesh and blood are *truly included;* how and where, leave thou to Him."

To the exhortation to believe and to exercise faith, Luther adds, in harmony with his conception of the significance of the sacrament, the exhortation to love—that each one should submit his life to the common interest of all. He declares that the natural body of Christ, without the spiritual, helps nothing in the sacrament; a transformation, he repeats, must be effected through love.

With this requirement of faith and love, Luther now turns to meet those who hold that the sacrament is *opus gratum opere operato, i. e.,* "such a work as is of itself pleasing to God, although those who perform it do not please Him." The sacrament, he affirms, works, upon the other hand, only injury, if it is merely an *opus operatum;* it must be the work of one who works (*opus operantis*), *i. e.,* it must be employed in faith. We must see to it that the sacrament is pleasing to God on account of our "faith and use" of it.

We call attention also, at this point, in connection with Luther's affirmation of the necessity of faith in the reception of the sacrament, to an incidental expression in the first section of the *Sermon*. Having there commended the administration of both elements to the laity, he adds: "Not because the one element is not sufficient, since, indeed, *even the desire of faith would alone be sufficient,* as St. Augustine says: Why do you prepare the stomach and the teeth? Only believe; so hast thou *already partaken* of the sacrament." The expression, although not repeated in this document, is yet in full accord with the underlying thoughts which we have just been tracing. That which the *Sermon* regards as the essential, spiritual benefit of the sacrament may also be appropriated by faith without the sacrament. The sacrament, or sign, is for faith a support and means of strengthening, which is, indeed, of the very highest value, but yet not absolutely indispensable. Thus, also, we have already heard Luther comfort those excluded against their own will from the sacrament (*supra*, p. 288).

Having briefly described again the "communion and love, by

which we are strengthened against death and all evil " as a fruit
of the sacrament, he would like to see how " the great glittering
Brotherhoods, of which there are now so many, compare and
tally with this."

Here, then, follows naturally the second and closely-related
Sermon vom Bann. In the main, the conception of excommunication is here also precisely that presented in the *Sermo de
virtute excommunicationis*. As Luther had there already dwelt
upon the distinction between the external and spiritual fellowship
(communion), so he now compares this distinction to that existing between the sign and the thing signified in the sacrament.
He declares that the spiritual communion, namely, the incorpora-
tion by faith, hope and love with Christ and all the saints, which
is, indeed, signified and given in the sacrament, can by no man
be imparted to nor taken from another. It is only from the
bodily communion, the approach to the sacrament and the reception of it in common with others, that bishops and Popes can
exclude, which is the excommunication authorized by Christ in
Matt. xviii. Again, as in the other discourse, he declares that
unrighteous excommunication does no harm. Excommunication
in itself does not deprive of the intercession, nor of all the good
works, of the Christian world. And he now refers expressly to
the sacrament : Even in case of excommunication, and, consequently, of exclusion from the sacrament, there yet remain, if only
faith and the love of God be in the heart, all the fruits of the
sacrament. The excommunicated man should nevertheless
" *spiritually go to the sacrament, i. e.*, he should heartily long
for it and believe that he shall spiritually partake of it, as has
been said in the *Sermon vom hochwürdigen Sacrament*." It
is further recommended, that those who have been deservedly
excommunicated be permitted still to attend the services of
the Church during the reading of the Gospel and the preaching,
in order that they may be benefited thereby.

If we now take a general view of the contents of the two dis-
sertations under review, we shall recognize as of the very highest
significance, first of all, the general idea here developed of the
communion of saints, which rests upon faith and love, and is to
be an actual and vital, as well as an inward and spiritual, fellowship. Luther has, in this term, described what is for him the true
nature of the *Church*, as the body of Christ, embracing all

believers and to be severed by no human decree. In it we see that Luther's principle, of a faith which is the affair of each separate individual, is yet as far as possible from isolating the believer. In it we recognize, still further, what of truth there is for Luther in the Roman Catholic idea of the *merits of the saints*, and of a treasure of their merits, which may be made available for the benefit of others: we may compare here, also, his declaration in regard to this treasure in his *Resolutiones* upon the indulgence theses (*supra*, p. 271). The most profound discussion of this idea as to the intercession of believers, or saints, for others will meet us again in the tract, *De libertate Christiana*. The blessing derived from communion with other believers and that derived from communion with the Redeemer are, in these discourses, still represented as upon one plane, which is not the case in the later discussions of the subject. Yet here already we see plainly what is to be attributed to the latter alone; and whatever is embraced in the former leads us back to the source of salvation in Christ, with no mention of any righteousness but the righteousness of Christ.

We must also give due consideration to the *relation which the communion of saints is said to hold to the sacrament of the altar*, and to the significance which is thus given to the latter. Already in the discourse, *Von der würdigen Bereitung*, published in 1518, whose main object is to urge a preparation through *faith*, "unity of heart" is described as a "work (*thun*) of the sacrament,"[1] reference being there made, as already noted, to the figure of the grains united in the bread. He there further discourses upon the words of Jesus recorded in John vi.: "He that eateth my flesh and drinketh my blood dwelleth in me," etc.; and in the conclusion he treats especially of the proper view of the *sufferings of Christ* (as a sacrament, and not merely an example: cf. *supra*, p. 285). He does not, however, here attempt a systematic combination of these conceptions. In harmony with the utterances of the writing now under review are those found in the *Sermon von Bereitung zum Sterben* (1519) and in the *Tessaradecas Consolatoria*, etc.[2] In the former, it is said of

[1] Erl. Ed., xvii, 55.

[2] Jen., i, 484 sq. The work was in already under the press in Dec., 1519 (Briefe, i, 378) and was issued early in February (Briefe, i, 407 sqq.).

the sacraments, more particularly of the sacrament of the altar and that of absolution,[1] that they are designed by God to be pledges and testimonials of all that Christ has wrought and gained for us by His life and sufferings, that through Him sin, death and hell have been overcome for us. To this he adds: We are, moreover, by these same sacraments implanted into one body with all believers, so that they with us die in Christ, bear sin and vanquish hell; the human body of Christ is a sign and pledge of the communion of all angels and saints—that they love me, care for me, pray for me, etc. The *Tessaradecas* again speaks of this communion with special fervency. He there magnifies the consolations which we find in the *ecclesia sanctorum*, where all goods (blessings) are in common, all evils commonly borne, and where every member suffers with his fellow-member. He even says of these saints: *Their merits shall remedy my sins.* This, he declares, is what the Apostolic Creed confesses; and he then quotes from the third article of the Creed, and immediately adds: This is just what the sacrament of the altar pictures to us in bread and wine, in view of which the apostle calls us one body, one bread.

But we have already learned, especially from our review of the discourse, *Von Bereitung zum Sterben*, that we dare not estimate the doctrine of Luther at this time upon the subject of the Lord's Supper merely from the ideas presented in the *Sermon vom hochwürdigen Sacrament.* In the former, far more than in the latter, the testimony to Christ's own work and the blessings secured through Him outweighs that touching communion with the fellow-members of Christ, the saints.[2] Here, too, impressive reference is made to the significance of the Word of God in connection with the sacrament. Although this had already been emphasized by Luther at an earlier period (cf. *supra*, p. 194 sq.), he finds no occasion to speak of it in the discourse upon the sacrament. Here, however, he explains the consoling power of the sacraments as follows: " For in the sacraments are Words of God, which enable them to show and promise Christ to us," etc.; and, further, we are to " believe it to be as the sacraments,

[1] Erl. Ed., xxi, 266 sqq.

[2] Cf. Ibid., xxi, 261 sqq., with which also the ideas embodied in the expressions touching the sacrament, Ibid., 266, stand in close relation.

through the *Word of God*, promise and pledge." The *Tessara-decas*, upon the other hand, contains no further discussion of the doctrine of the sacraments.

2. *Expositions of the Lord's Supper and the Sacrifice of the Mass in A. D. 1520.*

THE MASS A TESTAMENT—WORDS OF INSTITUTION ITS PRINCIPAL PART —ITS WORK—ITS SEAL—NO SACRIFICE—MASSES FOR THE DEAD AND PRIVATE MASSES.

We now pass on at once to those writings, of the early part of the year 1520, which more fully present and more definitely define the DOCTRINE OF THE LORD'S SUPPER. This forms the special subject of the *Sermon von dem neuen Testament, d. i., von der heiligen Messe*,[1] which Luther sent to Staupitz on August 3d, and which, we may accordingly infer, had left the press not long before.[2] The same fundamental ideas, however, occur in a discussion of the Third Commandment in the *Sermon von guten Werken*.[3] This tract was in course of preparation already in March, the dedication to Duke George being written on the 29th of that month, but it was still not quite completed on May 13th.[4] It is worthy of note how quickly this *Sermon* followed the *Tes-saradecas ;* but we must all the more on this account beware of severing the ideas here presented, in which there is certainly to be recognized an important advance in the foundation of Luther's doctrine, from their inner connection with his earlier utterances, and of regarding his entire earlier view as fully expressed in the representations of the *Tessaradecas*.

To the advanced position taken in the two publications now under review, Luther was led by a criticism of the Roman Cath-olic mass, as then celebrated, based upon the original institution of the sacrament as recorded in the Scriptures. This is perfectly manifest in the *Sermon von dem neuen Testament*, which begins with a denunciation of the numerous ecclesiastical ordinances, describes the holy mass as the only order of divine service insti-tuted by Christ, and then says in reference to the latter: " Now

[1] Erl. Ed., xxvii, 139 sqq.   [2] Briefe, i, 475.
[3] Erl. Ed., xx, 230 sqq.   [4] Cf. Briefe, i, 421, 430, 434, 447, 448.

the nearer our masses are to the first mass of Christ, the better are they, beyond doubt; and the farther from that, the more perilous." But the entire mass, with its whole nature, work, benefit and fruit, lies, according to Luther, in the *Words of Christ*, with which He celebrated and established it, and has commanded us to celebrate it. These words he quotes as follows: " Take and eat, this is my body (*Leichnam*) which is given for you; take and drink of it all together, this is the cup of the new and everlasting testament in my blood, which is shed for you and for many for the remission of sins." Upon these words the second *Sermon* also bases its argument.

Luther considers the words of institution, not as merely a formula of consecration, but as a promise of grace, to which Christians should cling; and, regarding them in this sense, he constantly describes them as the *principal part of the mass*. Christ, he thus explains, therein bestows upon us, according to the words, " cup of the testament," a new, everlasting and imperishable testament—a last, irrevocable will, in which He, in dying, arranges all His goods for distribution. The unspeakable treasure which is herein bestowed upon us is said to be, according to the words of institution, *the forgiveness of sins*. Christ says, as it were: I bestow upon thee, with these words, the forgiveness of all thy sins and everlasting life; and that thou mayest be sure that this vow shall remain for thee irrevocable, I will at once die and give for it my body and blood, and leave them both behind me as *a sign and seal* to thee, in receiving which (*dabei*) thou shalt remember me. Likewise, in the second dissertation, we read: Christ has made a testament, and in it has bequeathed, not temporal possessions, but forgiveness of all sins, grace and mercy unto everlasting life. Both discourses carry out the figure of a human will and testament still further, finding parallels also for the sign and seal. Thus especially the first-mentioned, in which we read: " It is also the case in worldly testaments, that not only are the words written out, but a seal and the attestation of a notary are also attached, in order that it may be valid and trustworthy. Thus also has Christ done in this testament, and attached a most powerful and most noble seal *to and in the words*, namely, His *own true flesh and blood under the bread and wine*." To this Luther adds, that God has commonly also in all His other promises given *with the Word also a sign*: as to

Noah, the rainbow; to Abraham, circumcision; to Gideon, the rain upon the ground and the fleece, etc. With this conception of the body of Christ in the sacrament corresponds the interpretation given in this *Sermon* to the elevation of the host, *i. e.*, when the priest elebates the host, it is not he who speaks to us so much as God, as though God should say : Behold, this is the seal and sign of the new testament, in which Christ has bestowed the pardon of all sins and everlasting life. The significance thus given to the words of institution leads to the demand that they be not spoken by the priest as secret words (cf. the opposite view formerly held, *supra*, p 204), but " sung as loudly as possible," and to the desire that masses might be read in German.[1]

The important points above noted are presented in this way by Luther *for the first time* in the two documents under consideration. Nor was there lacking in this case a special reason for the presentation of just these features of the subject. The ground of his opposition to the prevalent conception of the sacrament lay, at this time, not so much in its exclusive devotion to externals as in the fact that it made the very essence of the mass to consist in human presentations, human service, human sacrifice. The *Sermon von der Messe* presents at once the very opposite conception to this, and does so because basing its argument upon the words of institution. It proposes, at the outset, as a general principle : " If man is to have any dealings with God, and receive anything from Him, it must come to pass in such a way that the first step is not taken by man, but that God alone, without any petition on the part of man, must take the initiative and give to man a promise. This Word of God is the first thing, and upon it are built all the works, words and thoughts of man. This Word man must thankfully receive, and faithfully believe the divine promise." Thus God gave a promise immediately after the Fall to Adam, and afterwards to Noah and Abraham. This promise sustained Adam and his children in faith until the time of Noah, and afterward : just as Abraham was justified by faith in the promise, so were the children of Abraham sustained in the same faith until the coming of Christ.

The difference between the views of Luther upon the nature of

[1] Erl. Ed., xxvii, 152 sq.

the sacrament, as now expressed, and his earlier presentations of the same subject arises thus directly from the emphasis now laid upon the words of institution. The central place is accorded, not merely to the Gospel, or the Word of grace in general, which Luther had long been accustomed to adduce as fundamentally essential to the sacrament, but especially to the Word announcing the forgiveness of sins. This is advanced as the basis, and the very substance, of all communications of grace spoken of in connection with the sacrament, or with the new covenant in general. That which is received through Christ in communion with other believers, or with the saints, is no longer urged in these discourses. We are not to infer from this that the latter idea has come to be discredited by Luther, for his pamphlet *Von der Freiheit eines Christenmenschen*, and various later expositions of the doctrine of the Lord's Supper prove the contrary; but that it is now regarded as entitled to a place of but secondary importance, is quite clearly manifest. We shall shortly have occasion to observe also that Luther now presents the *collect* (cf. *supra*, p. 339) from a new point of view.

We must regard the opposition to the prevalent conception of the mass, and, still further, the emphasis now laid upon the *forgiveness of sins*, as at the same time an inner consequence of the fundamental principles which dominated the Reformer from the beginning, and by which, penetrating as they must through the whole system of saving truth, his entire further development must henceforth be determined. Purely receptive must ever be the attitude of man toward the prevenient and salvation-imparting grace of God, and what he needs to receive from it is, above all else, forgiveness—the pardon of guilt. The principal thing, therefore, in the sacrament always remains for Luther the offer and appropriation of the forgiveness of sins.

As to the other component elements of the doctrine of the Lord's Supper, the view in these two discourses still remains essentially the same as in the earlier writings of the Reformer.

On the one hand, Luther always recognizes the *true presence* of the body and blood of Christ in the sacrament (cf. *supra*: " His real [*wahrhaftig*] flesh and blood "). We may, perhaps, find some trace of variation from the Romish dogma in the fact that Luther, in the *Sermon von der heiligen Messe*, no longer, as in that *Von dem hochwürdigen Sacrament*, speaks only of the "*shape and form* of the bread," comparing this "form" with the water (not merely with the "form" of the water) in baptism,[1] but that he now says directly that the flesh and body of Christ are present "*under bread and wine*." Does there lie already at the basis of these forms of expression the view, that after consecration not only the form (*Gestalt, species*), but also the substance of bread and wine is yet present? (Cf. *De captivitate Babylonica*.) At all events, however, the presence of the body and blood is still firmly maintained.

But, upon the other hand, Luther here still conceives of the *body of Christ* essentially as a *sign ;* more definitely now, as a sign of the promise of the forgiveness of sins contained in the words of institution. Even now mention is made, not of any value which this body, as sacramentally imparted, is supposed to have in and of itself, nor of gracious influences (*Gnaden*) which are supposed to flow from this gift itself upon the believing recipient, but only of grace (*Gnade*), which is through it, as through a sign, still further and especially sealed, although having been already promised in the Word, and, in this promise, offered for reception to faith. The Word is " the principal part of the mass " (*Hauptstück*). This brings us back again to the general thought, that, not only in the words of institution of the sacrament, but in every sermon or announcement of the Gospel, this same offer is presented. The entire Gospel is " nothing else than an announcement of gracious divine blessings and the forgiveness of all sins, given us through the sufferings of Christ." Here, with the words of the testament, or sacrament, Christ has " embraced in a short summary " [2] the Gospel itself. Thus again Luther declares that the faith which leans upon the Word, although without it the sacrament would be of no avail, does *not absolutely need the sacrament;* " that the signs may, indeed, be lacking, but man nevertheless has the words, and may therefore be saved without the sacrament, yet not without the testament. I can daily enjoy the sacrament in the mass, if I only picture to myself the testament, *i. e.*, the words and vow of Christ, and feed my faith upon these." [3] The same statement was made by Luther, in the *Sermon von der Bereitung zum Sterben*, in regard to the sacraments

[1] Erl. Ed., xxvii, 28.   [2] Ibid., xxvii, 167.

[3] Ibid., p. 153; cf. also 164 sqq.

of penance and extreme unction, as well as that of the Lord's Supper. The dying believer should desire them, and receive them with confidence when he can secure them. But if this be not possible, the desire for them should be none the less comforting to him, since, according to Mk. ix. 23, all things are possible to him that believeth, " for the sacraments are nothing else than signs, which serve and stimulate to faith." [1] In the *Sermon von der Messe*, he says further, in regard to baptism, that it is to be observed, " although, without it, faith is sufficient." [2]

Wherein, then, it may be inquired, consists the *peculiar value* nevertheless attaching to the *sacraments as signs*, and hence also to the body and blood of Christ in the Lord's Supper? The reply furnished by the writings of the present period is, that, although the Word of God must first of all awaken faith, and faith must, upon its part, embrace the Word, yet the sacraments, as signs, in a special manner stimulate and strengthen this faith : " By the bodily looking upon and receiving of the sacrament we should more and more stir up and improve this faith." [3] And we stand, indeed, very much in need of this, since we are yet living on the earth and in the flesh. Faith, therefore, needs to be strengthened ever anew, and love to be ever warmed up anew. Hence Christ attaches to His testament also this sign and seal : " *For we poor men, since we live in the five senses, must have an external sign, along with the words*, upon which we may lay hold and concentrate our thoughts, yet in such a way * * * that we are drawn by that which is external to that which is spiritual." [4]

We have thus examined at length the fundamental outlines of Luther's doctrine concerning the proffer of the body of Christ in the Lord's Supper, and, at the same time, the proffer extended in every sacrament. When it afterwards becomes his task to defend the real presence of the body against assaults, and, at the same time, to estimate carefully its significance, still further important doctrinal points are developed ; but we shall find that those which we have now noted still maintain their place.

But we must now consider also more particularly the position taken by the *Sermon von der Messe*, in its doctrine of the Lord's Supper, against the Roman Catholic theory of sacrifice.

---

[1] Erl. Ed., xxi, 257.　　　　　　　　[2] Ibid., xxvii, 166.
[3] Ibid.　　　　　　　　　　　　　[4] Ibid., 148.

The principle involved we have already noted, *i. e.*, the essential character of the mass is not the offering of anything to God, but a proffer on the part of God to the believer. A testament, says Luther, is not a benefit accepted, but one bestowed.[1] The same thoughts had already at an earlier day, as he says in his *Operationes in Psalmos*,[2] claimed his attention : That the mystery has been established, not for the doing of a good work (by man), but for the employing of the righteousness of Christ and the exercising of the saving power of God.

Yet the *Sermon* in question speaks in such a way that, while the prevalent perversion of the mass, which made of it a sacrifice, is described as the most flagrant abuse, the conception of a sacrifice is yet not abandoned. This conception originated, it is said, through the custom of bringing food and other provisions for the needy, and consecrating them with prayer and the Word of God, as is done at our daily meals, and as Christ took the cup and gave thanks to God (Lk. xxii. 18). From this has been derived the term " collect "—properly a blessing and grace spoken over the collected food ; and also the offertorium and the elevation and offering of the unconsecrated host by the priest during the offertory hymn. This does not mean an offering of the sacrament upon our part, but a thanksgiving to God for the collected food, and the imploring of His blessing upon it. In the elevation of the consecrated elements, the priest says nothing of an offering : he elevates them, not before God, but before us, to remind us of the testament (cf. *supra*). Thus there remains then in the mass, says Luther, " nothing of the sacrifice, but only sacrament and testament." But, nevertheless, it is allowable and useful to call the mass—in another than the prevalent sense—a sacrifice, or offering. We should sacrifice spiritually, *i. e.*, ourselves and all that we have, with prayer ; and, moreover, we should not offer such prayer, praise, thanksgiving and sacrifice of self through ourselves, but lay them upon Christ, and let Him, as our priest, present them. The mass is called a sacrifice, therefore, not on its own account, but because we lay ourselves upon Christ with firm faith in His testament, and do not appear before God with our prayer, praise and sacrifice (cf. Heb. xiii. 15 ; the sacrifice of praise)

[1] Erl. Ed., xxvii, 155.

[2] Op. Ex., xv, 115 sq. (under Ps. ix.), published in 1520.

otherwise than through Him. *We* do not offer the sacrament, but by our prayer, etc., we give Him occasion to offer Himself for us in heaven, and us with Him. We do not offer Christ, but Christ offers us. According to this, the sacrifice of the mass, so far as there can be with Luther any thought of such a thing, is effected, not through the *priest*, but through the faith of *every Christian believer*. All those, he declares, are real parsons, and hold mass properly, who believe that Christ is a minister (*Pfarrer*) for them before God, and who offer their prayer, their praise, their wants and themselves, and then receive the sacrament and testament bodily or spiritually. *All* are parsons (priests), man and woman, young and old, learned or laity; there is here no difference, unless it be in the measure of faith. The expression, " bodily or spiritually," brings to view again the principle, that bodily participation in the sacrament is not absolutely required. In the same connection, he says further: And this kind of sacrifice a Christian may render everywhere and hourly, as Christ is, in Psalm cx., said to be a priest forever, offering sacrifice continually before God. " But we,'" he adds, " may not be at all times the same; therefore the mass has been instituted, that we may assemble with one another, and together offer this sacrifice." Here, says he, one stirs up, moves, inflames the other to earnestly press near to God, and we receive the things for which we ask.[1]

To the inquiry, what is then accomplished by the masses appointed *for the souls in purgatory*, Luther replies:[2] Custom or no custom, God's Word must be first (which teaches) that the mass is nothing but a testament and sacrament of God. He had, however, previously, in speaking of united worship, declared: If we would properly assemble ourselves in Christ's name, according to Matt. xviii. 19, 20, and pray, " the souls in purgatory would easily be delivered, and countless blessings would follow."

In the passage quoted from the *Operationes in Psalmos*, Luther has already expressed some doubts in regard to *private masses*, in which but one person reads and hears the Gospel, and but one partakes of the sacrament,—in which there is, therefore, no community (*communitas*) or mutual communication (*communicatio*). He will not condemn these, he now declares, for he knows, and has himself experienced, that they have been very

[1] Erl. Ed., xxvii, 162, 160.

[2] Ibid., xvii, 163.

profitable for some, though only when suffering from sore temptation; there are, however, hardly any persons to whom the prevailing usage may be found helpful.

The *Sermon* finally advises a reduction in the number of the appointed masses for souls, and that, especially in the towns, only one mass be celebrated, and that in the proper way, before the assembled congregation. If it is desired to hold more, the congregation should be divided into sections for their observance, in order that faith may be exercised upon such occasions, and prayer, praise and confession of need may be offered up in Christ.

3. *Further Points of Doctrine in the Writings of the Period.*

CUP FOR THE LAITY—NUMBER OF SACRAMENTS—BAPTISM—AURICULAR
  CONFESSION—GOOD WORKS—VOWS—SAINT WORSHIP—PURGATORY
  —UNIVERSAL PRIESTHOOD—BOHEMIANS.

If we now desire to trace the advance in Luther's views upon *other* points of doctrine also, as attested by the writings above cited and other smaller literary remains of the period, we must, first of all, before leaving the subject of the sacraments, call particular attention to the utterance already referred to upon the CUP FOR THE LAITY in the *Sermon von dem hochwürdigen Sacrament.*[1] Although, says Luther here, one element is in itself not insufficient, yet it seems to him that it would be well for the Church, in a general council, to again appoint both elements for all Christians. He appeals, in harmony with the fundamental idea of the discourse, to the fact, that the undivided communion of saints which is signified by the sacrament is very poorly represented by that which is merely a part of the sacrament, and expressly adds, further, that Christ instituted the two elements for the use of *all* Christians. With this agree the representations of the *Erklärung etlicher Artikel im Sermon vom heiligen Sacrament* and the *Autwort auf die Zedel, so unter des Officials zu Stolpen Siegel ist ausgegangen,* and also some statements made in the *Sermon vom neuen Testament.*[2] Christ, repeats Luther, is, indeed, present also under one element; and, he further asserts, no great importance is to be attached to the question of one

[1] Erl. Ed., xxvii, 28.
[2] Cf. especially Erl. Ed., xxvii, 70 sq., 81 sq., 168 sq.

element or both, because, at any rate, more depends upon the
Word than upon the signs. Individual bishops he would not
regard as authorized to introduce the distribution under both
elements; and he blames the Bohemians for not submitting to
authorities and resting satisfied with the one element. But yet,
says he, we dare not, on this account, denounce the Bohemians as
heretics; both parties should rather treat one another with forbearance. In the *Setmon von der Messe* we already find stronger
language. While here again repeating the remark, that no great
importance attaches to the subject itself, he now adds, that he
would like to know who gave the power to withhold the cup:
that if the Pope changes what Christ has established, he does it
without authority, as a tyrant—yea, as Antichrist.

The discourse just mentioned follows without question the prevailing theory as to the NUMBER OF THE SACRAMENTS, mentioning,
as other " sacraments besides the Lord's Supper," not only baptism, but also confirmation, penance, extreme unction, etc. The
Sermon vom hochwürdigen Sacrament had distinguished " baptism
and bread " as the two " principal " (*vornehmlichen*) sacraments.
But yet, so early as December, 1519, Luther had already written
to Spalatin, that no one need expect a publication from him upon
the other sacraments (besides the Lord's Supper, baptism—and,
no doubt, also repentance, upon which he had already written)
until he shall have first been taught by what passage of Scripture
he may justify them. He now already lays down the principle:
For no sacrament remains a *sacrament* for me, except where an
express divine promise is given, which may exercise faith; since,
without the *Word of the Promiser* and the *faith of the recipient*, it
is not possible for us to have any dealing with God. He then
adds: But as to the notion of these men concerning their seven
sacraments, thou shalt hear at another time.[1]

For the doctrine of CONTINUAL REPENTANCE and the FORGIVE-
NESS OF SINS AFTER BAPTISM (cf. *supra*, p. 326), a broader and
firmer basis is now laid in the independent discussion of the significance of baptism given by Luther in his *Sermon* upon this
subject, which appeared in November, 1519.[2] Inasmuch as,

---

[1] Briefe, i, 378. Cf. the utterance against the sacrament of ordination in the
latter part of the same letter.

[2] Erl. Ed., xxi, 227 sqq.

according to the views now presented, the sign in baptism, namely, the dipping beneath the water, signifies the entire work of renewal, for the accomplishment of which the baptized person submits himself to God, God binds Himself in a gracious covenant with the man, that He, from that hour on, begins the renewing and the mortification of sin by an inpouring of the Holy Spirit, and that He will no more impute to him the sins which yet remain. This recipient of grace is then, on the one hand, more and more to crucify sin in himself and allow it to be crucified, until at length the Judgment Day shall make him entirely a new man; and, on the other hand, as against the terrors of conscience, he is no longer to seek himself to render satisfaction, but boldly and freely to hold fast in faith to his baptism and the forgiving mercy therein promised. Thus the sacrament of repentance has its basis in the sacrament of baptism; and the latter is renewed in repentance and absolution. We observe here, that Luther, while demanding for the attainment of the continued forgiveness simply faith in the grace which is pledged in baptism, and which is dependent upon the intercession of Christ ("believest thou, so hast thou"), yet also declares, further, that God will not impute the yet remaining impurity, *in view of the purification already begun* (cf. *supra*, p. 328). As to the nature of the sacrament, he distinguishes here, in perfect keeping with the definitions of the *Sermon von dem hochwürdigen Sacrament:* as the first part, the outward sign of dipping beneath the water; as the second part, the significance of this sign, *i. e.*, "the blessed dying to sin and arising to the grace of God"; as the third part, faith. But we are to believe that what the sacrament signifies it also already begins and works. In how far this working actually begins through the very sacrament which signifies, he has not more definitely explained.

In regard to AURICULAR CONFESSION, Luther had already given public expression to his opposition, upon the ground of fundamental principle, to this ordinance of the Church. The institution itself he cheerfully acknowledges in his practical instructions. He constantly expresses himself as opposed only to the making of it a torture for the consciences of men, beclouding the grace of God, and imagining it to be possible to free one's self from guilt by a complete confession and by good resolutions. He warns against the idea that it is possible to recall to memory and confess all mortal sins. He emphasizes the axiom, that we should place confidence only in God.[1] Especially clear and impressive is his presentation of this prime duty in his *Confitendi ratio*,[2] in which he explains, that confession is for him, essentially and chiefly, a calling upon God to fulfil His promises, and an exercise of faith, which endeavors to lay hold of the promises without doubting, in order that to the Lord may be all the glory. He even gives, with appeal to Gerson, the seemingly paradoxical counsel: [3] We may now and then approach the altar with a scruple of conscience, *i. e.*, without first confessing, even if we have gone somewhat beyond proper bounds in eating, drinking or speaking: this we may do, in order to accustom our conscience to depend entirely and alone upon God, and not be alarmed at every falling leaf. Whether secret sins of the heart should also be confessed to the priest, or only to God, is an open question to him, and he is rather inclined to the former opinion. An assault made by Eck had already served to bring into view the open opposition of the principles of Luther to those of the Roman Church as to the validity of the entire institution of auricular confession. He was charged with having maintained that the sacramental confession had no divine right; [4] and, though he had not demanded the abolition of auricular confession, he yet now most positively maintains the position, that it was not appointed by God, but only by the Church. Even in the Church, he holds, it was not originally introduced, but only public confession, according to Matt. xviii. Finally, he repeats again, that he does not reject it, but only laments that it has been such a means of torture.[5]

In elucidation of the views now held by Luther upon the appropriation of salvation, or the significance of FAITH IN RELATION TO GOOD WORKS, it may here suffice simply to refer to the principal publication in which he at this time treated of the subject, namely, the *Sermon von guten Werken*.

With ever-increasing clearness is now unfolded the opinion of

---

[1] Von der würdigen Bereitung, etc., Erl. Ed., xvii, 54 sq.   Kurze Unterricht wie man beichten soll, Erl. Ed., xxi, 247, 251.

[2] Jena, i, 487 sqq.   Ibid., 490.

[4] Cf. Löscher, ii, 16.

[5] Contra malign. Eccii judicium, etc.—Löscher, iii, 880 sq.

Luther as to the character and value of those works which, amidst all outer diversity, may yet be regarded, in a general way, as the fruit of faith, and must, as such, be demanded. As every work is good only as a fruit of faith, and is otherwise only sin, so, he maintains, on the other hand, *all things are free* to the Christian through faith; and it is just in this freedom that the latter now serves his neighbor, and especially bears his infirmities. Without choice of his own, he freely accepts what is given him to do.[1] He is thus free from all *external ordinances*. He fasts and watches, but, in doing so, he fixes his attention, not upon the works of abstinence themselves, nor upon appointed days, nor upon any appointed variety or kind of diet, but alone upon his own inward requirements—upon that which the lust of his flesh requires for its restraint, and, on the other hand, upon that which it is able to endure without impairing the health, distracting the brain, etc.[2] Even the outward observance of Sunday, by bodily rest, is for him (cf. *supra*, p. 175) not expressly commanded, according to Col. ii. 16, 17. In and of themselves, all days are for him holy days, and, again, all days are working days. The special observance is only for the sake of the immature (imperfect) laity and the working people, in order that they may come to hear the Word of God. If we were all perfect and knew the Gospel, we might work or hold festival every day.[3] Yet more outspokenly than in the *Commentary upon Galatians* (cf. *supra*, p. 312) does Luther now express himself in regard to the use which may rightfully be made of this liberty as against even the express regulations of the Church. If one finds, says he, that he does not at present require such a restraint upon the flesh, or that he would by observing the rules for fasting ruin his body, he should omit the fasting, despite all requirements of the Church or of his Order.[4] In the *Operationes in Psalmos*, he treats at special length of the observance of the ecclesiastical ordinances and ceremonies in general,[5] declaring that we should not encourage carelessness in the observance of these upon the part of the young, who need outward discipline, nor on the part of the weak in faith, who have not yet been brought to an understanding of

[1] Erl. Ed., xx, 209.   [2] Ibid., 250 sqq.
[3] Ibid., 248.   Comm. ad Gal., iii, 324.   [4] Erl. Ed., xx, 251 sq.
[5] Op. Ex., xv, 277 sqq. (first printed in 1521).

Gospel liberty; we should endure the established laws in love and faith, however tyrannical they may be, just as in the case of political laws: but, he adds, he who realizes that he is placing his confidence in such works should be bold, and omit them now and then without first seeking a papal dispensation. We see here how close is the connection between Luther's view as to the inner value of Christian works and his recognition of the individual independence of the believer, as against the external appointments of the Church. He expressly asserts, in the context of the passage last cited, that nothing dare be appointed by statute which could in any way imperil faith, and that, in such matters, every Christian is to himself Pope and Church; still further, a Christian may in such cases not hesitate to take counsel with his neighbor, by virtue of the promise given in Matt. xviii. 19. In this consciousness of the liberty which should characterize the life of faith, Luther desires especially that there may be as few *laws* as possible for the government of the Church. He declares: " The less law, the more right living— the less commandment, the more good works "; and that the numerous laws of modern times in the Christian world have served only to promote dissimulation.[1] The *Sermon von der Messe*, in the introduction to which occurs the citation just made, concludes as follows: " Let us, therefore, beware of sins, but still more of laws and good works, and have regard only to divine promises and faith; the good works will then come of themselves:" What he understands by the " good works " against which he here warns, he briefly explains to Eck as follows: They have put good works *instead of works of the Law*, which are not necessary, but, on the contrary, injurious. Of the true good works he says: All good works whatsoever are necessary and salutary.[2]

Luther's present theory of the difference between *commandments* and *evangelical counsels*, which necessarily followed from his entire conception of morality, has been already presented in the preceding chapter. His theory as to the value of SPECIAL vows of holiness has at the same time been noted. We now have to observe the relation of the latter theory especially to the significance of baptism. No vow, says the *Sermon von der*

---

[1] Cf. also Briefe, i, 324 sq.   [2] Löscher, iii, 885.

Taufe, of chastity, spirituality, etc., is superior to the *baptismal vow,* in which we have all alike vowed, by the grace of God, to whom we surrender ourselves as clay to the potter, to crucify sin and become holy.   Beyond this vow, any person may now bind himself to some particular condition, or state, which he thinks may assist him in the fulfilment of the former, whether it be the state of marriage, with its activities and trials, or the state of chastity.   Each one may, according to his own personal require-ments, select the one path or the other ; but, in every state what-soever, each one should exert himself only for the fulfilment of the one baptismal vow, for the driving out of sin, etc.[1]   In the *Ratio confitendi,* Luther advises that general warning be given against the disposition to the making of vows ; since, compared with the fulfilment of the general divine commandments and the baptismal vow, whose requirements must be met in our relations with our neighbor, wife, children, etc., all vows of journeys to be undertaken,[2] fasts, prayers, etc., are to be accounted as nothing. Yea, he even wishes that there might be among Christians no vow whatsoever, except that of baptism.   Where, however, a vow has been made before God, he sees no possibility of a dis-pensation : the Pope can no more give such a dispensation than can any Christian brother, since a vow is a matter of divine right (jurisdiction).   He would make an exception only in the case of vows of chastity made before the age of puberty, which he would regard as invalid by their nature, since the individual assuming them does not know what he is doing.[3]

In relation to the WORSHIP OF THE SAINTS, the very foundation of which had been swept away by Luther's conception of Chris-tian life and its obligations in general, he now goes so far as to doubt the authority of the Pope in the matter of canonization, and even the significance, or benefit, of canonization itself.   He would like to know, he says, what passages of Scripture could be adduced in its behalf.[4]   He still, however, continues without any hesitancy to exhort his readers to call upon " the mother of God and all the apostles and the dear saints."

[1] Erl. Ed., xxi, 241 sqq.

[2] Cf. supra, citations from the Tessaradeca.

[3] Jena, i, 491.   [4] Löscher, iii, 867 sq.

[5] Sermon von Bereitung zum Sterben, Erl. Ed., xxi, 272; in Walch, the word " Christ " stands instead of " Saints."

He had, in the Leipzig disputation, questioned the scriptural warrant for the doctrine of PURGATORY. Returning now to this point in a letter to Spalatin, he advances to the bolder declaration, that it is certain that the doctrine of purgatory does not constitute an article of faith, and that the denial of it does not make one a heretic.[1] Yet, for himself, he still cherishes the idea of a purgatory. Thus, for example, in the *Sermon von der heiligen Messe,* when treating of the mass for the dead, he speaks repeatedly of souls in purgatory. To Spalatin he writes in a later letter :[2] " Concerning purgatory I have nothing more certain than a few Psalms, such as vi., xii., xxxvii., and certain others, which speak of that punishment." Evidently, he found in these Psalms reference to such anguish of soul as one may be called upon to endure in purgatory, and often already in the present life (cf. *Operationes in Psalmos,* vi. 6), without regarding the language employed as affording a sufficiently clear evidence to establish the existence of purgatory itself.

Returning now to the subect of the ecclesiastical organization, the priesthood, etc., we must once more call attention to the declarations of the *Sermon von der heiligen Messe,* in which Luther—for the first time to our knowledge—publicly proclaims the UNIVERSAL PRIESTHOOD OF BELIEVERS. We recall also his assertion, in controversy with Emser [3] (in which he had already rejected the special human priesthood of the Church of Rome, represented as parallel with the ancient Aaronic priesthood) that only Christ is for him a priest, in the sense of mediator between God and man. To this is now added the further assertion, that all Christians are priests, in the sense of appearing before God with offerings, and they are such only through Christ and in Him. But we are carried back to the declarations of the *Sermon von der Messe* still more directly by a statement of Luther in a letter written to Spalatin in December, 1519,[4] that he does not know what are the duties of the priests in regard to which the latter inquires ; for the more he considers over it, the less is he able to think of anything more than bare ceremonies. Moreover, the words of 1 Pet. ii. 9, and Rev. i. 6, according to which all Christians are priests, keep forcing themselves upon him. That priesthood, therefore, to which he and

[1] Briefe, i, 367.   [2] Ibid., i, 464.   [3] Supra, p. 304 sq.   [4] Briefe, i, 378.

Spalatin belong appears to be distinguished from the rank of the laity by nothing except the special ministry (*ministerium*), *i. e.*, the administering of Word and sacraments. In everything else they are alike, if we take away the ceremonies and human ordinances. He wonders, he declares, how the *order* attained the name of a *sacrament*, and hopes to discuss the subject further orally with Spalatin in the presence of Melanchthon, with whom he has had many and thorough-going conversations about these things.

That Luther no longer regarded the limits of the Roman ecclesiastical organization as, at the same time, the boundaries of the Church of Christ, we already know. He, therefore, now no longer shrinks from communication with the *Utraquists of Bohemia*, although he does not approve their separation from the Church of Rome. Already in October, 1519, he entertained two representatives sent by the latter, and presented to them a copy of his writings.[1] They had brought to him a book upon Huss. Luther appears now, for the first time, to have become acquainted with the doctrine proclaimed by this man, whom he had once so detested, some of whose chief principles he had, however, defended at Leipzig. With no scruple whatever on account of the ecclesiastical condemnation which had been visited upon the latter, he now allowed himself to be carried away in admiration of his spirit and his knowledge. He believed, said he, that he should yet discover that he himself, and even Staupitz, had without knowing it been teaching Hussite doctrine, and that even Paul and Augustine were literally Hussites.[2]

4. Nature of the Church, as Defined in the Tract, "Of the Papacy at Rome."

NO BODILY HEAD—A SPIRITUAL COMMUNITY—WIDER THAN ORGANIZATION—INVISIBLE—LIMITS OF HUMAN AUTHORITY WITHIN IT.

We have thus been brought back to the consideration of Luther's relation to the ORGANIZED CHURCH, and just at the point

---

[1] Briefe, i, 341, 350.

[2] Ibid., 428, 425. De Wette's estimate as to the time of the last-mentioned letter is probably correct.

of time which we have now reached appeared the publication which first records his view of the Church, in its complete and thenceforth unalterably fixed fundamental outlines, opposing the same directly to the papal hierarchy. We refer to the tract, *Von dem Papstthum zu Rom wider den hochberühmten Romanisten zu Leipzig*,[1] completed by Luther in the latter part of June, 1520.[2] The doctrines which he had just one year before maintained at the Leipzig disputation are here unfolded, followed to their logical conclusions, and clearly presented.

Again, as at Leipzig, the prominent question was, whether the Papacy was a divine or a human ordinance. The " Romanist," Alveld, of the Franciscan Order, had pursued a different course from that of Eck in the attempt to prove the necessity of an ecclesiastical, and hence of the papal, monarchy. Every congregation upon earth, he argued, must, to avoid dissolution, have a bodily head : the Church is a congregation upon earth ; it must, therefore, have a bodily head. Luther denies at the outset the validity of the major premise. He does not recognize the necessity of a monarchy even in civil organizations. The Roman Empire, and many another, enjoyed the very best government for a long time without a single head. The political leagues are still governed in this way. Further, we men are all members of but one race, and yet the various nations have their own heads. In reality, the mistaken inference of Alveld originated in the Middle Ages. The idea of the papal monarchy went hand in hand with that of a world-wide political monarchy. Yea, adds Luther, finally, and if there had never yet been any form of government in the world but the monarchical, who would yet hinder an association of men from selecting several rulers instead of one? But, however this may be, no inference could at any rate be drawn that would be applicable to the Christian Church ; for by no means is a " Christian community (*Gemeine*) like another and worldly community." This brings us to the principal subject, the real nature of the Church.

Luther had long been accustomed to define the Church, in the words of the Apostles' Creed, as the communion of saints. Only in

---

[1] Erl. Ed., xxvii, 85–139.

[2] Briefe, i, 459. It left the press, at all events, at that time, the printing having probably been begun in May (Briefe, i, 451).

this sense, he now declares, do the Holy Scriptures speak of Christendom (*die Christenheit*). This is called in the Scriptures an assembly of all believers in Christ on earth, as we pray in the confession of faith. It is the community of those who live in true faith, hope and love, with one baptism, one faith, one Lord, according to Eph. iv. 5. Although separated by thousands of miles from one another, they are yet *spiritually united*; and *this unity* is sufficient to make a Christendom, whereas, without this, no unity of place, time, person, etc., could make a Christendom. Hence Christ says that His kingdom is not of this world, and that it comes not with observation (John xviii. 36; Lk. xvii. 20 sq.), but that false prophets will say: "Lo here, lo there," etc. (Matt. xxiv. 23, 26). It is a horrible error to account the unity of the community, which Christ has severed from all bodily, outward cities and places, and located in spiritual places, as equivalent to "the bodily community, which must of necessity be bound down to locality and place." In the bodily assembly and unity are many who yet, by their sins, exclude themselves from the inner spiritual unity; and, on the other hand, the fact that one is outside of the Romish unity does not make him a heretic. It is true, indeed, that, as the body is an image of the soul, so also the bodily community (to the analogy of which Alveld had appealed) is a figure of the Christian, spiritual community. But from this it does not follow that the spiritual community must have a bodily head; but the true inference is that the former must have a spiritual as the latter has a bodily head.

This, therefore, is Christendom (or Christianity at large) according to the Holy Scriptures. But there is, Luther proceeds to say, a second way of speaking of Christendom, in which the word is applied to an assembly in a house, parish, bishopric or papacy, with outward exercises, singing, reading, vestments; and particularly to the clerical order, of bishops, priests, etc. With reference to the latter usage, he now declares: that the *words "spiritual" and "church" suffer violence when applied to this outward thing*. No single letter of Holy Scriptures indicates that *this* church, *when standing alone*, has been ordained of God. He would call it only a "bodily external Christendom." Yet he himself would not have us conceive of it as separate from the inward and spiritual Christendom. It is, says he, very much as we may, when speaking of a man, call him, in view of his soul, a spiritual man, and in view of his body, a bodily man. And inasmuch as he counts in the bodily Christendom all those who " in their outward life bear themselves as Christians," he includes " truly thorough Christians together with pretended Christians." Yea, he adds, although this community cannot of itself produce a single true Christian, since all its ranks can exist without faith, yet it is never found to be without some members who are also true Christians; and then still further says: " just as the body does not give life to the soul, and yet the soul lives in the body, and even, too, without the body." This last remark suggests the question, whether, since there are in this bodily community or congregation, also thorough Christians, *all* genuine Christians are not, therefore, to be found in an outward congregation? Can there also be genuine Christians without any outward communion or outward forms? But it must be borne in mind that Luther, in this passage, does not have in view the conception of an outward communion in general, or as such, but is thinking, on the one hand, specifically of the Roman communion, with its outward exercises and ranks, and, on the other hand, of the individual genuine believers, who may have been excluded from this or otherwise scattered throughout the world. Whether there would not arise also for these again a necessity for the establishment of outward forms, is a question which is not now considered. Those, finally, who hold a place in the bodily Christendom without themselves having faith, he pronounces dead in God's sight, and only wooden images of the true Christendom.

There is also a third way of speaking upon this subject, says Luther, in which houses built for the worship of God are called churches, and we hear thus of spiritual property or church property. The introduction of this misuse of language has wrought unutterable injury to the cause of Christianity.

Having then, upon these grounds, rejected the papal supremacy over the Church, Luther returns to the article of the Creed: I believe in a holy Christian Church, the community (*Gemeine*) of saints. He now expressly mentions, as an inference from this article, the *Invisibility* of the Church: "for what one believes is not bodily nor visible." Thus also, he says, no one can *see* who is holy, or who has faith. But he then explains in regard to this community of saints: " The signs by which we can outwardly observe where this Church is in the world are *baptism, sacrament* and the *Gospel*—not Rome, nor this or that place; for where baptism and the Gospel are, there let no one doubt that there are saints, even though they should be but children in the cradle."

We have evidently here already a clear recognition of the distinction between the *visible* and the *invisible* Church; and it is of great importance that we observe precisely how he here defines the latter, and, as we shall find, henceforth continues to define it. This invisible Church is for him something spiritual, and not bodily—something which is believed, and not something which is seen. Yet it is for him, at the same time, something truly real, existing in actual persons, founded and living in the real Christ. And as this community, although not of this world, yet lives in it, we can, therefore, in a certain sense, say of that which we cannot see, that we " outwardly observe where it is." It is clear from this also how essentially the " signs " by which it is said this Church is to be recognized belong to it; for they are not merely signs, but means of grace for the spiritual life itself. Thus by baptism at least " the children in the cradle " are sanctified (even though all the adults were unbelievers). What particular individuals, however, belong to this Church, is hidden from our view. It is, further, only to *this* community, which we cannot see, but for which we may know where to look, that Luther will accord, as we have seen, the name " Church." He refers to the custom of applying the term also to the bodily community, and the so-called spiritual orders, only to immediately and expressly disapprove it. The distinction between the visible and the invisible Church is, therefore, so far as the *terms themselves* are concerned, not according to his idea. He recognizes as " Christendom ", or " Church ", only *that* Christendom which is invisible, and which yet has a real existence in the world and manifests its existence in the means of grace. This remained Luther's conception of the Church, in opposition both to the outward and material and to the spiritualistic views. Melanchthon, in the *Augsburg Confession*, uses the expressions, " the Church broadly speaking " (*large dicta*) and " the Church properly speaking " (*proprie dicta*). According to Luther, we should have to substitute for these: Church, or Christendom, according to a purely erroneous, and Church according to the proper and biblical, use of the term.[1] It might be

---

[1] Cf. my discussion in " Luther's Lehre von der Kirche," 1853, sect. 5.

further asked, whether those baptized persons who have become unbelievers and fallen into sin do not also, according to Luther's doctrine of baptismal regeneration here announced, still belong to the body of Christ; and whether, accordingly, among Christian people, all of whom have been baptized, the spiritual body of Christ, or the spiritual community, does not coincide with the external and visible. Luther, during the period now under consideration, never departed from the above conception of baptism; but yet it is clear that he does not, therefore, by any means consider unbelieving and unfaithful baptized persons as members of Christ, or of His true " community." They are " dead in the sight of God," " wooden images," etc. This he afterwards constantly declares, and in even still stronger language.

With this conception of the nature of the Church, Luther now proceeds to prove, in refutation of Alveld, that it *cannot* have an earthly, human head. No man can even know who is a true believer, and thus a true member of Christendom; how then should any one rule over that which he cannot recognize or know? Further, it is the very nature of every head to infuse life and activity into its members. Thus, for example, a temporal ruler infuses into his subjects his own purpose and will, and sees to it that they do the work which he desires. But no man can infuse into another man's soul, or even into his own, faith, nor anything of the mind, will, or work of Christ, which are the chief matters in the Christian community. Only Christ can do this. Just as little is it possible for a man to become a vicar, or substitute of Christ. For a substitute must infuse the same work as his master would have infused. The Pope must, therefore, if he would be a substitute, infuse into a believer his Lord's work, namely, faith, hope, love and all grace. But, whatever may be thought of the validity of this comparison, we can at all events depend upon the declaration of Paul (Eph. iv. 15 sq.), in which he gives to Christendom only one head, to whom all the members must cling, and in union with whom they must grow—namely, Christ.

What was Peter, then, according to this? And what shall we think the Pope to be? Luther answers: Peter was, like any other apostle, one of twelve chosen messengers. Christ sent out all the apostles with equal power, namely, with His Word and His message, according to 2 Cor. v. 20 and 1 Cor. iii. 5. A messenger, too, the Pope should be, together with the bishops. Now, one messenger may be better or more capable than another ; but since they all carry one message, no one can be, by virtue of his office, above the rest.

We must, however, constantly remember that, in all these utterances, Luther has in view only the spiritual life of the congregation and its members. He would guard this from every suggestion of human supremacy. Here, all bishops are to work on an equal footing with the Pope (and, we may add, with every preacher), are to " pasture and rule " through the Gospel. This belongs to the very essence of church life ; this is of divine right. But he now also adds : " While all bishops are, according to the divine appointment, alike, I may yet acknowledge that one is by human appointment above the others in the external Church." Here, says he, the Popes may, indeed, infuse their purposes and their laws, in the outward control of the Church and with outward pomp. He describes their control, in so far as it extends only to this outward sphere, and does not intrude upon the relation of the soul to God, as not contrary to the divine will, since even he himself does not extend his conception of " divine appointment " to this sphere. But he again repeats, that no one is thus, *i. e.*, by virtue of outward ordinances, made a Christian, and no one becomes a heretic because not standing under such human ordinances ; " for there are as many customs as there are lands."

Luther in this publication treats, still further, of the claims of the Romanists based upon the office and position of the Old Testament high-priest and upon Matt. xvi. 18 sq. and John xxi. 15 sqq. In the " rock," in Matt. xvi., he sees, not Peter, but " only Christ and faith." The gates of hell, he says, have often had possession of the Papacy. Peter, he again maintains (with citation of Matt. xviii.), received the keys, " not as Peter, but instead of the congregation." He now opposes the idea that the power of the keys and the power to rule are one. The former has reference only to the binding and loosing of sins, spoken of in John xx. 23. The latter has to do also with the pious, who have to be bound or loosed ; and he includes under it, at the farthest, nothing but " preaching, admonishing, comforting, holding mass, imparting the sacrament, and the like." The scriptural declarations concerning the keys are to be considered as nothing more than " simply gracious promises given to the entire community (of believers), in order that poor sinful consciences may have a consolation when they are released, or absolved, by a man."

Finally, Luther declares that, inasmuch as we see that the Pope stands in his power above all the bishops, to which position he has not attained without the divine counsel (although, in Luther's opinion, as a result, not of the gracious, but of the wrathful counsel of God, for the chastisement of the world), he would not have any one resist the Pope, but rather that all should endure him with all patience, out of regard for the counsel of God. But for two things he is resolved to contend : first, he will not allow men to set up new articles of faith, and condemn others as heretics because they are not under the Pope ; and secondly, everything that the Pope appoints he will accept only in the sense that he will test it by the Holy Scriptures. If these two points are granted him, he will let the Pope alone ; yes, he will even help to exalt him as highly as any one may wish. But if these points be not granted, the Pope shall be to him neither Pope nor Christian, but he will freely declare him to be Antichrist. Others may make an idol of this Antichrist, but *he* will not worship him.

Section II. The Three Principal Reformatory Publications of A. D. 1520.

1. *Address to the Christian Nobility.*

THE SECULAR POWER MAY INSTITUTE REFORMS—PAPAL USURPATION —POINTS FOR THE CONSIDERATION OF A GENERAL COUNCIL— CHALLENGE TO ROME.

Luther cannot, of course, when he wrote as above, have still entertained any hope that his opponents, or the Pope himself, would surrender the doctrines and claims which he was resolved to combat to the utmost, without regard to consequences, as anti-christian. While still laboring upon the tract against Alveld, he was already engaged in the preparation of another work, which was designed to prepare the way for a reformation to be accomplished without the Pope, or, if necessary, in defiance of his opposition. He writes to Spalatin, not later than the early part of June,[1] that he proposes to publish an address to the Emperor

[1] Briefe, i, 453 sq.

Charles and the German Nobility against the tyranny and good-for-nothingness of the Romish curia. The letter which Luther soon after sent to Amsdorf, together with a copy of the *Schrift an den christlichen Adel deutscher Nation*, is dated June 23d. But yet Luther says, on the 20th of July, that the address is just then being published, repeating the same statement on August 3d. On the 18th of August, 4000 copies had already been disposed of.[1]

While Luther was engaged upon this document, the Bull condemning his writings was being prepared at Rome. He could already foresee that it would certainly be issued. On the other hand, certain of the German nobles, especially Francis of Sickingen, had offered him protection. He actually thought at one time of availing himself of this offer, writing candidly to Spalatin that he does not by any means think himself authorized, or able, to employ the secular arm of the nobles for violent intervention, but yet confessing that he, in his position at Wittenberg, feels himself under restraint in his conflict with the Pope in view of the possible consequences for his Prince and the University, and stating that a place now seemed to be open to him in which he would be free from all constraint of this character.[2] In various letters, he now declares that the die is cast; that he despises alike the rage and the favor of Rome; that they may, if they will, burn everything of his, and *he* will, for his part, publicly burn the whole papal law; that he will have no further fellowship with them forever; that he now fears nothing; and that he now no longer owes the Pope any obedience, unless it can be shown that he owes allegiance " to the born Antichrist." [3]

Under these circumstances, and in this spirit, he published the *Address to the Nobility*. Rightly did his friend Lange call it a war-trumpet. It struck even friends as an " atrocious and ferocious little book." He himself acknowledged that it was " full of liberty and impetuosity." [4] It is bold, dashing, vehement, and in its contents strikes out far beyond the sphere of the Church and into that of the state. There is nothing like it, particularly in the features last mentioned, in the earlier writings

---

[1] Briefe, i, pp. 470, 475, 478.   The address itself may be found in Erl. Ed., xxi, 274–360.

[2] Cf. especially, Briefe, i, 465 sq.

[3] Ibid., pp. 466, 475, 478.   [4] Ibid., p. 478.

of Luther. It appeared even to himself, as he says in his dedication to Amsdorf, as though he were now again just learning to cry out afresh : " The time for silence is past, and the time to speak has come." If any one feels inclined to accuse him, however, of stepping beyond his sphere, or of overstepping, within his sphere, the limits of his calling as a " sworn doctor of the Holy Scriptures " (cf. the letter to Amsdorf), let such critic first ponder carefully the intimate connection of all the points there discussed with the profoundest central truth of his most sacred evangelical convictions. How little he thought, in this bold assault, of claiming for himself the leadership in the divinely-demanded reformation, may be seen from a letter to Lange, in which he suggests that perhaps he may be permitted to serve as the forerunner of Philip (Melanchthon), preparing the way for him, like another Elijah, by throwing Israel and the followers of Ahab into terror and confusion.[1]

The object of the *Address* is thus briefly stated by the author to Amsdorf : he has brought together a few points, relating to the *improvement of the condition of Christian affairs*, for the purpose of laying them before the Nobility, in the hope that God may help His Church through the laity, since the clergy, to whom it more properly belongs, have become utterly careless. And it is not alone to the Nobility that he addresses himself, but to the Emperor as well. It is the " secular power " in general which he would arouse to undertake with the nobles the reformatory work.[2]

Luther's doctrine of the divine institution of the secular power, of a divine right inhering in it, and of the supremacy which belongs to it, as above even the spiritual orders, in secular affairs, have already become familiar to us from our examination of his *Resolutio* upon the *Thirteenth Thesis* of the Leipzig disputation. He still based it upon the apostolic declarations then cited. For this doctrine, so far as the independence of the civil power, as contrasted with the ecclesiastical and papal, is concerned, the way was prepared by that very conception of the nature of the Church and its officers which we have just seen more fully developed in his later publications. We must here recall also the *Inscription to Radhemius and Carlstadt*, in which he dedicates to them, in September, 1519, his *Commentary on Galatians*. He there re-

---

[1] Briefe, i, 478.   [2] Erl. Ed., xxi, 359 sq.

fers to the resolution of the Augsburg Diet in 1518, in which the
German princes refused to sanction a tax imposed by a Roman
council. He justifies them most fully in maintaining, as they do
in their resolution, that even a council and a Pope may err.[1] He
had already in January petitioned the Emperor Charles V. to
grant him protection against an unrighteous condemnation, by
means of which it was planned to destroy at once himself and
the Gospel.[2] He asks that it be granted only until he shall have
been permitted to prepare his defence in an orderly way, and
shall have come out of the transaction as either victor or vanquished. The authority of the *Emperor* to do this, he finds in
the fact that it is the calling of the latter to wield the sword in
the interest of truth, which is now threatened.

He now undertakes to prove, still further, that the Emperor
and the Nobility, as Christians, have authority to institute reforms even within the sphere of the Church itself. The basis of
the argument here employed is also already familiar to us, *i. e.*,
his doctrine of the universal priesthood of believers. This doctrine now reaches its full development, together with all its
natural consequences.

The Romanists, asserts the author of the *Address*, have hitherto built THREE WALLS about themselves, in order that no one
might reform them.

When the secular power is invoked against them, they build
their FIRST WALL in maintaining that the secular power has no
authority over them, but that, on the contrary, *the spiritual power
has authority over the secular*. But, says Luther, their idea
of the spiritual order, as they call the Pope, bishops, priests
and monks, has no foundation; for all Christians belong to the
spiritual order by virtue of one baptism, one Gospel and one
faith. We all become priests by baptism, according to 1 Pet.
ii. 9 and Rev. v. 10. There is here no difference of order, but
only a difference of office. *To exercise this office does not, however, befit every one; for, just because we all as priests have equal
authority, dare no single one, without our, that is, the Christian
community's or congregation's consent and choice, presume to
exercise the office for which all have authority.* Thus Luther is
now led by the very doctrine of the universal priesthood to discuss

<hr />

[1] Com. ad Gal., Erl. Ed., iii, 133 sq.　　　　[2] Briefe, i, 393.

the necessity of a special commissioning of individual believers. That there is a necessity for a special office, he takes for granted, *i. e.*, that the Word must be publicly and regularly proclaimed, the sacraments administered as a gift bestowed upon the congregation, the power of the keys properly and publicly exercised, and, still further, as lying in the very nature of the case, that this cannot be done by all, but only by persons designated for the purpose. A special calling of such persons is, therefore, demanded, just because the spiritual character upon which the authority for all these activities rest is possessed by all.

Accordingly, the consecration by a bishop, or *ordination*, has for Luther now no further significance than that the latter, in the place and person of the entire assembly, takes one out of the multitude who have all equal power, and instructs him to exercise this power for the others; just as though ten brothers, or princes, or heirs of equal rank, should select one of their number to manage the inheritance for them all. To make the principle still more plain, the case is supposed of a little band of Christians, without any ordained priest or bishop in their company, captured by an enemy and placed by themselves in a wilderness. Should these now elect one of their number, and confer upon him the office of baptizing, holding mass, absolving and preaching, such an one would be as truly a priest as though all the bishops in the world, and the Pope, had ordained him. Appeal is further taken to the fact, that in cases of extremity, any Christian is considered authorized to baptize and absolve. This would not be possible if all were not priests. The practice of the Ancient Church in the election of bishops is also again referred to (cf. in the *Resolutiones* as against Eck, *supra*, p. 302), *i. e.*, it is claimed, in accordance with principles maintained in the *Address*, that formerly the bishops and priests were selected by the people from the multitude, and were afterwards confirmed in their office by other bishops. If this is the true theory of the clerical office, it follows directly that a priest may be again removed from his office, and is then no longer anything more than an ordinary layman. The " indelible character " Luther pronounces a dream of the imagination.

We are thus, at length, led to see the position which should, according to these principles, be accorded to the *secular government* as over against the so-called spiritual orders. The so-called spiritual classes or individuals have nothing more than other

Christians, except "the handling of God's Word and the sacraments." But the government, on its part, has, none the less, an office of its own, namely, the sword and the rod, to punish the wicked and to protect the pious. Likewise every mechanic, farmer, etc., has his own office and work, although all are alike priests. It is, moreover, the duty of every member of Christendom to serve the other members by means of his own office and work. The office of the government should, therefore, be exercised unhindered throughout the whole body of Christendom— Pope, priests and monks not excluded. If the government is to be hindered because it is a lower office than that of the preachers, why are not mechanics also hindered in performing their peculiar work for the Pope and the priests? Luther has thus in the *Address to the Nobility* but maintained, in regard to the secular government, that which he had already claimed for it in earlier writings, namely, the right which belongs to it in its own sphere as distinct from that of the Church. But he deduces still further consequences from the doctrine of the universal priesthood.

If the attempt be made to rebuke the Romanists by quotations from the Scriptures, they then build their SECOND WALL by asserting that the *interpretation of the Scriptures belongs alone to the Pope*. In refutation of this claim, Luther quotes 1 Cor. xiv. 30; John vi. 45; 1 Cor. ii. 15; 2 Cor. iv. 13. In the Saviour's prayer for Peter, that his faith may not fail (Lk. xxii. 32), he sees a prayer, not for the Popes, who have in great part been without faith, but, on the contrary, for all the apostles and all Christians as well as for Peter, according to the plain words of the prayer in John xvii. 9, 20. We should all, as priests and spiritual men, promptly pass impartial judgment, according to our own enlightened understanding of the Scriptures, upon everything which the Popes do or neglect to do. There is thus established, finally, the right of Christian laymen to oppose ignorant, ungodly priests even in the sphere of the Church's special activity.

If the Romanists, says Luther, be threatened with a council, they build up their THIRD WALL by asserting that *only the Pope can call a council*. But, he maintains on the contrary, if the Pope does anything contrary to the Scriptures, we are in duty bound to stand by the latter, to rebuke him, and to control him, according to the command of Christ (Matt. xviii. 15: "tell it to the Church"). But if I am to bring accusation against the Pope before the Church, I must also call the latter together. There is nothing to interfere with my doing so except the laws of the Papists themselves, and these *can have no binding authority except in so far as they are not injurious to Christendom and the laws of God*. The council at Jerusalem (Acts xv.) was not called by Peter, but by all the apostles and elders. The Council of Nice was summoned by the Emperor Constantine, and many emperors since his day have exercised the same authority. " Therefore," he proceeds, " when necessity requires it, and the Pope is obnoxious to Christendom, *whoever first can* should see to it, as a true member of the body at large, that a really free council be held." And we are thus brought to recognize a right and duty inhering, under such circumstances and in such extremities of the Church, in *the secular government*, by virtue of its general character, even in matters pertaining primarily to the sphere of the Church. To the sentence last quoted Luther immediately adds : " which no one can so well do as the secular sword, especially since they, too, are now fellow-christians, fellow priests, with like authority in all things, and should freely exercise the office and work which they have received from God wherever its exercise may be necessary or beneficial." It would surely, says he, be a very unnatural procedure if a fire should break out in a city and all the citizens should stand still and let it burn, just because they did not have the authority of the burgomaster, or, perhaps, because the fire had started in the burgomaster's house. The Romanists boast of their power, which they claim it is not proper for any one to oppose. But a power that ruins Christendom and shuts out everything that could tend to improvement is a power of the devil and Antichrist, and we should withstand it with all our might.[1]

Luther then proceeds to enumerate the *separate points which should be the subjects of discussion in a council*. Popes, bishops and all the learned, he maintains, should give attention to these matters day and night ; but, if they neglect their duty, the people at large and the secular sword should take action.

In the " points " themselves which are thus suggested, we recognize again Luther's earnest endeavor to restore to the

---

[1] Cf. already, Sermon von den guten Werken, Erl. Ed., xx, 267 : We should hold the Roman authority in honor as our most exalted Father, and yet, since they have become frantic and demented, we should not grant them their requests, lest Christendom be thereby devastated.

Church its spiritual character and to protect the sphere of secular power against the encroachments of a secularized hierarchy.

The first thing which he denounces as offensive is the WORLDLY POMP AND GLORY OF THE POPE, or, in other words, his triple crown. He then speaks of the excessive number of cardinals, of the money which they consume, and of the expensiveness of the papal court, together with the exactions of money in all countries subject to the power of Rome. He demands that the princes interfere to prevent these. France has already begun to protect herself against the extortion; why do the Germans always allow themselves to be flayed and befooled? The civil authorities should forbid the payment of the Annates (the value of every spiritual living for the first year of the incumbent) to Rome. These were demands which, while, upon the part of the Reformer himself, most intimately associated with earnest desire for the welfare of the Church, must, at the same time, appeal in very wide circles to purely secular motives. The encroachments referred to had long been the subject of most grievous complaint upon the part of those whose interest was confined to the sphere of politics.

Luther's idea as to the organization of the Church itself finds fuller expression in the recommendations: that the BESTOWAL OF BENEFICES by the Pope in the separate national churches no longer be allowed; that it be forbidden by an imperial statute to look to Rome for the confirmation and the pallium of bishops; that the system approved by the Nicene Council be again introduced, according to which a bishop receives his confirmation at the hands of neighboring bishops or the archbishop; that the monasteries be no longer exempted from the jurisdiction of the bishoprics in which they were located; that the appealing of not only purely secular matters, but of questions relating to ecclesiastical investitures and benefices, to Rome for decision be forbidden, etc. It is Luther's theory that the separate national churches, under their own bishops, should secure that measure of independence which his rejection of the papal primacy left him at liberty to sanction, and which appeared to him indispensable for the welfare of the Church. The judges at Rome, he maintains, have, at any rate, too little acquaintance with the manners, laws and customs of the various nations to enable them to avoid the doing of injustice even unintentionally. He does not by any means propose the entire abolition of a primacy. In case the primates, or archbishops, should be unable of themselves to attend to any matter, or should fall to quarreling among themselves, such affairs, he grants, may be laid before the Pope. Besides the hearing of such appeals, the Pope should give himself to prayer, just as the apostles (Acts vi. 2, 4) desired not to leave the Word of God to serve tables, but to give themselves to preaching and prayer; whereas just the reverse is now the case at Rome. The German primate should then conduct a general consistory, before which all appeals from German churches should be laid.

Among Luther's further suggestions in regard to church ordinances and life, we must note especially his recommendation that the PRIESTS BE GIVEN LIBERTY TO MARRY. " Truly a noble, great and blessed state, the marriage state, if it be rightly observed," he had already declared a year before in a sermon.[1] He had then appealed to the divine institution of marriage (Gen. ii.) ; had, at the same time, called attention to the terrible misery connected with it when not rightly observed, with the remark that, if many a one would consider the latter, he would lose all craving for it; had declared celibacy to be still better for those who by the grace of God possessed the gift of continency, adding, however, at once that the latter gift is granted to but few, and that only by special divine favor. He now appeals to the actual state of affairs, to the degenerate condition of the priesthood, the multitude of poor priests overburdened with women and children, the troubled consciences to whom no one could bring relief. " If Pope and bishop," he declares, " suffer such things to go on, and do nothing to arrest such ruin, I will relieve my conscience and open my mouth wide." He maintains, that every town ought to have its priest, and that he should not be compelled to remain unmarried, as Paul writes, in 1 Tim. iii. 2 and Tit. i. 6, 7, that a bishop should be a man blameless and the husband of one respectable wife. It was so in the beginning. Afterwards, when great persecution arose, and conflict against the heretics, many of the Fathers willingly denied themselves the privilege of marriage, in order that they might the better devote themselves to study, and be at any hour prepared for death or conflict. But the Papacy at Rome has iniquitously made of this a universal law, under the suggestion of the devil, as declared in 1 Tim. iv. 3.

[1] Erl. Ed., xvi, 158–165.

Luther sees, indeed, that the entire system of church government, and the control of church property, must be changed if a
married priesthood be allowed. He declares himself willing to
allow Pope, bishops, chapters, priests and monks—none of which
have been appointed by God—to continue ; and if they have laid
burdens upon themselves, they may still carry them. But he is
now speaking of the pastoral office, which God has appointed,
and whose incumbents are to supply (rule) a congregation with
preaching and the sacraments, and to live in its midst, leading
an ordinary domestic life. To these pastors, at least, the liberty
to marry should be granted by a council. And he now gives bold
advice to the consciences of those pastors (parish priests) who
were otherwise pious and irreproachable in their lives, but who, in
their weakness, had entered into improper relations with the opposite sex. He advises every one in such circumstances, if he
cherishes heartfelt affection for the woman, to take her as his
lawful wife without any papal dispensation to ease his conscience,
even though the step must bring public disgrace upon him. He
urges those who have the faith needed for such a bold step to
take his advice, assuring them that he will not lead them astray.

Luther does not yet express himself as absolutely opposed to
the system of MONASTICISM. He recommends, however, a reduction in the number of the existing orders and a prohibition of the
establishment of new ones. He would like to see the chapters
and monasteries brought back again to their original character.
They were once Christian schools, in which the Scriptures and
good behavior were taught in a Christian way, and the young
were educated for civil positions and for the ministry. They
were all free, and each inmate could remain just as long as he
wished. It was only afterwards that this voluntary service of God
was fettered by vows, which were exalted even above the baptismal vow, and the institutions themselves transformed into places
of eternal imprisonment. The earlier liberty should be restored,
that the souls of Christians may no longer be bound by laws of
human invention. Thus, Luther would abolish the very central
and essential characteristic of monasticism. As to a possible
release from the obligation of monastic vows already assumed, he
makes as yet no suggestion.

Luther is very hostile to the *Mendicants*. He would have at
least ten of their cloisters combined in one, and then have their

begging prohibited. The right to preach and hear confession should, in view of the irregularities and offences which have been occasioned, be taken from them, except when individual members of their orders be regularly called and ordained. He had already at an earlier date, in a letter to Spalatin, expressed himself with great vehemence against these orders.[1]

He would have the PENALTIES of the canon law limited, the INTERDICT abolished, and EXCOMMUNICATION brought back again to the place and function assigned it in the Scriptures.

In the ecclesiastical MARRIAGE LAWS, he desires changes in the prescriptions as to the prohibited degrees of consanguinity, especially in those based upon sponsorship.

The observance of FASTS should be left free to every one. In Rome they are, at any rate, but a subject for ridicule.

So far as DISPENSATIONS from ecclesiastical requirements should be at all allowed, he desires that the authority to grant them may not be vested in the Pope, but extended to every pastor, and that they be granted gratuitously as a means of advancing the spiritual welfare of souls. In the whole business of papal dispensations, he sees a shameful public traffic.

The ANNUAL MASSES FOR SOULS, etc., should be abolished, or, at least, greatly reduced in number, on account of the present abuse of them, the vain babbling (contrary to Matt. vi. 7 ; xxiii. 14), and the greed for gold to which they minister. It would be better if a chapter or monastery should appoint all masses and vigils on one day, and then observe them with sincere earnestness.

We have witnessed the Reformer's zealous opposition to the then popular PILGRIMAGES even before the indulgence controversy. He now wishes that the pilgrimages to Rome, where the pilgrims at best witness only abuses, might be abolished, or permitted only to such as shall first prove, at an examination conducted by their pastors and the civil authorities, that they have some real occasion for making the journey. He does not declare the pilgrimages as of evil intent, but " they turn out badly in our day." He then reminds his readers, as he had before done, of the nearer obligations which always take precedence by far of pilgrimages.

The " WILD CHAPELS AND FIELD-CHURCHES," to which so many have recourse in his day, are especially obnoxious to him.

[1] Briefe, i, 423.

By these, the parish churches are weakened, false religion established, taverns and brothels increased, etc. It does not help the matter to appeal to the miraculous occurrences which are said to be witnessed there, as the evil spirit can also work wonders. If earnest steps were taken against the disorderly proceedings, the miracles would soon cease.

Evil results, both spiritual and temporal, are feared from the multiplication of FESTIVAL-DAYS. God is more provoked by drinking, gambling, idling, and all manner of other sins on these occasions than upon the ordinary working days. The working man is, moreover, thus·led to neglect his work, waste more of his means than at other times, and, besides, injure his bodily health. If it be thought desirable to retain the festivals of the Virgin Mary and the leading saints, they might be arranged to occur upon Sundays, or they might be celebrated merely by a morning mass, and the remainder of the day be devoted to ordinary labor.[1]

As the mendicant orders, so also MENDICANCY itself may and should, in Luther's opinion, be banished from Christendom.[2] Every town ought to care for its own poor, and strange beggars should not be allowed to pursue their avocation. To this end, a guardian for the poor should be appointed, whose duty it should be to make himself acquainted with their needs, and report accordingly to the council or the parish priest (pastor). Luther here then employs an argument based upon general economic principles, declaring that he has reckoned it out, that by means of the various mendicant orders, common beggars, pilgrims, etc., a town is laid under contribution about sixty times a year; and if to this there be now added the taxes of the secular government, and, finally, the booty that goes to Rome tò be there wasted, it is a real wonder how the people can continue to live and have anything to eat.

One of the chief matters of concern for Luther was at this time the relation of the Church to the BOHEMIANS. It is high time, he declares, that their cause be seriously and honestly examined. It must certainly be granted, in the first place, that Huss and Jerome were burned at Constance contrary to divine commandment, *i. e.*, in violation of safe-conduct and oath. As to the arti-

---

[1] Cf. Sermon von den guten Werken, Erl. Ed., xx, 247.

[2] Cf. already, Sermon vom Wucher, Erl. Ed., xx, 97.

cles of Huss, he does not propose at this time to express his opinion, although he can find nothing erroneous in them. But, however much of a heretic he may have been, we surely cannot expect the Bohemians to approve the violation of the safe-conduct. At any rate, heretics are to be vanquished, not with fire, but with arguments (*Schriften*); otherwise, hangmen would be the most learned doctors upon earth. In the second place, several pious, prudent bishops and learned men should be sent to the Bohemians, to examine into their belief and endeavor to bring about a harmonizing of their divisions. The Pope should also, on his part, surrender for a while his supremacy there and allow the Bohemians, in accordance with the statute of the Nicene Council, to select a bishop out of their own number, and have him confirmed by the neighboring bishops. Luther further advises, in harmony with the principles already adduced from his earlier writings, that the *use of the cup* be granted them. The new bishop should meanwhile only kindly admonish them, in order that disputings and mutual wranglings upon this subject might cease. Freedom should also be allowed them in questions concerning the priestly robes and other Roman ordinances, if they will only live aright in faith and according to the Scriptures. At this point, Luther now makes the assertion that *the doctrine, " that bread and wine are* [not] *essentially and naturally in the sacrament,"* is not an article of faith, but, on the contrary, a fancy of St. Thomas and the Pope. The article of faith is only, " that in natural bread and wine is true natural flesh and blood of Christ." He could not, therefore, condemn the Picards, if they should have no other error in their view of the sacrament of the altar than to believe that bread and wine are naturally present, yet, under these, true flesh and blood of Christ. It was here, then, for the first time, that Luther raised objection to the dogma of Transubstantiation. He expresses, in this connection, his desire that the parties to the dispute may exercise patience toward one another; for there is no danger in either view, whether or no the bread is believed to be present. We must make allowance for many opinions, provided only that they work no injury to faith. If, indeed, the faith of the Picards were not that here ascribed to them, he would " rather have [them] outside, but yet instruct them in the truth."

Luther, finally, attaches great importance, for the welfare of the

Church, to an improvement of the COURSE OF STUDY IN THE UNIVERSITIES, and especially in the INSTRUCTION OF THE YOUNG. Particularly does he now again express himself plainly against the domination of the " blind heathen master," Aristotle, whose books upon logic, rhetoric and poetry he however recognizes as helpful to study. He pronounces the " Ethics " the worst of his books, because it flatly opposes the doctrine of grace. In the discourse, *De anima*, he sees a denial of immortality. Much depends, he declares, upon the study of the Latin, Greek and Hebrew languages, mathematics and history. The theologians ought to be really teachers of the Holy Scriptures, whereas now the *Sententiae* of the Scholastics hold full sway. The number of books employed in theological study ought to be diminished, the best only being selected. The writings of the Fathers are now handled in such a way that those who study them remain in them and never come to the Scriptures, whereas the Fathers themselves only seek to lead us to the latter. In the lower schools, as well as in the universities, the Scriptures should be the chief text-book. He would like to see, not only schools for boys, but in every town also a school for girls, in which the children might learn the Gospel. Such had been, at one time, the laudable object of the monastery schools. He bitterly laments that now in Christendom the young people are left to languish, and miserably go to ruin, because they have not the Gospel.

We have, in the above, arranged under a few prominent headings the demands of Luther which relate to the inner life of the Church, without observing strictly the order in which he himself has presented them.

Returning now to the general conception of the nature of the Church and its power, upon the basis of which protest had been already made in the *Introduction of the Address*, against the ENCROACHMENTS OF THE PAPACY upon the sphere of the secular government, we shall find, in the enumeration of the points to be determined by a council, yet other complaints concerning definite abuses. Attention has already been called to the section in which protest is made against the carrying to Rome of secular matters, which should be left to the decision of the secular government. The same general conception of ecclesiastical sovereignty leads the Reformer to regard as a grievance the claim of the Pope to feudal supremacy over Naples and Sicily. The

Emperor, he says, should direct the Pope to attend to the Bible and prayer-book, allowing the secular officers to govern the land and the people. He expresses the same judgment in regard to the immediate papal possessions in Italy. Appeal is made to 2 Tim. ii. 4 : " No man that warreth entangleth himself with the affairs of this life." In this warfare, it is asserted, the Pope should be the foremost, as even Christ Himself, whose substitute the latter claims to be, would have nothing to do with secular government (cf. Lk. xii. 14). Already in February, 1520, Luther had in hand Laurentius Valla's exposure of the fraudulent character of the supposed *Donation of Constantine*, published by Hutten, and was incited by it to new expressions of his horror at the good-for-nothingness of the Romish apologists, and of his suspicion that the Pope is the real Antichrist.[1]

But Luther felt a very peculiar interest in the investigation of the VALIDITY OF THE ROMAN EMPIRE OF THE GERMAN NATION. He placed no confidence in the allegation of the Pope, who claimed that it had been received from the Greek Emperor and brought to the German nation. According to his view, the real Roman Empire foretold by Balaam and Daniel had been long since destroyed, as Balaam had prophesied, *i. e.*, that the Romans should come, destroy the Jews, and then themselves perish (cf. Numb. xxiv. 24). This had been accomplished through the Goths, through the Turkish Empire, through the downfall of Africa and Asia, and through the ascendancy of France, Spain and Venice. God, to whom it is a very little thing to cast about empires here and there, and who sometimes bestows them even upon men of evil character, did, indeed, make use of the Pope's wickedness to give to the German nation the present Empire after the fall of the first Roman Empire. But the Germans should now govern it, as given to them by God, just as long as it may please God to permit them to do so, in His fear, and free from the authority of the Pope. They won it honestly themselves. The language of Luther here attests that he felt all the pain which a true German must experience in view of the multitude of injuries and indignities which the nation and its emperors had received at the hand of the Pope. It is pitiful to tell, says he, how wantonly and haughtily many a noble Emperor

[1] Briefe, i, 430.

has in days past been persecuted by them. Through papal wiles, the Germans have already, also, paid all too dearly for their Roman Empire in the blood of countless multitudes, in the suppression of their liberty, in the robbery of their goods, and especially of their churches and benefices, in the endurance of unutterable deception and disgrace. They now have the name of the Empire, but the Pope has all its possessions, honor, body, life and soul. For a long time before the preparation of the *Address,* the soul of Luther had been stirred with indignation at the contemptuous treatment which the Germans had been compelled to endure at the hands of the Romanists. He had said in the preface to his *Commentary upon Galatians :* " What do they do except esteem us Germans mere blockheads, dullards, dolts and, as they say, barbarians and beasts, ridiculing even our incredible patience under their jeers and robbery?" [1] He himself knows how they are in Rome accustomed to speak of the " drunken Germans." [2] He speaks of these things repeatedly in the *Address,* declaring, for example, that the Papists have always abused the simplicity of the Germans, and have supposed that they could delude and befool the stupid Germans at pleasure. He would like them now to learn at Rome that the Germans are not always stupid and drunk, but that they have also, at length, become Christians, and, as such, do not propose any longer to endure the mockery of the name of Christ, under which the papal outrages are committed.[3]

In his zeal for the " improvement of the state of Christian affairs," he comes at length to speak also of various secular ordinances. When discussing the Universities, he complains of the present condition of CIVIL LAW. This, too, he declares, has become a wilderness, although, indeed, much better and more just than the ecclesiastical, in which there is nothing good at all. But there has come to be entirely too much of it. He would think it for the best, that, as every land has a character and calling of its own, it should also be governed by brief laws of its own. The extensive laws imported from distant lands serve only for the oppression of the people, and hinder rather than help in the settlement of disputes. He hopes, however, that this subject

---

[1] Comment. ad Gal., iii, 133.

[2] Erl. Ed., xxvii, 135.   [3] Cf. ibid., pp. 294, 307, 354.

has already received fuller consideration by others than he is able to give it. In the last section of the *Address*, Luther proposes, having said enough of spiritual wrongs, also to point out, in part, the SECULAR EVILS of the day. He deems it necessary that laws be enacted against *luxury* in clothing and diet, especially as so much money is sent out of the country for such purposes. The practice of *usury* appears to him the greatest calamity.[1] He takes offence especially at the conduct of the great merchants and capitalists, and would like to see a bridle laid in the mouths of the usurers and other like classes. He cannot understand, he says, how a man with a hundred guldens can gain twenty or more every year, and that not from products of the earth or from the increase of cattle, in which case it might be attributed, not to man's cunning, but to the blessing of God. It would be much more in accordance with the divine will, he thinks, to give more attention to husbandry and less to trade, as God has commanded men to work in the ground, and there is yet much land that has never yet been turned by the plow. Yet he merely commends this thought to the worldly-wise; it is his duty in the matter, as a theologian, only to criticise the evil and offensive appearance, according to 1 Thes. v. 22. Then follows a complaint of the *gormandizing and drinking*, which are accounted a special vice of the Germans, and which lead to murder, adultery and all manner of iniquities. Preaching has no longer any effect upon this evil; the secular sword must interfere to check it. Finally, reference is made to the *houses of ill-fame*. It will be hard, indeed, to abolish these. The frequenting of them is at least better than the assaulting of married women and pure girls. But a secular Christian government should seek to find some other than this heathenish way of protecting the latter.

All these points Luther had, indeed, already urged in his *Sermon von guten Werken*, being there led, in the discussion of the Fourth Commandment, to speak of the duties of the civil authorities.[2] He now refers the secular authorities and the Nobility to that publication, especially in view of the Christian

---

[1] Cf. already Dec. Præc., 184, 190; the two "sermons" upon Usury (of the year 1519), Erl. Ed., xx, 89 sqq.; the "sermon" on Good Works, Erl. Ed., xx, 221 sq. Also, further discussion, Bk. III, Chap. II.

[2] Erl. Ed., xx, 271 sq.

25

precepts affecting their own position and calling. He had there warned them not to give heed to sycophants: then, particularly, that they should not rush on in unbridled self-will; that, even in the best cause, they should not always dash forward recklessly, etc. Yet, after all, he adds, the secular abuses are not to be compared with those in the spiritual sphere.

In the *Conclusion*, Luther confesses that he may have pitched his voice in too high a key, suggested much that is impossible, and treated some points with entirely too much severity. But, he adds: "I am in duty bound to say these things; I would rather have the *world* than *God* angry with me. They cannot, at any rate, take more than life from me. I have already often attempted to make peace with my adversaries; but I perceive that God has been through them but compelling me to speak ever the more boldly. Well, if it must be so, I know yet another little song about Rome and her minions. If their ears are itching, I will sing that, too, for them, and tune my notes to the highest pitch. Do you understand, dear Rome, what I mean?" He closes with the prayer: "God grant to us all a Christian understanding, and especially to the Christian Nobility of the German Nation true spiritual courage to do the best for His poor Church. Amen."

Thus did Luther, in this publication, give right full and energetic expression to all that burdened his heart as a theologian, a Christian and a German. The peculiar ideas concerning luxurious diet, financial operations, etc., were certainly shared by a multitude of upright Christian men throughout the land. But was it not inevitable, that, by sounding the war trumpet so recklessly, and directing its terrific blasts against so many forms of evil at once, he should arouse unruly spirits of every kind, who should be tempted, in furtherance of their own separate schemes, and without discipline or order, to break loose against the existing social fabric under the pretext of aiding in the necessary reforms? And had even he himself a clear perception of the ways and means by which all his demands could be met under the existing ecclesiastical, as well as political and social, conditions? We reply: He had evidently but a very incomplete apprehension of the perils and grievances indicated; and even afterward, with all the sound judgment that distinguished him, he never manifested that type of special endowment which would have enabled him, on the basis of the lofty ideas and truths which lay in clear light before his mind, to suggest also in particular instances the measures and plans which were necessary, in view of all the actual practical conditions to be encountered, in order to effect the realization of his high ideals. But nothing could be farther from the truth than to attribute his present outburst to a malicious temper, or to the illusion of a shallow, sanguine mind as to the extent of the grievances assailed. It is, on the contrary, a spiritual impulse springing from the profoundest depths of his Christian life, which manifests itself now at length with all the more reckless energy, since it has for so long a time been held under restraint in hope of a peaceful solution of the difficulties. And it is, further, the unwavering and sacred conviction that, when the interest of human souls is at stake, all the powers and ordinances that persistently oppose must in the end themselves forfeit their claims to historical or divine authority, and must be destroyed as forces of sin. Due account, too, must be taken of his native individuality. This was marked primarily by a tendency to a cultivation of the inner life, which at one time seemed destined to hold him permanently under the spell of mystical Quietism. But when he is, at length, violently hurled into the activities of outward life and conflict, there is manifest also a natural vehemence, which throws itself into this world's strife all the more freely and boldly as the whole man feels himself driven into it by a call from above and by the adversaries of the heavenly kingdom, and as he is unhampered and unhindered by specific acquaintance with actual worldly affairs. Yet neither at this nor at any other time did he desire in any disorderly way to resist the ordinances which had thus grown hostile to the divine government. He recognizes also other powers, likewise ordained of God, which may and should here enter the conflict. When, therefore, he at a later day contends against the revolutionary demeanor of unauthorized individual subjects, he does not thereby change his principles in the least, but he only applies them in directions whence, it must be confessed, he had up to this time, in the high opinion which he entertained of the Christian world, failed to apprehend the really threatening perils. We must, therefore, conceive his position, apart from any apologetic interest, in a purely historical light. The idea that he now allowed himself to be diverted by *outside influences*, as by Hutten or other nobles, from the path marked out for him by his own development and experience, is so utterly lacking in historical evidence that we need waste no time in its refutation.[1]

2. *Prelude upon the Babylonian Captivity.*

TYRANNY OF ROME—CUP WITHHELD FROM THE LAITY—TRANSUB-STANTIATION—SACRIFICE OF THE MASS—BAPTISM—REPENTANCE—CONFIRMATION—MARRIAGE — ORDINATION — EXTREME UNCTION—SCRIPTURE TRUTH ATTESTED BY THE SPIRIT.

Luther's friend, Lange, had called the *Address to the Nobility* a war-trumpet. No less bold and significant in its way was the call to battle now issued in the *Praeludium de captivitate Babylonica*.[2] As church ordinances were treated in the former, so here it is prominent articles of doctrine, *i. e.*, those touching the sacraments, which fell under discussion. The new principles with regard to the latter, to which we have seen him advancing in various earlier writings, we here find systematized and developed. The book appeared in October. Luther had written it in full expectation of the appearance of the papal Bull against him, which had been already prepared, and which Eck in September began to publish in Germany.[3] In its *Conclusion*, he says that, if there be any truth in the report of the issuing of a Bull to compel him to recant, he wishes this little book to constitute a part of the coming recantation. He expects, he declares, to publish very shortly the remainder of the recantation, the like of which the Romish chair has never seen nor heard of.

He represents the Papacy as the Babylonian Empire, and proves the tyranny exercised by Rome chiefly with reference to the sacrament of the Lord's Supper.

He describes as the " FIRST CAPTIVITY " *the withholding of the cup from the laity*. He quotes the words of the Lord, " Drink ye all of it," and asks why the greater thing should be granted to the laity, *i. e.*, that Christ's blood was shed for them, and yet the less denied them, *i. e.*, that the sign of this blood is also here for

---

[1] None of the letters of nobles to Luther which have thus far been published make even an attempt to modify the formulation of his own principles.

[2] Jena, ii, 273 sqq.   [3] Cf. Briefe, i, 491.

them. Nevertheless, Luther does not here (as he had not done in the *Address to the Nobility*) think that the use of the cup should be obtained by violence, nor that it is a sin to commune in only one form, since there is no compulsory law upon the subject, and since Christ, indeed, had *commanded* neither form,[1] but merely said : ' As oft as ye do this," etc. He only insists that no one shall justify the tyranny manifested in the withholding of the privilege. Meanwhile, let it be endured just as one would a captivity among the Turks, where neither element could be received.

He sees the "SECOND CAPTIVITY" in the *doctrine of transubstantiation*. He now presents at length his objections to this theory, although well knowing that an assault upon it would, in the Romish Church, be fraught with the utmost peril. He now confesses who it was that had first awakened in his mind suspicions upon this subject, namely, Cardinal Cambray, Peter D'Ailly, whose works he had, according to Melanchthon's report, studied already upon every opportunity at Erfurt. He had there found developed, he declares, with great acuteness the opinion, that the recognition of true bread and wine, and not merely their properties, in the Lord's Supper has much more in its favor, and would assume fewer superfluous miracles, if only the Church had not decided against it. D'Ailly had maintained that the co-existence of the body of Christ with the substance of the bread by virtue of a *unio* could be at least as easily conceived as a presence of the body under a form, or under the properties of bread, whence the substance has been removed. Luther then proceeds to say that afterwards, when he saw what kind of a Church it was that had rendered the decision lamented by D'Ailly, *i. e.*, the Thomistic and Aristotelian, he became bolder, and is now thoroughly convinced in his conscience of the correctness of the view, " that it is manifestly *true bread and true wine*, in which are the true flesh and true blood of Christ no less than they (the Romanists) locate these under the properties of bread and wine." The opinions of the Thomists, even though approved by Pope and council, are still only opinions, and do not become articles of faith ; for that which is maintained without scriptural proof or well-attested revelation may be the basis for an opinion, but we are not compelled to believe it. But the opinion of Thomas in question is entirely

---

[1] Cf. also later, Erl. Ed., xxiv, 112.

without any scriptural evidence or reasonable basis (*sine ratione*), and does not even show an acquaintance with philosophy and dialectics.

We recognize here clearly enough the motive which prompts Luther in his opposition to this doctrine of the Church. It is the conviction that, in setting up this theory as an article of faith, the conscience is laid under the restraint of a purely human dogma, and one which, by virtue of its inherent weakness, must of itself awaken suspicions as to its validity. He himself declares that it is his only aim to remove scruples of conscience, so that no one may think himself guilty of heresy because he believes that there is true bread in the sacrament. He sees in the article merely an empty dogma, because it is not taught in the Scriptures; and he proceeds to say, further, that the plainest meaning of the words of institution is much rather against this dogma, and that we dare do no violence to the words of Scripture, but must, on the contrary, abide by their plainest meaning. The Evangelists clearly assert that *bread* was taken and blessed by Christ. Christ calls upon His disciples, after He has taken and broken the bread, to receive and eat it, since this very thing, namely, the bread taken and broken by Him, is His body. Likewise, Paul afterwards calls it bread ; he does not say, " in the bread," but *the bread*, " is the communion of the body of Christ." We are to understand true bread and true wine, just as a true cup : even the Thomists do not hold to a transubstantiation of the cup.

Luther appeals, also, to the Church before the rise of Scholasticism, when nothing was yet known of this dogma born of false philosophy.

Finally, he enters upon a consideration of the real inner nature of the sacramental act. Here, too, he can find nothing to justify theologians in robbing of their meaning the words of Scripture concerning the bread. He inquires, with D'Ailly, why Christ cannot cause His body to be contained (*corpus suum continere*) just as well within the substance of the bread as within its properties. He then employs, as an illustration, fire and iron, which are two substances, but which are yet so commingled in glowing iron that every part is *both fire and iron*. Why now might not, much rather, the glorified body of Christ be in every part of the substance of the bread? It will be observed that it is the *glorified* body of Christ, as such, for which Luther claims such a possibility. The

Thomistic theory of the properties has led also, in the sphere of philosophy, he maintains, to a perfect Babel of monstrous conceptions. It is a matter for rejoicing that the common people, at least, have retained a simple faith in the sacrament, *i. e.*, the simple belief that the body of Christ is here contained, without understanding or disputing about the theory of the schools.

Luther then turns aside to refute, by the use of their own dialectics, a logical argument of the Scholastics. They claimed, with appeal to Aristotle, that *an affirmative sentence must present precisely the same thing in the subject and in the predicate;* and therefore in the sentence, " This is my body," the bread can no longer be thought of as the subject, but only the body. To this he replies that, according to Aristotle, the specifications predicated of the properties would also have to be conceived as subjects, since he regards also this white, this great, etc., as subjects of which something may be said ; and thus the logical difficulty, on account of which it was sought to throw out the substance of the bread, would still remain, if we were to understand by " this " only the form of the bread. We would thus be compelled to accept, not only transubstantiation, but also transaccidentiation. If we can get beyond the accident, or property, so as, in the sentence, " This is my body," to find the real subject, not in the accident (but in the body of Christ), why could we not with equal ease dispose of the substance of the bread? The arguments with which Luther thus meets the Scholastics upon their own ground reveal to us how thoroughly at home he was upon this territory and among its distinctions and conceptions, so far more logically keen than valid, so often more subtle than true. But he never sought to draw positive arguments for *his own* views from any such sources. So now he returns to the Word of Scripture—" lest we philosophize too much." We shall hereafter find him dealing differently with such objections drawn from logic and grammar against his conception of the words of institution.[1]

Finally, he appeals, in support of his view of the relation of the bread and the body, to the *relation existing between the two natures of Christ.* For the bodily indwelling of the divinity in Christ, no transubstantiation of the human nature was required,

---

[1] Cf. below, what is said in the *Bekenntniss vom Abendmahl* (1528) in regard to the præmicatio identica.

but, without assailing the integrity of either nature, we assert : This man is God. Thus, while both the bread and the body remain, we may yet say : " This bread is my body."

In general, in this whole discussion, it is evident that Luther is concerned more for the refutation of his antagonists than for the positive presentation of any theory of his own. The fundamental drift of the argument is to allow no merely human theory, to which the consciences of men might be bound, to usurp the place of the simple Word of Scripture, and faith resting upon that Word. He does not, therefore, endeavor to dissuade any one from holding the scholastic view, but only insists that no one shall be forced to accept it as an article of faith. Of his own view, he says in conclusion : " Thus meanwhile I shall stand scrupulously for the honor of the sacred words of God, to which I shall not suffer violence to be done by petty human reasonings."

The third " CAPTIVITY " of the sacrament is for Luther the *sacrifice of the mass*, which is, indeed, by far the most iniquitous of all, and which has drawn with it an endless train of further abuses. He knows that he has here to contend with an evil that has been firmly entrenched for many centuries, which has received universal approval, and which cannot, indeed, be overthrown without changing almost the entire present organization of the Church and introducing an entirely different mode of conducting divine worship.

We are already familiar with the fundamental ideas which control this portion of the discussion. He, first of all, argues against the conception of the mass as the rendering of a good work. Starting with the words of institution, he reiterates the principles previously announced, and is thus led to speak of the significance of the presence of the body of Christ in the bread, which he still firmly maintains. The mass, or sacrament of the altar, is for him the testament of the departed Christ. This testament is the promise of the forgiveness of sins, confirmed by His death. The mass is essentially nothing more than words of Christ, in which He says, as it were : Behold, condemned sinner, out of pure grace I promise thee, before thou hast merited anything, the forgiveness of all thy sins and eternal life ; and, in order that thou mayest be perfectly sure of this, I will surrender my body and shed my blood, by which means I will by death confirm my promise, and I will leave behind me both my body and my blood as a sign and memorial to thee of this my promise. As oft as ye do this, remember me, extol my love, etc.—Thus God saves us, not by accepting our work, but by anticipating us with His promises. Nothing is required upon our part but faith, support-ing itself upon this divine Word. Upon faith, then, soon nat-urally follows the emotion of heartfelt love bestowed by the Holy Spirit, so that the spirit of the man casts itself upon Christ, and the whole man is renewed. From this consideration of the words of promise Luther is led again, just as in the *Sermons* already reviewed, to the peculiar nature of the sacrament as such. God is accustomed, under other circumstances also, to affix signs or memorials to His promises (*supra*, p. 347), and He has, accord-ingly, to the highest of all promises attached the very body of Christ as a memorial sign, as the Lord Himself says : " Do this in remembrance of me." The Word in the mass is the testament, the bread and wine (*i. e.*, together with the body therein con-tained) the sacrament ; just as in baptism the sign of dipping into the water accompanies the Word of promise. But the chief stress is still laid upon the Word, and the remark is again added, that we can *spiritually eat and drink* at any hour by nourishing faith upon the words of Christ. Of this spiritual reception of the Supper, Luther had already spoken in an earlier section of the tract, when discussing the question, whether any argument for the administration of both elements could be drawn from the words of Jesus in John vi. He had there very decidedly pronounced against the application of that passage to the sacrament, and in this connection had declared : It is not the sacramental eating, in which also the unworthy participate, but only the spiritual eating in faith, that quickens us ; and in this also children, the sick, and others who do not sacramentally receive the elements, participate. It is only this spiritual eating to which the words of the Lord, " whoso eateth not the flesh * * * hath no life in him," can apply. From this conception of the significance of the mass Luther now draws also the inference that it cannot be presented as a satisfaction either for the dead or for any condi-tion of distress ; for it is a promise, and, as such, can be applied to none but the believer, and to him only by virtue of his faith.

As an especial and yet greater offence Luther then, at length, designates the conception of the mass as a sacrifice offered to God, as it appears to be represented in the canon of the mass itself. Even Christ Himself, at the institution of the Supper, did not offer Himself as a sacrifice to God; but, sitting at the table, He announced to the individuals assembled there His testament, and offered to them the sign. The mass is the more thoroughly Christian under any circumstances the more nearly it resembles that first celebration, which was eminently simple, without any pomp of ceremonies. The term " collect " is again traced back to the apostolic custom of bringing food to the place of worship; and the elevation and presentation of the elements, to the Hebrew custom of elevating that which was to be consecrated by Word and prayer (cf. *supra*, pp. 348 and 352). Neither does the elevation of the elements after the consecration indicate a sacrifice, as there is no mention of anything of the kind in connection with this ceremony; but it originated either, like the one just mentioned, from a Hebrew custom, or it is intended to be for us an admonition to the exercise of faith in the testament, whose sign is held before our eyes.

That the mass, even when administered by an unworthy priest, is perfectly valid, he most readily concedes. Just so, he declares, is the Gospel also proclaimed by ungodly men; and to this he now adds: The mass is really a *part of the Gospel*, and, in fact, a *summary* and *short epitome* of the latter. For the Gospel is, in its whole significance, good tidings of the forgiveness of sins. But everything which can be said of this, or of the mercy of God, is briefly comprehended in the Word of the testament (cf. *supra*, p. 350). Hence, all sermons should be nothing else but an exposition of the mass.

The difference between a *sacrament*, or *testament*, and a *sacrifice* is thus concisely stated. The former comes from God through the ministration of the priest, and demands faith; the latter originates in our faith and ascends to God, from whom it demands a hearing. The latter, at least, he adds, requires a worthy, pious priest, inasmuch as God does not hear sinners.

In BAPTISM, likewise, to the discussion of which he now turns, he would have attention given, first of all, to the divine promise: "He that believeth and is baptized shall be saved." It is in the emphasis which he now lays upon these words of the institution that we note the advance in the present exposition as compared with the views presented in the *Sermon von der Taufe*, in which he had laid the main stress upon the sign of dipping beneath the water. In a similar way, we have already seen him, in the *Sermon von dem neuen Testament*, advance to a more prominent presentation of the words of institution.[1] In the present declarations concerning the perpetual validity of baptism and its relations to repentance, to human works of satisfaction, and to special vows, he now proceeds still further in the path pursued in the *Sermon* just mentioned. Faith, he asserts, must be exercised in the promise, for, without this, baptism is of no benefit. That promise should be continually proclaimed, and thus baptism continually repeated and faith incited ; for the promise, once bestowed upon us, retains for us its power during our whole life. Thus, also, penitence for sins committed after baptism and the forsaking of them is nothing else than a return to the power of (our) baptism, to the faith from which we had fallen away, to the promise which we had forsaken by our sin. This is the proper meaning of the maxim, that baptism is the first sacrament and the foundation of all the others.

Luther has thus laid down the positive antithesis to the leading error concerning baptism which he proposes to attack. He complains that scarcely any one in that day had any further thought of the baptism which he had received, since so many other ways had been discovered for securing the forgiveness of sins and attaining heaven. The occasion for this had been given by the dangerous saying of Jerome, that repentance after baptism is a board to be grasped after shipwreck—as though the ship, *i. e.*, the grace of baptism, had been lost. Hence come the vows, satisfactions, indulgences, etc. (Cf., upon the relation of vows to baptism, *supra*, p. 359.) There still remains, he claims, the invincible ship, namely, the faithfulness of the God who cannot deny Himself, extending the promise in the sacraments (2 Tim. ii. 13). Here is given to us that with which we may always oppose the adversary, the qualms of conscience, the terrors of the Law and death.

With this promise is also associated the " sign, or sacrament," namely, the dipping into water. But above all does Luther here insist that the sacrament effects nothing without faith, which is to be awakened by the very Word of promise itself, and which can save us even without the sacrament (hence Christ Himself does not add to the words of promise : " he that * * * *is not*

[1] Cf. supra, pp. 355 sq., 347.

baptized shall be damned "). Luther now represents it as the view of the majority, that there is in the Word and water a hidden spiritual power which works faith in the subject receiving the sacrament. According to the view of others, there is no power in the sacraments; but the grace is given by God Himself, who will always be efficaciously present at their administration. All, however, agree that the sacraments are effectual signs of grace. Otherwise, the sacraments of the new covenant would not be different from those of the old, and hence there is claimed for the former an efficacy even without faith, provided only that no obstacle be presented in the form of a purpose to commit further sin. In opposition to this claim, Luther now here repeats his discussion of the difference between the sacraments of the two dispensations.[1] He first cites those signs, or sacraments, under the old covenant in which God already in that age gave His promise and demanded faith. We recall his reference to these when discussing the doctrine of the Lord's Supper (*supra*, p. 348). He mentions the sacrifice by which God saved Abel, the rainbow by which He saved Noah, and circumcision by which He saved Abraham. In all of these, he sees signs equally significant with those of the New Testament. From both classes of sacraments he distinguishes the " figures of the Law," to which is attached no Word of promise requiring faith. These latter, which are meant to be indicated in the prevalent usage of the term " figures," were, he says, already fulfilled in the external act, even without faith; for they had reference only to external works. Of the Old Testament sacraments, which correspond to those of the New Testament, he declares that not they, as, for example, circumcision, were the justifying power, but faith in the promise with which the circumcision, etc., was connected. Faith fulfilled (*implebat*) what the circumcision signified. Just so, also, with baptism : it does not justify, but faith in the promise to which baptism is attached. " For faith," says he, " justifies, and fulfils what baptism signifies; for faith is the burial (*untertauchen*) of the old man and the arising of the new." Luther finds, therefore, no difference between the sacraments of the New Testament and those of the Old,[2] whereas the mere " figures " can be com-

[1] Supra, pp. 246, 265.

[2] Upon this subject Luther afterwards says, when discussing the sacrament

pared with neither, lacking as they do the Word of promise, which makes all the difference. With the ancient " figures " he compares the ceremonies, vestments, localities, etc., of the present day, which are figures of something that is to find its fulfilment in the spirit, and which, likewise, having no Word of promise, can be in no manner compared with the signs of baptism and bread, nor in any manner justify us. He pronounces untrue the doctrine, " that there inheres (*inesse*) in the sacraments an efficacious power of justification, or that they are efficacious signs of grace," adding, however : " unless the word ' efficacious ' be used to indicate that, *if undoubted faith be present*, they most certainly and most efficaciously confer grace." But these men, says he, do not mean only such an efficacy.

But what is it precisely, we may ask, which is signified by baptism—indicated by the sign, or sacrament? Luther replies : [1] Death and resurrection ; or, in other words, full and complete justification. This death and resurrection (cf. Rom. vi.) are called the new creature, regeneration, etc. And this includes also actual bodily death and resurrection ; for sin does not, in the full sense of the word, die, nor grace fully arise, until the present body of sin also perishes. Thus, again, baptism appears as something which continues perpetually in force. The experience which it signifies continues until death, and even until the resurrection on the last great day : for as long as we live, we die and rise again. Nor do we die only in a spiritual sense, renouncing sin and vanity ; but we begin in reality to forsake this bodily life and to lay hold upon the future life, so that there occurs a real, and even bodily, transition from this world to the Father. But the initiation of this process indicated by baptism is effected, according to Luther, by means of faith, without which the sacrament is inefficacious, and even already in this faith itself. When we begin to believe, we at the same time begin to die to this

---

of marriage: The Old Testament fathers also drank of the same spiritual drink as we, *i. e.*, out of the rock. which is Christ (1 Cor. x.). Grace is always the same, and faith is the same. But God gives at different times different signs, and likewise different promises of the same sin-forgiving grace. Thus, for example, it is only in modern times that he has given the keys in connection with repentance, although repentance itself has always existed, but, under the old covenant, sacrifice and other signs were attached to it (Cf. supra, p. 266).

[1] Cf. already, Sermon von der Taufe, Erl. Ed., xxi, 230 sqq.

world and to live in the future life, so that faith is truly death and resurrection, *i. e.*, the spiritual baptism spoken of. The peculiar employment of the word "justification" in this connection reminds us of the usage which we have observed in the earlier writings of the Reformer. As to the mode of baptism, he would prefer that it be performed, in keeping with the significance of the sign, by entirely immersing the subject. This, he says, is not necessary, but it would be becoming and appropriate.[1]

It is worthy of note, that Luther here, speaking of the *significance of the sign*, emphasizes a different thought from that which dominates in his presentation of the *perpetual validity of the promise*, whilst it is still, in the two cases, but different sides of one subject, *i. e.*, justification, which he has in view. He had above given prominence to the divine compassion, which accepts the sinner, pardoning his guilt, and to which the latter may afterwards, when distressed by sense of guilt and qualms of conscience, ever again return. Now he brings to view the inner, moral, and even natural, transformation of the personality, presenting, at the same time, the personal obligation assumed by the baptized. But even in the latter case, his chief aim is to offer comfort and encouragement, declaring of the sign, as of the promise itself, that it always retains its validity : " Baptism never becomes invalid so long as thou only dost not in despair refuse to return to salvation."

From this point Luther, having ventilated, in the section just considered, the Romish theory of repentance, turns his attention to the papal tyranny and its human enactments. By what right, he inquires, does the Pope set up his laws and take captive the *liberty* which is bestowed upon us by baptism? For our entire life there is no longer anything further required of us, but to become fully baptized, *i. e.*, to die to sin and to live again by faith in Christ. The Pope has, therefore, no right to impose upon us fasts and prayers, countless works of the Law and ceremonies. " Neither Pope, nor bishop, nor any man has the right to impose a single syllable upon a Christian man, unless it be with his own consent." But Luther does not, on this account, sanction outward insurrection against the existing papal power. Christians are free from all things ; but they should, without yielding their

---

[1] Similarly also in Erl. Ed., xxi, 229.

freedom of conscience, endure that which is laid upon them, knowing and confessing that they are suffering wrong, but enduring it with credit to themselves. They should be on their guard, however, neither to approve the course of the tyrant, nor, on the other hand, to murmur against the tyranny, keeping in mind the words of the apostle, 1 Pet. ii. 13. How this admonition can be made to harmonize with the right to institute reforms, which the *Address to the Nobility* claims for the laity, will be evident if we remember that the present exhortation is addressed only to individual believers as such. But he himself, Luther, must, since under the papal tyranny but few come to the knowledge of their Christian liberty, deliver his conscience and openly declare, that, if the Pope and his followers will not restore this liberty and allow it to be proclaimed, they must bear the guilt for all the souls destroyed through this captivity; and that the Papacy is nothing but the Empire of Babylon—yea, verily, the Empire of Antichrist, the man of sin and son of perdition, sitting in the churches as God (2 Thes. ii. 3, 4).

Specially important in shaping the doctrine of Luther is the discussion of *Infant Baptism*, to which he is here led by his requirement of faith in connection with baptism. We have already found, in a *Sermon* of the year 1518 (*supra*, p. 276), the assertion that a child is baptized upon the merit of another person's faith. In the first edition of the *Commentary upon Galatians* (A. D. 1519) he raised the question, how children could be baptized and saved, since they cannot as yet hear the Word, and since, without hearing, no one can believe (Rom. x. 14). He here assumes in advance that for baptism even children require faith. The question raised, he answers as follows : The Word must always, as it strikes the ear, at the same time inwardly communicate the Spirit. But the Word uttered above the individual baptized works through the Spirit the more readily in the case of a little child, since the latter is so much more receptive, and less pre-occupied (*quo patientior, nullis aliis rebus implicatus*).[1] According to this, it appeared as though faith were effected in the child by the very Word of baptism itself, upon the basis of a receptivity, which the child itself, even in its natural characteristic of childhood, brought with it to the ordinance. In the

[1] Comm. ad Gal., iii, 258. In the later editions the section is omitted.

present publication, we find the doctrine developed in the form
which in its leading features, though afterwards somewhat modified, it retained for Luther. It includes the faith of the children
themselves, effected directly by the divine Word, but effected in
view of the faith of the congregation presenting the children for
baptism. " Just as the Word of God is able * * * to
change even the heart of the wicked man, which is no less deaf
and incapable than any little child [there is here no further
mention of any special capacity in the child], so, through the
prayer of the Church offering and believing, to which all things
are possible, even the little child is, by the faith infused, changed,
cleansed and renewed." Even an adult may be thus transformed
by the prayer of the Church in any sacrament. Reference is then
made, as in the *Sermon* cited above, to the case of the paralytic,
Matt. ix. In this sense, Luther is even ready to grant the principle of the efficacy of the sacraments, and that even in the case
of persons who stubbornly interpose an obstacle. For what, says
he, should not the faith of the congregation and the prayer of
faith be able to overcome, seeing that Stephen conquered even a
Saul by this power. Yet he adds : Even here the sacraments still
do not work through their own power, but through the power of
faith.

In concluding the section of the treatise devoted to baptism,
Luther discusses the relation of *vows* to the latter in a similar vein
to that which we have already found in the *Sermon von der Taufe*
and in the *Ratio confitendi* (*supra*, p. 360). He now goes farther
in his warning against the prevalent abuse, and even presents the
fundamental ideas upon the basis of which he afterwards declared
the cloister-vows invalid, although he speaks here, in general, only
of public vows, leaving those privately assumed to the judgment
and conscience of individuals. He announces it as his opinion
that the public vows are perilous for the souls of men, since they
are a kind of ceremonial law and human ordinance, from which
the Christian is free. If there were no other ground of complaint
against the monastic vows, there would yet be weight enough in
the one objection, that they detract from baptism and faith, and
minister to the glorification of works. There is, indeed, scarcely
one person among a thousand who does not, when under such
vows, look more to works than to faith. The Scriptures furnish
no example of them ; and that which lacks such precedent is

always perilous, and, at all events, not to be commended. Indeed, he declares, he fears greatly that these monastic vows are also to be included under the saying of 1 Tim. iv. 3, which he had in the *Address to the Nobility* applied to the marriage of the priests. He therefore advises the great men of the Church (*magnates ecclesiarum*) to abolish all such vows, or, at least, no longer to recommend them. He advises all Christians against assuming them, unless they are well protected by knowledge of the truth, that in the sight of God the very highest works of the oath-bound orders stand on an equality with the labors of a farmer or housewife, and that God, under all circumstances, measures everything only by faith.

Two particular papal errors are pointed out in connection with vows: First, that the Pope arrogates to himself the right of granting dispensations from them; whereas, if any dispensation is possible, it may, by virtue of the keys bestowed upon all, be granted by any one, and if the vows be of divine right, it can be granted by no man whatsoever; and secondly, that the Pope shamelessly presumes to release from the obligation to fulfil a marriage vow, provided one of the parties desires to enter a cloister, whereas God's Word commands that such promises be kept.

Luther announces, finally, that he has in prospect the preparation of a more thorough exposition of this subject of vows, which he asserts to be very sorely needed.

For the doctrine of the THIRD SACRAMENT, that of REPENTANCE, he had already, when discussing baptism, presented, touching one important aspect, evangelical and reformatory principles. In the following chapter, which treats especially of this sacrament, he defines its nature as entirely analogous to that of baptism and the Lord's Supper. He represents it as consisting of the Word of promise on God's part (" What ye shall bind," etc., and " Whosesoever sins ye remit," etc.,) and faith upon our part. The Word of promise is here, just as in the cases of the first two sacraments, designed to awaken faith. But the entire nature of baptism, with its two constituent elements, has been rejected by the Papacy. Out of the service which those appointed to be stewards of the mysteries of God should render in repentance, just as in the administration of baptism and the Lord's Supper, it has made a lordship and tyranny. Faith it declares to be unnecessary.

26

Luther then takes up in order the *three parts* which the papal theory finds in repentance (penance).

He first of all charges that the prevalent doctrine in regard to *contrition* places it before and above faith, as though it were not a work of faith, but a meritorious thing, and that, in the presentation of the doctrine, no mention is even made of faith.   The theory of an *attritio*, which is converted into *contritio* by the power of the keys, he utterly rejects.   His own views he presents as follows : A contrite heart is a product only of a glowing faith directed upon the divine promise and threatening (*ardentis in promissionem   *   *   *   fidei*), which, in view of the unchangeable truth of God, alarms the conscience and makes it contrite, and which then lifts up again and comforts the contrite conscience, so that the believed truth of the threatening is the cause of the contrition, and the believed truth of the promise the cause of the comfort.   Faith is, therefore, first of all to be taught and awakened ; contrition and comfort will then follow of themselves. God does not then accept us on account of the contrition, but on account of the faith which we have bestowed upon His threatenings and promises.   We direct special attention here to two points, namely, that Luther places faith even before contrition, and that in the conception of *justifying* faith he includes also faith in the divine threatenings.   All things else, he says, are but works and fruits, which come of themselves, as a natural growth, in the life of the man made good by faith.

In discussing the second part of repentance, *confession*, Luther lays great stress upon the duty of the penitent to confess his sins. He not only demands a confessing before God and a general public confessing (according to Matt. iii. 6 ; 1 John i., and, especially, Matt. xviii. 15 sqq.), but he pronounces private confession, although he does not find it recommended in the Scriptures (cf. *supra*, p. 356), very useful, and even necessary.   But we now find presented with great precision the two principal points which mark the difference between private confession, as he conceives it, and that of the Roman Catholic Church.   In the first place, its essential significance always lies for him in the personal declaration by which the conscience of the penitent is to be encouraged ; and it is only in order that the divine Word of comfort from the lips of a brother may be received, that the conscience should be uncovered and the hidden wound laid bare in confidence before the latter.   Hence Luther here, with evident design, speaks always of the " brother," not of the priest.   It is through the brother that God speaks to us.   This idea Luther develops especially in assailing the attempt of the Pope to retain in his own hands the power of granting absolution for certain classes of sins.   He sustains his position, again, by an appeal to Matt. xviii.   It should be observed that he places the absolution which he has in view when treating of the sacrament of repentance and confession entirely under the general conception of the comforting assurance imparted by God through Christian brethren.

For a discussion of *satisfaction*, Luther refers to his earlier publications during the indulgence controversy.   The fundamental principle there enunciated meets us here again in the declarations, that true satisfaction is a renewal of the life, or a new course of conduct, and that the satisfaction which Christ imposes in the declaration of forgiveness is the crucifixion of the flesh.   Instead of this, it is the prevalent idea that the change of life is already completed in contrition and confession, and that it is now only necessary to render satisfaction for past sins.

These three sacraments, baptism, the Lord's Supper and repentance are the only ones whose validity as sacraments Luther is now willing to acknowledge.   He so declares in the *Introduction* to the treatise now before us, as he had already done in earlier utterances.   He here adds further, that, if we should follow the scriptural custom, we would have *only one* sacrament and three sacramental signs.   By the one he means the " mystery " of salvation in Christ Himself.[1]   In the *Conclusion* of the treatise, he · remarks that the conception of a sacrament might appear to be applicable to a very wide range of subjects, to everything to which a divine promise has been given ; as, for example, prayer, the Word, the cross of the believer, etc.   Yea, who can enumerate all the divine promises?   But, in the proper sense of the term, we speak of sacraments only where we have promises with signs attached to them.   We have seen how consistently he has applied this idea to the three sacraments named above.   But before leaving the topic he remarks further, that if we should speak strictly we could not call repentance a sacrament, since it lacks a

---

[1] Cf. the application of the conception of a sacrament to Christ Himself, *supra*, pp. 171 sq., 270, 285.   Also, the declaration concerning the sacrament of marriage.

visible sign appointed by God; but must confine the name to baptism and the bread, "since in these alone we see both a divinely-appointed sign and a promise of the remission of sins." Here he has once again, it will be observed, fixed the attention directly upon that which everywhere constitutes the fundamental content of the promise, and thus also the significance of the sacrament, namely, the forgiveness of sins. Thus the Lutheran doctrine of *two sacraments* has been now fully developed. We must, therefore, according to Luther's view of the matter, classify absolution, and with it the sacrament of repentance, which it essentially includes, under the dispensation of the bare Word of grace, the *nuda promissa*.

Turning to the four Catholic sacraments whose right to the name has thus been denied, Luther points out at once the absence of any divine Word of promise attaching specifically to CONFIRMATION. Christ, indeed, laid His hands upon many, and also transferred the laying on of hands for the healing of the sick to His apostles; but no one has ever sought to make a sacrament out of this. He therefore places confirmation, as an "ecclesiastical custom or sacramental ceremony," in the same category as the consecration of waters and other things. In this sense he allows its validity. If we consecrate other created things, says he, with the Word and prayer, why should it not be proper for us also to consecrate men in the same way? It is only as a sacrament that he refuses to acknowledge it.

In the so-called SACRAMENT OF MARRIAGE there is wanting, according to Luther, both promise and sign. As to the first, we nowhere read of an assurance of grace to every one who may marry. As to the second, we nowhere read that marriage was appointed by God in order to indicate something in a figurative way. Every visible act may, indeed, be employed as a figure, or allegory, of something invisible; but the usage of language will not permit us to consider every figure or allegory as a sacrament. Finally, the conception of marriage as a New Testament sacrament is refuted by pointing to the fact that marriage has existed since the creation, and thus, as well, among those who are not Christians at all. To meet the appeal of the opposite party to Eph. v., he explains that the Scriptures neither there nor elsewhere employ the word μυστηριον in the now accepted sense of the word sacrament, in support of which claim he adduces 1 Tim.

iii. 9, 16, and 1 Cor. ii. 7 ; iv. 1. Christ and the Church are in these passages represented as a *mysterium, i. e.,* as something hidden and great (*res secreta et magna*). This might, indeed, be done also under the figure of marriage, but marriage itself could not even in that case be called a sacrament.

Having thus maintained the sense of Scripture as over against human invention, Luther cheerfully concedes, and even advises, that even the usage of the term sacrament be tolerated, since it does not interfere with faith. We may observe that he himself had in the preceding year, in a *Sermon* upon the state of matrimony,[1] described marriage, in the traditional way, as a sacrament. He had there defined a sacrament as simply " a sacred sign, which indicates some spiritual, holy, heavenly and eternal thing." Thus, marriage is a sign of the very greatest and holiest things, *i. e,* the union of divinity and humanity in Christ, and the unity between Christ and Christendom. Of the requirement, that the sign, as such, must have a divine appointment and promise, he here says nothing.

In the present treatise, he raises objections against the Romish marriage canons. He first denounces the many obstacles placed in the way of marriage and the consequent trade in dispensations, not forgetting to include ordination, as then practiced, among these obstacles. He then treats of divorce, which he regards with horror, and in regard to the permissibility of which in general he does not, indeed, now venture to make positive declarations, although he goes so far as to assert that, according to the Word of Christ in Matt. v., marriage can be dissolved only on account of adultery, and hence the Pope errs in allowing it upon other grounds ; that, on the other hand, the innocent party in such a case may again marry, which is now, strangely enough, forbidden ; and, still further, that, as Paul in 1 Cor. vii., allows the person forsaken by an unbelieving partner to give up the latter and marry another, so he would like to see the same privilege now extended in case of desertion by a party who is in fact an unbeliever, although nominally a believer. It would be aside from our present purpose for us to dwell longer upon these propositions.

The sacrament of ORDINATION carries us back again to the

[1] Erl. Ed., xvi, 158 sqq.

doctrine of the universal priesthood. Luther denies to this sacrament also the possession of a special divine promise, and includes it, like that of confirmation, among merely ecclesiastical ceremonies, with the consecration of vessels, etc. He then asserts : We baptized persons are all priests ; the consecrated priests have only a ministry (*ministerium*), which is committed to them by our common consent, and they have no dominion over us except in so far as we willingly accord it to them. Ordination is, accordingly, nothing more than a certain form for the election of men to conduct assemblies in the Church (*ritus quidam eligendi concionatores in ecclesia*). Yet he would not on this account abolish the custom sanctioned by the usage of centuries. That for the public ministry of the Word a special call is necessary, is briefly proved in the same manner as in the *Address to the Nobility ;* and the doctrine of an indelible character attaching to the priesthood also in a similar way rejected. While thus making the priesthood a ministry of the Word, he declares of the *diaconate*, that it is not, according to Acts vi., an office for the reading of the Gospel and Epistle, but that its appropriate ministry consists in the distribution of the alms of the Church to the poor.

The sacrament of EXTREME UNCTION[1] possessed, according to the teaching of the Church, based upon Jas. v. 14 sqq., both promise and sign. Luther cannot refrain from again expressing, as in the Leipzig *Resolutiones*, his doubt as to the authority of this epistle. He observes that " many, with great probability, assert that this epistle is not from the Apostle James, nor in consonace with the apostolic spirit, but has by custom acquired such authority as it possesses." But his argument is not made to rest upon this negative foundation. He maintains that, even if the epistle be apostolic, yet an apostle could not, by virtue of his own authority, establish an ordinance, *i. e.*, give a divine promise with accompanying sign, but this lay in the power of Christ alone. Moreover, there has been a wide departure from the idea of the apostle, who speaks of unction, not as a gift for the sick *in their departure* from this life, but, on the contrary, as a means of

[1] In the Sermon, Von der Bereitung zum Sterben, A. D. 1519 (Erl. Ed., xxi, 256), Luther had, without expressing any suspicion as to the teaching of the Church, presented as elements of such preparation the "holy sacrament of the body of Christ and that of unction."

effecting their recovery. This ceremony must also, in order to
be entitled to the rank of a sacrament, be, according to the
common definition, an efficacious sign of that which in the
epistle it is said to represent and promise, whereas to-day, among
a thousand thus anointed, scarcely one recovers. Luther then
presents his own interpretation of the language cited, as follows :
The anointing referred to is like that spoken of in Mk. vi. 13,
and the laying on of hands in Mk. xvi. 18, which was customary
in the primitive Church in connection with miracles of healing,
and recommended by James upon the authority of the first-cited
passage in Mark. Luther does not believe that it was administered to all the sick, since the endurance of suffering is a chief
glory of the Church, but that it was merely appointed for those
who proved unable to endure sickness with patience. He
observes, further, that James attaches the promise of recovery
and the forgiveness of sins, not to the anointing, but to the
prayer of faith, whereas a sacrament demands, not the faith and
prayer of the administrant, but only the faith of the recipient.
And it is his conviction, he adds, that by such a prayer, *i. e.*, that
of the elders, or worthy holy men, or by any prayer of hearty faith,
the sick might be healed even now ; for what is faith not able to
accomplish ?

Yet Luther does not condemn the prevalent practice of extreme unction, of which nothing is said by James. He would
allow it to remain undisturbed, but regard it like any other consecration by the Word and prayer. He even admits that through
it pardon and peace may be bestowed, *i. e.*, by reason of the
faith of the recipient, in accordance with the words of Christ :
" All things are possible to him that believeth ; according to thy
faith be it unto thee."

Thus did Luther apply his doctrine of the sacraments in
opposition to the existing " Babylonian Captivity." It is everywhere the *Sacred Scriptures* upon which he bases as well his
conception of the nature of a sacrament, as such, as his concrete
application of that conception. He had not assumed the task
of presenting a special justification of this employment of the
Scriptures, nor any thorough instruction as to the relation
between the authority of the Scriptures and that of the Church.
Nevertheless, we find, in the section treating of the sacrament of
ordination, a discussion applicable to this subject, which, though

but brief, incidental, and rather loosely connected with the context, yet, on account of its peculiar and very significant ideas demands special notice at our hands.

The Church, says he, has not authority to institute new promises of grace, as is attempted by certain people who claim to be controlled by the Holy Spirit. The Church is, upon the other hand, herself born of the Word of promise, and cannot become the parent of her own originator. He then proceeds to assert, that it is certainly within the province of the Church to discriminate between the Word of God and human words. As to the way in which such a judgment is to be formed by the Church, he says: The soul is so laid hold upon by the truth itself, as Augustine says, that it judges everything by the truth, but cannot judge the truth itself, being simply impelled by unerring certainty to the acknowledgment of the latter (as, for example, to the acknowledgment that three and seven are ten); " truth being the judge, (the soul is) judged rather than judging." Just so the Church has also, through the illumination of the Holy Spirit, an inner apprehension in the judgment of doctrine, which she cannot demonstrate, and which has yet full certainty for her. As the philosophers agree that no one can pass judgment upon universal conceptions (*communes conceptiones*), but that all are judged by these, so it is, also, in the relation of the Spirit to believers, who judges them all and is judged by none. Here Luther checks himself abruptly with, " Of this again." But he still adds: Even if the Church could promise grace, it would not follow from this that ordination is a sacrament; for it remains a question, where that Church is which has the Spirit, since in the appointment of such ordinances but a few bishops and learned men are accustomed to participate, and these may not really belong to the Church and may altogether err, as whole councils have often erred. He lays down the principle: " That alone is reliably proved which is approved *by the Universal Church*, not only by that of Rome." Upon the natural inquiries, what is to be regarded as such a reliable utterance, and what relation is borne to it by that free judgment accorded by the Scriptures themselves to the individual Christian, he throws no further light. He evidently assumes that at least *such* an utterance cannot err. With this position we can reconcile his other declarations as to the judgment of the individual only by the further assumption that the Spirit in the individual believer will of itself surely agree, in the conception of scriptural truth, with the Spirit testifying in the entire believing Church.   But, in regard to this testimony of the Church at large, Luther was constantly led back to the statement, that it cannot be outwardly determined whether or no the true spiritual general congregation of believers has really spoken. Only this much can be safely said, *i. e.*, that a doctrine approved by all who make any claim to true Christianity cannot be false, inasmuch as the Spirit must testify, at least in some individual genuine believers, against any perversion of the truth of salvation. This principle we will find maintained also throughout the further development of Luther's views.

3. *Treatise upon Christian Liberty.*

THE POWER OF FAITH—THE INWARD AND THE OUTWARD MAN—THE THREE " VIRTUES " OF FAITH—FAITH FULFILS THE LAW—ROYALTY AND PRIESTHOOD OF BELIEVERS—EXERCISE OF THE OUTWARD MAN —ABUSE OF LIBERTY.

Just as the *Praeludium de captivitate Babylonica* was completed, the expected Bull of excommunication also arrived at Wittenberg. Nevertheless, Luther was induced, in accordance with the desire of the Elector, to countenance a yet further attempt at reconciliation made by Miltitz.   The final agreement was, that he should address another letter to the Pope, sending with it a short dissertation.   In the letter he was to present a report of the course of his affairs, and represent his assaults as directed, not against the Pope, but against Eck.[1]

The letter which he actually addressed to the Pope in pursuance of this agreement[2] leaves no room for any further thought of reconciliation with the existing *Papacy*.   We can regard it only as a final effort to personally admonish the present Pope himself to effect a radical severance of his relation with the Babylon over which he presided, however little we may suppose Luther to have himself anticipated any result whatever from such an effort.   He, therefore, takes the most charitable view of the position of Leo himself, comparing him to a sheep surrounded by

---

[1] Briefe, i, 496. The conference of Luther with Miltitz was held on Oct. 12th.
[2] Dated Sept. 6th, according to stipulation with Miltitz.   Briefe, i, 497 sqq.

a pack of wolves. He professes his own desire to cast himself
humbly at the feet of Leo with this, his warning and petition,
ready to endure everything that is not opposed to the Word of
God. Yet as strongly as in his most vigorous publications, does
he now denounce to the Pope himself the curia, or, in other
words, the entire structure and system of the Romish Church, as
a Babylon, a den of robbers, an empire of sin and hell, and even
the so-called vicars of Christ as genuine Antichrists. He renounces all possibility of recantation upon his part, since there is
one thing which he cannot endure, *i. e.*, that the Word of God
should be bound. He declares that he will challenge no one ;
but, if challenged, he will in fidelity to his Master, Christ, not
remain speechless.

The accompanying pamphlet, *De libertate Christiana*,[1] proposes, as the introduction to the Latin edition announces, to treat
of the power of faith, or, more definitely, of the truth, that the
Christian, just by virtue of his faith, " is a free lord over all
things, and subject to no one," and, at the same time, " a ministering servant of all things, and subject to every one."

We do not find this treatise pervaded by the spirit of conflict
and wrath which marks the letter. It is throughout a positive,
joyous testimony to the power of that faith which is " a living
fountain, flowing unto eternal life," and its aim is evidently to
inspire the reader with joy. Luther does not here propose to
address the learned. He aims to serve the plain people (*rudibus*),
and open to them the way of knowledge. He will speak as one
who has himself experienced in great and varied trials that to
which he testifies.[2] Most fervently, not in dialectical analysis, but in
comprehensive, mystical summary, he presents the unity with
Christ effected by faith, and the salvation thereby bestowed upon
the believer. From this profound apprehension of religious truth
flows naturally, and without constraint, the reformatory principle
of evangelical liberty. With the clear assertion of this principle
is, however, at once combined an admonition to loving devotion
to the work of relieving the want of Christian brethren, and to a
generous consideration for the weak and a self-denying restraint,
upon their account, in otherwise justifiable efforts for outward

---

[1] Latin, Jena i, 463 sqq. German, " Freiheit eines Christenmenschen,"
Erl. Ed., xxvii, 173 sqq.

[2] Cf. the Introduction.

reformation. Certainly a wonderful evidence of Luther's inner spiritual tendency was the preparation of *this* document in the midst of the greatest excitement of the conflict! And a remarkable and most significant act was the sending of *this particular document* to the Pope, in connection with the candid accompanying letter. We rightly place it side by side with the *Address to the Nobility* and the *Babylonian Captivity* as the third chief reformatory publication of Luther. He would, upon his own testimony, have most gladly devoted himself to the preparation of just such works as this. The Pope may, as he tells him in the letter, learn from this little treatise the kind of work in which he would gladly, and might be fruitfully, employed, if the unchristian Papists would but allow it.

We do not meet in the work before us any essentially new ideas, nor the development of any fresh antitheses to Romish theories or enactments. But the views already traced in earlier *Sermons* and publications here meet us in such rich and vivid combination as finds no parallel in other writings of the Reformer during this period. In this feature, indeed, no other writing of Luther, bearing upon the general truths here treated of, can be compared with this. It is on this account that we here briefly recall its contents.[1]

The two propositions, concerning Christian liberty and Christian servitude, were derived from 1 Cor. ix. 19. He prefaces them immediately with the statement, based upon Paul's expressions concerning the inward and the outward man in 2 Cor. iv. 16, that the first proposition refers to the former, or spiritual, inward man, known as the new man; and the second, to the latter, or outward, carnal man, known as the old man.

It is, therefore, the former, or spiritual man, whom he has in view when treating of the Christian's liberty. He inquires, in the first place, " *how an upright, free, Christian, that is, a spiritual, new, inward man arises.*" It is to be borne in mind that, throughout the entire work, he employs the terms " pious," " just," " righteous " (*fromm, gerecht, rechtfertig, bonus, justus, rectus*) as synonymous. Where, for example, the Latin copy has *justus*, we find *fromm* in the German edition.

In reply to the question raised as to the origination of the

---

[1] We quote from the Latin as well as from the German edition.

inward man, it is maintained that no external thing whatsoever, whether it be bodily health, or holy vestments, or formal prayers, fastings, or other works accomplished through the body, can make man pious or free, nor contribute anything to his *justitia* or *libertas*. He goes even further, declaring that " not even speculations, meditations, nor anything that can be contributed by the exercise of the mind (*per animae studia*), can profit anything." He means thus to include, as is quite evident, everything natural, worldly, or originating with ourselves, embracing even the entire natural, worldly and personal life, possessions and activity of the *soul*. We are reminded of the *Sermons* and *Theses* before the indulgence controversy (*supra*, p. 138), in which he expands the idea of the sensuous, or carnal, and sets in antithesis to it that which is " God Himself." The soul has, on the other hand, he proceeds to say, nothing in which to live and be free and pious but the holy *Word of God*, the Gospel of Christ, according to John xi. 25 ; xiv. 6 ; Matt. iv. 4. Comparing this with the *Sermons* above mentioned, it is significant to observe that he now always conceives of God directly as revealing Himself in the Word, and in that Word as a proclamation of grace. He was thus led to the placing of stronger emphasis upon the Word in this respect, purely through the increasing definiteness of his own inner apprehension of doctrinal truth, before he was called to witness the rise of a false and spiritualistic mysticism. If the soul but has the Word, he declares, it needs nothing else whatsoever ; in the Word it has full satisfaction, food, peace, justification, truth, liberty, everything that is good. It was for the preaching of this Word that Christ came, and that apostles, priests, etc., have been ordained. But this Word is the Gospel, in which God Himself speaks of His incarnate, suffering, glorified Son, and in which He teaches us that our own works avail nothing before Him, but that, on the contrary, we must with them be eternally lost. This Word, moreover, can be received and honored only in faith. To him who commits himself to Christ in firm faith, and confides boldly in Him, all sins shall be forgiven ; he shall be righteous, upright, filled with peace, pious, fulfilling all the commandments, and free from all things.

But how does it come to pass that faith alone makes pious or justifies? (As the German copy has *fromm* as the equivalent of *justus*, so also it puts *justificare* as synonymous with *fromm machen*). Luther presents his reply in the Latin copy (in which the subject matter is more systematically arranged under general headings than in the German) under three leading divisions.

He first points out the difference between the *commandments*, which only show man how incapable he is of fulfilling them, and the *promises*, which say to him : Dost thou desire to fulfil all the commandments, to be freed from thine evil lusts, as the Law demands? then believe in Christ, in whom I promise thee all grace, righteousness, peace and liberty. These promises, there-fore, he declares, give what the commandments demand, and fulfil what the commandments require. And that it *is just faith* which obtains these blessings, he establishes as follows : Since these words of God are holy, truthful, righteous, peace-bestowing, free, and full of every blessing, the *soul* which clings to them in unwavering faith becomes *so united with them*, so utterly and entirely absorbed, that all the virtues (qualities) of the Word become also those of the soul. As is the Word, so does the soul also become through it, just as iron by combination with fire be-comes also glowing-red like the fire itself. Hence, also, it is only faith, and no work, that can accomplish so much. No work clings like faith to the divine Word, nor can a work be in the soul. In the soul can reign only the Word and faith. This, now, is Christian liberty, *i. e.*, the faith that does not, indeed, make us indolent, but in view of which we need no work in order to obtain piety (*justitia*) and eternal blessedness.

In this *relation of faith to the Word*, and to the efficient power of the Word, Luther places the " first virtue of faith." The second he locates in the *glorifying of God Himself*, which is the essential characteristic of faith. " This is also the office of faith, that it worships Him whom it believes with the most reverent and highest possible apprehension of His excellence." When the believing soul accounts God true, good and just, it renders him the very greatest honor which it is possible for it to render ; just as unbelief is the greatest dishonor which can be manifested toward God, and just as, also, one man can render no higher honor to another than to esteem him a pious and true man. God then also honors the soul in return, esteems it pious (good) and true ; and it is also good and true, since the very act of ascribing to God truth and goodness is right and truth, and makes him who exercises it right and true. Faith *makes* truth and goodness (*justitia*, piety), rendering unto God His own.

The third and incomparable " virtue of faith " consists, finally, in the *union with Christ Himself* which it effects. Not only does the soul become like the divine Word, but it is bound up with Christ, as the bride with the bridegroom, in one body (Eph. v. 30). All that Christ has then becomes the soul's own—all His possessions and everlasting happiness. All that the soul has then becomes Christ's—all its iniquity and sin. But Christ is God and man without sin, and His goodness, or righteousness, His life, His everlasting happiness, is invincible, eternal, almighty; and inasmuch as He now makes the sins of the soul His own, just as though He Himself had sinned, suffering, dying and descending into hell, these must all be swallowed up in Him and drowned in a wondrous strife, since His righteousness is stronger than all sins, His life mightier than any death, His eternal happiness more unconquerable than all hell combined. Thus the rich, noble, good Bridegroom takes in marriage the poor, despised, wicked little whore, the soul, delivers it from all evil, adorns it with all His possessions. Of this Paul cries, in 1 Cor. xv.: Praise and thanksgiving be to God, who hath given us in Christ Jesus such a victory, in which death, together with sin, is swallowed up.

From this magnifying of the glory of God, Luther returns to the second characteristic of faith mentioned. Thou seest then, says he, upon what ground so much is rightly attributed to faith, *i. e.*, that it fulfils all the commandments and makes good (pious) without any other work; for faith alone fulfils *the First Commandment:* Thou shalt honor thy God. Therefore, faith alone is the righteousness of man and the fulfilling of all the commandments; since he who fulfils the first will also certainly and easily fulfil also all the others. Works, on the contrary, are dead things. They may, indeed, also be done to the honor of God. But we are here seeking for that which *is not done*, like works, but which is the doer and workmaster himself, honoring God and doing the works. This is none other than the faith of the heart. This is the head and whole being of goodness.

No one can fail to observe that Luther has, throughout this practical exposition, included again in the conception of justification or righteous-making, not only reception into the favor of God, but also as well the moral regeneration of the individual; and in faith itself he sees already the principle of the new out-

ward life.   Questions which naturally arise as to the mutual relation of these elements will at a later point require our attention.
They would be out of place in the consideration of the present
treatise, whose leading characteristic is the direct combination
of all elements.

Finally, there is presented an exposition of the *kingship* and
priesthood, of which believers become participants through this
union with Christ (1 Pet. ii. 9), to whom, as the first-born Son
of God, it originally belongs.   They are kings because they become by faith, despite all bodily oppression, lords of all things,
whom nothing can harm, whose everlasting happiness all things
must serve to promote (Rom. viii. 28; 1 Cor. iii. 22).   This is
their precious liberty and power.   A much greater thing than to
be thus kings is it that they are also priests, worthy to approach
God, to pray for one another, to teach one another what God is,
as praying and teaching constitute the office of a priest.[1]   In
place of the priestly order, of which it has been customary in our
day to speak, the Scriptures know only ministers, servants, work-
men, whose duty it is, because we cannot all do so, to preach
(*publice docere*) to others Christ, faith and Christian liberty.
"Who now can comprehend the honor and lofty dignity of a
Christian man?   Through his kingship he has power over all
things.   Through his priesthood he has power over God; for
God does what he requests and desires.   To these honors he
comes only through faith."

Thus much Luther has desired to say "concerning the *inward*
man, of his liberty and *chief righteousness*, which needs neither
Law nor good works"—of the *princeps justitia fidei*.   He now
turns to the other part, the *outward man.*

Man is inwardly, according to the Spirit, sufficiently justified
(*justificatur*) by faith; it remains only, in this respect, that this
faith and sufficiency shall continually grow until his entrance
upon a higher life.   But he must yet tarry for a season in the
life of the body, must rule his own body and associate with other
men.   This calls for the exercise of good works.

Luther here, first of all, speaks of this government, or discipline,
of one's own "body," or of "the flesh," in which the man still

[1] In the German copy, Erl. Ed., xxvii, teaching (p. 186) is not again expressly mentioned (cf. also p. 185).

finds a rebellious will, which must hence be " urged and exercised by fasting, watching, labors and all moderate discipline," the
amount of which must be determined by every one for himself.

At the same time, warning is again given against the idea that
works of any kind can make the Christian good and righteous.
These are rather to be regarded as the works of Adam, to whom
God assigned the duty of laboring in Paradise and keeping it, but
who had been created by God good and righteous (*justus et rectus*), without having been required first to become good and righteous (*justificari et rectus fieri*) by his own labors, but who would
still have had purely *free works* to do, in order to avoid indolence
and to please God (*beneplaciti divini gratia*). This would also
have been our natural state (had sin not entered). Just so is it
also now with the works of the believer, who has been by his faith
placed again in Paradise. He has them to do, that he may not
spend his time in idleness, and that he may labor upon his body
and keep it, only with the view of pleasing God. The distinction between the commandments and the promises is here again
brought to view. The former are to be proclaimed to terrify the
sinner and awaken penitence ; for it is from them that penitence
flows. The promise of grace is to be proclaimed in order to
teach faith ; for it is from it that faith flows.[1]

From works in general, and especially from those to be wrought
upon one's body, Luther passes to those which the Christian
should do in the service, and for the benefit, of other men. All
the works of the Christian should be done for the good of his
neighbor, just because he has enough for himself in his faith, and
hence all other energy and life is at his disposal, to be employed
in free love in the service of his neighbor. He has a pattern of
this in Christ, his Head, whom he should be like in disposition,
and who, though He was full of divine majesty (*Form*), and had
enough for Himself, and had no need of His life, works, or sufferings to make Him good and secure for Him eternal happiness,
yet emptied Himself of all this, did and suffered all manner of
things, looking only to our highest advantage, and thus, although
He was free, became a servant for our sakes. (The words *forma
dei, forma servi*, etc., in Phil. ii., are thus by no means to be ap-

---

[1] Compare with this exposition of faith the statements of the Praelud. de
capt. Babyl., cited above, p. 401.

plied to the two natures of Christ; but Paul means to say: " Christ, whilst He was full of the form of God, and abounding in all good things, * * * was nevertheless not puffed up nor elevated above us by these things, * * * but did thus, laboring, suffering, dying, that He might be like other men * * * all of which He did for our sakes, that He might serve us, and that all things which should be done in this form of a servant might become ours.")[1] As the duty of this serving love Luther mentions particularly the subjection, for the sake of the brethren, to outward ordinances, from which we would otherwise be free, just as Christ paid the tribute money, and Paul had Timothy circumcised. Boldly, at length, does he carry out the comparison of that which Christians should become for their brethren with that which Christ has become for them all—to the following most profound and comprehensive summary: " The blessings of God must flow from one into others and become a common possession, so that each one shall take the same interest in his neighbor as though his neighbor were himself. They flow from Christ into us: from us they must flow into others who are in need of them, and in such a way that I must place before God even my faith and righteousness for my neighbor, to cover over his sins, to take them upon myself, and act precisely as though they were my own, just as Christ has done for us all.[2] Behold, this is the nature of love, when it is genuine: but love is genuine wherever faith is genuine." This conception of the fellowship of Christian love reminds us of the earlier utterances of Luther concerning the communion of believers in and with the communion existing between them and the Saviour Himself. (*Supra*, pp. 271, 344 sq.) He affords us no closer nor mediating analysis of this interposing of self for others by the believer, just as he has not sought to further analyze the interposition of Christ Himself in behalf of believers and the absorption of their sins in Him. Only this much let us observe as clearly involved : At the basis of the theory lies the conception of the most profound sense of participation

---

[1] This interpretation is given by Luther already in the sermons in Erl. Ed., xviii, 199; Löscher, ii, 447 sqq., " de duplici justitia"; and Jen. i, 178 sqq. (all of A. D. 1518); and defended in Briefe i, 220 (A. D. 1519).

[2] Ut fidem et justitiam meam oporteat coram Deo poni pro tegendis *et deprecandis* proximi peccatis, quae super me accipiam et ita in eis laborem et serviam ac si mea propria essent.

27

in, and cordial sympathy with, the sad condition of one's sinning fellowmen and earnest effort to deliver them from it. The activity thus induced is described more accurately as intercession, and, still further, as toiling with the neighbor himself in devoted, ministering, soul-seeking intercourse with him. God is meanwhile conceived as not looking upon the sin of the neighbor, just because He beholds this sympathy, intercession and ministering activity in his behalf. That in all this the Christian interposes only with that which he has himself received, and is constantly receiving, from Christ is, of course, perfectly understood.

In the *Conclusion*, Luther sums up all in the brief statement, " that a Christian man lives not to himself, but in Christ and his neighbor: in Christ by faith; in his neighbor by love. By faith he mounts (*rapitur*) above himself to God; from God he descends (*libitur*) again below himself by love; and yet he remains ever in God and in divine love." * * * " Behold, this is the true, spiritual, Christian liberty, which sets the heart free from all sins, laws and commandments."

In the *Latin Edition* there is added, for the benefit of those of whom such good things cannot be said, and in order that they may not by their misunderstanding pervert the teaching, a declaration against *a carnal abuse of this doctrine of liberty*. He already anticipates such an abuse upon the part of a multitude of hearers: they (*quam plurimi*), when they hear of liberty, want to appear as free, and as Christians only in the despising of ceremonies, traditions and human laws, whereas the opposing party seeks to attain salvation only by the observance of these. He points, in illustration, to Rom. xiv. 3. The liberty in question he declares to be not a freedom from works, but a freedom from opinions about works, *i. e.*, from the opinion that we are justified by works. The Christian, he then says, must, in his conduct with regard to ceremonies, always have in view two different classes of men. The one class consists of hardened ceremonialists, who will neither endure nor understand liberty. In dealing with them, the proper course is to do directly the opposite of that which they demand, and offend them as boldly as possible. The other class consists of those weak in the faith, referred to in Rom. xiv. These should be spared and borne with until they are better instructed. To please them we should in love observe the fasts and other things which they esteem necessary. We cannot, he proceeds to say, live on earth entirely without ceremonies and works. Hot, impetuous *youth* requires these bonds, and every one needs likewise some chastisement of the body. A faithful minister of Christ must, therefore, in all such things endeavor so to rule and teach that no offence be given to consciences or to faith, and that, on the other hand, no idle fancy nor bitter root of work-righteousness may be permitted to spring up. In short, as Christian poverty incurs peril in the midst of wealth, fidelity and faith in the rush of business, humility in the enjoyment of honor, so also is the righteousness of faith endangered in the multiplicity of ceremonies. Nevertheless, we must live and move, as in the midst of wealth, business, etc., so also amid ceremonies, that is, in constant danger. Ceremonies should have no other place in the Christian life than is occupied among mechanics and artisans by the necessary preparations for building or other operations, which are prepared, not on their own account, nor for permanent preservation, but only because it is not practicable to build without them. When the building is finished, the scaffolding is laid aside.

The treatise upon *Christian Liberty* thus furnishes us with a complete expression of the views which Luther at all times and under all circumstances maintained and applied in regard to fasts and other similar external works—a complete presentation of the principles which he wished to have observed when the work of ecclesiastical reformation had been actually begun.

SECTION III. FURTHER DECLARATIONS AND WRITINGS OF LUTHER AFTER THE PUBLICATION OF THE BULL OF EXCOMMUNICATION: BEARING CHIEFLY UPON THE DOCTRINES OF THE CHURCH, OF FREE WILL, AND OF THE HOLY SCRIPTURES.

APPEAL FROM POPE TO COUNCIL—CLAIMS OF THE PAPACY—CUP FOR LAITY—MARRIAGE OF PRIESTS—UNIVERSAL PRIESTHOOD—RECOGNITION OF THE CHURCH—FREE WILL—INTERPRETATION OF SCRIPTURE.

As was to be expected, Luther's letter to the Pope had not the slightest influence in delaying the publication of the edict of excommunication. It condemned forty-one of his *Theses*, and demanded recantation within sixty days. Luther himself never even thought of pursuing any other course than the carrying out of the conflict against Antichrist, in the way upon which he had hitherto been divinely led, to the very last conclusion.

Repeating now his APPEAL TO A COUNCIL,[1] he in it solemnly depicts the Pope as a heretic condemned by the Scriptures (because boldly urging men to deny the necessity of faith in connection with the sacraments), and even as Antichrist, trampling upon the whole Scriptures. As in the *Address to the Nobility* he had instructed the secular power as to its rights and duty, so he now calls upon the Emperor, electors, princes, nobles, councilors, and all the authorities of the German nation, in defence of Catholic truth and in the interest of liberty and justice, to endorse his appeal for a genuine council, and oppose the wicked tyranny of the Pope, or, at least, to pay no regard to the unchristian Bull of excommunication. It has been charged upon him, he says, that he was trying to incite the laity against the Pope, the priests and the monks. To this he replies, that it would be no wonder if the princes, nobles, and laity in general should combine to drive these men all out of the land ; but that would not be his fault, but the Pope's.[2] At the same time, he warns Spalatin not in any event to rely upon princes, nor depend upon the judgment of men, whether they should approve or condemn his course, assuring the latter that he is not anxious to secure their protection, but only that they prove worthy to possess the divine Word, and that they through it may attain salvation.[3] To Hutton he writes,[4] that the Gospel dare not be defended with violence and slaughter ; that it is by the Word that the world has been conquered and the Church maintained, and that by this same Word the Church shall also be restored and Antichrist ground to powder.

The most striking evidence of his final breach with the Pope and the Romish Church was publicly given in his *burning of the Bull and the papal Decretals* on the tenth of December.[5]

His further publications in response to the Bull,[6] as well as the

---

[1] Jen. ii, 271 b sqq. Erl. Ed., xxiv, 28 sqq.

[2] Erl. Ed., xxiv, 42 sq.   [3] Briefe, i, 521 sq.

[4] Ibid., p. 543.   [5] Cf. Briefe, i, 542.

[6] Adv. execrab. Antichristi bullam, Jena, ii, 301 b sq. (Cf. Briefe, i, 521); Wider die Bulle des Antichrists, Erl. Ed., xxiv, 36 sqq.; Assertio omn. articulorum, etc., Jena, ii, 307 b sq. (Cf. Briefe, i, 543); Grund und Ursach, etc., Erl. Ed., xxiv, 52 sqq. (Cf. Briefe, i, 541, 561, 567); Warum des Papstes Buecher verbrannt sind, Erl. Ed., xxiv, 150 sqq.

other books issued soon afterwards (among which those against Emser,[1] particularly the *Antwort auf das überchristliche * * Buch Bock Emsers* and his *Responsio ad librum * * M. Ambros. Catharini*, etc.,[2] are for us the most important), display no essential advance in doctrinal development. They contain, however, more precise definitions upon many points, and the boldest possible expression of direct and thorough opposition to Romanism.

Luther still, as we observe, continues to represent his doctrine as the *Catholic truth*. He regards all the condemned *Theses* upon repentance as "Catholic doctrines" (*pro catholicis dogmatibus*).[3] Thus, for example, when referring to his *Operationes in Psalmos*, which appeared A. D. 1519–1521, he expresses the consoling conviction, that he has never in these comments done any violence to the pure and Catholic faith.[4] But his conception of Catholicity is very different from the traditional idea, just as he has come to hold a very different view as to the nature of the Church itself. As he no longer sees the Church, or Christendom, in the Pope, the bishops and the priests, nor even in the whole multitude of outward professors, but only in the true members of Christ, so the Catholic, or universal Christian faith, is for him only that which these true members of the Church believe. But, inasmuch as he recognizes as such only those who believe in the Word of Christ contained in the Holy Scriptures, it is a foregone conclusion, that only that can be for him Christian and Catholic truth which is derived from Scripture. The justification of his designation of this as " Catholic " truth must be sought in his firm conviction that there has always been, and still is, in the world a Christendom, or Church at large, resting upon the sacraments and the Word, which with one accord clings to the truth of Scripture, and that with this true Church his teaching is in harmony. His doctrine is, therefore, Catholic, and it is not some new doctrine, even though but few individuals in the outward visible Church recognize it, and none at all of the representatives of the Romish ecclesiasticism and theology. Verily, says he, when refuting this charge of teaching false doctrine, all Christian interests have gone to ruin among those who should have guarded them, *i. e.*,

---

[1] Erl. Ed., xxvii, 200 sqq., 205 sqq., 221 sqq.   [2] Jen., ii, 370 sq.

[3] Ibid., p. 307.   [4] Op. Lat., Erl., xvi, 235.

among the bishops and learned men ; but yet, no doubt, the truth has remained in the hearts of some, if it were only in babes in the cradle. Poor peasants and children now understand Christ better than bishops and doctors, just as, under the old covenant, the spiritual understanding of the Law was preserved only among a few humble souls, and not among the chief priests and learned men.[1] Even to the Fathers he openly attributes many errors, but declares that they are not heretics upon that account, since it is not error, but persistence in error and defence of it, that makes a heretic.[2] He is willing to grant that the Church, in his sense of the word, does all things rightly (*recte omnia facere*) and is controlled by the Holy Spirit. But that which his opponents call the Church is the school of Satan.[3]

As to the POSITION IN THE CHURCH CLAIMED BY THE POPE, Luther now not only reaffirms his earlier protests and again presents his own interpretation of Matt. xvi., but he has undertaken also a historical and critical investigation of the question, whether Peter, the reputed predecessor of the Pope, was really for twenty-five years Bishop of Rome, or whether he was even ever at Rome. These points are discussed in the above-named publication against Emser. The first question he answers in the negative. The second he thinks should be answered in the affirmative, although many openly hold the opposite view. He warns, however, against making of this supposed fact an article of faith, and considers it incapable of positive proof.

The necessity of a primacy in the Church he had already denied. He now asserts that the Church could, no doubt, exist without such a head better than with it, as she had certainly never yet derived any benefit from that source.[4] In this connection, he openly declares that he was led to recognize the scriptural truth upon this subect by the study of Huss' condemned book, which treats of the Church.

The suspicions as to the identity of the papacy and the dominion of Antichrist, which he had at first entertained with horror and inward alarm and then communicated, first in confidence to his nearest friends, and then in public words of warning, but which he had found more and more confirmed in the actual con-

---

[1] Erl. Ed., xxiv, 57. [2] Jen., ii, 373 b.
[3] Ibid. [4] Ibid., 321 b.

duct of the Pope, he now proclaims positively and without regard to consequences, and even announces as a doctrinal truth. He thus presents the subject in his book against Catharinus, in which we find an extended discussion of the prophecies of the Old Testament, particularly those of Daniel. He by no means denies, says he, the power of the Papal Church. Nay, of nothing else, outside of Christ Himself, do we have such testimonies in the Holy Scriptures. After the end of the four world-empires, the last of which was that of Rome, Antichrist was, according to Daniel, to arise; and thus the papal tyranny began just as the Roman Empire was hastening to dissolution. This is what Paul refers to in 2 Thes. ii. 6, 7, when he speaks of the κατέχων, after whose withdrawal the wicked one shall be revealed. It was only in name that the Roman Empire was extended over the German nation,[1] and yet, upon this pretext, that man has exalted himself above all kings and bishops, above heaven and earth. Hence, ungodliness has flourished, a brood of false prophets has arisen, Christ has been denied, etc. Rev. ix. 1 sq. is particularly cited as a prophecy of the unchristian theology which should prevail. In the fifth angel he sees the founder, or supporter, of the universities, although he is unable to name any single man who answers historically to this description. In the star fallen from heaven, who opens the bottomless pit, he sees Alexander of Hales, or, still more probably, Thomas Aquinas. In the progeny of the pit he recognizes dead philosophy, *i. e.*, in the smoke darkening the sun, the words of Aristotle; in the locusts, the multitude, born of this philosophy, clinging to and issuing from the universities; in Abaddon or Apollyon, Aristotle himself, the Light of Nature.

The Pope had condemned the *Thesis* of Luther which claimed that a council should restore the CUP TO THE LAITY. Luther now asserts the right and duty of every individual bishop to withstand the Pope in this matter. At all events, he himself now wishes to change the language of the *Thesis* referred to, and make it assert, that it is for every bishop in his own diocese, in accordance with the Gospel and in defiance of the Pope, to arrange for the restoration of the cup, since a bishop is under obligation to oppose the wolf in defence of the flock of Christ. It is only the laity whom

---

[1] Cf. supra, p. 383.

he regards as free from guilt in the matter, and he counsels them, as in the *Babylonian Captivity*, to endure the wrong, just as under the Turks one would be deprived of both elements. As it is, the laity should be content to receive one-half of the sacrament bodily and the other half but spiritually. To the claim of the Papists, that the *whole sacrament* is received under the bread, he replies : Christ also knew that everything could be received in the bread, but He nevertheless appointed both elements ; He even knew that everything could be received in bare faith, but He nevertheless appointed the sacraments.[1] In his reply to Catharinus he at once takes a still stronger position, asserting that, in his judgment, the whole sacrament is taken away when one part is taken, since bread and wine together constitute *one* sacrament, and the one part is left only in mockery. He who sins against God in one part of the sacrament is guilty of all, unless, indeed, God may have saved some in their *faith* in the whole sacrament, just as He can save, and has saved, many in faith alone, without the reception of either element. He here, it will be observed, represents the case as though consent to the withholding of the cup might be reckoned to all, even to the laity, as sin. Thus he is now led to the conclusion that it would be better to receive *neither* part rather than but one, in order the more certainly to escape the charge of mutilating an ordinance of Christ.[2]

As against the PROHIBITION OF MARRIAGE TO THE PRIESTS, he now not only, as before, still advises fallen, though otherwise pious, parish priests, to enter into lawful wedlock despite the Pope ; but he insists upon it as the duty of the entire body of the clergy to withstand the Pope in his imposition of a prohibition which an apostle has declared devilish, as they would withstand the devil himself, and to rend to tatters the enforced vow taken at their consecration. By this he does not, however, mean that in casting off this prohibition they must all actually marry. In support of this freedom from the obligation of the vows in question, he appeals to the canonical law itself, which says : " In promises wickedly made, it is not expedient to keep faith " (*in male promissis non expedit servare fidem*).[3]

[1] Erl. Ed., xxiv, 111 sqq.   Jena, ii, 319 b sq.
[2] Jena, ii, 395 b.   [3] Erl. Ed., xxiv, 290 sqq.

He even yet is unwilling to be quoted as having taught a dissolution of the monastic vow (cf. *supra*, p. 378). He declares it a malicious perversion, when Emser interprets his advice to the Nobility to diminish the number of cloisters as a summons to the inmates of cloisters to violate their vows and forsake the institutions. At about the same time, however,[1] he joyfully writes to a friend concerning his own personal position : " I am released and excommunicated by the authority of the Bull, from orders and from the papal laws." That he includes in the above also his monastic vow, is proved by the following words : "which I joyfully embrace, except that I do not relinquish my cloak (*vestem*, evidently his monastic garb) and my dwelling-place." These words can only be understood as indicating that he no longer felt under any moral obligation as resting upon him in consequence of the vows assumed, but that he still subjected himself to the requirements of his former position only in voluntary submission to the Church and its ordinances.

He has occasion to defend his doctrine of the PRIESTHOOD OF BELIEVERS, especially against Emser.[2] The latter had urged against it, that the apostle, in 1 Pet. ii. 9, is not speaking of the consecrated priesthood, the *sacerdotium ecclesiasticum*, but only of an inward, spiritual priesthood, and does not mean to say that all Christians should be priests, like those who have received episcopal consecration. In this objection Luther can see only blindness to the meaning of his own *Theses* and of the Holy Scriptures. He had never said that Peter spoke in that passage of the Church's priestcraft (*kirchischen Priesterei*), which is, at any rate, only an imaginary priesthood. That which is so called in our day is known in the Scriptures only as a *ministerium*, *servitus*, *dispensatio*, *episcopatus*, *presbyterium*, and never a *sacerdotium*. He then explains precisely what the German word *Priester* means, *i. e.*, " Elder," since the ecclesiastical government was formerly in the hands of the oldest persons, just as the senators of a city receive their name from their age. The word bishop he translates " guardian, or watchman on guard " (*Wartmann, Wächter auf der Warte*). Every pastor or spiritual ruler

---

[1] Briefe, i, 568 (March 5th).

[2] Auf das überchristliche Buch, etc., Erl. Ed., xxvii, 230 sqq. Cf. also Widerspruch seines Irrthums, etc., Erl. Ed., xxvii, 312 sqq.

should, therefore, be a bishop, *i. e.*, an overseer, or watchman, in order that the Gospel and faith in Christ may be built up. In support of his position, that priest, presbyter and bishop are synonymous terms, he again quotes Jerome. The so-called bishops of the present day, he declares, know neither God nor the Scriptures. The method of procedure in the appointment of spiritual rulers ought to be, as it formerly was, as follows: In every Christian city, where all are alike spiritual priests, one of their number, perhaps the most learned and pious, should be elected to be their minister (*Diener*), officer, provider, guardian in the Gospel and the sacraments, just as the burgomaster of a city is elected from the general body of the citizens. He traces the office of the present bishops to purely human laws and ordinances. Likewise, he designates the so-called priesthood as " the Church's " (*kirchisch*), because it "originated in the ordinances of the Church, and has no foundation in the Scriptures." Through the accursed law and government of the Pope it has come to pass that the precious names, " priest, spiritual," etc., have been taken away from the general body of believers and handed over to a very small number. Emser had appealed to custom; and it is, indeed, an ancient custom, since what had been authorized in the Old Testament was very early in the history of the Church applied to the New. But that which has been established by custom can just as well be abolished again, and, on account of its origin, cannot be regarded as a divine ordinance; " for a divine ordinance depends upon no changing custom, and cannot be altered by men." Luther is willing to let it pass as a human custom,[1] that only the smeared and shaven crowd have from ancient times been called priests; but we must be on our guard, and not allow the adversaries to force the Scriptures into an approval of their folly.

As to the NATURE OF THE CHURCH, he maintains against Emser, that it is bound to no place, person or time; and that we *believe* in it, and hence cannot see nor feel it.[2] As to the relation of that which in the Church is external, bodily, to its real nature, he makes most important declarations in his publication against Catharinus.[3] He notices the objection that, if the Church is entirely in the spirit, and a spiritual thing, no one can recognize

---

[1] Erl. Ed., xxvii, 317.   [2] Ibid., p. 303 sq.   [3] Jena, ii, 376 b sq.

where even a part of it exists in the world. To this he replies : Although the communion (*Gemeine, ecclesia*) lives in the flesh, it still does not live according to the flesh (Gal. ii.; 2 Cor. x.). It lives in a place, moves in the midst of things and works of the world; but it is not to be estimated according to these, for Christ banishes every place when He says that the kingdom of God cometh not with observation, but is within us. As the Church cannot exist in this life without food and drink, and yet the kingdom of God, as Paul teaches, is not food and drink; so, also, it is not without place and body, and yet place and body are not the Church, and do not even belong to the Church itself : and just as the Church and believers do not need a particular food, a particular drink, a particular kind of clothing, although they cannot live in the world without food, etc., but yet all things are free and equal to them (*omnia * * * indifferentia*) ; so also particular places and persons are not necessary, although the Church cannot exist without place and person. There reigns here that liberty of the spirit which makes everything bodily and earthly free and equal.

Speaking further of the cognizability of the Church, he grants that it must be in some way recognizable, and that there must be some sign by which it can be known : Some *visible sign* must be given, by virtue of which believers may assemble and hear the Word of God together. But, he declares : We have, indeed, signs, *i. e.*, baptism, the Lord's Supper, and, above all, the Gospel. These are the three symbols, tokens, brands, of Christians. Where thou seest these, at whatever place and among whatever persons it may be (cf. the maxim above, that the Church is bound to no place), there doubt not is the Church. For where there is one Gospel, *there* is also one faith, one hope, one love, one spirit. The Gospel is the principal sign of the Church (*Gemeine*), since through this are effected its conception, inner formation, birth, education, nourishment, clothing, strengthening, etc. In short, the whole life and being of the Church is in the Word of God, as Christ declares that man lives in every word that proceedeth out of the mouth of God. This is true, indeed, not of the written Word, but of the oral, preached Gospel (*de vocali evangelio*), and not of every sermon which is heard in a Church, but only of the genuine Word, which preaches the true faith. Luther introduces a peculiar comparison to illustrate these marks of the Church, finding them foreshadowed in the poles of the ark of the covenant, the ends of which extended out of the Holiest of Holies, and thus indicated the actual presence of the ark concealed within. Thus we may know by the oral and public voice of the Gospel where the Church and the mystery of the kingdom of heaven are to be found. The Church is, therefore, not seen, but only believed in by virtue of this sign of the Word, which cannot be sounded forth except in the Church through the Holy Ghost. We remark further, in this connection, that where the Gospel is wanting, Luther denies also the presence of the Church, even in spite of the observance of baptism and the Lord's Supper, declaring: We dare not doubt, therefore, that among the Papists and Thomists, although they baptize and eat of the altar, the Church nevertheless does not exist, except among the children and simple-hearted living in that Babylon.

In all other points, likewise, in which Luther had been pronounced heretical and condemned, he is ready to recant only in so far as to take still more advanced ground than that maintained in the condemned *Theses*. He recalls the statement that *indulgences* are only allowable and not beneficial. No, he now declares, they belong, on the contrary, in the category of deceitful and destructive things; yea, they are a hellish, devilish, antichristian fraud and robbery.[1] He recalls the statement that *some* of the articles of Huss condemned at Constance are genuinely Christian. He is now ready, on the other hand, to defend them *all*, although, beyond this, he is not prepared to endorse all that Huss teaches, nor all of his doctrines which the Papists accept.[2] He confesses that at the time of the Leipzig disputation he had unfortunately not yet read Huss; otherwise, he would then already have maintained all the condemned *Theses* of the latter.[3]

We must here note particularly the extreme to which he now carries his opposition to the acknowledgment of a FREE HUMAN WILL.[4] Condemnation had been pronounced upon his *Thesis:* That the will, since the fall of Adam, is an empty name, and when it takes its own way (does what is natural to it) sins mortally. He now defends this, primarily with reference to the state of man after the entrance of sin and before the impartation of grace.

[1] Jena, ii, 320 b. Erl. Ed., xxiv, 116.   [2] Jena, ii, 318 b.
[3] Erl. Ed., xxiv, 22.   [4] Jena, ii, 327 sq. Erl. Ed., xxiv, 143 sqq.

He here again explains, first of all, that man lacks freedom just
in so far as sin has enslaved him.   The heart of man is now at
all times, as testified in Gen. vi. 5 ; viii. 21, bent only upon evil.
The Scriptures call man entirely flesh ; and the free will, which
is entirely flesh, cannot follow after the spirit.   The expression,
" free will," had better never have been invented ; that which is
so called might more suitably be designated " self-will, which is
of no benefit." [1]   If it is wished to retain the word, it should be
applied to the regenerated man, who is certainly as free as was
Adam in Paradise.   He argues thus in the German tract, *Grund
und Ursach*, etc.   But in the Latin *Assertio*, etc., he goes farther,
not only declaring man unfree with regard to the sin reigning
within, but citing biblical language which would make his lack
of freedom a consequence of the general relation of man to God.
According to Jer. x. 23, the acts of man are not under his own
control, and it is in the power of no one to direct his way.   The
way of man, he explains, is what we are accustomed to call the
natural power of the will to do as it pleases.   But how can man
now prepare himself to do good, since it is not even in his power
to choose his *evil* ways?   For God *controls also the evil ways* of
the ungodly (Prov. xvi. 4 : The Lord hath made * * * even
the wicked for the day of evil) ; Rom. i. 28 ; Ex. ix. 16.   Under
Prov. xvi. 1, we have the explanation : That is, man is accustomed to propose many things, although his works are so little in
his own hand that he hath not even in his power words suitable
to the furtherance of his plans, being compelled by the wonderful
providence of God to both speak and do otherwise than as he
has thought.   It might appear from this that man may control
himself, at least, in his thoughts ; but we are immediately afterwards pointed to an experience which contradicts even that
degree of freedom : Who has not very often changed that which
he thought to do for another, though without knowing why he
changed it?   Luther cites the authors of the Bull as an example,
since, while intending to speak against him, they have but most
terribly disgraced themselves : Behold how this thought was not
in their will !   He then declares : Thus man is not in his own
hand even when doing or thinking evil, as Paul truthfully says in
Eph. i., *God worketh all things in all.* * * It is in no one's hand,

---

[1] Cf. supra, p. 146.

whether he will think of evil or of good; but all things are from God, against whom we are able to do nothing except in so far as He permits, or Himself does, the deed.   It is this that the poet wished to express when he said: " All things stand fixed by law." Luther has thus already advanced to deliverances which evidently reject the freedom of the will entirely, even when leaving sin out of the account.

We are led still further by a declaration which he immediately appends to the above touching the traditional theory of a general divine influence (*influentia generalis*) which God is supposed to exert upon men independently of the special influence of grace, and by virtue of which they are supposed to possess the capacity of exercising free will.   Upon this point he had already at an earlier day [1] expressed himself as follows : It is customary to attribute to this influence the ability to do those things which are natural to man, and which are called, neither good works nor sins, but neutral matters, or even " morally good " works (as distinguished from deeds lying beyond the sphere of nature, meritorious, and possible only through grace), *e. g.*, the ability to walk, work, eat, pray, and even to prepare one's self for the reception of grace. But Christ condemns (John xv. 5 : " without me," etc.) the theory of this general influence, since *nature can only seek its own*, abuse the divine gifts, and can do *nothing worthy before God* without the special influence of grace.   In this passage, Luther rejected, as will be observed, a free self-determination upon the part of the unregenerate man only in so far as this should involve the capacity for any genuinely moral action, without any reference to the question, whether there might not be such capacity at least in the sphere of purely natural external actions and in the free choice between various evil works.   He now makes the broad general declaration : That general influence also vanishes, by which they claim that it is in our power to perform natural acts (*naturales operationes*) ;   *   *   *   *   Behold, how stupid we are !   The very root of works, life itself, we know to be for no single moment in our own hand, and yet we dare to say that *any thought* is in our hand !   Could anything more absurd be said?   He, according to this, who has retained our life in His own hand, has placed our movements and works in our

---

[1] Briefe, i, 438 sqq. (April 13th, 1520).

hands! Far from it! In the sentences following the above, we find, at length, a mode of apprehending the subject according to which every thought of freedom springs only from the limitation of the view to that which is finite, and must, when regarded from a point of view in harmony with the truth, *i. e.*, with an upturned eye, vanish before the recognition of a general, divinely-ordained necessity, just as the theory of mere chance vanishes in a careful study of the world at large. He here says: "The inconstancy of human affairs, or, as they call it, chance, deceives these miserable men; for they bury their eyes in these earthly affairs themselves and the results to which they lead, and never elevate them to the view of God, in order to recognize the things that are above in God; for when we look downward things seem to be arbitrary and fortuitous, but when we look upward *all things are necessary*. The free will which, in view of ourselves and temporal things, seems to exist, disappears in the presence of God; for there, as James says, there is no variableness, neither shadow of turning, but here all things are changed and varied."

It is clearly manifest from this that we have not placed by any means too strict a construction upon the former utterances of Luther, especially those preceding the indulgence controversy, in regard to the lack of freedom in the human will and the all-embracing, all-pervading government of God.[1] We recall the reader's attention, also, to the remark which we deemed it necessary to append to the earlier declaration, that he did not wish to deny freedom in regard to inferior things (*respectu inferiorum*).[2] With the exposition now given, the teaching of his work, *De servo arbitrio*, will be found easily to harmonize. The views here advanced are in interesting coincidence, also, with the representations upon the subject in the first edition of Melanchthon's *Loci*, which was composed at the same time. Yet even now, upon the other hand, when we compare the entire volume of Luther's writings at this time, how solitary and apart do not the strongest of those comprehensive declarations seem to stand which lead us back from the peculiarly religious aspects of the subject to general metaphysical principles. How significant it is that the German treatise, *Grund und Ursach*, etc., which was de-

[1] Cf. supra, 112 sq., 122 sq., 167, 244, 286 sqq.

[2] Cf. supra, 122 sq.

signed to accompany the *Assertio*, does not repeat these utterances, but rests in the declarations of human depravity which
characterize the other writings of the Reformer. Even in the
Assertio, they are no further developed. It is particularly noticeable that the question, in what relation originally and before the
slavery of sin began, the freedom of Adam stood to the divine
universal agency, and how it became perverted to the service of
sin,[1] is not touched upon. And even in the *Assertio*, too, Luther
returns immediately from the passage above cited to his testimony, that we cannot by our own power win the grace of God,
asserting : " And we stupidly estimate divine things according to
these temporal affairs (*i. e.*, which are varied and changed), so
that we presume to anticipate God and extort grace from Him
as often as we wish, as though He were sleeping ; just as if He
could change places with us, and determine to do what He would
not otherwise have determined to do, and that by virtue of the
action and desire of our free will ! It is thus always zeal against
human righteousness and in behalf of the absolute nature of divine
grace which lies at the basis of his strongest utterances in regard
to the divine omnipotence and the changeless character of the
divine will in general. He does not deem it necessary to present
these statements at all to the plain Christian people for whom he
writes in German, as though realizing that they lead into depths
into which it is not necessary for the simple religious and believing mind at all to enter.

All these doctrines are maintained by Luther, it will be observed, despite the papal condemnation, upon the ground of the
supreme and only authority which attaches to the Scriptures.
For this employment of the Holy Scriptures, also, we find now
further important arguments. Particular attention is given to
the question as to the SOURCE WHENCE THE PROPER INTERPRETA-
TION OF THE SCRIPTURES must be derived, and in view of which an
independent use of them is to be accorded to every true Christian. Of this the *Introduction to the Assertio*[2] speaks, protesting
against the granting of a compulsory authority to the Fathers, in
so far as their doctrines are not proved from the Scriptures. We
must, says Luther, stand by the principle announced in the papal

[1] Cf. the Heidelberg Theses, supra, p. 284.

[2] Jena, ii, 308 b sq.

law itself, that " the Sacred Scriptures are not to be interpreted in any private spirit." The Papists have, indeed, so perverted this maxim that they have actually interpreted the Scriptures only according to *their* own spirit. He himself explains it as follows : Even Augustine and the Fathers had no right to thus privately interpret. *The Scriptures, on the contrary, dare be interpreted only by the Spirit, under whose direction they were written; and this Spirit is nowhere more truly present and active than in the very Scriptures written by Himself.* It is for us, therefore, laying aside all human books, to bury ourselves entirely in these with persevering application until we thus become sure of their own spirit. Thus imbibing this Spirit, every one will apprehend *His* interpretation, which is far exalted above all human writings, even those of the Fathers. That this is possible to every Christian, Luther is positive, because of his belief in the Spirit as yet granted to the Church. In support of the view, he appeals to Ps. cxix. 130 : " The entrance of thy words giveth light. It giveth understanding unto the simple." Understanding is given, therefore, by the sole words of God, as through an opening or entrance, or as through a first principle, from which we must set out, in order to attain light and understanding. Attention is further called to the duty of proving all things, accepting no other Gospel, etc. (1 Thes. v. 21 ; Gal. i. 8 ; 1 John iv. 1). Even the preaching of the new covenant had to be proved by the Scriptures of the Old Testament (Acts xvii. 11).

In the *Introduction* to the *Grund und Ursach*, Luther meets the charge that he was setting himself up presumptuously as a teacher above the whole Church. He asserts that he has not put himself forward, but that his enemies have drawn him into prominence in order, by vanquishing him, to gain credit for themselves. " And if it were true," he adds, " that I set myself up alone, that would not excuse them from giving heed to my message. Who knows whether God has not raised me up for this very purpose? Do we not read that God commonly raised up only one prophet at a time under the Old Testament? * * * Nor did He ever make the high priest or any other of high rank a prophet, but commonly chose some humble, despised person. * * * The godly of all ages have been compelled to preach against rulers, king, princes, priests and learned men, and to risk their lives in doing so. And the only defence of these great men

28

has always been, that they were the rulers, and that they, and not the poor prophets, must be obeyed. * * * I do not say that I am a prophet, but I do say, that the more they despise me and glorify themselves, the more reason they have to fear that I am such. There were many asses in the world in the days of Balaam, yet the Lord spoke through none but the prophet's beast." Thus, Luther makes no demand for the acceptance of his teaching because of any supposed superiority or authority in himself, but he simply proclaims the truth as he finds it in the Scriptures, and allows it to testify for itself.

He now further insists most emphatically that we must cling to the simple, clear sense of scriptural language, in opposition to arbitrary ALLEGORICAL INTERPRETATION. Thus he had already, in his work upon the *Babylonian Captivity*, maintained the plainest sense of the words employed in the institution of the Lord's Supper, and in the same connection [1] demanded that, in general, the actual grammatical sense of the words should, wherever at all possible, be retained. He treats expressly of the allegorical method of interpretation in controversy with Emser, [2] and it is there plainly manifest how completely he has now freed himself from the traditional view of the distinction between Spirit and Letter, which found its way even into his own *First Exposition of the Psalms* (*supra*, pp. 96, 110 sqq). Emser, he says, applies the words of Paul concerning the Letter that killeth and the Spirit that giveth life (2 Cor. iii. 6) to a double sense of the Scriptures, an outward, literal, and a hidden, spiritual sense. He himself rejects all such application of the words. By the Letter the Apostle means, on the contrary, the divine Law given in the Old Testament, which is called a letter because it remains for men a mere letter, does not make them better, does not grant them grace, but only makes demands upon them. The preaching office of the new covenant is called an office of the Spirit, inasmuch as all who believe its message shall receive the grace of God and the Holy Spirit. That which Emser would have regarded as the merely outward sense, Luther declares to be " the highest, best, strongest sense—in short, the whole substance, essence and foundation of the Holy Scriptures." He would rather not call this the " literal " sense, because Paul has something

---

[1] Jen., ii, 277, 297.   [2] Erl. Ed., xxvii, 255 sqq.

entirely different in view in his use of the term " letter ;" but, instead of this, he designates it the grammatical, historical or language sense, since it is understood by every one just as expressed by the language actually employed.   In this sense, says he, is found the proper dwelling-place and pasture-ground of all spirits. Even though the objects described in Scripture may also indicate something further, yet the Scriptures still retain this single sense, and whoever attempts to go beyond this must see to it that he do not, like the chamois-hunters, climb too high, as happened so often to Origen.   He then grants, that Paul speaks of " mysteries," *i. e.*, a hidden, secret sense, and sometimes even of " allegories " (Eph. v. 32 ; Gal. iv. 24).   But he denies that this is ever in the Bible called a *spiritual* sense, as that term is used by Origen and Jerome ; and he is not willing to allow men to invent mysteries themselves, but insists that they shall permit the Holy Spirit to reveal them, and shall prove them from the Scriptures themselves.   He, further, pronounces the so-called four-fold sense of Scripture a piece of folly.   More briefly, in the publication against Ambrosius, he again protests against the attributing of more than one sense to Scripture.   Only this one grammatical sense, he asserts, is to be employed in controversy. It must be confessed, however, that in this respect the Fathers have erred.[1]   He himself had even, at that time and afterwards, not hesitated in his practical expositions of Scripture, after explaining the primary sense of the text, to present also allegorical interpretations.   But he was always very well aware that these could not " stand the test," and was very careful not to employ them in controversy.[2]

With such a study of the Scriptures, and such a method of interpretation, Luther is perfectly convinced in advance that every genuine Christian will attain to one and the same conception of their divine contents—that, in other words, the principles of the supreme authority of the Scriptures will lead to One faith and thus to One Church.

It is remarkable that he should already anticipate the rise of errorists who, upon the plea of a higher, immediate illumination by the Holy Spirit, should no longer be content with the Scrip-

[1] Jena, ii, 272 b sq.

[2] Cf. Enarrat. Epistol. et Evangel. (A. D. 1521), Jena, ii, 368 b.

tures. But he contends that the Papacy could accomplish
nothing against such fanatical claims, because it itself does not
manifest due respect for the Scriptures. Thus, he asks Emser:
" If the Manichæan heresy were now to arise and assert that the
Scriptures do not furnish us sufficient instruction, but that the
Holy Spirit had revived it, how would you defend yourself against
the claim? Would you do no more than, instead of offering
a proof, point with your finger to your own doctrine? Or
would you say : " Ah ! you are too slow. We have ourselves
already found out that we must believe more than the Scriptures
give us?" [1]

Attention has already been called (p. 282) to expressions of
Luther in which he admits REASON along with the Scriptures as a
means of establishing positions taken. The Pope was challenged
to prove his declarations " with Scripture or reason." The doctrine of transubstantiation was rejected because " without Scripture or reason." [2] In a similar spirit, in his tract, *Warum des
Pabstes Bücher verbrannt sind,* he charges that the Pope has never
yet vanquished an opponent with " Scripture or reason," but has
always employed force alone.[3] Every passage of this kind adds
fresh confirmation to what has been said above as to the sense in
which Luther employed the word in such connections. It is
very evident, in the treatise on the *Babylonian Captivity*, that,
while denying all warrant in reason for the doctrine there combated, he would have been just as little inclined to acknowledge
as true any professed evidence from reason which should have
opposed the plain sense of Scripture, or refused to submit absolutely to this. Hear him in his treatise, *Von dem Pabstthum
zu Rom*, express his opinion of the " natural reason," when the
attempt is made by its aid to maintain the necessity of a bodily
head for the Church : " The Scriptures forbid us to follow reason,
for reason ever strives against the laws of God. Hence, to
attempt to establish or defend an ordinance of God by reason,
unless, indeed, reason have itself first been established and enlightened by faith, is as though I should attempt to illuminate the sun
with a little candle, or establish a rock upon a reed ; for Isaiah
(vii. 9) subordinates reason to faith, when he declares : " Except

---

[1] Erl. Ed., xxvii, 280.

[2] Supra, p. 390.   Jen., ii, 277, 277 b.   [3] Erl. Ed., xxiv, 163.

ye believe, ye shall not be sensible, nor reasonable." [1]   And we know what he regards as the foundation and source of this faith itself, *i. e.*, the Holy Scriptures, by virtue of the Spirit, in whom they are written and in whom they are to be interpreted.

Upon this basis of the Scriptures, whose authority and whose contents have attained for him an irrevocable, independent inner certainty, he, in the presence of the Diet at Worms, solemnly professes his adherence to the truth which he has hitherto preached and which the Church of Rome has condemned : " Unless I shall be convinced by proofs from the Scriptures, or evident reason (for I trust neither Pope nor councils alone, since it is certain that they have very often erred and contradicted themselves), I am bound by the Scriptures which I have adduced and my conscience is bound to the words of God.   I neither am able nor wish to revoke anything, since to act against conscience is neither safe nor right."   When, at a gathering in the residence of the Archbishop of Treves, to which he had been invited, the Elector of Brandenburg inquired whether he had refused to yield unless convinced by Scripture, he replied : " Yes, or by perfectly clear and evident reasons (*rationibus clarissimis et evidentibus*) [2]   But in regard to these " clear and evident reasons " [3] we must, in view of all that has been above noted, understand that he was thoroughly convinced in advance that such reasons as would shatter, or even in the least disturb, his confidence in the authority of Scripture could never be produced. A decisive point in the proceedings before the assembled Diet and those which followed upon it was his refusal to acknowledge the decision even of a council against a proposition which he recognized as scriptural.   The proposition which became the occasion for the assertion of this principle was the article of Huss, condemned at the Council of Constance and defended by Luther : " There is only one holy, universal Church, which is the number of the predestinated."   The council, he declares, in that instance condemned the Holy Scriptures, and also the article of the Catholic Creed, " I believe in a holy Christian

---

[1] Erl. Ed., xxvii, 94.

[2] Jena, ii, 438, 440.   The first declaration is repeated in the German reports, evidently with unclear and improper construction.

[3] Erl. Ed., lxiv. 382 : scheinbarliche und merkliche Ursachen.

Church." [1] Together with the doctrine of the Scriptures, he has, therefore, at the same time, undertaken to champion the true universal Christian Creed. He left the Diet with the declaration : " I will do everything which His Imperial Majesty may desire, but yet I will leave the Word of God unbound, as St. Paul says : ' The Word of God is not bound.' " [2]

[1] Cf. also particularly Briefe, i, 603.   [2] Ibid., i, 605.

BOOK III.

PRINCIPAL POINTS IN WHICH AN ADVANCE IS MANIFEST IN THE DOCTRINE OF LUTHER AFTER HIS RETIREMENT AT THE WARTBURG: DEVELOPED IN OPPOSITION, NOT ONLY TO ROMAN CATHOLICISM, BUT PARTICULARLY TO TENDENCIES WHICH APPEARED UPON THE TERRITORY OF THE REFORMATION ITSELF.

INTRODUCTORY.

RETIREMENT AT THE WARTBURG. THE NEW CONFLICT.

From the place at which Luther had declared his convictions in the most public and solemn form, and had more fully than ever before, concentrated upon himself the eyes of the entire nation, he was led away to the quiet retirement of the Wartburg, which he was himself fond of calling his "wilderness," his *Patmos*. It is customary to attribute to the season of confinement at the Wartburg a deep significance for the inner development of Luther, inasmuch as he now, after the conflicts into which he had already been drawn, and in the immediate prospect of a far wider expansion of the controversy embracing the entire sphere of the Church's and even of the nation's life, had opportunity to gather up afresh his mental energies, to establish yet more profoundly his convictions of the truth, and to clarify his turbid spirit in peaceful meditation. That quiet retirement must certainly have been very helpful in establishing more firmly and with greater certainty and clearness in his own mind the entire circle of his newly-won convictions. This process must have been greatly aided also by the fact that he felt himself thus providentially directed, through his outward circumstances and his exclusion from the field of public activity, entirely to the study of the Sacred Scriptures, to the translation of which he now addressed himself with all the energy of his soul. It was a circumstance of very great significance also that, when the reformatory spirit among his associates began to find public expression, partly in violent measures and partly in ways grossly erroneous, he was himself enabled first from his quiet watch-tower, with undisturbed and clear vision, to view and estimate the agitation as accurately as though he had been in the very midst of it, and then, upon his appearance at Wittenberg, to direct it into proper paths. But we are not to imagine that the outward quietude and inward meditation of the Wartburg led the Reformer to the least retraction of any of his earlier teachings or demands. The very fact that nothing of this kind occurred serves to demonstrate most clearly how completely, and with what inner logical consistency, his convictions had before this period already been matured. If he, indeed, now established himself the more securely, it was yet only upon the foundation which had been already laid. Not one of his declarations against the Romish ecclesiasticism and dogmas does he recall, but, upon the contrary, he in some particulars intensifies his opposition. In the arguments with which he now seeks to arrest the aberrations of the reformatory spirit we recognize but logical consequences and more accurate definitions of the very same principles which he had hitherto adopted. From these he does not suffer himself to be driven by alarm at any perils which seemed to be involved in his own teachings. Yet certain aspects of the truth, which, though not failing to arrest his attention at earlier periods, had not then been emphasized, are now presented in their relation to other aspects in a more thorough, precise and impressive way than hitherto. This was the case pre-eminently with the significance to be attached to the objective character of the Word and sacraments, yet without in the least weakening the former testimony as to the necessity of faith in the recipient. The same may be said of the estimate placed upon ecclesiastical order, and the necessary harmony of the newly-proclaimed doctrines with that which had been hitherto the unanimous belief of the whole Christian world.

Luther had, at the very first outbreak of these erroneous tendencies, at once recognized the significance and magnitude of the peril involved. It was just because he had done so, and by no means because, as some have supposed, he had overlooked or underestimated the danger, that he could reply so calmly and confidently as he did from the very beginning to a Melanchthon, when the latter was thrown into a critical state of excitement and agitation by the utterances of the Zwickau fanatics. He describes this danger in his tract, *Von beider Gestalt des Sacraments*, etc., with immediate reference to the violent Wittenberg reformers, in the following apt terms : Among ourselves, Satan is now trying to carry out his malicious designs. Since he sees that he cannot drive us to the left, he assails us upon the right hand. He used to make us altogether too popish ; now he *wants to make us alto-*

gether too evangelical.[1] Luther here recognized the new and grave responsibility which was from this time forward to rest upon him. Hence, when the Zwickau prophets made their early assault upon infant baptism, and Melanchthon was anxiously casting about for the means of meeting their objections, Luther did not for a single moment lose his self-composure, nor was he even surprised. He writes: I have always expected that Satan would touch that ulcer. Within ourselves and among our own friends this very grave schism arises mountain-like, but Christ will quickly crush it to pieces under our feet.[2] A great insurrection even, which might easily be induced by a carnal acceptance of the Gospel by the people, pictured itself even now as " alas only too certain " before his anxious vision. He held that the outbreak of such an insurrection was encouraged, to the extent of their ability, by those who were seeking to extinguish by violence the light of the Gospel itself, and thereby embittering the hearts of the people. He fears disorders in the midst of which princes and civil government shall be destroyed, together with the clergy, throughout all Germany. But he at the same time realizes that he dare not on this account take a single backward step in his testimony in behalf of Gospel truth, nor hesitate a single moment in his own conflict with the adversaries of the Gospel. So far as the latter are concerned, he says, it would be only an occasion for laughter if an insurrection should clear them all out of the world, according to the words of divine wisdom in Prov. i. 25, 26 : " I also will laugh," etc. Nevertheless, he would still like to do his part, in order that the judgment of God might, if possible, be averted or delayed ; he would like to set himself, as God commanded Ezekiel to do, as a wall of defence before the people.[3]

We enter, therefore, already with the years 1521 and 1522, upon that period of Luther's activity and doctrinal development, in which his testimony is directed chiefly against that spirit of error which, under the plea that it alone was applying the new light with real earnestness, seriously threatened to extinguish it altogether. But at the same time, and at the very outset of our investigations, we must trace yet further the particulars in which

[1] Erl. Ed., xxviii, 287.   [2] Briefe, ii, 128.

[3] Erl. Ed., xxviii, 149.   Briefe, ii, 149.

he was compelled to develop yet more definitely the consequences of his evangelical teaching in opposition to the dominant Catholicism.

We may, in this further and last period of our historical survey, treat these two aspects separately. The central point of his entire teaching, from which he always sets out for the combating of either form of error, remains the same as that with which we have already become familiar.

CHAPTER I.

FURTHER DEVELOPMENT OF OPPOSITION TO THE ROMAN
CATHOLIC CHURCH.

VOWS—THE MASS—PRIVATE CONFESSION—FASTS—IMAGES—INVOCA-
TION OF SAINTS—PURGATORY—FREE WILL—PREDESTINATION—
SCRIPTURE AND TRADITION.

LUTHER'S rupture with the doctrinal authority of the Romish
Church and every dogma which it held that could not be proved
from the Scriptures had now become for him final and complete.
With bold confidence and unwavering assurance, he opposes to
its teachings what he has learned to recognize as evangelical
truth. In his tract against Henry VIII. of England, for example,
written in the year 1522, he declares : I am certain that I have
my doctrines from heaven. He denounces not only those whom
he finds proclaiming doctrines of mere human invention, but no
less severely also such men as Erasmus, who with fear and hesitancy, like the skeptics and academicians, keep to themselves
their positive convictions. He likes to hear a positive affirmation
of the truth on the part of Christians. " Do away with the
assertion of your convictions, and you do away with (your)
Christianity." He has no further scruples on the score of mod-
esty, and will show no mercy in his dealings with Papists. In
vain, he declares, has he in the past humbled himself before
them ; he will now use his horns to rend Satan, until the latter
shall sink exhausted to the earth. He fully justifies the Bohemians in their separation from the murderers and Antichrists,
and is not afraid to be known as their associate, although he does
not approve everything which he finds among them. He wishes
to judge Pope Leo, as an individual, as charitably as possible, and
writes to King Henry VIII. that he is yet uncertain as to what
the former really thinks, and whether or no he still persists in

error.[1] When King Henry reproaches him with having frequently contradicted himself, he answers boldly, that all the world knows that he has always thought and taught the same things in regard to faith, love, works, and, in general, in regard to that which the Holy Spirit actually teaches in the Scriptures, except that he has advanced from day to day in his knowledge of these things. But it is true, he acknowledges, that in matters of which nothing is said in the Scriptures, as with reference to the Papacy, indulgences, masses, etc., he has advanced from timid opposition to complete condemnation. At first he was still willing to acknowledge the Papacy as a kingdom similar to other earthly kingdoms, but he now, with greater truthfulness, declares it to be the most " pestilential abomination " of Prince Satan.[2] In this passage, he expressly asserts that which we have traced in his writings as the actual course of his entire previous doctrinal development.

The next logical consequence of his opposition to Catholicism which it became necessary for him to further elucidate had relation to the sphere of practical life, being nothing less than the controverting of the prevalent theory in regard to celibacy. Here again we find, with all the assurance with which he pursues his way, yet also the greatest prudence and circumspection. He is satisfied with no logical inference, however advantageous it might be to him, unless it can be actually based upon the profound inner principle of evangelical truth. He proves all things more thoroughly than any of his associates in the reformatory conflict.

a. CELIBACY—MONASTIC VOWS.

That the requirement of celibacy in the priesthood was without any binding authority, Luther was now fully convinced, upon the grounds which he had already adduced. He found sufficient evidence in the declarations of St. Paul as to married bishops and as to the diabolic origin of the prohibition of matrimony. When the provost of Kemberg, Bernhard of Feldkirch, was married, he joyously applauded the step. He went so far as to declare at one time that, even if one had no desire to take a wife, he should do

---

[1] Jena, ii, 548 b; iii, 167.—Briefe, ii, 235 sq. Jena, ii, 551.—Briefe, ii, 232 sqq. Jena, ii, 554.

[2] Jena, ii, 548 b sqq.

it now, to grieve and spite the devil.[1] At the same time, he not only does not criticise the celibacy of priests among the Bohemian Brethren, but even applauds it; for, says he, it is there not compulsory, but voluntary. Yet he soon afterwards warns the Brethren that they are encroaching upon the Gospel when they urge their priests to live without marriage. He has evidently, in the meantime, heard other reports to the effect that they too had made celibacy a requirement for their priests. He reminds them that the married state is not to be despised, as though God could not be served in it, and that the gift of voluntary chastity is not so common as those of preaching and teaching.[2]

But the *unmarried state of the monks and nuns* appeared to him to rest upon another basis than that which controlled the celibacy of the priests. In the former case, he saw no compulsion exercised against a class of Christian people, but an obligation which the persons concerned had entirely of their own free choice assumed. He had long, as we know, been averse to vows, and would have rejoiced to be assured that no more would ever be assumed. But how should the word once pledged before God be canceled?

In Wittenberg, Carlstadt[3] had already, on June 19th, 1521, defended the *Thesis :* If monks feel a strong carnal desire, they may marry; they sin thereby, but the incontinent man who sins in his desire commits a greater offence than he who marries. He afterwards published tracts in which he justified the permission thus given to violate the oath of chastity. Luther, on the other hand, still cherishes scruples against such a course.[4] The priestly rank, he declares, has been appointed by God to be without restraint (*als ein freier*), but not so that of the monks, who of their own free will have offered themselves to God. He knows of no such divine utterance as that of 1 Tim. iv. 1–3 in behalf of the monks. Merely on the ground of carnal desire, liberty to marry could never have been claimed even for the priests. He rejects, as insufficient, the scriptural passages adduced by Carlstadt; as, for example, his appeal to the counsel of Paul (1 Tim. v. 9),

---

[1] Briefe, ii, 34, 9. Erl. Ed., xxviii, 194.

[2] Briefe, ii, 217. Erl. Ed., xxviii, 416 sq.

[3] Cf. Jäger, A. Bodenstein von Carlstadt, 1856, chap. vii.

[4] Briefe, ii, 34 sq.

that no widow under sixty years be elected. This advice, says Luther, is based not so much upon the unmarried state of these persons as such, as upon their condition as widows who were to be supported by the congregation; and, moreover, it does not apply to vows already assumed.[1] If it be proposed to base an argument upon the principle that the burning of carnal desire is an evil, he inquires: Who knows whether he will burn to-morrow as he does to-day?[2] Melanchthon thought that vows should be broken, if they could not be kept, to which Luther replies: Then it would follow that the commandments of God must also be disregarded. Or, he asks, does it make a difference, that the latter are imposed upon us, whereas the vows are voluntarily assumed? Then, he adds, they would be properly liable to violation, not because it was impossible to keep them, but because they had been voluntarily assumed. But that which has been voluntarily assumed has thereby become a divine law, according to the scriptural injunction: "Vow and pay."[3] He continually acknowledges, however, that he, too, heartily desires to find a way for the annulling of these vows. The attempt of Carlstadt was a very proper one, if only his writings were not so "lacking in light." Further, he declares, that he now desires nothing so much as to help the monks and nuns. He is concerned for their souls. He has no thought of himself making use of this liberty. "Good God!" he exclaims, "our Wittenbergers will give wives even to the monks; they shall not force any woman upon me."[4] And although he is not yet clear as to the proper arguments with which to justify the course which he is anxious to pursue, he yet already cherishes the firm conviction that Christ, if He were now upon the earth, would, as the true Saviour and Bishop of Souls, cast off these ridiculous things, make all vows invalid, and suffer no one to bear the pressure of an involuntary burden. He has certainly never given even the least intimation that He takes pleasure in these vows.[5]

But Luther very soon points out, also, what is the true way to the solution of the problem. He very aptly describes the task to be undertaken, when he advises Melanchthon: "You must rescind the vow *a priori*, and not *a posteriori*, that is, you must confute

---

[1] Briefe, ii, 37, 35, 42.   [2] Ibid., p. 35.

[3] Ibid., p. 45.   [4] Ibid., 35, 42, 40.   [5] Ibid., p. 39.

the *law of the vow* and its ritual." To this, he says, he has already sought to lead Melanchthon by his former objections to the arguments of the latter: " I wished to furnish occasion for you to apply yourself to the *root*, that is, to the law of the vow, and not to its fruit, or result." In the course which he now himself pursues, he proposes to follow the example of the Apostle Paul in dealing with the Galatians. The latter, he observes, had devoted themselves to God, in their circumcision and observance of the Law, in the same way as one now devotes himself by a monastic vow. But Paul releases them from this bondage, not in view of the fact that they have subjected themselves to the Law and circumcision, but in view of the fact that they have done so with a servile conscience. Thus Paul is for him an example, showing how we are to go down to the root of the matter. Hence, in dealing with the monastic vow, he lays the whole stress upon the *conscience* (*conscientia*), or, as he very frequently expresses it in German, the " idea " (*Meinung*) with which it was assumed. He briefly expresses his deduction upon the subject in the syllogism : Every-one who is living in pursuance of an intention (*Sinn*) opposed to evangelical liberty must be set free, and his vow is an accursed thing ; such is, however, the condition of him who has vowed with the intention of seeking salvation and righteousness through his vow : since, now, the great multitude of those assuming vows have almost without exception done so with this intention, it is evident that their vows are ungodly, and should be abrogated and pronounced accursed. Luther here fell into an agreement with a declaration found also in the writings of Carlstadt. The latter had asserted : The whole system of monasticism depends upon the idea (*Meinung*) that salvation rests in works. But here, too, Carlstadt was " lacking in light." The expression occurs amid a multitude of other arguments, some of which were altogether out of place and others, while correct in aim, failed to establish anything. He had not himself seen the real significance of the expression which he employed. Especially had he failed to show wherein lay the fundamental sin in the very idea which he designates. Whether now a vow had, in any particular instance, been taken with this " idea," must be left, according to Luther, to the decision of the conscience of the individual concerned. Whenever so assumed, they are contrary to faith and the Gospel, and are even idolatry.

29

With respect to vows of this kind which may have been assumed in a free and evangelical spirit, he adds: It is right also to observe them. But he does not believe that an evangelical conscience will ever dare, or has ever dared, to take such a step, unless resting under some delusion.[1]

Together with this letter, Luther sent to Melanchthon also a series of *Theses* for a disputation upon the subject, in which a vigorous line of argument leads to the same results.[2] In these he declares, for example : " Everything which does not originate in faith is sin. Faith is a firm opinion (*Meinung*) and an abiding sense (*conscientia*) of righteousness and blessedness. In it (faith) we believe, according to Heb. xi. 1, not in the visible, *i. e.*, in works done, but in the invisible, *i. e.*, in the promises of divine grace. The opinion, that one may through a work seek righteousness and blessedness is unbelief and idolatry. Vows are a law, and, as such, by their very nature take the conscience captive. Monastic life is essentially nothing but works of the Law. Paul's estimate of the Law and works applies, therefore, to it. There is in it no faith. The person who assumes a vow says : ' I vow to thee, O God, a sacrilegious ungodliness of my whole life.' It is probable that by far the greater number of those who have taken vows would not have done so if they had known that they could not thereby secure righteousness and salvation. Let him who is conscious of having vowed with this ' idea ' not look to papal authority nor regard the reproaches of the multitude, but be concerned first of all, for his own eternal happiness, and give up his vow." He is willing to grant that some, at least, may have assumed the vow with a better understanding. We do not desire hereby to condemn the vows of *all* monks, as Paul recognizes also a proper use of the Law. From the very same principle upon which he rejects the ordinary vow, he infers also the possibility of better ones : The conscience dare not be bound to any other work or law ; but, just in virtue of his liberty, it is the privilege of the Christian, of his own free desire and in such a way as never again to seek his salvation in works, but, on the contrary, preserve his conscience free from their bondage, to place himself again under laws. " The New Testament is a kingdom of liberty, but this liberty is a liberty, not of the flesh, but of the spirit or con-

---

[1] Briefe, ii, 45–48.   [2] Jen., i, 525 sqq.   (Sept. 9, 1521).

science." In this sense, he thinks, St. Bernhard and other pious men have assumed the rank of monks, *i. e.*, in such a way that, being justified by faith, they yet, without compulsion, desired to live in the monastic state. Likewise at present, he declares, any one who has discovered and renounced the ungodliness of his vow may yet, if he wishes to and can do so, carry out that which he had promised in his vow. The vow will, in such a case, be taken anew with a new " idea." But the former vow is in any event nugatory. Luther, in the *Theses* before us, presents it as a still further evidence of the invalidity of the present vows, that love, as well as faith, is denied in consequence of them. By vows and the rules of the Orders, the general duty of minister-ing to one's neighbor falls into neglect. It is, furthermore, wicked to forsake parents, relatives and friends so long as they need our services and we might be useful to them.

But the most comprehensive argument for the invalidity and reprehensible character of these vows is presented in the treatise entitled : *Judicium de votis monasticis*.[1] A briefer presentation of his arguments was given at about the same time in German, in the *Sermon for the Day of the Three Kings* (January 6) in his *Church Postils*, in which he treated of Herod's worship.[2]

In the above-named treatise, he introduces the subject with the assertion that the monastic vows have no scriptural authority, nor is there any example to justify them in the Holy Scriptures : They do not have Christ in their favor, who yet is alone the way and the truth ; they are not from God, but a form of worship invented by men. Throughout the discussion, Luther firmly maintains the ground that the directions of Christ are to be found only in the Scriptures. And the fact that the latter know nothing of such vows, but leave chastity, or virginity, as a matter of free choice to the individual, is of itself now sufficient to satisfy his mind. He pronounces open to condemnation " everything that is a matter of rules, statutes, etc., or that falls either short of, or aside of, or beyond Christ, even though it were brought by angels from heaven."

---

[1] Jena, ii, 504 sqq. (Dated, in the dedication to his father, Nov. 21st, 1521.)

[2] Erl. Ed., x, 416 sqq. That which the editions of Luther's works com-monly present as a separate work, under the title, " Bedenken und Unterricht von den Klöstern, etc. (Erl. Ed., xxviii, 1 sqq.), is identical with this long section in the above named sermon.

He then speaks again of the inner contradiction between these vows, on the one hand, and faith and evangelical liberty upon the other, and also of their interference with duties towards one's fellowmen, which God Himself has laid upon all.[1]

He repeats the declaration of Paul in Rom. xiv. 23 : " Whatsoever is not of faith is sin." We dare not here insert " conscience " (*Gewissen*) for " faith." Here, as elsewhere, it is nothing else than faith in Christ that is meant, namely, the faith that Christ is ours, and that we are for His sake acceptable to God. It is only in this faith that we can have such an assured conscience : without it, the conscience is wavering and full of doubts. And it is only from such a conscience that right works can proceed, as fruits of the forgiveness bestowed. Without this faith, no one can do otherwise than act against his conscience, since he never knows whether he is acceptable to God. The vows in question are, however, assumed with the idea that those who take them *thereby*, after the loss of baptismal grace, become not only good and free from their sins, but even better than other Christians. To become a monk is to fall from faith. Even the declaration of Paul concerning those who, having fallen from faith, forbid marriage (1 Tim. iv.), and which Luther had formerly applied only to the celibacy of the priests, he now believes to be applicable to all prescriptions of celibacy, and especially to that enjoined in monasticism.

With this opposition to faith is immediately connected also, in accordance with Luther's conception of evangelical liberty, a denial of the latter. Evangelical liberty is for him precisely that freedom of the conscience from the bondage of works which is claimed by the principle of faith ; not in the sense that no works are longer to be done, but in the sense that they are no longer to be trusted in, as though they must, or could, bring salvation. He says accordingly : " The form of a Christian vow would have to be this : ' I vow to thee, O God, a manner of life, which, in its very nature, is not necessary, and which cannot be accounted for righteousness.' But will not God reply : ' Then why dost thou vow, thou fool?' " But it is not even at all permissible, he claims, to bind one's self by such a vow ; for one thereby renounces a liberty which God Himself has given us. By virtue of the

---

[1] With the following summary, compare the sermon above-named.

baptismal covenant, we should always continue to enjoy the liberty to marry or to live in continence. God will not accept what is contrary to this His will. The same may be said also of all other vows which we might assume before God. Every monastic vow must hence, in order to be Christian, involve the liberty to recall it at pleasure. It must be understood to mean only : " I vow chastity, obedience, etc., until death, *with liberty*— *i. e.*, in such a way that I can alter it whenever I may see fit to do so." This may appear foolish and ridiculous ; but to just such foolish things do men come when they forsake the ordinances of God and follow their own judgment.[1]

The very fact that these vows are contrary to faith makes them also a violation of the chief commandments of God. The First Commandment, according to Luther, requires that we believe ; the Second, that we confess God's name ; the Third, that we allow God to work in us. In obedience to these requirements consists the proper and true service of God. But in these vows, on the contrary, we set up our own works, do away with faith, and confess our own name much rather than that of God.

But Luther charges also upon the monastic life and rules, as in the above *Theses*, that they are just as contrary to the commandments of the Second Table, which require love for one's neighbor, and especially to the obedience due to parents. On this account he regards his own vow, as he now confesses to his father, as not worth " a wild plum," because it led him to renounce the divinely-ordained authority of his parents. Nothing pained him more, he declares, during his own monastic life, than the denial of the general obligations of Christian love and mercy, in the neglect of the duty of visiting the sick, comforting the mourning, etc., outside of the cloister, for the sake of a minute observance of the monastic regulations.

Finally, he adduces, as an argument against the vows themselves, the impossibility of keeping them. We recall the objections which he had formerly raised against arguments based upon this idea. He himself now says : Even from the natural reason and the light of nature, it becomes plain to common sense that, in the assuming of a vow, an exception must always be made for cases

---

[1] Cf. also the expression in the Eight Wittenberg Sermons, Erl. Ed., xxviii, 264: "God has made it free, and dost thou, O Fool, dare to make of this freedom a vow contrary to the ordinance of God?"

in which fulfilment may be impossible.   But even here he would nullify the vow, to use his own words (p. 448), *a priori*, and not *a posteriori*.   He asserts, as a clear fact of experience, that we do not have under our own control the tyrant that dwells in our flesh. It is not in our power to avoid the natural impulses of carnal desire ; and yet (he assumes as unquestionable) in these the continence which is to be pledged in the vow is already violated. It is only by the special grace of God and a full measure of the Spirit that continence can be actually preserved.   It is, therefore, vowed to offer to God something which He must Himself first bestow.   Thus it was again proved that the theory of the vows was, in its very first principles, perverted and untenable.   To the objection, that the divine commandment of chastity, no less than the human vow of continence, involves an impossibility for us, and that, therefore, upon his theory licentiousness would be allowable, he replies : The state of marriage has been provided for us, in which fulfilment of the divine commandment becomes easy.   To the suggestion, that, upon his principle, the baptismal vow must also be rejected, since the keeping of faith and the divine commandments does not lie in our own power, but alone in the hand of God, he replies : The great difference lies in this, that in baptism we have a divine promise and proffer, which is not the case in the monastic vow—that, in fact, our vowing in baptism is nothing more than the acceptance of the proffered Christ.   He had afterwards to meet the further suggestion, that, although the keeping of the vow be impossible for man, the power to keep it may be received in answer to prayer, which he does as follows : We can, indeed, obtain everything from God by prayer ; but He will not allow us to tempt Him.   Christ might, indeed, have cast Himself down from the pinnacle of the temple, as the devil proposed, and so I might also by prayer obtain permission to live without eating or drinking of the fruits of the earth. But as there is no need of this, I must not tempt God by neglecting that which He has given, and, where there is no necessity, expecting something else which He has not given.[1]   That, in assuming the vow of continence, one sets himself in opposition to an original ordinance of God Himself, and that in this fact lies the explanation of the impossibility of keeping such a vow, is

<hr />

[1] Briefe, iii, 325 sq.

maintained especially in the tract, *Wider den falsch genannten geistlichen Stand*, etc. It is there asserted : When God created man and woman, it was not His desire that His law should be so commonly neglected, nor did He propose to be constantly abrogating it in such wonderful ways, but He designed virginity to be exceptional. He implanted the begetting of children as deeply in the nature of man as eating and drinking, and Himself gave to the body the appropriate members, arteries and fluxes. To prohibit this would be like forbidding nature to be nature, or forbidding fire to burn.[1]

Nevertheless, even yet, despite all his attacks upon the customary vows, Luther does not wish to be understood as denying the possibility of truly Christian vows. He even himself confesses that virginity is the highest state (*rem maximam*). But, in the assuming of such vows, there must be no thought whatever of meriting anything by them before God, or of being thereby elevated above other Christians. A virgin may thus prefer her present state to marriage, because a life in that state, being free from the cares and burdens of married life, leaves her more free for (the service of) God. She and all others should serve God with their peculiar gifts freely and without any thought of reward, always glorying only in Christ. Such a vow will pledge chastity, *as long as it may be possible*, with the reservation of the liberty to marry, whenever the individual concerned shall be unable longer to observe the pledge. Luther again expresses the conviction that such saints as Bernhard understood and kept their vows, without entertaining the present ungodly view of them, in a proper Christian spirit. Yet he does not hesitate to reply to those who appeal to the monastic life of these Fathers : Even the elect are liable to be led astray. God was able to protect Bernhard and others in the midst of the error prevailing around them, and God was able also to deliver them, in case they themselves had fallen into error. He has really suffered scarcely any great saint to live without error, in order that no one might depend upon the mere examples of the saints without the Scriptures.[2] Satisfaction is found especially in the reflection that Bernhard, at least at the close of his life, depended entirely and alone upon Christ, and acknowledged that his own life had been a lost one. His

[1] Erl. Ed., xxviii, 198 sqq.　　　　[2] Ibid., x, 438.

experience, it is suggested, was probably like that of the two hundred men who once, with good intentions, crossed over to Hebron with the rebellious Absalom (2 Sam. xv. 11) and certainly regretted their course when they understood the situation.

Luther, furthermore, does not at all desire that those who have hitherto been monks should now all at once enter the ranks of the laity, and seek salvation in secular, as they had formerly sought it in monastic life. He reminds them that before God neither condition avails anything. "Above thyself!" he cries, "above laymen, above monks, above (clerical) things, above secular things! Believe in Christ, and do to your neighbor as you believe that Christ has done to you! This is the only true way to be saved." Let him who feels himself weak, keep far away from monastic life. As a matter of principle, it will be sufficient, however, to abandon the false opinion that one may be saved through such a life: "First learn that the right way is to believe in Christ; then remain where thou art."[1] In harmony with the counsel thus given, he himself remained unmarried, and still wore his cowl until the year 1524. He writes to his father, in the preface of his *Judicium de votis*: "St. Paul says: All things are yours, and should I belong to the cowl, and not much rather the cowl belong to me? My conscience is free and delivered. I am now a monk, and yet not a monk." When, in 1522, his friend Lange left the monastery at Erfurt, he would have been better pleased to have the latter refrain from such exercise of his liberty, in order to leave no pretext for the slanders of the enemy, just as Paul waived his right to temporal support at Corinth.[2]

In presenting the principles of Luther in regard to vows, we have dwelt thus far mainly upon that of chastity. But the vows of *poverty and obedience* were also considered as sufficiently discredited by the fundamental objection, that they are opposed to faith and evangelical liberty. The principal objection which he urges against the obligation to monastic *obedience* is that previously advanced, *i. e.*, that the general obligations of Christian love are thereby forced into the background and denied, and also obedience to persons to whom it is by divine appointment

[1] Sermon upon the Epistle for New Year's Day, in the Church Postils, Erl. Ed., vii, 316 sqq. In the later editions the sentences here quoted are omitted.

[2] Briefe, i, 175.

due. In regard to the *poverty* included in the monastic vow, Luther refuses to acknowledge it as the *spiritual* poverty of which Christ speaks in Matt. v. 3. The latter cannot be the subject of a special vow, since it is a common duty of all Christians. It consists in dealing with one's possessions in a free spirit; not serving them, but ruling over them; not setting the heart upon them; not trusting in them; desiring nothing from them; using them for the good of one's fellowmen. The adherents of monasticism commit a double sin, since they make the injunction to spiritual poverty, which is given to all, a mere counsel, and then boast of themselves as being the only ones to observe it. But the bodily poverty which they vow is no poverty at all: it is, much rather, a general state of luxury, with which they are very well satisfied.

In these principles and deductions, Luther has now finally decided his relation to the vows of the Romish Church. It is only in the practical application of them that he afterwards advanced still farther, as the course of time and circumstances demanded. He very soon arrived at the conclusion, that there was no longer any reason why the monks in general should not be advised to actually leave the monasteries, in which there was no opportunity for a confession of the true faith and the " right opinion."

b. THE MASS—THE CUP—TRANSUBSTANTIATION.

The thoroughness with which Luther conducted his assault upon the MASS led to a breach with the entire worship of the Catholic Church, not only in respect to its form, but in respect to its very fundamental principle and its inmost spirit. Here he no longer felt any necessity of further investigation or confirmation as to the doctrine to be taught or the course to be advised. The declarations upon the subject of the supposed sacrifice which he now made, especially in his treatises, *Vom Missbrauch der Messe* and *De abroganda missa privata,*[1] introduce no new material, but

[1] The Latin copy is, in the dedication to the Augustinians of Wittenberg (Jena, i, 466), dated upon the Day of All Saints (Nov. 1), 1521, and is therefore the one to which Luther refers in his letter of Nov. 11th to Spalatin (Briefe, ii, 95). The German dedication bears the date (Briefe, ii, 108) of St. Catharine's Day (Nov. 25). Neither was published, however, until 1522, as Spalatin retained the former for some time.

merely present, elucidate and justify the positions previously taken. With the rejection of the current doctrine concerning the Sacrifice, the entire significance of PRIVATE MASSES had disappeared, so that the latter could, according to his conviction, be by no means longer celebrated with a good conscience by an evangelical Christian. As for himself, he writes to Melanchthon on August 1st, 1521 : " I will no more celebrate a private mass forever." [1] He feared that idolatry was practiced in the common daily mass.[2] He, therefore, upon his return to Wittenberg, cordially sympathizes with the demand that the hedge-masses be abolished, although, on the other hand, allowing liberty in regard to the forsaking of the monasteries and a life of celibacy. For, he declares : " The mass is an evil thing, and God is hostile to it, because it is celebrated in such a way as though it were a sacrifice and a meritorious work. There can be as little question here as there could be if one should ask whether God ought to be worshiped." In the celebration of the public mass he would have all words which express the idea of a sacrifice (*die aufs Sacrificium lauten*) excluded, and, on the contrary, the words of the institution freely used. He warns only against a wrong method of procedure in the rejection of the objectionable features. Here, too, he declares, Christian love must be on its guard against the employment of violence ; it is by the *Word* that we must operate upon the *hearts* of men.[3] But where the Word had been long proclaimed, his hesitancy upon this point was finally overcome. Thus, for example, he says to the canons of the Wittenberg cathedral, in August, 1523 : Since enough has been seen and heard of these things for almost two years, this whole abomination connected with the mass should now be done away with, without stopping to inquire further whether there may still be any persons who do not understand the matter.[4] At other places, where the truth had not been so long and faithfully preached, he even after this time admonishes not to " disturb the unenlightened multitude too quickly," but refers to his own treatise upon the subject as pointing out the evils connected with the mass.[5] It is evident that, in thus opposing the errors of the mass, Luther is thoroughly conscious, as upon other occasions, of the far-reaching significance

[1] Briefe, ii, 36.   [2] Ibid., p. 92.   [3] Erl. Ed., xxviii, 258, 262, 305 sq.

[4] Briefe, ii, 389.   [5] Ibid., p. 422.

of his assaults : " Triumphing over the mass, I think we triumph over the whole Papacy; for the whole Papacy, with its monasteries, bishoprics, offices and doctrines, strives in defence of the mass." [1]

He finally, at length, goes still further in his struggle against the hedge-masses, doubting whether the body and blood of Christ are present in them, and even asserting that they are not : for the order appointed by Christ is not found at all in them, nor the sacrament instituted by Him.[2]

The manner in which he sought to abolish the RESTRICTION OF THE LAITY TO THE ONE ELEMENT in the reception of the Lord's Supper was very similar to his course in opposing the mass. In the above-mentioned letter to Melanchthon, he declares that he has had it in mind first of all, upon his return to Wittenberg, to agitate the restoration of the ordinance of Christ in its purity; for he and his associates in the faith have now knowledge enough of the tyranny, and they are able to resist it. King Henry appealed, in support of the Church's right to withhold the cup, to the fact that it also permits the Supper to be celebrated in the morning instead of the evening, with water mingled with the wine, etc., thus varying from the method of the original institution. To this, Luther replies : These things are, so far as the Scriptures are concerned, matters of indifference, although the mixing of water with the wine had better be omitted. Christ gave no commandment concerning these things, but He did, on the other hand, Himself directly, and also through His apostle, Paul, institute *both* elements, and here no creature dare make any change.[3] Yet, in the practical application of this doctrine, Luther again urges the exercise of the consideration prompted by love. For this he was here at first disposed to leave more room than in the case of private masses. Certain as he was that pious hearts could not approve the spoliation, it yet at first appeared to him possible for a layman to whom the cup should still be denied by the tyrants, while entering his protest, nevertheless, under stress of the necessity, to accept the one element of the sacrament. This case was really different from that of one who saw in the very essence

[1] Jena, ii, 564 (Contra regem Angliae). Cf. De capt. Babyl., supra, i, 392.

[2] Erl. Ed., xxxi, 319, 324 sq., 355 sq., 386.

[3] Jena, ii, 554 sqq. Erl. Ed., xxviii, 362 sqq.

of the customary masses, *i. e.*, in the sacrifice, a species of idolatry, and who should nevertheless himself continue to hold them.
In proof of the position that the reception of the one element
under the circumstances supposed was not to be considered a sin
(cf. *supra*, p. 389), he again, in the above-mentioned letter to
Melanchthon, argues as follows: Christ has in fact *required*
neither of the two elements; just as baptism is not absolutely
required, in case some tyrant should forbid water for the purpose.
It was, moreover, the chief question, how to deal with those
whose own consciences had not yet been liberated from the
tyranny in question, *i. e.*, from the ecclesiastical authority refusing
the cup. This question Luther discussed particularly in his
treatise, *Von beider Gestalt des Sacraments*, etc.

Strongly as Luther had expressed and continues to express
himself in condemnation of the papal " spoliation of the sacrament," he yet insisted none the less strongly that the still weak
conscience of the ordinary man must be borne with in love and
led on to fuller knowledge. In forgetting this, the zealous reformers at Wittenberg had committed a serious error. It is not
both elements, said he, which make a Christian, but only faith
and love, and that, too, even without either element. Liberty
had lately been granted in Wittenberg to receive the sacrament
under both elements, or under but one ; but those who desired to
receive it under both elements should " do so apart from the
others, not at a common altar, nor at the same time when the
weak are employing their method." Evangelical Christians who
move to places in which the light has not yet even dawned he
advises to take the one element, without attempting to make
separate arrangements for themselves. He consoles those who
may be so situated by reminding them that they can yet, even
though receiving but one, or even neither element, still receive
what is the chief thing in the sacrament, *i. e.*, they can take the
words, and thereby the power of the sacrament. The guilt of
failing to observe the institution of Christ would not rest upon
them, since they would gladly do so were not one of the elements
held captive under that law of the Pope which serves to ensnare
weak consciences. Necessity knows no commandment, and
Christ cares more for love than for the elements of the sacrament.[1]

[1] Briefe, ii, 155, 159, 161.　Erl. Ed., xxviii, 274 sq , 305 sqq.

But already in January, 1523, the time appears to Luther to have come for a general distribution under both elements, as it is now almost exclusively stiff-necked opposers, and not weak consciences, that yet take offence. Nevertheless, as late even as the time of the Church Visitation in 1528, he still demanded for the weak so much consideration that, if they really had so little enlightenment and such timid consciences, the sacrament might yet for a season be administered to them under only one element. In the edition of the *Visitatoren Unterricht* published in the year 1538, the section treating of this point, which had been inserted in 1528 in pursuance of Luther's own judgment, was not again included.[1] He, however, continues to recommend patience with the weak, who are not yet instructed in the Word ; as, for example, in writing to the princes of Anhalt, as late as the year 1541.[2] To the proposition, that the reception under both forms is not a matter of indifference, but is a part of the institution and command of Christ, he strenuously adheres, even during the attempts at compromise which followed the Diet of Augsburg in 1530 : " For it is not a matter left to our choice to tolerate in the worship of God that which cannot be defended by the Word of God ; and that sacrilegious word, ' indifferent,' does not affect .me in the least, since by the use of this same word I might easily make all the laws and ordinances of God indifferent." [3] In opposing the stubbornness with which the Papists, upon their part, persisted in the withholding of the cup, he now knows nothing more of the permission formerly granted to evangelical believers to still, under protest, receive the sacrament under but one element. While he still desires to see exceptions made in the case of weak consciences in his own congregation, he does not hesitate to say plainly to the Christians at Halle, who had already been well instructed, and to whom their " tyrant," the bishop, had forbidden the cup, that it was no longer possible to do otherwise than acknowledge them to be in the right, since we must obey God rather than men.[4] To such as are, in disregard of their own desire, denied the cup, he expresses it as his deliberate opinion that for them the participation under but one element is not sufficient, but that it would be much better for them either

---

[1] Briefe, ii, 259; Jen., ii, 591-591 b; Erl. Ed., xxiii, 31 sqq.

[2] Briefe, v, 368.   [3] Ibid., iv, 146, 141.   [4] Ibid., iii, 305.

to seek out elsewhere some place where Christian liberty could be enjoyed, or, for the time being, to receive the sacrament only spiritually, by strengthening their consciences in faith by the Word of God, and meditating upon the sufferings of Christ.[1]

The advocacy of the dogma touching the Lord's Supper, *i. e.*, the doctrine of transubstantiation, by King Henry VIII. led the Reformer, not only to a further development of the arguments upon which his opposition was based, but also to sweeping condemnation of the entire doctrine. It might have been supposed, indeed, from expressions in the *Babylonian Captivity*, that he would perhaps allow the traditional teaching on this subject to pass without serious challenge, so long as no attempt was made to force it upon others. He himself says that he did not formerly consider it a matter of great importance whether one or another particular view was held in regard to the transformation of the elements. Now, however, since he has seen the excellent arguments of those who defend the accepted theory, he solemnly expresses his conviction that " it is impious and blasphemous to say that the bread is transubstantiated ; but it is Catholic and pious to say with Paul : The bread which we break is the body of Christ. Accursed be he who shall say otherwise, and change one jot or tittle, even though it be the new and distinguished Thomist, Lord Henry." The most excellent of the arguments referred to appears to him to be that which maintains that no other substance is worthy to be mingled with that which has created all things, and that, accordingly, the substance of the bread must be removed. That is as much as to say that the body and blood of Christ should be called a creatorial (*schöpferische*) substance. Thus, also, our faith would depend upon the worthiness or unworthiness of the substances, and we would have, on account of the unworthiness of human nature, to conclude that God is not man, and that the Holy Ghost is not poured out upon the hearts of righteous men, to say nothing of those of the wicked who still need to be justified.[2] In the presentation of his own view, Luther insists chiefly upon the argument, that the " this " of the words of institution refers to the bread, which is, therefore, yet present, and upon the words of St. Paul ; further,

---

[1] Briefe, iv, 160, 270, 364, 369. Erl. Ed., xxxi, 230.

[2] Jena, ii, 559, 558 b. Erl. Ed., xxviii, 371.

also, upon the illustration drawn from the union of fire with the iron which it heats to a glow. The details of his own doctrine we shall have occasion to examine more particularly hereafter, especially as developed in opposition to those who denied the real presence of the body.

c. PRIVATE CONFESSION—FASTS—PICTURES.

Among the other ecclesiastical ordinances and customs against which the reformatory spirit directed its energy, PRIVATE CONFESSION demands our special attention. The storm which arose at Wittenberg threatened to sweep this altogether out of existence. For Luther, however, this ordinance, although in the traditional method of its observance removed from the neck of evangelical Christians, still retained, when rightly administered, a very high value. Already in 'the summer of 1521,[1] he issued from the Wartburg his pamphlet, *Von der Beichte, ob die der Pabst Macht habe zu gebieten.* The aim of this publication was to conduct the reader away from the papal, hierarchical confession to that which was free and evangelical. This was followed by an exposition of the narrative of the ten lepers, with a dedication dated September 1st. After pointing out the perversity of the attempt to derive from this scriptural incident a commandment enjoining confession before the priest, he adds, that he does not, therefore, reject confession in itself, but, on the contrary, he heartily approves of it. He preached and wrote, also, in a similar spirit after his return to Wittenberg. He does not find private confession enjoined in the Scriptures; does not grant the Pope any authority to require it; guards, accordingly, against any attempt to make its exercise compulsory; and will no longer endure the torturing of consciences with the enumeration of all separate sins. But just at this point, when it appeared possible to abolish the confessional entirely, he testifies with impressive earnestness how highly he esteems it, when employed in an evangelical spirit. He declares that he " will suffer no one to deprive him of it, and would not exchange it for the treasures of the whole world," for he knows what comfort and strength he has himself derived from it. As its essential benefit, he always regards the declaration of absolution upon authority of the promise of Christ—a declaration

[1] The dedication to Sickingen is dated June 1st.

which no priest dare refuse to a soul longing for salvation, and which may be made by even an ordinary brother.[1] These are for him, as we know, no new doctrines; and we shall have occasion to return to a more careful examination of them when we come to estimate them in connection with the entire scope of his theology.

In regard to the PRESCRIBED FASTS also, we find Luther simply applying, as against the Papal Church, the principles which he had already clearly announced. The consciences of believers are free and unbound by such ordinances. Christians thus liberated should exercise patience toward their yet weak brethren, and be careful to give the latter no offence. If they require the food prohibited for the maintenance of their bodily health, they should freely partake of it. Finally, if the attempt is made to force upon them an observance of such ordinances, they should maintain and assert their liberty by boldly doing just the opposite of that which is prescribed.[2]

When it was proposed at Wittenberg to destroy the IMAGES in the churches, Luther viewed this subject also from the standpoint of evangelical liberty. He asserted that he had no liking for the images, and would rather have had them removed, since it is true that there is some peril connected with them. He did not, indeed, greatly fear that they would be actually worshiped as God, for he grants that this could very seldom happen. But his chief objection lay against the prevalent opinion that by providing these images a service was rendered to God. In this he saw a real idolatry. But he warns against the substitution of another " must " for the liberty already attained. Images were allowed also under the Law of the Old Testament, as, for example, the brazen serpent, the cherubim and the ark of the covenant, and only the worship of them was prohibited. Hence, we ought not now to create any disturbance about these things, but preach the Word to the hearts of men, and teach them that images are nothing. If the common man understands that the setting up of images is not a service rendered to God, he will of his own accord give up the practice, and only for his own pleasure, or for the sake of adornment, have them painted on the walls or make

[1] Erl. Ed., xxvii, 318 sqq.; xvii, 146 sqq.; xxviii, 281 sqq., 308 sq.

[2] Ibid., xxviii, 270 sq., 312.

other proper use of them without committing any sin. Even now, he says, there are at least some who do not share the popular delusion, but would be able to make a proper use of images and pictures.

We thus see already that, if once the perverted notion of merit associated with the use of images should be banished, it would be quite possible for Luther to overcome entirely his aversion to their employment. In fact, he very soon afterward declared that a psychological necessity leads naturally to the use of images. When we hear of Christ, the image of a man hanging upon a cross is pictured in our hearts; why, then, should it be a sin to have the image also before the eyes? He regards pictures representing scenes from Scripture or from the lives of good men as not, indeed, required or necessary, but " very useful." Indeed, it would not displease him if some one should have all the principal events of the whole Bible painted one after another in a little book, which might be used as a Bible for the laity. We cannot too frequently hold up to the view of the common man the words and works of God; and children and plain people can be more easily influenced by pictures than simply by word and doctrine to retain in memory the narratives of the divine Word.[1]

d. WORSHIP OF SAINTS—PURGATORY.

Among the articles of Christian faith in which Luther opposed the doctrine of the Romish Church, and in the apprehension and teaching of which he also now manifests a decided advance, we must yet mention, at least, the INVOCATION OF SAINTS and PURGATORY. It is particularly in his treatment of these subjects that we are led to realize by how entirely natural a process, through the pressure of an impulse from within, items of this kind, which he had at first in fidelity to his earlier faith retained in connection with his evangelical convictions, were by imperceptible stages quietly ignored, and finally abandoned.

He had still, in the year 1519 (*supra*, p. 360), spoken in unquestioning simplicity of the *Invocation of the Saints*, although he had already exposed the fallacy of the Catholic theory as to the meritoriousness of such prayers, and refused to give any counte-

[1] Erl. Ed., xxix, 158; xxx, 372; lxiii, 391 sq.

nance to the canonization of saints. As late as the year 1521, when undertaking to expound the Magnificat, he, in the same spirit in which it was customary, in the sermons of the day, to interject the *Ave Maria* as an ejaculatory prayer, expresses the devout wish : " Would that the same tender Mother of God might secure for me the spirit to properly and thoroughly expound this her song," etc. Yet, in this very work, he applauds especially the humility of the holy Virgin. She does not herself desire that we should honor her or expect to receive good from her. Only God should be praised in her. Although we are permitted to call her the Queen of Heaven, yet she is not a goddess, to bestow gifts or help. She gives nothing, but God alone gives.[1] The *Sermon* in the *Church Postils* upon the Epistle for the *Second Sunday in Advent* shows us further the path by which he advanced to a total rejection of saint-worship. He here avails himself (though in the Latin postil he had not yet done so) of the words of the apostle glorifying the Father of our Lord Jesus Christ, to emphasize a warning against any worshiping of saints in which the worshiper does not press on into the presence of God Himself. He is filled with anxiety lest an abominable idolatry may by such means be introduced. He grants that some employ the worship of saints and of the Mother of God in a proper spirit. Nevertheless, it seems to him to be a dangerous custom, which should not be observed in the general congregation. Though there were nothing wrong in the practice otherwise, it seems to him at the outset, a suspicious circumstance that it has the support of no scriptural text or example, but that it rather contradicts those passages which teach us to place all our confidence in God. With reference to the miracles, which were commonly adduced in support of the custom, and which he had still acknowledged in his *Unterricht auf etliche Artikel*, etc.,[2] he now declares, that we are to build, not upon these, but only upon the doctrine of Christ ; and that the miracles in question may have been wrought upon the saint-worshipers by the devil himself.[3] Luther, therefore, accords at once in principle with the Wittenberg agitators, who wished to have saint-worship entirely abandoned. He fears it more than the worship of images, which was at most but a rare

[1] Erl. Ed., xlv, 214, 245, 251.

[2] Erl. Ed., xxiv, 3 (February, 1519).   [3] Ibid., vii, 65 sqq.

occurrence. He wishes here too, however, first to see only such an efficient use of the Word as may set free the consciences of men. It would have been his desire, indeed, that this question might be allowed to rest for a while, since its agitation was not a pressing necessity, and Satan was already trying by useless questions to draw the attention of men away from faith and love. If it be only once established that saint-worship is nothing, it will fall into disuse without any special additional effort upon our part, and Christ will then remain alone upon Tabor. This, says Luther, was his own experience; he does not know how nor when he ceased to address prayers to the saints, contenting himself with the one Christ and God the Father.[1] In harmony with this is the advice given in 1522 to the Christians at Erfurt, among whom a dispute had been occasioned by " certain sermons upon unnecessary things, namely, upon the worship of saints." He writes to them that, although it is not necessary to honor the saints (that is, by invoking them), he yet does not think that one who does so should be condemned, if he only do not place his confidence in them, since what such a one does to them is done to Christ, because Christ is in them and they in Christ. We should, therefore, bear with the weak. We must, at any rate, all at last forsake the saints and ourselves, to know nothing but of Christ, and let all else go.[2] But when the evangelical teaching, which by its very nature could lend no sanction to saint-worship, had become thoroughly established in preaching and in the life of the people, and when, upon the other hand, such worship was cultivated but the more assiduously by the adversaries of the Gospel, Luther finally announced, as his position and advice, an entire and absolute rejection of the practice.

It is true, he still, in a *Sermon* upon the *Day of John the Baptist* (June 24), which he also included unaltered in his *Postils*, granted that one might say to such a saint as Peter, " Pray for me," and only advised that it would be better to address one's self to Christ alone, inasmuch as the Scriptures say nothing about such a prayer as the one mentioned, and we are only thereby led into a whole series of fruitless and improper questions concerning the condition of departed saints. But in the year

[1] Briefe, ii, 145, 188, 203 sq.

[2] Ibid., p. 221 sqq. Cf. also especially Erl. Ed., xv, 351.

1523, he expresses his decided approbation of the Bohemian Brethren for their course in not calling upon saints at all, but resting content in Christ. It was probably in the same year that he advised Urban Rhegius at Augsburg to abandon the worship of saints, because it was an uncertain thing, and we should confine ourselves to that which is certain. He gives this advice when sending to his friend a sermon of Carlstadt upon the intercession of Mary (which appeared in 1523), in which the latter had declared the invocation of Mary to be not only unnecessary, but " not good." [1] Moreover, he insisted that the invocation of the saints should no longer find a place in the regulations or hymns of the Church. [2] The opinion that, according to Lk. xvi. 9, the saints may " receive us into everlasting habitations " is combated expressly, in 1522, in a sermon preserved in the *Church Postils*. [3] It is, he maintains, the poor living with us upon the earth who are there spoken of, who are standing witnesses of the faith which we have manifested in our treatment of them. We are to serve them, and in general all our fellowmen upon earth. The saints require no service upon our part, no foundations, etc.

We afterwards find his view briefly summarized in a tract of the year 1530, *Vom Dolmetschen und Fürbitte der Heiligen*. The Papists had, as Luther here asserts, now been led to realize the abomination resulting from making gods of the saints. They were " secretly drawing in their horns " upon that theme and parading about with their *intercession* of the saints. But of this, too, he will hear nothing further ; for *since it is not becoming in us to undertake anything in the worship of God without a commandment of God*, and such an undertaking, if made, is a tempting of God, therefore we should not advise nor teach men to invoke the intercession of deceased saints, nor to teach others to do so, but we should, on the contrary, condemn the practice and teach men to avoid it. The light of the Gospel is now so widely diffused that henceforth no one who remains in darkness can have any excuse. He adds, that there is in such worship the further danger and offence, that the people may be-

---

[1] Erl. Ed., xv, 350; xxviii, 415. Briefe, ii, 593. Cf. Carlstadt, Jäger, 338 sqq.

[2] Briefe, ii, 389.   [3] Erl. Ed., xiii, 241 sq. Cf. Briefe, ii, 242.

come accustomed to place their confidence in the saints instead of in Christ. This offence, in view especially of the weakness of the people, so easily misled, he will not endure. Nature is at any rate only too much inclined to flee from God and place its confidence in men. We dare not paint the devil above the doorway. Thus, there is on the one side (in refraining from such worship), security; on the other, great danger and offence. But it is said: " He who runs into danger will perish in it," and, " Thou shalt not tempt God." [1] The *Smalcald Articles* describe the invocation of the saints bluntly as one of the antichristian abuses, which the knowledge of Christ abolishes, declaring that although the saints on earth, " or perhaps even those in heaven," pray for us, it yet does not follow that we are to pray to them.[2] In the sermon in the *Church Postils* for the *Second Sunday in Advent*, the later editions have omitted the sentences above quoted, and insert in their place merely a brief denunciation of the " abominable idolatry " which has been practiced with the departed saints.

Very similar to this was the course of Luther in dealing with the doctrine of PURGATORY. At first, he is convinced that nothing is said about it in the Scriptures, although he endeavors to interpret the doctrine itself in the most favorable sense possible, and thus tolerate it. Then, he becomes more and more impressed with the thought of the perils and offences incident to its acceptance; then, further, with the thought of the danger inevitably connected with the adoption of an article of faith not found in the Scriptures. Finally, he abandons it entirely and decisively, in order to fall back simply upon the inspired Word.

As we have thus far found him only in the first stage of this development, so now, in the *Assertio Omnium Articulorum*, to the opinion, that purgatory cannot be proved from Scripture, he adds the declaration: Nevertheless, I both believe that there is a purgatory, and I advise and urge others to believe it, but I do not desire to compel any one. The German edition already presents the matter in a milder form, merely testifying that Luther himself yet believed in purgatory, but without wishing to advise others in the matter.[3] In the *Exposition of Psalm xviii.*, which

[1] Erl. Ed., lxv, 119 sqq.   [2] Ibid., xxv, 121.

[3] Jena, ii, 3, 24. Erl. Ed., xxiv, 147 sq.

belongs to the same period, he still, as in earlier publications, discusses the question, whether despair also belongs to the punishment of purgatory.[1] In his pamphlet against Catharinus, he defends himself against the charge of having denied the duty of *prayer for the dead*, and affirms his rejection only of the dominion of the Pope over the dead.[2]

Luther's opposition to the theory of purgatory, which had been first awakened by the scandals connected with indulgences, was intensified by the relation in which it stood to the abominations of the mass. He was pointed to the great multitude of spirits who are said to have appeared after death, imploring their friends to deliver them from purgatory by the celebration of masses. This brings us again to the treatise, *Vom Missbrauch der Messe*, and especially to the *Sermon* for *Epiphany Sunday*, in which he had also woven in his denunciation of monastic vows. To the argument just referred to, he here replies : " Let wander what will " (*i. e.*, the supposed spirits), in no case does God wish us to look to spirits for a knowledge of the truth. Still further, if we regard the said spirits with suspicion, we shall not sin ; whereas, we are in danger of error whenever we regard any one of them as trustworthy. He himself does not hesitate to say openly, and he will prove it too, that they are not good spirits condemned by God to such punishment, but are following their own inclinations ; and that they are not the souls of men at all, but only a brood of the devil. The Word of God in the Scriptures, which alone must be our light, knows nothing of them, but, on the contrary, forbids us to believe such spirits (Deut. xviii. 11, 12 ; Isa. viii. 20 ; Lk. xvi. 29). The appearance of Samuel (1 Sam. xxviii. 11, 12,) he considers an apparition of the devil. This leads to a consideration of the general subject of purgatory. But it will be objected, says the *Sermon* above mentioned, that in this way purgatory itself will be denied. To this, Luther replies : If it is, that will make no man a heretic ; and it is better not to believe that which is not found in the Scriptures than to ignore what is in them (as the prohibition against the invocation of the dead). If any one wishes to pray for the dead, he has no desire to prevent it. For his part, he does not think that purgatory is such a universal experience as they make it, but that very few souls are sent there. But, as he has said before, one is in no danger if he do not believe in it at all. The treatise upon the mass declares simply : It is much safer to have no opinion at all about purgatory than, with a St. Gregory, to believe in the supposed appearances of the dead. In the latter case there is great danger ; in the former none. Similarly, in the *Sermon* upon the *Epistle for Christmas Day* in that year, Luther expresses his fear that the common teaching about purgatory " is entirely, or for the most part, a deception." Indeed, since it is always dangerous to accept what God has not taught, it would have been better if purgatory had never been invented or brought into the pulpit.[1]

Inasmuch as Luther now wished to rely entirely upon the Word of Scripture, the prevalent representations as to the *state of the dead in general* during the period intervening between their departure and the Day of Judgment also appeared to him unreliable. The scriptural mode of referring to the " sleep of the dead " inclined him to adopt the theory of a sleep of the soul, in which it shall not know where it is until the Day of Judgment. This he acknowledges, in 1522, to Amsdorf, who has asked him for his opinion upon the subject.[2] The conduct of those persons who were called back to life by Christ and the apostles, being awakened as out of sleep, appeared to him also to favor such a view. Yet, upon the other hand, in view of the appearance of Moses and Elias at the transfiguration of Christ, and the narrative of Lazarus and Dives, he did not venture to regard such a state of sleep as universal. It merely appears probable to him that the majority of the dead are in such a state. The inclination to this view must also have helped to undermine for Luther the very foundations of the theory of purgatory. Thus, he writes in the letter to Amsdorf, that purgatory is for him not a place, but an inner condition, namely, a foretaste of hell in this present life, such as Jesus, David, Job and many others experienced (in this world).[3] That such an experience may also befall souls out of the flesh cannot be denied, nor can it be proved. As opposed to the theory, that all souls tarrying between heaven and earth are in purgatory, he again points to the sleep which may be their condition. Very significant, as indicating how profound and full

[1] Erl. Ed., x, 335 sqq.; xxviii, 97 sqq.

[2] Briefe, ii, 122 sq.   [3] Cf. supra, pp. 230, 274.

was Luther's conception of the actual foretaste of hell upon earth, is his remark in this connection, that those who experience this agony while in the body are, indeed, so far as their real life is concerned, no longer in the body, but are already as good as dead. We are thus forcibly reminded of the experiences through which Luther confesses to have been himself led. We shall hereafter also have special occasion to recall these statements when we come to review the estimate which he places upon the sufferings of Christ.[1]

The *Circular* addressed to the *Christians at Erfurt* in the same year, discussing the subject of saint-worship, gives the admonition also in regard to " questions about the dead," that the preachers should let these alone, and try to turn the thoughts of the people likewise in other directions. This was now, indeed, the leading principle guiding the declarations of Luther upon the subject. Thus again, in 1523, he says to the Bohemian Brethren in reference to this question : " The judgments of God are hidden from us, and we are not commanded either to know or to believe them.[2] Nevertheless, he was again driven to more definite utterances, especially in reference to prayers for the dead. He therefore published in 1523 a *Sermon* upon *Lazarus and Dives*. In this he feels authorized " to hold to no purgatory," nor yet would he reject the idea. It is a matter that lies in the power of God. Similarly, he cannot deny that we should pray for the souls of the departed. We may pray in their behalf as follows : " Almighty God, I recognize Thy power. I pray for this soul, whether it be sleeping or suffering. If it be in suffering, I pray Thee to deliver it, if it be Thy divine will so to do." Once or twice we may pray thus, and then—stop ! [3] In precisely the same way he advises men to pray upon this subject, in the *Sermon* upon this text in the *Church Postils*, which did not appear until 1527, and in the *Sermon* preached upon the *Day of All Saints*.[4] He adds, that it is no sin to omit the prayers for the dead altogether, since God has not commanded them. But, on the other hand, although the Gospel, in relating the incident of Lazarus and Dives, does not

[1] Cf. especially, Operationes in Psalmos, xxii (A. D. 1521).

[2] Erl. Ed., xxviii, 414.

[3] Ibid., xviii, 268. Cf. the suggestions touching such prayer already in the "Sermons Preached at Weimar in 1522" (published by Höck in 1846), p. 84.

[4] Ibid., xiii, 13 sq.; xv, 466.

indicate an intermediate state, yet, from other items in the evangelical history, it appears to him certain that many dead have
been awakened who have not yet received their award ; hence
he is uncertain, also, as to whether all others have received their
eternal award.   Upon this uncertainty he bases the permissibility
of intercession in their behalf.   He now no longer mentions
purgatory.   When warning against belief in the supposed spirits,
he repeats again his favorite maxim, that God does not wish to let
us know how it fares with the dead.   Faith finds scope enough in
the declaration of the divine Word, that God saves believers
after this life, and destroys the unbelieving.   The possibility of a
purgatory is again expressly granted, for example, in the *Bekenntniss vom Abendmahl*, 1528,[1] where the positions taken above as
to prayers for the dead are also repeated.   To God, he says, all
things are possible, and hence, also, a torturing of souls after their
departure ; but God does not desire us to believe (that such an
experience has been appointed).   He adds : I know, indeed, of
another purgatory, but of this nothing is to be taught in the congregation, nor can anything be done against it by contributions
or vigils.   He evidently means that inward torture which is experienced when God permits an individual on earth already to
have for a season a foretaste of hell.

Luther was at a later day content to restrict himself to a simple
rejection and condemnation of the traditional conception of
purgatory, without making any reference to the possibility of the
existence of a genuine purgatory for the departed, refraining, in
general, from all representations concerning that intermediate
state in regard to which divine revelation is silent.   In the same
year in which the above-named circular upon the intercession of
the saints was published, 1530, appeared also his *Widerruf vom
Fegfeuer*.[2]   Here, as in the former document, he feels himself
impelled to bear further testimony in view of the manner in
which the " sophists " now bedeck themselves anew, and try, by
making a great noise, to conceal the falsity of what they preach.
Hence, he must " start up the old tune again " (*das alte Register
hervorziehen*) and "bring their praiseworthy virtue again to the
light of day."   He, therefore, takes up the passages of Scripture
and quotations from the Fathers, upon which they are always

[1] Erl. Ed., xxx, 370.   [2] Ibid., xxxi, 184-213.

drumming, in order to prove that the latter are no evidence of faith, and that the former have no reference at all to purgatory. The "fire" of 1 Cor. iii. 15 is not, he asserts, a purgatorial fire, but one by which Christian teachers and their doctrine must be tried upon the day of revelation. Not even by the passage in 2 Macc. xii. 43–46, even if that book were canonical, could the papal dogma be sufficiently proved. With this new refutation of the Romish lies he here rests the case, saying nothing further of a purgatory as still possible. From the text, Rev. xiv. 13, which was prominently used in the masses for the dead, he argues, on the contrary, as follows: If the dead who die in the Lord are blessed, why should we pray for them? And yet it is only for these that prayers are offered, *i. e.*, only for the souls of true Christians that are supposed to be in Purgatory, since the souls of unbelievers are already lost, and we can no longer pray for them. The subterfuge which represents such souls as blessed only as yet in hope he pronounces untenable, since they are said to rest already, to be in peace, as Isaiah lvii. 2 says of the righteous (and a Christian is righteous, according to Rom. i.). Thus the Scriptures testify also that Abraham, Isaac, etc., should die in peace; and hence, likewise, death is throughout the entire Scriptures called a sleep. The thief upon the cross presents, further, a powerful illustration of the blessedness of those who die in the Lord. He then applies to all who have died in the Lord what Augustine said concerning the martyrs, *i. e.*, that it is a shame to pray for them, since they are blessed.

The *Smalcald Articles* express themselves with peculiar severity upon the subject. They speak of purgatory as belonging to the vermin brood of idolatry, begotten by the tail of the dragon, *i. e.*, the mass, and declare that it is to be regarded, with all its pomp and show of worship, as a mere phantom of the devil.

In the sermon in the *House Postils* upon *the Rich Man*, preached at a later day, Luther does not touch upon the question of the intermediate state. The expressions which represent intercession for the dead as permissible are still found in the edition of the *Church Postils* prepared in 1543; but the declarations quoted above in relation to purgatory are omitted in some cases and altered in others.

Such was the development of Luther's ideas in regard to the state after death in the midst of the conflict against the scandals of

the traditional doctrine and practice, and especially those connected with masses for the dead. We shall have occasion to
observe more closely the formation of his positive views upon
the subject in our systematic review of his teaching. In regard
to his idea concerning the sleep of the soul, we here direct special
attention, not only to his letter to Amsdorf above referred to,
but also to the utterances cited from the *Widerruf vom Fegfeuer*.

e. FREE WILL—PREDESTINATION.

Upon the two subjects just considered, Saint-worship and
Purgatory, the views of Luther show a decided progress, both in
their more distinct opposition to the prevalent Catholicism and
in internal completeness and consistency, after the Diet of
Worms, although they were but remotely related to that central
point of his theory of salvation in which his chief interest was
always concentrated. He now advances, also, in combating the
Catholic theory, to a fuller statement of his convictions upon the
subjects of Grace and Free Will, which had from the beginning
stood in such direct connection with the vital centre of his doctrinal position. His controversy with Erasmus furnished the
immediate occasion for the treatment of these subjects, but the
views now presented had in their essential features been entertained by him long before. They accord especially with utterances in the *Assertio omnium articulorum*, as was remarked when
that work was under review, and they carry us back to the very
inception of the Reformer's evangelical apprehension of the truth,
as developed, in profound inner experience and amid sore temptation, under the influence of Augustinianism and Mysticism.

Luther's earlier utterances touching the absolute or UNCONDI-
TIONED DIVINE WILL, upon which the salvation of every individual
is dependent, find their closest parallel in his remarks upon the
temptations of Christians, found in the *Comments upon Psalm
xxii.*, written at the Wartburg.[1] He had already, in a passage
cited above from his *Exposition of the Psalms*,[2] called attention
in advance to that which he proposed to present when he should
come to treat of this Psalm. He now dwells especially upon the
alarming words (Ps. xxii. 8) : " He will deliver him, *seeing He
desires to have him*" (*quoniam vult eum*). What, he asks, should

[1] Op., xiv, 253. Supra, p. 329 sq.   [2] Op. Ex., xvi, 277 sqq.

the alarmed soul do when compelled to hear these words? It is
not said, " God can, or knows how to " deliver, but only, " He
desires to have ; " and not only, " He wills," but, with special
indication of the individual, " him." Now, although there be no
doubt that God can and will save, it yet becomes to the tempted
individual a matter of doubt whether He will (desires to) have
him. First of all, Luther warns his readers against disputing
with such thoughts and demons. We should rather say, with the
Hebrew children (Dan. iii. 16 sqq.) : " We are not careful to
answer thee in this matter. Our God, whom we serve, is able to
deliver us. * * But *if He will not*, yet be it known unto thee
that we will not serve thy gods." He would not have the pious
soul desire to know the secret counsel of God concerning it. Its
experience might otherwise be like that indicated in Prov. xxv. 27.[1]
He demands that we, on the contrary, carry on the conflict
against evil with the faith that is described as faith in that which
is not seen. We do not see, nor is it intended that we should
see, that God designs to save you and me. His design is here
for us unfathomable. Luther demands, further, such a faith as
shall not doubt that God always does what is perfectly right
(righteous), *whether He saves or destroys*.[2] We thus maintain
the glory of God upon our lips, when we ascribe to Him in every
ordering of His will nothing but righteousness, even though we
cannot see the righteousness therein, and although our own feelings protest vigorously against it. And, just in this connection,
the assurance of salvation is now given to such faith as this. It
is impossible, says he, that he who gives God the glory, and justifies Him in all the orderings of His will, should perish,—as He
Himself assures us in 1 Sam. ii. 30 : " Him that honoreth me,
will I also honor."

We observe here again [3] that he does not represent the matter
as though the secret counsels of the divine will embraced the
possibility of salvation for all, and it depended now upon us to
allow this possibilty to become a reality. Upon the contrary, we
must become reconciled to the thought, that the will of God itself
ordains destruction, and that such possibility is not at all pre-

---

[1] Supra, p. 300.

[2] Cf. also Op. Ex., xvi, 260.

[3] Supra, p. 288.

sented to you and me.   Yet, as he then still gives to that genuine faith which is displayed in the very act of unquestioning submission to God a positive assurance of salvation, he nevertheless exhorts us to the observance of a certain course of conduct, *i. e.*, to the exercise of such faith.   He does not further inquire, nor would he have any one ever inquire, to whom, then, the exercise of such a faith is actually possible.   Or, would he have us to understand it to be God's will that every one, at least every hearer of the Word, should receive (power to exercise) this faith, so that whether we actually receive it will, after all, depend upon our own acceptance, and, therefore, in so far, upon our own decision?   For testimony to the contrary, we need but refer to the passage cited above, which clearly teaches that the destruction of some men is to be traced to the divine will as truly as the salvation of others.

Upon the question, whether it was ever in any proper sense the divine will that those who now resist His gracious call should be saved, Luther expresses himself at about the same time plainly enough in the *Sermon upon Matt. xxiii. 37* (" How oft would I have gathered thy children," etc.),[1] preserved in the *Church Postils*.   He objects to the inference from these words that the will of man is free, and explains them as anthropomorphic, just as the Scriptures in other places speak of God as a man, attributing repentance to Him, although He cannot repent, and representing Him as descending, although He remains ever seated upon His throne, etc.   All this is said, he affirms, " according to our feeling and our notions of things, not according to the real state of the divine nature."   Accordingly, we are to understand from the above passage " that He (God) *so acted*, that no one could fail to think and feel that He would gladly gather them— acted as a man would act if he desired to do this."   We ought now to remain satisfied with this human way of speaking and of representing these matters—with this milk—and not trouble ourselves about high things, such as speculations concerning the divine nature.

The same thoughts which we have found in the *Exposition of the Psalms* recur again in Luther's letter to Hans of Rechenberg, in the year 1522, in reply to the question, whether God will not

---

[1] Erl. Ed., x, 224 sq.

save also those who die without faith.[1] It has appeared to many again in modern times, says he, as to Origen of old, altogether incompatible with the divine goodness, that God should thus cast men away and should have created them for eternal punishment, inasmuch as it is said in Psalm lxxvii. 8, 9, that He has not cut off His mercy forever, but, on the contrary, 1 Tim. ii. 4, that He *would that all men* might be saved. But Luther can only attribute such a question to the presumption which seeks to know the reason for the strict verdict of God, and which, if the verdict were not divine, would pronounce it unjust. On the other hand, appealing to Hebrews xi. 1, he esteems it the noblest virtue of faith, that it closes its eyes, does not desire to know the reasons of God, but regards Him as supreme goodness and righteousness, even when we can see only wrath and injustice in His ways. Whilst again warning the weak and those of ordinary intelligence not to worry over this subject, exhorting them rather to be content with the " milk," he now acknowledges also that there are men of profound and spiritual natures, assailed by strong temptations, with whom it may be proper to discuss the subject, and for whom, indeed, the discussion of no other subject could be so profitable. He then refutes the application made of the above-named passages. In 1 Tim. ii. 4, he sees merely the declaration, that it is the will of God that we should pray for all conditions of men and preach the truth to all men—that we should be helpful to all in things temporal and spiritual. In this sense (" since He so commands, and would have this done by us "), Paul rightly says that it is God's will that every one should be saved, since without His will this could not come to pass ; but it does not follow from this that He will save all men. Thus we find in Luther's exposition only the thought, that salvation is effectually wrought in no one without the will of God—and that we are to be instrumental in bringing it to all, and not at all the further thought, that it is the will of God Himself to make this service effectual for all. He closes with the warning not to allow our ambitious minds (*hoch-fliegende Geister*) to determine anything in such matters, but to bind them to the Mediator, Christ, and particularly to the humanity of Christ, where they may gather strength and advance in knowledge until they shall have grown sufficiently to deal with such subjects.

[1] Briefe, ii, 453 sqq. As to the date, compare Briefe, vi, 573, Anm., 5.

More briefly, but manifestly in the same spirit, he speaks, in 1522, in his *Preface to the Epistle to the Romans*,[1] under chapters ix.–xi., of the eternal foreordination of God, by which it is originally determined who shall believe and who shall not believe. He here bases Christian hope upon the very fact, that our salvation rests not at all in our own, but entirely in God's, hand. He again warns against beginning the study of the subject with an attempt to fathom the depths of divine foreordination, pointing to the course pursued in the Epistle itself, which, first of all, teaches us to recognize our own sin and the grace of Christ, and to contend against sin ; then, in chapter viii., brings us under the cross and suffering, which alone can give us a true knowledge of foreordination, and show us how comforting it is. Meanwhile, Melanchthon's *Loci*, with their strict theory of the absolute sovereignty of God administered in accordance with His predestination, appeared, and were joyfully welcomed by Luther.[2]

Yet it is thus far only in scattered passages that we meet, in Luther's writings, with such utterances in regard to the divine will, containing, as they do, only the opposite side of his fundamental doctrine of human inability and need of divine grace. They are always called forth by some special occasion, and he always wishes the reader to keep in mind " in what connection the matter is treated of." [3] He now, however, felt himself challenged by Erasmus to a comprehensive, connected and thorough-going presentation of his doctrine concerning the divine will, as well as that of human inability.

Erasmus had selected, for his assault upon Luther, a subject in which he would have the support of the Romish Church and the Scholastic theology, and yet might represent his own convictions and, at the same time, pose as the champion of a freer, humanistic and philosophical school of thought. His treatise, *De libero arbitrio*, appeared in September, 1524. It was perfectly natural for Luther, on the other hand, with his views of the doctrine of grace, to oppose and condemn the opinions of human philosophy, and of the natural reason in general, in regard to the human will, together with the positions of a Pelagian theory of faith. Thus, his warfare against such a theory of faith had been, at the same

[1] Erl. Ed., lxiii, 134 sq.   [2] Briefe, ii, 45 (Sept., 1521).
[3] Ibid., p. 455.

time, from the very first a warfare against Aristotle. Nor can there be any doubt as to the propriety of our examination of this reply to Erasmus in connection with the present chapter. Not only did Erasmus write at the suggestion of the *papal* antagonists of Luther, whose relations to the teachings of the Romish Church are now under consideration, but Luther himself was guided in his reply by the same impulse which had controlled him in his previous conflicts with Catholicism, and wrote under the distinct consciousness that in Erasmus he had again to contend against the same old fundamental error of the Pelagian theory embraced by Rome. His book, *De servo arbitrio*, is dated at the end of December, 1525.[1]

The controversy found a starting point in those declarations of the *Assertio*, etc., in which Luther had gone farther than in any other of his writings in maintaining an all-controlling divine agency—a general divine necessity, determining even our own wills—and had advanced from the truths immediately connected with the doctrine of salvation to the assertion of such metaphysical principles.

It is still everywhere the practical religious interest which controls him, as he now defends his views, and, in defending, is led to still further define them. Erasmus considered it a superfluous and presumptuous undertaking to investigate the relation of our will to the divine agency, foreknowledge, etc. He held that we should be content simply to maintain that the Christian should strive with all his might, and that the will cannot act except by the mercy of God. Luther, on the other hand, regarded these questions just as necessary as it is for a farmer to make himself acquainted with the nature of his land. We must certainly know, says he, for what we are indebted to God, in order that we may be able to thank Him. If only for this purpose, he demands an investigation of these questions, and reaches again the result : "*All things which we do*, although they seem to us to be done accidentally, are *really done necessarily and immutably*, if thou lookest upon the will of God." [2]

But he now approaches the question also from above, starting with the nature of God and of the divine life and agency in general.

---

[1] Jena, iii, 165 b, 238. Cf. Briefe, iii, 59.   [2] Jena, iii, 169 sq., 171.

The will of God is for him the *natural power* of God, His very nature itself—and therefore unchangeable, not subject to limitation from any source. The will of God does not, like that of man, rest after the accomplishment of its purpose. God is full of life, His omnipotence is ever active, working all in all. Even the natural reason must acknowledge that He by His liberty lays necessity upon us. The same inference is to be drawn from His knowledge and His purposing foreknowledge. If God, as the Scriptures teach, cannot err, then the inference, even for the common mind, is certain : " If He foreknows, it will necessarily come to pass." Our faith in God and our reverence for Him depend upon this, since otherwise His promises and threatenings would not be secure. We men, indeed, know in advance that an eclipse of the sun is coming because it is coming, and it does not come because we know in advance of its coming. But what have we to do with the divine foreknowledge? Thus, for example, if God foreknew the treachery of Judas, then it necessarily followed that Judas must become a betrayer, and it did not lie in the power of Judas to do otherwise, or to change his will (as Erasmus said). He acted of his own determination, indeed, and not under compulsion. But it was certain that this determination of his would be formed, since God foreknew it. His determination was his work, which God, however, by His omnipotence caused to be done, just as He brings all other things to pass. And this purposing foreknowledge and this foreknowing purposing are eternal and unchangeable, since they are the very nature of God (*immutabilis, quia natura, voluntas*). Thus, even Erasmus must acknowledge that the righteousness and gentleness of God belong to His nature, and that what belongs to His nature is unchangeable ; and the same is to be said of the knowledge and purpose of God. Precisely so is it, also, with the love and the hatred of God. Erasmus, he says, wishes to modify the scriptural statement, that God loved Jacob and hated Esau, because God does not love as we do and hates no one, since He is not subject to such emotions. He is right in maintaining that God does not love and hate *as we do*, for He loves and hates with an immutable nature ; His hatred is an everlasting hatred. If, now, God were to surrender anything of that which belongs to His nature, He would no longer be *good*. If God should cease to move by His omnipotence upon the hearts of the wicked (whose evil will He inwardly moves) in

3**1**

order that they might not become yet more wicked, He would thereby cease to be God. He would have to cease to be good, in order to prevent their becoming worse.[1]

We might, for ourselves, perhaps be disposed to insert among these propositions of Luther the further thought, that God may have so firmly fixed His unchangeable will from all eternity only because He foresaw from eternity that, for example, Judas would reject the grace which He might have granted even to him, and, refusing to be thereby moved to abandon his own will, would turn to do evil. This God may have known, in some way, indeed, inscrutable to us, and have accordingly determined (*gewollt*) that it should really be so. Thus, all would then come to pass without the possibility of variance at the present time from the course marked out in the foreknowledge of God, and yet in such a way that there is left to man a certain liberty of decision. But, whatever may be thought of such an attempted mediation, Luther, at all events, has not the remotest idea of accepting anything of the kind. It is an essential characteristic of *his* conception of the eternal, unconditioned and all-conditioning God, that in Him the purpose and the (fore-)knowledge are one and the same thing.

If we now take into view the entire course of finite affairs, together with human activity and purpose, we find Luther maintaining unconditionally the " paradox " : Whatever is done by us, is done, not by free will, but from *pure necessity* (*mera necessitate*). That which is called accidental in human affairs is so only in the sense in which anything " happens," so far as we are concerned, accidentally, or as by chance, or through our imprudence, because our will or hand seizes the opportunity afforded, as by chance, for doing that of which we had before had no thought or desire." But it is not so with the will and active omnipotence of God. This even the heathen have been obliged to confess. How often does a Virgil, for example, speak of " Fate "? It must not be forgotten, however, that the Fate of the Stoics is rightly rejected by Augustine.[2]

It was customary, as Luther remarks, to discriminate between logical necessity (*necessitas consequentis*), which arises from the *necessary* connection of a cause with its effect, and is alone an

[1] Jena, iii, 171, 209, 207 b, sq., 209 b, sqq., 211 b, 206 b.   [2] Ibid., 171 b.

absolute necessity,[1] and conditional necessity (*necessitas conse-quentiae*), in which anything arises from *accidental* and freely-operating, changeable causes, and hence must also be, and is, necessary in view of the divine foreknowledge, not by virtue of its immediate cause, but only because it now actually exists.   But for Luther, according to what has been already said, this distinc-tion loses all essential significance, since necessity, even in the last-mentioned sense of the word, completely annihilates free will. From the very fact that God knows a thing in advance, it is already absolutely necessary ; and a Judas, in whose case there was supposed to be merely a conditional necessity, since he had the power to change his will, cannot so change his will because of the foreknowledge of God.   Only that, indeed, is absolutely necessary which has necessary being (*essentiam*), that is, only God.   I am, for my part, accidental and changeable.   But, since the acts of God have necessity, everything comes to pass, although not necessary in its own nature, yet by necessity.   The whole distinction above noted is a miserable play upon words, and simply asserts, that all things come to pass necessarily, but yet do not so come to pass—even God Himself.[1]

It is, therefore, for Luther a fact beyond dispute, that man does not possess what is commonly understood by the term free will, *i. e., the power to act at pleasure in one way or the other* (*eam vim quae libere possit in utrumque se vertere*).   Indeed, the term should not, in his opinion, be applied to man at all. Erasmus had sought to define it as the power of the human will, by which man is able to apply himself to those things which lead to eternal salvation, or to turn away from them (*qua se possit homo applicare ad ea, quae perducunt ad aeternam salutem,* etc.). But Luther objects to this, not only because of its conflict with his general principle as to the universal agency of God, but because it appears to him to leave no sufficient room for the exercise of grace.   For, he argues, the " things " thus regarded or neglected are nothing else than the very words and works of God presented to man in the Law and the Gospel.   Hence, according to Erasmus, man can of himself choose or not choose, love or not love, the Word of God, and there is, therefore, no need for the agency of the Holy Spirit.[2]

[1] Jena, iii, 177, 210 sq.   [2] Ibid., 178, 180, 186 sq.

But how, we naturally inquire, is this *necessity consummated in the case of man ?* As remarked above, with reference to the case of Judas, it is not in any sense what we would call *compulsion*, nor anything in direct conflict with a man's own will. This is never the case when we speak of a necessity in the acts of God, nor is it to be thought of when we speak of a corresponding necessity in the acts of man. Even the will of man does of its own accord (*mit eigener Lust*) what it does. But man determines upon a given course of conduct by inward necessity, inasmuch as he cannot alter or change that course. There is here a *necessitas immutabilitatis.* So long as he is not moved by the Spirit of God, man, of his own choice (*sponte*), does evil. Just so, when he has been renewed and breathed upon by the Holy Spirit, he, purely of his own inclination, chooses the good. In the one case, we can choose only that which the god of this world, who reigns within us, chooses ; in the other case, we have become the possession of the Stronger One, and willingly do His will. The human will is like a saddle-horse, bearing either Satan or God, that always seeks to go, and does go, whither the rider directs.[1]

The will of man may yet be said to be free in relation to those things which are beneath it, or which have been subjected to it to be employed by it according to its own inclination (*respectu inferioris se rei,* etc. Cf. *supra,* pp. 150 sq., 431 sq.). This is the dominion referred to in Gen. i. and ii., where man is bidden to rule over the fishes of the sea, etc. ; these inferior creatures are to obey him, doing what he desires. By the exercise of this will man can attain to works externally good, to the righteousness of the civil law, or even that of the moral law (in so far as we understand by the latter merely a law of outward morality) ; but he can never thereby attain to the righteousness of God (*Gottesgerechtigkeit*). And even his own inclination, according to which he governs among these inferior things, is itself, again, entirely, in the hand of God. He is led by the inclination of God whither God desires to lead him.[2]

Only in one passage in this treatise does Luther grant that we may speak of a capacity of free will in relation to divine things

[1] Jena, iii, 171, 177 sqq., 209 b, sqq.
[2] Ibid., pp. 178, 189 b, sq., 229 sq., 235.

in so far as man is capable (*aptus*) of being touched by the grace of God and apprehended by the Spirit as a being created for eternal life or death. But this he regards as a purely passive capacity, or aptitude. When the actual apprehension by the Spirit occurs, it is entirely without self-determination or self-decision upon the part of man ; and Luther, having spoken of it, can immediately declare again that *we do all things from necessity*.[1]

Luther speaks further of a *co-operation* of God and man. But by this he understands only that inner agency of God, by virtue of which He is in such a sense within men that His will absolutely determines their conduct. Thus God works all in all (all things in all men), since He alone moves with His almighty impulse that which He alone has created, which impulse all men, each in accordance with his own God-given faculties, necessarily obey. Similarly does He also work by the Spirit of grace in the justified, and they, as new creatures, obey and work with Him, or, rather, they are, as Paul says, impelled (*getrieben*) by Him. Thus, the result is attained outside of the kingdom of God by His general omnipotence, and within that kingdom by the special power of His Spirit.[2]

Beyond question, the point in Luther's theory upon this subject which was most calculated to give offence, even to those who were inclined to accept his strictest statements touching the general doctrine of grace, was the *relation which he represented the universal divine agency as bearing to the ungodly*. But he, none the less, expresses himself upon this point most positively and openly—particularly, for example, in interpreting the scriptural language concerning the hardening of Pharaoh's heart. Here, too, he did not hesitate, as we have seen, to apply the maxim, that God works all in all. It is primarily only the *present* condition of man and the world, in which the entrance of sin is presupposed, which he has in mind ; and he declares of Satan, as well as of fallen men, that, since in them nature and will, although alienated from God, have yet not been destroyed, but still exist, God is no less the all-efficient and impelling force in them than in all other creatures. But He works in them in accordance with the character which He finds them possessing. Since they are evil, when they are driven into action by the impulse of His

[1] Jena, iii, p. 177 b.   [2] Ibid., p. 223.

omnipotence, they do only that which is evil. When, therefore, it is said that God hardens us, or works evil in us, it is not meant that God creates evil anew in us. It is not a creation, but the continual active agency of God in the creature, which is here spoken of. God does not act like a wicked householder, who should pour poison into a vessel, which can only, upon its part, receive whatever is given to it, but He deals with the wicked, by virtue of His universal agency, like a carpenter who saws poorly with a notched saw. God cannot cease the exercise of His efficient omnipotence, and the ungodly cannot change his condition of alienation from God. Hence, the above result must follow. The wicked sins from necessity, until the Holy Ghost renews him; the good God *cannot* work anything but evil with an evil instrument, although He then overrules the evil result to His own glory and our salvation. The process of hardening, in the case of the wicked, is thus described: Whereas, before, Satan held dominion over the sinner in peace, and the latter, unconcerned about his relation to God, sought only his own way, he is now, by a visitation of God, made to realize opposition and limitation in the enjoyment of his own way, and cannot do otherwise than rage against this interference. He can as little refrain from such raging as he can from seeking and desiring to have his own way; and he can no more cease to so desire than he can cease to exist, since he is a creature, even though a fallen creature, of God.[1]

If we were above taught that man is always necessarily impelled, either by the devil or by God, we have now further learned that, in Luther's own view, beneath such dominion of the devil there is yet also a continual and necessary impelling divine force, which is, however, not the impulse of the Holy Spirit as such.

Upon the other hand, the matter has thus far been presented in such a light that evil in itself appears to be a matter confined to man and Satan—the instrument which God employs being itself essentially corrupt. But we shall now very soon meet with declarations of much harsher sound.

For example, it is, in Luther's view, by no means in consequence of a new and real resolution upon his part that a man remains under the dominion of evil, or even that he becomes hardened

---

[1] Jena, iii, 205 b, sqq.

in his evil ways; but, left to himself, no other course is possible to him, although it still appears possible for God, upon His part, to free men from this condition, as He has actually thus freed a portion of the race. Side by side with the proposition, that God cannot work anything but evil with an evil instrument, we find the other declaration, that God can improve the instrument. Why then does God not improve also those whom He leaves under Satan's power? To this we might reply, that the explanation, at least in the case of those who have heard the Word of grace, is found in the fact that they do not obey. But Luther says: All hearing is in vain, if God do not Himself inwardly speak and draw. No one obeys—as a sheep obeys (follows) when a green twig is extended toward it—simply because God displays all the treasures of His grace. Such obedience is seen only in the case of those who have first, by the efficient inward agency of God, become true sheep. And such a speaking and drawing are acknowledged by Luther only in the case of those who are actually, and purely by means of this divine agency, renewed—not at all, therefore, in the case of others, to whom had been opened by such agency the possibility of obeying or not obeying, and, consequently, the possibility of such a turning one way or the other (*vertere in utrumque*), but by whom this possibility of obedience has been rejected. What is then, in view of all this, the reason why God leaves the evil will in so many men unchanged? Luther replies bluntly: " It is not for us to inquire about that, but it is ours to adore the divine mysteries. Who art thou, that thou shouldst call God to account? (Rom. ix. 20.)[1]

If we now endeavor to look back of the present condition of the sinner, and inquire, whence the individual has derived this character, we shall find Luther tracing it to the carnality of human nature in general, by which the latter has been marked ever since the first sin. God, he declares, has created evil men, as, for example, Pharaoh, out of evil material, out of corrupt seed. They must certainly be ungodly, who are born of ungodly seed (Ps. li.; Job xiv.). But from these same premises he deduces the further consequence, that the difference now existing between the pious and the ungodly, even those hardened in evil,

[1] Jena, iii, pp. 206 b, 196, 204, 235 b.

is a result of divine agency. He expressly repudiates the illustration of Erasmus, *i. e.*, that, just as the sun makes clay hard and wax soft, so God hardens one and converts another. All men, he claims upon the contrary, are in themselves like the clay; and out of precisely the same clay the Lord makes vessels for honor and for dishonor.[1]

But how, then, did sin originally enter? In a passage already cited, in which Luther discusses the statement that God hath made the wicked for the day of evil, he declares that he is not speaking of the (original) creation, and that God did not in such sense create the wicked, that He may be said to have created wickedness, or a wicked creature, but He formed the wicked out of wicked seed.[2] And we are led further still when we hear him speak, as he does, indeed, in but two or three passages, of the original fall. These passages, in view of their importance, we shall examine separately. In the first of them, Luther comments upon Sirach xv. 14–17. The freedom of choice which was, according to this passage, given to man at the creation, he applies, as we have seen, only to the lower orders of creation. He then proceeds to discuss the commandments which God gave to man with the attendant promise : If thou wilt keep the commandments, they shall keep thee. He denies that the ability to keep the commandments is here ascribed to man, and illustrates the passage by the conduct of parents, who sportively bid their little children come to them, only in order to show them that they cannot come, but must call for help. In just this way the divine Lawgiver would have us learn to realize our own impotency. This was true also, according to Luther, of the first man.[3] " Although he was not impotent when assisted by grace, nevertheless, in this precept, God sufficiently revealed to him how impotent he was in the absence of grace. Although *the Spirit was present*, he was yet not able by a new (resolution of the) will to choose the good newly-proposed, *i. e.*, obedience, because the *Spirit did not grant him* such new will (how much less, says Luther in passing, are we, who lack the presence of the Spirit which he enjoyed, able to do anything). In that man it is revealed to us what our free will, left to itself, and not continually

[1] Jena, iii, pp. 202 b, 205, 220 b.   [2] Ibid., p. 220 b.
[3] Cf. the Theses of A. D. 1518; supra, p. 284.

moved and strengthened more and more by the Spirit of God, can accomplish. He was not able to gain a fuller measure of the Spirit whose beginnings he had, but fell from the beginnings of the Spirit: how shall we, who have fallen, be able to gain the lost beginnings of the Spirit?" We cannot fail to catch the meaning of the above. Man would have at the first required a new working of the Spirit upon him to enable him to form a new resolution of obedience (in view of the newly-given commandment). This was not granted to him, although the Spirit was at that time with him, and although he, without such aid, could not by his own effort attain the required measure of the Spirit. The matter was permitted to take this course, by God's own appointment, in order that it might be forever seen how little the will of man, left to itself, is able to accomplish. Thus, God did not, indeed, directly create evil; but the natural impotency of man was yet a feature of his original nature, and from this it was a necessary consequence that, when now left to himself by God, the transgression would follow. In the same sense must we interpret the language of the Reformer's reply to the objection of Erasmus, that man, according to Gen. i., had been created good. True, he says, but Gen. iii. explains " how man became evil when *deserted by God and left to himself*" (*desertus a Deo ac sibi relictus*), and thus the seed of man is now corrupt, and only corrupt progeny can proceed from it. The words, " deserted by God," are not designed to indicate what man became through the fall, but how he came to fall. Nor, finally, can we, in view of all the preceding, explain in any other way the expression once employed by Luther: God permitted Adam to fall (*permisit ruere*). That which God permitted, by leaving Adam to himself and denying him the further aid of His Spirit, could not, according to God's own appointment, have happened otherwise. To the further question, therefore, why God permitted Adam to fall, although He might have preserved him, there is here no answer, except that which Luther now gives: We dare as little inquire about that as we dare ask why God does not again make good the will that has become evil. " This belongs to the secrets of majesty, and it is not for us to ask about it, but to adore these mysteries.[1]

[1] Jena, iii, 190 sqq., 205, 206 b.

If, now, man is in this whole process so immediately and absolutely controlled by the omnipotence of God inwardly operating upon him, the question naturally arises, what can then be the significance of the mediation by the Word, which God Himself employs in the revelation of Himself to men; and, especially, how can God continually give commandments, if the fulfilment of such commandments is purely His own work, and if, in the case of the natural man, no fulfilment is at all possible?

The latter question is largely discussed in Luther's treatise. He replies to it in the same way as in the above utterances concerning Adam and his experience. God imparts His commandments to Adam, much more to us sinners, not with the expectation that we shall be able to keep them, but in order thereby to awaken in us such a sense of our own incapacity. The language of God is to be understood in the same way, when He says hypothetically: If thou doest thus or so, thou shalt live, etc. But, at the same time, He is seeking to show us what, by virtue of His energy, might be wrought in us, and what can and shall (in those whom He creates anew) one day be accomplished.[1]

Luther expresses himself less fully in regard to the significance of the words through which God grants (to those to whom He at the same time inwardly speaks) His Spirit. Reason, says he, may sneeringly ask, why God employs such words, inasmuch as the words effect nothing, since the will can turn neither to the one side nor to the other, and since, without the inwardly-moving Spirit, the will can, despite the hearing of the Word, accomplish nothing more; whereas, if the Spirit be present, everything then at last depends upon the Spirit alone. He points, in reply, to the design of God to make men among their fellows co-workers with Himself in His saving work—a design which always retained for the Reformer a peculiar significance, exerting a marked influence upon his entire conception of the Christian life, and upon his doctrine touching the communion of saints and the Church. He says: Thus it pleased God to give the Spirit, not without the Word, but through the Word, so that He might have us as fellow-workers, whilst we sound abroad what He Himself alone breathes within wheresoever He may wish to do so—all of which, indeed,

[1] Jena, iii, 190 sqq., 198, 209 b.

He would be able to do, but does not desire to do, without the Word.[1]

The most important utterances of Scripture which Erasmus had cited against Luther were those in which God expressly declares, that He desires not the death of the wicked, but that he turn from his wickedness and live (Ezek. xviii.), and, from the New Testament, especially the address of Christ to Jerusalem (Matt. xxiii. 37). Would God, says Erasmus, bewail the death of the wicked, if He Himself causes it? If God does not desire our death, then it must be ascribed to our own will; and how is this possible, if we are ourselves able to do nothing? Might not the Jews have retorted with the inquiry, why the Lord had sent them prophets, if it had not been His will that they should hear them?—or, why He should charge upon them that which had come to pass according to *His* will, as something which was upon their part necessary?

In replying to this challenge, Luther now carries out his principles to the utmost extent of their possible development. He discriminates between the God and divine will preached and presented to us, and worshiped by us, in the revealed Word and the *God not preached nor revealed*, who is not an object of worship for us. He appeals, in support of this distinction, to the words of the apostle in 2 Thes. ii. 4, according to which Antichrist shall exalt himself " *supra omnem Deum praedicatum et cultum*," whereas an exaltation " above the God not worshiped nor preached, as He is in His nature and majesty," is not possible. Of this God, he says : God concealed in majesty neither deplores nor abolishes death, but He works life, death and all things in all. Neither has He at all limited Himself by His Word, but has kept Himself free above all things. In this sense it is, then, that we must interpret the declaration of the *Church Postil* upon the words in Matt. xxiii., which are said to be spoken " not according to the essential state of the divine nature." He now proceeds to say : He (Erasmus) deceives himself in his ignorant diatribe, since he does not discriminate between God as preached and as concealed, that is, *between the Word of God and God Himself.* God does many things which He does not

---

[1] Jena, iii, 200 b. It is evident that the co-operation here spoken of is something entirely different from that referred to above (p. 485). Cf. also 223 and the citation there made from 1 Cor., iii, 9.

show to us in His Word, and He, accordingly, wishes many things which He does not in His Word show that He wishes. Thus, he does not, according to His Word, wish the death of the sinner, but He does wish it according to His inscrutable will. But if we now inquire for the content and fundamental character of *this* will, how it is related to the revealed will, or how we can be assured that there is no conflict between the essential will and that expressed in the Word, Luther would have the veil drawn at once over *this* will and all further questionings in regard to it excluded. It is enough for us to know, he says, *that there is* in God an inscrutable will. With anything further than this we have nothing to do. The maxim: "What is above us, is no concern of ours (*Quod supra nos, nihil ad nos*) has here a fitting application. God Himself does not desire us to treat with Him as He *is* in His majesty and in His own nature, but only as He has clothed and revealed Himself in His Word. Thus, also, we may say: God does not bewail the death of the people which He Himself works in them, but He bewails the death which He finds prevailing among the people, and which He labors to banish. Human presumption, he says further, seeks to penetrate into that secret will with which we have nothing to do, and, at the same time, neglects that which is necessary. It is with the incarnate God, on the contrary, that we have to deal—with the crucified Christ, in whom are hidden all the treasures of knowledge. Through Him we possess in abundance all things that we are to know or not to know. This incarnate God weeps over the ruin of the ungodly, whilst the will of the divine Majesty by its own decree passes by and rejects some, so that they perish (*ex propositione aliquos relinquat et reprobet, ut pereant*). It is not for us to inquire why He does so, but to worship God, who can and will do such things.[1]

Thus, in general, the subject now under consideration should, according to Luther, be kept free from all presumptuous questionings of human reason. Nor is it only questions concerning the secret will of God which are thus condemned, but those, as well, which challenge the acts of His revealed will. Among the latter is named especially the question as to the *righteousness* of

[1] Jena, iii, 195 b to 197 b. Cf. upon "aliquos," ibid., pp. 175 b, 176 b, where the *salvation of few* is spoken of.

the divine dealing with those, on the one hand, who are saved, and with those, on the other hand, whom God, according to the express declaration of His Word, hardens. We have already heard Luther reply with the challenge: " Who art thou, that thou shouldest call God to account?" Men, he declares, dare not, in any event, apply their laws to God. He is not bound to explain to us His reasons for doing that which seems to us to lack all appearance of righteousness. We must leave to Him His own secrets. It belongs, in fact, to the very nature and idea of God, according to Luther, that no rule nor measure of any kind can be prescribed to the divine will, since nothing is equal or superior to it, but it is itself the rule for all things. " If it had rule, measure or cause, it would on that very account cease to be a divine will; for that Which He determines is not right because He ought so to do or to determine, but, on the contrary, that which comes to pass must be right because He so determines." Reason and cause are prescribed for the will of man, but not for the will of the Creator. Luther does not mean hereby, so far as we can see, to exclude the idea that God Himself may limit His own will in a perpetual, consistent, and therefore perfect manner. But he denies that we are at liberty to lay down postulates for the conduct of God Himself upon the basis of the principles which He has prescribed for the moral government of us as His creatures. The idea, that the ways in which God upon His part chooses to proceed, and which are, therefore, good, must correspond with these prescriptions for our conduct, simply because the latter also come from Him, never appears in the writings of Luther; or, at least, it may be said that he knows nothing of any ability upon our part to actually recognize a relation of correspondence between the two. That which is true in regard to divine righteousness, is true also in relation to the goodness of God. Reason, says Luther, cannot submissively accept the faith, that the God who hardens is yet good. It wants to apprehend God as good, and not terrible. It could understand, if it were to be said that God hardens and condemns no one, abolishes hell and future punishments, and saves all men. But faith and the Spirit have a different opinion; they believe that God is good even though He should destroy all men.[1]

[1] Jena, iii, 206 b sq., 213 b, 204 b sq.

Such is the doctrine with which Luther opposed the "free will" of Erasmus. We again call attention to the fact, that he did not wish to be understood as having taken up the gauntlet in the spirit of scholastic controversy, or for the sake of philosophical argument, but it was his aim to teach that which Christians need to know in the interest of their piety, faith and Christian life (cf. *Introduction* of the treatise). He wished his views, therefore, to be proclaimed without reserve before the ears of all. The unchangeableness of the divine foreknowledge and will is for him the basis of the assurance with which faith may now trust in the divine promises. In the hardening of Pharaoh's heart, at which reason stumbles, he sees confirmation and consolation for believers. It was meant that the Israelites should know that God wrought even the insolence of Pharaoh in order to perform so much the more glorious miracles in their behalf. Luther regards it as essential to our faith that we should realize especially that God does not bind Himself to the conception which human reason forms concerning righteousness ; for woe be to us if God should, as that conception demands, deal with us according to our desert.[1] Erasmus warned against allowing the statement, that all things occur from pure necessity, to gain currency among the common people. For what a door would thus be opened for iniquity ! Who would then still seek to reform his life? To this question, Luther calmly replies : No man will or can do so ; but the elect and pious will be reformed by the Holy Spirit, and the others will perish unreformed. He then presents two reasons why this doctrine should be preached ; first, for the humbling of our pride and the recognition of divine grace ; and second, the nature of Christian faith itself, which is essentially a faith in that which is not seen. Yet more strongly and bluntly than we have found in any earlier writings is the latter argument urged. " In order that faith may have an existence, everything believed must be hidden. But it cannot be more deeply hidden than when the exact contrary is presented and experienced. Thus, God makes alive by killing. Thus, He conceals His eternal mercy under eternal wrath, His righteousness under injustice. This is the highest stage of faith, to believe Him to be merciful, who saves so few and condemns so many ; to believe Him to be just,

[1] Jena, iii, 171 b, 207, 213 b.

who by *His own will makes us subject, of necessity, to damnation (necessario damnabiles facit)*, so that He appears, as Erasmus reminds us, to delight in the miseries of the wretched and to be worthy of hatred rather than of love." In another passage, he confesses that he himself had more than once taken serious offence at this, especially at the course of God in abandoning, hardening and condemning men purely of His own will (*mera voluntate sua*), and that he had been thereby brought to the verge of despair, and wished that he had never been created a man. But he at once adds : until he recognized how wholesome is this despair, and how near it is to grace. He found it wholesome, no doubt, just because it had driven him in absolute humiliation and with renunciation of all his own righteousness and reason, to a pure and simple apprehending of the salvation revealed in Christ with a faith that mounted above all apparent contradictions.[1] That which is, even according to the most stringent views of Luther, to be carefully avoided, is not reflection upon the to us so offensive necessity of all things and upon the existence of a secret divine will, but only the opinion, that we should and can penetrate into the problems thus presented to our minds, and the general disposition to meddle further with the secret things, instead of simply acknowledging them and then immediately turning our attention entirely to the preached and incarnate God.

He guards himself, moreover, expressly against the suspicion that he has been led unawares in the heat of strife to the adoption of the views here maintained : " There are themes and problems (here) in which I have always up to this very hour asserted that there is no (place for) free will— convinced by the truth and compelled by argument, I have thus felt and written." [2]

It was, therefore, the truth and the nature of Christian faith which led him, in his defence of the grace upon which our salvation rests and in opposition to all thought of man's own righteousness, to now advance to the argument before us touching the universal divine agency and the relation of the absolute will to the finite and created as such. And yet we must not fail to note again, even in this treatise, *De servo arbitrio*, which is far more extreme than any other upon this topic, that it is, after all, not the relation of the absolute to the finite and human, as such,

---

[1] Jena, iii, 175 b sqq, 209.　　　　　[2] Ibid., p. 224.

which riveted his own interest, but the relation of man, as actually
lying in sin and needing salvation, to that God who alone can
save. In evidence of this, we may recall the fact that, in the
writings already reviewed, he always aims at the latter, and from
every digression returns again to it. But we find peculiarly significant testimony to this, as the real point of interest for the
Reformer, in a further examination of the treatise before us.
What has thus far been cited has been selected almost entirely
from the introduction and the first two chapters of the book, in
which he rebuts the arguments of Erasmus for the freedom of the
will and then defends his own arguments which had been assailed
by the latter. It is only in the third chapter that he addresses
himself to the special and positive task of contending " against
free will in behalf of the grace of God." Here he proposes to
" bring up our forces," and, while keeping in view what he has
already said, lead the apostles Paul and John upon the field.[1]
He again declares that the arguments drawn from the plan of
divine grace, from the divine election, etc., are in themselves,
indeed, sufficiently clear and strong to disprove the theory of a
free will.[2] But, while proposing to review these arguments, he,
instead of doing so directly, presents in substance the contents
of the first chapter of the Epistle to the Romans, *i. e.*, the testimony of experience to the condition of sin and wrath under which
all men are actually found, and in consequence of which they no
longer have a striving after that which is good *(conatus ad
bonum)*, and can attain righteousness only by the grace of God
through faith. From the Gospel of John he cites the words of
Jesus to Nicodemus (i. 16), the declaration that Jesus is alone
the way, the truth and the life, etc., and then also vi. 44 (cf.
what is said on p. 487 of the inner drawing and speaking). His
own deepest interest in the theme is clearly expressed in his
confession : [3] " Even if it were possible, I should not desire that
free will should be granted to me, nor that anything at all should
be left in my hands by means of which I could secure eternal life
through my own effort : for then, even were I not subject to the
many threatening dangers that surround me and to the assaults
of the devil, I should still always labor in uncertainty, since my
conscience could never, though I were to live and labor forever,

[1] Jena, iii, 186, 224 b.   [2] Ibid., p. 231 b.   [3] Ibid., p. 236 sq.

be certain and fully satisfied as to how much it was necessary for me to do in order to satisfy God.   Such has been the experience of all self-righteous persons, and I myself, to my great injury, had for many years a full enough experience of the same kind. But now, since God removes my salvation from my will, and places it in His own, and has promised to save me, not by my working and running, but by His grace, I am calm and secure, because He is faithful and powerful and great.[1]   Hence it comes to pass, that if not all, yet at least many, are saved, whereas by the power of free will no one at all could be saved."   This brings him again to the difficult question of the goodness and justice of God, in regard to which he now expresses himself at least somewhat more mildly than in the earlier portion of the discussion.   He now traces the necessity, under stress of which the reprobate sin, only to the nature ruined through the fall of Adam, without indicating any cause for Adam's sin.   He then proceeds to say : The most gracious God is to be glorified in those whom, although themselves utterly unworthy, He yet justifies and saves, and we ought certainly to leave some little room for the exercise of the divine wisdom, by believing in His righteousness when His ways appear to us unjust.—He points faith onward to the light which shall arise for us upon this darkness in the world of glory.   The darkness which in the light of mere nature rests in this life upon the ways of the righteous God is already illuminated by the light which grace sheds upon the future life with its compensations. For the present, even under this light, we have no solution of the problem, how God can condemn one ungodly person and save another who is perhaps more ungodly still ; but the third light, that of glory, will reveal this also as the *most exalted righteousness* (cf. what has been said above, as to the interpretation of the statement, that for God there is no law). ·

The earnest spirit of the entire work, and particularly of the general discussions concerning the divine will, knowledge and power, is again clearly shown in the *Conclusion*, and at the same time, just as clearly, the great object held in view, *i. e.*, to prove that without Christ we would be utterly lost.   Here we find again the propositions : " God foreknows and foreordains all things " ; " reason itself being the witness, there can be no free will in man

[1] Cf. Introd. Ep. Rom.

nor in an angel nor in any creature "—then, references to the dominion of Satan, to original sin, Paul's testimony as to both Jews and Greeks, etc.—and, finally : If we believe that Christ redeemed men, we are compelled to confess that the whole man (that is, not only the lower part of his nature, the higher part still retaining power to do good) was lost : otherwise, we make Christ either superfluous or the Redeemer of the vilest part, which is blasphemy and sacrilege.

Our examination of this treatise must have fully convinced us, as well of the natural connection of the principles here enunciated with those of Luther's earlier writings (a fact to which he himself refers in rebuttal of the positions of Erasmus) as of the very special importance attaching to the document in view of the development of these principles in a way entirely peculiar to itself. It remains for us merely to call attention, further, to such utterances of the period as bear most closely upon the same themes.

In the controversy between Luther and Erasmus, the discussion was chiefly, so far as scriptural evidence was concerned, upon the proper understanding of the hardening of Pharaoh's heart by God. At the very same time, Luther had occasion, in the series of *Sermons upon Exodus*, begun on the nineteenth Tuesday after Trinity, 1524, and continued into the year 1526, to express his view upon this subject before the congregation. He did so just as unreservedly as in his controversial writings. Just as God then stirred up Pharaoh against Israel, so, he declares, does God now stir up the devil, and through the devil wicked men, against His own people. For the latter, he finds again the same consolation before offered them, namely, that, since they know that God has stirred up the devil, they know also that He holds him in the hollow of His hand. Here comes again the question of reason, how God can condemn the man whom He Himself compels to do evil—and how, in general, He can incite to evil. Appeal is again taken to the fact that we dare *not prescribe law, measure, nor aim* to God : " God gives out the law (to us), but He does not take it up again (to be Himself bound by it)—God will do as He pleases and must do so, for His will is the law, and it cannot be otherwise." The contradiction which reason finds at this point, and before which it can do no more than stand in silence, is still presented without any attempt at disguise. The language of the *Sermon* sounds almost more severe than that of the controversial treatise : " God in this [impelling to evil] does well, and nothing wrong. But he who is thus impelled does wrong, for he has before him the commandment of God which forbids him to do so, and yet the devil impels him so to act. [As to the relation of this impulse from the devil to the impelling power of God, see page 484, and also the sentence here following.] If thou shouldst now ask : Is then the will of God against itself?—that is going too far. The will of God is here, but how this can be, I am not permitted to know." Instead of asking any further questions, it is said again, in conclusion, we should bring down our thoughts to the will of God revealed in His Word and to the incarnate Christ.[1] The exhortations to this effect here given are far more explicit and urgent than in the former document.

Luther speaks no less plainly in his *Briefe an die Antwerpener*, published in 1525.[2] The object of this letter was to warn against certain errorists, who taught, among other things, that the Holy Ghost is our own reason ; that he who is without the Holy Ghost can have no sin, because he has no reason ; that there is no perdition for souls, but that they all have eternal life.[3] One of these men had visited Luther. Of him, the Reformer now declares : He " would not acknowledge that God, although He does not will sin, yet *ordains that it shall come to pass* "—he wanted to understand how God can *not will* sin and yet, by His ordaining, *will* it ; he, in short, would recognize only the one will in God. But to the men of Antwerp Luther himself declares, that he does not teach, as his visitor may slanderously report, that God desires to have sin, but that He has forbidden it, and does not desire it ; that this will has been revealed to us, and it is necessary for us to know it ; but, on the other hand, how God ordains and wills sin belongs to the mystery of divine majesty—we are not to know it, and dare not call God to account in regard to it (Rom. ix. 20). He concludes : " We all have to work hard enough all our lifetime to learn God's commandments and His Son, Christ. When we shall have learned these thoroughly, we will be ready to inquire further in regard to the hidden matters which this false

---

[1] Erl. Ed., xxxv, 160–175. [2] Briefe, iii, 60 sqq.

[3] Cf. the opinion which Luther had occasion to controvert, already in 1522, in his letter to Rechenberg.

spirit now needlessly agitates." For further instruction upon the subject, he refers to the Epistle to the Romans, and his own *Introduction* to it.

Luther's firmly-maintained distinction between the Word of God preached and heard, and the inward speaking of God which especially accompanies the latter in the case of those who are vessels of grace, and only in the case of such, is all the more noticeable at a time when he was engaged in conflict with those who placed a low estimate upon the external Word in general, and depended upon the inward word which they professed to have received. He was also well aware, as we have observed, that these men might draw from his own teachings the inference that the mediation of an external Word is superfluous. Nevertheless, he does not attempt to modify his teaching. Especially in response to the question, why some among the hearers of the Word believe and others do not, he continues to maintain that the Holy Ghost gives faith where and to whom He will. This maxim he employs without hesitancy in opposition to these very Fanatics, and also in his tract against the " Heavenly Prophets," in the beginning of the year 1525, declaring in the latter : " In the same Word comes the Spirit, and gives faith where and to whom He will." [1]

We shall hereafter have occasion to investigate the precise form attained in the later writings of Luther by these doctrines, whose bold development has hitherto been influenced by direct opposition to the Roman Catholic repudiators of the doctrine of grace. But however much or little further modification we shall find in them will no longer be attributable to the opposition of Catholicism, but must, on the contrary, be viewed in connection with the entire doctrine of the means of grace and with the general conception of the nature of God. This fact has determined us to postpone the further consideration of the subject until we shall meet it again in our final systematic review.

The further exposition of Luther's doctrine of justification will also there find its appropriate place. One of the most important of Luther's writings upon this subject called forth in response to Catholic opponents, *i. e.*, his *Ratio Latomica*, was written at the Wartburg. But we shall find in it, as also in his later writings, a

[1] Erl. Ed., xxix, 212.

repetition of that form of the doctrine which has already grown familiar, although a somewhat keener light is afterwards thrown upon a few separate phases of the subject.

f. SCRIPTURE AND TRADITION, ETC.

Before leaving the discussion of the views of Luther as developed in direct opposition to Catholicism, we must yet endeavor to apprehend clearly the position which he now finally claims for THE HOLY SCRIPTURES. We have observed that, in all the points of doctrine thus far examined, he has insisted upon their exclusive authority. Now that the dominant Church has at length fully opened his eyes to her own corruption, he falls back upon the Word of Scripture with an exclusive devotion, to which he was, despite all his previous reliance upon that Word, but gradually led. As, from the time of his adoption of evangelical principles, he had contended against everything which he saw to be in conflict with the contents of Scripture, he now strenuously urges the view, that nothing belongs to saving truth except what is positively and clearly contained in Scripture, and that every other doctrine and ordinance which claims the recognition of believers is without divine sanction, and even contrary to the divine will. The Scriptures are for him the only *supreme rule* of saving truth, in the sense that truth must be seen to flow from them as the only divine source.

Thus, for example, we have already heard him in his treatise, *De Votis*, denounce everything which "falls either short of, or aside of, or beyond Christ"; and, in so declaring, he assumes in advance that the testimony and example of Christ are divinely set before us only in the Scriptures. In the same book, he designates as a lie the maxim of the Papists : Not all things have been declared and instituted by Christ and the apostles, but very many things have been left to be declared and instituted by the Church.[1] He here again discriminates between lower and higher affairs (*res inferiores et superiores*). In the former, upon which divine service does not depend, and which are pursued alike by the ungodly and the pious, God permits us to do also what He has not expressly commanded ; but in the latter—in our relations with Himself—we must always have an expressed commandment

---

[1] Jena, ii, 506 b, 544 (supplement to p. 539 in this Jena edition).

of God. That which is not commanded is, by that very fact, prohibited—*eo ipso contra deum, quod sine verbo Dei*.[1] In support of this position he is accustomed to quote especially Deut. iv. 2 : " Ye shall not add unto the word," etc. He treats of this principle expressly in the pamphlet of the year 1522, *Von Menschenlehre zu meiden*.[2]

It would, therefore, be utterly false to say that Luther up to that time tolerated also TRADITION along with the Scriptures as a subordinate source of authority. Nor did he afterwards in any degree relax the rigor of his position upon this point. On the contrary, we have—for example, in regard to the doctrines of purgatory and prayer for the dead—witnessed an increasing positiveness in the presentation of it.

Nevertheless, what has been said in itself suggests the inquiry, in how far, according to the views of Luther, human ordinances and voluntary human exercises and customs may have and retain a place in Christianity. Whilst it may be conceded that, in everything bearing upon the plan of salvation and the relation of the soul and conscience to God, absolutely " nothing dare be added " to the Word of Scripture, yet the divine worship appointed by God in His Word has also an external, earthly, local embodiment (*Einkleidung*) which is, just because of its unessential character, variable, and left to the choice of Christian liberty. That which is to be rejected when presented as an essential part of the plan of salvation may, therefore, be tolerated by the believer as a purely external work, and may even, in the exercise of the brotherly love which should actuate in dealing with such external matters, become his duty. Luther expressed himself in this way, for example, in regard to the external usages connected with the Lord's Supper, in his reply to King Henry VIII. He likewise, under peculiar circumstances, recommended the observance of the rules for fasting, and even a continuance under monastic regulations. The important point is only that the Christian shall no longer regard matters of this kind as belonging to the higher order of things (*superiora*). As the original papal institution of these things was contrary to God's Word, so, likewise, would he act in opposition to that Word, who should make salvation depend upon the neglect of them. It is in this sense

[1] Briefe, ii, 291 sq.   [2] Erl. Ed., xxviii, 318 sqq.

that Luther now again says : Beyond the Scriptures, nothing must
be appointed (*statuendum*), or, *if anything be appointed*, it must
be regarded as voluntary and not necessary; all things which
Christ has not appointed are voluntary and unnecessary, and
hence, also, not injurious (referring to outward ceremonies in connection with divine worship).[1] The resistance to a form of compulsion from a direction opposite to that against which the
Reformer has hitherto had to contend, displayed in this citation,
will fall under our observation again when we come to study his
testimony against false reformatory tendencies. Thus he still
allowed many things to stand as free articles of faith, but, as indicated by the designation itself, no longer articles of *saving* faith ;
as, for example, a possible purgatory, such a state of the departed as made it permissible to pray for them, and, at first, also
the acceptance of the theory of transubstantiation. But he
became more and more impressed with the danger involved in
these additions to the proper Christian faith, especially in view of
their origin in a spirit that paid little regard to scriptural authority ; and he always watched with great solicitude every movement
in the line of practical ecclesiastical enactments, lest there be any
further open or secret encroachment upon the sphere of the
" higher things."

With this recognition of the Scriptures as the only source of
saving truth goes hand in hand the assertion, that the authority
of the Church, or of the Ancient Fathers, dare not even in the
interpretation of Scripture be placed upon an equal footing with
the Word itself ; but that, on the contrary, the Scriptures themselves present their testimony with sufficient clearness. Nothing,
says Luther, is clearer than the sun, *i. e.*, the Scriptures ; and, even
when a cloud passes over it, there is still behind the cloud
nothing but the same clear sun. Therefore, if we happen to find
a dark saying in the Scriptures, we ought not to doubt that the
same truth lies behind it as that which is clearly seen at other
places. Let him that cannot understand the dark passage be
content to dwell upon those that are light.[2] The conviction of
the Reformer is briefly summarized, in a passage in his tract
against Latomus, as follows : The Scriptures are common to all,

[1] Jena, ii, 562. Erl. Ed., xxviii, 69 sq.
[2] Erl. Ed., xxxix, 133-136 (A. D. 1521).

sufficiently clear in everything required for salvation, and also sufficiently obscure for contemplative minds; let every one study his own part in the most abundant and most common Word of God.[1] We have thus a more precise definition of his meaning in the passage before quoted, *i. e.*, it is the saving truth, which men need to know, which he represents as so clearly revealed. At the same time, there is a clear statement of the natural inference as to the use of the Scriptures, *i. e.*, liberty of access for all to this fountain of truth, and the independent understanding of the Word attainable by every believer. Luther maintains against Erasmus this clearness of the Scriptures also in regard to those doctrines which the latter regarded as superfluous, but which he declared to be necessary. Whereas Erasmus appealed to the fact that God Himself had here left many things dark, Luther maintains: Many passages are dark, it is true, but not on account of the majesty of their contents, but only on account of our ignorance of the words and grammar; and not in such a sense as to lay a designed obstacle in the way of our knowledge of all things in the Scriptures, nor as to justify us in declaring the matters themselves dark on account of a few dark words. How could it be otherwise, since the very highest mysteries are here revealed, *i. e.*, the incarnation of the Son of God, the Trinity, the sufferings of Christ for us? It is only our own hearts that are darkened. There is, indeed, an *obscuritas in cordis cognitione sita*. No man, indeed, who has not the Spirit of God can truly understand even an iota of the Scriptures. But yet everything is objectively fully displayed before our eyes in the ministration (*ministerium*) of the Word. It is in this way, therefore, that Luther defines respectively the clearness and the obscurity of Scripture: the one is external, located in the ministration of the Word; the other lies " in the apprehension of the heart." [2]

Of the FATHERS AND SAINTS, on the other hand, Luther now openly declares that, while they themselves lay claim to the confidence of their readers only in so far as their teachings are supported by Scripture, they are not safe authorities in the interpretation of the Word, but have often been themselves ensnared in error, and have, time and again, overpowered by the flesh,

[1] Jena, ii, 423 sq., 434 b.
[2] Ibid., iii, 168–169.

spoken and labored according to the flesh.[1] Moreover, before acknowledging the authority of the saints, it would first be necessary to inquire whom we dare recognize as actual saints. There is truth in the proverb, that many pass for saints on earth whose souls are in hell. Love, indeed, requires us to regard others as saints (Luther evidently means by " saints " all true followers of Christ) but it can never become for us an article of faith, that certain other persons are holy.[2]

Perfectly futile, and even reprehensible, appeared to Luther the appeal in behalf of traditional dogmas to an antiquity of a thousand years, or to the vast multitude of men and nations who had professed them. In this way, he writes to King Henry VIII., even the Turk might fortify himself in his religious views.[3]

But in what light, according to the above, is the AUTHORITY OF THE CHURCH in connection with the Scriptures regarded? Even now that Luther has fully realized that the breach between himself and the Romish Church is irreparable, he still maintains that the Church cannot be left in error by God—that it is the foundation (*Grundfeste*, 1 Tim. iii. 15) of the truth. His reply to Erasmus here again furnishes us interesting material.[4] In it he goes so far as to acknowledge that the Church, since Christ is with it, and the Holy Spirit rules it, cannot err even in the least article. He even extends this activity of the Spirit to all individual believers, declaring that in not one of the latter has God tolerated the error of (an imagined) free will. He presents this thought still more definitely in this passage and in many others, affirming that, although believers should spend their whole lives under the dominion, of erroneous views, to which they are liable in consequence of their carnal nature, they would yet, of necessity, be brought back to the right way at least before their death (*vid supra*, p. 455). He endeavors further, in a very noteworthy and delicate way, to establish a distinction between that which such believers may have perhaps said in controversy about free will, and the disposition which has been operative in their actual feelings and impulses—in their *affectus*, and has controlled them in their prayers and, in general, in their intercourse with God. He undertakes to show that, as often as holy men

---

[1] Jena, ii, 422 b sq., 553. Erl. Ed., xxviii, 32. Jena, iii, 179.

[2] Ibid., iii, 179, 182. [3] Ibid., ii, 552. [4] Ibid., iii, 180 sqq.

draw near to God to pray to Him or serve Him, they will draw near inwardly, forgetful of their free will, despairing of themselves, etc., as was frequently the case with Augustine, and with Bernhard also as he realized that the time of his death was drawing near. He, therefore, lays down the principle : " Good as well as evil men are to be measured, in fact, rather by their disposition than by their speech " (*ex effectu vero potius quam ex sermone*).

But Luther constantly returns to the question : Where then is the Church? Who are the Christians, or " saints," whom the Holy Ghost controls? He reminds us that at one time in Israel, when kings, priests and prophets had fallen away, only seven thousand souls had been preserved by God. Who, he asks, then recognized in these seven thousand the people of God? He considers it possible that God should at present also allow the great mass of professing Christians, together with their leaders, the men holding public name and office, to fall away ; that He should permit all the larger congregations to walk in their own ways, as did the heathen formerly ; and that He should perpetuate His Church among those who are not regarded as belonging to the Church, but are burned like Huss. And, even in regard to those who may really be true saints of God, we yet cannot affirm as an article of faith, that they are such. Even in their case, we must again first inquire, in how far the Spirit has dominated in their utterances and in how far the flesh has intruded, and we can decide such a question only by the authority of the Holy Scriptures.

There is no contradiction between the position here assumed by Luther, in meeting the appeal of the Papists to ecclesiastical tradition, and the spirit in which we shall presently find him himself appealing, in support of the doctrines of infant baptism and the Lord's Supper, to the constant and universal endorsement of the Church.[1] The relation of the ideas is as follows : As the Scriptures are " common to all," each separate Christian may and must base his faith upon his own knowledge of their contents, and is authorized, and in duty bound, to test by them whatever is presented to him as doctrine. For this purpose, the eye must be opened by the Spirit, who makes inwardly clear that which is objectively clear in the scriptural presentation. " Every one must

---

[1] Vid. the next chapter; also supra, pp. 408 sq., 421.

believe only because it is God's Word and because he inwardly realizes that it is truth." " It belongs to each and every Christian to recognize and to judge concerning doctrine, and it so belongs to them that he is accursed who shall have assailed this right with a single javelin." In support of these claims, Luther quotes Matt. vii. 15 ; John x. 4, 5 ; 1 John iv. 1 ; 1 Thes. v. 21 ; 1 Cor. ii. 15 (with the remark : but any (*quilibet*) Christian at all is spiritual by virtue of the spirit of Christ) ; 1 Cor. iii. 22 (" that is, you have the right of judging concerning the things said and done by all ").[1]

If we now, finally, ask how, in view of all this, certainty is to be attained in regard to the highest truths of Christianity and a true judgment to be formed in regard to the various spirits that may appear, we shall find in Luther's treatise against Erasmus a reply which is based entirely on the principles above noted, and must be interpreted in harmony with them, but which, nevertheless, calls for a few explanatory remarks.[2] He here notes a *two-fold estimate of the spirits*, to correspond with the two-fold clearness (*claritas*) of the Scriptures above explained. The one is the inward judgment, in which each individual Christian, by virtue of his possession of the Holy Spirit, judges all doctrines, etc., for himself with perfect certainty (1 Cor. ii. 15). This belongs to (subjective) faith, and is necessary for every Christian, even among the laity. This is that *interior claritas scripturae* which has been spoken of (here, too, Luther means, therefore, an inner assurance and illumination through the Spirit, in so far as the latter opens to the mind and seals upon the heart the contents of Scripture). But this judgment, he proceeds to say, benefits no one else (except him who already experiences within himself this discriminating agency of the Spirit ; not, therefore, those who do not yet accept the truth). The second judgment is the external, in which we also, for the good of our fellowmen, judge spirits and doctrines. This is a matter pertaining to the public ministration of the Word and to external office, and belongs chiefly to the leaders of the Church and preachers of the Word. It is to be exercised for the strengthening of the weak in faith and for the refutation of opponents. This is what has been called

---

[1] Erl. Ed., xxviii, 339 sqq. Jena, ii, 562 b, sq.

[2] Jena, iii, 182 b, sqq.

the *externa claritas scripturae.* By this, Luther evidently means to designate the external employment of the Word, through which, by virtue of its objectively inherent clearness, it is presented also to others. And he now again expresses his firm conviction that, as a matter of fact, everything needed for the confutation of errorists is clearly enough taught in the Scriptures, and may and should be held up before them by means of the public ministry of the Word. In special illustration of this principle, he instances the scriptural teachings upon the subject of free will, in the defence of which against the assaults of Erasmus he is at the very time engaged. So clearly are these doctrines presented in the Scriptures, that, despite all the exertions of the adversaries, the inability of the latter to withstand the evidence is apparent to all, and that, in fact, by the judgment of the " common sense," their counter arguments amount to nothing. But if it be asked why the adversaries do not then accept this clear scriptural truth, the explanation can be found only in their inward, carnal blindness, in the hardness of their hearts, and in the dominion of Satan over them. And their very blindness must (according to the will of God) serve for the further glorifying of the scriptural doctrine of free will.

It is perfectly evident, from all the above, that Luther, in maintaining such an " external judgment " by the ministers of the Word, has no idea of again establishing an external human tribunal, with authority to render official decisions (in matters of doctrine). It is not in any such authority that he locates the force of the judgments pronounced by the ministers of the Word, but solely in the Word of Scripture itself, whose ministers they are. It is, according to his view, always possible that they may themselves become unfaithful to the teachings of Scripture, and hence their external presentations of scriptural truth must, in turn, be tested in the light of the Scriptures themselves by every individual believer through the Spirit granted personally to himself. It is to be observed, moreover, that Luther assigns this duty of external judgment only " chiefly " (*maxime*) to the regularly-appointed preachers of the Word. It may fall to the lot of any individual Christian, as well, to exercise this office privately in relation to his neighbor. Especially is the " strengthening of the weak " always among the duties of every private Christian.

Thus the investigations of the Reformer lead to the clear conclusion, that there is, according to the divine order, *no external, tangible, final decision in matters of faith.* To the individual have been given, as means by which he may be convicted of error and convinced of the truth, the external Word and its external pro- clamation by his fellowmen, chiefly by those regularly ordained to the preaching office. But only the Spirit, whom he must for himself receive from God, can give him actual inner conviction and certainty. We must not understand even the declaration concerning the " common sense " as implying that the latter can work faith ; but, even if an objective witness of the controversy between the clearly-revealed truth of Scripture and its adver- saries be compelled, by virtue of this " common sense " alone, to acknowledge that the scriptural testimony is clearly against the latter, he will still require the gift of the Holy Spirit, in order to attain, despite the opposition of the natural heart to this clear revelation, to an inward personal acceptance of the truth. Upon the question, what course was to be pursued in case any party should refuse to acknowledge the authority of the Scriptures in general, and should, therefore, require to be convinced, first of all, of their divine character, Luther had no occasion to enter.

The establishment of saving doctrine upon the Scriptures as its only rule and source, in opposition to the authority claimed for the Church and hierarchy, remained with Luther a fixed principle until the end of his life. He never afterwards sought any further ground of assurance for those who already cherished saving faith, or for the conviction and refutation of errorists.

But, even in the writings already cited, he does not speak as though insensible in any degree to the dangers which might be thought incident to such a view. We have already seen how clearly he recognized from the very beginning the new spirit of error which threatened to assert itself as soon as appeal should have been openly taken from the acknowledged ecclesiastical authority to the simple Scriptures. He refers, in his argument with Erasmus, to the hard battle which he had already waged with the Fanatical Spirits, " who subject the Scriptures to their own spirit for interpretation." But he can see nothing better than this in the Papacy itself, *i. e.,* the same exaltation of the human spirit above the Word of God. It may, indeed, be asked, he writes to King Henry, how it would be if the multitude of persons thus authorized to sit in judgment should disagree among themselves. He asks, in reply, how much harmony there would be among those who should suffer themselves to be coerced into submission to the judgment of the Pope; and whether harmony is attained by the mere fact of union under the external name of the Pope. For who, he inquires, *is certain in his conscience* that the Pope judges rightly? And without this certainty there can be no unity. In fact, there is, under the Papacy, a real Babel of confusion beneath a show of outward harmony, in which there is no agreement of heart with heart. He calmly relies, on the contrary, upon the inward Spirit from on high, to enable all those who are taught of God (John vi. 45) to dwell together in harmony.

The restlessness and revolutions prophesied as the sure result of evangelical preaching do not frighten him from his course, even after these fears have been justified by the frightful outbreak of actual violence. Indeed, he declares that he should have been greatly mistaken in his estimate of the Gospel if it should not excite tumult in this God-opposing world—if we should not be called upon to witness the fulfilment of Christ's prophecies concerning the sword and fire which He would send. The abuse by many of the Gospel and of the liberty which it brings is no reason for impeding the progress of the Gospel itself. The world was just as wicked before, but its wickedness is now just being revealed to the light, " and, even if not all can be saved, yet those for whose sake the Word of God has been given will, in consequence of these disorders, live but the more fervently and be bound together in a more sacred union in one spirit." Luther indignantly rejects the subterfuge of Erasmus, urged against the public preaching of the doctrine of the Scriptures, *i. e.,* that there are diseases, such as leprosy, which can be more easily endured than the measures required for their cure. Luther can see, as a threatening result of the efforts to purge the Church of the present leprosy, nothing worse than *temporal* evils, disorders, etc., and he hence reverses the above sentence, and declares, that this leprosy of temporal evil had much better be endured than that we should, in order to escape it, allow the souls of men to be hurled into everlasting perdition.[1]

Luther did now, however, in view of the encroachments, from the opposite direction, of those errors in which his enemies sought

[1] Jena, iii, 182 b; ii, 563 b; iii, 173 b, sq.

to trace such terrible consequences of his teachings as would lead to their abandonment, endeavor all the more zealously to protect the divine Word, for whose exclusive authority he had contended against the Romish Church, from the assaults, on the other hand, of a purely human spirit, from the carping criticisms of the ordinary reason, and especially from the assumptions of the professed divine spirit of the Fanatics. But we are not to imagine that it was only or chiefly through the new form of opposition now encountered that he was led to guard his position against such perversion. This prudent precaution had been taken from the very first, and became all the more manifest as he was led from time to time to rely the more absolutely upon the Scriptures in antagonizing the authority of the Church. How conscientiously, and even anxiously, for example, does he not, in combating the theory underlying the monastic vows, seek to avoid every argument not drawn strictly from the Scriptures; and how strictly did he not, from the very beginning of his assault upon the dogma of transubstantiation, base his argument on that subject upon the very letter of the Scriptures.

In the relations into which Luther is now led with the new class of errorists, we shall see his views attaining greater precision, especially with regard to the objective means by which God brings, not only the truth, but His entire salvation as well, to men, and which now for Luther assumed the place of the traditional mediation claimed in favor of the entire Romish ecclesiasticism; with regard, also, to a fixed order of ecclesiastical activity and official position as still necessary, although no authority of binding the souls of men was longer conceded to any ecclesiastical officials. It was only thus that his entire doctrine concerning the Church attained its final and complete form. Yet, with this new development, the antagonism of his teachings to the doctrines of the Romish Church remained, without any retraction or abatement, the same as we have hitherto found it.

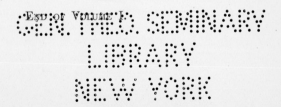